1-09

IN THE PEOPLE'S INTEREST

A Centennial History of Montana State University

Robert Rydell • Jeffrey Safford • Pierce Mullen

ISBN 0-9635114-0-8

Foreword

After more than 30 years as a historian of Montana and the West, the prospect of a comprehensive work of my own institution, Montana State University, filled me with fascination, curiosity, and admittedly a bit of apprehension.

My fascination stems from the prospect of learning much more about the roots of this institution, which is so much a part of the fabric of Montana. I had read and learned much from Merrill Burlingame's Diamond Jubilee history not long after I arrived at MSU, but it whetted my appetite for more. MSU is Montana's land grant university and was the first of the state's public institutions of higher education to be created. Its history can tell us much about ourselves and our state.

Wisely, I believe, we entrusted the task of researching and writing this history to three seasoned historians: Robert Rydell, Jeffrey Safford and Pierce Mullen. They spent more than four years recording oral histories and researching the primary and secondary source materials of our past.

Oftentimes, university histories such as this one take the form of "coffee table books," which are more useful for kindling nostalgia or promoting public relations than as serious histories of an institution. The authors, quite correctly, have rejected this approach. They have done an exceptional amount of research and they have produced a history that records the institution's dark hours as well as its days in the sun, that reflects its problems and failures as well as its triumphs and successes.

We must remember that Montana State University did not become a comprehensive academic institution of substance without controversy and without failure. After all, it is the creature of a state that has had a history of booms and busts. While we might cringe today at some of the things that happened in the past, we must remember that those who came before us faced problems that, in many ways, were more formidable than most of those we face today.

As the tenth President of Montana State University, I am indebted to my colleagues for the history that they have produced. It is fine reading for all, and it has already taught me much. We shall all learn from it, be inspired by it, and be encouraged by it. Learning from what came before, we can position ourselves better for the Second Century. And finally, there is always the nostalgia that comes from reflecting back upon the past of an institution that means so much to all of us.

Michael Malone
President
Montana State University
July 1992

Acknowledgements

In the course of our research and writing, we have acquired numerous debts. The Centennial History Project was fostered initially by Montana State University President William Tietz, sustained by his successor President Michael Malone, underwritten through the generosity of the Montana State University Foundation, and shepherded along by Marilyn Wessel, director of university relations. We are grateful for their unflagging support.

This chronicle of our university's past would not have been possible without the cooperation of many students, both graduate and undergraduate. Participants in research seminars focused on the history of American higher education and wrote papers, some of which are cited in the endnotes, on various aspects of MSU's history. Other students served as research assistants. To John Darnell, Timothy LeCain, Mike Leslie, James Pritchard, Kiki Leigh Rydell, Lisa Tritz, and Richard Wojtowicz we offer our deep gratitude. We are especially indebted to John Darnell for his perseverance in tracking down the records of the College of Engineering. And we wish to thank Richard Wojtowicz not only for his contributions to certain vignettes but for sharing the knowledge of the campus he gained while preparing a separate history of the Strand Union Building.

Several colleagues read and criticized chapter drafts. We are grateful to Rob Kroes, Jonathan McLeod, Michael Malone, Michelle Maskiell, Thomas Nopper, Richard Roeder, and Bruce Shively for their suggestions for improvement.

In the Merrill G. Burlingame Special Collections and Montana State University Archives we compiled a list of debts that can never be adequately repaid. We thank Minnie Paugh for her years of dedicated service to a department she loved. In the beginning, Rolf Swensen and Marlene Anderson kept us constantly supplied with materials. More recently, Nathan Bender, Marjorie David, and Deborah Nash have come to the rescue. One of MSU's treasures is the University Archives, and we are eternally grateful to the aforementioned individuals for sharing its wealth of information with us and our student investigators. Other keepers of records who deserve our thanks are Steven Jackson, curator of art and photography at the Museum of the Rockies; Dale Johnson, university archivist at the Mansfield Library in Missoula; and David Walter, librarian at the State Historical Society in Helena.

Many individuals around the state and nation shared their knowledge of the university. Almost 200 persons consented to interviews and/or consultations, some more than once, and a few repeatedly, and we are exceedingly grateful to them for providing us with their recollections. Some of those we consulted supplied documents and records that improved greatly our ability to recall MSU's past. It goes without saying that we, not they, bear responsibility for interpretations made of the interviews and resources they so kindly contributed.

This project demanded a great deal from history department staff, especially Dee George, Nancy Evans, and Lynne Peachey, and provided a constant source of bemusement to our colleagues in history, philosophy, and religious studies. For all of the extra work we demanded of our administrative assistant and secretaries, we apologize; for all of the amusement we afforded our colleagues, we expect eternal deference.

We are especially indebted to our gifted copy editor, Ursula Smith, for beyond-the-call devotion to the manuscript and its improvement. Always upbeat, always constructive in her criticism, she was able to meld three quite different styles and smooth many passages. Allan Smart, director of communication services, and his able associates, Bruce Eng and Caroline Zimmerman, brought skill, artistry, and an active partnership to this work. The handsome product of that collaboration is in your hands.

Finally, we wish to acknowledge the support of our wives: Kiki Leigh Rydell, June Billings Safford, and Margaret Montague Mullen. They shouldered more than their share of the centennial history project and we thank them dearly for having helped bring it to fruition.

Photo Credits

Victoria Enger: cover photo. **MSU Archives:** All photos in Chapters One through Three except top photo on p. 28; pp. 56, 62, 63, 69, 70, 71, 75, 78, 87, 91, 93, 99 top and bottom, 103 middle, 106, 107, 112, 113, 119, 127, 132, 140, 146 bottom, 152, 162 top, 185, 187, 203 bottom, 208, 217, 218, 236, 241 bottom, 256, 259 bottom, 278, and 307. **MSU Communications Services:** pp. 68, 92, 94, 97, 99 middle, 100, 101, 102 bottom, 103 top and bottom, 108, 109, 114, 121, 125, 129, 138, 142, 143 top, 146 top, 155, 157, 158, 162 bottom, 163, 164, 165, 168, 169, 173, 175 top, 179, 182, 183, 184, 186, 188, 191, 192, 195, 196, 198, 201, 204 top left, 205, 209, 211 top left and bottom right, 212 right, 213 top, 215, 216, 224, 226, 227, 230, 231 top and bottom left, 232, 233 top, 237 bottom, 238 bottom right, 240, 242, 243, 244, 245, 247, 249, 253, 257, 259 top, 260, 261, 264, 266 top, 267, 270, 271, 273, 276, 277, 279, 280, 281, 284, 286, and 287. *Montanans* **(yearbooks):** pp. 64 (1954), 66 (1957), 72 (1952), 74 (1948), 79 top (1958) and bottom (1959), 80 top left (1961) and top right (1960) and bottom (1959), 82 (1972), 85 (1961), 86 (1961), 102 top (1967), 104 (1959), 115 (1970), 117 (1970), 118 (1972), 144 (1965), 145 (1956), 147 bottom (1978), 154 (1977), 174 (1985), 189 (1980), 203 top (1972), 204 bottom right (1952), 210 (1962), 211 bottom left (1968), 214 (1969), 221 (1985), and 223 top (1985). **MSU Athletics:** pp. 204 bottom left, 212 left, 213 bottom, 231 bottom right, 237 top, 238 top and bottom left, and 241 top. **MSU Alumni Association:** pp. 131, 143 bottom, 147 top, 190, 200, 223 bottom, 233 bottom, 262, 268 bottom, and 283. **Montana Historical Society:** pp. 89, 120, 134, 135, 136, and 175 bottom. **Museum of the Rockies:** pp. 160, 161, and 202. **MSU International Education:** p. 166. **MSU Foundation:** p. 177. **Mansfield Library, University of Montana:** p. 28 top. **Cliff Davis:** p. 252. **Pierce Mullen:** p. 254 **Hayden Fergusen:** p. 255. *Medicare Northwest,* **Spring 1992:** p. 265. **Gary Strobel:** p. 274. *Corona,* **vol. II:** p. 275. **Janet Bignell:** p. 235.

Introduction

Not many histories of a university can begin with a registry book anchored to a 10,000 foot mountain peak. But that is an appropriate starting point for this centennial history of Montana State University.

Several years ago, when plans for this history were just developing, one of the authors followed the well-worn path up the east side of the Bridger Mountains to the summit of the mountain called Sacagawea. Anyone who has taken this walk knows that there is more than one reason to catch your breath on the top. The scramble to the peak affords dizzying views of a veritable sea of mountain ranges that make the human settlements and the university in the valley below seem utterly out of place. Like many mountain summits, Sacagawea boasts a registry for hikers to record their names and observations. Among the many signatures and inscriptions, one written several days earlier caught the author's eye: "Thanks M.S.U. for four great years."

Two decades before this student penned her or his note, a former English department faculty member, Robert Pirsig, recorded his memories of what then was called Montana State College in *Zen and the Art of Motorcycle Maintenance* and they conveyed a distinctly different impression:

> The school was what could euphemistically be called a "teaching college." At a teaching college you teach and you teach and you teach with no time for research, no time for contemplation, no time for participation in outside affairs. Just teach and teach and teach until your mind grows dull and your creativity vanishes and you become an automaton saying the same dull things over and over to endless waves of innocent students who cannot understand why you are so dull, lose respect and fan this disrespect out into the community. The reason you teach and you teach and you teach is that this is a very clever way of running a college on the cheap while giving a false appearance of genuine education.[1]

As Pirsig knew only too well, "the college on the hill" was not exactly an ivory tower and had been rocked on more than one occasion by the reverberations of Montana politics.

Point and counterpoint—the exhiliration of a student and the vertigo of a dedicated teacher. These episodes convey a partial range of experiences that we have uncovered in assembling this centennial history of Montana State University. The word "partial" is crucial. This is not a definitive history. It is not the last word on the subject of Montana State University or on the Montana system of higher education. Our four summers of research and writing have reminded us of the complexity of this university and we have agonized about omissions of departments and individuals who played a role in shaping the university that has done so much for the state of Montana. To help round out the story of the university's development, we have added to our historical narrative a series of vignettes about significant people and interesting events in the university's past and included an appendix containing information about campus buildings. There are still gaps and omissions in our story. But it has never been our intention to write just an internal history of the institution, in part because very good departmental histories already exist—at least through 1968—and because much of this information is provided in Merrill G. Burlingame's seventy-fifth anniversary history of MSU.

More importantly, we believed when we started this project, as we do now, that an internal institutional history would miss the forest for the trees. From the moment MSU originated as a college in 1893—a year remembered as the date of a nationwide depression, of a world's fair in Chicago, and of Frederick Jackson Turner's famous paper concerning the significance of the frontier in American history—the institution has been integrally connected to the social, political, and cultural history of the state and the nation. The task we set for ourselves then was to highlight the points of intersection in order to support the simple proposition that MSU has more than a past to be remembered; it has a contextual history that needs to be understood.

That history begins with a chapter that takes the founding of the "college on the hill" not as a beginning, but as the culmination of a series of developments reaching through the era of the mining frontier, through the Civil War and back to the Lewis and Clark expedition. Put another way, the college carried the freight of history and bore the unmistakable impress of its recent past, including the wars against Native Americans that opened the American West for white settlement. It also reflected the heady conviction of its founders that, far from being mere products of history, they could make history by inscribing their dreams on an institution of higher education.

Precisely because the future was at stake, higher education became one of the most hotly contested issues in the early history of the state. Should a state the size of Montana have one institution or several? The first chapter traces the early history of these debates, while the second examines the result of the decision to decentralize the university system and the efforts of MSC administrators, especially presidents James Reid and James Hamilton, to carve out an identity for their college that would distinguish it from the university in Missoula. The shift from Reid's emphasis on "culture and skill" to Hamilton's insistence on "education for efficiency" was a pivotal moment in the history of the college.

Once "education for efficiency" became the institution's official trademark, it remained for Hamilton's successors to work out the details of his vision during a period between the wars that historian Merrill Burlingame aptly called "years of bleakness."[2] Chapter 3 calls attention to the hard times that befell the college during Montana's two decades of depression and notes the rising dominance of the College of Agriculture and the College of Engineering. The chapter concludes by noting the growing movement to turn MSC into a university that would value research as well as teaching and vocational training.

At the close of the Second World War, if not shortly before, Montana State College reached a crossroads. How would the school accommodate the large number of veterans returning from war? How would it meet its land grant outreach responsibilities in a state and world suddenly shaped by iron curtains and cold war mentalities? The task of finding answers to these questions fell to the liberal New Dealer Roland Renne, and chapter 4 chronicles the clash of Renne's policies with the conservative politics of the 1950s and early 1960s.

The next three chapters examine the presidential administrations of Leon Johnson, William Johnstone, Carl McIntosh, and William Tietz, and touch on the school's first year under Michael Malone. Chapter five treats of the transition of MSC to MSU in the Johnson/Johnstone period, and discusses the rapidly growing university in the context of the youth movement of the '60s and the Vietnam war. The sixth chapter examines the Carl McIntosh administration, the impact of the new state constitution of 1972 on higher education, and the troubled relationship produced thereby. Chapter 7 chronicles the lengthy and remarkable administration of William Tietz, a period of both euphoria and disappointment as the state at first liberally supported higher education, but then, beset by burgeoning fiscal problems, progressively withdrew its commitment to the system. On the eve of MSU's centennial celebration the university's new president, Michael Malone, pledged himself to reverse the trend, but it was difficult to know to what extent circumstances would allow recovery.

Within this broad chronological overview, three aspects of the institution's history have been given additional emphasis: the evolution and place of athletics, the growth and development of the sciences and engineering, and the increasing significance of the arts and humanities. Chapter 8 deals not only with the university's athletic history, but the cultural, political, and economic factors shaping the special character of sport at MSU. Chapter 9 offers an overview of the tradition of science on campus and the reconfiguration of that tradition, while chapter 10 examines the nature of the humanities and related professional schools.

In a recent book about contemporary American culture, French critic Jean Baudrillard likens history itself to one of those outside rearview automobile mirrors that bears the notice: "Caution, objects in this mirror are closer than they may appear."[3] Our collective goal in writing *In The People's Interest* is to outfit MSU with such a mirror, to supplement the inside mirror that Merrill Burlingame provided when he wrote the seventy-fifth anniversary history of the college. As we drive toward the second century of MSU's existence, it is our hope that, thus outfitted, the university can meet the many challenges that the new century—and the new millennium—will present.

Three historians from the department of history and philosophy co-authored this volume. We read and criticized drafts of each other's chapters, but each author bears primary responsibility for specific sections of the narrative that follows. Robert Rydell wrote the first three chapters, Jeffrey Safford authored chapters 4 through 8, and Pierce Mullen contributed the two concluding chapters. We dedicate this book to future generations of MSU students, faculty, administrators, and staff and to the example set by two distinguished colleagues, Merrill G. Burlingame and Robert G. Dunbar, who made Montana history in the course of teaching and writing about the subject.

Robert W. Rydell
Jeffrey J. Safford
Pierce C. Mullen

Bozeman, Montana 1992

Table of Contents

Vignettes

IN THE PEOPLE'S INTEREST

A Centennial History of Montana State University

Robert Rydell • Jeffrey Safford • Pierce Mullen

Chapter One
Beginnings In Bozeman

Origins

Beginnings have beginnings. On February 16, 1893, Montana Governor John E. Rickards signed the bill establishing the Agricultural College of the State of Montana in Bozeman. But Rickards' signature, formally creating a land grant college that would develop in the next century into Montana State University, marked as much the culmination of events as the starting point of Montana's first state-supported college.

In July 1806, Meriwether Lewis and William Clark returned to the headwaters of the Missouri River en route from the Pacific Ocean to report the findings of their expedition to the anxiously awaiting Thomas Jefferson. On a frosty summer morning, at the confluence of three rivers they had named the previous year for President Jefferson, Secretary of State James Madison, and Secretary of the Treasury Albert Gallatin, the explorers parted company. Clark, guided by the Shoshone Indian woman, Sacagawea, followed the east fork of the Gallatin River toward a pass in the mountains to the east. As they followed the banks of the river, Clark could hardly escape noticing the spellbinding terrain his party traversed. Behind them loomed jagged mountains that sliced the sun's afternoon descent. To the north, the rising plane of the valley floor seemed inseparable from the sky. Straight ahead rose a rocky mound of pine- and fir-speckled hills, while to the south, Tayabeshockup, or the "Valley of the Flowers" as Native Americans called it, met foothills that buffered towering, snow-capped peaks.[1]

Clark, anxious to return to the east coast, made few references to the valley and made no record of any thoughts he might have had concerning the future of this niche in the vast Louisiana Purchase Territory. He could certainly never have dreamed that eighty-seven years later and two miles or so to the south of the path he followed across the valley a college would be established that would include buildings named for himself and Lewis, though none would bear witness to the woman who helped make their trek possible.

If Montana's first state-supported institution of higher learning had its distant origins in the era of national westward expansion launched by Lewis and Clark, its more immediate past developed in the maelstrom of intense political and economic conflict that accompanied efforts to rebuild the nation after the Civil War and to industrialize the American West. In addition to bearing the stamp of these struggles, the college bore the impress of several other intersecting forces. First, the college owed its existence to the Morrill Land Grant Act of 1862 that set in motion a movement that ultimately resulted in the creation of sixty-eight land grant colleges around the country and its territorial possessions. Second, the college bore the unmistakable impress of the searing political struggles that characterized Montana's transition from territorial status to statehood. Finally, the college was shaped by a group of southwestern Montana community builders whose lives had been shaped in an age that witnessed what one historian has called the "incorporation of America"[2]—an age alive with changing ideas about the meaning and future of higher education in a nation that had been transformed by corporate capitalism.

From these beginnings in the convergence of national, regional, local, and private histories, a college developed that, along with the other units of the Montana university system, would give form and substance to the cultural geography of a land Joseph Kinsey Howard prosaically described as "high, wide, and handsome."[3]

The Land Grant Acts

Before the Civil War, especially after the 1849 gold rush to California, the American West loomed large in the imagination and politics of white Americans. The West, most Americans could agree, would play a pivotal role in the nation's future. What was less certain was whether the lands acquired first by purchase and then by war would be open to slavery. In 1856, as Congress debated the expansion of slavery, as national political parties collapsed, and as the country teetered on the brink of a bloody conflict that would kill more Americans than any subsequent war, Vermont's representative, Justin A. Morrill, introduced a bill to underwrite, through the grant of 6.3 million acres of federal lands to the states,

> the endowment, support and maintenance of at least one college in each state where the leading object shall be, without excluding other scientific or classical studies, to teach such branches of learning as are related to agriculture and the mechanic arts, as the legislatures of the states may respectively prescribe, in order to promote the liberal and practical education of the industrial classes in the several pursuits and professions of life.[4]

This was a momentous idea and reflected the changed circumstances of the American nation since the founding of the republic.

The Industrial Revolution had ushered in a period of corporate capitalism that was radically altering the circumstances that had led Jefferson to envision a republic composed primarily of yeoman farmers. Instead of becoming an agrarian republic, America was quickly becoming a republic driven by profits generated by southern, African-American slave labor that were reinvested in northern manufacturing and western agriculture. As tensions between the North and South grew, the nation turned its eyes to the future and asked, in Abraham Lincoln's words, whether the country "could endure half slave and half free." As antislavery forces in the North stepped up their attacks on the insitution of slavery for its degrading effects on white laborers, proslavery southerners responded by condemning the emergence of industrial capitalism and wage slavery in the North. Morrill's concern about the emergence of "industrial classes" was not unique. Neither was his solution.[5]

Six years before Morrill introduced his bill in the U.S. House of Representatives, Jonathan Turner, a farmer and former professor at Illinois College, presented a proposal at the Illinois Teachers Institute to apply monies the state received from the sale of federal lands to endow a state university for the express purpose of educating the "industrial classes." Morrill, in short, rode the crest of a wave to reform American higher education and make it relevant to the changed economic circumstances of American life. His initial efforts secured narrow support in both houses of Congress only to crash on the shoals of sectional politics. In 1859, President James Buchanan vetoed the land grant bill, claiming that the costly act represented an unwarranted intrusion on states' rights. Morrill's reply reflected his view that a strong national government was necessary for the nation's progress:

> If we can legislate for the insane, may we not legislate for the sane? We have granted lands for railroad purposes, for military services, and we have granted lands to the several States for the promotion of health; that is, we have granted to the States the swamp and overflowed lands within their limits. Now, sir, if we can grant lands for the promotion of physical health, can we not grant them for the purpose of promoting the moral health and education of the people? . . . Cannot we grant them for education, and for the education of the great mass of the country; and a class, too, which has received no special benefit from any act of Congress?

Despite its eloquence, Morrill's rhetoric failed to persuade Democrats in Congress to desert their president and override his veto.[6]

Had the Civil War not intervened, Turner's dream and Morrill's act might not have materialized. But the war eliminated southern Democrats from Congress and gave the Republicans the opportunity to consolidate their economic program for the stepped-up industrialization of the country. During the war, the recently formed Republican Party passed a series of interrelated measures—including a high tariff on foreign imports devised to encourage domestic manufacturing, an immigration act drawn up to encourage the migration of potential laborers for the nation's burgeoning industries, a transcontinental railroad bill intended to increase domestic markets for industrial and agricultural products, and a homestead act designed to settle the West with producers of agricultural goods for eastern markets and consumers of industrial goods from those same markets. Morrill's land grant legislation fit in perfectly with these broad aims of his party. The increasing pace of industrialization demanded a trained work force and the application of science to agriculture promised a cornucopia of produce for the railroads to haul to distant markets.

Such visions of national growth and development, of course, were predicated on a northern military victory in the Civil War.[7] But early reports from the battlefields were less than encouraging. As Union defeats mounted, it was apparent that the North lacked military leadership. Less than six months after the fall of Fort Sumter, Morrill added to his bill the provision that each college created from the federal grant of lands include training in military strategy and that territories as well as seceded states be excluded from the act's provisions. In 1862, Morrill's measure passed both houses of Congress; on July 2, President Abraham Lincoln signed it into law.[8]

The North's eventual victory in the Civil War ended slavery and cleared the way for the Republican economic program for national expansion. For the next half century, with the exception of Grover Cleveland's split terms as president, Republicans maintained control of the presidency and generally controlled at least one house of Congress.[9] By the close of the century, Morrill's plan for land grant colleges, a fixture in national politics, was anchored to the national cultural topography as surely as the railroads.

Like the railway lines that sprouted spurs and trunks as they evolved into a massive national transportation network, Morrill's Land Grant Act spawned additional legislation intended to promote the rapid development of colleges around the country. The most important of these measures extended land grant eligibility to territories and former Confederate states, specified the length of time states had to organize a college after accepting the terms of the land grant, and gave states greater flexibility in investing land grant revenues. More dramatically, the 1887 Hatch Act authorized the sale of additional public lands to endow agricultural experiment stations at land grant colleges and the so-called Second Morrill Act of 1890 appropriated $15,000 to each land grant college and an additional $1000 per year until the sum reached $25,000.[10] By 1890, the various land grant measures had attained a momentum that seemed impossible to derail except through inertia on the part of state legislatures. In Montana, the unimaginable almost happened as the politics of state building nearly derailed plans to develop a system of state-funded higher education.

The Politics of State and University Building

In 1889, after a twenty-five year struggle to secure statehood, Montana entered the Union as the forty-first state when President Benjamin Harrison signed the official proclamation. Harrison might as well have embossed the document with a match. Over the course of the next decade a political fire storm swept the state, leaving in its wake charred dreams, smoldering ambitions, and a fledgling university system that survived more by dint of local courage than by state support.[11]

At issue in the formative years of Montana was the political control and direction of the state. The two political parties shared about equal support: the first legislature was divided equally between Democrats and Republicans; the governor was a Democrat; and the state's single congressman was a Republican. What a classical political theorist might have regarded as an ideal balance between contending forces rapidly degenerated into open warfare as the two parties traded charges of fraud and corruption over the election of five state representatives from Silver Bow County. The stakes were great. Until 1913, state legislatures, not the electorate, selected U. S. senators. The party that won the majority of Silver Bow seats would be in a position to select its candidate for the Senate. Neither party budged on the Silver Bow question; rather, the parties organized themselves into two separate houses of representatives. The situation resembled a circus and governance took a back seat to entertainment. The Senate deadlocked on bills submitted by the separate houses and each party submitted the names of two candidates to the U.S. Senate. This result made the state look ridiculous and, more ominously, rendered it liable to gross manipulation by contending corporations that vied for control of its natural resources.[12]

Despite the intrigues that remained at center stage of this theater of the politically absurd— which culminated in the election of "copper king" William A. Clark to the U.S. Senate in 1900— Montana's political leadership did make headway in creating an institutional infrastructure for the state. One of the consequences of political gridlock in the first legislative session was the continuing loss of some of the best public lands in the state to homesteaders and corporations. Under the terms of the 1881 Land Grant Act, 46,000

acres had been deeded to the territory of Montana to help endow a university. The land had been promptly surveyed by Robert Howey, farsighted superintendent of public instruction. Seven years later, the Enabling Act, "enabling" Montana to become a state, provided an additional 140,000 acres for a college of agriculture and mechanic arts. But the act left the location of the lands to the State Board of Land Commissioners, which made no effort to survey those lands until the second legislature, under prodding by Governor Joseph K. Toole, worked out a compromise on the Silver Bow representatives and passed a torrent of laws, including one authorizing the governor to appoint a land agent to survey the remaining public lands and determine which site should be acquired for purposes of establishing a land grant college.[13]

The second legislative session continued to simmer in the heat of partisan politics, but found ample diversion in trying to fulfill the terms of Montana's constitution, which authorized the legislature to appropriate funds for "Education, reformatory, and penal institutions, and those for the benefit of the insane, blind, deaf and mute, soldier's home, and such other institutions as the public good may require."[14] The one prize the legislature took out of its own hands and left to the voters was the location of the state capital. Other state institutions, however, were up for grabs within the legislature, and politicians wasted little time tumbling over each other trying to secure one or another of these lucrative plums for their own districts. Twin Bridges demanded the state normal school; Missoula wanted a state university; Bozeman lobbied for the agricultural college; White Sulphur Springs pushed for the asylum. Meanwhile, Great Falls promoter Paris Gibson complicated matters by demanding consolidation of university and college in one institution located in his city. Gibson's proposal—endorsed by leading educators around the nation and by the state teachers' association—sent representatives from other towns into orbit. They argued that Gibson was conspiring with Helena's capital lobby to divide the locus of state power between the two cities and managed to defeat the proposal. Ultimately, the second legislature failed to agree on the location of any of the state institutions, but it drew the battle lines for the next session, which met in January 1893.[15]

In the interim, voters winnowed the contenders for the capital to two sites—Helena and Anaconda. To make the final decision on the issue, another election was scheduled for 1894. Communities that had lost their bids for the capital site, including Boulder, Bozeman, Butte, Deer Lodge, and Great Falls, renewed their lobbying for the remaining institutions and found themselves competing with rivals from Billings and Miles City as well. Pressure on the legislature to make a decision was acute. Under the terms of the Second

Morrill Act, the state was already losing $30,000 per year in federal funds because of its failure to create a land grant college. Prodded by raw economics, the "tournament of cities"[16] began anew under the canopy of the big sky.

Under these circumstances, Great Falls developer Paris Gibson renewed his proposal for consolidation, arguing that separate colleges would be too costly and reduce the quality of education. As historian William Lang relates, to sweeten the proposal, Gibson added that Great Falls would set aside 320 acres of land and provide a $100,000 endowment for the college cum university. His offer met a flood of opposition from representatives of communities that, since the previous session, had built a powerful coalition to oppose the consolidation plan. Opponents pointed to the size of the state and the need for students to have easy access to educational institutions from their farms; they noted that in most states the educational units were divided; and they argued that higher education in Montana would require the support of a coalition of representatives with a vested interest in supporting institutions in their home counties. Equally important, opponents of consolidation gained support of the Montana Farmers' Alliance, thus joining anti-urban sentiments and eastern Montanans' unease with concentrations of political power in the western half of the state to the crusade against consolidation.[17]

Faced with defeat, Gibson denounced the forces arrayed against him: "I believe we are about to commit, I might say, a great crime." Advocates of separate institutions, he declared, "will nail up the coffin in which will be buried the educational institutions of Montana." Then, in a concluding rhetorical flourish that was remarkably prescient, Gibson berated his colleagues: "I know everything is working beautifully and harmoniously now among these gentlemen who want to divide these institutions up. But how will it be two years from now? You will then have three separate lobbies, each working for his particular institution and against the other."[18] Gibson lost the battle, but the movement was not dead. It would lie dormant for two decades until, in a peculiar twist of fate, the winds of consolidation would begin to blow in from Missoula.

The 1893 legislature failed to resolve the political dispute over Montana's representation in the U.S. Senate, but it accomplished the dispersal of its political plums with great relish, situating the reform school in Miles City, the school for the deaf and dumb in Boulder, the school of mines in Butte, the state university in Missoula, the orphanage in Twin Bridges, the soldiers' home in Columbia Falls, the normal school in Dillon, the state prison in Deer Lodge, another penitentiary in Billings (which was never built), and the agricultural college in Bozeman.[19]

The last assignment was due in no small measure to the political acumen of Bozeman's political and civic leaders who formed a coalition of interests within a broader network of empire builders. Their success in gaining a college for their community contrasted sharply with Paris Gibson's failure. In the war of the spoils, as Lang points out, Great Falls was clearly the loser.

Bozeman's Builders

Bozeman's success in securing the agricultural college capped three decades of feverish community building by a group of individuals bent on incorporating the Gallatin Valley and southwestern Montana into the national industrial economy and the national cultural landscape.

With Civil War raging to the east, a series of gold and silver strikes in southwestern Montana sparked a rush of immigrants to the newly discovered field of dreams. Led by John Bozeman, trailblazer and pioneer real estate developer, a wagon train of immigrants descended into the Gallatin Valley in 1864 to establish a town that would service the needs of miners and immigrants en route to Pacific shores. Bozeman envisioned the community that would bear his name as one "standing right in the gate of the mountains ready to swallow up all the tenderfeet that would reach the territory from the east, with their golden fleeces to be taken care of."[20] Bozeman and his cohorts proceeded to encourage the development of homesteads, flour mills, and mercantile establishments on land that had historically been the shared hunting grounds of the Crow, Blackfeet, and Shoshones. Three years later, while developing a ferry crossing over the Yellowstone River, Bozeman was murdered, allegedly by Native Americans.[21]

The assumption that Bozeman had been killed by Indians proved a pivotal development in the history of the community. With the Great Plains already erupting in open warfare as Native Americans made a last-ditch stand to halt the invasion of their territory, the U.S. army decided to construct Fort Ellis three miles to the east of Bozeman as part of its effort to subdue the Indian uprisings. Fort Ellis and the Indian wars did for Bozeman what the mining fields had only promised to do. As historian Merrill Burlingame explains: "The presence of 200-300 men and as many horses provided a market for the great variety of goods which could not well be shipped by overland train such as hay, grain, fresh meats, milk, butter, eggs, and fuel which were supplied locally with large profits."[22]

An equally pivotal event in the life of the town occurred when troops from Fort Ellis were designated to escort a Northern Pacific railway survey team along the Yellowstone River. When the troops were turned back by Indian attacks,

Bozeman merchants mounted a citizen army of their own to defeat the Indians and keep the roads to the east open to immigrant traffic. The Yellowstone Wagon Road and Prospecting Expedition of 1874 resulted in a disastrous defeat for Bozeman's vigilantes and helped to escalate conflict between whites and Indians along the frontier to such an extent that the army, under General George Armstrong Custer, was forced to intervene. Custer's subsequent defeat in 1876 in southeastern Montana stepped up the pace of the war practiced against the Native Americans and opened the upper Great Plains to the advance of the Northern Pacific Railroad. In 1883, the Northern Pacific cut through the Bridger Mountains and arrived in Bozeman, transforming a backwater outpost into an agricultural entrepôt and gateway city to Yellowstone National Park, which had been created as the nation's first national park by an act of Congress a decade before.[23]

The prime movers behind these developments were a group of fortune seekers who, like

Peter Koch, member of the college's governing board

John Bozeman, met frustration in Virginia City's mining fields but found economic paradise in the Gallatin Valley. One of these figures was Peter Koch. Born in Denmark in 1844, Koch attended the University of Copenhagen before leaving his native country in search of opportunity in the United States. He arrived in New York right at the end of the Civil War and promptly journeyed to Mississippi to live with a relative. Though he met there the woman he would eventually marry, Koch never put roots down in southern soil. Tales of mining fortunes being made in the Far West set his head spinning and he departed Mississippi for Montana. In 1870, disappointment in mining led

him to Bozeman where he gained employment first as a civilian sutler and surveyor at Fort Ellis and then as a disbursing agent in the quartermaster's office at Crow Agency. In 1873, he came to Bozeman, first finding employment in the department store operated by Lester Willson and Charles V. Rich and shortly thereafter joining Bozeman's most influential citizen, Nelson Story, in founding the Gallatin Valley Bank. From this position, Koch launched a career in banking and built a reputation as an expert financial manager—a reputation that led, in 1893, to his appointment by the governor as a member of the Local Executive Board of Education, which had oversight responsibilities for the recently created land grant college in Bozeman.[24]

Nelson Story, the man who ushered Peter Koch into Bozeman's world of power and high finance, was born in 1838 in Ohio. Unable to complete his college education for financial reasons, he taught school until he earned enough money to take him west to the Virginia City goldfields. Unlike John Bozeman and Peter Koch, Story hit pay dirt, earning some $30,000 from his mining claims. But Story was not satisfied with a modicum of wealth. As was the case with Bozeman and Koch, he set his sights on developing services for miners. With his Virginia City capital, he launched a series of mercantile ventures that by the early 1870s had put him in an excellent position to serve the needs of troops at Fort Ellis—and to defraud the Indians under their charge. According to the U.S. army, Story had established himself as the godfather of Bozeman's notorious "Indian Ring," a group of prominent citizens dedicated to building a community and their private fortunes at the expense of Native Americans.[25]

Along with other Bozeman entrepreneurs, including Charles Rich, Story had developed a lucrative contract in the early 1870s with the U.S. government to supply Crow Indians with the foodstuffs they were entitled to receive under treaty arrangements. A military officer at Fort Ellis accused Story of fraud. According to the report, Story double-sacked flour, put his brands on cattle belonging to the Crow, and stuffed barrels that supposedly contained ham with offal. In one particularly grim episode, he allegedly enlisted the help of a civilian working in the quartermaster's office at the Crow agency to unload essential foodstuffs from a supply wagon intended for the Indians and to replace them with sugar and coffee. That civilian was none other than Peter Koch. With tensions between Indians and whites already at a fever pitch, the army tried to put a stop to Story's racketeering and brought charges against him before a grand jury in Virginia City. To the amazement of government officials and the presiding judge, the jury decided not to indict Story. But the decision is rather easily explained. Story's point man, Peter Koch, evidently bribed a key government witness not to volunteer information to the grand jury; Story himself boasted of spending over $10,000 to fix the jury. Whatever its basis, the decision to exonerate Story preserved the Indian Ring's profits. Story invested heavily in ranching and real estate operations throughout the West. He bought downtown property in Los Angeles and, like Montana's notorious robber baron, William A. Clark, acquired an impressive second home for his family in southern California. In addition to developing banks, department stores, and flour mills in the Gallatin Valley, he also donated 160 acres for the establishment of the agricultural college and joined Koch on its governing board in an advisory position.[26]

No evidence has surfaced suggesting that the other driving force behind the creation of the college, Walter A. Cooper, was involved in the racketeering schemes of his fellow board members. He could afford to stand one step removed from such activity if only because he was drinking from another trough—one watered by Butte mining magnate William A. Clark. Cooper was born in New York in 1841. As a youngster, family circumstances forced him to move ever farther

Nelson Story, advisor to the college's governing board

Walter Cooper, member of the college's governing board

west until, with the nation at war, he reached Colorado, where he served in the First Colorado Regiment. There he also fell under the magnetic spell of Virginia City and its fabled Alder Gulch. Heading north in 1864, he tried his hand at mining, but like Story and Koch, soon realized that the path to riches lay in other directions. He developed a freighting operation between Fort Benton and the mines before turning to the mer-

cantile trade and settling in Bozeman in 1867. Here he rapidly became one of the town's leading developers and an influential voice in the effort to secure the Northern Pacific railroad route through the community. With the aid of money loaned by Clark, Cooper developed a logging empire in Gallatin County and rich coalfields outside of Cooke City and Red Lodge as part of his effort to convince railroad authorities that there were ample natural resources to sustain the railway line in southern Montana. In the 1880s, Cooper became involved in local and state politics and, at the time of his appointment to the Local Executive Board of Education, was one of the state's leading Democrats.[27]

Another charter member of Bozeman's inner circle was Lester S. Willson, who traced his ancestry to the fabled knights of the Round Table. Born in 1839, Willson fought in the Civil War, eventually joining Sherman's command on its march through Georgia and earning the rank of brevet general. After the war, he was appointed quartermaster general of New York before receiving a similar appointment to the territory of Montana. Here in the West, he linked his economic fortunes to Story's, joining the latter in founding the Gallatin Valley Bank. Whether he participated in the Indian Ring is unknown, but the absence of an affidavit from Willson condemning Story's activities strongly hints at the kind of silence that implies knowing consent. As a member of the Bozeman Board of Trade, along with Walter Cooper, Willson played a key role in the economic development of the town. Not surprisingly, he joined Koch, Story, and Cooper first in the fight to secure the state capital and then in the battle to win the land grant college. He too was a charter member of the college's Local Executive Board.[28]

By the mid-1880s, the centrifugal forces generated by Bozeman's self-selected economic and political elite were apparent for all with eyes to see. They had put the town on the map and chartered a course for its development that would persist well into the next century. Cast in the role as merchant princes vying for power and prestige with Butte's copper kings, they were a force to be reckoned with in Montana politics and business. When they failed to gain popular support for locating the capital in their fiefdom, they quickly adjusted their sights on the land grant college. Kings they might never be, but the status of cultural barons was within their grasp. In 1892, they picked themselves up from defeat in the capital fight, recalled their collective experience with mining, Indian wars, and railroad building, and, at the urging of their wives, determined to build a college.

Though the exact influence of Nellie Koch, Ellen Trent Story, and Emma Willson is hard to trace, the women were hardly idle while their men

Lester Willson, first president of the college's governing board

were engaged in the relentless pursuit of economic profit. They took it upon themselves to organize social clubs and church societies to clothe frontier rawness with the attributes of civilization.[29] With respect to the founding of the college, none was more influential than Emma Willson, who urged her husband forward, arguing that the college would be the center of all "civilizing" influences in the Gallatin Valley, especially of music and the fine arts, two of her most passionate interests.[30]

Having spent the better part of three decades contending with some of the most monumental forces in American history—the Civil War, the passing of the mining frontier, the Indian wars, and the industrialization of the American West—Bozeman's elite began dreaming of a college that would transform their town into "the Athens of the West."[31] The prospect of laying claim to the civilizing influence of a college might have paled in comparison with some of their other schemes, but a college promised stability—and held out the larger promise of bestowing a measure of legitimacy to their own rise to positions of influence and power.

Chapter Two
The College Takes Form, 1893-1919

Civilization has reached its highest levels and most sublime sweep in semi-arid and rather harsh climates, where there is pure air, beautiful scenery and exhillerating [sic] temperature. The dry unyielding Judean hills produced a race of men who taught religion to twenty centuries of the world's most enlightened nations. . . . As I look down the vista of the near future, I see the forces of civilization, the best in literature, art and philosophy . . . assembling along the eastern slopes of the Rocky Mountains, the great continental backbone, there to reproduce another Judea, another Scotland, another New England, all rolled into one.

James Hamilton[1]

The First Year

In February of 1893, when Bozeman's leading citizens secured Governor Rickards' signature on the bill awarding the land grant college to Bozeman, they confronted the awesome task of giving form to an idea. Deadlines imposed by federal and state laws made the magnitude of the job even greater. The Second Land Grant Act of 1890 had mandated that instruction had to begin before July 1, 1893, or the state would lose $33,000 in funds, while the state bill creating the college required that a site for the school be selected in ninety days.[2] If these concerns were not pressing enough, the national economy had stagnated. Concern turned to panic when, in a grim reminder of the industrial depression of the 1870s, the economy collapsed.[3]

In this context of government-imposed deadlines and a tumbling economy, the organization and direction of the college acquired a heightened degree of urgency. Not surprisingly, many Montanans, including many Bozeman residents, failed to understand why funds should be spent on building a college in the midst of a worsening depression.[4] When the legislature, responding to the debilitating state of the economy, refused to appropriate any state monies for operating costs and the State Board of Examiners disallowed the appropriation for buildings, it would have taken a high-stakes Virginia City gambler to wager on the college's success. But Bozeman, as we have seen, had its share of risk takers educated in the Virginia City school of venture capitalism. Shortly after signing the college bill, Governor Rickards appointed Walter Cooper, Peter Koch, and Lester S. Willson to the college's governing body, the Local Executive Board of Education. Rickards also selected Livingston banker E. H. Talcott and Manhattan (Montana) malting executive George Kinkel, Jr., to the board. These board members were to be assisted by an advisory committee, consisting of the omnipresent Nelson Story, Dawson County attorney Henry J. Haskell, and Butte educator Robert G. Young. Control of the college was vested in the Local Executive Board "subject only to the general direction and control of the State Board of Education." When the local board elected Willson as its president, Kinkel as vice president, and Koch as secretary-treasurer, the control of the college was firmly in the hands of prominent men of influence.[5]

Robert G. Young, advisor to the college's governing board

Their stature and substance notwithstanding, the local board members, along with the state advisory committee, were in a terrible bind. By law, no monies from the federal Land Grant Act could be used to purchase land for college buildings or to construct the buildings. And the failure of the state government to allot funds appropriated to the college by the legislature left local board members with few options. Furthermore, they had to select a site for the college quickly or lose a significant amount of federal money. The local board agreed to consider three prospective locations: a section of land set aside for schools north of town near Belgrade, the military station at Fort Ellis that some board members felt the federal government would be willing to donate for purposes of a university, and forty acres just south of town that had been set aside as a possible site for the state capitol. All of these locations presented problems. The site near Belgrade was simply too far out of town. Fort Ellis seemed more promising, but there was no guarantee that the

George Kinkel, Jr., member of the college's governing board

Luther Foster, acting president of the college, 1893

military could turn over the post in time to meet the deadline. And the forty-acre site south of town was small, with the added disadvantage of being adjacent to the 160-acre county poor farm. This latter site, however, had two advantages. Bozeman had constructed a boulevard (now 8th Avenue) to the proposed capitol site as part of the effort to attract the seat of state government to the community. And the poor farm rested on land that several board members regarded as prime property for an agricultural experiment station. Furthermore, there was additional land available around the site that could be purchased for possible future expansion of the college. At the urging of Bozeman's most prominent citizens, the county commission agreed to make county poor-farm lands available for the college and to launch a campaign to raise funds to buy the original forty-acre site from the city. The ailing economy—and some profound doubts among Bozeman residents about the value of the college—dampened any enthusiastic response to the appeal for funds. With time running out, Nelson Story, perhaps recalling his own thwarted ambitions to finish his education in Ohio, bought the remaining lands for about $1500, no small sum in the depression year of 1893, and donated them to the college.[6]

While they were trying to secure land for the erection of college buildings, the local board had to figure out a way to meet the other land grant deadline—commencing formal instruction before July 1. Since there was no way to construct buildings on "the hill" south of town in time to comply with the terms of the Land Grant Act,

Bozeman Academy building, the college's first home

board members had to come up with an alternative. Obviously, the only buildings available for classes were located downtown. Fortunately, a downtown roller-skating rink had recently been converted into a private school, the Bozeman Academy. More fortunate still, two of the academy's directors were Koch and Willson. And the building's owner was none other than Story. After Koch and Willson conferred with Story, the latter agreed to allow the first college

Benjamin Maiden, member of the first faculty

classes to meet in his building without paying rent.[7]

With all of these arrangements in place by late March 1893, the local board announced that the agricultural college would open on April 17 for a ten-week session and that Luther Foster, a Union veteran, graduate of the first class of the Iowa State College of Agriculture, and professor at the South Dakota Agricultural College, would serve as acting president. The board also announced that Foster would be aided by three faculty: S. M. Emery, a former regent of the University of Minnesota turned nursery salesman and good friend of Walter Cooper; Homer G. Phelps, a private business school entrepreneur and instructor; and Benjamin F. Maiden, an instructor at the Bozeman Academy. Eight students, already attending the academy, were coerced into enrolling in the college's first courses. One of the students recalled how he and his peers suddenly found themselves attending college instead of prep school. Probably reflecting wider community feeling, the student regarded the upstart college as "an annex to a barber college" and was sorely vexed at being forced to switch loyalties from the Bozeman Academy to the recently created college. Students, however, were supposed to be seen and not heard. As far as the federal government was concerned, the local board had students attending classes at the college and that was sufficient to qualify for funding. The Agricultural College of the State of Montana had begun.[8]

So had the depression. As conditions worsened, as the money supply shrank, the future appeared grim. In July, Koch, who quickly established himself as the most powerful individual on

Frank W. Traphagen, member of the first faculty

the Local Executive Board, was forced to close the doors of his bank because so much money was being withdrawn.[9]

Yet, as serious as the depression was becoming, the cascading economic misfortunes of the summer held hidden benefits for the fledgling college. The source of those benefits lay in the college-building boom that swept the country in the years following the Civil War. In the late nineteenth century, college building became one of the most popular national pastimes. Well over 100 new colleges were founded and ten state-supported colleges were established in the last two decades of the century. In Montana several colleges antedated the founding of the agricultural college. As early as 1878, prominent citizens of Deer Lodge raised funds to organize the Montana Collegiate Institute. In the 1880s, the Presbyterian Church took control of the institute and renamed it the College of Montana. With funds from copper king W. A. Clark, who was interested in developing a technical training school for his mining operations, the College of Montana built an international faculty that, for a short time, included on its staff Irving Babbitt, in later years a professor at Harvard, and a leading conservative

What's in a Name?

Over the course of its hundred-year history, Montana State University has had several names, most of them being variations of one another. The February 16, 1893, piece of legislation that established the state's university system referred to the school as The Agricultural College of the State of Montana. And the law that established the chancellorship of the university system on March 14, 1913, referred to the Bozeman school as Montana State College of Agriculture and Mechanic Arts. However, neither of these pieces of legislation was designed to name the school; the legislators were simply applying the title most commonly used at the time.

The Local Executive Board itself once promulgated rules for the "Agricultural College and Experiment Station of the State of Montana," probably the first and only use of that particular title. The first consistently used formal name for the institution was Montana College of Agriculture and Mechanic Arts, which appeared in course catalogs from 1893 to 1896 and was used by the college newspaper from 1895 through 1901. In 1897, course catalogs began using "Montana State College of Agriculture and Mechanic Arts," while agricultural extension bulletins variously referred to the school as the College of Agriculture of Montana, the Montana College of Agriculture, the Agricultural College of Montana, and Montana Agricultural College. This last name, abbreviated MAC, was probably the name most familiar to Montanans in the first two decades of the twentieth century.

Then, in 1921, the college catalog first used the name of Montana State College, the name the then-president, Alfred Atkinson, preferred. Gradually that title became more and more widely used, though the masthead of the *Exponent* continued to use "Montana State College of Agriculture and Mechanic Arts" and even at times "Montana State College of the University of Montana." On July 1, 1965, with its elevation in status, the school was finally and officially designated Montana State University by act of the thirty-ninth legislative assembly of the state of Montana.[1]

1.   Nathan Bender to Robert Rydell, 19 November 1991.

cultural critic. The school's economic underpinnings appeared impressive (there were even reports that railroad magnate James J. Hill was preparing to make a large monetary contribution to the college), but, in fact, the College of Montana was always on shaky financial grounds. When the depression hit, the college received a mortal blow from which it never recovered. As funds dried up, nervous faculty members began looking elsewhere for employment. The announcement of a new state-supported college across the mountains to the east seemed like a godsend.[10]

Three College of Montana faculty members jumped ship immediately. Augustus M. Ryon, professor of mineralogy and holder of a Ph.D. from the Columbia College of Mines, accepted the Local Executive Board's offer to replace Luther Foster as president of the agricultural college. Frank W. Traphagen, another Ph.D.-holder from Columbia, agreed to assume responsibilities for teaching chemistry and natural science courses. And music teacher Kate M. Calvin agreed, perhaps at the urging of Emma Willson, to take on that post at the college in Bozeman.[11]

The task of finding faculty for the new college was only one of many confronting local board members in the middle months of 1893. Equally pressing was the job of crafting a curriculum—the intellectual scaffolding—for the college. What exactly should the college be teaching? What role should it play in Montana? These questions took form in the context of sweeping changes occurring in higher education in America. Church-sponsored colleges, like the College of Montana in Deer Lodge and the smaller Montana University, founded in 1890 and located just north of Helena, were already losing their positions of prominence. Beginning in 1876, with the founding of the Johns Hopkins University, the development of higher education in the United States began veering in the direction of specialization and research, with a growing emphasis on postgraduate instruction. Put simply, the revolution in the sciences, associated primarily with Charles Darwin, contributed to an explosion of knowledge, or, to put it more accurately, to an explosion of awareness that knowledge was increasing so rapidly and becoming so complex that no one individual could master it all. This development cut at a right angle to the role of the traditional sectarian and liberal arts college where knowledge—indeed, truth itself—was presumed to be fixed and where faculty took it upon themselves to teach a variety of subjects, having as their goal the imparting of permanent moral truths. With the advent of graduate study in the United States, generalists rapidly gave way to specialists, and research, or the generation of new knowledge, was perceived as fully equal, if not indispensable, to teaching.[12] At the undergraduate level,

Augustus M. Ryon, first president of the college, 1893-1894

sweeping changes were also occurring. As historians John S. Brubacher and Willis Rudy explain, between 1890 and 1920 "the old disciplinary theory of education was disintegrating."[13] At the urging of Charles W. Eliot, president of Harvard, the classical curriculum was giving way to a curriculum that included a large number of electives, organized, at least in theory, as satellite courses in support of a specialized major field of emphasis chosen by the student.[14]

Layered into these changes was another shift associated with the development of land grant colleges and technical institutes. As already noted, the land grant colleges took form in response to the pressures of America's rapid industrialization in the nineteenth century. Likewise, a series of technical institutes, including the Massachusetts Institute of Technology (1864) and the Stevens Institute of Technology (1885), were founded to meet the growing technical requirements of industry. They demanded research, required knowledge of advanced mathematics, and demanded training in theoretical sciences. Paralleling the development of these "school"-oriented institutes was the growth of "shop"-oriented, polytechnical institutions like Worcester Free Institute and Rose Polytechnic Institute that emphasized applied science and concentrated on training skilled machinists, not research-minded engineers.[15]

For the men and women involved in securing the agricultural college for Bozeman, these developments—the rise of research universities, curricular reform, and the debate over the relative merits of "shop" and "school" cultures—seemed as far away as Baltimore, Chicago, and Boston. To the extent they thought about these issues, Bozeman's college promoters tried to push them aside. They envisioned an institution that would combine the traditional denominational college's function of teaching permanent moral truths with the land grant college's emphasis on sound agricultural practice and training in a variety of trades.[16]

This vision, never terribly sharp before the summer of 1893, underwent important modifications with the arrival of the faculty from Deer Lodge, who were trained at eastern universities involved in the debate over the future direction of higher education. The pivotal figure in the trio of Ryon, Traphagen, and Calvin was President-elect Ryon. Only 31 years old, this New York City native had already established himself as the leading authority on mining engineering in Montana. He had arrived in the state with the specific understanding that he was to organize a college of engineering at Deer Lodge to train young men for employment in W. A. Clark's operations. When the depression hit, Ryon left the College of Montana, where he had implemented the first professional engineering curriculum in the state, to pursue his ambitions in Bozeman. During the

spring and summer of 1893, he presented his convictions about the function of a land grant college to the Local Executive Board. His ideas differed from those of the board in important ways. Where the board members had been content with giving the college an agricultural focus, Ryon overwhelmed them with numbers showing that few students in agricultural curricula remained in farming after graduation. Where board members nurtured a view of the mechanical arts that conjured up images of trades, Ryon convinced them to be more modern in their thinking.[17]

For Ryon, a professional engineer, the outmoded emphasis on the "mechanical arts," if included at all in the college, had to be subordinated to the demands of professional engineering. He persuaded the Local Executive Board that everyone's interests would best be served by making engineering conterminous with agriculture in the college curriculum. The board not only agreed with Ryon's argument, it appointed him to a committee composed of former college president Foster and English instructor Maiden and gave the committee two days to design the first curriculum for the college.[18]

That curriculum, designed in haste but not without thought, framed the early intellectual underpinning of the college. Courses (in this context, a four-year program of study) took form in three general areas: agriculture, applied science, and domestic economy. The local board, reflecting Koch's strong conviction that Montana students were ill-prepared for college (in 1890 there were only a dozen high schools in the state), also insisted on including a preparatory department to bring prospective students up to speed in the sciences, liberal arts, and mathematics.[19]

There was more to this curriculum, however, than met the eye. The first catalog explained the overall philosophy that shaped the curriculum:

> These courses have been carefully arranged with the view of furnishing, so far as is possible, such instruction as will be most beneficial to Montana students and to Montana interests in general, and it is believed that in one or the other of these courses the majority of the young men and the young women of the State will find a line of work suited to their tastes and abilities.[20]

But how was it determined what courses would be "most beneficial to Montana students and to Montana interests in general"? What were "Montana interests in general"? Why, in the middle of the worst depression of the century, would anyone think that the majority of the state's young people would, as a result of their education at a college that had been in existence for less than six months, "find a line of work suited to their tastes and abilities"? The first college catalog did not answer these questions so much as reflect the heady conviction of the local board and early faculty that they could shape the future course of the state's development.

What would the future look like? As the catalog made clear, college founders expected agriculture to play a dominant role in the state's future. But this was 1893. The agricultural sector of the economy was depressed, and pundits blamed farmers for the overproduction that had contributed to economic collapse. To steady the course of agriculture, the college promised training that would be thoroughly scientific. Throughout their four years, students would be required to take courses in the natural and physical sciences. A course in bookkeeping would also be required, evidently to prepare students for surviving the vagaries of industrial capitalism. And, reflecting the importance affixed to farmers as the backbone of American civilization, students would be required to take courses in the "history of civilization" and constitutional law as well as a capstone course in ethics in their senior year.[21]

If there was nothing surprising about the prominence given agriculture in the curriculum, the applied science course was full of surprises. The older association of the mechanical arts with trades evaporated. As Ryon envisioned the state's future needs and the college's role in meeting those needs, training in engineering was the key to success. And the course of study he designed was aimed at the training of professional engineers, not of shop workers. Prospective engineers in their first year would be required to take courses in mathematics, natural sciences, English, and bookkeeping—the latter requirement reflecting the growing conviction among engineers that members of their profession should be trained in sound business practices. When the local board hired R. E. Chandler from the Stevens Institute of Technology to teach mechanical engineering and mathematics, it was even more apparent that Ryon wanted to align the future of the state with the future of engineering.[22]

Perhaps the strength of Ryon's conviction worried the merchants on the Local Executive Board. At a time when few colleges anywhere included training in business practices, the first college catalog announced that a division of business would be included in the preparatory department that would educate Montana's young people in "Book-keeping, Commercial Arithmetic, Commercial Correspondence, Penmanship, Commercial Law, Business Ethics, etc."[23]

In addition to incorporating scientifically trained farmers, engineers, and businessmen into their vision of Montana's future, curriculum designers gave a prominent place to homemaking under the heading "domestic economy." Like engineering and business, domestic economy was a thoroughly modern and recent curricular inno-

vation in higher education. It reflected the growing need of colleges to satisfy the demands of women for a college education while still satisfying the dictum of a patriarchal society that a woman's primary place was in the home. Since Montana's legislature, bowing to the demands of the Second Land Grant Act, had removed gender and racial barriers to admission to the agricultural college, the local board, anticipating a sizable enrollment of young women, made the domestic economy program one of the original substructures of the college. In so doing, they established an important niche for women in the future development of the state: women would become professional household managers who would be guardians of "the laws of life and health." That the men on the board felt uncomfortable with the prospect of educating women was reflected in their failure to select a faculty member to teach courses in domestic economy until 1896, some three years after the department was created.[24]

The local board and its first faculty awaited the opening of the fall term with trepidation. The first catalog listed several faculty positions as "to be supplied in the near future" and the campus boasted only one partially constructed building, the agricultural experiment building. Despite the college's scant physical and intellectual resources, 139 students seized the opportunity to attend classes in the fall of 1893.[25]

There were deep sighs of relief heard in Bozeman's stately homes. But the sense of relief was tempered by the ongoing reality of the depression and the emerging contest of wills between Peter Koch and A. M. Ryon. The depression, which would cast its shadows over the middle third of the decade, cut deeply into the lives of Montanans and further decreased the already low enthusiasm of state legislators for spending money on the agricultural college. In the absence of state monies, the local board turned to student fees to keep the college afloat.[26]

In addition to these festering economic hardships, the college suffered from growing disagreements between its ambitious young president and its equally strong-willed bursar. The roots of the conflict between Ryon and Koch are not hard to pinpoint. Temperamentally, each man had the flexibility of a hungry badger. Intellectually, each gravitated toward a different constellation of ideas about the future of the college. Ryon, through the prism of his experience at Columbia, saw the college as a training ground for expert engineers, well versed in theoretical sciences. Koch, on the other hand, drew on his experience in Denmark with a system of education that, as Merrill Burlingame explains, "held that through education a greater loyalty to the homeland could be fostered, and, more important, the youth could be educated in a scholarly and practical manner which would enable them to cope against any aggressor."[27] In retrospect, the conflict that developed between the two men seems inevitable. Shortly after Ryon accepted the position of president, he clashed with Koch over the preparatory department. Given the woeful state of secondary education in the state and his own belief that education and patriotism went hand in hand, Koch insisted on a preparatory department for underprepared students. When asked by one faculty member if the ratio of seven subfreshman to one college student would change, Koch replied, "Not in your lifetime."[28]

James Reid, president of the college, 1894-1904

Ryon, on the other hand, feared that the preparatory department would drain resources from the college and worried that Koch's interest in utilitarian education would impede the theoretical studies necessary for engineering. Before the end of the 1893-1894 term, the simmering disagreement between Ryon and Koch led the former to tender his resignation as president. Within two years he would resign his professorship in another, even more bitter, conflict with the local board.[29]

"Culture and Skill"

Koch's brief and unpleasant encounter with Ryon led him to seek a successor cut of different cloth. When Ryon resigned, the local board, having already raided the College of Montana for

faculty, set its sights on that school's president, James R. Reid. In 1894, Reid became the president of the agricultural college and for the next ten years provided much-needed stability while molding the institution's image around his own conception of higher education as a finely honed balance between culture and skill.

Unlike Ryon, Reid's background was thoroughly religious. Born in 1850 in Reid's Mill, Ontario, to parents who had emigrated from northern Ireland to Canada in the 1820s, Reid was raised in a strict Presbyterian household along with ten siblings. After his father's death, Reid determined to enter the ministry. He attended the Collegiate Institute in Hamilton, the University of Toronto, and McGill University before entering Union Theological Seminary in New York City and, later, Presbyterian College of Montreal. His first ministry was in Bay City, Michigan, where he simultaneously served as head of the local high school. In 1890, at the age of 40, the unmarried minister accepted a new position in Deer Lodge, Montana, as both minister of the Presbyterian church and president of the Presbyterian-controlled College of Montana. For the next four years, Reid did his best to put the College of Montana on sound footing. His impressive administrative efforts earned him selection to the State Board of Education—a position that introduced him to most of the college builders in Bozeman. In 1894, Bozeman's cultural barons persuaded Reid to resign his position at the College of Montana and to accept the handsome—by contemporary standards—annual salary of $3000 to succeed Ryon as president of the Agricultural College of the State of Montana.[30]

Reid was well suited to the needs of the college board. Like its members, he had his feet firmly planted in the shifting sands of a Victorian world caught between the seeming fixity of the past and uncertainty of the future. He clung to his religious values and, like many American intellectuals, sought to reconcile them with the increasingly scientific temperament of the times. A Republican in politics and a cultural conservative, Reid was anything but a neanderthal. He committed himself to reconciling religion and science in the belief that the result would assure continuing national material and moral progress. Comfortable with being described as a "progressive," he felt at ease in the company of local business leaders who paid hard cash to insert their autobiographies in a spacious volume called *Progressive Men of Montana*.[31]

Reid articulated his ideas about higher education in an article that appeared in the first issue of *The College Exponent*, the college newspaper, under the title "Education! What Is It?" He carved his answer to that question out of an ideology that historian David Hollinger has aptly termed "the moral efficacy of scientific practice."[32] At the

Early campus panorama

and observation came greater knowledge of nature. And, as Reid emphasized, a "correct and thorough acquaintance with nature and its laws must have a tendency to elevate character." Consequently, he assured his readers, the college "teacher of today who has no interest in the development of moral character is not in sympathy with the prevailing trend in education." At the same time that higher education had to be scientific and moral, it had to be practical: "A man may have a mind stored with knowledge, but we do not consider him educated unless he is at the same time gifted with the practical faculty of applying means to the end he desires to attain, and to resort to means or to seek ends that are selfish, dishonorable or base is to prove that he is not educated in any true sense."[33] Reid's philosophy of education was tailor-made to suit the specifications of the local board. By establishing the moral authority of the college, Reid would also shore up the board's own moral standing in the community. Wedding science to morality, in other words, was more than a formula for success; it served as a formula for stability and for lending legitimacy to the authority of Bozeman's aspiring culture barons.

outset of his article, Reid made clear that education—inseparable from mental discipline—assisted the "development of the ethical and spiritual faculties, and the formation of habits of right thinking and doing." The problem with higher education in the United States, he claimed, was not its emphasis on mental discipline, but a fundamental misunderstanding of what mental discipline required. The problem, he insisted, was that educators had insisted on "the development of the memory, while ignoring the growth of the faculties of research and observation." These faculties were important to nurture because with research

While Reid set to work providing the intellectual mortar for the growing college, the buildings themselves slowly took form. The first official building, the brick-veneered agricultural experiment station building, was completed in 1894 at a cost of $4000 (provided by the Hatch Act) and

Early Campus Buildings

The agricultural experiment station was, appropriately enough, the first building to be constructed on the campus. Completed in the summer of 1894, at a cost of $4000, it provided living

Agricultural Experiment Station Building (Taylor Hall)

quarters for S. M. Emery, the first station director, as well as offices, machine shops, and veterinary classrooms. After the turn of the century it became the "biology building," housing the zoology-entomology department with its labs, herbarium, insectary, and greenhouse. In 1923 when the biological sciences moved to Lewis Hall, the newly remodeled building was given to the Cooperative Extension Service. Sixty years later, almost ninety years after its construction, the extension building was officially dedicated in honor of J. C. Taylor, the county extension agent who had led the Montana Extension Service through the droughts, depressions, and labor shortages of the 1920s, 1930s, and 1940s.[1]

In 1897, the drill hall, a one-story frame structure, 60 by 100 feet in dimensions, was erected just to the southeast of the agricultural experiment building. Basically just four walls and a roof (in the beginning it lacked even a floor), it was intended to provide shelter in inclement weather for military drill, but it was soon pressed into use as a gymnasium and for campus social activities as well.[2]

Main (Montana) Hall

In 1898, more than four years after the agricultural experiment station building was completed, and fifteen months after the ceremonies that marked the laying of its cornerstone, Main Hall was opened. During the next nine months, students and faculty helped to move classroom and office equipment from the college's temporary downtown quarters to the imposing structure. In 1914, the building was renamed Montana Hall and today serves as the administrative center of the university.[3]

Just west of Main Hall stood the chemistry and physics building. Built the same year that Main Hall

opened, this structure was crowned with twin observation towers that gave the first home of the sciences on campus the look of a medieval castle. An explosion in a lab in October 1916 sparked a fire that destroyed the building and threatened Montana Hall. Students and faculty were able to rescue the chemistry library, the chemicals, the mineralogical collection, and most of the meteorological data. The chemical and physical sciences were studied under make-shift conditions at Gallatin County High School until a modern, fireproof structure was completed in 1919. In 1968, the building was renamed for F. W. Traphagen, the school's first chemistry instructor.[4]

Hamilton Hall, dedicated in 1910 and named by the faculty to honor Emma Hamilton, the late wife of President James Hamilton, served as the first and only student residence on campus for many years. As "a home away from home," the residence hall consisted of a music room, library, guest room, "fudge kitchen," and laundry rooms as well as two floors of dorm rooms. The administration expected all female students from outside the Bozeman area to room in Hamilton Hall, where they were supervised by the dean of women, who resided there herself. Later, as other living arrangements opened to women students, males were also housed in Hamilton. In 1965,

Chemistry and Physics building aflame, October 20, 1916

Hamilton Hall, women's residence

the building was fully converted to office spaces.[5]

Built between 1908 and 1912 at a cost of $80,000, the building variously called Morrill Hall (after the Morrill Act that established land grant colleges) and the "ag building" answered the growing need for instructional, laboratory, and office space on campus. The three-story building contrasted starkly with other campus buildings, boasting a light-colored rather than a brick exterior. In September 1968 the ag building was formally renamed Frederic Bertil Linfield Hall in honor of the early director of the experiment station and dean of the College of Agriculture.[6]

1. "Dedication, J. C. Taylor Hall, Montana State University, 22 September 1983," f. A6.1.Taylor, MSUA; "Extension Building 1896-," in Montana State University Quick Facts, MSUSC; "Montana State University and How It Was Built," Louis True Papers, Acc. 88-032, Box 1, f. "M.S.U. 75th Anniversary Slide Program," MSUA; "The A. M. Ryon Engineering Laboratories," f. FA6.1.Ryon Laboratories, MSUA; *Montana State College of Agriculture and Mechanic Arts Fifth Annual Catalogue, 1897-1898,* 13-14; *Tenth Annual Catalogue,* 1901-1902, 14; *Fourteenth Annual Catalogue, 1906-1907,* 10,11; *Fifteenth Annual Catalogue, 1907-1908,* 10, 11.

2. *Montana State College of Agriculture and Mechanic Arts Fifth Annual Catalogue, 1897-1898,* 13; *Montana Collegian,* Spring 1966, 2.

3. *Weekly Exponent,* 3 February 1931; "Montana State University and How It Was Built," 88-032/1, f. "MSU 75th Anniversary Slide Program," MSUA; *State College of Agriculture and Mechanic Arts Fifth Annual Catalogue, 1897-1898,* 11-12.

4. *State College of Agriculture and Mechanic Arts Fifth Annual Catalogue, 1897-1898,* 5; *Exponent,* October 1897, May 1898, 15 September 1911, 27 October 1916, 10 November 1916, 17 November 1916, 24 November 1916, 13 April 1917, 7 June 1918, 16 January 1920.

5. "Hamilton Hall, Montana State College," f. A6.1.Quad, MSUA; "MSU Residence Hall History: Housing and Feeding Students Major Function," *Montana Collegian,* 41:3 (Autumn 1965), 4; *Montana State College of Agriculture and Mechanic Arts Seventeenth Annual Catalog, 1909-1910,* 12; *Eighteenth Annual Catalogue, 1910-1911,* 9; *Nineteenth Annual Catalogue, 1911-1912,* 12.

6. *Fourteenth Annual Catalogue Montana State College of Acrigulture and Mechanic Arts, 1906-1907,* 12; "Agricultural Building Dedication," in Montana State University Quick Facts, MSUSC; "Some Other Major Buildings at M.S.C.," *Montana Collegian,* 2:7 (August 1926), 3.

Agriculture building (Linfield Hall)

housed a limited number of agriculture and engineering classrooms as well as faculty offices. In the continuing absence of state construction funds, however, the bulk of the classes continued to be held a mile downtown in the Bozeman Academy and the Ferris Block, with the president's office located in the newly constructed high school building. To correct this situation, the State Board of Education recommended that the legislature issue bonds on the security of 50,000 acres provided by the land grant acts. In 1895, the legislature agreed to issue $100,000 in bonds to finance the construction of a main building and a heating plant as well as buildings for laboratories, veterinary science, and military drill.[34] Though the state attorney general would ultimately declare the issuance of these bonds null and void, thereby forcing the state to issue its own bonds in 1905, the creative use of federal land grants in 1895 permitted the construction of college buildings that otherwise would not have been built until the turn of the century when the state's economic fortunes improved. The building program provided a tremendous lift to local spirits; it also provided an opportunity for Reid to become a master builder in his own right.[35]

The official rebirth of the college came on October 21, 1896, with the laying of the cornerstone for the Main Building (renamed Montana Hall in 1914). On that drizzly afternoon, well over 100 college students joined an equal number of local Masons in a grand procession from downtown to the campus grounds. Led by the "Free Silver Band," the parade made its way through a community muddied by rains and debate over whether silver should replace gold as the standard against which national currency was measured. The noisy procession came to rest around the site selected for a building that would dominate the campus from that day to the present.[36]

Speech making was the order of the day and orations continued despite a torrential downpour that sent most of the audience running for shelter. Governor J. E. Rickards delivered the keynote address. Entitled "The Relation of Education to Good Government," the governor's message was not lost on anyone familiar with the circuslike atmosphere of state politics. "Under such conditions," Rickards intoned,

> a day like this becomes an event in the history of the state. It means the creation of a permanent home for a factory of ideas, whose handiwork will leave its impress upon generations yet to come.... It places well disciplined leaders at the head of an orderly rank and file. It fights the battles of good government with the weapons of equity and justice, and the wrongs are righted in the forum of legislation instead of upon the bloody fields of war.

Rickards' image of the college as a "factory of ideas" that would discipline society was grafted onto a set of historical images articulated by State Superintendent Eugene A. Steere. Steere waxed eloquent. "This is a progressive age," he said, one that flowed naturally from heroic antecedents: "Columbus opened the way for a new continent, and Jefferson, wishing to `open up overland commercial relations with China and India,' sent out Lewis and Clarke [sic], who blazed a highway through this state and through this valley." Precisely because of its heroic lineage, the college had special responsibilities. "Mr. Chairman," Steere concluded,

> the teachings of this institution will be carefully guarded, and we trust the results will be found in the highest types of manhood and womanhood in those who go forth from this college into the marts of trade. May the flag of this glorious Union ever float over the aspirations, the inspirations and the ennobling thoughts engendered here.... Then, sir, we can rest assured that our homes will be benefited, this institution of learning revered, our state honored, and humanity blessed.

Eugene A. Steere, state superintendent of schools, 1896

The ceremonies concluded with the laying of the cornerstone on top of a time capsule—a box marked with the Masonic emblems of the compass and square that contained newspapers, copies of the *Exponent*, college catalogs, blueprints for buildings, proceedings of Masonic lodges, lists of Masonic members, a silver dollar, and various private cards.[37]

Through their words and mementos, state and community leaders placed an awesome responsibility on the college. They expected it to become a factory of learning, a source of social order, a custodian of Victorian cultural values, and, in Steere's carefully chosen words, a bridge

Mountains, and the whole of the beautiful Gallatin Valley. All the laboratories and offices are furnished with gas, and the whole building will be lighted with electricity from our experimental plant in the basement.[39]

Main (Montana) Hall

between the "pilgrim from the East and the '49'er from the West."[38]

The first visible sign that the college would reflect the admonitions of state political authorities was in the design of the building that rose on the site dedicated that rainy October day. When it was finally completed in May 1898, Main Hall, designed by architects John Gustave Link and Charles S. Haire, loomed large as jubilant testimony to the ability of the college to reconcile functions of workshop and secular cathedral. As the college catalog described it,

It is three stories. It has a large, well lighted basement which furnishes quarters for the Mechanical Laboratory, Domestic Science Department and two class rooms. The first floor contains the Library, four offices, and three large class rooms. The north half of the second floor is devoted to the Art Department, the arrangement being such that the three large rooms can be thrown together, by sliding doors, for exhibition purposes. The south half of this floor is fitted up entirely for the use of the Business Department, the arrangement being that of the best Business Colleges. The third floor contains the large Assembly Room, a draughting room, the Biological Lecture room, and five laboratory and music rooms. The building . . . commands a magnificent view of the Bridger and Gallatin

With its basement power plant humming, Main Hall—on one level, a veritable machine in the garden—sounded indeed like a factory of ideas. Reid, together with Koch, had little doubt that it could be made to function like one.

When Reid assumed the position of president, he immediately joined Koch's corner in the fight over the preparatory department and agreed to turn it into a three-year program of remedial education that could prepare students for college as well as provide the student not bound for college "the opportunity to obtain a sufficient knowledge of English for the ordinary work of life, and such an acquaintance with the sciences [that would] develop within him the faculty of observation and bring him more closely into touch with nature."[40] As Reid saw it, the college existed, at least in part, "to take in the young people of the rural, ungraded schools and give them something beyond that point because they were often over-age and even unwelcome in a few towns or county high schools of the state."[41] As if to underscore his commitment to giving the college a less theoretical focus than it had under Ryon's direction, Reid determined to make a fundamental change in the original curriculum and splintered the applied science course into separate courses in general science, chemistry, and mechanical engineering. Not all faculty were sanguine over these developments. The institution's two former presidents, Luther Foster and A. M. Ryon, had returned to teaching in agriculture and engineering, respectively. Ryon was particularly vociferous in objecting to the turn away from applied sciences as an umbrella for mining engineering and Foster apparently was less than pleased with plans to introduce a short course—two five-month terms—in agriculture. Foster and Ryon were joined in their dissatisfaction by English instructor Benjamin Maiden, who disapproved of changes in the preparatory department.[42]

Amidst growing animosity between the different factions, the local board, backed by the State Board of Education, determined to give "a lesson to all" and demanded resignations from the entire faculty. Only those of Ryon, Foster, and Maiden were accepted. When the three appealed their case to the Local Executive Board, they received a hearing that confirmed the absolute authority of the board over the college. "We have received your letter referring to the matter of your resignation," the board told the appellants. "We have made and make no charges against you. We have simply after mature deliberation come to the conclusion that it would best serve the interests of the institution that your resignation should be accepted. We have therefore no explanation or apology to offer." The college, in other words, had become a fiefdom of local culture barons and faculty had been put on notice that the bounds of inquiry and dissent did not extend to the management of the college. As Koch put it: "There seems to be a disposition in some quarters to imagine that an appointment to this College carries a life position to be forfeited only by the preferment of formal charges, a regular trial, the right of appeal, etc." Nothing, in Koch's eyes, could have been further from the truth. In one stunning act of arrogance, Koch, backed by the State Board of Education, asserted his control over the college and set a horrible precedent for the university system as a whole. With the Ryon case, as one historian has noted, "the State Board of Education was embarking on a forty-five year spree of star chamber proceedings, book-burning, suppression of academic freedom, and the firing, without hearings, of both professors and presidents."[43]

As far as Reid was concerned, the termination of dissident faculty had been a positive step and opened the way for him to fashion the college in accordance with his vision of higher education—a vision that dovetailed nicely with that of state and local authorities. Reid had no difficulty persuading the board to give the sciences greater prominence in the curriculum than they had under Ryon and Foster. And he met with agreement in trying to bolster the practical side of the students' education as well as their powers of observation by requiring additional laboratory work. Indeed, within two years of Reid's appointment, students were expected to take the bulk of their "course"-related classes in the morning and devote the better part of their afternoons to sharpening "faculties of observation" in drawing, laboratory experiments, and shop work. Since, in Reid's eyes, education was inseparable from instruction in moral and cultural values, he also instituted a collegewide assembly. At 9 a.m. sharp every Monday morning, students and faculty gathered in Main Hall's assembly room for lectures on ethics, devotional exercises, and musical performances. Like other college presidents of his day, Reid also shouldered teaching responsibilities in "mental and moral sciences" as well as in political science and astronomy. He took it upon himself, in short, to reconcile the demands of state political leaders for a factory of ideas with his own commitment to adapting the ideals of liberal culture to the modern age. As he explained his efforts to the Local Executive Board:

> Recognizing that a truly scientific and practical education must be based upon a knowledge of scientific facts more or less thoroughly combined with a culture more or less liberal, your faculty has been trying to preserve the golden mean, avoiding on the one side the mistakes of those who ignore the practical or manual training feature; and on the other, the equally fatal error of making instruction chiefly technical.[44]

As if to underscore his commitment to maintaining this balancing act, Reid coined an unofficial motto for the college—"Culture and Skill."[45]

For the remainder of his term as president, Reid struggled to maintain this golden mean. The problem area of the college was agriculture. Given the location of the college in a valley described by some as "the Egypt of America,"[46] and the interest of the state in promoting its agricultural development, it came as a surprise that so few students enrolled in agriculture courses. The situation was so bleak in 1897 that Reid felt compelled to explain why the agricultural course failed to attract more students. "Various courses conspire at present to turn the attention of our student to the mechanical arts," Reid informed the local board. "They hold out to him greater promise of prosperity and usefulness under present conditions. Agriculture does not invite him."[47] More to the point, Reid told the board, the state had not done enough to "improve" the land. Of the state's 90 million acres, only 300,000 were under cultivation. To remedy the situation at the college, the local board hired Robert S. Shaw, the son of James J. Hill's agricultural advisor and a graduate of the Ontario Agricultural College, as professor of agriculture. Enrollments in agriculture, however, remained far below expectations until another graduate of the Ontario Agricultural College, Frederic B. Linfield, took charge in 1902.

Reid viewed education as a whole way of life. "A president of a college does not know what duties the day may bring," he once wrote. On one day alone, Reid recorded that he met with students who were in danger of being expelled from the college, helped prepare the school's state fair exhibit, oversaw repairs to a building, and taught his psychology class. In 1897, he helped organize and presided over the Contemporary Club, a reading and discussion group for faculty. He also traveled widely throughout the state, advertising the college to rural Montanans, and he served on a variety of state education commissions, including the commission that selected textbooks for the state's growing number of public schools. Reid suffused all of these activities with a high sense of moral purpose that, while perhaps befitting a Presbyterian minister (Reid continued to deliver Sunday sermons around the state while he was college president), enveloped him in controversy.[48]

Concern for the moral uprightness of his students and faculty led Reid to launch a crusade against gambling establishments in Bozeman and to put an end to student dances. The latter, he wrote, were "the most hurtful and demoralizing form of amusement among students" and needed to be offset by greater involvement with athletics and physical culture.[49] He also joined with temperance forces in the community and advocated closing Bozeman's fifteen saloons. If these crusades were not enough to raise the ire of some commercial interests who feared the economic consequences of Reid's reforms, he also campaigned to close down the town's red-light district. In response to these activities, one of the local newspaper editors raised the matter of sectarian domination of a public college. Reid replied in high-toned fashion: "I am proud of some of the enemies I have made."[50]

Reid had little difficulty weathering these local tempests. A far greater source of aggravation were personnel changes on the Local Executive Board and the grind of lobbying the legislature in Helena. Increasingly, Reid believed, the governor was appointing men to the local board who were toting less than full seabags. As Reid confided in a letter, Governor Joseph K. Toole "put men on boards who have no more fitness for such positions than children as they know nothing whatever about educational matters and don't care to know. We have to bring one of them from a neighboring saloon as a rule where he plays 'poker' most of the time, and when he does come he is no help whatever but to make a quorum." Professional politicians—Reid described them as "prompted by sinister and unworthy motives"—were no better. Even his fellow Republicans discouraged him: "The ways of politicians are dark and mysterious. The more I know of some men, the better I like dogs."[51] The problem for Reid, as

for every subsequent president of the institution, was that politicians had to be courted for support of the college. In one week alone, an exhausted Reid reported, he had met with more than seventy of the ninety-eight legislators to plead for improved funding levels for the college.[52] Obdurate legislators were frustrating, but the slide of the local board toward mediocrity troubled him deeply.

Compounding these worries was trouble from an unexpected source—the 1904 graduating class. When Reid refused to allow two students to graduate because of their academic performance, all but one of the remaining students refused to appear on the stage during commencement exercises. The president simply refused to confer diplomas on the protesters.[53]

Reid's stands on these various issues were principled. They were also informed by developments in his private life. Reid was a bachelor—for the better part of his term as president he lived alone in an apartment in the Bozeman Hotel and walked two miles to and from his office on campus. While on vacation in the summer of 1902, he met and fell in love with Ella Holden, a woman twenty years his junior. She refused to leave Montreal and he was unwilling to quit the college that had been so much a part of his life until he was satisfied that an acceptable replacement would be appointed. In September 1904, after receiving assurances that his long-time acquaintance at the state university in Missoula, James Hamilton, would replace him, Reid tendered his resignation and moved to Montreal.[54]

Reid left a multi-tiered legacy. Under his guidance, a college campus had taken form. The grounds were planted in clover and blue grass and dotted with Carolina poplars. While landscaping provided outward and visible signs of the college's mission to tame Montana's land, buildings also began to proliferate, underscoring the mission of the college to civilize the state's inhabitants. Under Reid's administration, Main Hall became the dominant structure on the college campus. A gymnasium was constructed in 1900 and fields were laid out south of Main Hall for athletics and military drill. (The latter was part of the land grant requirement and an opportunity to demonstrate the college's commitment to discipline.) A power house was built in 1901.[55]

In keeping with the physical growth of the college, the number of students and faculty increased—in 1904, the year James Reid tendered his resignation, the student body numbered 356, the faculty 32—and the curriculum continued to expand. Home science, an outgrowth of domestic economy, became a four-year course and biology was divided into two departments, zoology and botany. Reid also developed plans for a four-year course in civil engineering. And, to underscore his commitment to liberal arts, he outlined plans for four-year courses in modern languages, English, and history.[56]

Despite his confrontation with the senior class and his moral crusade against students' leisure-time activities, Reid was held in grudging respect by the students. For all of the starch in his clothes, he enjoyed sitting in on students' cooking classes and joining them on excursions down the Gallatin Canyon toward Yellowstone Park.[57]

Confronted by state and community authorities who wanted him to build a "factory of ideas,"

President Reid on a field trip

Reid did his best to accommodate their desires with his own ideals of liberal culture. The result was an institution dedicated to establishing the moral efficacy of technology.

"Education for Efficiency"

Reid's successor to the presidency of the Agricultural College of the State of Montana was the short, dapper, congenial James Hamilton. Born in 1861 to Scotch-Irish parents, Hamilton was raised in Illinois where, at age 18, he started teaching in rural schools. His interest in furthering his education led him to Union Christian College in Indiana where he determined to become a public school administrator. After serving as a superintendent of schools in Sumner, Illinois, he learned of a vacancy for a similar position on the other side of the continental divide in Missoula, Montana. He served for two years as superintendent of schools in Missoula before the fledgling

state university, in 1901, invited him to become professor of history and economics.[58]

In Missoula, Hamilton wasted little time establishing himself as an authority on public education. In 1893, he was selected to serve on the State Board of Education during the crucial developmental years of the state university system. For almost a decade, Hamilton helped the university system develop and became intimately acquainted with institutional entrepreneurs in Bozeman, Butte, Missoula, and Dillon. A professional educator and an expert on matters of administration, Hamilton was also a visionary. He regarded the presidency of the agricultural college as an opportunity to put into practice a set of ideas that were firing the imagination of a broad range of reformers around the nation. Carried forward by the new scientific management movement, those ideas centered on the concept of efficiency.

The scientific management movement came of age with the period of progressive reform. In the face of growing national concerns about a burgeoning urban population, powerful concentrations of capital, corrupt politicians, fluctuating national economic fortunes, and increasing class conflict, a generation of middle-class reformers sought to bring a modicum of order to American society. Among the reforms they advocated were the better management of American cities (the growth of cities, the reformers believed, could be planned), the better management of American political machines (corruption, reformers argued, could be eliminated through processes of initiative, referendum, and recall), and the better management of American industry and agriculture (waste in a land of abundance, reformers insisted, could be eliminated by improved methods of production). In their emphasis on better management methods, the social reformers found themselves aligned with a growing number of businessmen and engineers whose goal it was to make American industry and society more efficient.[59]

One of the institutions targeted for reform by scientific management enthusiasts was the public school. As early as 1900, the president of the National Education Association (NEA) forecast that "the real educational leaders of the age whose influence will be permanent are those who have the business capacity to appreciate and comprehend the business problems which are always a part of the educational problem."[60] These pressures for incorporating businesslike procedures in education, together with the growing pressures to educate the children of millions of immigrants, made it increasingly easy for educators to regard the school as a factory. What distinguished Montana was that its leaders were already thinking of its land grant college in these terms. Its public schools, thanks to the State Board of Education, were not far behind.

James Hamilton, president of the college, 1904-1919

Emma Hamilton, wife of the president

Montana educators hitched their wagons to efficiency's star right around the turn of the century and placed their faith in wagonmasters—and NEA members—like James Hamilton. Hamilton joined the NEA in 1895 and helped organize its Montana affiliate, the Montana Education Association. Like promoters of professionalization for other disciplines, Hamilton saw professionalization as a vehicle for enhancing the prestige of educators, for standardizing education requirements, and for securing the public trust. Winning and maintaining public trust was Hamilton's forte. A kindly and forceful man who on more than one occasion reached into his own pocket to provide loans for students, Hamilton had always been an advocate of making public education practical. When he was invited to become president of the agricultural college he had long since been converted to the cause of utilitarianism and the need for industrial education in institutions of higher learning. What appealed to him about the presidency of the Bozeman college was the possibility it afforded for linking the land grant college's traditional emphasis on "applied" training to the modern call for efficiency.[61]

For progressive reformers around the country, efficiency was a buzzword signifying, in the words of historian Henry May, "the sum of all good things."[62] Carrying explicit moral meaning, efficiency became an ideal to be implanted in students with the same care as the virtues of hard work, thrift, and moral rectitude. Educating students efficiently, in other words, was only half the battle. The more important half was educating them to live up to the ideal of efficiency—an ideal that implied "disinterestedness, rigor, and a method employing the power of laws of nature which would make the appeal to conscience of the old-style uplifters unnecessary."[63] At once a method

and an ideal, efficiency represented nothing less than an ideology legitimizing the place of the expert in American society. "The time of the self-made man has passed," Montana's lieutenant governor declared in an article written for the *Inter-Mountain Educator*. "The time of the expert is at hand."[64] Under Hamilton's direction, this way of thinking gained legitimacy at the agricultural college and spiraled into the political culture of the state as a whole.

Once he assumed the presidency of the college in Bozeman, Hamilton wasted no time pursuing his dream to transform the institution into a "high grade technical college."[65] As he envisioned it, the final result would be the "M.I.T. of the West" which would complement the transformation of the state university in Missoula into "the Harvard of the West."[66]

Constantly looking over his shoulder to developments in Missoula, Hamilton quickly determined that the most pressing problem confronting the state system of higher education was the matter of duplication. "The Normal College and School of Mines had kept well within their particular fields of instruction," Hamilton wrote, "but the University and the College of Agriculture had invaded each other's distinctive lines of work which resulted in a large amount of duplication." The problem, according to Hamilton, was self-evident: "Montana with its small population and limited taxable property could not afford this waste and the distribution of the small available funds over such a variety of curricula with inadequate facilities and faculties was bound to lower the quality of the work."[67]

To remedy the situation, Hamilton opted to jettison Reid's ideals of liberal culture. Because they supposedly duplicated offerings at the state university, Hamilton eliminated independent literature and history majors, combining these into a single history-literature course. He also combined mathematics and physics into a single mathematics-physics course and eliminated the four-year course in agriculture and replaced it with majors in agronomy, animal industry, horticulture, and dairy. More momentous were a series of decisions about the business department. Shortly after assuming the presidency, Hamilton decided to eliminate the business department because it required only an eighth-grade education for admission and was draining funds from college-level courses in agriculture and engineering.[68] Shifting funds to these disciplines, however, created an unanticipated problem inasmuch as the business department had attracted young women interested in careers outside the home. Without business offerings, Hamilton discovered that the enrollment of women in the college was stagnating. In 1912, he refashioned the business department into a curriculum in secretarial studies with courses in "typewriting, stenography and book-

The Evolution of the Montana University System

Historian of education Lincoln J. Aikens notes that the Montana system of higher education was "unique" as it took form in the early twentieth century. "This uniqueness," Aikens writes, "was due to the retention by the units of the university of fully autonomous freedom of operation on the local level within a framework of integrated administrative control under a chancellor, the executive officer of the State Board of

control bred much political mischief and contributed to the distinctive and embattled history of the Missoula campus.[2]

The early history of Western Montana College also bears notice. During the legislative debates about the locations of various state institutions, including colleges, most Montanans assumed the state's normal, or teaching, college would be located in Twin Bridges where a private normal school already existed. But, at the last minute, some characteristic shenanigans in the legislature thwarted the Twin Bridges plan; Dillon's representatives, backed by Butte magnate Marcus Daly, secured the necessary votes to locate the normal college in their town. None were more surprised by this turn of events than Dillon's own residents. According to Aikens, they showed little support for the college and through the years this ongoing lack of interest slowed its growth.

In the topsy-turvy world of college building, it is hardly surprising that the origins of the School of Mines at Butte were tumultuous. The legislature awarded the college to Butte in 1893, but for two years there was no effort on the part of Butte's civic leaders to take any action to build the college. As delay followed delay, the State Board of Education forced action. Finally, in September 1900, the college opened its doors to thirty-nine students.

The existence of so many colleges led to the charge that the campuses were simply duplications of effort—an absurd charge since

Montana State Normal College, Dillon

Education."[1] In its early years, the university system included Montana State College at Bozeman, Montana State University at Missoula, Montana State School of Mines at Butte, and Western Montana College of Education at Dillon.

Technically, the state university at Missoula was founded in the same year as the college in Bozeman, but plans were not developed for opening the university until 1895 and buildings were not erected until 1897. Through a quirk in the original legislation, there was no provision for a local executive board, similar to the one at Bozeman. Consequently, the State Board of Education appointed one, thus giving the state board much more control over the Missoula campus than it ever had over the Bozeman school. As Aikens notes, the state board supervised "such routine university affairs as the purchase of library books, employment of janitors, reimbursement of the president for postage expended, furnishings for the library, textbooks to be used by faculty, authorization for annual catalogs and the like." Such

College of Mineral Science and Technology, Butte

it was physically impossible for faculty at the different colleges to replicate each others' offerings. Even so, in the context of the growing drive for efficiency, the State Board of Education, in 1903, launched an investigation "with the object in view of eliminating any duplication of work in their courses of study." This investigation, together with the loose structure of universitywide administration, led to a "running jurisdictional fight between the local executive boards . . . and

Eastern Montana Normal
College, Billings

the State Board of Education." Not surprisingly, these tensions proved fertile ground for nurturing earlier arguments that the entire university system should be consolidated at one campus. When it became clear that Missoula interests were leading the fight—and gaining public support through a petition drive—for locating the consolidated university in Missoula, opponents of unification, led by Bozeman professor William F. Brewer, carried their opposition around the state and defeated the consolidation measure by a 3-2 margin. The legislature, dominated by Missoula supporters, nevertheless passed a consolidation bill. Only Governor Samuel Stewart's veto saved the day for the institutions beyond Missoula.

Stewart also insisted on implementing a chancellor system whereby the four college units would retain their autonomy but operate under a single administrative unit. Precisely because it threatened the power of the legislature to control the colleges, the office of chancellor never gained a firm political hold in the state, and during the Second World War, criticized from all sides, it came unhinged.

While the chancellorship system was developing, Havre civic leaders began a drive to secure an "agricultural and manual training school" in the northern part of the state. In 1925, northern and eastern Montanans joined forces to lobby for the creation of colleges in their respective regions. The northern Montana group relentlessly pursued its aim and argued that the increasing population of the region and the distance from other university units made it imperative that a college be created in Havre. The legislature agreed. In 1929, Northern Montana College became part of the greater university system.

Similar arguments were heard for the creation of a normal school for training teachers, especially elementary teachers, in the eastern part of the state. In 1922, the State Board of Education agreed to open normal schools during the summers in several eastern Montana towns and place them under the supervision of the normal school at Dillon. With pressure building to locate a permanent normal school in the east, the state board asked an outside commission of three experts to select a site for a permanent college. The commission considered applications from nearly a dozen eastern Montana towns, including Glendive, Culbertson, and Roundup, before unanimously deciding on Billings. In 1927, Eastern Montana State Normal School was established.

1. Lincoln J. Aikens, "The Montana System, An Experiment in Integrated Education," Ph.D. dissertation, Montana State College, 1958. The information that follows about other colleges is drawn from Aiken's work.
2. For the history of the University of Montana, see H. G. Merriam, *The University of Montana: A History* (Missoula, 1970).

Northern Montana College, Havre

keeping" that were intended to train women for gender-specific secretarial positions in the world of business. Because he feared this curriculum was intellectually suspect, Hamilton tried to combine it with the history-literature course under the rubric of "vocational English." That experiment lasted only one year before being abandoned in favor of shifting secretarial offerings to divisions of the college set aside for "women's work."[69]

So sweeping were these changes that in 1911 the student newspaper exclaimed: "A year ago the college entered upon a revolutionary period. New methods were adopted, new enterprises started, new organizations perfected, new policies promulgated."[70] Just to be certain that no one could possibly miss the full import of this revolution, Hamilton, borrowing a phrase from Harvard President Charles W. Eliot, coined a new motto for the college: "Education for Efficiency."[71]

Hamilton's drive to suffuse the college with the gospel of efficiency carried important implications beyond the area of curricular reform. It further augmented the moral authority of the faculty by making them appear to be disinterested experts in matters of public concern. One consequence of this development was to tighten the Anaconda Company's grip over the affairs of ordinary Montanans.

In 1905, farmers in the Deer Lodge Valley brought suit against "the Company," claiming that the Anaconda Copper Company's smelter had deposited large amounts of arsenic in the soil, resulting in damaged crops, dead livestock, and lethal doses of arsenic in the milk of cows. The Company, attuned to the implications of the suit for its smelting operations around the state, brought in a variety of expert witnesses, including Frank W. Traphagen, one of the original faculty members of the state college who had recently left for a faculty position at the Colorado School of Mines, and Joseph Blankenship, Harvard-trained member of the state college faculty. Traphagen, a long-time "company partisan" holding "heavy investments in mining and smelting," assured the court that the sulphur dioxide emissions from the smelter were well below levels that would cause danger to crops and livestock. Blankenship was more innovative in his testimony. Far from being the result of toxic pollution from the smelter, Blankenship argued, the source of the problem in the Deer Lodge Valley was biological. Crops and livestock, he told the court, were suffering from the "drying up disease"—a disease that Blankenship claimed existed only near the communities of Anaconda and Great Falls, sites of the Company's smelters. With the help of expert testimony from the college, the Company defeated a potentially devastating legal challenge. While it would be untrue to claim that the college, under Hamilton, became a think tank for the Company (that distinction probably belonged to the School of Mines in Butte), at least some state college professors, sensing their growing authority as experts within the cult of efficiency, were serving as its intellectual underwriters.[72]

However beneficial the cult of efficiency

Faculty, State College of Agriculture and Mechanic Arts, 1909

Campus panorama, 1910. Major buildings include (left to right): Main (Montana) Hall, Chemistry and Physics Building, drill hall, Agricultural Experiment Station (Taylor Hall), and Agriculture Building (Linfield Hall)

was for maintaining the Company's grip on Montana, it had pernicious consequences for the development of higher education in the state. As efficiency increasingly became the touchstone for educational reform, the university system, perennially confronted by legislators equally short on funds and vision, developed an obsession for avoiding duplication of courses and curricula. In the first decade of the century, the logic of this argument led campus administrators to specialize the functions of their campuses. Hamilton, in other words, could easily endorse the development of the state university into the Harvard of the West, providing it left the state college to develop into the M.I.T. of the West. What Hamilton failed to anticipate was that an argument based on principles of efficiency could also disgorge the ghosts of the consolidation movement that had so haunted the college founders in the previous decade.[73]

In 1912, the state university in Missoula hired a new president, Edwin B. Craighead. To Craighead's way of thinking, the logic of efficiency argued less for specialization of function than for consolidation of the entire system in one unit. When Craighead's ideas resulted in a ballot initiative that threatened the very existence of the state college, Hamilton, evidently with no sense of irony, turned for assistance to a faculty member in one of the departments he had earlier tried to eliminate, enlisting William F. Brewer of the English department in a public relations campaign that rehearsed arguments heard two decades earlier and resulted in the defeat of the initiative.[74]

Proponents of consolidation, however, did not so much acquiesce in defeat as shift the terms of the argument. In 1913, the legislature, acting on an idea first proposed by *Anaconda Standard* editor George Durston, passed bills mandating an end to duplication of courses and creating a chancellorship system that would centralize administrative functions in a single office. The latter proposal fired a new round of intense public debate. Craighead and his backers still insisted that the state should have one centralized university, while Hamilton endorsed the chancellorship

proposal as a compromise.[75]

Rather than refight the consolidation battle, the ever-astute Hamilton took a step that caught his opponents completely off guard. He resigned. The effect of this action was twofold. It generated a wellspring of support for Hamilton from around the state, including editorials urging the State Board of Education not to accept his resignation. Resentment over Craighead's position became so great that when he refused the State Board of Education's request to cease campaigning for consolidation, the board fired him outright, begged Hamilton to continue as president of the state college, eliminated the engineering curriculum at the state university, and, as a token gesture to the university, transferred the college's pharmacy program to Missoula. Weary from the fight, Hamilton served until 1919 as president of the college before resigning to become its dean of men—a position he held for another two decades.[76]

Hamilton's victory over Craighead represented more than a personal triumph. It represented the triumph of a way of thinking about higher education that, during the First World War, would attain absolute hegemony in the state. Thenceforth, the cult of efficiency would spread, cancerlike, into public discourse on higher education, reducing every argument about improving the quality of education in the state to a debate over the "function" of the different units of production. Put in the position of casting sidelong glances at one another's efficiency and productivity, the colleges would develop in an atmosphere of mutual suspicion where growth would easily be confused with progress, competition with health, and jobs for graduates with a college's "worth." In such an environment, the winners would seldom be the universities. Rather, the gospel of efficiency became a secular religion perfectly suited to the rise of corporations to positions of state and national power.[77] However appropriate to an assembly line, the conversion of the state's system of higher education into "units" of production had a shattering effect on higher learning that would reverberate throughout the century.

Edward C. Elliott, first chancellor of the university system

The First World War and the Campus

In 1917, Edward C. Elliott arrived from the University of Wisconsin to assume the post of chancellor of the state university system. More specifically, he assumed a position created by the legislature to oversee the efficient operation of the different units of the university system. He was well equipped for the task. An educator with the soul of a businessman, Elliott had established his reputation on the basis of his work on the financial problems of education and on his research into measuring teachers' efficiency. A high priest of the gospel of efficiency, Elliott regarded the chancellorship as the perfect post for realizing one of his longstanding dreams: transforming the American university into the servant of the state. "In the past," Elliott asserted in a 1913 speech, "the ebb of energy has been from the state to the university. Today the flow is from the university to the state." Put another way, Elliott proclaimed: "Service to the state is no longer a matter of choice on the part of public schools and universities."[78] Exactly what Elliott had in mind became apparent when a momentous event—America's entry into the First World War—unshuttered a world of opportunity for efficiency-minded experts.

When news of the Archduke Ferdinand's assassination reached Bozeman in the summer of 1914, the shadows of war in Europe occasioned an eight-cent price rise in wheat, but little excitement otherwise.[79] Indeed, a young French instructor at the college who spent her summer vacation in Europe reported that she "had a very pleasant vacation" despite "a few inconveniences caused by the European war."[80] This carefree attitude persisted during the academic year as campus life was dominated more by sophomore class concern that first-year males wear their green beanies on campus than by the thunder of guns in Europe. In 1914-1915 the penalty for not paying attention to events abroad seemed highly abstract, but the penalty for not wearing your beanie was a summary haircut by attentive guardians of campus traditions.[81] By the following autumn, first-year males were still wearing their beanies, but apathy about the European war was giving way to concern over America's possible entry into the conflict.

What role should the college play in the growing preparedness effort? People in the state were divided. Many immigrant homesteaders in the eastern part of the state opposed America's entry into the war, as did miners in Butte who would soon rally around the slogan "a rich man's war and poor man's fight."[82] The position of the state university system was exactly the opposite. In his first official act as chancellor, Elliott ordered each unit of the system to fly the American flag every day.[83] If there was ever any doubt what this gesture meant as far as the college was concerned, it was laid to rest when Elliott announced plans to put the institution on a "war footing."[84] That spring of 1916, a full year before President Woodrow Wilson declared war on Germany, between fifty and one hundred young men formed a volunteer militia on campus and drilled under the tutelage of two volunteer faculty officers, an entomologist and an agronomist. (See the section on military science, Chapter 10.)

It is difficult to recapture the enthusiasm for war preparedness that gripped the Bozeman cam-

The "M" Club, 1917

pus and other colleges around the country. One historian has recently suggested that this enthusiasm for combat in the First World War was informed by the heroic myths surrounding the conquest of the American frontier. War was still perceived as a noble cause, a heroic pursuit, and, above all, as a civilizing mission.[85] Unless they were unusually adept at recognizing the mass destruction of Native Americans that the nation's

"M" Day, firing the cannon

westward expansion had occasioned, students at the college and their faculty mentors had no reason to anticipate the horrific slaughter of human beings occasioned by the First World War. Theirs was a world animated by the rhetoric of reform. War seemed like a crusade and a great reform movement all rolled into one. It demanded pageantry and sacrifice. The theater of combat seemed like a show not to be missed. Little did any of them realize the full measure of its horrors.

As preparations to shift the campus to a war footing proceeded, students responded with a rousing show of school spirit. While some young men were marching to and fro across the campus under the tutelage of their volunteer drill instructors, the sophomore class realized the earlier ambitions of students to leave a permanent mark on the Gallatin Valley. In the spring and autumn of 1916, after receiving a permit from the U.S. Forest Service and carefully marking the lines, sixty young men went to work on the west face of Mount Baldy that rises in the Bridger Mountains just northeast of Bozeman. They pried stones loose from the mountainside, passed them by hand, and formed them into a 240-foot by 160-foot "M" that they intended as an enduring "monument of college spirit for coming college generations."[86] When the freshmen—who else?—were recruited to whitewash the rocks, a campus tradition was born that would be reenacted for many years to come.

The same spirit that drove students to leave their mark on the mountainside animated a desire

to leave their mark on the world. When the local national guard was mobilized, hundreds of students organized a parade to accompany them to the train station. College regimental band members were so moved at the prospect of mobilization that they volunteered to enlist as a unit, though it must be said that their enthusiasm waned when they learned that they would be on active duty for three years and serve another three on reserve. Students at the college also joined with students at other campuses in the system in sending a supportive telegram to President Wilson.[87] When they returned to classes in the autumn of 1917, students organized a massive parade to show support for local men drafted into the service. This time, the parade culminated in a rousing show of speech-making with President Hamilton featured as the keynoter.[88]

While students enthusiastically supported war preparations, they did not exactly relish the thought of becoming cannon fodder. As rumors circulated that the draft age would be lowered to 18, young men flocked to enlist so they could avoid the infantry. All of the males on campus were enthusiastic about the war effort, the student newspaper explained, but they were equally positive "that there is one branch of service for which they are not fitted and that branch is the infantry."[89] By the start of the 1917 academic year, with the ranks of males from the junior and senior classes being rapidly depleted, student concerns about fighting in the infantry were somewhat allayed by Hamilton's efforts to develop a war-training curriculum at the college as the necessary first step toward securing a permanent Reserve Officer Training Corps (ROTC) component on campus

The "M"

Una B. Herrick, dean of women, 1911-1932

that would, in effect, allow male students to defer enlistment until graduation and reward them with commissions as officers.

Students were not alone in their excitement about a ROTC program. Since taking the helm of the college in 1905, Hamilton had tried, without much success, to upgrade the military training capacity of the college. In part, Hamilton's interest in military training reflected his understanding of the historical mission of the land grant college. And Hamilton saw military training programs as one way one way to obtain badly needed laboratory equipment that the state legislature refused to provide. But more importantly, Hamilton regarded military training and discipline as central to his own efforts to render the college a modern technical institution and to further the cause of industrial education in the state. When, in 1916, Congress established ROTC training under the provisions of the National Defense Act, Hamilton saw a golden opportunity for realizing his ambitions. In early 1917, he asked the War Department to establish a ROTC program at the college, noting that the school could immediately train 500 young men for the military and would gladly meet the War Department's stipulation that a military training curriculum be incorporated on campus. The following year, Hamilton rushed to embrace the Student Army Training Corps (SATC) program—a program established by the War Department's Committee on Education and Special Training (CEST) that effectively put most male students on reserve status while training them in vocations deemed necessary to America's war effort.[90]

It is important to emphasize that Hamilton's welcome embrace of ROTC and SATC was more than a patriotic gesture and that CEST represented far more than a run-of-the-mill government bureaucracy. The curricular requirements of ROTC and SATC actually provided Hamilton with the ammunition to complete his drive to render the college an efficient educational plant, while those same requirements served the interests of powerful industrial consortia that were trying to tailor college curricula to meet corporate industry's needs. "In reality," one historian has written, "the educational work of the military during the war was placed in the hands of the educational directors of A.T.& T., Western Electric, and Westinghouse and the leading advocates of the corporate reform of engineering education."[91] Marching under the banner of "Efficiency as a War Measure," educational reformers like Hamilton and Elliott, with the cooperation of influential faculty and administrators like William Cobleigh, professor of chemical engineering, and Una B. Herrick, dean of women, brought the "efficiency" movement to a powerful climax at the State College of Agriculture and Mechanic Arts by overseeing the development of the school

into a training camp for corporate industry.[92]

Between 1916 and the end of the war in 1918, college officials took several steps to make "efficiency" the intellectual bulwark of the institution. In addition to seeking and implementing military-training programs that put students under the authority of the War Department, the college announced plans to standardize its evaluation procedures. "Recognizing that the value of college students to their employers after graduation is often measured by qualities not represented by their grades in college work," the *Bozeman Weekly Courier* reported, "the State College authorities have devised a system of rating college students by which those who wish to employ them may judge of their general personal character." That system, which would be brought to a stage of perfection in ensuing decades, involved judging "ability, honesty, application, thoroughness, attitude, punctuality, reliability, neatness in work, personal appearance, command of English, industry, and cheerfulness."[93]

Women, no less than men, were subjected to this intensified campaign in the name of efficiency. In the heat of war, the university system issued a booklet that urged women "to organize into great armies of non-combatants" with those studying home economics taking the lead.

> The young women of today must recognize these facts. They must prepare themselves so that they can take their places along these highly efficient men who are to reconstruct and strengthen the American democracy. Today one of the most important fields in the world's struggle for democracy is the field of home economics. Schools of home economics headed by the great organization known as the food administration are teaching the women and men of the world every possible means of contributing to the world's food and clothing supply. This is as important a branch of the allied organization as is the artillery, or the infantry. No woman today is considered educated who does not know food values and nutrition.[94]

Under the leadership of Una B. Herrick, dean of women between 1911 and 1934, women on the Bozeman campus signed a sugar pledge: "Recognizing the present shortage of sugar available to our allies in the war, we, the women of Montana State College, are glad to join the food administration in efforts to reduce sugar consumption in the United States, and to this end pledge ourselves not to use more than one tablespoon of sugar a day, and not to eat more than six pieces of candy a week, from the present date (November 6, 1917) until January 15, 1918." "It is agreed," the women pledged, "that these pieces shall not be larger than the equivalent of one inch square and one-half inch thick." To those who ridiculed their efforts, the women responded: "The girls are doing their share, the boys should too. If they cut back on tobacco, beer, and liquor, it would save a lot of sugar, barley, and corn for the men at the front."[95] This jibe at the hedonism of their male peers was good-natured, but also reflected the growing sense of power among this army of noncombatants who were spearheading bond drives, raising funds for the YMCA and YWCA, wrapping packages of toiletries and bandages for the Red Cross, and training to become nurses.[96]

Empowering women with the precepts of the efficiency movement was one of Herrick's chief goals. A remarkable woman, friend of progressive reformer Jane Addams, Herrick preached the gospel of efficiency as a way for young women to develop skills that would give them an independent source of income before marriage and render them competent scientific household managers after marriage. Unlike her friend Addams, who opposed American involvement in the First World War, Herrick saw the war as an opportunity for middle-class women to prove their worth outside their home as responsible citizens and as responsible workers capable of filling clerical positions that men had vacated to fight the war. Seizing on the logic of efficiency, Herrick stressed the importance of organization. She arranged the first Women's Vocational Congress—one of the first such congresses in the country—and helped college women organize the Women's League, forerunner of the more powerful Associated Women Students, an organization that would exist on the Bozeman campus until, in the 1960s, the university determined that its fee-based membership discriminated against men.[97] As evidence of women's growing power on campus, Mary Egan would be elected student body president in 1922.[98] And as evidence of men's growing concern about these developments, Alfred Atkinson, a professor of agronomy and future president of the college, told the Women's Vocational Congress gathering, "If Mr. Jones was a farmer, Mrs. Jones was a necessary adjunct, not to farming, but to Mr. Jones."[99]

To offset fears that women were stepping out of line, Herrick encouraged young women in recitations of "A Creed for Women." Written by reformer Laura Drake Gill, the creed affirmed "that every woman needs a skilled occupation developed to the degree of possible self support" and "that every woman should expect marriage to interrupt for some years the pursuit of any regular gainful occupation."[100] Exactly what Herrick had in mind became clear in the two-track program she developed for women during the war. To underscore the centrality of women's work for the war effort, the home economics department developed senior electives in "War Breads," "Peanut Butter in War Dishes," and "Conservation as Applied to Clothing." At the same time, a "war course" offering in secretarial studies trained women in secretarial work, typing, and accounting procedures.[101]

On one level, Herrick's reforms certainly liberated women from the set of conventional ideas that they had no place in the business world. But on another level, Herrick's energies chained women to an efficiency ideology that specialized their labor in gender-defined home management positions or clerical roles well removed from the managerial world open to young men. If Herrick had a role model in mind for her students, Jeannette Kelly fit the bill. Kelly, a 1917 graduate, was hired by General Mills to help organize its Betty Crocker Institute.[102]

The ideology of efficiency permeated the campus in other, more insidious ways. In 1917, Governor Samuel Stewart, taking his cue from Woodrow Wilson's administration, organized the Montana Council of Defense to act as a propaganda and fund-raising agency. In no time at all, the Council of Defense turned into the state's thought-police, sniffing out expressions of pro-German sentiment, which could range from the aromas of German cuisine to criticism of Montana's mining tax that afforded "the Company" a carte blanche to plunder the resources of the state.[103]

The Council of Defense soon turned its attention to the Bozeman campus. In a gross affront to the manifest patriotism of students and faculty, the council organized a student Council of Defense chapter on campus to ferret out "slackers."[104] "This college should be considered an intellectual reserve training camp," the student newspaper explained, and the "members of it should consider themselves candidates for commissions in an army of brains."[105] When this campaign of intimidation bogged down for lack of dissenters, the council, carrying the fury of anti-German feelings to new heights, zeroed in on two surefire signs of German subversion on campus—German-language books in the library and instruction in the German language itself.[106]

Paralleling similar episodes in other states, the Council of Defense persuaded Chancellor Elliott that to avoid being tarnished as unpatriotic he should order German-language books removed from the library and end German language instruction immediately. Elliott complied, as did Hamilton. Both men were trapped by their own deep involvement in Council of Defense activities and by the logic of their own arguments about efficiency.[107] Had Elliott argued that the college should show its mettle by being a servant to the state? The Council of Defense asked him to make good on his word. And like so many of his contemporaries around the country, he did without so much as a whimper about the loss of intellectual independence.[108]

Significantly, the Council of Defense, which had such bad luck in its search for dissenters on the Bozeman campus, actually generated some dissent on its own. The student newspaper, in what can only be termed a courageous act of reasonableness, protested the decision to terminate German instruction and the instructor. More pointed was one of those marvelous episodes of reality-testing that are prone to engage the talents of college students. In the early hours of a May 1918 morning, with the campus still abuzz over Elliott's decision to abolish the German language in the classroom and the library, several early risers in Hamilton Hall—the women's dormitory named for the recently deceased wife of the college president—looked out their windows only to see a replica of a German U-boat setting its sights on Montana Hall. The women tried to rouse their housemates, but before the submarine could sink the flagship of the college fleet, a dutiful custodian removed the enemy vessel from the grounds. In the absence of any confessions, the student newspaper disingenuously blamed the incident on the pro-German crowd in the community.[109]

If dissent was a scarce commodity among students, it was rarer still among faculty. For the most part, faculty dutifully followed marching orders received from Elliott and Hamilton and, more ominously, from the Montana Council of Defense, which met with the chancellor in Bozeman in 1917. As a result of their deliberations, faculty and farm extension agents were sent to address Farmers' National Defense meetings around the state. In particular, faculty were expected to become propaganda agents for the war effort. According to the program developed by Elliott and the Council of Defense, faculty were supposed to lecture on the dangers of neutrality, the need for stepped-up food production, the profitability of increased food production ("we can probably grow rich in the returns from our toil as producers of food"), the humanity of the American effort, and then to conclude their remarks with a rousing exhortation to sacrifice. By the end of the war, faculty from the state college had addressed 380 defense meetings and spoken to some 80,000 people around Montana. But not all of the institution's speakers came across as mindless nabobs of patriotism. Much to the horror of Council of Defense types around the state, some extension agents, according to the editor of the Fergus County *Argus*, were not only less than enthusiastic in their patriotic oratory, but were inviting representatives of the Non-Partisan

League to address farmers' gatherings. These allegations came as no surprise to the editor of the Miles City *Star* who was convinced that Fred S. Cooley, director of the Agricultural Extension Service, had "Socialistic leanings." In response to these charges, Elliott immediately launched an internal investigation at the institution, but turned up not one shred of evidence supporting allegations of disloyalty among college faculty members.[110]

In this climate of rabid patriotism, internal investigations, and general militarism, the college celebrated its silver anniversary. For the occasion, Hamilton invited his predecessor and old friend, James Reid, to participate in the ceremonies. To a packed opera house in downtown Bozeman, the former president explained his hatred of the Germans: "The German mentality is unspeakable, unutterable, simply inexorable. Their religion is void of any Christian element whatever. What would you do with such a people? What should you do with a mad dog?" Leaving no doubt about his position on the subject, Reid proceeded to declare his own conversion to the ideology of education for efficiency. "Efficiency is the thing that counts," Reid empahsized. And the responsibility of educators was clear: "We should control our education while giving free play to individual energy and develop to the utmost the efficiency of every citizen and the resources of the community."[111] The significance of Reid's speech should not be underestimated. Representing the authority of the past, Reid added an important layer of legitimacy to Hamilton's reforms and ratified the college's shift in emphasis from "culture and skill" to "education for efficiency."

The college would emerge from the war in full possession of its newfound identity as a "high grade technical college" ready to undertake the industrial training of Montana's young people. But it would soon lose its president. In 1919, Hamilton relinquished the power and influence of his prestigious office to concentrate on shaping the consciousness of students from the newly created post of dean of men—a position he would hold until his death in 1940. For the next two decades he would watch, as his successor in the presidency, Alfred Atkinson, adjusted the ideology of efficiency to the changed social and economic circumstances of Montana. The old decade ended not with a bang, but a sneeze. And the new decade began with the wrenching sounds of a slowing economy.

Chapter Three
The Interim Years, 1919-1943

Two misfortunes are pressing upon us just now. One of these is the weather. . . . The other catastrophe is the legislature.
Alfred Atkinson, February 2, 1937[1]

We have been watching the reports on that man, Hitler, and it seems as though that fellow may have possibilities in world affairs. We have two young Ph.D.'s here from German universities in our Department of Economics just now, and in talking with those fellows, they made out that Hitler would never get any place. They said he didn't have any influence, and it was all talk about what he was apt to do.
Alfred Atkinson, December 16, 1930[2]

The end of the First World War ushered in two of the most perplexing decades in American history. "The most interesting phase of American history since Valley Forge" was how one contemporary described them.[3] They were "years of bleakness" another recalled.[4] There was, to be sure, a sense of euphoria over the allied victory in 1918, but it was tempered by a devastating influenza epidemic and anxiety about the Russian revolution. Concern over the latter event fed the fires of the "Red scare" of 1919 and rekindled the drive to impose racial quotas on immigration that culminated in the 1924 Immigration Restriction Act. The decade of the 1920s was a time of uneven national prosperity fueled by mass production and mass consumption on an unparalleled scale. The economy ballooned until, in 1929, the stock market crash exposed its structural flaws. The ensuing depression quickly became the worst national crisis since the Civil War. Only the reforms of the New Deal and the conversion of the economy to a wartime footing righted the ship of state.[5]

Montana stood in peculiar relationship to these national and international events. As if to underscore the state's vulnerability to outside forces, 5000 Montanans, most between the ages of 18 and 45, were among the 5 million Americans who lost their lives in the flu pandemic that swept the world between 1918 and 1919. Then history got ahead of itself. The northern plains entered a cycle of drought that desiccated crops and destroyed farmers' hopes for a share in the markets of war-ravaged Europe. In Montana, unlike most of the nation, the Jazz Age was actually accompanied by a depression in what seemed, in retrospect, a strangely rehearsed jam session for the Great Depression that followed.[6]

Between the world wars, the school, renamed Montana State College in 1921, remained a provincial institution—its average annual enrollment stood at just over 1200 students—in a state colo-

nized by outside corporate interests, especially "the Company," the Anaconda Copper Mining Company (A.C.M.). The college's provincial status, reinforced by the state legislature's decision to expand the university system to include units in Havre and Billings during the worsening farm crisis, led MSC officials to concentrate on consolidating the achievements of Hamilton's administration by refining the "education for efficiency" ideology in the context of what historian David O. Levine calls the emergent "culture of aspiration" that took hold of the nation's colleges between 1915 and 1945. According to Levine, "institutions of higher learning were no longer content to educate; they now set out to train, accredit, and impart social status to their students . . . . The campus became a center for the ethos of an emergent white-collar, consumption-oriented middle class."[7] Provincial though it was, MSC, driven largely by its Colleges of Agriculture and Engineering, played a key role in grooming students and the state for modernity.

The Ascension of Atkinson

For the better part of the interwar years, the college was in the hands of Alfred A. Atkinson. A native of Seaforth, Ontario, Atkinson graduated from the Ontario Agricultural College and attended Iowa State College and Cornell before arriving at MSC as an instructor in agronomy in 1904. The next year he received an appointment as professor of agronomy, a title he would hold until his appointment to the presidency in 1919.[8]

An expert on dryland farming, Atkinson quickly established a reputation for his work on grain varieties suitable for Montana's harsh environment. Through his work in the extension service, he also gained statewide recognition that contributed to his selection as the state food administrator during the First World War. This administrative experience brought him to the attention of the State Board of Education and helped persuade the board that he was the right person to fill the presidency of the college when Hamilton resigned to become dean of men.

In addition to his experience in education, agriculture, and administration, Atkinson possessed other attributes that contributed to his selection. The year 1919 found the Board of Education engulfed by its controversial firing and subsequent reinstatement of state university economist Louis Levine who had called attention to the special treatment the Company received under Montana's mining tax laws.[9] Caught off guard by the national storm of protest over its handling of the Levine case, the Board of Education was anxious to ensure stability at the other

Alfred Atkinson, president of the college, 1919-1937

*Civil engineering students,
ca. 1901*

"We have substituted the three 'H's—the head, the heart, and the hand—with a rather marked emphasis on the training of the hand." And, in a sentence that might well have served as an epigram for his presidency, Atkinson announced that Montana State College had "one great purpose to so direct its affairs that 'it best serves its constituency under the conditions prevailing.'"[12] Right at the start, Atkinson established the accommodationist tone that would characterize the campus under his stewardship. It was perfectly in keeping with an age so brilliantly satirized by Sinclair Lewis in *Babbitt* and wholly conducive to one of the most important developments to occur at MSC during the interwar period—the triumph of engineering.

wing of the state's system of higher education. Atkinson fit the bill perfectly. "He was innately conservative and highly apprehensive of adverse public opinion," historian Merrill G. Burlingame has noted.[10] A close friend of Henry C. Gardiner, land agent for A.C.M., Atkinson was situated near the center of the state's political and economic power. Put charitably, Atkinson could be expected not to incur the wrath of the Company. Despite his obdurateness—Atkinson "might be wrong, but he was never in doubt" was how entomologist and future MSC president A. L. Strand described him—Atkinson was the ideal caretaker to oversee the consolidation of Hamilton's efficiency measures at the college.[11]

Atkinson's presidential inauguration ceremonics foreshadowed the tenor of his nineteen-year regime. Politicians, including Governor Stewart, academicians, including university presidents from around the region, Chancellor Elliott, and the MSC faculty, joined the students to fill the drill hall to capacity for the ceremony. They heard the head of Cornell's College of Agriculture, Liberty Hyde Bailey, former head of Theodore Roosevelt's Country Life Commission, deliver the keynote speech on "The Rank and File." Atkinson's own panegyric, filled with encomiums to the gospel of efficiency, was a model of accommodation. "We have come a long way from the three 'R's,'" Atkinson told his audience.

"Techno Kampus":
The Triumph of Engineering

From the college's beginning, engineering had been one of the pillars of the curriculum, but its light was often buried under the bushel of MSC's reputation as an "ag college." In the years immediately preceding Atkinson's inauguration, this situation had begun to change. In the first place, James Hamilton's drive to turn MSC into a "high grade technical institute" paid off when the legislature, during the heated battle over the consolidation of the university system, decided to shift engineering instruction from the Missoula to the Bozeman campus. In the second place, the legislature also agreed to provide funds for a new engineering building on campus. Excavation for this structure began during Atkinson's first year in office and gave added weight to his insistence that "America must have more trained men who can direct the forces that increase man power. We hold that the engineer must become more important as this phase of society becomes more complex."[13]

Engineering lab, ca. 1906

The Engineering Buildings

In response to increased engineering instructional and research needs on the Bozeman campus, the 1911 legislature appropriated $60,000 for what would much later be dedicated as William Milnor Roberts Hall in honor of one of the state's earliest and finest civil engineers. Bozeman architect Fred T. Willson designed the building and W. R. Plew, professor of architecture and head of the school's physical plant, supervised the construction. At its completion in 1923, the new building was described as a "fine specimen of modern architecture" and praised for its "fine grade of terra cotta" in ornamental trimmings and its "red Tennessee marble and floors of red quarry tile." The building provided offices, classrooms, and drafting rooms for all engineering departments. Civil engineering occupied the first floor; electrical engineering and the engineering library the second, and architectural engineering the third. Sharing third-floor spaces with the architects was the physical plant division.[1]

Just south of Roberts Hall, and under construction at about the same time as the larger building, was the A. M. Ryon Engineering Laboratories building, with its distinctive monitor-style roof designed to withstand heavy snow accumulation. Initially, Ryon's shops and labs accommodated electrical engineering and engineering-materials testing facilities, pattern and machine shops, student lockers, and the most modern of cleanup facilities. Later, as financing permitted, two new wings were added to the original structure. The state highway laboratory was soon operating out of the building, and for years the older part of the building continued to serve as a steam- and gas-engineering facility. Named in 1939 for MSC's first president, it was the first campus building to be named for a living person.[2]

Roberts Hall

Ryon Labs

1   *Montana State College of Agriculture and Mechanic Arts Eighteenth Annual Catalogue, 1910-1911,* 10; "Engineering Building and Shops Building," in "State College Statement to December 1, 1922, of Expenditures from Educational Bond Funds," f. PA6.2.Buildings, MSUA; "Roberts Hall" in Montana State University Quick Facts, MSUSC; "State Completes Bond Issue Building Program This Year at the State College in Bozeman," *Montana Collegian,* 2:7 (August 1926), 1; "New Home of Engineering Department—Best in the Northwest," *Weekly Exponent,* 10 March 1922.

2   "The A. M. Ryon Engineering Laboratories," in *Commemoration of the Ceremony of Naming the Engineering Laboratories the A. M. Ryon Laboratories,* October 27, 1939, f. A6.1.Ryon Laboratory, MSUA; "Ryon Laboratory 1923" in Montana State University Quick Facts, MSUSC; "State Completes Bond Issue Building Program This Year at the State College in Bozeman," *Montana Collegian,* 2:7 (August 1926), 1; "New Engineering Shops," *Weekly Exponent,* 28 November 1922.

Electrical engineering students, 1910-1911

These local developments coincided with a set of developments on the national level centering on the growing effort by a new generation of professional, reform-minded engineers to "bring education into line with . . .the new realities of modern industry."[14] Spearheading this drive was the Society for the Promotion of Engineering Education (S.P.E.E.), first organized in the wake of the World's Congress of Engineering at the 1893 Chicago World's Columbian Exposition. During the decades before the First World War, the S.P.E.E. endeavored to reorient higher education generally and engineering education specifically toward meeting the demands of industrial corporations. The movement to bring higher education into line with the requirements of industry received additional momentum during the war with the decision by the federal government to create the National Research Council to coordinate the wartime efforts of government, industry, science, and engineering. By the 1920s, a full-blown reform movement was underway in engineering schools across the country that, according to historian David Noble, was "aimed at gearing engineering education for the production of both efficient and loyal corporate employees and competent and dedicated 'leaders of industry'; they were at once the work of a profession in search of power and recognition, and of corporate leaders in search of their subordinates and successors."[15] At MSC, a number of dedicated engineers did what they could to bring the College of Engineering into conformity with S.P.E.E. dictates. In so doing, they left a powerful impress on the school as a whole.

The task of modernizing engineering education at MSC under Atkinson's presidency ini-

tially fell to Earle B. Norris. Educated as a mechanical engineer at Pennsylvania State University, Norris worked in industry before turning his talents to higher education. Between 1908 and 1916 he rose to the rank of professor at the University of Wisconsin, writing several textbooks on industrial and mechanical engineering. During the war, he received a commission as captain in the ordnance department and was promoted to the rank of major. In 1919, he resigned his post as chief engineer at the Rock Island arsenal and became dean of the College of Engineering at MSC.[16]

An active S.P.E.E. member, Norris was in tune with the movement to equate service to the engineering profession with service to industrial corporations and was in complete sympathy with the S.P.E.E. aim to bring higher education into line with industrial processes. When he informed Atkinson of the Carnegie Foundation-backed S.P.E.E. study of engineering curricula at the nation's colleges, he identified the study as a "plan to determine whether the engineering curricula are meeting the needs of modern industry with the view to making the curricula of the different engineering colleges more nearly uniform at the same time so that they will be adjusted to the needs of future industrial leaders."[17] And Norris was instrumental in securing a visit to the MSC campus from William Wickendon, the director of the S.P.E.E. investigation of higher education.[18] With a zeal usually reserved for religious enthusiasts, MSC's well-connected dean of engineering relentlessly sought to implement the S.P.E.E. agenda of "retooling American higher education 'processes' to meet industrial demands."[19]

To accomplish these ends, Norris moved on three fronts. First, he attacked the engineering curricula, making all phases of the engineering major more science-based. Second, he set his sights on engineering the personality of his students, instilling in them a professional ethos that would make them conform to the dictates of industry. Third, he became a zealous propagandist for the industrialization of the state of Montana, stressing the contributions that MSC graduates could make to the process.

The first phase of Norris's program was announced in the *1920-1921 Annual Catalogue.* Engineering courses, Norris informed students, would conform to "the accepted practice in the leading engineering colleges of the United States, the aim being to instruct the students thoroughly in the fundamental sciences upon which all engineering rests and to impart such special and technical knowledge of the various branches of engineering as will fit the graduates to embark upon successful careers in their chosen fields."[20] The next year, Norris introduced the curriculum in engineering physics to train students for "research work in the laboratories of the large engineering corporations" and broadened the mechanical engineering curriculum to acquaint students "with present-day industrial problems and

Earle B. Norris, dean of the College of Engineering

with the modern business methods in industrial organization."[21] By 1924, when Wickendon visited the campus, S.P.E.E. curricular reforms, centering on training in scientific research, had been locked in place and the college had renewed its commitment to the use of public funds for the support of private industry.

Norris's curricular reforms were momentous—engineering physics laid the basis for the creation of the modern physics department and for the subsequent transformation of MSC into a university after the Second World War—but they are only part of the story. Of equal, if not greater significance, were his efforts to complement curricular reform by shaping students into the mold of the professional engineer.

What exactly was a professional engineer? This question had been nagging engineering societies since before the turn of the century. After the First World War, the urge to resolve the question once and for all intensified and the S.P.E.E. assumed responsibility for developing guidelines that would help colleges make professionals out of their engineering students. Wickendon's Board of Investigation and Coordination, the S.P.E.E.'s most powerful committee, developed a set of criteria for the "professional life" that Norris, and his peers around the country, embedded in their programs.[22]

Among the attributes of the professional, according to these guidelines, were possession of scientific knowledge obtained through professional schools, a "recognition of status by colleagues or by organized society," and "organization of the professional group, based on common interest and social duty." Additional attributes included "a standard of qualifications . . . based on character, education, and competency" as well as a "standard of conduct . . . based on honor, courtesy and ethics."[23]

When this S.P.E.E. report was issued in 1924, Norris was already taking steps to place Montana State College at the cutting edge of the movement to mold students into professional engineers. With curricular reforms already in place that would ground students' knowledge in science, Norris proceeded to devote a great deal of attention to imprinting students with the stamp of good character, competency, and an appreciation for the importance of status. On one level, he sought to accomplish these aims through the pressure that only a student's peers can generate. Beginning in the early 1920s, Norris actively sought to diminish the role of the traditional, but loosely arranged, campus engineering societies by securing a chapter of the prestigious—and hierarchically minded—national engineering honorary society, Tau Beta Pi. After his initial requests were denied, Norris began a letter-writing campaign to persuade his peers around the country that MSC had sufficient numbers in its graduating class to qualify for membership and that the college had sufficient physical equipment, and "a very able faculty."[24] Furthermore, Norris emphasized to a colleague in Michigan: "You can appreciate that the young men at MSC are of much the same stock as the men in your own institution. They are practically all of native born American stock and

The Blue and Gold, to the Engineer

You have loudly sung our praises,
You have cheered us on field and floor;
But, tell us, Sons of Tubal Cain,
Are we colors and nothing more?

When your college score is finished
And you're out in the world at last,
Will we lead you to high endeavor
Or be symbols alone of the past?

There's the blue of lumniferous ether,
The Key to the vast unknown
Will you be one to explore it,
Or rest on the things that are done?

There's the blue of steel that is tempered
To ease the burden of toil,
Of mountain lakes and rivers,
To quench the thirsty soil.

There's the blue of lightning's flashes
You have harnessed to serve man's need;
The symbol of power triumphant
O'er toil and sweat and greed.

There's gold the king of metals,
By fume or stain unsoiled;
The symbol of honor and virtue,
The reward of those who have toiled.

There's the golden light of the furnace,
The glow of intensive fires
That make the metal plastic
To the engineers' desires.

There are golden oils and greases
That smoothe and ease the way
To the humming wheels of commerce
Through endless night and day.

Let these be the engineer's symbols
As he journeys forth on earth,
The Blue of Loyal Service
And the Gold of Honest Worth.

Earle B. Norris
Dean of Engineering, 1925

we are absolutely free from the Hebrew problem which has become so serious in so many eastern schools."[25] With these words, Norris bared an important racist subtext in engineers' discourse about professionalism. Encoded in the emphasis on "character" was a racial litmus test that would assure the status of engineering as a male-dominated, Anglo-Saxon profession.[26]

How could the character—racial and otherwise—of engineering graduates be assured? In 1924, Norris laid plans for the inclusion of a personnel and placement service within the College of Engineering that would take responsibility for molding and evaluating a student's character. When it began functioning late in the decade as a "service" to students, the profession, and industry, the personnel service added another layer of social control over prospective engineers during their years in college. In the meantime, to assure the requisite intellectual and social discipline of his future engineers, Norris relied on the student engineering societies, supplemented in 1925 with the acquisition of a Tau Beta Pi chapter, the rigors of science-based course work, and his own gift for inspired utterance.[27]

For the 1925 yearbook, Norris composed "The Blue and Gold, To the Engineer." A lengthy ode to engineering graduates, this poem accurately reflected how campus traditions could be employed to develop one of the character traits most prized by industry: loyalty. "Let these be the engineer's symbols/As he journeys forth on earth," the last stanza trumpeted, "The Blue of Loyal

Service/And the Gold of Honest Worth."[28]

Norris had every reason to address the engineer's journey in the context of the 1920s. The simple fact of the matter was that jobs for engineering graduates within the state of Montana were scarce. Norris laid out his solution to this problem in an address delivered to the local Kiwanis Club that he titled "Moving Pittsburgh to Montana: The Ultimate Way out of Montana's Financial Difficulties." No fool, Norris understood the consequences of his proposal for Montana's natural beauty. But, in his eyes, Montana's pristine environment could be improved through engineering:

We are prone to consider scenic beauty only as it may revive the spirit through recreation or feed the soul through inspiration. . . . In addition, it presents to the engineer the inspiration to high endeavor, the far-seeing vision to plan, and the challenge to dare. In glaciers and eternal snows, in mountain lakes and rivers, he may see waters to be fed to the fertile valleys and plains. In the secret depths of the mountains and upon their timbered slopes he may find in abundant variety the materials of construction and industry. In mountain pass or deep crevasse he may find a challenge to his construction skill. And so, in gratitude for the material and spiritual bounty of "Scenic Montana" we may well say with the psalmist: "I will lift up mine eyes unto the hills, from whence cometh my help."[29]

Montana, in Norris's opinion, was a state just waiting to be engineered and he was prepared to put all of the resources at his disposal toward that end.

There was a rub, however. While Norris was poised to throw the weight of his college behind a movement to bring Pittsburgh to Montana through the untrammeled exploitation of Montana's natural resources, the college's own financial resources kept dwindling. In 1928, this starry-eyed missionary of engineering education and industrial development tendered his resignation to become dean of engineering at Virginia Polytechnic Institute. "I will regret exceedingly leaving my many loyal friends at the Montana State College and throughout Montana," he wrote. "However," he continued in a refrain that would echo through the corridors of the institution over the course of the century, "it must be apparent that any increase in salary must eventually come out of the operating funds which are already on a starvation basis. In fact it is this condition more than the personal financial advancement which has been the deciding factor." As for his colleagues, Norris had nothing but praise.

> The Engineering Faculty has been very loyal in trying to make the best of an impossible situation, but patience has almost ceased to be a virtue. Our budget for 1927-1928 was actually less than we had 7 or 8 years ago, while the registration has almost doubled. The ratio of our funds to our teaching load has steadily decreased until it is now only 65% of what it was at the outset of my administration.

"With nothing but discouragement facing us," Norris concluded, "I am sure that I am justified in making a change that offers greater opportunity for constructive accomplishment."[30]

Norris's abrupt departure came as a blow to sagging college morale, but Atkinson moved quickly to fill the dean's position with one of the most trusted members of the faculty, William M. Cobleigh. Born in 1872 and raised as the son of a minister, Cobleigh came of age in North Dakota just when authority of religion was declining in American life. Like other young men of his generation in search of a calling, Cobleigh turned to one of the new professions, engineering, and found in the College of Montana an institution that combined what to his mind seemed the best of all possible worlds: training in religion, science, and engineering. With the demise of the College of Montana, Cobleigh followed his mentors, F. W. Traphagen and A. M. Ryon, to Bozeman before embarking on graduate education at Columbia. Over the course of his distinguished career, Cobleigh studied at Harvard, Chicago, and M.I.T., eventually earning election to the American Academy of Sciences. He worked as a

chemist for A.C.M. and served as director of the state's water laboratory and chair of the Montana Sewage and Industrial Water Association. At MSC, he would serve as head of three departments and make the College of Engineering indispensable to the industrial development of the state. A gentle and forceful man, Cobleigh was remarkably well connected at the college. He married zoology professor Robert A. Cooley's sister-in-law and lived in close proximity to the Atkinsons. During Atkinson's administrative reorganization of the college, Cobleigh became one of the president's inner circle, a group that had tremendous influence over college affairs that extended from matters of hiring and promotion to textbook selection.[31]

William M. Cobleigh, dean of the
College of Engineering

Given Cobleigh's distinguished academic credentials and his niche within the college power structure, it came as no surprise that he was selected to replace Norris as dean of the College of Engineering. In 1929, with his appointment to the dean's position, he joined the S.P.E.E. and for the next twelve years continued Norris's general policy of building bridges between college and industry, refining one aspect of Norris's program—the personnel service—to near perfection.

The personnel service had been allowed to languish in Norris's last years as dean. Now, with the fervor of a Sunday school teacher with limited time on his hands, Cobleigh set out to revive the service as a means to shape the personality of his charges and prepare them for their future reward as professional engineers in the service of industry. As he explained to Atkinson, the personnel service was modeled on the "Purdue procedure," which insisted that "Upright character, correct living, service to society, agreeable personality, and, good citizenship are the objectives in the training of the engineer." Without diminishing the significance of the other objectives, Cobleigh sought to pare the Purdue procedure to its core. "Personality development," he informed Atkinson, "is the chief purpose of the personnel service. By means of personality ratings and performance records the service focuses the students' attention upon the importance of good traits of personality."[32]

Under his direction, the personnel service functioned as nothing less than an industrial sociology department similar to the one utilized by Henry Ford to control the behavior of his workers. The service worked this way. Initially only first-year students were required to "meet with the Dean in relation to the personnel service of the college of engineering."[33] But by 1930, "all engineering students" were admonished to discuss the importance of personality development with Cobleigh.[34] Exactly what Cobleigh told students can only be inferred from the records that survive. He probably told them that the service would be monitoring their character development as closely as their intellectual growth and would generate files on each of them that would be used to assemble a personnel dossier for their prospective employers. What he may or may not have told them is that the service would include relevant information from high school files and build a cumulative "personality rating scale."

Among the criteria used to evaluate a student's personality were appearance ("How do his appearance and manners affect others?"), initiative ("Does he need constant prodding or does he go ahead with his work without being told?"), leadership ("Does he get others to do what he wishes?"), emotional stability ("How does he control his emotions?"), and purposefulness ("Has he a program with definite purposes in terms of which he distributes his time and energy?"). In response to the latter, evaluators were asked to check a box that most accurately described the student. Each evaluator was given a range of possible responses: "Aimless trifler; Aims just to 'get by'; Has vaguely formed objectives; Directs energies effectively with fairly definite program; Engrossed in realizing well formulated objectives."[35] Another form asked for information about a student's "loyalty"—possible responses here ranged from "Considers his and the company's success as synonymous and builds up morale" to "Hypocritical and faultfinding,"—and about a student's "personality." For this latter, all-inclusive category, evaluators were asked to circle one

of four possibilities: "A. Unusually pleasing; B. Pleasing; C. Somewhat displeasing; D. Repellant." Finally, evaluators were asked to assess the "[m]oral character and personal reputation" of the student and to comment on those "OUTSTANDING traits" that would prove to be an advantage or disadvantage in later life.[36] This information was assiduously compiled by Cobleigh and made available to employers on request.[37]

Students were not left out of the process altogether. In the early 1930s, the personnel service helped the senior class produce "Senior Personnel Leaflets" that included information on "parentage," "health," and "physical defects" in addition to information about high school and college activities. By 1936, Cobleigh's new assistant, Merrill R. Goode, a local Sunday school superintendent and scoutmaster who had worked in personnel departments at Northwestern Bell and Western Electric, could boast:

> The advantages of pre-information on available seniors goes without question. Industry is served better and the ultimate effect will be more intelligent placement of our own students. This placement service has grown until now it has become almost a tradition among the seniors in engineering, and each year our industrial contacts look eagerly toward receiving their copy of our "SENIOR PERSONNEL LEAFLETS."[38]

The success of the personnel service in making students acceptable to industrial employers was remarkable. Louis Bender of A.C.M. called the leaflets "a very good thing and reflex [sic] great credit upon the school for getting up the record of the senior class of the College of Engineering."[39] Other companies were similarly impressed. During the hard times of the interwar period, due in no small measure to Cobleigh's innovative personnel service, the MSC College of Engineering built a solid reputation with leading industrial corporations like Westinghouse and General Electric for turning out professionals who were fit for the task of engineering America.[40]

No doubt the personnel service served the needs of industrial corporations. Whether it served the best interests of students is another matter. That personality ratings were a poor predictor of future performance became clear when one professor was forced to concede about a former student: "The [student's] weak point while he was with us was his personality. . . . Since graduation he has been with the Westinghouse Company and evidently has made good." Rather than acknowledge the shortcomings of the rating scale, however, the professor took another tack: "[The student] must have developed his personality a good deal since he left the institution."[41] Still more problematic was the conversion of the personnel

Merrill R. Goode, director of the personnel service

service into an internal intelligence-gathering unit that could thoroughly discredit students on the basis of hearsay and innuendo. "Information in regard to [one student] comes through a report from his counselor with the following statement: 'Fellow freshmen report that he thinks it smart to act dumb and to brag about drinking.'" The long arm of the service could even reach into a student's home community. Regarding another student, Cobleigh wrote: "On a personality rating scale, a business man in the young man's home town states that he is inclined towards drinking too much liquor. I have no evidence that he is drinking here, but apparently the tendency has been known to his neighbors at home."[42] Cobleigh fed such information to President Atkinson. Atkinson, who was prone to "sinking spells"[43] over the public perception of the college, saw the potential of the personnel service to play Big Brother within the institution, and informed Cobleigh of his thoughts: "It is probable that in the personnel records of individual students being built up by the teaching deans there sometimes appears information of personal conduct which would be of interest to the Dean of Men."[44] Cobleigh was clearly of the same opinion and kept his eyes open for behavior that college authorities—and potential industrial employers—considered deviant.[45]

If Cobleigh seems like a vintage technocrat, he was just that. In a 1939 paper presented to the Quest for Knowledge Club, he bared his soul to a group of colleagues: "A leader of men is one who creates illusion," he declared, while "a thinker is one who destroys it." Continuing, he explained, "everything, including all education outside the pure sciences, becomes a racket." For Cobleigh, only scientists and science-based engineers could know reality. Only they were free of illusions. Only they were "thinkers." The rest, "the majority . . . [were] inevitably wrong." Before he finished his address, Cobleigh elaborated on the implications of his reasoning: "[D]emocracy cannot operate by decisions made by the voters." Rather, democracy, not to mention colleges, was best run by experts who had been baptized in the waters of pure science.[46]

That Cobleigh's own faith might have been more illusory and ideological than true and correct never occurred to him. The virtual absence of women graduates from the College of Engineering, for instance, seemed to him to be in the natural course of things, and the high rate of unemployment among engineering graduates during the Great Depression only raised the heights of his rhetoric rather than causing him to question whether the welding of higher education to the interests of industrial corporations was anything but desirable. For Cobleigh, it came as high praise when his engineering students began dubbing MSC a "Techno Kampus."[47]

The Triumph of Agriculture

Despite the manifest rise of engineering to preeminence during the 1920s and 1930s, most Montanans, when they thought of MSC, thought of the school as the "ag college." In certain respects, this perception was on target. The institution did have the only College of Agriculture in the system and the campus barns could give the air a pungent quality. But most MSC students did not major in agriculture. Indeed, as a list of graduates from 1893 through 1930 made clear, degrees in agriculture lagged behind those in engineering, household and industrial arts, and applied sciences. What made the "ag college" label stick was the institution's original name (the Agricultural College of the State of Montana), the rural background of many of its students, and the work of MSC extension and experiment station agents around the state. What made the image unfortunate was that it obscured the deep immersion of the College of Agriculture in the gospel of efficiency and its work in applying principles of industrial efficiency to rural life.[48]

The seeds for this commitment were sown in 1893 when the state legislature authorized the creation of the state's first agricultural experiment station as part of the legislation locating the land grant college in Bozeman. The purpose of the station was clear from the start. Its overriding mission was to help develop the agricultural resources of the state by making information derived from scientific research and experimentation available to farmers and ranchers. Less than a year after its creation, the station began providing information about disease control, crop diversification, and irrigation problems. Between 1898 and 1904, bulletins on the feasibility of growing sugar beets stimulated the production of that crop and the building of the state's first sugar-beet processing plant in Billings in 1906.[49] (See more on the experiment station in Chapter 9.)

These contributions notwithstanding, the experiment station and agricultural program at the college remained a shoestring operation. Staff turnover was high, enrollments were ridiculously low, and finances were so limited that the first experiment station director had to depend on donations of equipment and supplies. Indeed, the first state appropriation for the experiment station came only in 1901, eight years after the legislature created the station to take advantage of federal funds made available by the 1887 Hatch Act.[50]

The reason for the reluctance of the legislature to fund the experiment station was the limited amount of agricultural development in the state. According to historians Michael P. Malone and Richard B. Roeder, at the beginning of the twentieth century "the eastern two-thirds of Montana lay wide open, with a settlement or Indian village

Experiment station nursery, 1895: Frank Traphagen (left), S. M. Emery (right)

Frederic B. Linfield, dean of the College of Agriculture

here and there, occasional herds of cattle and flocks of sheep, and nearly everywhere vast expanses of vacant public lands."[51] Had these conditions persisted, the experiment station no doubt would have continued to languish. But Montana was standing on the brink of a revolution. Beginning about 1905, the dryland farming movement, which originated in South Dakota, picked up momentum in Montana and led to the passage of federal homestead acts in 1909 and 1912 that made millions of acres of public land available for settlement.[52]

The effects on the state were staggering. Between 1900 and 1910, Montana's population increased by a third while the number of ranches doubled. By 1910, agriculture had outpaced mining as the state's leading industry. For the agricultural experts at the college, this was their moment in the sun. In the course of nurturing and criticizing the dryland movement, they did more than provide food for thought. They transformed thought into food. In so doing, they fueled the homestead boom, shouldered partial responsibility for its failure, and ultimately placed one of their own in Franklin D. Roosevelt's administration as undersecretary of agriculture.

The driving force behind these developments was Frederic B. Linfield. Born in Newfoundland in 1866, he moved to Ontario as a youngster and attended the Ontario Agricultural College. He obtained a job with the college dairy as a traveling demonstrator before attending a short course at the University of Wisconsin. Upon returning to Ontario, Linfield was informed by Professor Thomas Shaw, soon to become railroad financier James J. Hill's agricultural expert, of a job opening at the college in Logan, Utah. In 1893, Linfield and his wife moved west. Over the next several years, Linfield made a name for himself as the leading authority on the Utah dairy industry, and

in 1899, he became head of the department of agriculture at Utah College. His tenacious efforts to secure larger appropriations for his department evidently generated sufficient hard feelings so that when, in 1902, he was offered a professorship at MSC he eagerly decamped.[53]

What Linfield found in Bozeman was nothing less than an academic rodeo. He had been brought to MSC "to become a potent factor in building up [Montana's] infant industries so products such as butter, cheese, poultry, and hams, now supplied by Utah, may be produced by our own people."[54] But first he had to rectify the zany state of affairs that existed on campus among his colleagues. Not long before his arrival, S. M. Emery, the original director of the experiment station, had been asked to resign because of his ongoing disputes with the college administration and the Local Executive Board. When Emery refused to resign, the board took matters into its own hands and passed the directorship to Samuel Fortier. Fortier, under cover of darkness, hoisted a student on his shoulders, enabling the fellow to clamber through a window into the experiment station building and padlock Emery's office door.[55] The embattled director got the message and left. But this incident typified the state of the agricultural division of the college prior to Linfield's arrival. What Linfield added was a steadying hand and a gift for institutional entrepreneurship, and over the course of his thirty-year tenure at MSC, he built the College of Agriculture into a nationally respected source of expertise on applying industrial principles and scientific knowledge to agricultural expansion. Before he retired in 1937, Linfield could point with pride to any number of programs commenced under his directorship that netted millions of dollars for Montana's farmers and agricultural businesses. These ranged from grasshopper eradication programs to improved irrigation methods to research by entomologist Robert A. Cooley that would lead to the development of vaccines against Rocky Mountain spotted fever.

The key to Linfield's success was his talent for hiring and retaining bright faculty committed to the scientific management of agriculture. Initially, the mainstays of the agricultural division were Linfield and his fellow graduate of the Ontario Agricultural College, Alfred Atkinson. Joined by extension service director Fred S. Cooley and influenced by their former mentor and James Hill's chief advisor on agriculture, Thomas Shaw, Linfield and Atkinson hitched their wagons to the dryland movement. They accepted research money from Hill's Northern Pacific to find crops suitable for dryland farming and authored several bulletins promoting the need for moisture conservation and summer fallow. In this respect, they were better scientists than company men inasmuch as their advice on farming the dry lands ran contrary to the deep-plowing propaganda circulated by the railroad. Nevertheless, their disagreement with Hill was never whether dryland farming should be carried on, but how.[56]

One of those attracted by the new farming opportunities in eastern Montana was Milburn Lincoln Wilson. A native of Iowa's corn country, Wilson studied at Iowa State College and left with an abiding commitment to scientific management and to making the latest scientific information available to farmers. His early experience in Montana was less than positive. Iowa farming

scarcely prepared Wilson for the conditions of eastern Montana. After a fire destroyed his home near Fallon, Wilson might have thrown up his hands in despair and left the state for more promising climes. Instead, he set out to improve the methods of dryland farming.[57]

Wilson's keen intellect caught the attention of experiment station staff and in 1911 he was appointed to the position of Farm Institute lecturer. Two years later, after the state legislature authorized counties to pay a portion of the costs of a "county agricultural lecturer," Wilson assumed that post in Custer and Dawson counties, effectively becoming the state's first county extension agent. In the wake of the 1914 Smith-Lever Act that provided federal funds to establish a cooperative extension service, Wilson was selected by college authorities to train extension agents.[58]

Over the next five years, the extension service took root in the state. Wilson's agents carried the latest thinking of experiment station scientists to rural Montanans—ideas about everything from better livestock breeding and soil conservation to rodent control and fertilizers. They started boys' and girls' clubs—forerunners of the 4-H Clubs—around the state and helped organize state fair exhibits. Meanwhile, home extension agents focused on the home, especially on providing information about food and clothing preparation. By the time America entered the First World War, the extension service was a smoothly running machine that played a pivotal role in encouraging agricultural production, food conservation, and

Greenhouses and Agriculture Building (Linfield Hall) in foreground, World War I barracks in background

loyalty to America's war aims. At war's close, when the influenza epidemic hit, extension agents took a leading role in organizing hospitals and clinics in rural Montana. They became an extension of Montana State College, carrying the gospel of efficiency and scientific expertise into the farthest reaches of the state.[59]

Milburn L. Wilson, head of ag economics department

At war's end, as those far-eastern Montana plains became progressively drier, Wilson, with his gift for seeing around corners, took steps to address the economic and social disaster that he foresaw. In 1919, he set out to redress imperfections in his own education. By 1923, he had received a master's degree in agricultural economics at the University of Wisconsin and had taken advanced training at the University of Chicago and Cornell as well. Studying with the likes of University of Wisconsin economist John R. Commons and University of Chicago philospher James Tufts, Wilson produced work which was as much philosophical and social as it was technical and scientific. Indeed, these years of advanced study crystallized Wilson's own ideas about the relationship of democracy to science and higher education. For the rest of the decade, as head of the newly created agricultural economics program at MSC, Wilson put into practice ideas that would greatly influence the course of American agriculture for the rest of the century.[60]

The cornerstone of Wilson's philosophy was his Jeffersonian-inspired faith that the future of the republic depended on the well-being of small farmers. Layered on top of this conviction was a scientific pragmatism acquired through his advanced studies.[61]

Upon his return from graduate work, Wilson issued his famous "Dry Farming in the North-Central Montana Triangle." Surveying an area bounded by Havre, Great Falls, Cut Bank, and the Canadian border, Wilson examined the reasons for the success and failure of the region's farmers and laid down five fundamental principles for dryland farming:

1. Build reserves of soil moisture, feed, and cash during good years for use in unfavorable seasons;

2. Adopt a diversified farming base with shelter belts, farm gardens, milk cows, chickens, turkeys, and pigs to provide supplemental income when wheat crops are low;

3. Graze on a large scale when tillable lands are unavailable or marginal in productivity;

4. Use the largest units of tillable land possible with wheat as the principal crop; use teams or tractors and improved tillage methods to enable one farmer to cover a large acreage efficiently;

5. Develop dryland irrigation wherever possible through the use of flood and waste water.[62]

Managed scientifically, Wilson suggested, dry lands could become profitable farmlands.

To implement these principles, Wilson devised a grand experiment in social engineering that attempted to wed his faith in scientific pragmatism and the gospel of efficiency to the Jeffersonian conviction that small farmers were the backbone of American democracy.[63] His experiment turned on organizing a corporation that would purchase foreclosed farms and "throw these farms into regional units of machine-workable size and man their larger units with tenants who in the crash of 1920 or thereafter had gone broke." The idea was to "farm thousands of acres under modern principles of large-scale centralized management and make it pay." As Wilson explained it: "Our central idea was to put the weapons of industry—land with an adequate plant and equipment, financial and managerial assistance, accurate knowledge, adequate reserves—into the hands of men who had lacked the advantage of land." The result, Wilson believed, would be to help "capable men climb the ladder from tenancy to ownership."[64]

The immense scale of the farms required to realize this goal did not phase Wilson. "The economy of immensity," he argued, would result in "a new and 'fair way' of purchase-partnership between landlord and tenant" that in turn would "wipe out the remaining differences, distances, and distinctions between country and city people." "Within twenty-five years," he added, "the increased mechanization of agriculture and improved communication will make of the American farmer a town or city dweller."[65] In Wilson's eyes, yeoman farmers, informed with the latest scientific knowledge, could reestablish themselves under the umbrella of "corporation farming" and "restore as the buttress of our national structure the freehold, one-family farm." Astride their powerful tractors, plowing immense tracts of soil, these farmers would realize Jefferson's pastoral dream of America's future in the dry lands of northeastern Montana.

These ideas struck some as absurd, others as ingenious. John D. Rockefeller, Jr., stood in the latter camp. He found Wilson's ideas so compelling that he agreed to underwrite them with a loan of $100,000. In 1924, Wilson set up nine "Fairway Farms," including a 3000-acre experimental tractor farm at Brockton that was intended to convince farmers of the viability of becoming "factory farmers." Since most Montana farmers could not afford to travel to Brockton in the state's remote northeast corner, Wilson, with the support of the Great Northern Railroad, organized a fifteen-car demonstration train that transported "everything except the land" around the state. Mon-

Field lecture and demonstration near Glendive, 1912

tana State College agronomists traveling with the train told crowds what to grow, while engineers lectured about the tractors on display. The demonstration even included a motion picture and lectures about the totality of the Fairway Farms concept.[66]

Initial interest in the Fairway Farms project quickly gave way to the harsh reality of drought and to accusations that Wilson was mismanaging the farms. To keep the experiment alive, Rockefeller invested additional sums over the next several years. But financial difficulties, coupled with the worsening drought conditions in the 1930s, proved disastrous for the project. For Wilson, on the other hand, the Fairway Farms secured his reputation as one of America's foremost agricultural thinkers and contributed to Franklin D. Roosevelt's decision to invite him to

join his administration. In later years, Wilson would argue that the failures of the Fairway Farm project had been exaggerated and that the experimental farms had sewn the seeds for important federal programs like the Jones-Bankhead Act, the Farm Security Administration, and the Agricultural Adjustment Program.[67]

There were other consequences of the Fairway Farms project. During the interwar period, Wilson and Linfield, among others, tried to accomplish for Montana agriculture exactly what James Hamilton had accomplished for higher education. Where Hamilton set out to convert the college into a factory of learning, MSC farm experts set their sights on transforming Montana's agricultural lands into factories in the fields.[68]

In so doing, they generated a storm of protest that no doubt heightened the frequency and depth of Alfred Atkinson's "sinking spells." In the early 1920s, a group of merchants and wholesalers, facing bankruptcy from the dire agricultural conditions, banded together and formed the Montana Development Association. They became convinced that at the heart of their problem was the advice farmers were receiving from the farm experts in Bozeman about summer fallow. Over the next decade, this opposition continued to build and eventually became part of a nationwide movement led by the Chicago *Tribune's* Robert McCormick to curtail government funding of extension programs.[69] Between the mid-1920s and mid-1930s, opposition remained sufficiently strong in Montana that bills were introduced in the Montana legislature to eliminate all state funds for extension work.[70]

As the financial condition of the state continued to worsen and Atkinson was forced to terminate some faculty and to ask remaining faculty to forego one day's pay each month, the prospect of further cuts brought on by the concerted opposition of some business interests to the extension service and experiment stations was simply untenable. At the same time that Atkinson defended his staff to the chancellor, he also established two committees, one to examine the perceived involvement of MSC faculty in politically energized reform movements, the other to reexamine the philosophy of education for the college.

The Committee on State Problems and College Policy, chaired by Augustus Leroy Strand, included Merrill R. Goode, who, as director of the personnel service, knew one or two things about the influence of special interests on college policy.[71] This committee issued a stinging rebuke to agricultural staff who had been active in shaping and implementing Agricultural Adjustment Act measures. "Our non-partisan position and reputation as a source of unprejudiced opinion should never be compromised no matter what may be the exigency of a particular situation, nor how clear the path to worthwhile reform may

John T. Hays, Jr.,
Rhodes Scholar, 1935

Robert Tichenor,
Rhodes Scholar, 1938

appear to some *individual*," the committee declared, evidently overlooking the College of Engineering's own bedding down with corporation-based educational reformers. "Reforms," the committee added with a wag of its finger and no hint of hypocrisy, "have a way of producing side reactions and by-products entirely unforeseen and unexpected."[72]

While Strand's committee expressed concern about the alleged partisan reform activities of College of Agriculture staff, the committee on "philosophy of education" sought refuge from political heat in the cooler climes of the library and laboratory. As Frederic Linfield, chair of this committee, put the matter:

> . . . we as a faculty should consider in our philosophy of education the university ideal which we shall all I think agree is an inner thing. . . . It is an appreciation of learning which in its highest sense is a quest for something new, a process of creative discovery. It is a means by which modern man discovers those new truths he is in need of. . . . Higher education is built on the spirit of inquiry—original research . . . A university cannot maintain this ideal or transmit it effectively, unless it has a faculty of practicing scholars imbued with the spirit of scientific and humanistic inquiry, and the desire and skills to transmit this spirit through research and teaching.[73]

Original research, not political reform, was the true mission of higher education.

Perhaps in another state, at another college, the emphasis placed on original research by the Linfield Report would have been unnecessary. But at MSC, Linfield's sentiments reflected a growing undertow of faculty resentment over the college's vocational reputation and its "class C" rating.[74] Particularly grating was the worsening

condition of the library—a condition aggravated by the destruction of books ordered by the head of the library.[75] Although it was issued without much fanfare, the Linfield Report heralded the beginnings of a reform movement within the college that would continue to gain momentum after the Second World War and ultimately transform MSC into a research-oriented university.

Faculty, it needs to be emphasized, were not alone in clamoring for change at the college. Perhaps feeling boxed in by the precepts of "education for efficiency," some students in the 1930s began demanding a broader general education—a movement that took heart from the prestigious Rhodes scholarships that John Hays, Charles Jelenek, and Robert Tichenor earned in the years between 1935 and 1939.[76] Throughout the interwar years, moreover, students fostered a culture—a student culture—that helped bring the college increasingly into the national mainstream.

Student Life Between the Wars

Between the world wars, as historian Paula Fass points out, college students around the nation became agents of reform as they increasingly found earlier Victorian values out of step with the modern age.[77] At MSC, the 1920s and 1930s witnessed the emergence of an increasingly self-conscious youth culture with values that appeared shocking to an older generation of parents and college administrators. But, as historian Keith Walden cautions, what was woven into this youth culture was "not a self-confident peer society busily defining new standards of permissiveness and augmenting the authority of the young . . . but a conservative, insecure group increasingly susceptible to adult pressures."[78] Theirs was not a culture in open rebellion like the student culture of the 1960s. They were, as Fass puts it, "'naughty,' not angry." But, for the most part, their rituals

Bobcat Band, 1935

Engineering Society

Hamiltonia Literary Society, 1908

were liminal exercises easing their entry into the hierarchical world of corporate capitalism and its governing professional ethos.

Prior to the First World War, student life had been relatively unstructured on the MSC campus. Life beyond the classroom was governed by clubs, with students, for the most part, boarding in private homes and pursuing pleasure in Main Street establishments. It was precisely this lack of control of students, especially of women students, and the conditions of private boarding establishments that led to the construction in 1910-1911 of Hamilton Hall. The opening of this dormitory for women students motivated several male students to organize a Greek-letter fraternity, and in November 1911, Delta Chi came into existence, followed four months later by Kappa Nu.[79]

The surge in fraternities alarmed some faculty members who feared they would foster unwarranted social divisions among students. President Hamilton, despite his own membership in Sigma Chi, agreed with faculty hard-liners and in 1913 insisted that students respect the ban on Greek-letter fraternities handed down by the State Board of Education, a ban imposed on the college campus though not on the state university campus.[80]

However onerous, the ban on fraternities and sororities was short-lived. Student enrollment increased by 22 percent over the 1913-1914 academic year. And as the housing crisis became acute in Bozeman, pressure mounted to lift the ban. In May 1916, Chancellor Elliott agreed to allow the establishment of fraternities and sororities at the college. The next year, Alpha Omicron Pi was organized as the first sorority on campus and was quickly followed over the next seven years by Chi Omega, Pi Beta Phi, Alpha Gamma Delta, and Kappa Delta. Fraternities similarly expanded. Between 1919 and 1939, Sigma Alpha Epsilon, Alpha Gamma Rho, Kappa Sigma, Pi Kappa Alpha, Lambda Chi Alpha, and Phi Sigma Kappa were established.[81]

Cliolian Literary Society,
ca. 1897

Dramatics Club, 1918

New Student Facilities

In 1922, a new gymnasium replaced the overcrowded facilities of the old drill hall, enabling the college to expand its physical education, intramural, and intercollegiate sports programs. The building, which was officially named in the autumn of 1973 for G. Ott Romney, once the director of physical education as well as an outstanding basketball coach, included handball courts, a tanbark running track, a swimming pool, and a gymnasium that seated 3000 spectators at basketball games, assemblies, dances, and conventions.[1]

The Quad

Completed in 1926, under the direction of W. R. Plew, supervising architect of the college, Herrick Hall was designed to relieve the pressure of classroom space in Linfield Hall for the expanding home economics department. The first floor of Herrick Hall afforded students several research laboratories, including a "rat room" for nutrition experiments, a small dining room, and two classrooms. Clothing laboratories, administrative offices, a seminar room, a kitchen and dining area, and the "fireplace room" (the fireplace was finished only after students, seeing that construction monies had run short, launched their

Herrick Hall

own fund-raising campaign) filled the second floor, while the third floor accommodated lecture rooms and five studios. Named for Una Herrick, dean of women and director of the College of Household and Industrial Arts, the building was the first on campus to be dedicated immediately upon completion and only the second—after Ryon Labs—to be named for a living person.[2]

Because the number of women students increased dramatically at the end of World War I, Dean of Women Gladys Branegan pressed for new living facilities to be financed through Public Works Administration funds and a federal loan. Her plans were initially opposed by President Alfred Atkinson, who saw the scheme as an unwarranted expenditure of public funds. However, Atkinson eventually lent his support to plans for a quadrangular complex to be built at Cleveland and 7th, site of the College Inn. Once known as the Bobcat Lair and a popular socializing center for the campus, the College Inn was consequently relocated a few blocks away and converted to a grocery store. Completed in 1935, the Alfred Atkinson Quadrangle provided "superior accommodations" for its women students—three separate fireproof Tudor-style buildings each housed twenty students and a "house mother," while a central kitchen in the north building supplied service to the units through a tunnel system. Reasonable rates combined with a clublike atmosphere drew much of the campus social life to the Quad in the absence of the proposed student union building.[3]

1. "Gymnasium," Louis True Papers, Acc. 88-032, f. "MSU 75th Anniversary Slide Program—MSU and How It was Built," MSUA; "Gymnasium Building," in "State College Statement to December 1, 1922, of Expenditures from Educational Bond Funds," f. PA.6.Buildings, MSUA; "Gymnasium Aids Students," *Montana Collegian*, 1:1 (December 1924), 3.

2. "Home Economics Offices Are Moved to Herrick Hall," *Montana Collegian*, 2:9 (November 1926), 3; "New Building Will Accommodate Women's Division," *Weekly Exponent*, 5 January 1926.

3. Mark Dotson, "History of Residence Halls and Family Housing," f. A6.1.Quad, MSUA; "New Building Started," *Montana Collegian*, 10:3 (September 1934), 2; "College Inn Moved," *Montana Collegian*, 10:4 (December 1934), 4; "Residence Halls for Women, Montana State College, Bozeman," f. A6.1.Quad, MSUA; "MSC's New Resident Hall Only One of Kind in U.S.," *Weekly Exponent*, 26 September 1935

On one level, these fraternal and sororal organizations were simply a response to the growing pressure for adequate boarding facilities in the community. On another level, fraternities and sororities were seen by college administrators as wholly compatible with the drive to educate students for efficiency. As one faculty member explained, Greek-letter organizations would prepare young men and women for a world "where men and combinations of men of different classes meet, mingle and clash."[82] With their elaborate initiation rites, rituals, and codes of behavior, fraternities and sororities became a dominant force in the social life of students, preparing them as much for the efficient pursuit of pleasure as for professional careers.

No less important and probably more intrusive was Septemviri, an honorary society established in 1920 by the conservative Atkinson to safeguard campus traditions. Consisting of seven senior men recommended by the faculty, Septemviri, together with a sophomore unit of enforcers known as the Fangs, instilled values of hierarchy and social deference in their peers. Under the watchful eyes of the Fangs, who often assumed sentry posts at the main entrances to campus, first-year men were required to wear green beanies while women were required to wear green tams. Among other things, first-year students were prohibited from using the main entrance of buildings, walking on campus lawns, sitting on upperclass benches, wearing high school emblems, and sporting mustaches. They were also required to help athletic managers when requested to do so and enjoined from dating until the "M" had been painted. Violators were compelled to appear before the Septemviri who could order punishments that ranged from summary haircuts to paddling to late night dunkings in the muck of the frog pond.[83]

However harsh, these officially sanctioned hazing practices need to be understood in the context of rapidly shifting social relations that took the nation by storm after the First World War. Dean of Women Una B. Herrick captured the response of her generation to the shenanigans of young people when she reflected:

> Many old fashioned ideals were shattered according to the "Olders" of the generation. The whole world of "Younglings" seemed to say: "Here, you pressed us into war to 'save the world for democracy,' now the order is going to change." But what and how, the "Olders" inquired. The "Younglings" could not reply. They only knew by doing, by trying it out. Social precedent changed; many customs were eliminated, but the hearts of the "Younglings" were honest and fine.[84]

Among the fads that college students were trying out were wild and crazy dances like the Charleston. More threatening to campus "olders" was the growing practice of "necking" and "petting." Under the headline, "Necking—Chief Campus Sport," the editors of the student newspaper observed:

> Neckers . . . You can find these strange creatures wherever there is room to sit down and often when there is not . . . fraternity house stairs, park benches, cars parked anyplace anytime, benches, anywhere that is fairly convenient and comfortable. . . . Anyhow, we must commend the general tendency toward privacy in these oscilatory [sic] activities. Necking and petting have gotten to be about as common as eating and sleeping and about on a par as far as excitement is concerned as well.[85]

The collapse of moral restraint was exaggerated (according to a 1938 poll of women students by the *Exponent,* 96 percent of the respondents said they did not believe in premarital intercourse), but many parents nevertheless expected the worst of their rapidly maturing children.[86] The father of one fraternity member complained to Chancellor M. A. Brannon that at a fraternity party at the Baxter Hotel the dining room "was very dimly lighted with the exception of the place where the orchestra was playing." As the chancellor informed Atkinson, the young man's father "was able to discover from the shadow dancers that many of them were making use of the deep shadows for decidedly active necking and unseemly behaviour and he was quite certain that liquor was being used freely notwithstanding the fact that two faculty members were acting as chaperons." Atkinson immediately consulted with Dean Cobleigh and reported that the parent had evidently confused a sorority dance, which Atkinson and his wife had chaperoned, with a public cabaret held at the Baxter the evening before. The relieved chancellor replied: "I am very happy to know that the functions sponsored by any of the State College organizations have clean and satisfactory records."[87]

It was precisely this spiraling concern about the collapsing moral structure of the nation's college youth that led the Atkinson administration to empower students to control peer behavior through organizations like Semptimviri, the Fangs, and Spurs—the latter, the women students' counterpart to the Fangs. A similar drive for social control inspired the growing fetish for physical education and intercollegiate athletics at the college.

Prior to the First World War, physical education had been equated primarily with military preparedness in the college curriculum. The allied victory only lent validity to this equation and

M. A. Brannon, chancellor of the university system

fueled demands after the war that the wind-blown and frosty drill hall be replaced with a modern gymnasium. As supporters of the new gymnasium put it in 1920, "One of the lessons impressed by the war was the very great need for physical education by the young people of the whole country."[88] In the eyes of college administrators, there were other compelling reasons for a new gymnasium. As Chancellor Brannon explained, the gymnasium would be "a shrine to be used for the development of good sportsmanship. Sportsmanship is needed not only in college athletics, but also in the game of citizenship." Atkinson took a slightly different tack, drawing a line between physical education and career preparation, when he noted that "although people may

have a very broad education, if they have not the physical machine to carry them through, they will never get very far." At the same time that they rationalized the $5 million dollar gymnasium on grounds of citizenship training and professional preparation, campus administrators never lost sight of another advantage of the structure: it would allow college authorities to centralize and monitor student social activities, especially dances.[89]

The ritual and ceremony of athletics perfectly complemented the social function of physical education. Between the wars, MSC's intercollegiate athletic teams, especially the men's basketball and football teams, came of age and played out the academic rivalry with the state

Rivalry on and off the Gridiron

Rivalries between Montana State College and the state university at Missoula ran deep. MSC's distinguished alumnus Henry C. Gardiner, Jr., related the details of one extraordinary escapade:

For several years after I entered Montana State, the annual football game between the Bobcats and Grizzlies was held on our respective campuses, alternating. Then it was decided that they could probably do better from the standpoint of receipts and convenience if they held it in Butte, which was, of course, midway between Missoula and Bozeman . . . It so happened that . . . the second year [of this arrangement], I was

president of the student body in Bozeman, and the president of the student body in Missoula was from Anaconda. We'd been in high school together, so there was that interesting coincidence, and I had talked to him . . . on the telephone about the arrangements for the game. . . . And it was agreed as to which band was to play first and that each team would parade their respective mascot. The university had a bear at Missoula, and we had a bobcat. Now our bobcat for a while was kept here in Bozeman, but he was not a tame bobcat and was something of a problem. So . . . we sent him over to the Columbia Gardens Zoo in Butte

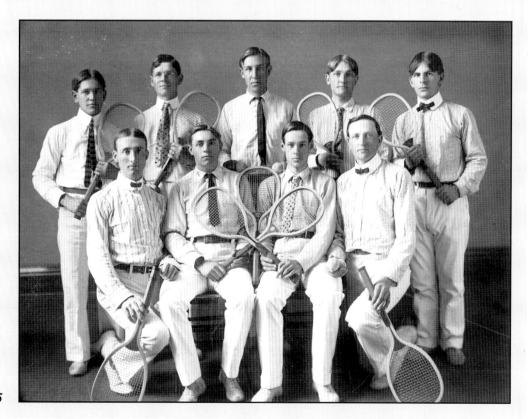

Tennis team, 1905

*Women's basketball team,
1912*

with the understanding that we could have him anytime we wanted him. . . .

For the occasion of this particular game, I went over to Butte the afternoon before on the train with the football team . . . [my] mother was meeting me in Butte with the family car from the ranch. When I got off the train, I was met by the head of our alumni in Butte, and the first thing he said to me was "Did you authorize the release of the bobcat today?" And I knew without another word what had happened. I realized that these smart university students had gone up there and gotten our bobcat. . . .

Well, I went uptown and talked around there a little bit, and made some inquiries if anybody knew anything about the Grizzlies' bear. . . . Was it in town yet? No, it was coming in on a special train that was due in the next day just in time for the game. But somebody said, "You know, there's a bear at a filling station just west of Butte, and we heard that they might be renting that bear, and not bringing one over." Well, that was a possibility. But I felt that if they had stolen our bobcat, they certainly would have their bear protected.

In any event, I drove down there in that big old Hudson we had. . . . And I went up to this filling station, and I saw this little bear tethered out there on a chain, two chains, matter of fact . . . and I said to the attendant, "You know, I'm from the University of Montana. We just hijacked the college bobcat and we heard that they might try to come out here and get your bear tonight, rather than wait until the morning." . . . [The] young kid there at the filling station . . . said, "Well . . . we've

agreed to rent our bear tomorrow." "Well," I said, "I'd like to get him tonight, because surely [the Bozeman people will] be out here any minute to pick him up." "Oh," he said, "I couldn't let you have it." . . . But I said to this boy, . . ."[H]ere's ten dollars for the bear. You let me have him, and we'll return it to you unscathed, unharmed, after the game." "Well," he said, . . . and unhooked this bear.

The bear had a collar with two chains on it, so [it] could be kept in position and wouldn't be hiding all the time. And I started out with that bear, with another boy on the other chain. . . . And we started out in the dark to get away from the filling station on the assumption that if this was their bear they'd come and get it any minute. That was at Rocker, . . . [a] sort of an abandoned mining community; there were holes around there—old shafts—and we were dodging those in the dark. We finally got far enough away, and we tied this bear to a telephone pole. And then I went back and told my mother to go to the ranch and get the foreman there to come back with a truck, because we couldn't put this bear in the car. . . . Now here we have this bear staked out to the bottom of this post, and the dogs in the area are just raising cain. And I was so sure that anytime up would come the university crowd looking for their bear, and would hear this rumpus. . . . [Meanwhile], the bear had scooted up to this crossarm on the telephone pole, sitting there. . . .So I sent this one boy to buy all the chocolate, all the Hershey bars he could, at some little

Interclass basketball champions, 1910

place down the road. . . .Well, we coaxed the bear down with a piece of chocolate. He clambered down and gobbled this chocolate, and . . [as] soon as he put that chocolate away, he started up the pole again. . . . [T]o keep him down, or to get him back down, we had to keep feeding him these chocolate bars. . . .

"Well, it seemed an eternity, but finally here comes our ranch foreman with a truck and with a sheep crate on the back of it. So we load him in that and take him off and put him in the barn at Willow Glen. We were reasonably sure that if they started to look for him they wouldn't look for him down there. Then we went back into Butte and got on the telephone. At that time there was a Mr. Lemon who was superintendent of the Anaconda smelter and whose daughter was a student at Montana State. They had a zoo at Anaconda. So we . . .told him what the

Rifle team, 1924

situation was. 'We have a bear, and we think we have the bear that the university was going to use. But they may suddenly decide that they have to find a bear, and might come up there and try to get your bear at the zoo. . . .'" "I'll see to it that . . . nobody gets any bear . . . ," he promised us. And we did that with several places. We called every place we could think of who might have a bear in that section of the state.

[But] we were still concerned that [the Grizzlies] might have their bear on that special train they were coming in on from Missoula. Well, students do a lot of screwball things. At that time, the Milwaukee Railroad, before it went into the Durant Canyon, went through a grade crossing near Gregson. . . . So we went down there and put some red fuses on the track. . . . And when the train was about to come in there we lit these fuses. Well, the train came to a stop, and we had a crew [of students] on hand to take that bear by force. . . . Of course, [when the train stopped], the conductors came up and wanted to know what the hell was going on. And while that confusion was on—the few minutes the train was stopped there—we got into the baggage car. [N]o bear. So the train took off.

So, now we're down to game time practically. And there was a big to-do when out comes the university band, and no bear. And out comes the college band, and no bobcat. . . [W]hat they had done with the bobcat was to put him in a crate and ship him on the Milwaukee to Spokane, where they had someone pick him up there. And subsequently they shipped him back, consigned to us, actually, freight collect, with the crate all painted in university colors.[1]

1. Henry C. Gardiner, Jr., interview, 27 July 1988.

university in Missoula on the gridiron and court. The centerpiece of the athletic program was the basketball team that came to be known as the Golden Bobcats, coached first by Ott Romney and subsequently by Schubert Dyche. Renowned for introducing the fast break, or "fire-engine" style of play, the Golden Bobcats, with a host of talented players, including J. Ashworth "Cat" Thompson, John "Brick" Breeden, Max Worthington, and Orland Ward, won the 1928-1929 national collegiate championship. During the dire economic times of the late 1920s, their team became the rallying point for the college and a source of immense pride around the state. (For further discussion of the Golden Bobcats and the development of the school's athletic program, see Chapter 8.) Sustaining a winning tradition, however, entailed consequences that sometimes undercut the educational mission of the college.[90]

In 1930, Atkinson, who, as much as anyone, basked in the glory of the Golden Bobcats, received a letter from Coach Dyche asking that a failing grade received by one of "his boys" be removed from the official transcript and that the student be allowed to substitute another course.[91] Twenty-one years later, when allegations of scandals in the athletic program forced Dyche's resignation as athletic director, the coach defended his actions by claiming that athletics had become nothing less than "a business."[92] In an important sense, Dyche was absolutely right. No less than courses in business and engineering, the rituals and practice of big-time college athletics, with their emphasis on winning, team play, loyalty, and, on occasion, tolerance for cheating, prepared one for entering the brave new world of corporate capitalism.

But student acceptance of this new bureaucratic and hierarchical order was far from complete. For all of their elaborate systems of social control, including the personnel service, administrators were still plagued by worries about student conduct. Among their concerns were smoking (between classes, smokers used to dash for the cover of a fence located along the north side of campus), hoboing (students constantly hopped trains), secret student marriages (marriage was deemed grounds for suspension), and the consequences that followed from giving students a measure of control over their own social space in fraternities and sororities.[93]

These latter consequences came to light in an episode that made national news. In 1930, Dean Herrick, who had been at the college for two decades and had, to be charitable, a Victorian attitude toward student conduct, decided to put an end to student carousing after dark. On November 11, Herrick, without consulting students, announced that henceforth college women had to be in their rooms by 11 p.m. on weekends rather than by midnight, as had been the custom. With

Atkinson out of town, Herrick's decision caused an immediate uproar. By that same evening, a Tuesday, her efforts to rein in youthful hormones had generated a powerful backlash in sororities and fraternities as students determined to issue an "appeal for freedom" from administrative controls. Before the end of the week, students had organized a boycott of classes that lasted four days and received coverage in *Time*. When Atkinson returned, he let students know in no uncertain terms that he found their actions intolerable, that Herrick's decision would stand, and that the administration would continue to draw up guidelines for student conduct without consultation with students.[94]

By comparison with contemporary student activism at other colleges and universities—centering mainly on the Oxford Pledge never to fight in another war—the 1930 student strike at MSC may seem relatively insignificant.[95] But it did reflect a growing sense of autonomy in student culture during the interwar period and attested to the limits confronting college authorities who wished to mass-produce students for machine-age America.

As if to underscore the reservoir of student resistance that continued to plague MSC's corporation-minded administrators, the 1933 college yearbook came off the press. Brainchild of two students, Dave Rivenes and Chris Schlecten, the *Montanan* was a delightful parody of "education for efficiency." As Merrill Burlingame describes it:

> The Bobcat basketball team had not been outstanding and the usual team picture was that of 10 candy bars—"Butterfingers." The introductory page to the society section was a superbly photographed setting of "Anti-B.O." soap and a bottle of mouthwash. The story of the year in drama was introduced by an equally well photographed grouping of premium hams. The usual group picture of a leading sorority was replaced with a picture of the house with a generous sprinkling of Sunkist-brand lemons scattered on the lawn.[96]

The yearbook brought Atkinson just the kind of attention he most feared—public laughter. And the prize the yearbook received for being the best college annual of the year deprived him of the pleasure of suspending Rivenes. But most importantly, the yearbook spoke volumes about the contradictions of the "life of the mind" at Montana State College. If, as historian Keith Walden argues, "[I]ndustrial capitalist society was not likely to concede any real power, except consumption, to such a potentially volatile group as the young," consumption itself could provide a vocabulary for developing a critique of the dominant order.[97]

The 1933 Montanan

The 1933 student yearbook brightened an otherwise dismal year. With its sarcastic and irreverent look at college life, it generated equal doses of mirth and anger before winning a national prize for the most creative student yearbook production of the year.[1]

As ingenious as it was, the '33 yearbook was not without precedent. Earlier college annuals—for instance the 1910 edition of the *Montanan*—had poked fun at professors, administrators, and students. And the earlier yearbooks had certainly reflected the bawdier side of student life. But the '33 yearbook stood in a class by itself.

Two individuals, Dave Rivenes and Chris Schlecten, had actually hatched the idea for an alternative annual while they were still in high school. When Rivenes gained election to the post of yearbook editor at MSC, the idea became reality. Rivenes' pal Schlecten took all the standard yearbook photographs of students, student organizations, faculty, and administrators, but he also photographed another friend, Bill Rider, dressed as a cross between a rodeo clown and hobo. (Rider, as Rivenes later revealed, agreed to be photographed in this garb "never fully understanding the purpose.") Schlecten then proceeded to superimpose pictures of Rider, renamed Clarence Mjork, onto the regular yearbook photographs. Rivenes, meanwhile, attended to the copy, rejecting student contributions and, with the help of a local printer, substituting in their place excerpts from *The Rover Boys Go to College*.

The finished yearbook captured the attention of the college community. As readers turned the pages, they found each class section introduced with a photograph of a jug filled with an unidentified liquid. As they followed the progression of classes toward graduation, the level of the liquid in the jug decreased until, at the outset of the senior-class section, the jug stood empty. The photograph of the student association president showed the fellow hitching a ride on a freight train, while the photograph of the women students' association president depicted her sitting on Mjork's lap. In the caption to another photograph, readers learned that the fictitious Mjork was the "campus playboy." The caption for the photograph of the women's basketball team read: "They beat [the men's team] in a three-game series. It seems the boys couldn't last the full game—they usually gave out about in the third quarter." Schlecten and Rivenes similarly satirized fraternities and sororities, interspersing photographs of cows and sheep with shots of fraternity and sorority members.

All of this might have been dismissed as innocent fun except for one problem. President Atkinson had written the introduction to the yearbook without ever having seen the copy, and Atkinson, as might be expected, penned a sober introduction, linking student traditions to confidence in economic recovery:

> During periods of business depression it is important that insofar as possible, there should be continuing records of attainment and general group activities that have proven valuable under normal conditions. It is gratifying therefore, that the present Montanan staff has maintained the customary high standards in this year's Annual. It reflects the confidence of the oncoming generation in the soundness of America's opportunities. Such confidence is essential in bringing about economic recovery.

In a final flourish, Atkinson praised the yearbook staff. "I commend your sound optimism," he wrote.

Exactly how Atkinson secured a copy of the yearbook's first printing is unclear. But he did secure one and immediately made his displeasure known. He might have ordered Rivenes and Schlecten to abandon the entire enterprise, but he saw the folly—and expense—of ordering the press to destroy the entire run. He did insist on purging several photographs, but he allowed the censored version of the yearbook to circulate. In 1990, Rivenes donated a copy of the uncensored version to Special Collections at the MSU library.

The 1933 Montanan episode raised many questions. At issue were basic concerns of freedom of speech as well the degree to which the ideology of education for efficiency had taken hold in the minds of students. Perhaps the central lesson of the 1933 Montanan was that the overall effect of education for efficiency was never so absolute as to render its target, the students, passive cogs in machine-age America.

1. From "Mjork Goes to College," *Billings Gazette,* 5 March 1991; Louis True, "The 1933 *Montanan*," ca. 1970; and the 1933 Montanan, all in Acc. 90056, MSUSC.

A. L. Strand, president of the college, 1937-1942

The Strand Years and Another War

The Atkinson era in Bozeman came to an end just before the shadows of agricultural depression began receding across the state. In 1937, Atkinson resigned his position at MSC to assume the presidency of the University of Arizona. Under his presidency, it had become impossible to think of modernizing Montana apart from the college's involvement. Atkinson's replacement, A. L. Strand, proudly bore the imprint of his MSC education. Born in 1894 in Texas, Strand was raised in Butte and Helena and came to the Bozeman campus as an undergraduate. He distinguished himself as a writer for the student newspaper, as the editor of the campus yearbook, and as a leader in the fight to establish fraternities on campus. After a stint with the military, Strand completed graduate work in entomology at the University of Minnesota before returning to MSC in 1931 to head the department of entomology. He quickly established a statewide reputation for his effective practice of chemical warfare against the devasting grasshopper invasions of the early 1930s.[98] Like his predecessor, Strand shared Hamilton's vision of Montana State College as the M.I.T. of the West and shared the basic precepts of Hamilton's "education for efficiency"

Flight officials, army air force training program

philosophy. Restoration, not innovation, was his byword, and over the course of his five-year presidency, Strand did his utmost to help the institution recover from the calamities of the depressions of the 1920s and 1930s. Yet, as was the case with the nation as a whole, it required more than one person or one set of programs to put the college on the road to recovery. It required the

impact of an external force so great that the institution, like the nation as a whole, would be jolted to its very core. That force was another world war that, far from restoring the institution, helped transform it from an ideologically land-locked college into a fledgling university.

The Second World War, no less than the first, brought rapid changes to the campus. Five hundred soldiers from the Army Air Forces Training Command were trained at the college, putting enormous pressures on the limited housing available for students and requiring food services on a scale that only the recently opened Student Union Building could provide.[99] As was the case with the First World War, disciplines across campus rapidly converted to a wartime footing. The nursing program helped fill the void left by the departure of so many professional nurses for military hospitals; the home economics department once again played a vital role in food conservation programs around the state; and college agricultural specialists concentrated on enhancing the yield of Montana's fields for the war effort. In the autumn of 1942, in response to the onset of unexpectedly harsh weather and the acute shortage of agricultural labor, male students were excused from classes to harvest sugar beets in the eastern part of the state. (During subsequent harvests, Japanese-American internees at the Heart Mountain, Wyoming, relocation center replaced MSC student labor in the fields.)[100]

The impact of the war was felt everywhere on campus, especially in the College of Engineering. In 1941, the U.S. government launched the Engineering, Science, and Mangement Defense Training Program (ESMDT) to supply the armed forces and the nation's industries with trained personnel. When the government called for production increases of, in some cases, 3000 percent, William Cobleigh, then dean of the College of Engineering concluded: "What government and industry wanted was the mass production of engineers for design, construction, supervision, maintenance, teaching of operators, and research work to develop new defense equipment ahead of the rapid obsolesence inherent in war activities."[101] Cobleigh wasted little time implementing radio training courses and formulating a proposal, ultimately accepted by the military, to develop radar detection courses that would train individuals for industry. These curricular changes accompanied another, more profound change in the College of Engineering. For the first time in its history, the college recruited a significant number of women to fulfill the terms of the ESMDT program, which specified that men and women be included in the short courses developed to train qualified technicians for the nation's industry.[102]

The spirit on campus during the Second World War was aptly captured by the program developed for the annual high school week re-

Wartime Harvests

In the fall of 1942, as war raged in the European and Pacific theaters, Montana's sugar beet growers confronted an acute labor shortage, with many young men away in the service. Since sugar beets were the only cash crop for many Montana farmers, the harvest was critical to the state's economy.[1]

At the request of the growers and at the insistence of Montana Governor Sam Ford, the state's colleges agreed to mobilize their male students for work in the beet fields. For the better part of two weeks, nearly 800 young men from MSC labored in the fields, pulling in the harvest. In return for their labor, they received a dollar a day, free room, and $1.05 per ton of beets harvested. Once in the fields, students worked with local residents, including high school and junior high school students, as well as racially segregated work crews that included African-Americans, Mexicans, Native Americans, and Japanese-Americans from the relocation camp at Heart Mountain, Wyoming. Their collective labors saved the beet crop and helped the state avoid a devastating economic blow.

Racially segregated work crews were nothing new in Montana, but the presence of Japanese-American crews was a sign of the times. In February 1942, President Roosevelt had issued Executive Order 9066, depriving Japanese Americans of their civil rights and forcing them into relocation centers for the duration of the war.

Montanans, like most Americans, generally supported Roosevelt's decision. The governor went so far as to exclaim: "One damned Jap in this state is too many!" Bozeman, moreover, had never been a bastion of racial tolerance. But during the war, one fraternity rallied around Victor Ohta, a Japanese-American student from the Livingston area. This fraternity,

unlike others, had no racial exclusion clause in its constitution and, despite the protests from alums around the state, invited Ohta to join. Over the course of his student career, Ohta completed a premed curriculum. When he graduated in 1946, he joined the military, compiled a distinguished record, and became a respected physician in southern California.

Ohta's career gave lie to the racist rationale that underlay the forced relocation of Japanese American citizens during the war. And the actions of the fraternity challenged the college to live up to the demands presented by America's multiracial society. In 1944, some students rose to that challenge and asked Paul Robeson, a renowned singer and political activist, to write a dedication for the yearbook. Robeson, who had visited Bozeman a year earlier, complied with their wishes and wrote a letter to MSC students reflecting on the role they would have to play in shaping the peace that followed the Second World War. "The basic principles," Robeson declared, "are clear—the decisive one—the indivisibility of Freedom. All men, including the hitherto oppressed, have been promised a greater measure of liberty and the opportunities for a richer life." He concluded with this admonition: "I would dedicate myself and hope that these students would dedicate themselves to working toward such a realizable ideal."[2] With these words, Robeson gave voice to a solid strain of idealism on the campus that three decades of education for efficiency had been unable to erase.

1. Information on the beet harvest can be found in Ray B. Haight's presentation before the Montana Institute of the Arts, History Group, Acc. 491a, MSUSC.
2. 1944 *Montanan.*

cruitment drive organized in 1942. Taking as its theme "Keep 'Em Training," the program included the usual speeches and campus tours, but with a definite wartime twist. It featured a "surprise attack" barbecue picnic held outside the entrance to the campus air-raid shelter, located in tunnels connecting Traphagen Hall, Bridger Hall, and the old music building.[103]

Whether he knew it or not, Cobleigh, who served as interim president of MSC in 1942-1943 after Strand resigned to become president of

Oregon State University, was presiding over a college that would never be quite the same. Returning military personnel would boost enrollments, bolster demands for a larger faculty and new facilities, and question the need for green beanies. Just as important, the atomic bombs dropped on Japan ushered in an era in which science, especially physics, would take command. Within the short space of twenty years, Montana State College, under the direction of Roland R. Renne, would be transformed into a university.

Chapter 4
The Renne Years, 1943-1964

A Liberal Comes to Office

The extraordinary transformation between World War II and the mid-1960s of Montana State College into Montana State University, the flagship institution of the state's higher educational system, was unquestionably one of the most significant developments in Montana's educational history. Numbers alone illustrate the dramatic change. In 1944-1945, at the close of the war, MSC's enrollment was 1155 students. By 1964-1965, enrollments had risen to 5250. Faculty had increased in number from 132 to 389. During the same period the physical plant grew in leaps and bounds, campus acreage more than doubled, and the number and extent of undergraduate and graduate curricula mushroomed. Research and public service programs increased impressively. By the time the school assumed the title of Montana State University on July 1, 1965, Bozeman's "cow college" had come into its own as one of the Northern Rockies' leading educa-

Roland R. Renne, president of MSC, 1943-1964

tional institutions. It was no coincidence that these remarkable developments coincided with the administration of Dr. Roland R. Renne, MSC's president from 1943 to 1964. The least that can be said of Roland Renne, or Rollie, as his friends knew him, was that he was an absolute dynamo, an acknowledged workaholic—"a slave to work" is how his family described him— who committed his life with extraordinary zeal and dogged determination to transforming MSC into a true university and Montana's leading public service agency.

Born in 1905, Renne grew up on a marginal truck and dairy farm in the remote Pine Barrens of southern New Jersey. Reared in a devout Presbyterian family, he attended small, rural schools before being admitted in 1923 to Rutgers University, New Jersey's land grant institution, where he majored in agriculture. Upon receiving his degree, summa cum laude, from Rutgers in 1927, Renne was admitted to graduate study at the University of Wisconsin, from which institution he obtained the Ph.D. in agricultural economics in 1930.

From his Rutgers and Wisconsin experiences, Renne developed a philosophy of education closely identified with the land grant college tradition. A champion of public education, he enjoyed scoffing at the stuffiness of the great private institutions, whose elitist enrollment policies violated his sense of justice. His family still recalls the old Rutgers jingle he taught them: "'Don't send my boy to Harvard,' the dying mother said. 'Don't sent my boy to Harvard; I'd rather see him dead.'" [1] Instead, Renne's sympathies and attachments were clearly linked to the midwestern state universities, and particularly to the University of Wisconsin, which was acclaimed in Renne's time as the epitome of the land grant college.

To understand the impact of Wisconsin on education in Renne's time is to understand not only Roland Renne, but twenty-one years of Montana State College history, for one of the major dictates of Renne's way of running MSC was the so-called Wisconsin idea, a philosophy of education which permeated that institution when Renne enrolled there in the late 1920s. This ideal, forged in the 1890s and refined in the years before World War I, articulated a philosophy that would become acknowledged as the educational credo of the progressive movement that swept America in the first twenty years of this century, and of which Roland Renne was a devout follower.

The key tenet of the Wisconsin philosophy was service to the state. As a historian of the movement observed, the public university had a responsibility to "remain hospitable to every form of creative endeavor in the humanities, the natural and social sciences, and the practical arts, sending into the community a steady stream of dedicated citizens who [would] lead the way to constructive advance in every realm." [2] Defined further, service to the state was "the provision of expert leadership in a great variety of spheres and the extension of new knowledge gained in the university's research programs to as large a segment of the population as possible." [3] As one of Wisconsin's early presidents remarked: "I shall never be content until the beneficent influence of the University reaches every family in the state. This is my ideal of a state university." [4] Such ideals deeply impressed the young graduate student from New Jersey and shaped the central axioms of his faith in higher education as an agent of democracy. [5]

The Wisconsin ideal of service to the state had taken its earliest shape in the field of agriculture. Over the years a distinguished array of educators gave form and substance to the university's effort to upgrade the state's livestock, dairy, fruit, and vegetable industries. Wisconsin's efforts in the social sciences were fully as distinctive. The creation in 1892 of the School of Economics, Political Science, and History represented one of the nation's first concrete efforts to institutionalize scholarship in the social sciences. Its founder, Richard T. Ely, was one of the nation's foremost economists, a man strongly attracted to the problems of American labor, and a leader in the so-called social gospel movement of that time. German-trained, he had broken with classical, individualistic, laissez-faire economics to formulate a philosophy of cooperation wherein "the truths of science and religion were complementary, and all the institutions of men—church, state, family, school, industry, should work together to advance human progress." [6] It was a middle-of-the-road philosophy that espoused neither capitalism nor socialism, but a "new individualism," a cooperative outlook that fell midway between the two ideologies. [7] When Ely came to Wisconsin in 1894, his development of "the social law of service" attracted the attention of a wide circle of educators, many of whom came from thousands of miles away to study and then extol the virtues of the Wisconsin system. When young Roland Renne arrived in Madison for graduate study in 1927, the septuagenarian Ely, still teaching, was Wisconsin's most widely known faculty member, and he had a significant impact upon the Wisconsin student body.

While Ely influenced Renne, the inspiration of the equally renowned economist, John R. Commons, was even greater. Commons had come to Wisconsin in 1904 as Ely's assistant. A political scientist and sociologist as well as an economist, he served as a leader in espousing nonpartisan commission government "as a device for uncovering public needs and formulating solutions to meet them." [8] Under the leadership of Commons and others, Wisconsin faculty "increasingly became advisers to the state administration, in the sciences, engineering, finance, education, and agriculture." [9]

Commons was America's pioneer historian of the country's labor movement, an "easy-going, sober, tolerant" reformer who believed that cooperation among contending forces could be achieved only by the application of strong leadership and strong administration. Commons actually held that scientifically enlightened and expert administration ought to replace legislation as the fourth arm of government. [10] The "need to impose order" in society was another important ingredient of his view on life. Although Commons advocated collective bargaining in the marketplace, it is important to note that he had no intention of undercutting the authority of the managerial system. Instead, "he warned the enthusiasts of industrial democracy that labor could not and did not want the responsibilities of managing industry." It was "immoral," he thought, to encourage labor in this expectation. The members of a corporation, Commons argued, could not function without strong executive leadership.[11]

Renne responded enthusiastically to Commons' teaching. He conducted his graduate research under Commons' direction, and acknowledged a lifelong indebtedness to his mentor. Put together, the concept of service, coupled with strong executive leadership, nonpartisanship, and the separation of politics from administration, all of these at the very center of the progressive reform movement, indelibly shaped the actions of the young social scientist who arrived on Bozeman's campus as an assistant professor in agricultural economics in 1930. Other offers had been placed before him, but he wanted to broaden his experience by becoming acquainted with the West and its agriculture. [12] Moreover, the Treasure State, as a predominately labor-intensive region, provided him with an outlet for his emotional attachment to the laborer generally, and to the small farmer specifically.

Although progressivism and its educational philosophers theorized about a nonpartisan application of the "social law of service," putting this idea in practice was more difficult. As an avid supporter of a particular approach to life, framed within an identifiable political structure, Renne could not help but proceed naturally from the ideology of progressivism into the ideology of its successor, the highly politicized New Deal of Franklin Delano Roosevelt. As a member of MSC's faculty, Renne did not hesitate to throw his support and energy fully behind the economics and philosophy of the New Deal. During the 1930s he addressed groups all over Montana and the West extolling the AAA and the NRA, in the process lauding Keynesian concepts of government pump priming and government direction of the economy. FDR's fiscal policies were the right antidote for curing the depression, Renne insisted before many groups in many communities. As department head of agricultural economics in the late '30s, he worked closely with the WPA. Unlike MSC's depression-era president Alfred Atkinson, who resisted federal funds for campus dormitory construction, Renne proved adept at securing New Deal support for educational purposes. As chairman of the Bozeman city school board, he promoted a plan to pay for three new elementary schools—Hawthorne, Irving, and Longfellow—with federal funds. When town conservatives blocked Renne's building plans on the grounds that the New Deal was socialistic, Renne persevered almost single-handedly, and Bozeman was able to get construction under way at great savings. [13] In 1942, during World War II, it made sense for a man like Renne, who supported strong governmental initiatives in economic decision making, to accept a position with Montana's Office of Price Administration and Civilian Supply, the Roosevelt administration's effort to protect consumers by controlling prices and establishing a system of rationing.

Renne's arguments and actions on behalf of a regulated, cooperative, and, if necessary, controlled economy left no recourse for advocates of unfettered private enterprise, Montana's political conservatives, but to brand him a committed liberal and a Roosevelt New Dealer and to see him as a danger to their cause. When Renne left the OPA in 1943 and was appointed acting president of MSC on September 1, alledgedly at the insistence of the chancellor of education, Ernest O. Melby, an observer summed up conservative attitudes when he notified the Republican governor, Sam C. Ford, that

> [The Republicans] don't like Dr. Renne because he is a new dealer. The story they are telling is that Melby made the state board of education promise that he could name the president of the state college and that he picked a new dealer similar to himself. They feel that Renne and Melby both favor federal interference in agriculture and education. I guess Wes is pretty burned up and Zales is also. The general situation appears to be that some of the university people are not in key with the public. [14]

The "Wes" and "Zales" who were disturbed with Renne's appointment were Wesley D'Ewart, Montana's eastern district congressman from Wilsall, and Zales Ecton, from the Gallatin Valley, who would, in 1946, win election to the U. S. Senate. Ranchers both, D'Ewart and Ecton epitomized the existence of a major resistance to Renne's presidency, the Montana Stockgrowers

Association. To the stockgrowers, and to conservatives generally, Renne and the philosophy he espoused were simply not consistent with the Treasure State's prevailing political climate. The 38-year-old acting president had, by his actions and philosophy, declared his politics as liberal and in conflict with those espoused by the political right. This identification with liberalism would be one Renne would have to contend with his entire administrative career. Of all MSC/MSU's presidential administrations, Roland Renne's would prove the most politically contentious.

Following a year as acting president, Renne was appointed to MSC's presidency in 1944. His inaugural address, given during ceremonies that were postponed until April 1945 because of the war, most likely disappointed his ideological adversaries. The new president said little about liberal economics, but much about a liberal education. Entitled "The Future of the Land-Grant College," his address first worked its way rather subtly through several developments which Renne found bothersome. One of his major concerns was with overspecialization and fragmentation in knowledge, of particular concern at a technical institution like MSC. Technical and scientific specialization, Renne argued, quoting the philosopher Jose Ortega y Gassett, too often produced all the talents "except the talent to make use of them," while fragmentation fostered skepticism, detachment, and a lack of perspective and judgment. Renne wondered in this line whether the nearly 1000 courses listed in MSC's catalog weren't excessive. He spoke also to complaints he had heard all too often on campus and on his many travels about "too narrow a curricula, turning out agricultural graduates who slaughter the English language, home economists who cannot spell, and engineers who have had so little biology that they do not know… 'how or why they are born.'" The important question, he then posed, was how to "best organize our teaching, research and extension programs to turn out well-rounded effective citizens and best serve our state and nation." [15]

Renne paused at this moment to speak about the role of the college, any college, as "a creation of a democratic form of government." Then he became more specific:

> As "democracy's college" we must not fail to meet the test and to make the adaptations which are necessary if we are to continue our position of leadership in higher education. The spirit of the land-grant colleges can be characterized as one of pioneering, of progress, of service and of democracy. If we can continue to exercise this spirit we will fulfill our highest function. Those institutions which most completely surrender themselves to the state and nation in a spirit of service will be the greatest among us. [16]

Romney Gym, c. 1950

Awaiting registration numbers, 1948

Renne then proposed a course of action that must have both surprised and impressed his audience. Launching into the "big controversy which is now raging and has raged for a long time in education," Renne declared war on a state educational system that denied MSC a "liberal arts and classical type of education." "I do not feel," he remarked, "that either the strictly liberal arts institutions or the strictly technical and professional schools have any right to feel that either of these two types of education alone will fill the bill. Our aim should be to try to combine the best in both and eliminate the worst in each." Renne went on to argue that proficiency in the applied fields and natural sciences was "not enough if our graduates are to be outstanding leaders and our research and extension programs are to be most useful in the development and well-being of Montana and the nation." Renne would not go so far as to demand majors in the humanities and social sciences, but he insisted that MSC had to "incorporate" these fields into the curriculum to overcome criticisms leveled against the school as "over-technical and excessively narrow." Pointing out that MSC allocated only 16.9 percent of its instructional budget for the humanities and social sciences, Renne called for a substantial increase of outlays for the liberal arts. It was time, he said, for "a more realistic appreciation of the values of the humanistic-social science subjects and the improvement of all our services in the interests of serving the general welfare." [17] As Merrill G. Burlingame observed in his seventy-fifth anniversary history of MSU, Roland Renne had just "laid the groundwork for the projection of Montana State College into Montana State University." [18]

Taking the Helm

Renne's immediate and more visible actions were less idealistic and liberalizing than they were pragmatic responses to problems brought on by the conclusion of World War II. Of these, the need to construct classrooms and student housing necessary to serve the requirements of veterans returning from that conflict occupied a large portion of his time. Encouraged to avail themselves of the remarkable G.I. Bill, which provided dollars to support the veterans' right to a good education, men and women released from military service flocked to the nation's campuses. MSC's student body almost doubled in 1945-1946, increasing from 1155 to 2014. Another huge increase took place the following year when

Some of the trailers brought in to house World War II vets and their families

At the 1952 groundbreaking. From left to right: John Hurst (math), A. J. M. Johnson (physics), P. C. Gaines (acting president), and Frank Cotner (dean of the division of science)

surplus wooden-frame buildings for single- or double-family occupancy; numerous quonset huts; and one large barracks that became a men's dorm housing 376 students. [19]

Together, the new instructional buildings and student dorms provided much-needed emergency facilities, but just how efficient they were was questionable. As one professor recalled: "You wouldn't believe the classrooms we had to work in. . . . One could prepare well and with great expectation for a class, but all of one's enthusiasm for teaching could be lost when entering these barracks." [20] The two-story wooden barracks between College and Cleveland were ill-repaired, possessed faulty steam heating and lighting, and extremely poor blackboards. They were also feared as fire traps, and another instructor had repeated nightmares of barracks infernos. [21] Student-faculty housing was also primitive. The wooden frame buildings were heated by leaky coal stoves, the land about the dwellings was unimproved, and when it rained faculty and students had to "wade through a sea of mud." [22] While all of these structures were erected in a state of emergency and were considered temporary solutions at best, virtually all of them became fixtures on campus for more than a quarter century, not to be removed until the 1970s and 1980s.

In the meantime, it was not difficult to sell the campus housing shortage to the authorities in Helena. Fortunately, the state had cut back many services during the war; the result was a surplus of some $4.5 million, a goodly portion of which was allocated by the legislature to provide state agencies with needed buildings. MSC used its share of this surplus to construct a new brick library and make improvements and repairs to the physical grounds and plant. To accommodate these additions and changes, a new campus plan was adopted, one result of which was the removal of the crescent drive that had formerly approached Montana Hall on the north from Cleveland Street.

With the exception of the Quad, built with reluctance by President Atkinson during the depression, substantive construction of major buildings had not taken place anywhere in the university system since the late 1920s. In 1948 the voters of the state, persuaded of these realities by the State Board of Education, authorized raising the educational mill levy from 3 1/2 to 6 mills, and approved a $5 million bond issue for building programs. Unfortunately, the monies appropriated were not distributed for four years. High-Line politicians, angered that the Board of Education's allocation did not sufficiently reward Northern Montana College, successfully pressured the State Board of Examiners to withhold release of the voter-approved funds. Two legislative sessions passed before the politicos were satisfied and the monies were released. In the meantime, fast-rising inflation in building

3591 enrolled. This figure increased slightly again in 1947-1948 to 3664.

Renne moved quickly to meet the need. He did so by applying perhaps his greatest strength—imaginativeness, boldness, and shrewd use of monies. Using as a base some $50,000 acquired from the federal government for on-campus military service programs run during the war, he purchased a substantial number of large frame buildings formerly employed at a federal chrome mining project near Columbus. These were adapted for use by a variety of disciplines, including physics, chemistry (a lab), nursing, education, engineering, agriculture (the wool lab), psychology, and music. Living quarters for the many new students were met in creative ways by importing house trailers (some 125 of them); prefab war-

Acting president P. C. Gaines and J. Hugo Aronson, governor of the state of Montana, 1952-1960, break ground for the new men's dorm, 1953

costs had eaten away a substantial percentage of the fund's purchasing power. When, finally, in 1952 MSC did get its portion of the state allocation, the college constructed a mathematics-physics building (now A. J. M. Johnson Hall), an animal husbandry addition to Linfield Hall, a lab for veterinary research, an addition to the Ryon engineering laboratories, two greenhouses, and a service shop. [23]

Even though enrollments had fallen to 2331 in 1954, due primarily to the decline of G.I. students, pressure for permanent dormitory space, substantiated by national studies predicting large increases in enrollments in the decade ahead, enabled President Renne that year to persuade the Board of Education to authorize a $4.5 million bond issue to construct dormitories for 634 men and 304 women and an addition to the Student Union, including a bowling alley, an enlarged bookstore, a small auditorium for theatrical use, and a health service wing. Revenues obtained from the use of these structures were to serve as repayment of the bond. No state monies were required to fund the building program. [24] Renne was a whiz at arranging creative ways of funding construction; he measured his financial capabilities as one of the major successes of his presidency. His success in purchasing at bargain rates land on the college's peripheries was another thing he took great pride in. Over the objections of many, including those who opposed the land sales because this would result in the withdrawal of taxable lands from the county's tax rolls, Renne

was able to extend the campus a full mile to the west, and one-half mile to the south. [25] The current 1170-acre campus is in large part the product of his vision, as well as his fiscal capability.

The large increase in student enrollments demanded that MSC also augment the size of its postwar faculty. Renne played a part in all hiring decisions. Between 1945 and 1950, the number of faculty almost doubled, from 132 to 257. Graduates of land grant institutions were in an overwhelming majority. MSC degree holders predominated, but roughly 20 percent of the faculty had degrees from either the University of Minnesota or the University of Wisconsin. Faculty with degrees from the universities of Nebraska, Iowa, and Illinois were sprinkled throughout the ranks. Salaries were modest, but the transition to twelve-month contracts with eighth-quarter leaves for professional growth proved attractive. As always, the beautiful natural environment of southwest Montana helped in luring quality candidates. The small town atmosphere—Bozeman was populated by only 11,252 souls in 1950 and was not much larger than Livingston—appealed to yet others.

Faculty who came in the late '40s and early '50s spoke not only of Bozeman's qualities, but of an ambiance in the campus community they enjoyed immensely. When Charles Bradley, fresh out of Wisconsin as a geologist, arrived in 1950, he was impressed with what he saw. Salaries were low, but faculty spirit was high. "Here they were, working like the dickens. . . taking on impossible jobs. . . . They all knew each other; they all liked each other. Everybody seemed to be getting some zest out of what was going on, rather than threatening to leave. I found that really a wonderful spirit to come into." Bradley associated that "zest" with the warmth and zeal of Roland Renne. [26]

Renne's ritual orientations for new faculty characterized the president's sense of purpose. Held two evenings the first week of classes, these get-togethers featured two speakers per night followed by light refreshments. One such orientation in the early 1950s was structured as follows: Renne opened the first evening's meeting with his standard, "This is MSU: Organization, Administration and Service." He was followed by Cy Conrad, from the art department, who gave a talk titled, "This is a Good Place to Live," which described "cultural, religious, educational, recreational and service opportunities" for new faculty and their spouses. The second evening featured Charles Bradley from geology who talked about the "Origin and History of the Gallatin Area," followed by Maurice Brookhart, head of testing and counseling, who lectured on "The Students We Work With," covering the background and training of MSC's student body, the work of the testing and counseling service, and the competence of Bobcat graduates. Department heads were responsible for bringing all new staff and spouses to the meeting and introducing them. These orientations were a common means by which Renne introduced both himself and the spirit and sense of community he desired to instill in MSC's faculty. [27] This ambiance was not experienced by faculty only; students felt very close to a president who made every effort to identify with them. Renne seemed to have eternal youth; he chatted with students regularly on his campus meanderings, put them in increasing numbers on advisory councils, and even challenged them to a vigorous game of handball or tennis, at which he played with all the ferocity associated with that of the college's mascot. [28]

On the other side of campus a young agricultural economist, Edward Ward, another Wisconsin graduate, recalled that inasmuch as the faculty and staff were small, "everybody knew everybody." There was no need for annual flowery curriculum vitae to justify promotions; whether a faculty member was productive or dogging it was common knowledge. Cross-fertilization between departments was considerable and fruitful. [29] When a department desired to hire and had Renne's go-ahead, there was no reason to go through the hassle of a national search. Department heads just singled out their candidates and got them. The success or failure to make good hires determined the department heads' continuity in office. Teaching loads were heavy, with fifteen hours, or five courses per quarter, the norm. Teaching, research, and service were the maxims by which personal industry was measured. In the sciences, particularly, research activity was strongly encouraged. But the "publish or perish" ethic that would later characterize calibrations of faculty capability was not a fixed policy. Similarly, whereas in later administrations service to the state would be demoted to a lower priority, under Renne, outreach was given significant weight in determining salary and promotion—memberships on State committees and commissions, for example, were deemed as important as publications. [30]

This commitment to service proceeded naturally from the outreach example Renne himself set. His own scholarly output and the roadwork he undertook to keep MSC in the public eye were perfectly awesome. Take 1949-1950. Addressing innumerable groups and conferences visiting the MSC campus, he also spoke to various assemblages in Billings, Butte, Great Falls, Hamilton, Miles City, Three Forks, Eden, Joliet, Circle, Forsyth, Glendive, Helena, Hardin, Whitehall, Judith Gap, Ekalaka, Baker, Lodge Grass, Dillon, Livingston, Lewistown, Fort Peck, Sidney, and Martinsdale, not to mention many meetings in Bozeman. Renne echoed the philosophy of his Wisconsin mentors, and it seemed clear that he would "never be content until the beneficent influence of the University reache[d] every fam-

ily in the state." Outside of Montana he made presentations at conferences in Wyoming, Washington, North and South Dakota, Minnesota, Iowa, California, Arkansas, Missouri, and Colorado. He visited the nation's capitol at least four times in the course of the year. When President Harry Truman appointed him to the federal Water Resources Policy Commission in January 1950, Renne spent almost the entirety of June and July attending hearings all over the country. His presentations and involvements throughout this period covered a wide array of subjects: from water resources, water conservation, and river basin development to banking, farm economics, land management, Indian affairs, and Christian stewardship. On top of this, in 1949-1950 Renne published six articles and reviewed two books. [31]

This was an awesome act for anyone else to follow and laid out impressively what Renne thought a land grant employee ought to be gauging his worth by. And if all of this wasn't sufficient to bury a normal man, the Rennes had their own eighty-acre working farm on Sourdough Road, where the president and his wife, Polly, ran most everything, from horses and cows, to sheep, hogs, and chickens. Colleagues recall his rushing breathlessly home during the evening hour to eat and carry out farm chores, then rushing back to the campus to carry on at the office. When time was short and the chores imposing, one or more of Renne's deans might be pressed into service as a farmhand. [32]

Despite Renne's announced determination to broaden the humanities, in 1950, five years after his inauguration, the liberal arts and social sciences, while increasing in size, still functioned primarily as service departments—providing enrichment for the sciences and engineering, but offering no degrees. In many cases "service" meant simply serving up courses requested by the engineers, the botanists, the biologists, or the bacteriologists. Research was not expected of service department faculty. To be sure, the time required to be productive was seriously limited not only by the large number of hours entailed in teaching five courses, but by the attitudes of many nonhumanists. These attitudes were perhaps best characterized by the jaundiced views of the crusty dean of the division of science, Frank Cotner, who told one geologist that he didn't "give a damn" about research in that discipline; Cotner believed, as one professor of speech put it, that "English, Speech and Drama were necessary evils that had to be endured, along with History." [33] As might be expected, service departments were quite limited in scope and size. Art could be offered only as "Applied Art." Sociology was linked to economics, psychology was joined to education, and speech was found within English. Geography/geology was a one-man operation. History and modern language each had a staff of four. Such departments as political science and philosophy didn't even exist.

The inability of the liberal arts to expand in a manner consistent with that called for in Renne's inaugural address of 1945 was due in part to his belief that such change should be achieved only with care. Renne had the authority to govern the pace of change. When attempts were made to speed up the humanizing process, Renne would balk and urge patience, not because he opposed disciplinary expansion in this area, but because he feared conflicts with Missoula over duplication and the negative impact these would have on his efforts to secure continued state funding for MSC. In short, Renne was obliged, in his estimation, to adopt an evolutionary, rather than revolutionary, attitude toward improving the liberal arts and social sciences. Progress was made slowly, but a 1960 accreditation review criticized the prevailing "service" character of the humanities and social sciences. The latter, the report noted, were virtually "orphans" in the academic field. [34]

On campus, Renne, like his predecessors, possessed almost dictatorial powers. The understanding that this was Roland Renne's college, that President Renne "ran the college out of his hip pocket," was a reality every faculty member had to come to grips with sooner or later, and the sooner the better. When one junior faculty member suggested in 1951 that MSU salaries were not up to par, Renne's response was to the point: "No assistant professor's going to tell me how to run this college," he said. [35] The outcome, in fact, provided practically no salary enrichment and even a reduction in full-time equivalents, or FTEs. Calling it an "adjustment" required by declining enrollments, Renne arbitrarily slashed ten faculty positions in 1951, six of them from the arts and humanities. [36]

Virtually every decision affecting promotion, tenure, salary, travel, even the assignment of class materials, came under Renne's purview. Nothing seemed to escape his eye. There was no systematic way of determining how one merited any kind of recognition; these decisions were made, some thought capriciously, some thought justifiably, by virtue of some kind of insight or intuitiveness Renne had about the quality of any particular employee, project, or proposal. This had its pros and cons.

On the pro side, Renne's desire to be the decision maker in every aspect of college administration saved departmental heads, and faculty, many hours of what he considered unnecessary labor. There was no need, for example, for faculty to worry about college governance. Renne did it all, having such a high regard for his own administrative capabilities that he sought to spare others the effort involved. Faculty meetings were held primarily, it seemed to those who attended, not for mutual discussion of campus policy, but as press conferences during which Renne laid out his ideas and policy. One of his administrative counterparts at the University of Montana, had heard, for example, and he put credence in the rumor, that Renne's scheduling of faculty meetings at 5 p.m. was intended to discourage faculty participation, the staff being tired and hungry after a hard day's work (in Missoula, such meetings were held at 3 p.m.). [37] Many faculty applauded Renne's one-man administration since the system of unilateral decision making relieved them of onerous tasks best suited for the professionals. This attitude was quite conspicuous

The Deans Council, 1957. From left to right: Val Glynn, Leon Johnson, Frank Cotner, E. W. Schilling, P. C. Gaines, Roland R. Renne, Maurice Kelso, James Nickerson, Katherine Roy, and Martha Hawksworth

amongst the faculty from the professional schools—engineering, business, and agriculture in the main.

But the fact that the sharing of governance at MSC came very slowly, and hardly at all during Renne's tenure, can also be looked at negatively. Even his deans complained about not being consulted. The Deans Council was at best a sounding board; it had no authority whatsover. If it did desire to develop a point, and Renne didn't agree with the point, "he'd simply cut off the discussion, just like that." [38] Many faculty believed that the most important person on campus, besides Renne, was not an academic, but the business manager and treasurer, Bernard Copping. Department heads and even deans were often completely frustrated in their ability to determine the level of funding to be allocated to their operations, so thoroughly did Renne control the budget. As one dean reminisced, "I'd submit my departmental budgets, and my dreams and justifications. After a long period of silence the budgets would come back with no apparent correction to what we'd put in. No explanations. Nothing. Mostly what happened was a slight percentage increase across the board. . . . It was a kind of desperate feeling of not getting anywhere." [39] Another administrator put it this way: "Renne ran this institution out of his back pocket. He'd just go into the closet with Bernie Copping. . . and decide how much there was in the budget and then just come out and announce things. . . . Leon [Johnson] once told me that he was with Renne and he just went down the list, 'yes,' 'no,' 'yes,' 'no,' and that was that." [40]

Renne's virtually complete control of MSC's administration was a reflection of the power he had developed in Helena. In 1943, the State Board of Education had restored the old chancellor system by appointing to the office Ernest O. Melby, on leave from the presidency of the state university at Missoula. It was Melby, it will be recalled, who, in one of his first acts in office, appointed Roland Renne acting president of MSC. The Board of Education, and the politicians who favored the restoration of the chancellorship, including the governor, Sam Ford, no doubt honestly believed that an administrative position of this kind was necessary to harness the contentiousness that existed among the university units. Melby worked hard to control the divisiveness, but failed. For one thing, he had to contend with a long tradition of hostility in both the legislature and university system toward the chancellorship form of administration. The suspicion that Melby was still a Missoulian at heart was another factor that worked against his cause, as did his espousal of a unified budget for the university system. A fourth factor contributing to his downfall was his association with the Montana Commission on Higher Education. Appointed in 1943, the com-

mission published a report two years later that insisted Montana could not afford to finance six university units. Although Melby had not endorsed the commission's conclusions, he had supported similar recommendations, adding that he favored a single institution with branches. The smaller units, including MSC, feared a power play by the university and rebelled. [41] Consequently, the legislature refused to act on either the Melby Plan or the commission's recommendations, preferring instead to request individual budgets from each of the system's units. This was a departure from traditional practice, and it opened a leadership opportunity for the aggressive president of MSC who, because of numerous administrative changes at the other units, particularly at the state university, became the senior member of the Presidents Council. When the chancellorship was phased out in 1950, Renne's influence increased proportionately. [42]

For all practical purposes, Renne served during the 1950s as the unappointed representative of all six units to the Board of Education and state legislature. As senior member of the Presidents Council, coupled with his natural penchant for leadership and a remarkable capability for salesmanship, Renne assumed responsibility for meeting the needs of not only his own institution, but of those of the other units as well. This involved budgeting, finance, bond issues, millage needs, and a variety of other issues relevant to higher education. Renne was on the road incessantly, addressing groups on the significance of aid to higher education. At home he organized conferences for the purpose of educating the state's politicos on the intricacies of university budgeting, for many of the legislators were too apathetic, insufficiently informed, or ill-organized to grasp the complicated ways in which, for example, varying teacher-student ratios and graduate versus undergraduate teaching loads impacted budget formulas.

Renne labored hard to bring the legislators into a positive relationship with the university system. During the 1950s he was able to secure considerable support for the system generally, and for MSC specifically. His way with the politicians was shrewd and compelling. He developed a reputation as a kind of persuasive giant. "[Renne] was incredibly efficient," observed a legislator/banker from Victor. "I went down to a committee on education [once]. . . with a specific purpose—to take some money out of the [education] budget. . . . I made the four [other presidents] mad. Very, very mad. They left. And Renne finally took me on head to head, and when they [MSC] got through they whipped me so bad it was beautiful. They took me apart with cold hard logic and ended up getting most of what they needed." [43]

Renne's battles before the Board of Education with Carl McFarland, president of the univer-

sity, were just as legendary. Encouraged by their respective constituents, the two fought like "pit bulls." [44] McFarland despised Renne; he would not acknowledge him in public. He correctly perceived that Melby's failure had turned to MSC's advantage, and he scrapped ferociously to prevent Renne from besting him. If Missoula couldn't obtain an objective, then the tactic was to deny it to Bozeman. A "master of bad human relations" is the way one university faculty member described his president. [45] McFarland's successes, and those of Harry Newburn, who followed him, were mixed. The Missoula school was able for many years to hold on to academic areas it claimed as its own bailiwick, particularly in the arts and humanities. But in other areas MSC gained materially. Ph.D. programs were authorized in chemistry and chemical engineering, a division of education was created in 1954, and four years later a graduate program, including a doctorate in education, was approved. This latter gave much-needed formalization to the training of teachers, which had been going on at MSC for many years. Progressively, the department of commerce was expanded into what would later become the School of Business.

No matter what the opposition, Renne always seemed able to increase the size of the campus plant. A major instructional and office building, Reid Hall, was put in partial use in 1958. A new dairy center followed in 1959, and one year later a medical science research building was constructed with federal funds. A number of dormitories were constructed, including Langford, Culbertson, and Mullan halls; others were planned. (The extraordinary field house he financed in the late '50s is described in Chapter 8.) At the same time, Renne continued to increase campus acreage. While some branded this expansion program an example of profligate spending, others viewed it as an awesome achievement.

In Missoula it prompted nothing but envy. The competition between the two units was so strong that one way of viewing the activity of the 1950s is to see it as a championship boxing match, a match that Renne won rather decisively—if not by a knockout, then by a convincing decision. Renne's success in securing funding for MSC projects was unrivaled; it threw a sense of paranoia into Missoula's officials, who kept a close eye on the MSC president, always fearing that if they didn't, "he'd get into your pockets." [46] Given Renne's repeated successes, it was not surprising when a new member of the legislative council in Helena recalled how stunned he was when the redoubtable president of MSC was first pointed out to him. The diminutiveness of Renne, but 5 feet 5 inches in size, absolutely shocked him, as he had been convinced by what he had heard that this was a person of great physical size. [47]

Religion at MSC/MSU

From its very beginnings, the college possessed a strong religious character, making it rather unique among the nation's rural land grant schools. Indeed, MSC was virtually founded on a religious base, as the initial faculty in 1893 came almost in its entirety from the Presbyterian College of Montana in Deer Lodge. MSC's first permanent president, James Reid, was an ordained Presbyterian minister, and William Cobleigh, the first chemistry instructor, who later served both as dean of engineering and as acting president, was a leader in the Bozeman Presbyterian church. In the early days, faculty appointments with Presbyterian connections were made with regularity. So strong was the relationship between this faith and the college, that the description of MSC as a Presbyterian academy was not taken lightly. [1]

Students from industrial arts constructing the Danforth Chapel

But the heavy Presbyterian influence did not prevent the development of congenial relationships between the campus and other churches in the community. In the mid-1930s, the Gallatin County Ministerial Association ran a series of weekly seminars, involving four to eight local pastors, through MSC's history department. These seminars were well received and were gradually expanded so that classroom instruction by community pastors was a part of the campus curriculum for the next thirty years.

Religious Emphasis Week (REW) first evolved in the 1940s. Mirroring a national campus trend, it received funding from both the college and the ministerial association. The program was run initially through the department of history, but soon became significant enough to be transferred to the office of student affairs under the direction of the campus religious coordinator, Patricia Stenhjem Anderson. Providing a full week's program of panels, speakers, and exhibits, REW became an institution at the Bozeman campus from the 1940s through the late 1960s. [2] Catholics and Jews took some part in the activities, but Religious Emphasis Week was primarily a reflection of the mainline Protestant background of rural Montana and the students it sent to MSC. The demise of REW in the late 1960s resulted in part from the emerging conflict between these traditional Protestants and the new evangelicals over control of the program. [3]

Another development that underlined the quasi-Protestant character of MSC was the college's affiliation with the Danforth Foundation, a nondenominational, but Protestant-oriented, benevolent enterprise of William H. Danforth and the Ralston Purina Company. The Foundation sponsored Danforth Associates, faculty who served as touchstones for student spirituality, and Danforth Graduate Fellows. Clyde McKee, dean of the College of Agriculture, was appointed the first Danforth Associate at MSC in 1940, and Patricia Stenhjem became MSC's first graduate fellow when in 1950 she was tapped for a year's training in religious leadership in Alabama. [4]

The Danforth Foundation also underwrote the construction of chapels on campuses across the nation, and shortly after World War II, Roland Renne became very interested in building a Danforth Chapel at MSC. To secure the Foundation's grant of $5000, the college had to raise $20,000 in private local monies and guarantee student commitment to the project. It was a major undertaking, but the response was extraordinary. Architecture students took on the task of designing the exterior of the chapel. A Jewish student, Emanuel Milstein, a senior in architecture, actually spearheaded the design project. The horticulture department advised on location of the chapel and its landscaping. The art department designed the interior, its furnishing, and the stained-glass window. Students from industrial arts performed the actual construction. Electrical engineering and mechanical engineering students designed and supervised the installation of lighting, heating, and ventilation. The *Exponent* kept everyone informed on progress. Fiscal support came willingly, if in small amounts,

Danforth Chapel

from Protestant churches throughout the state. Perhaps the biggest boost came when W. H. Danforth himself contributed $5000 to cap the drive. Ground was broken for the Danforth Chapel in May of 1950, and the first service was held (by Mormons) in May of 1952. The following month W. H. Danforth himself was present for the structure's dedication. [5]

The spirit that brought forth Danforth Chapel has been manifested in many other, and largely ecumenical, ways on the campus. During the 1940s and 1950s an Inter-Church Council coordinated activities for Protestant students. In time, various faiths began to assign chaplains to the campus. The first two, Paul Krebill, a Presbyterian, and Gerald Thrush, a Methodist, came in 1958. Two years later Herbert Strom, a Lutheran pastor, arrived on campus. Father Joseph O'Donnell, rector of Holy Rosary Church downtown, served the Roman Catholic students on a part-time basis, supervising Newman Club activities.

In 1965, the Presbyterians, Lutherans, and Episcopalians first began to talk of combining their resources and purchasing a residence to serve as a campus Christian center. These plans were forwarded in 1967 when Chaplain Jack Jennings took up the call to serve not only the Presbyterians, but the American Baptists, United Church of Christ, and Disciples of Christ as well. In the meantime, the Methodists built Wesley House on South 8th, on the northern fringe of the campus. The first experiment of its kind in the country, Wesley House afforded a dormitory for forty students, a chapel, meeting rooms, several offices, and food service. Though it was a model of Christian community, on the practical level it was an exceedingly expensive undertaking. In 1979, when the experiment proved to be financially unfeasible, it was abandoned and the building sold to the campus Christian center consortium. The structure was thereupon renamed Christus Collegium—Center for Campus Ministry.

In the meantime, the Catholic Newman Club petitioned their diocese in Helena for permission and funds to build a parish center on campus. In 1976, Resurrection Church, a handsome, modern facility, was built just southwest of the field house. Almost overnight Resurrection attracted hundreds of students and townspeople—eventually membership reached 2000 parishioners—and President William Tietz praised it as a "vital campus force." [6] The parish has been served by several personable and intellectual priests, among them Fathers Michael Miles, Cornelius J. Kelly, and Thomas P. Haffey. Bishop Raymond Hunthausen's willingness, in 1973, to press the limits of Vatican II by allowing Father Miles to marry made Resurrection and its parishioners party to a challenge to clerical celibacy that had no equal in any location in the United States. For five years it appeared as though the experiment would be allowed to proceed, but when Bishop Hunthausen was elevated to an archbishopric in Seattle, more traditional church authorities terminated Father Miles' ministry. [7]

Through all of this the college itself was moving toward a more pluralistic religious environment than was evident in the early days of Presbyterian influence. In 1968, religion moved directly into academia when Irving Dayton, vice president for academic affairs, created a new teaching position in religious studies. Although the local ministerial association had long provided classroom instruction on campus, Dayton sought to elevate religious studies to the status of an academic discipline. Seeking a highly qualified professional to establish the program, he brought in Marvin Shaw, who had a degree in divinity from Union Theological Seminary and a Ph.D. from Columbia University. [8] This course of study, strengthened by a second full-time position in the mid-1980s, is attached to the department of history and philosophy and has become one of the most popular in the humanistic field.

The campus ministry itself was frequently involved in social action in response to the events of the 1960s, 1970s, and beyond. Political tensions between right and left during the Nutter-Babcock administrations of the 1960s had their own peculiar effect on campus ministers, and three of them found themselves on the John Birch Society proscription list because of their views. During the Kent State-Cambodian crisis of 1970, the campus ministry held services to calm student emotions, and during the Iranian crisis of 1979, Christus Collegium was one of the very few places in the country that remained hospitable to Iranian students. [9]

The evangelical movement, which accompanied a growing conservatism, became increasingly apparent on campus in the late '70s and '80s, though it seems to be in a period of decline as MSU approaches its centennial year. In fact, though the facilities and the spirit are still in place, campus religious involvement is entering a muted phase, reflected in the decline of student participation in all religious activities—mainline Protestant, evangelical, and Roman Catholic. The somewhat conservative agenda that marked the role of religion on campus only a few years ago has yielded to an agenda defined more by secularism. Time will tell whether these developments are of a cyclical or a permanent character.

1. Merrill G. Burlingame, Patricia Stenhjem Anderson, and William G. Walter, *The Danforth Chapel and Religious Activities at Montana State University, 1893-1991* (Bozeman, 1991), 25-27.
2. Ibid.
3. Reverend Herbert Strom interview, 2 August 1988.
4. Burlingame, Anderson, and Walter, *The Danforth Chapel*, 6, 8.
5. Ibid.,10-25.
6. Tietz to Eldon Curtiss, Bishop of Helena, 3 January 1978, 82031/6, "R" file, MSUA.
7. This experience and its outcome is documented by Father Miles in *Love Is Always* (New York, 1986).
8. Irving Dayton interview, 27 June 1988; Molly Jane McAuliffe, "A History of Religious Studies at MSU," history seminar paper (1990).
9. Rev. Herbert Strom interview. At various times Christus Collegium has housed students from East Germany, West Germany, Pakistan, Iran, Iraq, Turkey, Egypt, Nigeria, Malaysia, China, and Hong Kong—students who traditionally have difficulty in finding housing in Bozeman.

Homecoming parade, 1953

Painting the "M", 1951

MSC, McCarthyism, and Academic Freedom

One of the most controversial issues of Roland Renne's presidency concerned the issue of academic freedom. Unquestionably, with the exception of the First World War, no period in American history was fraught more with controversy over the right of the academic community to free speech and open thinking than that covering the years from the end of World War II through the 1960s, a period virtually identical with that of Renne's administration. Unlike the World War I era, when for the most part Germans, and Germanic imperialism, were the source of the public's fear and enmity, in the two decades following World War II a majority of Americans came to view communism, and its perceived association with Soviet imperialism, as one of the deadliest threats to internal security the democracy had ever faced.

From the perspective of the 1990s, this interpretation represented harmful exaggeration, if not bald error. As the historian Ellen Schrecker points out, "Whatever perils the Cold War might have brought on the international level, the danger that a few thousand American Communists, acting on secret instructions from Moscow, were about to take over the United States was not one of them." Nevertheless, the public image of communists as part of a deadly foreign plot, coupled with the employment of that image as a way of coping with the intangibles of the Cold War, led many Americans to support, or at least condone, a witch hunt that brought with it often irrational thinking and sometimes fearsome result. [48]

Events in the late '40s and early '50s seemed to corroborate the feeling that the Soviet Union under the leadership of Joseph Stalin was capable of the most dangerous and sinister undertakings. The dropping of the so-called Iron Curtain over Eastern Europe, the Berlin Blockade, Stalin's brutal purges, the "loss" of China, the development of Soviet atomic capability, and then, to cap it off, the communist invasion of South Korea, seemed to certify the belief that communism was inexorably on the march, and that its ultimate objective was world conquest.

That American communists, leftists, and liberals were responsible for such developments was, when viewed in the face of evidence, ludicrous. Yet the politics of the situation demanded that people of such persuasion be countered domestically as well as overseas. When the Truman administration acceded to the hysteria and sanctioned the passage of the loyalty oath rider to the Truman Doctrine in 1947, the crusade against communism was enlarged to contain the threat not only abroad, but to exterminate it within. While Republicans, particularly, pounced on whatever they defined as undemocratic or unpatriotic, both parties endorsed the effort to extirpate communism at home. The outcome was that anybody left of center stood in danger of being labeled a Soviet agent, contriving to introduce subversive ideas or, perhaps, communicating state secrets to the Kremlin. While the methods for containing communists varied, there was a broad consensus that leftists, socialists, and liberals had to be monitored carefully, so immense was the perceived danger. Some believed these myths sincerely, while others merely sought to make political gain from them. Nevertheless, the pressure from the right became intense, especially on the campuses of the nation's state universities and colleges, for it was a maxim of these troubled times that America should be free of those who were not conspicuous followers of the conservative, patriotic movement. [49]

Montana State College was not immune from the critics who claimed to see communists behind every stack in the college library. Liberals and freethinkers on the Bozeman campus were deeply disturbed by the attacks being made upon them, which they interpreted not as genuine expressions of concern with communism but as means by which conservatives, capitalizing on the communist threat, could attack the New Deal at home, the Truman administration's foreign policy abroad, and liberal ideas generally. While antiliberal crusades directed at MSC did not make headlines nationwide, the Bozeman campus had its share of "Red scares," the first of which took place in 1951 as the result of the Korean war. The issue involved conscientious objection, or the right, guaranteed by the Bill of Rights, to hold true to a religious conviction forbidding military participation. At stake were the rights of Montana's Hutterites, who, on the basis of their religious beliefs, resisted the authority of the state to compel military service.

Montana is a medley of nationalities and ethnicities. Immigrants in large numbers shaped our state—mining its minerals, turning its soil, felling its trees. Most came individually or as families in the late nineteenth and early twentieth centuries, while others came in groups, some considerably later than the mainstream. Within the latter category were the Hutterites, German-speaking agriculturalists who lived in isolated and closed colonies. Persecuted for their Anabaptist beliefs ever since the Reformation, the Hutterites wandered about Europe until they began to migrate to America in the late 19th century—first to South Dakota, then to Canada, and finally, when Canada passed discriminatory legislation against them during and directly following World War II, to Montana. By 1950, or coincident with the outbreak of the Korean war, approximately a thousand of them had settled in eleven colonies in the state, almost entirely in the central and northcentral agricultural areas.

Under normal circumstances, the Hutterites might have been allowed to quietly practice their pacifist faith, but they had the misfortune to migrate to Montana almost simultaneously with the rise of McCarthyism—that conservative, nationalistic movement that rose to prominence coincident with the Korean war. To many Americans the Korean war certified their belief that Soviet communism had a master plan to conquer the world. For a while, the initial shock of the war was replaced by euphoric contemplation of complete victory, and American patriotism enjoyed one of its finest hours. But this was a short-lived celebration—the subsequent entry of the communist Chinese into the conflict and the retreat of the allied forces to the 38th parallel turned seeming victory into humiliating defeat—*The retreat From Victory*, as Senator McCarthy titled one of the books he wrote condemning American policy.[50]

At home, the defeat damaged faith in American invincibility and resulted in terrible traumas. One manifestation of these traumas took form in Helena during the 1951 legislative session when the state's politicians drafted a bill to punish the Hutterites as pacifists and conscientious objectors (COs). When the essence of the proposed bill, which would have deprived COs of their draft-exempt status, was publicized in the state's newspapers, a small group of nine concerned MSC faculty, faculty wives, and graduate students took action. Their protest, in the form of a letter written to the editor of the *Bozeman Daily Chronicle* in mid-February 1951, was hardly inflammatory, but it raised a storm of controversy and presaged a number of similar confrontations between Gallatin County's conservatives and freethinkers on the MSC/MSU campus over the next twenty years. The letter began:

> Recent items which have appeared in Montana newspapers indicate an attitude of opposition or hostility to conscientious objectors to war, especially to the Hutterites. It is maintained by those who want to alter the present legal status of the conscientious objector that each person in the country is given certain rights by the government and that hence he should be willing to bear arms whenever the government requests him to do so.

The letter went on to contend that the Declaration of Independence guaranteed that certain rights were inalienable and that according to the Constitution, "the government shall not take these rights away." Among these inalienable and constitutionally protected rights was the "principle of religious liberty." In recognition of that, the government had created the 4-E classification "for all men who can demonstrate that their opposition to participation in war is based on their religious beliefs." The authors of the letter then cited the constructive activities men in the 4-E classification had performed during World War II, undertaking soil conservation projects, working in mental hospitals, serving as "human guinea pigs" at medical research centers, and, in Montana and other northwestern states, risking their lives as smokejumpers. The letter concluded:

> Should a man be imprisoned simply because he acts in accordance with his religious beliefs? The United States has in the past opened its doors to the religious minorities which other nations have persecuted. It would be most unfortunate if the people of Montana were to urge their national government to secede from the basic principles of religious liberty. [51]

To right-wingers in Gallatin County, this letter, despite its temperance, represented an unpatriotic declaration, and they took after the authors with ferocity.

At the center of the controversy was MSC geographer, Nicholas Helburn, a Quaker and a conscientious objector who had done graduate work under Renne in the early 1940s, and later additional graduate study at the University of Wisconsin. During the war Helburn had performed compulsory duty in a CO camp in Glendora, California. When, eight months after the war had ended, however, he and his fellow COs were not released from service, they went out on strike. When the Truman administration in response tightened its authority over the COs, Helburn and eighty others walked out of the Glendora compound and established a center for sending CARE packages to war-torn Europe. This was a more useful service, Helburn thought, than the leaf raking to which they had been detailed in the CO camp. Nevertheless, he and his campmates were indicted for their defection. The case had not been settled when Renne hired Helburn as a one-man department of geography. That Helburn was still under indictment when he signed his contract with MSC was known only to a very few. On Renne's part, it was an act of courage and a certification of his respect for Helburn's integrity and scholarship. As Helburn recalled, "Roland Renne's loyalty to Civil Rights was very strong." More than that, Renne respected Helburn's right to his religious beliefs and acted courageously to bring to MSC a man with the desirable scholarly credentials and with a penchant for service. Renne's move was vindicated when the charges against Helburn were subsequently dropped. [52]

It might have ended right there but for the letter to the editor in 1951. It is a testimony to the intensity of McCarthyism and its impact on educational funding that Renne, who felt strongly about the right of academics to free expression and who could have stayed on the sidelines, decided instead to enter into the fracas, asserting, in a counter letter to the editor, that the Helburn group had not spoken for the majority at MSC. As Renne put it, Helburn and his eight co-signers, "representing only a small fraction of one percent of total staff, have, by their selfish and untimely action, cast a shadow upon the loyalty and good standing of the entire faculty of Montana State College." [53]

Helburn and his colleagues had expected the intolerant response of the right wing; they had not anticipated Roland Renne's disclaimer. As they saw it, Renne's letter was not only an admonishment to them, it was a veiled threat of worse things to come—promotion failure, salary reduction, or, worse, tenure refusal. That Renne, a practiced liberal, was bowing before the state's

conservatives, stunned them. At the request of MSC's fledgling union, the American Federation of Teachers (AFT), an off-the-record confrontation with Renne was held before a full house in the lounge of the Student Union Building. With the press absent, it was, in one participant's memory, "a pretty hot meeting." [54] The faculty emphatically informed Renne that his intervention had been interpreted as a threat. In response, Renne backed off some, admitting that perhaps he had overreacted, but he left his faculty with a sober reminder of the consequences of public controversy:

> The future of this school depends not just on what the staff does; it depends on what the townspeople and state do and their reaction to what the staff does. These are things that are political facts that have to be dealt with, and when it becomes too difficult, then the school loses, or will lose. We can't escape being part of the community we're in. [55]

It is interesting to note that Renne, very shortly thereafter, took a one-year leave of absence, subsequently extended to a second year, to accept a Truman administration ministerial post to the Philippines with the responsibility to assist Philippine agricultural recovery so as to strengthen that nation's resolve against insurgent communism. Ironically, in some ways it was easier to combat communism abroad in the 1950s than it was to protect democratic principles in the hysteria at home. Given the almost stifling conservative climate of the time, and the genuine concern that an unfettered liberalism on campus would prejudice administrative abilities to obtain services and support for education, one can understand, if not condone, Renne's action. And Renne was certainly not alone. All over the country liberals on college campuses were, as one freethinker dismissed from Temple University put it, discovering in the midst of right-wing criticism that the "speed of flight was hotter than their love of liberty." [56] The facility with which administrators and faculty alike accommodated themselves to conservative pressure is one of the striking features of McCarthyism's impact upon the academy. It was exceedingly difficult for academics to stand up to the right wing in those years.

One of those who did so at MSC was Robert G. Dunbar, professor of history and another Wisconsin Ph.D. Before coming to Bozeman, Dunbar had taught for ten years at Colorado State University where he had become an expert in western water policy and law. Renne had always seen water issues as absolutely primary to Montana's economy and, in keeping with his concept of cooperativism and federalism, had supported the late-'40s effort to apply the Tennessee Valley Authority (TVA) concept to the Missouri River.

Nicholas Helburn

In 1947 Renne convinced Dunbar to come to MSC. Within a week of his arrival, Dunbar witnessed in Dillon a particularly hostile reaction to efforts made by Montana's Democratic Senator James Murray to build support for a Missouri Valley Authority (MVA), which would have extended government supervision to that river and its tributaries in a manner similar to that then existing under the TVA. These hearings demonstrated to Dunbar that conservative elements in Montana were prepared to go to great lengths to discourage forms of governmentalism that touched upon private property. And it corroborated something he had already learned in Colorado—water-user districts were predictably core centers of that conservatism. As a critic of the doctrine of prior appropriation, or unregulated capitalism, Dunbar was set on a collision course with conservative advocates of the sanctity of private property from the moment he arrived on campus. [57]

To add to the difficulty, Dunbar was an academic who placed a great deal of faith in international cooperation as a way of breaking down barriers to world peace. This put him solidly in the camp of those who, like Roland Renne and Mike Mansfield, supported the United Nations. As the Montana Republican Party's right wing were inveterate enemies of the United Nations, Dunbar, and any who favored the organization, were on their "enemies list" from day 1. Shortly after the CO fracas, Dunbar gave a talk to the local Rotary Club. Entitled "Facts Forgotten about Russia," the speech attempted to bring balance to reality by giving credit to the Soviets for their efforts in defeating Nazism in World War II. In the audience were rancher and turkey expert Harvey Griffin, editor of the archconservative *Gallatin County Tribune*, and Malcolm Story, another long-time resident of Bozeman and descendant of one of the town's founding fathers. At the conclusion of Dunbar's address, Griffin and Story condemned his "sympathetic" treatment of the U.S.S.R. In the wake of the speech, Frank Cotner, the abrupt, conservative dean of the division of science, which in those days included the history department, called Dunbar into his office and accused him point-blank of having gotten his ideas from Joseph Stalin, of having some kind of "direct relationship with Uncle Joe." The accusation reflected the wild rhetoric of McCarthyism. [58]

While Senator Joseph McCarthy made only one appearance in Montana (in Missoula), his political roadmen made periodic contributions to state politics. One of the most notorious of these unprincipled scoundrels was Harvey M. Matusow, called in by Republican extremists in the fall of 1952 to smear Mike Mansfield, then running for the U.S. Senate against the incumbent Zales Ecton, rancher-legislator from the Gallatin Valley. The race was extremely tight, and Ecton's supporters

Robert G. Dunbar

sponsored Matusow for a series of talks in nine different Montana communities. Matusow's extremes embarrassed even the extremists as he sought to link Mansfield with a soft-on-communism philosophy. Nor did he reserve his condemnations for Mansfield alone; Matusow was prepared to expose the entire state, which, he alledged, contained "more Communists per capita than any other." [59] In late October 1952, Matusow appeared in Bozeman's Rialto Theatre and, acting as the McCarthy clone he was, pointed to a satchel at his side and asserted that it contained a list of all the communists on MSC's campus. Like Senator McCarthy, Matusow never did produce the list for public scrutiny; intimations were made with impunity. [60] Months later Matusow was indicted for perjury and in a confessional autobiography published shortly thereafter admitted to the battery of lies he had employed against liberals in Montana as well as across the nation. [61]

Campus liberals would be involved in scrapes like this for better than a decade. Local redbaiters thrived on producing "enemies" lists such as those waved about by the McCarthyites. Charles Bradley recalled being cited with a number of other campus "subversives" in the mid-'50s in a right wing "Blue Book." His crime had been to sign a petition calling for the cessation of atmospheric atomic testing after a shot in Nevada had sent its radioactivity to Montana. Although geiger counters went wild in Montana for three days, the right wing chose to view Bradley's endorsement of a test ban, not as an ecological stance, but as an act of softness towards the Soviet Union on the part of a campus "pinko." [62] On another occasion, Bradley drew flak from the right for having made favorable remarks about Linus Pauling, the eminent Cal Tech chemist who had won the Medal of Merit for World War II rocket research, but had antagonized the right by opposing McCarthyism and supporting the American Peace Crusade. [63] Later in the '50s, the unwary signers of a liberal petitition circulated by one of the town's conservative preachers ended up as Griffin's "Most Wanted MSC Professors" list. [64]

On still another occasion, in 1957, the American Legion attacked MSC for hosting Bayard Rustin, secretary of the War Resisters League. Rustin had been invited by the International Cooperation Center, a pro-United Nations group supported by Renne, Nicholas Helburn, local Judge W. W. Lessley, and Harvey Battey, a former professor at the American University in Beirut, Lebanon, and an old acquaintance of Renne's. Rustin arrived, but sensing the right-wing pressure being put on MSC, in this case by the American Legion, offered to leave town immediately. Renne persuaded him to stay, arguing that withdrawal was exactly what the right wing was counting on. But Renne was deeply troubled over the incident, and he ordered Helburn to leave

Montana for Mexico, with pay and with classes covered, until the matter cooled. Any campus action that could compromise his success in getting appropriations for the college greatly disturbed the MSC president. [65]

Dunbar, in the meantime, had incurred the enmity of the right once more by serving as host to Eleanor Roosevelt, wife of the former president, and another noted American despised by ultraconservatives for her strong identification with the United Nations and opposition to movements, such as McCarthyism, that defined national interests on the basis of blind fear of communism. Mrs. Roosevelt had come to Bozeman at the invitation of the same International Cooperation Center that had brought Bayard Rustin to town, but on this occasion Renne capitulated to conservative pressure and denied her permission to speak on campus. The event was then scheduled for Willson Auditorium. Robert Dunbar was asked to preside at Roosevelt's presentation, and he later recalled the rudeness with which the stateswoman was received. Whoever set the stage, for example, had draped the table in red cloth and had acquired red chairs for Roosevelt and Dunbar. The next noon Roosevelt talked to Rotary. As usual, Harvey Griffin was there and subsequently blasted her as a communist in his newspaper. [66] Dunbar did not ingratiate himself any further with the right by offering courses in Russian and Asian history during a decade when conservatives expressed hatred for anyone who viewed the Soviet Union and Communist China with less than loathing. [67]

Despite his efforts to avoid controversy, Renne was himself a periodic recipient of Griffin's vicious barbs. There were facets of Renne's leadership the editor applauded, particularly the president's strength of character. But Griffin had grave doubts about his "Americanism." Griffin's attacks on Renne became sufficiently abusive that one young lawyer in town, Hal Bollinger, threatened to bring a libel suit if the loose-with-facts editor didn't cease fabricating news items about the MSC president. Griffin backed off some, but his desire to be in the middle of any confrontation touching upon conservative-vs.-liberal issues was so great that it was a temporary retreat at best. [68]

MSU's freethinking faculty, while linked in liberalism with Renne, began to chafe at his tendency to defer, when expedient, to outside criticism. They were, moreover, critical of his unwillingness to incorporate the faculty in college governance. Renne's penchant for unilateral decision making irked them, and some of them determined to gain a voice by unionizing. The result was the creation of a campus chapter of the American Federation of Teachers (AFT), which was affiliated with the state AFL/CIO. Carl Kraenzel, a rural sociologist and Wisconsin man,

had been instrumental in establishing the AFT on campus in the late 1940s. As noted, the organization had been involved in the CO controversy, and later, in 1961, it would become embroiled in another case of academic freedom—the Leslie Fiedler incident. But in the 1950s, its main objective was to impress Renne with the need to listen to MSC faculty on matters of campus concern, most notably salary and benefits. It was not an easy task; at one of these early confrontations Renne had emphatically suggested that junior faculty members, unionized or not, weren't going to tell him how to run MSC. Nevertheless, the tiny union persisted, a group of probably not more than twenty-five to thirty members at any one time. After all, Renne himself had often espoused the cause of labor, and there was reason to believe pressure from an organized union on campus would eventually prove fruitful.

At the root of the local AFT's existence was its belief that unionization was the only way to improve laboring conditions. This was consistent with the acknowledged goals of the union movement nationally. The AFT, therefore, maintained a close relationship with its parent, the state AFL/CIO; members regularly attended meetings of the local trades and labor council. The group also associated with the Montana Farmers Union, the liberal farmers' association. One AFTer explained that he had joined the union "because I felt that. . . labor's liberalism should have a pipe-line to the universities of this country. The survival of liberalism in this country rested upon the American labor movement." [69] "We were," another recalled, "very much part of the labor movement." [70]

Conditions for faculty and staff at MSU did warrant pressure for improvement. Salaries were insufficient, definitely below the peer average for the Northern Plains and Rockies. Moreover, there was no satisfactory health insurance program or sick leave policy. Retirement benefits were also subpar, and sabbatical leaves were nonexistent. Social security had not been adopted by the MSC administration, despite the passage of the act in 1935. Teaching requirements were high, with some faculty in the humanities responsible for eighteen hour course loads. Faculty faced a shortage of housing in Bozeman, and desired assistance. The AFT worked hard toward improvement in all these areas, helping to make gains in some, especially in the area of housing, but not always without resistance. For example, in 1955 conservatives on campus fought hard against initiating social security benefits. B. L. Johnson, a chemist of the "old school," the stereotype of the classic academician, marshaled forces against its introduction at MSC. He argued for the old frontier notion of self-sufficiency, urging his colleagues to disapprove any form of federal assistance, which was seen by conservatives as a form of federal intervention. Ultimately, President

Griffin's "Reluctant Admiration"

Under the simple headline, "Dr. Renne," Harvey Griffin, conservative editor of the *Gallatin County Tribune*, assessed the performance of the president.

. . . .Talking to some Oregon people not long ago, the conversation veered to a mutual friend, A. L. Strand, former president of MSC and now head of the Oregon State college. These Oregon people were high in their praises of Strand, his administrative ability and particularly the rather summary manner in which he disposed of several socialistic minded travelers who had crept unheralded into his faculty. Instinctively, comparison of the public view of Strand's leadership and that of the present administration of Montana State became our concern. Comparisons are always odious. No one ever collects all the facts, all the cross currents, all the twisted threads from which we weave the tapestry of our lives. So much depends on appearances; and appearances are always deceitful. Nevertheless, sometimes we come to a corner that needs turning. . . .

We have in Dr. Renne a personality; brilliant, interesting, exasperating perhaps, and at times inspirational, with a strongly developed instinct to keep out of difficult situations rather than to get out. He is widely acquainted over the state and nation and well liked both for his unfailing tact and his genuine interest in people. A personable man, with little humerous gleams in his eyes and a swift, rare smile that lends his face a peculiar eagerness, he everywhere makes friends for himself and the institution. There is no question but that Dr. Renne wields a strong influence in Montana affairs and even his enemies—and Renne is too positive a personality not to have made enemies—regard him with reluctant admiration.

We use the word "reluctant" advisedly, for Dr. Renne, with all his ability and charm is, like most of us, afflicted with an Achilles heel—in his case an apparent softness toward fellow travelers and socialist-teaching professors. That a few such men and women are members of the faculty at Montana State college is well known to the students, the faculty, to men and women whose sons and daughters absorb their radical teachings in the class rooms; to the friends of the institution, to the friends of Dr. Renne himself. And Dr. Renne is the positive head of the college.

The enigma of the situation does not lie solely in the fact these radicals are allowed to remain as members of the college faculty. With the growing awareness of the thinking public to the dangers of subversion, with the growing realization on the part of conservatives, regardless of political party, that the time is fast coming for America to clean house, the tenure of these "pink" profs is bound to be short here in Bozeman. The danger in the situation lies in the fact the housecleaning may be too thorough.

The pity of the picture lies in what the situation may do to Dr. Renne himself. We do not intimate that he will absorb radical teachings, even though Shakespeare did write something about the dyer's hand taking the color of what it works in. But here is a man with a tremendous potential for constructive work in Montana. He does not hold himself aloof, but knows his students and their problems. He has immeasurable energy. He is a gifted orator who can make even dull columns of statistics read like golden prose. People all over the state, and particularly here in Bozeman, recognize his ability. And yet in any conversation concerning Dr. Renne and the college, there creeps in that thread of concern. . . .

Dr. Renne is the positive head of the college. The fact these people remain as faculty members attests to Dr. Renne's decision to run the risks of possible social, political and economic harm to young minds in exchange for supporting the principle of academic freedom. In the light of changing world philosophies, inimical to our national interests, perhaps Dr. Renne might properly reappraise the picture.

Montana State college had a great president in Dr. A. L. Strand. Montana State college has a strong president in Dr. R. R. Renne—who could become the greatest. Higher education in Montana needs the best of leadership to instill that loyalty to free American citizenship in the next generation. A "Strand" of decisive action would remove the adjective "reluctant" and leave only admiration for Dr. Renne. [1]

1.   Editorial, *Gallatin County Tribune*, 12 February 1959.

Renne felt obliged to allow faculty to decide the issue themselves, and a large majority voted in favor of adopting social security. [71]

But Renne would not let himself be pressured by those who sought to leverage salary scales. For every fact marshaled by the AFT, Renne shot back a counterfact. His argument was standard; MSC faculty were doing quite well, and he could produce all sorts of data to back up his arguments. Renne was not unsympathetic to his faculty's concern for good wages; in the early stages of the Great Depression he and his family

MSC campus, 1955

had suffered greatly with other MSC staff when salaries had been cut as much as 20 percent across the board. But he was adamant that he could provide better salaries by administrative lobbying in Helena than the AFT could manage through union pressure. Renne would not be the first, or last, MSC/MSU president to take this position. A large majority of MSC's faculty agreed with him. AFT members, while vocally strong, were weak in numbers, and it was understood that a strike would not be productive. Picketing was sometimes considered, but even this tactic was not tested. In the end, the AFT's power of persuasion was limited. Unions have not had a history of dramatic success at the Bozeman campus.

Nevertheless, organization had its advantages. When another issue of controversy arose over dropping Saturday morning classes from the instructional system, the AFT took the initiative. For years, faculty and students had been lobbying for the elimination of Saturday classes. Students, characteristically lethargic in the 1950s, as were their peers across the country, never demonstrated against the five-and-half-day week, but their lack of attendance at Saturday classes was a proven fact. Inevitably, they headed for home on Friday to help with farm and ranch work or, having stayed in Bozeman for the weekend, were too tired to attend classes, their instructors surmised, because of partying the previous evening. Faculty not only disliked conducting class for a

few, but loathed the six days per week needed for class preparation. Merrill Burlingame, head of the history department, recalls that for years his Friday evenings were spent, not in the pursuit of normal pleasures, but in preparing for four consecutive Saturday morning classes. In 1955-1956 AFT members worked out a five-day schedule and convinced the registrar, Martha Hawksworth, that it was feasible. The new class program was tried for a quarter, after which a referendum was held. Faculty and students voted in large majority to continue the new system, and the experiment was repeated winter quarter with even heavier support. But the favorable vote had coincided with a legislative session, and President Renne ultimately vetoed the program because he was concerned that it would be interpreted in Helena as a cutback in MSC faculty workloads. Saturday morning classes remained for another twelve years, being phased out finally in 1968. Although Renne did not oppose a five-day class week in principle, this was another one of those cases where his reluctance to change the system stemmed from his awareness that many members of the public simply did not understand how college instruction was carried out. MSC instructors had worked five-and-half-day work weeks for so long it could be interpreted that any reduction would mean they were loafing. This was bad P.R. for the college, and Renne's reluctance was, to him, a necessary and prudent response.

"We Needed Something like That"
The Great MSC Panty Raid of March 7, 1957

The prediction was made by a student columnist in the *Exponent* on the first of March, 1957:

> We'll choose a dark night sometime next quarter and if all goes well the most stupendous feat of unlawful devilment ever to take place on this campus will come about. We're going to have a panty raid.

The reality was reported by the *Bozeman Daily Chronicle* exactly a week later.

Student Mob Fights Officers Two Hours

Police and sheriffs' officers resorted to anti-riot tactics last night with the use of tear gas in breaking up a howling mob of Montana State College male students whose "panty raid" on Hannon Hall reached riot proportions. A crowd estimated at 1,000 college boys converged on Hannon Hall, women's dormitory on the campus.

All available sheriff's deputies and police officers were called to the scene at 11 p.m. last night. . . . More than two hours was required to quell the milling throng. Rocks, ice and beer cans were thrown both at the officers and through windows of both stories of Hannon Hall. . . . For more than two hours a continual fight and scramble continued with the officers dispersing the throng, which then reorganized and the fights began again.

Trouble started . . . when . . . lights were out when a transformer had to be changed. Lights were out for more than a half hour at one time during the fight and again for about ten minutes, hampering the efforts of officers trying to get the students under control.

Dean Val Glynn . . . aided officers in bringing the situation under control. . . . Names and identifications were taken . . . but no arrests were made.

Dr. R. R. Renne, MSC president said today that "last night's affair was a regrettable incident. It was unfortunate that the lights were to be off and that word of it leaked out. What started out as a prank got out of control. It is too bad that young men sometimes do not act like men. . . ."

One participant, who admitted to having been inside Hannon Hall, said, "no one touched the girls, in fact, some of them seemed to be enjoying the whole thing. . . . We needed something like that on the campus to stir things up a little. It's too dull up there, terrific lack of spirit. Nothing but a few assemblies and we needed a little excitement."

According to the penal code of Montana, persons participating in a riot are punishable by a prison term of ten years and a $2,000 fine or both. A riot is defined as a gathering of two or more persons whose actions result in property damage or disturbance of the peace, or injuries to others.

"Go Western Day," 1958

Generating school spirit: the annual pie-eating contest, 1958

Frosh woes, I, 1960

Frosh woes, II, 1960

Junior Prom, 1959

Fiedler, Nutter, and MSC

All of this tugging and pulling between liberalism and conservatism, between academic freedom and academic restraint, came to a head in the last four years of Roland Renne's administration. Although Renne was at heart a committed liberal, he had labored to downplay that liberalism during the difficult 1950s. Perhaps because of that, and because he was dealing with governors who were not ideologues, he had gotten along quite well with the conservative Democratic Governor John Bonner (1948-1952) and the Republican Governor Hugo Aronson (1952-1960). Even Renne's worst critics had granted him "reluctant admiration." But the election of 1960 changed all of that dramatically, the result of which was that Roland Renne, by force, found himself and MSC cast as principal participants in Montana politics for the next four years.

The election of the ultraconservative Republican Donald G. Nutter to the governorship in November 1960 is seen to this day, more than three decades later, as one of the bleakest moments in the history of higher education in this state. Nutter's political ascendancy represented the final flowering of Montana's postwar right-wing political movement. Gaining momentum in the late 1940s coincident with the development of the Cold War, this movement witnessed in the 1950s the rise to political power of a group of ideological conservatives, some of whom possessed strong leanings first toward McCarthy and then toward the Goldwater wing of the Republican Party. These men came from a variety of backgrounds, but they shared one trait in common: an antagonism toward what Roland Renne symbolized—a vigorous role for the college as an agent for strong federal involvement in the administration of the state, politically, economically, and socially. The Big Sky was much more Taft-Eisenhower than Truman-Stevenson-Kennedy country. Large numbers of Montanans shared the assumption, as an analyst of conservatism expressed it, "that all personal liberty rested on economic liberty, that activist presidents and the bureaucratic regulatory state represented the most serious threats conceivable to the American tradition, [and] that the handout state inevitably would undermine the work ethic and cripple the entrepreneurial spirit that had made America great." The conservative contention that the liberalism of the New Deal was "taking America down an irreversible road from welfarism to socialism to totalitarian Communism" was merely the next step in that argument. [72]

In 1960-1961, in the midst of a brief but worrisome national depression, this crusade against liberalism culminated in the election of Donald Nutter to the state's highest office. While the senate retained a Democratic influence, the house of representatives was controlled by conservatives. Nutter staffed his administration with right-wingers, and his leadership expressed itself in antiliberalism, with MSC and President Renne becoming a focus of conservative dissatisfaction. As one legislator recalled:

> '61 . . . was the most conservative session in years and years. There were drastic fiscal cutbacks, the lashing out against education . . . the resolution of censure against the prof, the animosity against Bob Dunbar, the hassle over the "Vital Issues" program in the Extension Service at Bozeman. . . . It just seemed to me that we were in the middle of a right-wing revolution. [73]

Two particularly important developments preceded the election and colored it in a way inimical to MSC's interests. These developments document the split personality in MSC's administrative leadership. On the one hand, there was Renne's long commitment to vigorous public outreach, or the Wisconsin idea, a philosophy identified with progressive liberalism. On the other hand there was Renne's periodic tendency to muzzle free expression on campus in order to avoid or placate right-wing criticism, which, if allowed to fester, could seriously damage MSC's prospects for continued state funding and outreach success.

The first of these two events was the decision in 1959-1960 to engage MSC's Cooperative Extension Service in a public service project entitled "Vital Issues." The actual brainchild of the new director of Cooperative Extension, Torlief Aasheim, Vital Issues was an ambitious effort,

grant-supported to the amount of $40,000 by the Ford Foundation's Fund for Adult Education, to encourage the interest of Montanans in public affairs and public responsibility. It was in every way the logical and proper application of the Cooperative Extension Service mandate: "The development of people themselves to the end that they, through their own initiative, may effectively identify and solve the various problems directly affecting their welfare." [74] Six topics were selected as "vital issues":

1. Education—What Goals for Montana?
2. How Can Montana Grow?
3. Welfare in Montana—What Needs? Whose Responsibility?
4. What Do We Expect from Government?
5. How Should Montana Finance Public Service?
6. What Can Montana Afford?

These topics had been "identified and spelled out by scholars and other experts from Montana State College and other Montana institutions" as representing some of "the most critical problems facing the state in the next decade." The Vital Issues program was shot through with Renne's commitment to social science and to making the land grant concept work through public outreach.

Materials to support the program were distributed in the spring of 1960. The issues were widely and vigorously discussed at public meetings. Inevitably, participants in the discussions expressed a concern for improved education and public services and called for revenues to support them. Once this trend became clear, politics entered the scene, as critics of enlarged governmental services questioned the capability of the state to produce the required funds. The Montana Taxpayers' Association, for example, held that the state could not afford added services and argued that the Vital Issues program was raising false hopes. The state Republican organization took it another step. It identified possible political motives in the program and asserted that the discussions, "financed in part by public funds and directed by state employees, supported the Democrats." In short, critics of Vital Issues interpreted the discussions as an effort on the part of the Renne administration to indoctrinate the public with its own political brand of federalism, a position they saw as closely aligned with New Deal philosophy. Thus, Vital Issues became part of the political campaign of 1960. [75]

Another development that embroiled MSC in controversy on the eve of the 1960 campaign was the decision of MSC's AFT chapter to invite to the Bozeman campus Leslie Fiedler, professor of English at the state university. Fiedler had a national reputation for literary criticism; a book he had just published, *Love and Death in the*

American Novel, was receiving widespread attention. He had appeared at MSC before, proving to be a stimulating lecturer when he spoke on Judaism during Religious Emphasis Week. Fiedler's reputation was prejudiced, however, by his left-wingism, his homosexuality, and his irreverence toward values many Montanans held dear. Since 1958, Fiedler had suffered almost constant harrassment from conservatives in western Montana. In a widely circulated tract by an ultraconservative from Bigfork, Fiedler was accused of immorality. Anti-Semitism also crept into the controversy. The university received a great deal of criticism for harboring so-called perverts and communists such as Leslie Fiedler.

Leslie Fiedler

These factors did not prevent the AFT chapter at MSC from inviting Fiedler to speak at the Bozeman campus on April 19, 1960. To the AFT, Fiedler's nationally endorsed credentials and his status as a fellow academic in the same university system were sufficient cause to justify an invitation. On the surface, the invitation appeared an innocent-enough endeavor to bring first-class scholarship to MSC. But when Renne vetoed Fiedler's appearance, the issue became a *cause célèbre*. What the public understood through news coverage was that Renne had denied the AFT its on-campus sponsorship on the grounds that it was in conflict with two other major events being held

the same week and to which the president assigned a priority. These were the middleweight title boxing match scheduled for April 20 between Joey Giardello and Gene Fullmer at the field house, and the appearance on campus the following day of state university president Harry Newburn. As Renne expressed it, it was his policy to prevent three major events from being scheduled on the MSC calendar on successive nights. Multiple events prevented "full participation" of students and faculty, and the fight and presidential visit had been scheduled prior to the Fiedler invitation. [76]

The AFT thence arranged to move the event downtown to the First Methodist Church, but the furor of protest on campus following Renne's veto alarmed the congregation, which withdrew its offer in order to be spared the controversy. Renne was then presented by the AFT with several alternative dates for the following weeks, but the president turned these down on the same reasoning applied to his initial veto: the MSC spring-quarter calendar was already too full. [77] Fiedler came anyway; he spoke for two hours before a packed audience at the Lambda Chi Alpha fraternity house. But the off-campus appearance hardly satisfied the offended sensibilities of those who had hoped to have Fiedler speak on campus. There was no question in their minds but that the professor's controversiality, and particularly his conflict with conservatives, was the main reason behind Renne's rescission of the AFT invitation. Their sentiments were perhaps best expressed by a member of the student body:

> Renne was on the spot. If he accepted one of the alternative dates, the ultra-conservative elements in Bozeman would damn him as a radical. If he rejected all of them, college and university personnel throughout the nation would damn him as a reactionary. It boiled down to a question of whether the traditions of the college as a liberal, freedom-loving institution were to be upheld, or whether a small percentage of the Montana population was to be placated. [78]

The heralded Montana author A. B. Guthrie expressed it this way:

> Montana State College could accommodate the spectacle of a fist fight. It could not accommodate the appearance of Dr. Leslie Fiedler, a distinguished if controversial literary critic and a University teacher whom, however one may disagree with his judgements, Montana is lucky to have. Hail, Brawn! Down, Brain! Hurrah, Education!" [79]

Renne was infuriated by such reactions. He had been pushed into a corner by a small group of campus activists who had chosen to create controversy at a time fraught with political sensitivity. He did not dispute their right to free speech, but their timing was perfectly awful. What the public could not know was that Renne and the AFT had spent many hours in advance of April 19 attempting to work out an agreeable compromise, but that the AFT, on the understanding that Fiedler preferred the original date (he wanted to stay the next day to attend the boxing event), was not inclined to revise his schedule. Renne was angered by the manner in which the Fiedler event had been scheduled in the first place; the invitation had been extended while he was out of state (in Ethiopia, in fact), and he was perturbed that the Fiedler event coincided with the visit to MSC of Fiedler's boss, Harry Newburn, president of the university in Missoula. Newburn had been the subject of much harassment because of Fiedler, and Renne believed Newburn's visit to campus should not be complicated by the presence of the controversial English professor. In closed discussion with the AFT, Renne had pointed out that High-Line conservatives were putting a great deal of pressure on the university to get rid of "Fiedler types," and that an invitation to Fiedler at this time was "politically inadvisable." Renne and the majority of his administrators agreed that while, in the main, they had no personal objections to Fiedler's appearance, it was "poor public relations" in an election year already tilting toward extremism to invite a man of such controversial reputation. [80]

Renne had been put between a rock and hard place. He did not want to go on public record as opposing Fiedler because of the English professor's controversiality—that ran against his own liberal grain and would have been a concession to the right wing. He could hardly have failed to sympathize with chemist Charles Caughlan's reminder that, "no great university has ever been built by allowing reactionary pressures to control its action." [81] But his better sense, the practical political sense, said that the timing was all wrong. Consequently, when the AFT would not back off, he took a middle course between the two extremes by employing a tactic emphasizing conflict with other campus events. That this avoided coming to grips with the real issue was quite obvious. In private, Renne was deeply disturbed with the AFT, a number of whose members he had personally recruited to the faculty, and who now had unfairly forced him to compromise his belief in free speech. He felt that they had willfully pushed him into a corner and had jeopardized the good standing of the college at a time of heightened political tension. To two Missoula professors who had boycotted a Bozeman meeting of the Montana Academy of Science as a protest over the handling of the Fiedler incident, Renne wrote that the AFT had "handled the whole matter in a highly irresponsible manner." "Apparently," he went on, "they have a burning desire to be 'martyrs' to an imagined case of 'academic freedom' even at the expense of being honest with me or the public. Needless to say, until they prove in future dealings that they are honest, responsible, and fair, I will be in no frame of mind to be particularly sympathetic to any program or personality they may sponsor." [82] Most of Renne's faculty and staff sympathized. Leslie Heathcote, head librarian, expressed it thusly: "There is a sort of bitter irony in a situation where charges of dictatorship and breach of academic freedom are leveled against a man who has been outstanding in his liberal viewpoint, in his adherence to the best traditions of academic practice, and in his willingness to confide in his faculty because he had faith in their integrity. For a large majority of the faculty this faith is not misplaced." [83]

It was a difficult moment for both Renne and the AFT. Earlier in March, Duane Hill, president of AFT, had protested that his organization had not intended to embarrass Renne. He admitted, however, that the membership had been quite "unaware of [Fiedler's] power to stimulate responses, both pro and con." Hill believed, nevertheless, that "if we are no longer free to offend, there is little freedom left in America." In conclusion, Hill admitted to Renne that everything had devolved into a "crazy, mixed-up affair." It was a prescient observation. [84] Later, Howard Dean, then president of the AFT, would claim that although the battle over Fiedler had developed "unfortunate heat and bitterness," it had "served a useful purpose favorable to freedom of expression." Dean doubted whether a fellow faculty member would "ever again be refused the right to speak on the campus." [85]

Renne saw things quite differently; "academic freedom" had to be considered in the light of the state's 1960 political climate. Could not the academics see this? Could they not see that any attention drawn to campus events deemed antithetical to conservative values in a most conservative state could produce repercussions far more damaging than that caused by one man's inability to speak? It was the classic dilemma of the liberal.[86] Renne labored intensively in the summer and fall of 1960 to prevent Republicans from winning the governorship. From outward appearances it often seemed that the real political contest was not between Nutter and his Democratic opponent, but between Nutter and Renne. [87] When the votes were counted in November, Nutter had won. The ultraconservatives were in, and drastic fiscal cutbacks in education were virtually guaranteed.

But even these realities were not sufficiently appreciated on the Bozeman campus; the damage done by the Vital Issues program was compounded shortly after the election by the Cooperative Extension's adoption of a new variation on the same theme—public discussion of sensitive political issues—but with an international rather than state focus. Entitled "Great Decisions," the program was obtained from the liberally backed Foreign Policy Association and included eight topics:

1. Deadlock over Germany
2. Soviet Challenge and World Leadership
3. France and Western Unity
4. Japan—The Future of an Asian Ally
5. The U.N. in Explosive Africa
6. The Americas in Jeopardy
7. Arms and Survival
8. Blueprints for the World Economy

As Burlingame and Edward J. Bell, Jr., document in their history of the Cooperative Extension Service, "a storm of protest broke over the state almost as soon as the program was announced." The protest came mainly from the John Birch Society, which argued that the discussion materials contained unpatriotic criticism of the United States. Other groups joined in the chorus, maintaining that the extension service, a tax-supported agency, should not be involved in public affairs issues. Labels of "insidious" and "subversive" were applied to the Great Decisions instructional materials. [88] Aasheim was absolutely disgusted with this response, which suggested that the sole function for the Cooperative Extension Service should be purely agricultural—or "corn, hogs, and manure," and nothing else, as the director colorfully expressed it. [89] This controversy continued as the state legislature met to discuss, among other items, the budget allocation to higher education. To compound matters, Robert Dunbar got into another tiff with the John Birch Society over a talk he gave in Bozeman on the value of the United Nations and international cooperation. Threats were made upon his life, and for several weeks he and his family lived in constant fear. MSC's association with liberal policy and liberal protest could not have come at a worse time. [90]

In the legislative session of 1961, Donald Nutter and the Republican-dominated house made a point of challenging the university system's budgeting. They had campaigned on a platform of fiscal austerity; now they had the occasion to put it to work. Moreover, some conservative legislators saw this as a chance, finally, to challenge Renne, to make him more fully accountable for his deeds, to reverse his earlier ability to wheedle monies out of an ill-informed and outmanned legislature. This view was put quite succinctly by a key Republican legislator-stockman from Roscoe:

> Roland Renne, Whoo! All I can remember, when he was in his hey-day . . . there'd be five of us . . . three from the House and two from the Senate . . . . And here'd come Roland Renne and

[Bob] Pantzer. And they'd each have about six guys with them. And then . . . there'd be . . . Dillon, and . . . Havre, and the School of Mines, and Eastern. And they'd all have their staff there so that the total would be about 30 of them and about five of us. And Renne would be kind of a spokesman . . . . And I really think all he was trying to do was to confuse us on what the needs were, and where the money came from . . . so that toward the end of the session we'd say to them, "Well, just how much can you get by with." . . . And I never thought it was very intelligent, that way of doing that. Now that's one thing I wanted to change. I didn't want to see that system . . . . These university guys with their business managers and accountants and so on, they thought we were just a bunch of stupid rural guys . . . who didn't even know what they're doing. [91]

The Republican house majority leader in 1961, a Hardin rancher, explained it this way:

> We had a real aggressive guy at Montana State [College] at that time by the name of Dr. Roland Renne, and we had to put a few strings on him to hold him down. He built up a terrific physical plant and, of course, anytime you've got a physical plant, it takes increased appropriations to run the thing. Well, I've been accused many times of hurting education, but I don't feel that I ever did. I think anybody has to live with a balanced budget, live within their income and estimated expenditures. I think if they get all the money they want they get too careless in the way it's spent. [92]

With that reasoning and the strength of a majority in the house, Nutter set out to cut back the state's educational appropriations to the bone. Many agencies were targeted, as the projected fiscal deficit was estimated at $6 million. The university system, however, took the major brunt of the backlash, and MSC seemed to have been singled out specifically.

Nutter, the archconservative, had little use for Renne, the liberal. Earlier, the two had clashed head on in Sidney, Nutter's hometown, during a public forum. Nutter had made some statements that Renne believed were incorrect. Throwing caution aside, Renne had pulled out all the stops and, as an onlooker observed, "completely demolished everything Nutter just said." The hostility between the two was so intense that one MSC official who had accompanied Renne to Sidney anticipated Nutter would, if he had the opportunity, take his revenge. [93] The hatchet fell when the new governor announced in his inaugural address that MSC was overstaffed and that he was going to demand a significant reduction in personnel. When the State Board of Education made budget recommendations less stringent than Nutter desired, he rejected these (there were reports he burned them in the Capitol's furnace) and substituted an alternative that would have forced MSC to cut forty-five faculty positions out of a total of 280, a 16 percent loss of staff. Cuts as deep as 15 percent for the entire college, 62.3 percent for the experiment station, and 42.8 percent for the extension service were announced. When Renne protested the faculty cuts, the governor callously suggested that he simply reduce all salaries to $2,500, maintaining that at that level enough MSC faculty would quit to meet the quota. [94] Nutter and his budget director then began to bypass the Board of Education completely, directing from the governor's office all the board's functions—handling negotiations, presenting information, and making recommendations. Each unit president was called separately to Helena to justify in person to Nutter and his budget director an absolute "rockbottom" estimate of costs, from light bulbs to toilet paper. The old system of a Renne-led team of unit educators lobbying for support before an outmanned legislative appropriations committee was effectively ended. [95]

Donald G. Nutter, governor of the state of Montana, 1960-1962

At the same time, Nutter set about changing the character of the Board of Education, appointing conservatives to positions as they opened. The new chairman of the board's curriculum committee, Gordon Doering, was convinced the university system was too large. In his determination to reduce state revenues assigned to higher education, he pushed through a proposal to penalize unit administrators if they attempted to make up for lost revenues by swelling their enrollments through expanded recruitment. [96] Doering also disliked Renne. Consequently, Renne lost much support from the board, a body he had been on good working terms with for better than a decade.

No one doubted for a moment that Nutter had not purposefully reconstituted the board for just that purpose. To add insult to injury, Nutter appointed Harvey Griffin to MSC's Local Executive Board.

But the resolute and wily Renne fought tooth and nail to soften the blows. When the legislature found itself undecided on final appropriations measures for the public school and university systems, a record-breaking overtime session had to be scheduled. Some legislators blamed Renne directly for the impasse. According to the house majority leader Clyde Hawks, a "gentlemen's agreement" had been reached between the six university units and the appropriate senate and house committees that the available funds would be split in a particular way. But then Renne had thrown a monkey wrench into the works, demanding a supplementary $600,000. Harriet Miller, state superintendent of schools, and a former Republican who had switched parties, then joined Renne in making additional demands. Renne, it appears, had shrewdly sought compromise in the house, where the Republicans reigned, but changed his pitch when the appropriations measure reached the senate, where the Democrats had the votes. As Hawks put it, "All of our negotiations and presession planning went up in smoke." Renne had "thrown us into a turmoil." This put the legislature into one of the longest and most difficult overtime sessions in memory. Legislators did not receive pay for overtime, and there was bitterness in the minds of some conservative members. Renne had, they felt, gotten the better of them once again. [97]

Renne was able to get approximately one-half of his requested additional $600,000. Still, the college had been hit hard (180 employees received termination notices) and, unquestionably, in a discriminatory manner. Although MSC now exceeded the university in enrollment by better than 200 students, and although an agreement had been reached that all the system's units would be funded equally on a basis of student enrollment, the Missoula school received a budget increase of 8.9 percent. In contrast, MSC took a 2.8 percent cut, while three of the four remaining units suffered even more. Overall, higher education was reduced 4 percent. At the same time, public welfare funding was pared 7.3 percent, and the custodial institutions 13.9 percent. In a classic understatement, historian Merrill Burlingame suggested that this particular legislative session had not been "socially conscious." [98] Taking the entire austerity program at its fullest, covering all state agencies, Malone and Roeder, in their history of Montana, concluded that the "wholesale cuts of 1961" were still evident in the "budget problems and erosion of state services" in the late 1970s. [99]

Even the 2.8 percent cut didn't reveal the true extent of the damage done to MSC. Nutter's budgets crucified the experiment stations and the Cooperative Extension Service. The former was targeted for a cut of 34 percent, the latter 51 percent. When Renne threatened to close the experiment station at Sidney, Nutter's home, the governor retaliated by maintaining the previous biennium's budget for Sidney, while drastically decreasing still farther those for stations elsewhere. Although fiscal efficiency was explained as the cause for the reductions, there was ample evidence that Nutterites viewed extension agents as political front men for the federal government and for Renne's economic philosophy, and they sought to limit the potential for such ideological subversion. Even the Bozeman Chamber of Commerce endorsed Nutter's cuts of MSU's agricultural extension services. [100]

Research activities were also hard hit; for some programs research was cut completely out of the budget. When Renne sought an explanation for these omissions, Nutter's budget director responded "that research and extension were in a category which could be placed on the shelf and picked up two years from now if funds were available." [101] When the losses to the experiment stations and extension service were added to those of the college, MSC had been cut back in total dollars substantially more than the total sum of all cutbacks for all state government services—$1.5 million to $1.1 million. [102] Fortunately, Renne was able to cover some of the agricultural losses with federal and county supports, reducing the cuts to 20 percent in extension, and 27 percent for the experiment stations. But the cuts, even when softened, made shambles of the research programs in these services, and caused a terrific decline in morale. It took years to overcome the loss of twenty positions and numerous research projects in these two divisions. In a signal display of displeasure, MSC's department of agricultural economics placed its entire staff on the market. Some thought this overly dramatic, but the department had been so devastated by the Nutter cuts that it concluded the future in Montana was

The Exponent, *January 21, 1961*

sufficiently bleak to warrant its members looking for positions elsewhere. Viewed nationally, there was much to be said for this interpretation. Across the nation, only Montana and Alabama had cut their educational budgets in 1960-1961. Elsewhere, the average state allotments for education had risen 22.5 percent. Montana was not in the educational mainstream.

MSC's students, as they had with the Fiedler affair, took more than casual notice of these events. There were in excess of 4000 of them now on the Bozeman campus, and significant numbers of them were beginning, after a decade of laid-back spectatorship, to make their concerns known. In the spring of 1960 some 300 had signed a petition backing Fiedler; now, a year later, as many and more agitated against the cutbacks. A special edition of the *Exponent* was devoted to the budget crisis and made available to the parents and friends of MSC students. This brought widespread condemnation from the conservative press, which accused Renne of having provoked student rebellion against the authority of the state. When a delegation of students, led by student body president Arjay Godston, visited with Nutter to register their concerns, the governor led them to believe his intentions were not hostile, and the delegation returned to Bozeman urging patience.

Later, when the newly constituted Board of Education applied a legislatively approved increase of $10 per quarter in student fees, the students felt they had been deceived. [103]

Governor Nutter's remarks that he was planning another budget cut for 1963 seemed to cast a truly dark shadow on the future of Montana's higher education. In Bozeman there was genuine fear that the Sidney lawyer was out to get Renne; his attempt to reduce presidential contracts to annual appointments, although defeated, seemed to indicate that MSC would suffer as long as Nutter remained governor. The state's liberal newssheet, *The People's Voice*, published out of Helena, was convinced of this:

> There seems to be little question that Governor Nutter is hell bent on getting rid of Dr. Renne, either because of personal vindictiveness or because of pressure from the radical right and especially one powerful corporate interest or all three, and together these forces spell dynamite.[104]

Nutter's shocking death in an airplane accident in January 1962 spared Renne further attacks from the governor, but Nutter's allies did not diminish their attempts to restrain the university system and make it more accountable.

MSC's 10,000th graduate, 1960

Pirsig, MSC, and Zen

[MSC] was what could euphemistically be called a "teaching college." At a teaching college you teach and you teach and you teach with no time for participation in outside affairs. Just teach and teach and teach until your mind grows dull and your creativity vanishes and you become an automaton saying the same dull things over and over to endless waves of innocent students who cannot understand why you are so dull, lose respect and fan this disrespect out into the community. The reason you teach and you teach and you teach is that this is a very clever way of running a college on the cheap while giving a false appearance of genuine education. [1]

There is a strong, if not unimpeachable, probability that more millions around the world know our land grant institution by this description than any other printed or pronounced. For these are the words of Robert Pirsig, professor of English at MSC, 1959-1961, as he immortalized that two-year experience in his 1974 bestseller, *Zen and the Art of Motorcycle Maintenance.*

Seventeen years later, in 1991, a review of Pirsig's work spoke in glowing terms of the significance of the book:

> Robert Pirsig's first book, *Zen and the Art of Motorcyle Maintenance*, appeared in 1974 . . . and the memory of it still lingers, green and cheerful, in the mind. It was a byproduct of that low-tech, do-it-yourself movement which produced, under the auspices of *The Whole Earth Catalogue*, a rash of adventuresome lifestyles and fantasies of the same. Pirsig, his motorcycle, and his son formed a peripatetic commune of three—a triangular—motorized polis, enroute from a nonorigin to a nondestination, snatching along the way at philosophical problems allied with the phantom of self-definition. [2]

The end of the '50s and the early '60s, the period of Pirsig's tenure at MSC, was a period when English department faculty were moving in and out with some regularity. Pirsig was one of these transients, a "real eccentric," as one colleague remembered him, who came to Bozeman as an instructor following ten years in India in the study of oriental philosophy. Colleagues also remember him as being consumed with a quest for "quality." He was an exceedingly intense person who approached everything with a certain fanaticism. His teaching methodologies intimidated students, and not a few people on campus thought he was perhaps going a little crazy. Eventually, Pirsig accommodated them; after leaving MSC in 1961 to pursue graduate work in the Midwest, he was hospitalized because of a severe breakdown, though, in time, he recovered.

Among the philosophic musings in *Zen and the Art of Motorcycle Maintenance* are Pirsig's personal reflections on how difficult it was to teach in an institution where the liberal arts and the humanities were relegated to service roles; where individual professional initiative was discouraged by the all-consuming chore of providing classes to meet the freshman English requirement and the curricular interests of the aggies, engineers, and scientists; and where service departments taught six days a week, while engineering taught only five.

Pirsig's *Zen* also serves MSC's history as a documentary of the influence of politics in college operations. Employed at the school during the period of confrontations between President Renne and Governor Donald Nutter, Pirsig suffered, as MSC suffered, from this liberal-conservative feud. The English department paid a particular toll, in Pirsig's view, since Renne liberally passed on to that department—which had got him in trouble by vocalizing too often and too loud on issues of academic freedom—a disproportionate share of Nutter's budget cuts. Pirsig had not been idle during this time; he had been a member of AFT and had called for the withdrawal of MSC accreditation, so concerned was he that standards had been lowered by the budget crunch and the crackdown on civil liberties. [3]

Colleagues of Pirsig's do not recall him as quite the rabble rouser suggested in *Zen*, but agree that his description of the burdens of teaching in a service department at MSC and his memory of the trauma caused by the political turmoil of the times reflect the reality accurately. They also agree that no other work produced in MSC/MSU letters has had as significant, lasting, and universal appeal.

1. Robert Pirsig, *Zen and the Art of Motorcyle Maintenance* (New York, 1974), 140.
2. Robert M. Adams, "The Floating Operetta," *New York Review of Books*, 19 December 1991, 59.
3. Pirsig, *Zen*, 140-142; interviews with John Parker and Kenneth Bryson, 4 August 1987 and 4 January 1992.

Renne Runs for Governor

On February 15, 1964, Roland Renne resigned as president of Montana State College and four days later declared himself a candidate for the governorship of Montana. This announcement did not come unexpectedly. Exactly a year previous, he had been granted a year's leave of absence by the State Board of Education to fill the new position of assistant secretary of agriculture for foreign affairs in the Kennedy administration. While Renne labored in Washington, D.C., and overseas to implement the nation's agricultural foreign-aid programs, rumors circulated in Montana that he had become a fixture in government and would not return to Bozeman. Renne did return, but not to retake the helm of MSC. Instead, he concluded that he had an opportunity to unseat the Republican regime, now under the leadership of Tim Babcock, who, as lieutenant governor at the time of Nutter's death in 1962, had been elevated to the chief executive's job in Helena.

Tim M. Babcock, governor of the state of Montana, 1962-1968

Just when Roland Renne decided to run for public office is not clear, but by the late fall of 1963, or just after President Kennedy's death, his supporters back in Montana began to press him for a commitment. The 58-year-old Renne seemed to enjoy the attention; the excitement and challenge promised by a political campaign suited him. In early December 1963, he came home to canvass the possibilities. He was encouraged by what he saw. Not only would the state Democratic Party throw its full weight behind his candidacy, but he got some "very real encouragement" from "some of the more able and forward looking

Republicans in the state." [105] John L. Fischer, head of MSC's agricultural economics department, had been canvassing the state: "Everyone feels that hope for the Democrats is pretty dim unless you run for Governor. They want you in the worst way." [106]

Renne accepted the call. In February of 1964, he came home, resigned his MSC presidency, and declared. Signs were there for a successful campaign. "I have never seen such intense interest in a Governor's race," wrote a follower, adding that prospects of getting disgruntled Republican support appeared good: "So many people, and not all of them Democrats, are very dissatisfied with Babcock." [107] The fact that this was also an election year for Mike Mansfield, a perennial favorite with Montanans, seemed a good omen, promising a kind of coattail reaction that would help Renne into office. Others saw it exactly the opposite way; Renne's strong visibility in the state should boost Mansfield's efforts, they figured. Either way, prospects looked good.

The Renne campaign commenced on a strong note. Early reports suggested he enjoyed as much as a three-to-two margin in popularity. He won the Democratic primary easily, beating his opponent by 15,000 votes. On the Republican side, Tim Babcock won without opposition.

Despite Renne's optimism, disillusionment began to creep into the Democratic camp. Renne, it was proving, was not a seasoned public office seeker, and his speeches lacked the necessary punch. All too often what dominated was his overemphasis on dull academic and fiscal logic, loaded with statistical data—an approach that bored his listeners and diluted their enthusiasm. Many who attended Renne's campaign talks can recall the pedantic character of his speeches and the kind of washed-out feeling that followed. They had come with enthusiasm to hear him but, having been deluged with tiresome detail, had lost faith in his ability as a candidate. His style on the campaign trail seemed in stark contrast to the reputation he had achieved as a man of force and action in Helena and in Bozeman. Fear that he might not be able to pull off a successful gubernatorial campaign became pervasive. "When Renne returned to Montana people were enthusiastic about his campaign," summed up one party stalwart, "but the lackluster campaign in the primary convinced many that he could never beat Babcock. These . . . people are throwing away the best opportunity the Democrats have ever had to elect a Governor." [108]

The Republicans believed that Renne's actions and beliefs made him eminently vulnerable. They turned his interests in educational consolidation for fiscal efficiency into a bias against smaller units and the communities in which they existed. They used against him his periodic leaves of absence to take on government jobs: "I will not let him forget that in time of need he left the leadership of Montana State College to others because the glamor of a federal position lured him to Washington," charged Babcock. [109] They challenged his economic philosophy. His adherence to the so-called Kennedy New Economics simply wasn't acceptable to the fiscal conservatives holding power in the Treasure State.

Taking it a step farther, conservatives identified Renne as a socialist who would substitute for free enterprise a controlled economy. They took as their major source Renne's own book, *Land Economics*, published originally in 1947 and revised in 1958. By freely employing quotations taken out of context, Renne's detractors were able to link the former MSC president with a federalism abhorrent to the champions of unfettered free enterprise and far to the left of where the former MSC president actually stood. This tactic proved very effective.

Others hardly required statements taken out of context on which to base their opposition to Renne. One such group was the Montana Stockgrowers Association (MSA). A past president of the MSA observed later that in all his years he had never seen the Stockgrowers Association more unanimously opposed to a candidate, whom they saw as "entirely too socialistic." [110] The position of the Stockgrowers Association was linked historically to that of the Montana Power Company. Long allied in opposition to liberalism, and particularly to any candidate who championed the notion, as Renne did, that "through social control, property rights must be modified from time to time, so that property may improve the general welfare rather than enrich too greatly the fortunate or aggressive few," [111] the Stockgrowers Association and the Montana Power Company combined resources to campaign against the Bozemanite. Renne tried to work out an understanding with the Company, the most powerful corporation in the state. In the summer of 1964 the Rennes spent an evening in Butte at the home of J. E. Corette, the utility's president, and an old acquaintance through Rotary. The two men retired to Corette's den where they went "round and round and round." Later Renne confided to his wife that Corette had told him that "frankly they never let anybody in [the governor's] office they couldn't control." [112]

Throughout the campaign, Renne, the Kennedy-Johnson New Deal liberal, stood in stark contrast to Governor Babcock, the right-wing disciple of Nutterism and outspoken supporter of Barry Goldwater, the extremist Republican candidate for the presidency that year. Applying liberally Goldwater's provocative argument that "extremism in the defense of liberty is no vice," the Republicans and their allies embarked on one of Montana's greatest political smears. There seemed to be agreement among

conservatives that if there had ever been an opponent worth defeating, Renne was that person. Linking him with Soviet communism was the primary tactic. Charges and countercharges characterized the campaign as it headed into the heat of summer. Renne, stung by charges that he was a communist sympathizer and by concern within his own party that his campaign style lacked energy, made a major switch in tactics. He dropped his scholarly approach to vote seeking and opened up a blistering attack on his adversaries. His campaign speeches became shriller and filled with invective. He adopted the hyperbolic tactics of his adversaries. "Crushing the five B's—Babcock, Battin, Blewitt, Barry and the Birchers" became his campaign theme. He did everything he could to link Babcock with Goldwater, who was, as the public polls documented, much too far to the right to suit most Americans. Babcock, like Goldwater, Renne pointed out, was anti-labor, anti-social security, anti-civil rights, and anti-education. Babcock had become, in Renne's words, "a new echo satellite" for Goldwater in Montana, "beep[ing] his echo of the reactionary radical right-wing program of Senator Goldwater and his Birchite friends." [113]

But Renne's efforts to counter his opponent's smear tactics were not effective. They were, in fact, counterproductive. Even voters who were too smart to be taken in by innuendo were, it was becoming clear, concerned about what Renne might do if he achieved office. If Barry Goldwater was too far to the right, it appeared that Roland Renne was too far to the left. Renne's lead began to melt away. His efforts to persuade Montanans that he was moderate in his liberalism were not as effective as his opponent's efforts to convince the voters that Babcock was conservative in his conservatism. By late summer the race was deadlocked. As the campaign progressed, Renne's supporters came more and more to the realization that Renne himself was the key factor in the decline of his popularity. Lee Metcalf, Montana's other Democratic senator, lent what support he could, and Hubert Humphrey and Ted Kennedy showed up to stump for the Bozeman pedagogue. Mike Mansfield, in a tactic that came to be questioned, only jumped into the campaign late in the fray. In any event, it was too late to save the Renne candidacy.

Roland Renne lost the 1964 gubernatorial election by 7000 votes in one of the closest races ever run in the state's history. On the election eve, many of his supporters actually believed their man had won; his staff had gone to bed late that evening firmly convinced of victory, only to rise in the morning to find that the slow-in-arriving eastern Montana rural county votes had thrown the election to Babcock. [114] It hurt particularly that Renne had lost in his own county, and by a substantial margin, getting only 42.8 percent of

*Running for governor:
Roland Renne with Senator
Edward Kennedy, Missoula,
1964*

People who knew Roland Renne said that he never recovered from this defeat, that he never got back his former vitality and fiery liberalism. He had lived a life of hard-earned success piled upon success, and this was likely the first time he had ever tasted such defeat. His family noted a lapse into despondency, during which time he sat in stoic silence before the fireplace, or stood in the barnyard, burning his many sensitive private papers. It was a sad ending to a truly extraordinary university career.

Yet, from a quarter-century's retrospect, many who supported Roland Renne in 1964 wonder whether he would have been a successful governor. More to the point, many wonder whether Roland Renne could have continued successfully as president of Montana State College. No one doubted his forceful ability, extraordinary work ethic, and consistent devotion to his college and its land grant ethic. No one denied him his achievement in building, almost from scratch, the state's most extensive and creatively funded university plant. And no one could take from him his successful effort to direct the college toward true university status.

But taking into account the dramatic developments of the 1960s, including the influence of a deeply conservative state government, the doubling of enrollments at MSC, and the campus rumblings as students and faculty responded to issues of academic freedom and the Vietnam war, one can question Renne's ability to have commanded successfully in those circumstances. As they weighed realities in the years that followed, those close to Renne suggested that he could not have worked with a conservative, hostile Board of Education and governor's office, that his insistence upon controlling all information would have overwhelmed him as the college grew, and that his dictatorial style would have been severely tested by the outbreak of faculty and student activism. They suggested also that Renne's insistence upon commanding exclusively every function of university governance would have taxed him beyond human capability. While his political defeat in 1964 was an all-too-tragic culmination of a truly remarkable public career—the most personalized in MSC's history and one that still today evokes emotional praise—substantial change was in the air, and it would require new forms, new ideas, and new kinds of people to lead the way.

the vote. Gallatin County had always been deeply conservative, but he had not anticipated it would abandon him so thoroughly. It hurt him to the core. He had barely won in Missoula County. The strong labor counties—Silver Bow, Cascade, Deer Lodge, and Lincoln—had supported him, but he had been soundly throttled in rural Montana, especially in eastern Montana, Nutter's and Babcock's stronghold. Even Petroleum County, whose form of county government had been reorganized by Renne in the early 1940s with great savings and efficiency, gave him only 40 percent of its votes.

Chapter Five
Growing Pains, 1964-1970

A New Man, a New Name, a New Spirit

This University has always been over-extended and it will continue to be so for a long time to come. We seem to work best under these circumstances.

Leon Johnson, February 10, 1966 [1]

Leon H. Johnson, president of MSC/MSU, 1964-1969

It was with an air of relief and expectation that members of the MSC community received the news on February 16, 1964, that Dr. Leon H. Johnson had been elevated from acting to permanent president of the Bozeman institution. Distracted since 1960 by harsh and sometimes perfectly ugly political confrontations, demoralizing budget cuts, and bothersome uncertainties about the future of the college's administrative stability, the community looked to the new president to

provide the leadership that would depoliticize higher education, provide MSC with a strong and predictable economic base, and enable the college to meet the sometimes awesome and bewildering changes that seemed to be taking place on a consistent and even revolutionary basis in this most extraordinary decade—the 1960s. In retrospect, the new president proved to be just the leader the college needed to tackle these problems.

Leon Johnson had long been headed for a college presidency. Born in 1908 in Minnesota, he received his B.A. degree in chemistry from Concordia College and his Ph.D. in biochemistry from the University of Minnesota. Before coming to Montana, he had taught chemistry, physics, and music at high schools in Killdeer and Mandan in North Dakota. He had joined the MSC faculty as a biochemist in 1943. Four years later Roland Renne appointed him executive director of the new Endowment and Research Foundation. Then, in 1955, Renne named Johnson dean of the Graduate School, but continued his appointment as head of the Foundation, recognizing the strong link between the Foundation and graduate research. In 1963, when Renne took leave to join the Kennedy administration, Leon Johnson was named acting president. A year later, when Renne resigned to run for the governorship, the Board of Education appointed Johnson his successor.

Politically, Leon Johnson was a conservative. A good friend described him as a "Wall Street Republican." [2] The new president did not flaunt his politics, but it was obvious that he strongly disliked extremes, whether left or right. On domestic policy Johnson was deeply concerned with the deterioration of the nation's cities and with poverty and civil rights problems. On foreign policy he described himself as "much more a 'Hawk' than a 'Dove' by several orders of magnitude." If anything, he wrote a friend in the waning hours of 1967, "I would have escalated the air war much more rapidly than was done and much sooner." He was not, as he put it, a "murderous hawk," but felt that "our position on Viet Nam has been right." [3]

Johnson was a no-nonsense, straight-up intellectual of Norwegian ancestry, in which tongue he was fluent. If he did not share his predecessor's politics, he shared his warmth of character. Meeting Johnson on the street, one would confront an average-sized, genial, alert man in formal clothing, clutching in hand or teeth the ubiquitous pipe that was his personal trademark. Johnson absolutely loved university life, especially the challenge of research, about which he could wax eloquent. "[T]he responsibility of the university is not the dissemination of knowledge alone," he remarked in 1958 before an alumni homecoming gathering, "but also its acquisition." It was just as important to be exploring the frontiers of knowledge as it was to be instructing students about the past explorations of these frontiers. "Research," he continued, "is the creative efforts of men's minds. . . . It is not confined to the laboratories alone but is found everywhere that intelligent men grapple with problems." [4] Even after becoming president, Johnson could not be detached from his old discipline; faculty fondly recall the way in which he would drop in on research labs at any time of the day or night, with his predictable "Hi, what's happening?" The new president also periodically attended student science club gatherings. [5] Johnson was a generous leader, sharing his presidential perks with grace. If, for example, the army might invite him, at government expense, to visit the Presidio in San Francisco, there was every probability he would take a faculty member along, or send one as his representative. [6]

Although a trained scientist, Johnson was unquestionably the best friend of the arts of any president in the university's history. Renne had rationalized the need to expand the humanities, but had ignored the arts, which he saw as strictly a service area. In contrast, Johnson and his deans of education, James Nickerson and Harold Rosé, pushed hard for degrees in the arts and inaugurated a campaign for the construction of a new creative arts complex. Johnson nurtured a special love for music; he saw it as not only a major source of cultural and pleasurable entertainment, but as one of the school's finest outreach programs. Band tours under Lester Opp and Carl Lobitz, and choir tours by the regionally famous "Montanans," under the direction of George Buckbee, Maurice Casey, and Lowell Hickman, received his all-out support. When the head of the music department, Creech Reynolds, and others created the Bozeman Symphony Society in 1968, Johnson supported it enthusiastically and was one of the society's very first benefactors. Johnson's dedication to cultural outreach could also be seen in his fondness for the Museum of the Rockies. When the decision was made to move the museum from the old barn on South 11th to the current site, Johnson kicked off the building campaign with a substantial contribution. He measured his sponsorship of the museum as among

The Bozeman Symphony Orchestra and Chorus in the Ellen Theatre

the most important things he could do as president, for he was convinced that the museum would provide Montana with an incomparable program of scientific and historical enrichment.

Johnson was an avid hunter, sportsman and horseback rider; he just loved to commune with the land. Possibly his favorite social occasion was the long fall hunting trip he took annually with a band of campus loyalists to the far eastern reaches of the state. Understandably, Johnson had a strong liking for rodeo; he provided major support to its development, and insisted the program report to him personally. Its earthy character appealed to him as a living symbol of the institution's link with the land. [7] For Johnson was deeply imbued with a sense of MSC's responsibility as a land grant institution; he was emphatic that its byword be "service." He never ceased to think of MSC as the "people's university," with its major role to serve its two constituencies: the public and the students. "Education," he believed, was "everybody's business," and the future of Montana and the nation depended upon it. [8]

Among Leon Johnson's first presidential chores was to secure the renaming of Montana State College. For two decades, Renne had been calling for recognition of the school's university status. Boards of review that had visited the campus in both 1958 and 1960 had pointed out that MSC was in every way a true university, and lacked only the name to verify that status. Some members of the review teams had allowed, in private, that MSC, with its divisions of engineering, business, education, agriculture, and nursing, was in truth more a university than its counterpart in Missoula. [9] Renne's call for legal recognition of the situation was not unusual; all across the country the land grant colleges were being renamed state universities. MSC, in fact, was one of only a very few land grant colleges in 1960 that had not yet been elevated in name. A measure was backed by Renne during the tumultuous legislative session of 1961, but was rejected. The response to the measure in Missoula, as one might have expected, was extremely hostile. Moreover, the timing was unfortunate, and the proposal, and its presentation, were less than adequate.

The changing of names, while on surface a matter of truly minor significance, proved to be quite complex. History has demonstrated over and over how resistant humans can be to change, however justified the change might be. MSC's rival in Missoula surely proved this maxim; its representatives cited numerous justifications for denying the name change, even blatantly basing their resistance on the simple discomfort of change. Under the chancellorship, the higher educational system itself had been called "The University of Montana." The Missoula school was Montana State University, and Bozeman was Montana State College. Now it had been recommended that MSC become MSU, and MSU become UM. What would happen to the name of the system itself? That was enough to cause pause to everyone, it seemed. [10] Missoula carried its foot dragging to extreme lengths, lamenting mightily over this so-called momentous undertaking, making mountains out of molehills, stooping so low as to cite as major justifications the costs and bother of changing the wording on diplomas and letterheads, for example, and citing the burdens entailed in removing MSU stamps from library books. [11] Some of this might have been genuine, if overinflated, concern. Yet it was hard for friends of MSC not to believe that these rationalizations were based less on issues of efficiency than on some self-serving desire to deny official university status to the so-called cow college in Bozeman.

It should be acknowledged, however, that Missoula's response was not unusual; it merely replicated similar responses to name changes around the country. The "violent objection" in the mid-50s of the University of Michigan to the elevation of Michigan State College to Michigan State University is one case in point. [12] The same contentiousness had occurred in Colorado and Washington, yet, in short order, all three of these state colleges became superb examples of the successful conversion from college status to fully accredited university.

MSC's second attempt to gain university status, made during the legislative session of 1963, was better timed, better organized, and, as the consequence, better received than the first. Led by acting president Leon Johnson, MSC representatives were able to persuade the Board of Education and the legislature that the failure to change names would not only deprive the school of a status appropriately earned, but would once more leave the state in the rear guard with respect to national educational developments. Everywhere, the land grant colleges were being converted in name to universities. The Idaho and Dakota state colleges had already received legislative name-change approval. Popular support swelled, and Johnson was not surprised when the appeal received endorsement from representatives of agricultural communities. Basically conservative, these legislators were pleased with MSC's rise in status—in the dramatically changing 1960s they were beginning to think of the Missoula institution as a refuge for radicals, whereas MSU was seen as a place to learn and pursue a career. [13]

The Johnson team also made shrewd use of reverse psychology to win its point. Missoula alumni had protested vigorously the change in names, but over the months an MSC campaign to persuade its rivals, particularly graduates of the Missoula law school, that state universities across the nation were now identified as the primary grantors of agricultural, engineering, and nursing degrees, and not law degrees, finally turned the tide, as UM's barristers did not want to be identified with an agricultural or nursing college. In the fall of 1963, the Board of Education approved name changes for all of Montana's higher educational units. With formal ratification, the system itself would be called the Montana System of Higher Education. MSU would become UM, MSC become MSU, The Montana School of Mines become the Montana College of Mineral Science and Technology, and the colleges of education at Havre, Dillon, and Billings become, respectively, Northern, Western, and Eastern Montana Colleges. [14] The official name changes took place on July 1, 1965, when MSC became the last of the northern land grant colleges to undergo the transition. Johnson celebrated the event at the faculty meeting that opened the fall quarter that year: "I got you the name," he lectured his staff in his gravelly, booming bass voice, his forefinger pointed emphatically in their direction, "and you're going to live up to it." [15]

Achieving the right to award bachelor of arts degrees in the humanities and social sciences was one of the first steps. English and history were the first to receive recognition, with degrees activated in the fall of 1964. In rapid succession modern language, music, government, and philosophy were allowed degree granting privileges. The social sciences were also recognized, with economics, psychology, and sociology choosing to award the bachelor of science degree. An honors program was established under the direction of Harry Hausser, professor of philosophy, and initially, seven departments offered honors courses.

Graduate study burgeoned. No other area of study developed with such rapidity. Much of this was the fruit of Leon Johnson's direction of the graduate division between 1955 and 1963. In 1965 Johnson was able to note with pride that the previous decade had seen the greatest advancement ever made in graduate education at the school. Whereas in 1955 MSC offered doctoral degrees in only three fields, in 1965 that had increased to sixteen. Moreover, during those ten years the institution had awarded better than half of all the graduate degrees earned in its entire history. [16] Simultaneously, research support, almost exclusively graduate-connected, had increased from a few thousand dollars to more than $2 million.

Much of this expansion was made possible by the extraordinary growth of the student body, which throughout the 1960s was increasing at an average rate of 8 percent per annum. The fees produced as a result generated an extra $1 million a year, which was used to underwrite the expansion of programs and the contracting of faculty to staff them. An indication of the rapidity of expansion in these years can be measured by the number of phones in service. In 1957 it had taken 168 phones to service the staff and faculty. In 1965 this number had increased to 268, and two years later to more than 350.

Teaching conditions improved immensely. In the fall of 1968 the hated Saturday morning classes were finally stricken from the class schedule. Although salaries remained well below the average of those of Rocky Mountain peer institutions, they were moving upward. Entry-level salaries were competitive and the university was adding some excellent hires. A very positive development was the drop in teaching loads. Whereas a decade earlier most loads were as much as fifteen hours, the averages had dropped to twelve for service courses, and nine, and even less, for research-directed and graduate-related disciplines. As always, the degree of subject flexibility allowed faculty, especially in the liberal arts and social sciences, was remarkable. By comparison with other institutions nationwide, MSU faculty had a wide range of choice in course offerings. Old graduate school friends teaching elsewhere in the some of the most prestigious institutions envied the innovation and experimentation encouraged in MSU instruction. These same faculty waited years to receive permission to offer their first upper-division—no less graduate—course. At MSU this opportunity came soon and often. Promotions also came more quickly at MSU. Leon Johnson was instrumental in the improvement of all of these areas, and soon came to be known among the resident instructional staff as "the faculty's president."

The continued extraordinary growth of the student body, while giving MSU much to be proud about, also caused concern on the part of many that the growth was getting out of control. Student services personnel were sufficiently sensitive to increased public discussion of the problem that in 1967 the deans addressed themselves to the issue. "You may be wondering if MSU is becoming so big," they wrote the parents of 2000 incoming freshmen, "that students are being handled on a mass 'assembly line' basis, with little consideration for each one as an individual." Assuredly not, the message continued—MSU would continue to make every effort to take care of the students as it had in the past by augmenting and extending student service capabilities. Yet, the message was clear—growth and change brought an overextension of services and a concomitant sense of unease. [17]

Another example of the difficulty with which change was wrought is evidenced by the vicissitudes of a proposal put before the Board of Education in 1964. This proposal to grant a bachelor's degree in history can be seen as a commentary on how psychologically arduous it was for some humanists to throw off their instinctive need to

Married student housing, 1968

presence of these students in our classes, however, makes our staff members steadily aware of the important relationships between the cultural, political, social and the scientific, technical and applied fields. [18]

It is impossible to say whether this reasoning was instrumental in history's receiving its degree. The English department, in contrast, developed a justification with a different emphasis. Until very recently, the English department stated, MSC had "put almost exclusive emphasis on technological training," with the humanities relegated to "service responsibilities." The need now, however, was "to teach young men and women to live and think as citizens in the mid-twentieth century, instead of training them simply to earn a living in it." [19] Inasmuch as both proposals were approved, one cannot say whether one approach was superior to the other. But history's did demonstrate how difficult it was for one department to justify its coming of age without deferring to the scientific-technological imperative. The maturation of the institution was not accomplished without considerable agonizing.

Once MSC acquired its new name and the degrees to support it, Johnson set about salving the wounds of many years of infighting, overt and covert, between the Bozeman and Missoula institutions. There was little object, to his way of thinking, in the continuation of the feud that had existed throughout the Renne years. When UM's new president, Dr. Robert Johns, attacked him at their first meeting in Helena, a livid Leon Johnson cornered Johns that evening and demanded an end to the internecine warfare of years past. Johns was surprised; he had understood this was a tactic expected of his office, if by tradition alone. Together, the two presidents succeeded in burying the hatchet, and a series of administrative get-togethers was arranged. The first was held in Bozeman, with eleven representatives from each unit in attendance. Johnson set the ground rules: each issue would be discussed for five minutes. If no agreement was reached, the issue would be dropped. At this first meeting perhaps thirteen or fourteen issues were brought to the table. One staff member who took part in the proceedings recalls the intensity of the gathering as akin to "the Grizzlies and Bobcats lined up against each other on the gridiron." Two issues did result in some understanding and were brought back for further consideration. [20]

A number of months later a second meeting has held on the Missoula campus, where administrative counterparts were paired off for discussion. By contrast with the initial meeting, this one was much more polite. Following the meeting, the conferees adjourned to President Johns' house where it was discovered that agreement had been achieved in several areas. The result was that both

justify their own worth vis-a-vis the position enjoyed for so long by the scientists and technocrats. History's "Statement of Emphasis" read as follows:

> The History of Civilization includes considerable content related to the influence of the great inventions, the commercial and agricultural revolutions, the impact of scientific discovery, and the development of technology. Similarly, instructors teaching the American History survey are particularly aware of the importance of land and land laws in the advance into the American West, of mechanical invention, and of other economic influences. We have courses in the History of American Agriculture and the Philosophy of Science, to meet interests and demands in special areas. A large enrollment in the course of The Industrial History of the United States is another indication of direction of interest. We have just employed a young man whose special training is in the area of the History of Science. . . . Many of the departments in Engineering, and those of Physics and Pre-Medicine . . . because of the social implications of the work of graduates trained in these fields, are under constant pressure from national accrediting agencies to include more history and social science subjects in their curricular. Neither the staff nor the students in these departments want subject matter unduly slanted toward their interests. The

administrations began to comprehend the value of a united front before the Board of Education, rather than appearing as two factions vying with each other. [21] Subsequently, Johnson and Johns undertook together a very successful trip throughout Montana and the nation, addressing joint alumni gatherings in eleven major cities. When President Johns resigned in 1966, his successor, Robert T. Pantzer, carried on the new cooperative relationship. Pantzer and Johnson talked regularly on the phone regarding matters of mutual interest, with particular concern for the avoidance of program duplication. Pantzer recalls that despite the success at cooperation, some UM faculty, unable to divorce themselves from the past, criticized him for "fraternizing with the enemy." [22]

Johnson was likewise successful in ending the animosities that had existed formerly between his predecessor and the conservatives in Helena. Johnson carried none of the liberal ideological baggage that Roland Renne had been proud to flaunt; it certainly never occurred to him to seek office as a means of throwing out men and ideas judged inimical to his view of higher education. Rather, Johnson sought to demonstrate "prudent stewardship" of MSU. "We demand," he wrote to Governor Babcock, "that every program and every effort must be justified by meeting two basic criteria—that it will help Montana or Montanans, and that the expected returns justify the cost." [23] Johnson insisted that the state support its primary industry, agriculture, and that the politicos back the experiment stations in their effort to provide new ideas and improved agricultural methods. Arguing that the universities were the "principal catalyst" for new industries, Johnson called on the governor to acknowledge the significance of MSU to the economic health of the state. In return, Johnson pledged to submit "realistic budgets" and promised to "muster [the] total resources" of MSU for solutions of the state's industrial needs. Babcock seems to have taken Johnson's commitment to heart; he developed strong confidence in the president's nonconfrontational, moderate conservatism; the two respected each other and worked satisfactorily throughout Babcock's term, which ended in 1968.

Johnson also enjoyed a good relationship with the Board of Education. Although the board was now composed of many Nutter and Babcock conservatives, Johnson mollified much of the concern they voiced, or were expected to voice, about unaccountable growth and expenditure in higher education. And he watched with satisfaction as the board matured. In the fall of 1965 he wrote one of the regents that whereas only shortly before this had been a board "dominated by suspicion and Macchiavellianism," it was now "growing in stature . . . [and] is rapidly becoming the lay people's advocate for a sound, strong educational program for our young people." [24] It was hard for the board not to respond to that kind of support. Even Gordon Doering, Governor Nutter's most conspicuous right-wing regental appointment, warmed to Johnson. One regent summed it up thusly: "All the presidents were not above feeding us malarkey, but we took Johnson more at his word; we figured he wasn't pulling the wool over our eyes as much as some of the others." [25]

Funding for Montana State University was a critical problem in the mid-'60s. In 1961, the Nutter regime had put a moratorium on university system construction projects. With enrollments having jumped since 1960 at better than 8 percent each fall, the expansion of MSU's facilities and buildings became a major concern. In 1965, President Johnson estimated that in order to keep up with demand, a ten-year building program of close to $10 million would be necessary. Previously, Renne had built many structures with the use of student fees, open-ended bond issues, and private support. But private funds were not materializing as anticipated. The students and their parents were beginning to raise objections to fees imposed upon them, and the state had always been uncomfortable with the way Renne had bypassed its authority with bond issues. In 1965, the legislature, responding to obvious needs, lifted its moratorium and established for the first time in its history a prioritized plan for the construction of state buildings. Four million dollars was appropriated to put the plan into effect, and 5 percent of the state's income tax and corporate tax was set aside for the same purpose. Governor Babcock and his staff gave strong support to the building plan, but in order to prevent it and other needed educational construction projects from consuming established revenues, Babcock advocated the continuation of a tax about to lose its purpose, a three-cent cigarette tax initiated in earlier years for soldiers' bonuses. In a referendum vote in the fall of 1966, the voters of Montana approved the continuation of this tax. MSU alumni played a significant role in securing its passage.

In some ways, Leon Johnson's internal administrative style did not differ measurably from that of Renne. Johnson could be as abrupt and as arbitrary as his predecessor in making decisions. For example, Johnson's appointments of Roy Huffman, dean of the School of Agriculture, to the research vice presidency, and Irving Dayton, head of physics, to the new office of vice president for academic affairs, came virtually out of the blue. There were no discussions, no consideration of the appointments among the deans or faculty, just an announcement.

But, even if the appointments were made without consultation, major changes were taking place administratively that had the effect of opening up decision making on a scale previous presi-

William Johnstone, vice president for administration, 1964-1976

Irving Dayton, vice president for academic affairs, 1966-1976

Roy Huffman, vice president for research, 1965-1977

dents had never considered desirable. First, the Deans Council was replaced by an executive council, which was to serve not merely as a sounding board, but as a true advisory board for Johnson. The Executive Council consisted of twelve members: the three vice presidents, the five college deans, the dean of student affairs and services, the business manager, the registrar, and the coordinator of extension and community services, with the director of information sitting in as a nonvoting member.

The concept of vice presidencies was essentially new. There had been a single vice president in past administrations who served only to act for the president during his absence. Johnson felt, however, that MSU could no longer afford to operate without a substantial enlargement of administrative offices and authorities. MSU was now "a much more complex institution requiring a different administrative organization," he claimed. [26] The deans would continue to have direct access to the president but would now be primarily responsible to the Executive Council and through it to the president, and the vice presidents would handle matters on broad bases that would enable the president's office to devote time to other matters of importance. The vice presidencies established under Johnson remain today MSU's primary executive offices.

The vice president for administration, as chief fiscal officer, was closest to the president, and would therefore be the person to replace the president in his absence. Responsibility for the university's physical plant also resided in this office. William Johnstone, from the School of Education, was chosen for this slot. The vice president for research, Roy Huffman, dean of the College of Agriculture, coordinated the total research effort of the university and served as an expediter for it. This vice president maintained a close liaison with the various agencies of the federal and state government as well as with private foundations and industries. All university research grants and contracts were to go through this office, which would be third in command. The vice president for academic affairs, Irving Dayton, former head of physics, was charged with governing curricular matters, instructional methods, student advising and counseling, faculty tenure and promotion, and other matters pertaining to the purely academic. When the president and other vice presidents were absent, he would act for the president. None of these officers were expected to be mere functionaries or "yes men." When Johnson announced to the Executive Council that he had appointed Irving Dayton to the vice presidency for academic affairs, the audible groan around the table delighted him, for under Dayton the physics department had become one of the most vigorous, and Johnson knew he had chosen someone who would

"rattle cages." [27] Finally, the coordinator for extension and community services, Ernest Ahrendes, was responsible for the coordination of those academic and service activities occurring off the campus and at branch stations. The community service activities of MSU would be his special responsibility.

Johnson propounded a simple philosophy of administration. "[T]here should be as little of it as possible and what there is should be unobtrusive." Administrative organization was "not an end in itself but an expediter for the efficient operation" of the campus. Johnson used the analogy of the Minnesota loggers whose object was to get the logs from the forest down the river to the mills as quickly and efficiently as possible. "Ineptness and inattention," he pointed out, "frequently resulted in monumental log jams that took much work and more emotional frustration to dislodge." But efficiency was not itself sufficient—real leadership was demanded of the members of the Executive Council. "Proficiency in the process of persuasion," Johnson termed it. [28]

Johnson's successes in bringing MSC/MSU into the mainstream caught the attention of higher educational systems in other states, and in the summer of 1966 he was asked to apply for a presidential position in the California State College system. Johnson was flattered, but cordially refused. His response sums up not only his own reasons for staying at MSU, but says something also about the relatively benign state of affairs in Bozeman on the eve of the great campus upheavals of the late 1960's.

> I am flattered . . . by the notion that I would even be considered for a presidency elsewhere . . . . But . . . my place . . . is here in Montana. We are facing a critical legislative year with a brand new inexperienced legislature as a result of reapportionment. The state is without assertive educational leadership and unless someone assumes it with courage and vigor this state's higher educational system could well suffer a setback of serious proportions.
>
> Frankly, I am challenged by the intellectual lethargy and the incipient attitude of despair which seems to prevail. There is too much good stuff here to let it go down the drain without a struggle. I have faced skirmishes before and I have had more than my share of victories but this is a battle I want to win.
>
> We have attracted a faculty of surprising ability. True, it is young, but it is aggressive and there is a remarkable amount of real talent. Since I was in a way responsible for bringing much of it to the campus, I am not about to desert it now.
>
> Perhaps when this battle is won I might look at something different. I seem to be developing a "second wind" and I need big problems to sustain me. [29]

MSU campus, 1968

The Campus Stirs

Of problems at MSU sufficient to "sustain" Leon Johnson there were many. But it is doubtful whether the president and his staff had in mind those that ultimately came to consume their energies in the late '60s. Whereas Johnson spoke largely of problems in terms of a legislative lack of leadership, an intellectual apathy in the state, and the need to sustain and gratify the energies of a talented and aggressive faculty, the problems that soon grabbed his attention were those based on an entirely different set of issues. They were the same issues found on all the nation's university and college campuses, issues that centered on new social, economic, and political phenomena, and that resulted in the remarkable civil rights, antiwar, and environmental movements of this era.

Although Roland Renne's campaign in 1964 to push Montana in a liberal direction had not succeeded, the state's support at the presidential level for Lyndon Baines Johnson represented an acknowledgement that Barry Goldwater's brand of extreme conservatism did not adequately address the country's growing problems of poverty and injustice. As the decade progressed, domestic unrest was supplemented by debate over the war in southeast Asia and a deepening concern about U. S. foreign policy, which significant numbers identified as unwise, if not imperial in nature. The exposure of these ills created concern in every segment of the American population. But in no segment did the need to reorganize American society ring more resonantly than among the maturing children of the post-World War II baby boom. Members of the baby-boom generation came of age in the 1960s; in 1963 they constituted the single largest group in the country— 27 million Americans were then between the ages of 15 and 24. By no means did all of these young people take part in the so-called youth movement of this era. Many, particularly those of rural and working-class upbringing, stuck to the conventions of their more traditional heritage. Others "dropped out," joining the flower children and hippies of an American counterculture. But the overall number of the nation's youth was so great that what agitated a modest, or even small, percentage of them was sufficient to command the most serious consideration. That the youth movement of the 1960s centered on the nation's campuses proceeded naturally from demographic phenomena associated with post-World War II affluence. Many of the baby boomers, notably from the immense and prosperous middle class, were able to go on to higher education after graduating from high school, more so than in any previous generation. By the end of the 1960s, college enrollments had increased by a factor of four times what they had been at the close of World War II. (At MSU the rate of growth between 1945 and 1968 was even greater, nearly 600 percent—from 1260 to 7200.)

ley, among others, banned on-campus discussion of the issue and employed police action to make its point, the free-speech movement was born. The ferment at Berkeley quickly spread to other campuses; nationwide students began to demand a significantly enlarged involvement in university affairs. [30]

To say that MSU students were immediately caught up in this movement and that they demonstrated with every bit the fury of their fellows at other institutions would be to overstate the case. In fact, the Bozeman students not only entered the lists belatedly, they did so on terms that paled beside those expressed on other campuses, including the sister institution in Missoula. As one MSU administrator recalls: "MSU was probably

Montana Hall

Revelations of poverty, which were incongruous with affluence, and violations of civil rights, which were contradictory to democracy, were the initial issues challenging youthful idealism. An early manifestation of this disillusionment was the creation in 1960 of Students for a Democratic Society (SDS). Its manifesto identified vast social and economic disparities in America, condemned modern life, and called for the creation of an aggressive and antiestablishment "new left." When hundreds of college students attempting to implement the new Civil Rights Act of 1964 were met in the South with violent resistance (three were murdered, eighty beaten, a thousand arrested) and the University of California at Berke-

as unaffected [by the 1960s controversies] as any university. In fact, we had the interesting situation where students would transfer from MSU to Missoula to get where the action was, and students from Missoula would come here to get away from the action. . . . In terms of a university this was as quiet as you could be." [31] Of disruption on campus there was comparatively little, and of damage absolutely none. There were no forced class cancellations, no armed occupation of buildings, no arson attempts. Nevertheless, there were activist undertakings on campus in the late 1960s and very early '70s, which, while perhaps not as newsworthy as student actions elsewhere, were extraordinary in many ways.

Signs of student unrest had been evident somewhat earlier in the decade. As noted in the previous chapter, several hundred MSU students supported Leslie Fiedler's right to appear on campus in1960. A year later a student group had gone to Helena to demand an accounting from Governor Nutter on educational budget cuts; simultaneously, they had gone statewide in a publicity campaign to air these grievances. The effects of the Nutter-Renne feud were all too apparent among students, many of whom felt that Renne's determination to slug it out with the university system's conservative adversaries was

The legendary stocks—Freshmen Orientation Week, 1966

a true act of courage, and in 1964 a group of them created "Students for Renne" in an effort to assist the president in his run for the governorship. The willingness of MSU students to support the liberal agenda of their college president was in some ways an offshoot of the election and subsequent assassination of John F. Kennedy. The large majority of students at MSU in 1960 had been Nixon Republicans, but they became more and more moderate as they felt the influence of Kennedy's idealism. For example, the Peace Corps summer training program which was awarded to MSU in 1963 was received with enthusiastic campus sup-

port. (See Chapter 10.) Kennedy's assassination late that year only fostered increased sympathy for liberal causes on the part of many of MSU's student body.

At the same time, the students began to direct their energies toward eliminating much of the arbitrariness of the many conservative rules and regulations that governed student life in the early to mid '60s. There was good reason for students to express concern. At the turn of the decade the university still accepted the traditional roll of in loco parentis and monitored student life rather strictly. With rare exception, all women had to live on campus, all female and all freshman male students were held to dorm hours, dress codes were strictly enforced, alcohol was prohibited on campus, social events required chaperones, marriages had to be reported to the registrar, and "campusing" was a way of life. All freshman and sophomore men had to adhere to mandatory military training. Students were expected, and sometimes pressured, to attend campus convocations and take active part in special events such as Religious Emphasis Week and "M" Day. All sorts of rules governed frosh behavior, including the time-honored requirement they wear silly and demeaning beanies at specificied times. In front of the SUB were stocks for freshmen caught without this headwear.

When students disobeyed campus codes,

The Spurs, custodians of campus traditions, help a freshman settle in.

Max Worthington, director of alumni, 1948-1963; dean of students, 1964-1973

Marjorie Paisley, dean of women, 1963-1974

Edward Hanson, dean of men, 1964-1978; associate dean of students, 1978-1989

hearings were held before the old Deans Council, with probation or suspension possible verdicts. If students ran into trouble downtown, the university, not the city, for the most part, took disciplinary action against them. By mutual and benevolent agreement, students who got into scrapes with the law were protected by the local police, who would turn them over to campus authorities in order to spare them a criminal record. The county attorneys also favored this policy, much preferring that the university discipline its own students. [32] In the main, the offices of the deans of students were administered by well-meaning but conservative alumni—two of the deans (Val Glynn and Max Worthington) had been Golden Bobcats in the late 1920s and early 1930s—who had matured in an environment of conventions and conformities, who thought these conventions worked, and who were prepared to stand by them. No dean was anxious to rush into a dramatic liberalization of standards. To be sure, most students themselves, especially the women, were quite conservative and comfortable with traditional patterns. [33]

Nevertheless, the students began to openly express their concerns in the mid-1960s. As a result, the old restrictions governing dorm hours and dress codes were gradually phased out and consideration was given, if slowly, to student agitation for open dorms and the right to drink on campus. Compulsory military training came into question, as did attendance at convocations and other campus events. An interesting and telling development was the appearance in 1963 of an "underground" newspaper, the *Stiletto*, created to challenge the *Exponent*, which was, for the most part, identified with conventional thinking and was run for and by members of the Greek fraternity system. The first issue of the *Stiletto* was run off anonymously on the history department's mimeo machine in a darkened room. This newspaper for Sanctimonious Omphaloskepsists, as it described itself, was dedicated to raising questions about campus conventions. The fourth issue, for example, covered Religous Emphasis Week. Picking up on growing criticism of the event, the editors did not call for its elimination; rather, they urged students to participate actively in it so as to convert it from a week of complacency and dogmatization into a "forum of philosophical exchange and discovery." [34] Students responded enthusiastically to this alternative newspaper, and its editors had no difficulty in securing contributions. [35]

The concept of the university in loco parentis was gradually abandoned. By 1968-1969 students who got into trouble downtown were no longer hauled before conduct committees. The deans' offices came to consider off-campus behavior out of their province. Administrative control of learning also underwent change. Whereas the old dean of the faculty, P. C. Gaines, had regularly reviewed class text requirements, and applied a rule that, for reasons of cost, no instructor should assign any class more than a prescribed number of books, Irving Dayton, now academic vice president, removed that limit, arguing that cost factoring had to be subordinated to overall educational experience and exposure. Also terminated was the exclusive right of higher administration to pass judgment on the content of texts; departments would now exercise that responsibility. This was an important step, but the mandate was left just vague enough as to cause difficulty later, as we shall see. In 1966, a new conduct committee, composed of administrators more professionally engaged in student life, was formed to replace the old Deans Council. The dean of students, Max Worthington, worked to streamline office responsibilities so that more time could be devoted to student needs. A manifestation of this was the decision to increase the number of students and faculty on the conduct committee, while removing from the committee the deans of women and men. [36]

Students continued to enjoy access to faculty, despite the rapidly growing size of the institution. This was both refreshing and rewarding, and it spurred critical thinking on the part of the students. Many departments contained faculty who prided themselves on being available for consultation, whether personal or intellectual. These "mentors" were receptive to the changes students believed necessary on campus. History had its Merrill Burlingame and English its Paul Grieder; math had its Adrian Hess; theatre its Joe Fitch. Fitch himself provides a good example of the mentor at work. A southerner who combined a World War II Marine Corps experience with a Yale master of fine arts degree, Fitch revolutionized theatre at MSU and enriched the lives of hundreds of students from every branch of inquiry. He also introduced summer theatre to Bozeman, which he thence transformed, with the indispensable support of Bozeman's foremost philanthropists, Herbert and Marguerite Kirk, into the popular Loft Theatre. At the same time, he used his summers to train Montana schoolteachers in the art and performance of theatre. Fitch was particularly successful in attracting to his program students from virtually every discipline; it was not unusual for his casts to feature a chemical engineer, a football player, or a home economics major. He introduced theatre-in-the-round and theatre of the absurd. No season was complete without a serious Shakespearian drama. He also championed controversial theatre; he staged both Koestler's "Darkness at Noon," a study of Stalinism and its purges, and Kramer's "Inherit the Wind," the Broadway classic attacking the 1920s Tennessee law prohibiting the teaching of evolution.

Inherit the Wind.
1959 production

The strength of the faculty did not spare the campus its measure of discord. Drugs had arrived in the Northern Rockies, and Bozeman was not immune. In the fall of 1966 a "hippie" and avowed LSD user from Berkeley, "Charlie Brown" Artman, beguiled the student body and infuriated the administration with his efforts to organize a psychedelic intellectual campus revolt against authority. Artman, who resided in a tepee made of parachutes, enticed some students into his fold, but not many; MSU students (86 percent of the total student body, and 90 percent of all freshmen, were home-grown) had little use for him. The administration put him under surveillance and he soon left Bozeman. That next summer of 1967, however, the campus and its community were shocked when nine Bozemanites, including Sid Kurland, a member of the art department, were arrested and indicted for use of marijuana. Because Montana law deemed marijuana a narcotic, the accused stood to receive jail sentences of up to five years. For a short period much was made of the incident, as the press was able to touch upon the fears of those Montanans who perceived drugs as the tool of subversives and/or the devil. [37] The charges were ultimately dropped, although local newspaper editor Harvey Griffin would not temper his determination that marijuana users suffer the death penalty, whether MSU faculty or not.

The most controversial development on campus at this time involved yet another instance of "academic freedom." Twice in the school's history the right to free expression by faculty had been challenged by the administration. The first, in 1951, concerned the right of faculty to support the cause of conscientious objection. The second, in 1960, involved the right of a so-called radical, Leslie Fiedler, to speak on the MSC campus. Both incidents were highly publicized. So too, in the late '60s, was a new issue of academic freedom, the right of a faculty member to assign textual materials of his or her own choosing.

James Myers had been hired in the fall of

1967 as an instructor in English. Fresh out of UCLA graduate school with a master of arts degree, he was bright, verbal, and innovative. He could also be abrasive, and he was prone to confrontationalism. In numerous ways he was a prototype of the angry, impatient intellectual of the 1960s whose mission was to challenge established value systems. [38] Teaching a freshman literature course that was required of almost all MSU students regardless of discipline, Myers chose to assign black author James Baldwin's controversial novel, *Another Country*. Transparently autobiographical, the novel expressed Baldwin's overwhelming sense of rage against white racism and his vociferous anti-integrationist views. The subject matter and the use of vulgarity disturbed established sensitivities. Should freshmen be required to read this book? Were black nationalism and racism a meaningful way by which to introduce American literature? Conventional custodians of culture thought not. [39]

Memories of a recent incident only added weight to the consternation. Another young instructor in the English department who shared many of Myers' antagonisms toward conservative conventions, Douglas Lien, had become embroiled with downtowners when portions of a hippie newspaper, the *San Francisco Oracle*, which Lien had recommended to the very conservative son of an even more conservative Gallatin County rancher, were copied and circulated on Main Street as illustrative of the degenerate character of MSU's faculty. One the one hand, Lien's position that the student had a responsibility to view his self-selected assignment—an examination of the counterculture—from the radical as well as the conservative point of view made perfect sense, [40] but Lien had not taken into consideration the sensitivity of the valley's ultraconservatives, including the ever-vigilant Harvey Griffin, who, as usual, quickly placed himself in the middle of things. Leon Johnson handled the resulting town-gown tension quite capably, simply stonewalling

Griffin and facing down Griffin's crowd. [41]

While this altercation had been resolved in Lien's favor, the incident remained indelibly fixed in the minds of the senior members of the English department, and they did not savor a repeat episode. After some heated departmental debate, in which politicking and manuevering played an inordinate part and in which normal support for academic freedom was eroded by personality issues, Myers was told by his chair that he could not assign Baldwin in Freshman Lit. [42] The president's office and the Executive Council strongly endorsed the decision. But Myers would have none of it; he pursued his grievance in various ways, openly attacking the administration, and Leon Johnson personally, protesting his case to the American Association of University Professors (AAUP), soliciting the assistance of faculty and students, and in general doing what he could to keep the issue burning. In these actions he had the support of some members of his department, and of faculty from Arts and Architecture, almost all of them young, idealistic instructors like himself. In short order, Myers, and the issues he defended, attracted statewide attention and became a highly disconcerting and irritating thorn in Johnson's side.

Beset, Johnson vacillated. On one day he could inform the AAUP that this was not a case of academic freedom, but a case of academic responsibility—he rejected the notion that Myers had an "absolute right" to do anything he chose to do in the classroom—though he assured the AAUP that he hoped to reform Myers and retain his services. On the next day he could assure a concerned valley resident that "We sometimes obtain teachers who are less than desirable," but, as was the established practice, "we terminate the employment of these as quickly and as quietly as possible." [43] To a regent he wrote that he had the matter "under control," that the students and faculty, the majority of whom he felt supported him, had learned that he didn't "push" easily. [44]

Concern over the Myers issue continued, much of it confirming Johnson's conviction that he had the campus behind him. The Faculty Policy Advisory Committee (FPAC) debated the issue extensively in February, but declined to make a statement. Many faculty, who might under other circumstances have been supporters, were put off by Myers' arrogance and belligerence and sought to distance themselves from his cause, however righteous. The student senate spent considerable time on the controversy during winter and spring quarters of 1968, but a resolution to support professors "striving on behalf of academic freeedom" failed. [45] A committee was created to work up a statement. In time, it produced a document supportive of academic freedom and the right of instructors to chose their own materials. The committee's chairman, Duane

Roll, felt strongly about its work and expressed the belief that the experience certified a "need for a beginning of students to voice their opinion in an organized, forceful, and constructive manner, especially when it concerns the quality of their education." [46] Such aspirations were rudely jolted when President Johnson subsequently persuaded the university bookstore to ban the sale of controversial newspapers associated with radical persuasions. [47]

The cause for academic freedom simmered down during the summer and fall of 1968 in Bozeman, but not statewide. In Missoula a similar controversy broke out at the university with results that differed markedly from those that pertained at MSU; the case illustrates the fundamental difference between the two institutions on matters concerning the professorial right to free inquiry and the unfettered use of instructional materials. This was the so-called Student-as-Nigger affair, the furor that arose over a UM instructor's decision to assign a highly controversial essay, laced with obscenities, during the UM summer session. The public was outraged. Conservatives distributed over 100,000 copies of the essay, and the Board of Regents demanded an accounting from the university. But Robert Pantzer, UM president, stood his ground on the principle of academic freedom and refused to punish the instructor. Pantzer anticipated losing his job over the issue, but the regents and Governor Anderson backed off. When Pantzer gave his "state of the university" presentation that September, his faculty rose in tumultuous applause, cheering and yelling their support. [48] It would have been hard to imagine the great bulk of MSU's faculty cheering a Leon Johnson decision to support Jim Myers, so emphatically different were the two faculties in political disposition. Still, the repercussion from the incident badly damaged UM's public image, and, much to MSU's advantage, the university would have to wear this albatross around its neck for another decade and more.

Some MSU faculty continued to view Myers' position favorably, but they were running against the grain. When in early 1969 an FPAC arbitration committee voted 3-2 to permit Myers to use Another Country in the freshman literature class, with the understanding that if students didn't like it, they could transfer to another section of the course, Johnson did not appear perturbed. In truth, he had already decided to terminate Myers, confident that his stand on the matter had been correct. "[T]he subject of 'Another Country' is now passe," he wrote that spring. "To dredge it up now for more discussion would serve no useful purpose. It is like keeping a dead horse." [49] But it was not a dead horse. Myers' termination was to cause many more months of controversy, but that puts us needlessly ahead of the story here.

"75 Years of Investment in People": MSU's Diamond Anniversary

It was a cold, cloudy winter's morning in Bozeman, with a forecast for scattered snowshowers. Students catching the radio or TV news, or reading a newspaper, perhaps in the SUB, caught a glimpse of gloomy international developments. In Czechoslovakia the moderate Alexander Dubcek was struggling against hardliners to consolidate his control. In Moscow massive preparations were underway for the celebration of the fiftieth anniversary of the USSR armed forces. In the Middle East the Israeli-Arab war of the previous year had turned that region into a powder keg. In Vietnam the communist Tet offensive of the previous weeks had been broken, but repercussions stemming from the unexpected attack had thrown grave doubts upon America's ability to win the war. In Washington, D.C., candidates in the upcoming presidential primaries exchanged charges and countercharges on their war positions. Such was the state of the world on Friday, February 16, 1968.

The rest of the world was really quite remote from MSU that morning, however, as developments of greater local importance were about to take place. Notices had been posted about campus that classes between 10 a.m. and noon would be canceled to enable students to attend an assembly in Romney Gym. Assemblies, common events on campus in the Renne years, had become almost extinct in the late 1960s. But this was a special occasion and merited the student's attention: it was Founders Day, and not just any Founders Day, but the diamond anniversary—the seventy-fifth—of the university's founding in 1893.

Much preparation had gone into making the

President Johnson and the 75th diamond anniversary logo

year a very special one. It was not only the seventy-fifth year of MSU's existence, but a year for another six-mill levy vote, and the university's administration had determined to make the celebration politically as well as historically significant. The former head of the history department, Montana's premier historian Merrill G. Burlingame, had been commissioned to write the official diamond anniversary history, and each department had been asked to produce historical information for incorporation in the text, with specific directions to list all the "most important achievements... over the years starting with when [the department] was first formed" and including evidence to show that the department was "ahead of its time." [1]

A general theme for the year had been adopted—"75 Years of Investment in People"—and the anniversary was not to be confined to a single day's celebration but would be officially observed at three separate functions: Founder's Day, the seventy-first commencement in June, and Homecoming in October. A two-day program had been decided upon for the first of these celebrations, commencing Thursday evening, February 15th, with a dinner address by Governor Tim Babcock. The popular and affable governor gave a speech deploring politics in education and reiterated his strong support for the six-mill levy and a sales tax referendum. Following the banquet, a play, "The Physicists", was presented for guests in the SUB theatre.

The Friday morning assembly, to which the entire campus was invited, commenced with an invocation by Reverend Herbert Strom, Lutheran campus pastor, and was emceed by President Leon Johnson. The featured event was the awarding of four honorary doctoral degrees, three of which went to distinguished alumni with backgrounds in engineering, nutrition, and agronomy. The fourth went to a member of Montana's Crow community, Barney Old Coyote, coordinator of the Jobs Corps office in the Department of the Interior. Old Coyote delivered the main address, a speech in which he emphasized our need to embrace environmentalism and spoke of the special plight of Native Americans. Following Dr. Old Coyote's address, the Alma Mater, "Fair M.S.U.," was sung, accompanied by the MSU Wind Ensemble, Larry Sowell, director.

That afternoon the colleges of Agriculture, Engineering, Letters and Science, and Professional Schools put on symposia of two hours' length. Roy Huffman, vice president for research, had early recommended an overall theme of "Man and His Environment," with each college putting on a symposium emphasizing scientific development. But Charles Bradley, dean of the College of Letters and Science, had pushed for one campuswide event, protesting the idea of separate symposia as tending "to perpetuate the old A and M image we are rapidly outgrowing." [2] Bradley lost his argument, however, partly because the ASMSU representatives to the committee believed students would respond better to disciplinary programs. Nevertheless, Bradley attained part of his goal when Letters and Science and Professional Schools combined to host a discussion of "MSU and the Small High Schools

in Montana." Following these programs, each college held an open house until 9 p.m.

The day had passed rather quietly. In the days previous, the *Bozeman Daily Chronicle* had devoted much space to the upcoming celebration, but editions following the event did not mention Founders Day at all. It seems that MSU had come of age, and there was no reason to make more than was necessary of that obvious fact.

1. Louis G. True directive, undated, 75th Anniversary Loose-Leaf file, MSU Alumni Office.
2. Charles Bradley to Joe May (alumni director), 26 October 1967, ibid.

The Library: This building and Reid Hall were built in stages— framed in and then completed floor by floor as funds became available.

A Taste of Campus Radicalism

To be a war correspondent today is to move among the college battlefields. . . . You would have to tear yourself apart to get to all the college wars. Yesterday it was Cornell and Harvard, the day before yesterday Columbia and San Francisco State and the Sorbonne; the day before that Berkeley. Today it is Columbia again and various city colleges. Tomorrow it will be somewhere else. [50]

In early October 1968, with the Myers case presumably settled, Leon Johnson was questioned by a state legislator about MSU campus stability. Johnson responded that all was well—the campus was quiet, absent of any "important controversy . . . around which students would rally." If there was a problem, it concerned not academic freedom, but automobiles—the 4000 of them that MSU's 7274 students had brought to Bozeman that fall. Together with those of an ever-expanding faculty, there were 800 more vehicles registered on campus than there had been the year before. This was the kind of irritant, with its potential to grow into a major problem, that was worrying Johnson. [51] The president's observation that all was quiet on the western front was certainly verifiable. Arriving new faculty were amazed at the tranquil nature of affairs at MSU, particularly the six new hires in one liberal arts department who came from Rutgers, Columbia, Yale, Wisconsin, Oregon, and Washington State, institutions that were the centers of intensive, and in some cases highly disruptive, antiwar student and faculty agitations. They were amazed to find that most of the excitement at MSU that fall seemed to center on the exploits of a scrappy football team, the ritualistic hazing of freshmen, who were still compelled to wear those ridiculous beanies, and the statewide campaign to secure passage of the six-mill educational levy. For a president to point out that automobiles were his chief concern at a time when elsewhere in the nation campuses were in a state of extraordinary political and social upheaval is a remarkable statement indeed, and serves as a poignant example of just how remote Montana State University seemed to be in what Johnson himself termed the "sizzling sixties."

Romney Gym

"What We Faced": The Six-Mill Levy Fight of '68

Late in 1968 the coordinator of the Referendum 65 Committee, Charles Stauffer, filed a report with the president's office that summarized campaign efforts for the six-mill levy for higher education. In his report Stauffer pinpointed the groups most adverse to the passage of the levy.

Selling a levy—even one with the long history of the University Levy—is always difficult in Montana and becomes increasingly so with each successive campaign. The reasons are fairly obvious: A large state with a small population is forever faced with the problems of raising sufficient tax revenues to meet demands of its citizens. Due to inflationary trends of recent years, these problems are compounded and pose a bitter pill to real and personal property taxpayers, who must meet the brunt of governmental expenses. Consequently, many are reluctant to vote for any levy, despite its merits.

We encountered numerous citizens throughout the state who felt that a negative vote would not hurt education since "the legislature will come up with appropriations from someplace." None, however, could pinpoint that elusive 'someplace' . . . nor could our state's foremost fiscal experts.

Others believed a sales tax was "inevitable" and money could be derived from this revenue income for support of higher education. . . .

Perhaps the most predominant objection to the levy resulted from controversial campus events, students and professors. Although Montana has experienced little of this type agitation, the accent which newspapers and television placed on such flare-ups as Berkeley and Columbia undoubtedly left a marked effect on citizens in every state who concluded that most students were developing into hippies and yippies while, at the same time, instructors were becoming increasingly militant and "odd-ball."

I personally feel that our most stubborn opposition—as well as least recognized—stemmed from that faction of the population which has no college or university training, no background in education whatsoever, and little if any association with teaching and administrative personnel of our University System. These were evident, particularly, among small businessmen who enjoy boasting that "I've made a success of my business without all that nonsense which you're teaching at the colleges." This is a tough nut to crack and his ranks comprise a significant portion of the electorate.

We were also confronted with an "extremist" or ultra-conservative rightwing element which sincerely believes that our campuses and faculties are being invaded by subversives, that many organizations and instructors are actually "planted" within our educational systems for the express purpose of eventually overthrowing this nation. . . There is no concrete foundation for this conclusion—but the aroma of Birchism was in our nostrils on countless occasions during this campaign. . . .

There are also those who subconsciously are envious of the salaries and positions which University System personnel enjoy. These are principally wage-earners in the $5,000-$7,000 class who undergo a daily struggle and ofttimes long hours to barely make ends meet. Most are "experts" on what's wrong with education today. Given the opportunity, which they occasionally are, to point their fingers at an isolated bit of campus scandal or demonstration, their day is made when they can comment, "Look what those nuts are doing now!" Some of these people are eventually converted through their children-students but few ever overcome completely this inborn antagonism toward "those who live in their ivory towers, draw big wages, and bitch at a 15-hour work week."

Ranchers and farmers, understandably, harbor a natural opposition to all taxes and levies, simply because they are the large landowners and, consequently, the large taxpayers. However, many of them are graduates of this University System or have children attending one of the units and I cannot believe they comprise a significantly adverse factor in this campaign.

All of these segments of Montana society provided our barriers. [1]

Despite the opposition, the campaign was hugely successful; the final vote—127,625 for, 89,396 against—represented the largest plurality for a tax levy in the state's history.

1. Charles Stauffer (Statewide Coordinator, Referendum 65 Committee), "Summary: 1968-Six-Mill Levy Campaign," December 1968, 79026/3, "Leon H. Johnson General Correspondence" File, MSUA.]

The central event in the 1960s, which came to supercede the issues of civil rights and poverty, was the intensification of war in southeast Asia. Lyndon Johnson's decision in 1964 to escalate the war to North Vietnam and to augment enormously American forces in the war zone caused serious repercussions in American society, particularly among college-age students whose already demonstrated concern for socioeconomic problems at home was quite naturally extended to concern for the inhumanities of war. Student response to the southeast Asian conflict resulted in the commencement on many campuses in early 1965 of so-called teach-ins, or around-the-clock peace forums. For many students, the war in Vietnam, with its almost indiscriminate slaughter of human beings and utter disregard for the environment—"destroying the country to save it," as one of LBJ's military commanders described it—brought the grim and cruel realities of the Cold War into clear focus. Moreover, students were well aware that this was a war being fought, not by the college-deferred, but by those who chose not to or could not further their education. Protests against the war intensified, and during 1967, huge antiwar marches, participated in by tens of thousands of college students, were organized in such places as New York City, Washington, D.C., and San Francisco. In each instance, the marchers were met with some form of organized police or military resistance.

Anti-war protests were joined and even overshadowed by black protests. The nation cringed with the news of terrible riots in Newark and Detroit. In 1968, protest increased by a substantial and, to many, an alarming degree. The assassinations of Robert F. Kennedy and Martin Luther King, Jr., further intensified activist frustrations. Campus takeovers commenced. Organized by radicalized students and faculty, the first occurred at Columbia University in New York City. That summer, radicals, including large numbers of college students, protested the Democratic Party's prosecution of the war by congregating in Chicago to lobby the party's presidential nominating convention. When Mayor Richard Daley ordered Chicago's police to establish order among the protesters, a bloody riot ensued which served to radicalize even more students. The idealism of many an American youth was seared by these experiences, and the campuses of America became major battlegrounds upon which issues of national and international significance were vigorously and vociferously debated, and where disillusionment and frustration, and the reaction to these, were too often exercised in irrational and destructive ways.

Montana State University was affected by many of these events, and although the repercussions on the Bozeman campus were on a different order of magnitude than at, for example, Colum-

bia or Berkeley, during the late 1960s and into 1970 MSU was the site of a degree of political and intellectual fervor uncharacteristic of the institution's previous seventy-five years' experience. One of the first documentable antiwar activities at MSU took place in the fall of 1966 when a small group of students under the advisorship of John Langenbach, a young activist philosopher, formed a club called the Organization for the Advancement of Cultural Understanding (OACU). Designed to "serve as a vehicle to publish controversial subjects that could not ordinarily be expressed," the group engaged in a number of activities, one of which was the distribution of antiwar pamphlets. [52] OACU did not support confrontationalism; under Langenbach's leadership it maintained a moderate profile, its essential concern being to "combat student apathy." At times as many as 200 students participated in meetings.

In December of 1967, another alternative newspaper appeared, The *Nonnewspaper*. Sponsored by the Young Democrats, its faculty advisor was history professor Pierce Mullen. Its student editors hoped that it would become "the information center for radical ideas." The *Nonnewspaper* took stands on the Myers case, restrictions on student rights and government, the draft, and the Vietnam war, and enjoyed a limited circulation. Five issues were published, the last leaving the press in April 1969. [53]

The *Nonnewspaper* and the Viet Nam symposium organized by faculty and students in May of 1968 as a forum to discuss the many sides of the issue served to set the stage for a series of events that marked an eighteen-month period from the end of 1968 to the summer of 1970 when the MSU campus came closest to being truly activist. While the Vietnam war controversy was always powerfully represented in the debates and activities of this remarkable period, other important developments expressing faculty and student concerns attracted equal, and sometimes even greater, levels of energy. Sometimes it was hard to determine where these energies were coming from, where they were going, and which cause was favored over another. But that there was an abundance of emotional energy was indisputable.

It is critical to note, moreover, that these eighteen months coincided with what might be appropriately called an "interregnum" in MSU administrative history. In October 1968, Leon Johnson suffered a severe heart attack. He would die of another massive attack the following June. In between, Johnson tried to carry on—his determination to do so was amazing. But he was hindered seriously by a slow recuperation, and by surgery in April of 1969, which kept him out of state for medical care. The consequence was that an acting administration, under the leadership of the vice president for administration, the institution's chief budget officer, William Johnstone, handled matters throughout Johnson's illness and for almost one year thereafter until a permanent appointment was made in May 1970. Johnstone found himself in an exceedingly difficult situation. From October 1968 through April 1969 he was an on-and-off chief executive. From April through June he was basically acting president, but he communicated his moves to Minnesota, where Leon Johnson was recuperating. Following Johnson's death that June, Johnstone served for the next eleven months as the officially appointed acting president whose task it was to keep the wagon on the road until a new president took the reins.

Leon Johnson was still in Montana and still recuperating from his first heart attack when a series of unanticipated controversies developed. A growing antagonism toward favoritism for athletics sparked one. Throughout the 1960s, MSU's varsity athletic program had done exceedingly well. The overall sports program, particularly in football, basketball, wrestling, and skiing, was the cream of the crop of the newly constituted Big Sky Conference. While the major sports, basketball and football, enjoyed a mutuality in success, they did not share an equality in facilities. Whereas basketball operated out of the magnificent 8000-seat field house, football functioned on Gatton Field, an antiquated, mostly temporary-bleachered field of perhaps 6000 capacity. It stood to reason that a new facility was required, and plans were drawn for a bowllike stadium south of campus, with permanent seating for 16,000, expandable to 30,000 by the addition of two upper decks. If all went well, funding sources would be organized and construction commence in the spring of 1969, with first use of the new stadium scheduled for fall season 1970. [54] Students were not consulted in the architectural planning stage, but they were apprised of its development, as it was clear that the stadium could not be built without their willingness to provide funds matching those raised from the private sector. Neither the administration nor the coaches had reason to believe there would be any problem in gaining student support; a little more than a decade earlier the students had not objected to being assessed a "use" fee to help in the construction of other athletic facilities, including the field house itself. Student fees, in fact, had become an accepted way of life, or so it seemed. Optimism was high—a "Stadium for State," as the fund-raising campaign called itself, seemed assured.

The administration's and athletic department's expectations were dampened, however, when the students, in December 1968, narrowly voted to reject the new stadium proposal. Stadium boosters pushed aggressively for a reconsideration. A study of the vote revealed that the students had turned down the proposal on two grounds. First, the stadium proposal did not meet what many students thought a far more important priority—the construction of adequate recreational and physical education facilities. Second, there had been a general feeling that the issue had been "railroaded through" by the administration and the athletic department. [55] Consequently, efforts to get the students to reconsider immediately failed. The student feeling of being pushed around solidified when the administration and athletic department attempted to link the two projects together on one ballot, anticipating that the students' desire for new PE facilities would pull the stadium through on its coattails. This tactic the students adamantly rejected. They insisted on separate ballots and made the decision to delay a second vote for an entire year. Naturally, this put a serious crimp in the stadium campaign. Here was another circumstance in which students were beginning to rebel against administrative decisions made without their input. (See Chapter 8.)

Almost simultaneously another development challenged established authority. Progressive student government officers resented what they felt was an overrepresentation of faculty and university administrators on committees involved in student affairs, and agitation for a new constitution and bylaws to reflect these and other concerns commenced in the winter quarter of 1969. The first draft of the new bylaws alarmed the administration—it called for significant reductions of faculty membership on all committees (cultural affairs, dramatics, forensics, information and public relations, social affairs, field house, and bookstore); it also contained a preamble setting forth student rights that Johnstone and Irving Dayton, vice president for academic affairs, were extremely critical of. The preamble made no mention of student responsibilities nor did it acknowledge any other source of authority. Other portions of the rewritten constitution revealed how determined the students were to gain control over student fees, particularly the fee for athletics. [56]

Simultaneously, the protest movement against closed dorms heated up. This movement had been started originally by the men's residence association. Not unexpectedly, the Associated Women Students, always the more conservative element, opposed open dorms, as did the deans of students, the student affairs committee, the local Executive Board, a large number of parents, and MSU's administration, particularly Bill Johnstone. But there was no denying that open-dorm policies were in effect on campuses all across the nation, and Johnstone was forced to admit that MSU's conservative on-campus living policies were not in keeping with the times. Yet, in May 1969, when another group calling itself the Independent Students for Independency organized a mass meeting in front of Montana Hall to protest the

A 1969 student protest in front of Montana Hall

van Teylingen, campus architect, the barn was saved. Today it provides vital recreational services and stands as a tribute to the resolve and foresight of the student body.

Omnipresent was the war issue. In May of 1969 The Citizens for a Peaceful World Committee, a group of faculty wives, students, housewives, and teachers, organized a Peace Fair. Although its organizers claimed that it was "not a demonstration or protest, but a charitable event to raise money for the war injured children in Viet Nam and the under-nourished children in Biafra," and although artistic expression outwardly appeared the fair's major thrust, the fact that the fair featured an information booth providing draft counseling and advertising the interests of various peace groups marked it as a form of antiwar protest. The Bozeman community feared the worst—concerned citizens patrolled the fair's perimeters, and city police scrutinized the affair closely from cruising squad cars. [58]

This was paralleled by a sad set of confrontations between a number of self-proclaimed patriots, most of them cowboys, and hippie types, to whom the reactionaries took exception, whether they were antiwar protesters or not. In one ugly instance, some student cowboys roped a hippie and cut off his hair with sheep shears. One of those involved in the incident became a kind of folk hero with the patrons of the Main Street bar he frequented; they actually bought him a saddle in recognition of his antihippie exploits. The same bar advertised free drinks for a "lock of hippy hair." Another counterculture student was molested in his dormitory. The persecuted could only take so much of this; some of them warned the administration that they planned to retaliate. Posters with a telling message appeared on campus trees: Join the KKK—Kill a Kowboy for Khrist. Johnstone was greatly exercised by these developments. While he harbored a personal distaste for "long-hairs," as he often referred to them, he abhorred the actions of their antagonists, the self-proclaimed vigilantes from Linfield Hall. He and the deans worked hard to head off confrontations of this sort. Leon Johnson had already taken a step in this direction, appointing antiwar philosopher John Langenbach as an assistant to Irving Dayton. Langenbach's job was to serve as the administration's pointman with the counterculture—to keep in touch with it and cool down passions on that side of the conflict. This he did quite effectively. [59]

Johnstone was exhausted by these developments: "The role of president is almost too demanding for a mortal man in the universities," he lamented. [60] As for academic freedom, he thought it better described as "Academic Anarchy." [61] He could not have known that he was on the edge of an academic year that would make the one just concluded pale in comparison.

administration's dorm policy, Johnstone treated the rally as if it might escalate into a bloody battle: "The County Attorney and Judge are ready in case there is any disruption or violence or destruction at any time. We will use injunction and the courts and/or Conduct Committee action if needed," he reported to President Johnson. Johnstone's reaction showed his determination to keep the school from becoming another Berkeley, another Columbia, another Cornell. But the mass meeting was conducted without incident. [57]

Still other controversies broke out. A petition to recall the student senate almost succeeded. The senate had recommended an ill-advised alteration of the manner in which the annual yearbook, *The Montanan*, would be paid for and distributed, and large numbers of students rebelled. The incident caused much anxiety in Montana Hall, as Johnstone had developed a good working relationship with certain officers within the student senate and feared their expulsion from power. Then a campaign got underway to rescue from administrative demolition one of the last of the truly magnificent barns located just west of South 11th, in this case the beef barn built in 1926. Entitled the Save Our Barn campaign, or SOB (which acronym students simultaneously employed as a pejorative aimed at the administrators who advocated the barn's destruction), the effort attracted hundreds of protestors. After much agitation, and with the invaluable support of Andy

ever have the urge to **save a barn** ??

You have? Well, isn't that a coincidence; the students at Montana State University just happen to have one that needs saving.

This one is a 1926-vintage beef barn that nestles, a little incongruous-ly, in the shadow of a big, highrise dormitory on the campus. It isn't in use anymore and school officials were about to tear it down.

That's when the kids at Bozeman started to protest. Not the kind of student protest you read about in the newspapers so distressingly often. In fact, construction, not destruction, is the object of this uprising.

The students feel that if they can come up with $75,000 somewhere, they can save the barn for useful purposes (art gallery, little theater, child day care center, folk-dancing hall, etc.) while preserving a symbol of MSU's agricultural heritage, in the bargain.

This isn't the kind of student arousal that makes national headlines. But you've got to admit, it's a whole lot healthier than occupying the Dean's office (which no one appreciates more than our Dean).

Want to join the protest? Fire off a check or some cash (any amount will help and it's tax deductible) to SAVE OUR BARN, Montana State University, Bozeman, Montana 59715.

(Run as a public service by this newspaper)

A Major Milestone

Campus events of a more controversial and volatile nature almost totally obscured an institutional accomplishment of real note. In the summer of 1969, MSU granted its 20,000th degree. The 10,000th had been awarded in 1960. In less than one decade, the school had doubled its alumni. In the same nine years, it had awarded two-and-a-half times the number of master's degrees and eight times the number of doctoral degrees that it had awarded in all of its previous sixty-seven years.

Accommodation and Confrontation

William A. Johnstone was born in 1916 to ranching parents in Fort Benton, Montana. A 1937 graduate of MSC, he became that year a teacher of history, mathematics, and science in Belgrade. Eventually he moved into school administration as a superintendent, first at Highwood and then at Fort Benton. In 1951 he obtained an master's degree in public school administration from Missoula. Seven years later he returned to his undergraduate alma mater as an associate professor of education. At various times thereafter, Johnstone was director of institutional research, acting dean of education, and director of the summer quarter. All of these were under Roland Renne. When P. C. Gaines became ill during Renne's absence in 1963-1964, Johnstone became acting dean of the faculty. Johnstone's excellent way with numbers, budgets, and planning earned him praise in these positions. When

William A. Johnstone, acting president of MSU, 1969-1970

Leon Johnson became president on Renne's resignation in 1964, Johnstone was appointed vice president for administration, and when Johnson suffered his debilitating heart attack, the Fort Bentonite also assumed the responsibility of acting president.

William Johnstone was, and remains, the only native Montanan to ever hold MSU's presidential reins. Johnstone had faith in the system the way it was and accepted change only with reservation. He had a penchant for talking about change in the context of its accomplishment "within the system." In Montana, that meant a very conservative system, and Johnstone was a typical Montanan. He revered Leon Johnson, but he was not as flexible as the Minnesotan, nor as intellectual. More a managerial type than an academic, Johnstone's major concern was to run an ordered shop.

Johnstone's conservatism played an important role in the 1960s as support for education was measured and remeasured under the Babcock regime. Because he could be counted upon to exercise the utmost in fiscal integrity, Johnstone, as vice president for administration, got along well with the state's legislative conservatives who believed he was doing his best to ensure that the state got the biggest return for its appropriated dollars. Accordingly, Johnstone's budget requests gained the respect that Renne's had lost, and overcame much of the antagonism that had characterized the relationship between MSU and Helena. Legislators appreciated his straight-forward, businesslike approach. Many who had formerly distrusted Renne, or had been put off by him, found the acting president a refreshing realist, a welcome alternative to the academics with whom they had often felt uncomfortable. His willingness to state his prejudices, particularly his dislike for confrontation of any kind, placed him in accord with the social disposition of the majority of the state's politicians. Bill Johnstone's earthiness further bolstered his image. He was a gregarious, tall, lanky guy with one of the broadest smiles in Big Sky country. He was the genuine thing. He was a son of the soil. He'd worked his whole life in small Montana towns with tight budgets. And he had another thing working for him—in the 1930s and '40s he had acquired a reputation as one of the state's premier semiprofessional baseball and fast-pitch softball players, on one occasion leading a Bozeman squad to the national finals.

Johnstone's personality was both well suited and ill suited for the events taking place on MSU's campus during his acting presidency, 1969-1970. Put succinctly, his conservatism pleased conservatives, but displeased liberals and radicals. Since liberals and radicals were the primary source of campus activism during this period, Bill Johnstone posed considerable difficulty for them. Conservatives, however, were in the large majority, and Johnstone met their needs with resoluteness and often creativity. One of the early steps Johnstone took to stabilize the campus was to set up a cooperative and positive relationship with student leaders. His experience in working with the students on the stadium issue and on the rewrite of the constitutions and bylaws had led him to the conclusion that he had to have their support to survive. The officers of ASMSU now had an open line to Montana Hall. Johnstone put a lot of stock in student, staff, and faculty get-togethers. In September 1969, before classes commenced, he organized a conference on university governance at the 320 Ranch in the Gallatin Canyon. Bob Brown, president of ASMSU, Bob Quinn, vice president, and Bert Tarrant, editor of the *Exponent*, were among the group of ten invited to participate. A good working relationship developed there on the guest ranch that was to continue throughout this crucial year. Johnstone and Brown were particularly close; they shared a basic political conservatism and an abhorrence of disorder. There has probably been no student-president relationship to match it in MSU's history.

The improvement of on-campus living conditions was another of Johnstone's concerns. Under the direction of Glenn Lewis, director of on-campus living, food service received special attention; meal hours were staggered, more than doubled, and menus increased in their variety. This was not only good for morale; it made it possible for the administration to utilize mealtime hours for instructive purposes and better maximize space. Student participation in curriculum planning, accomplished departmentally, also developed. Chemical engineering, for example, created a student-faculty advisory committee, and a host of other departments, including ROTC, inaugurated variations of this model. This policy of accomodating students touched every corner of the campus. One self-described "shaggy campus radical" recalled asking Bud Purdy, field house manager, if that facility could be used for a Peace Fair. Purdy had been a paratrooper in World War II and an ultraconservative legislator during the McCarthy era, and the student expected the worst. But Purdy was extremely cordial. "Why sure," he responded, "this is a place to be used by the students." And radicals who expected Campus Security to obstruct them in every way found to their astonishment that Don Skerritt's crew could be quite accommodating. [62]

Other developments paved the way for the curtailment of student unrest. In December, a second vote on the PE complex and football stadium took place. This time administration abandoned its effort to ride the stadium in on the same ballot as the PE complex, and the students responded by reversing their previous vote and

giving their approval, if by narrow margin, to student-fee subsidization of the new stadium. Thus was salved a major source of irritation. At the same time, student leaders rewriting the new constitution labored to create a document that reflected reason and compromise in place of the strident demands they had put forth the previous spring. In short, the Johnstone administration made and influenced many adjustments to ease campus tensions. But the work was hard, and William Johnstone came to the conclusion that these months were the toughest of his life.

Some will argue that if Ronald Perrin had not been hired in 1969 to teach philosophy at MSU things would have been different. Others have argued that if Leon Johnson had lived things would have been different. Either position might be hard to support. Nevertheless, if there was ever a time when one individual came closest to standing the university on its head, or when, perhaps more properly stated, people thought this institution was about to be stood on its head, this was that time.

Ronald Perrin

Perrin was the closest MSU ever came to possessing an out-and-out dedicated radical activist. He arrived in Bozeman in 1969, a full-blown Marxist with ideological leanings one could see at work at Columbia or UCLA, but which were quite foreign to Montana. This hardly fazed the University of San Diego-trained professor. Most likely, he viewed this opportunity to radicalize a small town and its vocationally oriented campus as one of the most exciting challenges of his life. A native of New Hampshire, who had studied at Northwestern, Perrin had been caught up in the civil rights and antiwar movements of the early 1960s and concluded that teaching was where he really desired to place his life's emphasis. Consequently, in the mid-1960s he entered the graduate school at the University of San Diego to obtain a Ph.D. in philosophy.

Perrin chose San Diego in order to study there under Herbert Marcuse, an elderly refugee from Nazism whose reverence for Hegel, Freud, and Marx inspired many of the early members of the youth movement. In his books Marcuse preached that the individual in American capitalistic society was severely repressed, a condition that could be relieved only by political revolution. But he understood the fruitlessness of rebellion in a society so overwhelmingly committed to the work ethic and the competitive marketplace. Therefore he stressed the necessity for individual freedom, for it stood to reason that a revolution could never succeed until its members first achieved their own liberation. Liberalism this was not, for liberals, the Marcusians believed, acted out of guilt to relieve others of oppression, while radicals understood themselves as the oppressed. The object then was to attack the institutions that oppressed them. It followed that students were victims of oppression, for universities trained their students to become servant/slaves in the workplace. "Students fighting for control of the universities," as a historian explained Marcuse, "would soon see that the issues of dorm hours and Viet Nam were connected and that corporate liberalism was the system responsible for both." [63] If revolution was unreasonable, resistance was not. Liberals might protest, but radicals resisted. The purpose of resistance was not to seize power, but to transform lives. As one Marcuse student put it, "People are capable of doing extraordinary things when they are in resistance. . . . In the process of resistance . . . there is a rediscovery of the self in the midst of a dehumanizing society." [64] This was the philosophy Ronald Perrin was steeped in, and the philosophy he brought to MSU from Heidelberg, Germany, where he had been working on his dissertation and observing the German student movement.

Perrin's appointment was received with mixed feelings. The administration, and especially its deans of students, was greatly disturbed, for anyone who saw little difference between conservative dorm hours and the federal government's Vietnam policy was someone to be feared. On the other hand, less restrained thinkers within the academic community found much to applaud. Perrin's department, history, government and philosophy, believed strongly, whether its faculty were conservative, liberal, or radical, that diversity of thought and behavior had to be an important part of every student's experience. The foremost advocate of this approach was Perrin's section leader, philosopher Harry Hausser, a "pot stirrer" who consistently sought to foster intellectual controversy. The luxury of possessing a Marxist philosopher produced a great deal of excitement in Hausser and others, for it promised interesting dialogue and debate over controversial philosophic issues not normally available for discussion in Montana's conservative climate. The department encouraged Perrin to speak out freely and in an effort to prevent false images from being created helped him organize a public presentation so that the community could see what he was and what he stood for and against.

Perrin was amazed to discover just how conservative MSU was. In his opinion, the students and staff demonstrated "an almost total lack of political consciousness." [65] The absence of an active faculty organization also surprised him. Although the AFT had been quite active in the 1950s and early 1960s, those who remained in the late '60s found it almost impossible to recruit younger faculty to their ranks. There were reasons for this. The Fiedler affair had damaged the group's image. Some of the membership were chagrined at the way the organization had pushed Renne. As one of them recalled: "We just dug a hole and covered ourselves." [66] The university's new and forceful emphasis upon professional development, such as publication and advanced-degree status, was also consuming energies formerly put into campus activism. And this was a period when labor unions were in ill repute; the working-class ethic behind the AFT was not accepted with enthusiasm by this growing, professionally oriented faculty.

Whatever the reasons for the lack of ferment, Perrin set out to create the political consciousness he longed for. In October, just weeks after his arrival, he became involved in an MSU peace moratorium. The October 15th Peace Committee had been organized by Perrin's fellow philosopher John Langenbach and patterned on a national student peace movement. To influence administrative acceptance of the idea, Langenbach produced a petition of 522 signatures calling upon the administration to set aside a day so that students and faculty could "express to Washington their dissatisfaction with the Vietnam War." This would take the form of morning classroom discussions of Vietnam and its implications, and a cancellation of all afternoon instruction for the purpose of supporting a Vietnam teach-in. The petition was not really a request, but an ultimatum, as certain faculty, including Langenbach, were pledged to observe a moratorium on classes whether the administration authorized one or not.[67] The Johnstone administration rejected this appeal at once. A serious discussion of the war and its significance was a "legitimate university activity," provided it was "dignified," "planned," "informative," and "objective." A cancellation of classes, however, was out of the question. Students who desired to benefit from courses ordinarily scheduled for that day could not be deprived of that right. More to the point, it was not proper, Johnstone informed the university community, "to force participation in this sort of program upon members of the University community who do not agree with the Vietnam Moratorium Committee." [68] A program, including a flag-lowering ceremony to honor those who had been killed, and would be killed, in Vietnam, was in order, but no class was to be canceled. Montana Hall had stated its position clearly—it would not take a position supportive of antiwar sentiment, and it would not allow itself to be pushed around by what it considered a distinct minority. The moratorium was conducted peaceably without instructional disruption, and a second national student strike, called for November, received no notice at MSU.

Vietnam Moratorium, 1969

That Langenbach, once associated with Leon Johnson's and Irving Dayton's offices as an administrative assistant responsible for forging peace between campus extremes, was involved in this challenge to Montana Hall attests to the impact Perrin had upon certain of his peers. Langenbach came from a conservative background—his grandfather had been a career military man, and his father was a state highway engineer with gunsmithing as a hobby. After an undergraduate stint at Berkeley, Langenbach had enlisted in the army, ending up as a Green Beret military advisor in Vietnam in 1957. As it would for many Vietnam veterans, the experience left Langenbach with serious questions about the advisability of American involvement in southeast Asia. Leaving the

army, Langenbach brought his growing dissent to the University of Maryland where he commenced a Ph.D. program, commencing a dissertation on the liberal philosopher John Stuart Mill. At Robert Dunbar's recommendation the department had hired Langenbach in 1965, and soon after, the young professor gained recognition as the campus's foremost critic of the southeast Asian conflict. [69]

A big, full-bearded, gregarious, earthy fellow, Langenbach related easily to people, including many Main Street entrepreneurs who honored his military background, liked his outdoorsy demeanor, and were content to overlook his political philosophy. Langenbach's liberal-socialistic tendencies were radicalized by Perrin, however, and after only a short period of exposure to MSU's new Marcusian, the former Green Beret was transformed into a believer. In reality, Langenbach was ripe for transformation. Leon Johnson's death had crushed him—the philosopher and the chemist-president had enjoyed a special relationship and Langenbach was not sure the Johnstone administration would make the same effort to accommodate campus activism. Consequently, his ties with Montana Hall, and particularly with Irving Dayton, deteriorated rapidly. He moved ever more to the left. While Marcusian logic was not quite his thing—Mills' gentler approach always lurked in the back of his mind—he joined his cause with that of Perrin. It was a difficult conversion; Langenbach did not relish playing second fiddle to Perrin, and he envied his colleague's worldly experience and superb intellectual qualities. These factors seemed to tear at him relentlessly; a more visceral and emotional participant, Langenbach attempted to upstage Perrin with radical outbursts. His frustrations eventually turned to bitterness and even irrationality. Within a year he would leave the profession, one of the unfortunate victims of campus radicalism in the 1960s.

That Perrin had a gift for persuasion is clear. Students who became enamored of Perrin's approach talked later of his unique capability for drawing them into his philosophical and activist circle. One result of his persuasive talents was the radicalization of Langenbach's old Organization for the Advancement of Cultural Understanding (OACU). In the fall of 1969 it was decided that the title simply did not convey the kinds of things Perrin and his following desired. Consequently, OACU with its moderate approach was disbanded, and a new group, the Radical Student Union (RSU), was formed on Marcusian resistance principles. [70] Its founders thought of it as a kind of rump student government. Lindy Miller, a psychology-to-art-to-philosophy student from nearby Harrison, became president. Miller, now a successful potter and ceramicist, recalls:

The brains of RSU was Ronald Perrin. The membership trusted his judgment and trusted him as an individual. Perrin was no "primrose path" leader. . . . RSU involved a lot of kids sticking their necks out. It was a war on the home front. Many of the members were willing to sacrifice all for what they believed in those days—that people were somebody, that people shouldn't be manipulated, that the worth of the individual was important. There was a vision here of the making of the new society. [71]

RSU leadership was almost entirely Montana-born; they came from small towns like Harrison, Deer Lodge, and Stevensville. They had come from backgrounds emphasizing traditional values. Now they were radicalized, some of them from having taken Perrin's courses or having taken part in the regular get-togethers he held at his home (often under police surveillance); some from being disenchanted with administrative regulations they felt outdated and inflexible, or with the administration's seeming disinterest in the world outside Montana. They might have come, the better part of them, from provincial backgrounds, but they were bright and industrious and excited about the exposure they were getting to new and bold ideas. But membership was not only local; at one time a number of black athletes were involved. Women's liberation also generated supportive energy, and a good number of RSU's members were Vietnam veterans who felt better working with a cause emphasizing discussion of the war than they did with the so-called stay-home types harrassing the antiwar movement. For a short period RSU put out its own newspaper as an alternative to the *Exponent*. Drugs were decidedly discouraged. This could not be completely curtailed, but Perrin's and Miller's philosophy that one couldn't be an effective activist while a "druggie" prevailed.

Perrin's association with controversy became a consuming topic on the Bozeman campus and in the community. Every time one of his radical associates or friends came through town—and Perrin entertained many of these—there would be some sort of reaction. His friendship with members of the Black Panthers, and with the radical black activist Angela Davis, placed him in a position of notoriety. It was understood that he and others were a conduit for draft evaders attempting to reach Canada. Evidence of local police, FBI, and CIA surveillance was abundant. Speculation on Perrin's motives, often grossly exaggerated, was a constant on Main Street, in administrative circles, and in the more conservative university divisions and departments. Fears were expressed that Perrin was the point man for a larger influx of leftists who would attempt to radicalize the campus. "Perrinoia," merely a play on words for some, was to others a serious reality.

The radical movement at MSU never actually made any serious attempt to recruit outside help or to relate its activities to student movements elsewhere. Perrin did make several efforts to forge a relationship with radical elements at the university in Missoula, but his efforts failed. [72] Missoula's large out-of-state enrollment (generally in the vicinity of 30 percent of the student body and more) seemed to foster an elitism in UM's radicalism that was alien to the largely Montana-rooted activism in Bozeman. Members

of the movement in Missoula appeared to look down at the ag school's efforts, labeling RSU activists "stumpjumpers—hicks over their heads." MSU's student radicals were nonplussed. A unified effort with UM mattered little to them. The more confrontational character of the Missoula campus's resistance didn't fit the mellower nature of RSU's strategy, anyway. What counted was the cause, and the cause, for most of MSU's radicals, was the Vietnam war. Lindy Miller, RSU's first president, was "rabidly" opposed to the war and "totally consumed" by the antiwar effort, the righteousness of which, he felt, gave him a sense of infallibility. But "infallibility" didn't make RSU an agent of disorder. Miller was a devotee of peace—he abhorred violence and advocated passive resistance. On occasion RSU members could become agitated over issues and advocate disorder, but Miller and the leadership were always able to diffuse these excesses, favoring cooperation and community over carnage and carnival.

A rally to protest the termination of English professor James Myers, 1970

But it wasn't the antiwar protest movement that brought the campus's one eventful claim to activist fame. Instead, it was a revival of the old Myers case. At the beginning of the fall quarter of 1969, the campus community learned that Myers had been given a terminal contract, and that as of June 30, 1970, he would no longer be in MSU's employ. Protest sprang up at once and mushroomed into an attempt to reopen the case—to give Myers another reading. The head of Myers' department, the dean of his college, and sizable numbers of faculty and students—1300 of them in all— petitioned Johnstone to do so. The acting president refused. [73] Myers then exercised his right of protest to the Faculty Service Committee, which proceeded under its own mandate to hold many meetings and interviews. In January 1970,

the committee unanimously recommended "reconsideration of the dismissal" of Myers, arguing that the punishment, banishment from teaching at MSU, did not fit the crime—"errors in judgement" and actions which "may have been somewhat damaging to the public image of the University." The positive attributes of the instructor, his "professional competence, teaching ability and proficiency," the committee felt, outweighed the negative. [74]

The reopening of the controversy was intensified by other campus events of note. Herbert Marcuse had been invited to speak at MSU in April as part of the honors program lecture series, and Bill Johnstone was receiving, as the result, a lot of abuse from the state's ultraconservatives. April's calendar also featured Earth Day, a day of environmental dedication. Ironically, some activist faculty were distressed by the observance of Earth Day, thinking that the emphasis given environmentalism would draw attention away from the southeast Asian war. Some students and faculty saw the Myers affair in much the same light. Leaders of the Radical Student Union were not pleased by the attention being given the freedom-of-speech issue, for it promised to divert focus away from their major cause, the antiwar campaign. In an effort to resolve this dilemma, leaders of RSU asked Myers and his wife to meet with them. But the Myers insisted that RSU's concern was insignificant compared with their own.

Events boiled over on April 1, 1970, when the administration rejected the Service Committee's recommendation and reiterated its decision to terminate Myers. The announcement produced an angry, dramatic response unlike any that had preceded or would follow. On April 2, approximately 250 students and faculty carried out a sit-in, an occupation of Montana Hall. The principle at stake for many now went beyond the Myers question, for now that the appeal verdict, which favored Myers' retention, had been rejected, what avenue was there for student and faculty input in decision making? The sit-in had been organized in a day's time by faculty supportive of Myers and the issues he epitomized. The Radical Student Union also played a role of importance, previously preparing for events of this kind by creating a "committee for spontaneous demonstrations." But no violence of any kind took place during the sit-in. It was not a seizure of a building, although the cluttering up of halls and staircases with bodies did hamper administrative mobility. Students and faculty were very unsure of what the administration's response would be. There were justifiable fears that students might be expelled and faculty fired. At one point, when the demonstrators thought they might be forcibly evicted, they called in one of the campus pastors to lead a prayer vigil, trusting that the administration would not try to break up a religious service.

The sit-in at Montana Hall, 1970

Forrest H. Anderson, governor of the state of Montana, 1968-1972

Considering all, the administration responded in a very constrained way, but it was determined to prevent the affair from escalating. When a local radio operator/owner attempted to set up a news center in the president's office, he was promptly evicted. Irving Dayton, vice president for academic affairs, tried to arrange a voluntary evacuation of the building, but the demonstrators refused. The result was a private negotiation between several RSU officers and Johnstone and Dayton. Dayton controlled the meeting: "We're not going to let this turn into a circus," he said at the outset. He was, in a student leader's estimation, "a tough cookie, intellectually and emotionally. You couldn't manipulate him, he put up real resistance, and succeeded in keeping the lid on. He wasn't intimidated by long-haired, shaggy, ill-clad students." [75] But the students did gain a concession; in exchange for their evacuation of the building at the end of the workday, the administration agreed to hold an open hearing in the very near future. Although some demonstrators weighed the plausibility of staying on throughout the night, they accepted the compromise and left Montana Hall peaceably at 5 p.m. The following week a few particularly disgruntled faculty members held their own sit-ins, but these attracted little, if any, support. In the meantime, Johnstone was buoyed greatly by the receipt of a petition signed by 750 students who supported Myers' dismissal. [76]

Glorietta

In an interesting footnote to the Myers affair, most of the faculty who left MSU combined to establish Glorietta, an experimental school situated high in the mountains of northern New Mexico. There they pooled their meager resources, purchased property, and constructed, by hand, adobe school buildings. Financial resources were slim, and they were forced to live communally. It was a tough experience for most of them, communal living being alien to their previous lifestyle. The natural environment proved inhospitable, particularly the winter's cold, and students were hard to come by. A few came down from MSU, brought mostly by curiosity, but they left in disappointment. One of these was Lindy Miller, once the president of RSU. There were just "too many poets and not enough carpenters," Miller would say of the experiment. Gradually the members drifted away, and Glorietta became history. [1]

1. Lindy Miller interview, 22 August 1988; Sam Curtis interview, 8 October 1991.

That the "sit-ins" had not served their purpose was made evident a week later when the promised hearing, held in a packed classroom in Reid Hall, failed to budge the administration's determination to fire the English instructor. Claiming that it had no authority to act on the Service Committee's report, the administration referred Myers' supporters to the Board of Education. This angered the group immensely. As most everyone knew, the regents had from the beginning backed Johnson's, and then Johnstone's, determination to release Myers. Naturally, those opposed to the instructor's release felt that the hearing had been conducted deceitfully and by way of tokenism. In truth, the acting president had long lost any ability to compromise. The Board of Education's stand on Myers was emphatic. Members of the board had periodically reminded MSU officials that they would not tolerate any backtracking on the issue. The chairman of the board had actually come to Bozeman to emphasize that point. Moreover, the regents had the absolute backing of the new governor, Forrest Anderson, who more than once had reassured Johnstone of his commitment to Myers' release. [77] While these sentiments had not been voiced in public, Myers' supporters had a good sense of them. Their allegations that the April 1970 hearing had been held in less than good faith were quite accurate. One of their number emphasized the impact this had among the protesters:

> The prevailing atmosphere on this campus is one of anger and frustration. Rumors are rampant that other untenured controversial faculty members will not have their contracts renewed next year. Many are considering leaving this university in favor of teaching somewhere where they will have both academic freedom and freedom of speech. [78]

This was no idle threat—eight faculty resigned as a protest against the administration's action. The majority of these were colleagues of Myers' from English, but architecture and art contributed resignations as well. For almost all of them this was a decision of remarkable extremism, one that would change their lives forever. There was a saying in the 1960s that the acid test of a radical was his or her willingness to sacrifice security, a job, a home, for a cause. By that measure, one might say that these eight men, and their wives, rank among the few in MSU history who can claim true radical stature.

Bill Johnstone considered the outcome of the Myers affair an important victory for the administration. "We have had a somewhat difficult spring in trying to establish who is running the University," he wrote a valley resident. "I think we have made some gain in making the termination of Mr. Myers stick." [79] With his budget committee he discussed the plausibility of taking action against those faculty who had organized the sit-in. Salary dockings and suspension without pay were mentioned. [80] To Governor Anderson he extended thanks for his support in dismissing Myers. [81] To an inquiry from the ever-vigilant Harvey Griffin, who wanted to know if the administration required any assistance, Johnstone replied that as far as he was concerned the Myers case was over and that interest had "declined." One of the good things to come out of it, he said, had been the "nearly unanimous" backing of the community and the state of Montana. There had been "general" and "reasonable" support on campus as well. He appreciated Griffin's interest, but added diplomatically that as the university now had everything under control, he would be pleased to be spared "the pressure of further outside action." [82]

But as events would tell, the confidence in having passed through a crisis stage was once more misplaced. That very month, President Richard Nixon would announce that the war had been extended beyond Vietnam's border and that American troops had invaded Cambodia: "You have to electrify people with bold decisions," he would remark. [83] When demonstrations erupted on campuses across the nation, and protesters were shot at Kent State University and Jackson State College, MSU's students were indeed electrified.

Cobleigh Hall under construction, 1969

In the Wake of Kent State

The first full week of May 1970 will remain one of the most unforgettable in American history. As the significance of the killings at Kent State and Jackson State sank in, student strikes broke out at over 400 colleges and universities, or on better than a third of the nation's campuses. While students on most campuses demonstrated peacefully, some dissent was expressed in violent forms. A national antiwar student strike was called. Classes were disrupted, many campuses were temporarily shut down, and a few were actually closed for the remainder of the academic year. Not unexpectedly, the violent, rather than the peaceful, nature of the student response received the most publicity.

MSU was not immune to these developments. When the first news of student strikes broke on May 5, President Johnstone was in Billings, preparing to board a plane for a meeting in Washington, D.C. At the airport he received a call informing him that the meeting had been canceled and that he should return to his campus as quickly as possible. The Deans Council went into immediate session upon Johnstone's arrival. One of those invited to the meeting was Bob Brown, president of ASMSU. Brown expressed his concern that some form of positive action be undertaken before campus radicals, meaning those associated with the Radical Student Union, reacted and forged their own responses. This was, in essence, an effort to beat the RSU to the punch. A comprehensive, and, as it turned out, well-worked-out plan was devised. Part of it was to establish an ASMSU wire service to enable students to send telegrams free of charge to their congressional representatives, or to the White House, as they preferred. The free telegram service would not be limited to those protesting the war's expansion; those who supported it would be encouraged to participate as well. The whole idea was to produce as quickly as possible a mechanism by which students could "blow off steam." The plan's second part provided for a memorial service to be held at 3 p.m. the following afternoon, May 6, at the campus flagpole. The service would honor both the war dead in Vietnam and students killed in campus antiwar demonstrations. The campus ministry was invited to organize the observance. In keeping with the solemnity of the affair, the flag would be lowered to half-mast. Classes at that hour would not be canceled, but the administration requested that faculty not penalize students who chose to attend the service. [84] The ASMSU officers rushed to get out the word.

Whether the plan would work was anyone's guess. But Brown felt strongly, with the administration, that a peaceable alternative to violence had to be put in place. That afternoon he learned that the Radical Student Union had called a meeting. He attended it; without invitation or introduction, amid hisses and boos, he took the stage to explain his position. He announced that he sympathized with RSU—Kent State was a national tragedy. Informing the group of the memorial service to be held the following afternoon, he invited RSU to send three representatives, people who would not only attend, but speak out. He then described the establishment of ASMSU's telegram service. Having said his piece and without waiting for an answer, he left. Only later did he learn that RSU, after much debate, and for lack of a better alternative, accepted his offer. It had been one of the most daring, and in some ways frightening, things he had undertaken in his young life.[85]

In the meantime, Bill Johnstone sought to defuse campus dissidence by drafting a telegram to Senator Mansfield. "May I express my personal concern and that of this University regarding the expanded military involvement and the implications for all young Americans. We urge adherence to the announced doctrine of early and consistent withdrawal of young Americans from South East Asia," he cabled. [86] The next day he made a campuswide appeal:

> While universities encourage dissent they cannot exist in any desirable form during violence, destruction and disruption. Violence begets violence. The university is dependent upon rational discussion and action by responsible members of the university community who recognize that we are judged by our actions and accomplishments in many arenas. [87]

That afternoon the memorial service was held without incident. In the next two or three days over 2000 students took advantage of ASMSU's telegram service. Though tension was tangibly reduced, the 2000 student petitioners represented little more than a quarter of the total student body. ASMSU observers noted, moreover, that the preponderance of telegram users were antiwar, and that those who reserved opinion or supported President Nixon's strategy did not avail themselves of the service. Sensing that a sentiment counter to the national trend prevailed on the Bozeman campus, ASMSU, with the assistance of the testing and counseling service in the College of Education, worked up a questionnaire for distribution the following week testing opinions on the war. The questionnaires, distributed during a targeted class hour, reached roughly 3200 students, or about 45 percent of the student body. The results confirmed Brown's and the administration's suspicions—the student opinion generally supported Nixon's invasion of Cambodia. To the question, "Do you agree with the decision to dispatch U.S. ground troops to Cambodia?" 43 percent answered "no," but 48 percent

answered "yes." Other responses paralleled Montana's conservative penchant for order and the willingness to use force to preserve it. Forty-two percent, for example, did not disfavor the use of lethal weapons on campus, and only 10 percent opposed the use of the National Guard for maintaining campus order. On the other hand, 71 percent favored the continuation of educational draft deferments.

The opinion poll's results boosted President Johnstone's morale considerably. They vindicated his conviction that the MSU campus desired to resolve problems peaceably and suggested that his year-long effort to hold a conservative line and to prepare for such emergencies had paid off. He could not have missed the marked contrast that existed between MSU and UM in their respective responses to the crisis. In Missoula, the student strike had forced the campus to shut down for better than three days. In Bozeman, not a single class had been canceled. In Missoula, protesters had occupied the ROTC building with a sit-in and had forced the closing of its offices. In Bozeman, there had been a few anticipated crank bomb threats, but not one instance of disorder. In Missoula, the UM Foundation was picketed for having invested in military-related corporations. In Bozeman, no agency of the university was pressured in any way. The striking difference in campus mood was obvious to Ronald Perrin, who visited Missoula that week in May. Upon returning to Bozeman, he acknowledged that the contrast between the two campuses was "extraordinary." [88]

One of Johnstone's fears had been that students from some of the closed campuses across the country "would come out here and find out that Montana hadn't done anything destructive and help [cause trouble]." One group of outsiders did attempt to encourage a student uprising against ROTC, but MSU police hustled them off campus without incident. [89] Sensing the advantages that could be gained in showing MSU to be an oasis of peace amid nationwide disorder, Johnstone conceived of the idea of publicizing the campus situation in Washington, D.C.. Here was an opportunity to inform the White House and the nation's legislators that at least one school had acted responsibly. As Johnstone saw it, on other campuses radicalized students had seized the day. In contrast, at MSU a strategy had been designed to enable all voices to participate in the debate. And a valid opinion poll had revealed the true character of MSU's student sentiments—a preference for things the way they were and a predilection for order above all. Here one could see the rewards of working through the system. Why not publicize it for all it was worth? [90]

Accordingly, Johnstone sent Bob Brown, ASMSU vice president Bob Quinn, and ASMSU president-elect Kelly Addy to Washington, D.C.,

Cambodia and Kent State: MSU Student Opinion Poll

Reprinted here in its entirety is the May 1970 questionnaire that sampled campus student opinion on the Cambodian invasion and the Kent State affair. Some 3200 students responded to the poll.

1. Do you agree with the decision to dispatch U.S. ground troops to Cambodia?
    (1) Yes   (2) No   (3) No opinion
       48%   43.2%   8.8%

2. Do you feel we should:
    19%   (1) Withdraw immediately
    55%   (2) Withdraw as soon as it is safely possible
    17.2% (3) Fight to our best military advantage
    8.8   (4) Win the war by any means necessary

3. Do you feel troop committal in Cambodia is justified:
    5%   (1) Under any circumstances
    50%   (2) If it is necessary to protect announced policy of withdrawl
    24.1% (3) It is too early to tell
    20.9% (4) Under no circumstances

4. Do you feel the National Guard should:
    10.2% (1) Enter the campus under no circumstances
    78.8% (2) Enter the campus only at the University president's request
    11%   (3) Enter the campus without the University president's permission

5. If the National Guard is called on a campus do you feel they should be permitted to use:
    5.6%   (1) No riot equipment at all
    52.6% (2) Only non-lethal riot control equipment
    3.8%   (3) Live ammunition
    38%   (4) Whatever they deem necessary

6. How far would you go to express your opinions:
    7%   (1) Would do nothing
    44.6% (2) Writing a letter to elected representatives
    42.8% (3) Participate in non-violent demonstrations
    5.6%   (4) Participate in violent demonstrations if necessary

7. U.S. combat forces should be committed to military action only if Congress declares war.
    (1) Strongly agree   (2) Agree   (3) Disagree   (4) Strongly disagree
        22%   40.8%   31%   6.2%

8. National referendum should be held in the U.S. concerning S.E. Asain involvement.
    (1) Strongly agree   (2) Agree   (3) Disagree   (4) Strongly disagree
        28%   49.5%   18%   4.5%

9. Educational draft deferments should be eliminated.
    (1) Strongly agree   (2) Agree   (3) Disagree   (4) Strongly disagree
        10.8%   18.2%   36.5%   34.5%

10. The occupational draft deferments should be eliminated.
    (1) Strongly agree   (2) Agree   (3) Disagree   (4) Strongly disagree
        10.8%   25.7%   44%   19.5%

11. The lottery system is fair.
    (1) Strongly agree   (2) Agree   (3) Disagree   (4) Strongly disagree
        10%   53%   25.7%   11.3%

12. The U.S. should establish a volunteer army.
    (1) Strongly agree   (2) Agree   (3) Disagree   (4) Strongly disagree
        31.7%   41.3%   18.8%   8.2%

13. The Montana Congressional delegation is out of touch with Montana students.
    (1) Strongly agree   (2) Agree   (3) Disagree   (4) Strongly disagree
        26%   48%   23%   3%

to advertise the campus situation. It was an extraordinary experience for these young student officers. They had lots of company in the nation's capitol. Washington was, as Brown recalled, "under siege by students who were jamming the halls of Congress and accosting their legislators in the halls." Mike Mansfield, who was opposed to military escalation, greeted them with inscrutable noncommitment. Arnold Olson, Democratic representative from Montana's western district, who had also come out against the war, was visibly disturbed. But Brown, who had his own political aspirations (he had just filed for the state legislature from Flathead County) hoped to get into the Oval Office. Actually, he got as far as one of the president's special assistants who was so delighted when he saw the poll the ASMSU officers carried that he provided them access to certain conservative legislators and even took them down on the floor of the Senate. The poll made history when Senator Hansen of Wyoming had it inserted in the *Congressional Record.* [91] For Kelly Addy the trip to Washington was a real education. Quite a bit less conservative than Brown, he reported to the student senate upon his return that, compared with students in the East, "the students of Montana seemed very isolated from the world." [92]

There is very little debate among those who participated in or witnessed the events of spring quarter 1970 that the failure of the Myers protest movement and the conservative response of large numbers of students to the Cambodia invasion and the Kent State affair took the wind out of the sails of the campus youth movement and the faculty who supported it. Radical Student Union membership declined significantly thereafter. A substantial number of the most dissident of the faculty resigned, including those who protested the Myers case. John Langenbach, who left that summer to go back to graduate school, was informed in his absence that his contract had been voided. Ronald Perrin saw the writing on the wall and would be gone in two years—to Missoula, in fact, where the intellectual atmosphere was more receptive to his activist philosophy. Finally, the presidency was soon filled with a new chief executive who could not be held accountable for prior policies. When staff, students, and faculty came back to school in the fall of 1970 it was almost as if nothing had ever happened. The events of the months before were now just a part of the past.

What explained the failure of radicals to exert more influence on the Bozeman campus? Two MSU sociologists, Robert Harvie and Patrick Jobes, examining that question in 1973, concluded that MSU, as a small public university situated in a small western city with a decidedly vocational outlook toward education, was typical of other institutions of the same character in that its protest movement was essentially "conven-

tional," that is, geared to protest through conventional, rather than unconventional means. MSU's social environment was the basis of this conventionality. Students at MSU came "from more traditionally based types of social systems," the sociologists reported. They were "more rural and agricultural." By national comparison, their parents "occupied more traditional roles," were less educated, and represented "more modest income backgrounds." Their children's career expectations were "similarly modest." The authors concluded that MSU's peculiar social environment did not discourage student organization, but that where organizations did exist they were socially and educationally career-oriented and conspicuously absent of "political activity directed towards social change." [93]

Leon Johnson had earlier anticipated something similar. In assuring a state legislator that he need not worry about campus disruption at MSU, Johnson offered, in explanation, two unique Montana characteristics. First, the Montana student was generally "much too independent to become involved in a monolithic, dogmatic structure such as SDS." Second, since MSU was located in a small community, it was spared the kinds of "racial and nonstudent problems" that had caused so much unrest elsewhere. [94] (MSU's student body was almost 99 percent caucasian and better than 80 percent Montana-born at this time.) Marge Paisley, dean of women during most of the 1960s and early 1970s, would endorse this view. Although the deans had worked tirelessly to maintain student calm, they could never have accomplished it without the students' natural predisposition toward order. [95]

Jobes and Harvie touched briefly upon another aspect of note. Where campuses were large, where environments were more urban and cosmopolitan, and where systems for student expression were cumbersome and impersonal, protest had frequently broken out in forms of bitter frustration and even violence. This had not occurred at MSU because the smallness of the institution, coupled with the socioeconomic homogeneity of its student body, fostered a level of communication that enabled it to survive crises. [96] This observation, of course, covers essentially the antiwar movement and does not cover other causes of unrest. For there were two crises at MSU in the turbulent spring months of 1970, and they brought dissimilar responses. One was the Myers case, which resulted in MSU's only demonstration. The other, the invasion of Cambodia and the Kent State killings, did not incite protest. What explains this? In the former case an administrative decision was made largely without reference to faculty and student input, while in the latter every effort was made to provide fair means for the expression of student and faculty sentiments. When presidents Johnson and Johnstone arbitrarily decided to terminate Myers, they closed avenues to free expression and, in effect, imposed upon a large number of faculty and students a two-year period of frustration and bitterness that led, ultimately, to a demonstration—the sit-in at Montana Hall. In contrast, the invasion of Cambodia and the Kent State killings, while on surface capable of producing a far more passionate response that could have fed on frustrations built up over the Myers case, instead brought no disturbance, largely because the administration and student leaders provided the campus community with meaningful avenues for emotional and political expression.

There is, of course, still another way of looking at all of this. In the Myers case, the arbitrariness of the dismissal decision, formulated and prosecuted by two conservative presidents, and backed from the start by a conservative Board of Regents and a conservative governor, reflected a determination to deny campus liberals a victory on the issue of academic freedom. In the Cambodian-Kent State affair, where a conservative reaction could be counted on, the administration provided for expression of that conservatism. Still other interpretations might be advanced. What emerges is clear, however. MSU's basic response to the disruptive issues of this era was quite constrained and rarely departed from conventional lines.

Chapter Six
The Politics of Education, 1970-1977

The higher educational system in our state was politically conceived, and its future is going to be guided through this process.
       Mike Mansfield, August 13, 1974 [1]

Holding the Line

The new president of MSU, Carl W. McIntosh, had been in office for less than twenty-four hours in early June 1970 when he received a memo from Bill Johnstone. The former acting president wanted to recommend a strategy for maintaining campus order. Recalling the "tension-ridden days of May," Johnstone enclosed a copy of an old Montana law he thought could be used "to curb inflammatory statements which might lead to property destruction or personal harm." This was the notorious Sedition Law of 1918, passed by the Montana legislature during World War I to crush the antiwar movement. This piece of legislation, which became the model for the federal act of the same name and year, pro-

Carl W. McIntosh, president of MSU, 1970-1977

vided for a one-to-five-year imprisonment, or fine, for uttering, printing, writing, or publishing anything "calculated to incite or inflame resistance to any duly constituted Federal or State authority in connection with the prosecution of the War." [2] Had this act been applied, several MSU faculty who had openly suggested that cause existed for violent action against the Nixon administration could have been indicted and sent to prison.

There is no record of a response by McIntosh to this extraordinary recommendation. Even if there had been, one can speculate with fair certainty that the new president would have downplayed the possibility of anarchy and would have refused to apply such an extreme and aggressive action. For this simply was not the new president's style. Excessive actions such as these did not fit his character. They were abhorrent to him. This gentle Californian believed that he had learned important lessons from more than twenty years of college and university administration, and that the cardinal of these was to avoid precipitous action.

Carl McIntosh had been born in Redlands, California, in 1914. After receiving his A.B. from the University of Redlands, McIntosh obtained his master's and Ph.D. degrees in speech and communications from the University of Iowa. Following two years of teaching in Missouri, he settled in at Idaho State (then the University of Idaho Southern Branch) in 1939. After a stint of war service, he returned to Pocatello in 1946, and a year later, at the remarkable age of 33, was appointed president of the newly renamed Idaho State College. Here he remained for twelve years, or until 1959, when he moved into the presidency of California State College at Long Beach.

McIntosh's experience at Long Beach State seems to have been a major shaper of his administrative style. Long Beach State was hardly a small institution; its 28,000 students composed a body larger than all of Montana's higher educational institutions combined. Many of these students were not as laid-back as those customarily found in Montana, being much more active and much more aggressive in their demands. During the 1960s, for example, Friday afternoon demonstrations at Long Beach State were not uncommon. The student and faculty tendency to believe that problems were administratively caused bred defensive administrative strategies. Moreover, McIntosh's presidency at Long Beach State coincided with Ronald Reagan's governorship of California, and the confrontation between the governor's well-established anti-intellectualism and the state's educational system did not make the administration of the state's universities an easy one. Simply keeping a ship's bow into the waves, and not becoming too concerned with headway, was to some administrators the best way to handle the 1960s.

If Carl McIntosh hoped a presidency at MSU would provide a refuge from the unrest and controversy he had experienced in California, this notion was almost immediately dispelled when he arrived in Bozeman. In retrospect, his seven year's at the MSU helm seem to have brought an almost ritual repetition of crises. The first of these presented itself to the new president only days after his arrival. Among the first persons McIntosh met in Montana Hall was a team of four accountants from Helena, employees of the state office of the legislative auditor. They had been at MSU for five months through the period of the Myers sit-in, and would stay yet another month, poring through seventy-seven years of records. They had not come on a friendly mission, and their report substantiated their suspicions. Presented confidentially to McIntosh on June 30, it strongly criticized the university for running an antiquated and inefficient bookkeeping system. For almost eight decades, the auditors reported, the school had made "no substantial changes" in its accounting, modifying procedures only in a "piece-meal fashion" and then only when absolutely needed. A complete and immediate revision of MSU's accounting system was required. [3]

MSU's administrators pushed other work aside and pitched into the laborious task of formulating a response. McIntosh took the confidential audit in stride—it was a time when external controls were being brought to bear on all kinds of public institutions by governmental authorities at all levels, and it was clear that a significant number of changes were in order. But the audit had uncovered aspects of the university's history of a positive, as well as a negative, nature, and McIntosh took great satisfaction in those findings. What struck the new president most was the auditors' discovery that not a single instance of fiscal impropriety could be found in seventy-seven years of bookkeeping. McIntosh thought this absolutely remarkable. Here was proof of a degree of integrity and honesty at MSU at all levels, integrity and honesty he had not found characteristic of many other institutions with which he had familiarity, and he believed that these findings would balance out, if not subordinate, the negative report on bookkeeping methods. [4]

But events would not permit the new president this satisfaction, for when the university's response was finally delivered—almost seven months later on January 22, 1971—the legislative session for that biennium had commenced in Helena, and the report was made and received in highly politicized circumstances. McIntosh had anticipated criticism to a certain degree, but he was deeply disappointed when the media chose to emphasize the negative and ignore the positive. Instead of giving credit to MSU for having conducted its affairs in sincerity and with trustworthy integrity for three-quarters of a century, the news services created a climate in which MSU was viewed as having been "profligate" and "irresponsible" in its fiscal affairs. The results, McIntosh lamented, had cultivated "reservations concerning, suspicion about, or hostility toward the University." [5]

Simultaneously, the legislative session proved to be a great disappointment for higher education in general. Fiscal concerns predominated; revenues were down and significant cutbacks were predicted. Moreover, the sociopolitical atmosphere was charged with anti-intellectualism. Colleges and universities throughout the nation were being subjected to criticism on a scale hitherto unknown. The Nixon administration's attacks on higher education, conducted through the vice presidency of Spiro Agnew and its crude assault on so-called educational effetes, helped to poison the atmosphere. Although not as coarsely applied in Montana, the effects of this rhetoric could be sensed in and around the halls of the Helena capitol.

It was McIntosh's first Montana legislative session, and he did not like what he saw. "[I]n my judgment," he informed the MSU advisory council in late January, "the University System is in trouble. I have no basis of experience in Montana for judging whether the trouble is serious or 'normal,' but I am not sanguine concerning the eventual outcome unless there is more confidence in and support for the University's program than is thus far apparent." McIntosh was struck by a legislative "preoccupation with lack of resources." [6] Early in the session the universities had been told directly or indirectly that "even if we raise money, you won't get any of it." To this, one prominent senator had added, "The people don't like your product—at least they don't like the image of your product." [7] These were not auspicious beginnings for McIntosh; they presaged difficult times ahead, with budgetary problems not easily solved. Back from one legislative session in March, he informed the faculty flatly that the days of great postwar growth in educational budgets were over and that the decade of the 1970s would be one of significant scarcity in financial support for higher education. [8]

From the start, then, the new president was obliged to design strategy geared to austere fiscal imperatives. This is not what McIntosh had come to MSU for, nor is it what MSU had anticipated. It was difficult for the university community to grasp these new realities, so accustomed had it become to the easy money and impressive growth made possible by the previous decade's increased enrollments. Stabilized enrollments and shrinking economies were obviously much to blame. But should not leadership accept some responsibility? Renne had somehow managed in the terrible fiscal crisis of the early 1960s. His legacy was strong. Johnson had led the university out of that crisis into a period of unparalleled expansion. Now things had slowed down. Could the problem be laid to fiscal stringency alone? Was it just the legislature's fault? Or were there other causes to be factored in?

Increasingly, MSU staff, faculty, and students came to ascribe a good portion of the difficulty to McIntosh's leadership style. It was so different from that of the presidencies of the preceding decades. Its deliberateness and seeming lack of aggressiveness confounded, and sometimes deeply disturbed, the campus. Talk commenced early on about a discernible slowdown. For some the administration appeared to be "spinning its wheels" rather than forging ahead—a kind of powerful machine revved up but with its gears disengaged, a university with enormous energy, but driverless. Some discerned movement, but thought it more "crablike" than direct, a style that proceeded in a sideling and oblique, rather than direct and frontal, manner. An administration of "missed opportunities" was a description heard increasingly. Others were not nearly so kind, labeling Montana Hall as the citadel of "no decision," as the repository of the philosophy that

Montana Hall

the best decision is often no decision at all.

McIntosh's strongly applied philosophy of government by committee seemed to fit all of these descriptions—a scheme of decision making that encouraged a democratic process but that also created a terrific amount of faculty and staff obligation to meetings and paperwork, wearing down and discouraging the participants. Committees, boards, and councils proliferated during the McIntosh years (there were sixty of them in 1971-1972: twelve boards, forty standing committees, and eight councils), all of which met periodically and seemed to produce too little for the personnel-hours required. Getting off a committee was almost as frustrating as serving on one. A member of the presidentially appointed library committee reported that it took more than a full academic quarter of appeals and paperwork, channeled through six committees and/or administrators, before the resignation received presidential authorization. [9] Many administrators and faculty learned quickly to avoid confronting the president with problems or proposals for fear an answer would be deferred in favor of yet another committee. Although well intended, McIntosh's administrative technique had the overall effect of slowing down the administrative process from its brisk pace of the 1960s. [10]

Some faculty members were so concerned about the president's deliberative character they wondered whether his appointment had not been a calculated regental effort to restrain MSU's development. With the exception of the institution's very first presidents, all other executive officers had come up through the ranks. During the search process of 1970 there had been varying levels of support on campus for Bill Johnstone, Roy Huffman, and Richard McBee, dean of the College of Letters and Science. But the regental search committee, conducting the first-ever national search to fill an MSU presidency, rejected these sentiments and chose a candidate, not only from outside of the state, but a rhetorician whose administrative style did not seem to complement the no-nonsense, forward-looking approach of the Bozeman university. As the new president's deliberate and cautious character made itself known, all sorts of rumors developed to explain his appointment. The worst of these, still believed by many to this day, was that he had been, either consciously or unconsciously, appointed to harness the MSU steamroller, which was accelerating at a rate so rapid as to threaten not only to overtake but to bolt ahead of the University of Montana. Ever since Renne's success in expanding the physical plant, legislators and regents had expressed increasing concern about the need to contain MSU's growth, to keep it in balance with its sister institution. Remarks by legislators and regents about "holding the line," about preventing the university system from overexpanding, increased concern in Bozeman. Although the main impetus behind these remarks was logically fiscal, many staff and faculty at MSU resented the restraints being put upon them, and it was hard for some to accept the reasoning, once McIntosh's conservative style became known, that his appointment had not been made with that in mind. Unfortunately, this attitude, not substantiated by fact, would fester throughout McIntosh's administration and beyond.

Even McIntosh's love for words worked against him. Language was everything to him; there was no questioning his rhetorical skills. Consider a paragraph from his opening remarks to the faculty in September 1970, the paragraph he selected for publication in the annual yearbook:

> When I joined this University community, I did not bring change with me, prepackaged in the latest synthetic wrapper, a product to be peddled by either a hard sell or subliminal persuasion. The forces of change were already here, easier to sense than to measure and felt by many, not without cause, as more of a threat to the cherished and familiar than a promise of an even brighter future. We have a paradoxical responsibility to preserve as well as to change, to change as well as to preserve, and to seek with restless urgency that perspective which will guide and clarify our often misunderstood efforts. [11]

If McIntosh had a charismatic quality, it was his way with verbage. Like President Woodrow Wilson, during whose administration he had been born, McIntosh's rhetoric perfectly soared, and he had a sense of power when given the chance to convey his feelings orally. Given time, he told his staff, he believed he could settle any conflict with words. He loved to communicate—in 1974-1975 his presidential signature was fixed to over 3000 letters and memoranda. Public speeches were his bread and butter; he averaged better than one every other week throughout his entire administrative career. And they were bright, witty, and engaging.

But it is also an unfortunate truth that McIntosh's flourishes bred impatience and irritability on the part of the university's many "can-do" types whose notion of progress championed action and a minimization of debate and oratorical overkill. Complaints that he talked over the heads of his listeners were common. More common were convictions that he used verbiage to generate clouds of incomprehensibility, like the Wizard of Oz.

These and other concerns were expressed strongly during spring quarter 1971, or less than a year following the new president's arrival, when a variety of frustrated campus groups demanded that McIntosh explain his decision-making process and make his positions clear or clearer. Graduate students and liberal arts faculty were upset at rumors that the master's of science degree program in applied science was to be terminated. Undergraduates and faculty were incensed at the rumored termination of the honors program. Faculty were up in arms about sharply increased faculty-student teaching ratios and reports that the president had advocated twelve-hour teaching loads. Yet another group, including the heads of AAUP, honors, various departments, and the student body, blasted McIntosh's budget-reduction priorities, claiming that faculty and student views were "totally disregarded . . . and priorities determined in star chamber fashion by the administrative budget committee." [12] Another memorandum charged that an "administrative dictatorship" was developing at MSU, "answerable to no-one but themselves," and that their "autonomous decision making" was a blow to the academic prestige of the institution. [13] A Faculty Policy Advisory Committee report opened with a telling clause: "Whereas there has been evidence of a communication gap between the administration and the faculty and student body of Montana State University. . ." [14] An ad hoc Student-Faculty Coordinating Committee, claiming to represent more than 600 faculty and students, charged that the new president's entrenchment policies represented "a betrayal" of the students of MSU and the citizens of Montana, who had held such high expectations of the school. [15]

Quite understandably, McIntosh was disturbed by these developments. Early in winter quarter of 1971 he had asked faculty members to get in touch with students for a discussion of problems. Only one faculty member had responded formally, and then to report that he had invited thirty students to a rap session, but only three had attended, and none had voiced any grievance. [16] Now dissension was rife. But was it justified? McIntosh felt not. Many of the complaints were unfair, or were based on false assumption or on incorrect information, he asserted. Yes, he had advocated twelve-hour teaching loads, but only for those who did not engage in research. [17] Yes, he had questions about continuing the honors program, but only because it had dwindled to next to nothing in departmental and student support. Yes, he favored the elimination of certain graduate degree programs, but as Irving Dayton, academic vice president, expressed it for him, many graduate programs were of extremely poor quality, while others were too expensive. Faculty members had to face these realities and cease being "obsessed with the idea" that departments could not function without graduate programs. There was no place for "status symbols" in a period of fiscal austerity. [18]

Despite the logicality of these responses, one

of the tragedies of McIntosh's presidency is that no matter how hard he tried, his constituency seemed always reluctant to accept his arguments. It is a fact that the California native suffered through his term realizing that his credibility would never receive the degree of sympathic support he believed it deserved.

McIntosh's relationship with the University of Montana suffered much the same fate. Hard times, combined with his administrative style, ruffled his relationship with UM president Robert Pantzer. A personal compatibility existed between them, but from the first Presidents Council meeting, Pantzer learned that it was hard to gauge just what MSU's new leader stood for and where he was going. [19] And the competition between the two universities to maintain progress and programs in a period of shrinking resources caused friction between the two institutions. Following a long and hard 1971 legislative session, in which both universities had their budget requests cut considerably, UM nevertheless ended up with half a million dollars more than MSU, even though the enrollments of the two institutions were identical. When it was made clear that UM's much larger out-of-state enrollment-fee payments would account for 40 percent of this half million, Roy Huffman, MSU's VP for research, blasted the legislature and UM before an alumni gathering in Butte. MSU, he charged, was being penalized "for educating more homegrown Montana students." [20] Pantzer was disturbed by Huffman's outburst; he registered his disappointment with McIntosh that the cooperation he had developed with presidents Johnson and Johnstone was being jeopardized. He hoped the old Renne-McFarland days weren't returning. "If there is anything that some people would like to see happen, it is certainly active warfare within our system," he wrote to his counterpart in Bozeman. [21]

McIntosh resigned himself to the worst: "This year's efforts [at cooperation] have every appearance of being an exercise in futility," he responded, not because a conflict existed between the two institutions, but on account of his conviction, generated from his recent experience in Helena, that a distinct antiuniversity sentiment prevailed in the legislature. McIntosh saw little hope for an immediate resolution:

> Neither our students nor faculty are apt to respond with instant crew cuts, clean shaves and the substitution of Edgar Guest for the editorial columns in the Kaimin or Exponent. This does not do justice to the depth of the misgivings nor perhaps to the validity of some of them but the incredibility gap between what seems to be expected and what the faculty and students believe universities are all about is of staggering proportions. To some degree a vocal and visible proportion of students have said, "We don't like your hypocritical, money dependent, special interest oriented society, we will establish a different life style reflecting our own set of values and beliefs;" and through their chosen representatives the people of Montana have said: 'Not with any more of our money you won't."

McIntosh then concluded prophetically: "We should have an interesting two years ahead of us, as Custer said shortly before leading his troops out into the wilds of Montana." [22]

MSU campus, c. 1970

Rationalizing the University System: Starts and Stops

The state of Montana should never have had a six-unit university system. The current system is more the result of political fighting in the war of the Copper Kings than any kind of logic. The system was birthed by politics; it has lived by politics, and we can only hope it will die by politics. [23]

The frustration the higher educational system was experiencing in the early 1970s as it struggled within itself and with the legislature over image and needs was not a problem confined to the universities. For many months Montanans had become increasingly aware that the astounding post-World War II growth of education into a major agency of state government had overextended seriously the capacity of the existing forms of educational administration to manage that

Loading the Bridger Bowl ski bus

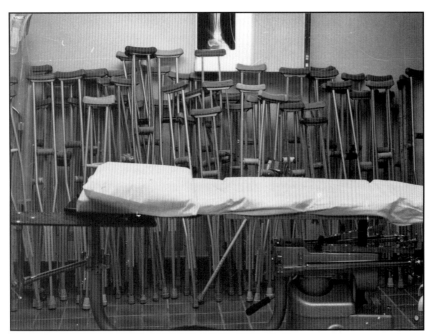

Swingle Student Health Center

Executive Outreach

Carl McIntosh enjoyed sharing presidential ups and downs with other chief executives. When one of these, the president of the University of New Mexico, was reported in the news as having been physically injured as the result of a run-in with a rabid basketball fan, McIntosh sent the following tongue-in-cheek admonishment:

Dear Bud:

One of the predictable spinoffs of painful misfortune is the unwelcome hilarity of friends who assume that because an injury is not fatal, the victim is fair game for all manner of presumably good natured jests. I confess that having learned of your recent dispute with a basketball fan, I contemplated questioning, not your judgement or ability, but your eligibility. Some of us have mixed feelings about your ability to expand the normal hazards of the president's office. We admire your courage and commitment to comprehensive participation, but you are setting a standard which causes some of us to have misgivings.

Quite apart from all of the unsolicited commentary which you will by now have received, I am dismayed that such things can be. I hope your antagonist was prominent, wealthy, and vulnerable. Everyone can use an extra annuity these days, and I would encourage you to turn the incident into a substantial long-lasting fringe benefit. [1]

1. McIntosh to William E. Davis, 18 February 1977, 80040x/2, "Outgoing Correspondence" file, MSUA.

growth efficiently and effectively. As has been documented, many previous attempts had been made to rationalize the system. The chancellorship experiments of two earlier periods had sought that end but had been rejected, the last in 1950. What had followed is what had preceded these efforts—controversial duplication of programs and internecine warfare among the units as they lobbied, often bitterly, to secure legislative and regental support for their respective needs. As we have noted, those institutions with the most aggressive leadership profited best from the absence of a unified system of higher education, while the less ably represented units suffered. Sheer frontier Darwinism often prevailed, and if it pleased the competitive instincts of some, it displeased those who believed in coordination, cooperation, and the most efficient use of the taxpayers' revenues.

Other attempts at rationalization had been the periodic efforts at consolidating the units themselves by either eliminating one or more of them, or by creating one major institution with the others in a subordinate relationship. Over time, however, efforts along these lines had invariably been crushed by partisan politicians in continually depressed economic environments who were reluctant to see a source of valuable state assistance slip from their communities' assets. Efficiency of management meant little in these circumstances—political protectionisn and/or the sheer desire to survive inevitably spelling the difference.

Developments in the 1950s and 1960s only made the failure at modernization more obvious. Following the steady increase of enrollments in the 1950s, and then their explosion in the 1960s, the entire university system grew at a rate that would have been inconceivable to an earlier generation. Montana State College, for example, grew into a university almost overnight, and together the two universities, in order to accommodate the growing student numbers, expanded and improved their facilities dramatically. Despite the increased costs associated with these developments, the state did not discourage, but encouraged the proliferation and development of even more centers of education. With federal assistance, in 1969 Montana established five vocational-technical education centers in Billings, Butte, Great Falls, Helena, and Missoula. Two years later the legislature made the extraordinary decision to provide partial state funding for Montana's three community colleges in Glendive, Kalispell, and Miles City. Previously two-year institutions run locally, these colleges were now incorporated, along with the six four-year institutions, under the authority of the Board of Regents. The postsecondary system had now grown to fourteen units, which gave Montana more state-supported institutions of higher education per capita than any other state in the union.

If there has ever been a time when circumstances seemed most propitious to address the need to develop a coherent, efficient, and, if possible, nonpartisan system of educational administration, it was the late 1960s and early 1970s. As Malone, Roeder, and Lang point out in their superb history of Montana, this was a period of "rapid social, economic, and political change," based on nationalizing trends which were breaking down Montana's "local peculiarities" and were drawing the state "into the main current of American life."[24] Key to these developments was the erosion of the state's rural influence and the growing power of the urban centers and the middle class that resided there. Reapportionment in 1965 gave increased representation to the cities, which now began to flex their muscles, while the rural regions resisted change and became even more conservative. The middle class was neither right nor left, but composed a growing political centrism, "less provincial and more cosmopolitan," and infinitely better informed. Not surprisingly, these developments were paralleled by a striking new interest in the reform and improvement of society and government. "Not since the Progressive Era had Montana seen such widespread popular participation in politics as that which blossomed in the early 1970's."[25]

Although the 1971 legislative budgetary allocations for higher education were criticized by the university system as inadequate, other developments were shaping which would address the problems of higher education in extremely significant ways. While turning down increased funding for education, the legislators, many of them representing a profile of political consciousness hitherto unknown in state politics, accomplished some remarkable things. Tough environmental laws, executive reorganization, the state's first minimum wage law, and a referendum to bring the controversial sales tax issue directly before the people were among them. But none was as dramatic a pronouncement of the new politics as the final preparations the 1971 legislature made to convene a constitutional convention.

The argument that the 1889 constitution needed rewriting was almost as old as the argument that the educational system needed rationalization. For sixty years, however, little was accomplished. Then, in the 1950s and '60s, interest in governmental change increased as a new Legislative Council and various citizens groups examined the legislative and judicial systems.[26] Finally, in the November 1970 election a referendum was approved authorizing a constitutional convention. At a special election the following November, Montana's voters selected 100 delegates to attend a convention to draft a new constitution. In the same election the referendum on the sales tax was addressed, and soundly

The Montana Constitutional Convention delegates, 1971

defeated by a whopping 2-to-1 margin. This issue, coming at the same time as the election of the constitutional convention ("Con-Con") delegates, resulted in a backlash against the Republican Party, which had run on a sales tax platform, and resulted in the election of an "exceptionally liberal-minded group of delegates to the constitutional convention." [27]

Once assembled, the delegates produced a constitution which was praised nationwide as a "model document" and a triumph of "grass roots democracy in action." Among the most significant innovations in the new constitution were single-member legislative districts, annual legislative sessions (since repealed by a special referendum vote in 1974), statewide property tax assessment, significant efforts to strengthen the powers of the legislature (including new auditing authorities), and several major provisions to rationalize the university system. Governor Forrest Anderson, who had already reorganized the executive branch, strongly supported these efforts. Through the MSU community services program, historians Pierce Mullen and Richard Roeder (the latter a Con-Con delegate and its official historian) prepared a tabloid newspaper supplement

that was distributed statewide and provided information on the new constitution in an effort to assist voters in making "coherent and wise" decisions when entering the polling place. [28] After a hard-fought campaign that generally "pitted urban interests in favor of the constitution against rural interests in opposition," the document passed by the slender margin of 116,415 in favor, 113,883 opposed. A conservative effort, spearheaded by the Farm Bureau, to strike down the new constitution on technicalities barely failed. [29]

What the new constitution did for education is extremely significant. One aspect of reorganization separated control of higher education from that of public education. Whereas formerly the Board of Education, when it discussed university issues, merely changed its hat, so to speak, to become a Board of Regents, the new constitution created two separate agencies—the Board of Public Education, with exclusive responsibility for kindergarten through high school (K-12), and the Board of Regents, with exclusive responsibility for higher education. The reasoning behind this was elementary—the delegates felt that higher education had become too complex for one board to administer, no less comprehend. The Board of

Regents would have "full power, responsibility, and authority to supervise, coordinate, manage and control the University System." To oversee the Board's responsibility to control and coordinate the universities, the delegates created a commissioner of higher education with powerful authority. To assure the authority of this new office, the commissioner was made a constitutional officer. There was also a determination among the delegates to create an officer who would supercede the old Presidents Council and terminate the fighting that had gone on ad infinitum between the system's units. Some of the delegates were prepared to go as far as a chancellorship, but they were sensitive to the past failure of such systems and called it instead a commissionership. [30]

Secondly, constitutional delegates felt that the Board of Regents should be freed from former restraints in directing the university system. This was based on two codependent assumptions—that in order to develop a coordinated and efficient system, governance of higher education had to be given, as much as possible, independence from former legislative authorities, or as the first chairman of the Board of Regents put it, "from the sometimes capricious influence of politics." [31] Ever since statehood, there had been an unfortunate tendency of legislators to intervene in the day-to-day life of the university system, and the constitutional convention delegates hoped that the new authority of the Board of Regents would discourage its continuation.

That the delegates were deeply concerned to provide the Board of Regents with an extraordinary degree of autonomy is clear. Some favored complete autonomy, but a somewhat lesser system of authority was recommended as a compromise for fear the public would not accept the total absence of legislative restraint. Nevertheless, a critical component of the educational article of the constitution was the limitation imposed upon the legislature's former ability to mandate how and where monies appropriated for education were to be spent. The delegates had no intention of circumscribing the auditing authorities of the legislature, and under the new arrangement, the legislature would continue to hold the purse strings—the appropriation of monies for education—but the specific allocation of those monies within the university system would be the responsibility of the commissioner and the Board of Regents. [32]

These developments brought a great sense of unease to certain members of the legislature. Many legislators, particularly fiscal conservatives, were resentful of a system that deprived them, as representatives of the taxpayers, of the former authority they had in denying or bestowing fiscal support to education, for the ability to allocate or not allocate monies to specific programs or campuses had been a major means of forcing accountability from the university system. A substantial number of legislators openly stated their opposition to the new constitutional article, and fought, and still fight, to strip the Board of Regents of its autonomy and to recapture the board's decision-making authorities. For some legislators the educational question was less significant than the simple fact that a new arm of government had been created with authorities that had formerly been the exclusive province of the lawmaking branch. So immediately intense were legislative efforts to regain these authorities over educational expenditures (in one instance the legislature attempted to fix the salaries of the university system's presidents) that the new Board of Regents felt compelled in 1973 to bring suit against the legislature. This suit the regents won, but the result sparked a kind of guerrilla warfare between the legislators and the board that continues to this day.

No sooner had the new state constitution with its reorganization of higher education been put into effect—on July 1, 1973—than a major effort was made by the new Thomas Judge administration to create a long-range plan for education, including governance and "role and scope" guidelines for the various campuses. To accomplish this, Governor Judge created the Commission on Post-Secondary Education. Popularly called the Blue Ribbon Commission because of the high quality of its membership, the commission set out to accomplish the governor's mandate—to combine three critical elements, "quality control, expanded educational opportunity, and fiscal responsibility," into a set of recommendations and implementation plans that would ensure the state's college students "the best possible set of options for quality education that the taxpayers of Montana can afford." [33]

Thomas L. Judge, governor of the state of Montana, 1972-1980

Governor Judge and Commissioner of Higher Education Lawrence K. Pettit with the Blue Ribbon Bill, 1973

Senator Mike Mansfield

Under the directorship of Californian Patrick M. Callan, the commission quickly concluded that of all the ills in Montana higher education, the most fundamental was the state's commitment to fourteen units—far too many units given Montana's sparse population and limited fiscal capability. This concern intensified as the commission completed its research and began to comprehend the costs of program duplication among the many units. On-campus visitations demonstrated, moreover, that faculties and staffs were being held back professionally at every school by the across-the-board dispersion of monetary support for education. Faculty salaries at MSU, for example, were 15 percent below the peer average for other Rocky Mountain state universities, and at or near the bottom on a national scale. [34] Then there was the embarrassing example set by sister-state Wyoming which, with only two-thirds of Montana's population, spent more on one four-year university than Montana did on six. The commission concluded that a major overhaul of the system was required and that the best means to this end necessitated a concentration of four-year programming in the two major universities, with Montana College of Mineral Science and Technology and Northern Montana College converted into community colleges and Western Montana College closed completely. These recommendations flew in the face of the myopia and pork barrelling that for decades had kept the postsecondary system in a perpetual state of inefficiency; obviously the commission hoped that once and for all their impartial and scientifically proven documentation would convince the units

themselves, and the communities in which they were located, to accept the plan for reorganization. In order to carry its appeal as broadly as possible, the commission held eleven public hearings across the state and published thirteen different progress reports.

But in the end, $300,000 and tens of thousands of hours in labor were spent fruitlessly. In 1974 the recommendation of the commission to subordinate the smaller units was met with such strong political opposition that the commission backed off, revised its thinking, and, in the winter of 1974-1975, conceded defeat. The commission's recommendations were sensible and, in their assessment of the historic ills contained and multiplied within the system, intelligent and constructive. But as constructive as the recommendations were, the commission's expectation that they would be adopted proved to be extraordinarily naive. No manner of appeal to reason and to concepts of educational efficiency was going to move the small-college communities to sacrifice a major element of their economic welfare. This was particularly so as it related to the commission's recommendations for Butte, which pulled out every stop to defend its own college. Surely no manner of warning of the influence of politics in higher education in an economically depressed community could have prepared the commission for the concerted attacks made upon it by Butte and its allies when the preliminary report became public on June 6, 1974.

The report was plagued from the start. First of all, bad timing accompanied its release. Four days before, Senator Mike Mansfield, Butte's number-1 booster, had given the commencement address at Tech's annual graduation exercises, an address in which he treated at length the role Tech should play in new technogical developments, particularly in energy and environment. Back in Washington, D.C. on June 5, Mansfield had his address inserted in the *Congressional Record*, prefacing it with laudatory remarks covering Tech's expansion from mining engineering into letters and science. Tech was, the senator insisted, "the best mining school in the world, without exception," and he hoped that it would continue to "grow and expand." [35]

Understandably, Mansfield was shocked to hear that the Blue Ribbon Commission advocated Tech's relinquishment of its engineering program and its conversion to a community college. The senator wasted no time in informing the powers in Montana that he was amazed, given his known and newly reiterated support for Tech, that the commission would even consider downgrading the institution. He felt much the same way about the closure of Western. To Governor Judge, he wrote, with copies to others influential in state education and communication, that he was "very disturbed" with the commission's recommendation that Tech be downgraded. Tech was a good school, providing important services in a state "dependent upon its natural resources." It was also extremely close to his heart. He had a "very close attachment" to Butte; he honored Tech for providing him the opportunity to begin his college education, and for providing him "many fond memories" as well. The letter to the governor conveyed a sentiment to be considered seriously, coming as it did from the state's most powerful politician: "When I delivered the commencement address at Montana Tech on June 2 I had no idea that it was the beginnings of an era to dismantle one of Montana's fine institutions of higher learning. I will not be associated with any such effort and I would hope that the present staff recommendation will be reversed." [36]

Mansfield's response was mild compared with Butte's. The city was enraged. A radio editorial from Butte's KBOW provides a good example of the intensity of the mining community's reaction:

The recent announcement of the staff report of the Blue Ribbion Commission on Higher Education was and is a devastating blow to this community. In the report they recommended to close Montana Tech, transfer the engineering courses to Montana State University and convert the facilities into a community college. . . . The plain intent of the staff report was to completely emasculate the higher education system in Butte. . . . . Not only will the State of Montana be a loser because of the loss of one of the finest mining and minerals engineering schools in the country, but Butte would be a big loser on the economic side. . . . More than $2,500,000 is spent annually for the operation of Tech in wages, supplies and other items. Additionally, another two million is spent by students, faculty members and staff personnel for personal living expenses; all of it in this community. The dollar figure would not be replaced by a community junior college. Here's another grabber; right now Tech is fully funded by the Higher Education System. If a community college were to be put in its place, by law they are partially funded by local money. This would be at least a 30% increase in Silver Bow County property taxes. It is ironic too that a community like Butte which loves and supports Tech is being stripped of courses. They are being sent to the cities of Bozeman and Missoula where there is a strong feeling of distrust and resentment between the "downtown" units of the community and the universities. . . . Once more it is time for the citizens of this community and surrounding area to rise up and protest. We urge you as individuals and groups to express your opinions. . . . Let us vigorously oppose actions of "Asphalt Jungle Exiles" . . . to destroy this noble institution. [37]

Two particularly important issues relevant to higher education in Montana are touched upon in this editorial. One takes into consideration the significance of Montana's colleges and universities to the economic well-being of the communities in which they are located. A closure or downscaling of any would seriously depress that community (Butte had been economically depressed for years), in which context educational efficiency had little meaning. A second touched upon the pride with which the smaller-unit communities attached themselves to their institutions of higher learning. The editorial's observation that Silver Bow County took Tech truly to heart, while Gallatin and Missoula counties had a long record of antagonism toward their own institutions of higher learning, touched upon another element that had much truth in it and which elevated visceral reaction over statistical reasoning. When commission director Pat Callan responded that the "hue and cry" over Montana Tech would resolve a basic issue—"whether politics or policy considerations will determine the future of education in this state"—Mansfield and Butte answered unequivocally in support of the former. [38] As long as their politicians had a say, Tech would not be downgraded nor Western closed. Educational efficiency was of secondary importance to economic stability. Mansfield was in full agreement with the Tech faculty member who argued: "Here we are in a population center, surrounded by the sons and daughters of laborers who cannot afford to go elsewhere and pay board-and-room and we are to be shut down. . . . [I]f the University system is to serve the people of Montana, Tech is the one institution that should be forced into growth—in all areas, but particularly in the Humanistic area, unless Labor is interested in going back and shivering on the docks of Liverpool." [39]

When a member of the Blue Ribbon Commission protested Mansfield's intervention, the senator acknowledged that Callan was indeed "completely objective," and neither "politically, economically, nor sentimentally attached to the state," but that he himself was "politically, economically, and sentimentally attached to the state," and that he decried the severe damage already done to the reputation of the two colleges. He wanted Western maintained and Tech reinforced and expanded. Abandonment of the Butte campus would be an "absolute waste of funds." His complaint with the commission was that its report was "far more negative than necessary," and that the commission itself seemed "preoccupied with a concentration into a few large units." He preferred that Tech's mineral and energy research disciplines be developed and then coordinated with programs at MSU. [40] Mansfield wanted to emphasize his rejection of the commission's effort to keep the issue on an objective level: "The higher educational system in our state was politically conceived and its future is going to be guided through this process," he informed another commission member. [41] In Washington, Mansfield marshaled the energies of the Montana delegation to secure federal funding for the design and planning of a commercial-scale engineering test facility in Montana, called MHD (magnetohydrodynamics), a coalfield project centered at Tech, but in cooperation with MSU. [42] One way to ensure Tech's continuity was to secure for it appropriations for new programs.

Throughout the summer, forces allied with Tech and Western pounded home their message. Butte became hostile territory, so antagonistic that members of the commission and their allies, including the governor, hesitated to visit the community. The awesome power of the Butte political delegation worked in remarkable ways. The presses of southwestern Montana were almost incendiary in their attacks. So virulent was their

position that commissioner of higher education Lawrence K. Pettit concluded facetiously, but on the mark, that Patrick Callan's open-minded approach was, in the view of the opposition, "his most grievous error." Prejudices were determining the outcome, not reason. [43]

By late summer of 1974, however, Pettit and the commission were clearly bowing to the realities of Montana politics—Mansfield was adamantly opposed, Governor Judge was feeling terrific heat from the small-college towns, the state legislature that would make the final decision was not sympathetic, and the Board of Regents, at first supportive, had begun to back off. In early October the commission openly acknowledged Mansfield's influence. [44] On October 23, by a tight 15-13 vote, the commission backed down completely on Tech and promised a review of its recommendations on Western. [45] When in the 1977 legislative session the Butte delegation was able to secure a $1 million appropriation for a new library for Tech, the writing was on the wall—the consolidation recommendations of the commission were dead.

Members of the commission and their allies were crushed by the refusal of Montanans to support a system that was clearly better suited to the state's fiscal and population support capabilities. And they were deeply disappointed by the inability of the communities concerned to place the state's welfare above their own parochial interests. This applied also to the administrations of the smaller colleges involved. Some of this failure was caused by the commission's inability to communicate its message, but the basic psychology of the situation—the existence of strong regional parochialisms—was the final determinant. In looking back from the ever-deepening fiscal conservatism of the 1980s and early 1990s, the adherents of consolidation lamented even more the fact that if ever a period had recommended itself for change, it had been the early-to-mid-1970s. Never before, or since, given the more liberal nature of the legislature and the general statewide disposition toward reform at that time, has the atmosphere been more politically conducive to educational modernization. Today, so poor is the economy and so strong are the dispositions favoring the smaller units, that it would be an utter waste of energy and resources for anyone or any group to advocate streamlining the university system by downgrading or eliminating units. If the example of the past is to serve as instruction, Montanans will make no change until they are utterly prostrated by economic catastrophe. In the meantime, the state seems reconciled to paying, at the lowest possible rate, for what each community wants to retain. The politics of jobs, not efficiency, nor learning, is what Montana education is all too often reduced to. [46]

Campus Doings

Perhaps it was just as well MSU was spared the animosity that assuredly would have risen had Tech been emasculated and some of its programs, including engineering, transferred to Bozeman, for the land grant institution had many other problems to contend with. As noted, the 1970-1977 administration of Carl McIntosh coincided with a legislature determined to assert its authority by clamping down hard on university- system cost accounting. Consequently, the university system found itself besieged by a spate of new bureaucratic fiscal regulations that forced it to account for the expenditure of virtually every penny. Tom Nopper, business manager during the McIntosh years, recalled the impact of some of these changes:

One of the great state pastimes [in the 1970s] was reading state legislative audits. There was much controversy over them. During those years, every month there was some state agency that caught hell for something, and a big argument with the legislative auditor. We went through many of them. At the same time the legislative fiscal analyst was established. So the legislature . . . mushroomed in their function, and in many respects . . . took over functions that had been primarily within the executive branch. And the executive branch . . . had been the main power on the board of regents. So all of that changed. And McIntosh was right in the middle of that . . . . Our accounting system was taken away from us . . . we had to comply with the state accounting system. We had our own personnel system. . . [now] there was a state personnel system. We had our own investment program; now there became state investment offices. We had all of those things at Montana State prior to the [new constitution], but when they took them over everything was centralized and the units really had little to say about how the state ran them . . . . [T]hat . . . happened during McIntosh's era. And I think that's pretty reflective of the problems that he had. [47]

To this, MSU's business manager could have added yet another fiscal category now accountable to the state—purchasing. In previous years the business office could acquire, for example, fifty desks and chairs overnight with no questions asked. Now state regulation governed such acquisitions, and the process of requisitioning office equipment was tedious and involved enormous amounts of paperwork. What infuriated MSU's administrators and personnel was that prior to the new authority of the state, in such matters MSU had run a commendably clean and efficient program of acquisition and accounting, and resented the implication of distrust and potential wrongdo-

ing suggested by the creation of new state offices. [48] The tremendous imposition of bothersome, cumbersome, and time-consuming bureaucratic red tape kept everyone in a state of frustration, if not resistance. "The mere idea of involved central record-keeping," McIntosh informed a west coast colleague, "is as repugnant to [MSU faculty and staff] now as the disappearance of the free range was to some of their forebears." [49]

One area in which the university responded slowly to change during the 1970s was in the field of affirmative action. With respect to personnel, hiring and firing procedures were changed dramatically by new federal mandates. The old method of picking up a phone and hiring someone was most definitely over. Now it took long months of effort and paperwork on the part of selection committees to fill a position. Affirmative action, based on the Equal Rights Amendment of 1964, was unquestionably a very positive and necessary process. But the new rules, which required that women and minorities be treated equally with white males in employment and employment benefits, slowed decision making enormously, caused considerable expense, ran up against strong prejudices, and, consequently, were applied with reluctance. Even when the state embodied the principles of equal rights in its new constitution of 1972, MSU proved reluctant to institutionalize these. That the state's legal offices did not enforce compliance in the university system was also a factor.

Women faculty at MSU were the first to challenge the inequities in the system. In 1974, after having failed for two years to get voluntary compliance from the McIntosh administration, five MSU women faculty members sued the Board of Regents, MSU, and its president, for having violated the Civil Rights Act of 1964. These faculty were Helen Mecklenburg from biology, Ellen Kreighbaum and Betty Lowry from physical education, Jeanne Claus from nursing, and Eleanor Pratt, an adjunct instructor in modern language. Specifically, the charges read that MSU had for years "underutilized" women in staff and academic positions and had "discriminated against [women] in the areas of promotion, tenure, salary, and appointment to important university committees." [50] The period of litigation lasted a full two years, 1974-1976, and, although the suit could have been settled out of court, the administration allowed the heated controversy to proceed to its conclusion. This resulted in a clear-cut decision in favor of the women, a verdict that, when applied to all women at MSU, cost the university system over $400,000 in back wages, not to mention retroactive promotions.

McIntosh's rationalization for pushing the suit to its conclusion is noteworthy, as much hassle could have been avoided, and considerable savings effected in legal costs and actual settlement, had the suit been settled out of court. But McIntosh determined to seek a court conclusion for two reasons. First, he felt that an out-of-court settlement would not produce the legal verdict he believed the school needed upon which to structure its compliance program. Without a legal verdict, he argued, there was little to prevent another class-action suit from being filed six months down the road. He wanted to know what was right by the law. Second, McIntosh wasn't sure who would pay the bill. Would the regents

provide the funds, and, if so, under which condition—a negotiated out-of-court settlement or a decision dictated by the court? He concluded that a court-dictated settlement would more likely produce regental support than a negotiated settlement. His assumption was correct; the regents provided the $400,000 fine above and beyond normal funding formulas. This established an important precedent for the entire university system, and McIntosh was largely responsible for that. [51] It is worthy of note that prior to the constitution of 1972, the state enjoyed a legal sovereignty that clothed it with immunity against suits such as these. Five years earlier the plaintiffs in this case could not have sought damages from the state. [52]

Times were definitely changing. Within the year a new program, Focus on Women, headed by Scottie Giebink and Sue Sincell, secured office space on campus and organized the first of a series of "Women Aware" conferences. These services would be revamped in 1981 when Focus on Women became the Women's Resource Center, with Jan Strout as first director. The center functions as a division of Student Affairs and Services and has done much to address the unique issues facing females, whether on campus or not. [53]

Fiscal woes accompanied bureaucratic afflictions. McIntosh's 1971 warning to the faculty that the decade ahead would be economically depressed had set the tone. Salaries were kept to a minimum, and capped entirely later that year

Painting the "Hello Walk," 1972

The President's Rhetoric

Carl McIntosh possessed a refreshing ability to laugh at himself and his assorted plights. His "Charge to the Graduates," class of 1976, highlights his way of making light of adversity, in this case the "commandment of accountability:"

> Each year, about this time of year, I have the privilege of talking for five minutes to the members of the graduating class, before the degrees are conferred and the diplomas awarded. There is no consensus as to whether this is a valuable tradition, a harmless indulgence, or a pernicious custom, but it will probably be continued as long as the time limit is strictly observed.
>
> By completing the requirements for your degrees, you have also demonstrated your ability to survive in an increasingly bureaucratic world. We are all to some degree the victims of increasingly complex regulations and procedures, and our responses may range from resignation to rage depending upon the circumstances. Even the very young are con-

> scious of this development. About four years ago, a periodical which crossed my desk contained a series of very short letters from children to God. One of these letters read: "Dear God: How come you only have ten rules but our school has millions." God's response was not recorded.
>
> Excellence was the educational war cry of the early 60's, which gave way to the slogan of relevance, only to be followed by the commandment of "accountability." Each a valid concept, used for both constructive purposes and curious aberrations, including now a prodigious amount of procedural razzle-dazzle. Assuming that we all survive the superior judgment of distant statisticians, perhaps we will enter an era of significance. No doubt it would also be corrupted in time by its most fervent disciples, but it would come to us as a welcome relief nonetheless. [1]

1. McIntosh, "Charge to Graduates," 81033/2, "1976 Commencement" file, MSUA.

when the Nixon administration placed a moratorium on federal wages. When the moratorium was lifted MSU salaries did not recover, but fell steadily behind until by 1974 they had dropped 15 percent below their Rocky Mountain state university peer averages. In the spring of 1972 the axe began to fall on academic programs. University honors was one of the first to go—allowed to declare itself bankrupt in June of '72. McIntosh was distressed; it seemed inconceivable to him that the university could not muster adequate student and departmental interest in the program, and he found it "difficult to believe that there is not some solution within even our limited resources that can support an honors program of merit." [54] But the resources were not allocated and the program was allowed to die, not to be restored until the inauguration of a new president. Although the demise of honors was much more the failure of leadership at the faculty and department level, it is an unfortunate fact that McIntosh received most of the blame. Such was the president's plight; when things went wrong between 1970 and 1977, it was not uncommon to assume that Montana Hall was at the root of the problem.

In the fall of 1972 projected legislative allocations were so low the university adopted an emergency "hold-the-line" budget wherein any new program costs or necessary increases in existing programs were financed by cutbacks in other programs. Several important curriculum decisions were made to effect savings. The aerospace program in engineering was dropped, industrial and management engineering were merged with the computer science department, and agricultural education was merged with industrial arts. Then the controversial termination of graduate programs was finalized, with three master of science degree programs, three doctorate of philosophy programs, and fourteen categories of master of science in applied science degree programs terminated. [55]

The decision to terminate the applied science degree graduate programs caused much anger, particularly in Wilson Hall, which housed the humanities and social sciences. Most faculty acknowledged that this degree program left much to be desired but feared that, once terminated, graduate-degree granting privileges for the humanities and social sciences might not return. Despite these reservations, the administration prevailed. Although Montana Hall made much of the need to clear the path for new degree programs of more substantial and professional quality, the fears of the humanities and social sciences were in the end confirmed. Today, only history and government offer advanced degrees. It seems incredible, but it is true that students in English, speech, theatre arts, philosophy, psychology, sociology, and modern language cannot earn an MSU graduate degree in those disciplines. On the positive side,

the humanities and social sciences could count on an excellent friend in Roy Huffman, vice president for research, who was always receptive to good research projects, which he invariably encouraged with travel and per diem funds.

In early 1973 McIntosh identified yet another assortment of economic "disasters" for the Board of Regents. President Richard Nixon's austerity budget had resulted in serious decreases in federal funding critical to various MSU programs, including nursing, social justice, weather modification research, and environmental health engineering. Financial aid programs for students also were hard hit by the reduction of federal support, and the agricultural experiment station and Cooperative Extension Service were likewise affected. [56] The weather modification program, for example, which provided important information to farmers and ranchers all over the state, and the meteorological group at MSU that performed these services, was entirely dependent upon federal funds. This group, touted as one of the finest in the country, faced a shutdown in July if not otherwise supported.

The social justice option program within the sociology department faced a similar fate. Understandably, the discipline of sociology had become extremely popular with undergraduates in the late 1960s, and social justice and social welfare were two options developed within the department to satisfy demand. The social justice program was inaugurated in 1970; it interfaced and shared services with the state Law Enforcement Academy, also situated on the campus. By winter quarter 1973 the program had grown to 154 students. But it was a soft-money program, supported entirely by federal monies allocated from the governor's Crime Control Commission. Now the program was jeopardized. [57] Fortunately, MSU's administration worked out ways to save both programs, the latter getting a special line-item allocation from the legislature, which felt strongly about the need to prepare students for employment in law enforcement, correctional agencies, and social service organizations. But these were the kinds of fiscal worries that McIntosh and his administrators had to deal with on persistent bases virtually throughout his seven years.

Problems were so prominent in the early-to-mid 1970s as to often obscure positive developments of real significance. Advances in the area of science were outstanding; despite austerity, energies on the instructional and research level were sustained and much progress achieved. One of the most interesting enterprises of the period was MSU's contract with the National Science Foundation to conduct a comprehensive multidisciplinary study of the Gallatin Canyon. Called for by reason of the planned construction of Chet Huntley's Big Sky project at Lone Mountain, the study became highly controversial and politically sensitive. Over time the project was given due credit for having brought disciplines together and for having contributed to the development of many environmentally associated programs of study currently active on campus. [58] (See Chapter 9.)

A Wally Byam caravan

But the most remarkable undertaking, the one that stood out beyond all others, was the university's successful 1972 bid to get the WAMI medical program situated on the MSU campus. A cooperative program between Washington, Alaska, Montana, and Idaho, WAMI enables twenty students each year from Montana to commence their medical education at MSU and complete it at the University of Washington. The presumption had been that WAMI would be situated in Missoula, but MSU's strengths in medical science, built up over the previous decade and a half, coupled with the intense competitiveness and enthusiastic and extraordinary preparation made by the MSU team, convinced the visitation committee to select the Bozeman campus. (See Chapter 9.) This decision validated MSU's argument it had superior staff, facilities, and initiative, and produced a result considered by many to this day as the most important ever made for science in the state of Montana. [59]

The esthetic appearance of the campus was always high on President McIntosh's list of priorities, and he made landscaping improvements when and where possible. When members of his administration lobbied for a major reduction in groundskeeping as a means to balance budgets— one of the arguments being that legislators and townspeople might begin to take the university's fiscal woes seriously if they saw parched lawns— he understood, but always took exception. The campus was a home to over 8000 students and he wanted to be able to say that "we value this environment, we believe in the esthetics of a campus, that [it] is a place where people like to

spend their time because there are esthetic pleasures about it." More trees, not less, was McIntosh's wish, and he was remorseful that the budget would not properly permit him that pleasure. Consequently, it delighted him no end when he was able to persuade the Wally Byam Caravan Club International, headquartered on campus the summer of 1973, to make their memorial gift to the university a park on the southwest corner of College and South 11th—the Wally Byam Caravan Club Grove, as it was officially named. The club had at first recommended the installation of a pair of flagpoles in front of the field house, but McIntosh saw the improvement of campus landscaping as a higher good, and jumped at the chance to influence the Byams in that direction. [60]

Despite the paucity of monies for the instructional budget, an above-average rate of construction prevailed on campus during these years. The Reno H. Sales Stadium and new health and physical education center (named almost a decade later for Marga Hosaeus, long-time director of the women's health and physical education program) were dedicated on the south side of campus in 1974. The former opened to large crowds and was the home field for one of the most exciting Bobcat football teams of the decade—the national NCAA Division II championship squad of 1976. The Creative Arts Complex, composed of three separate buildings housing art (Haynes Hall), architecture (Cheever Hall), and music (Howard Hall) and situated on South 11th, was opened in the fall of 1974. (Haynes Hall was named for Jack Ellis Haynes, a pioneer photographer-artist noted for his pictorial works of Yellowstone Park, while Cheever Hall was named for Hurlbert Cheever, dean of the College of Arts and Architecture, 1945-1961. Howard Hall was dedicated to Louis L. Howard, who came to MSU in 1908 and served as band director for thirty-eight years.) Unfortunately, during the process of planning the complex was impacted badly by inflation and by a debate over whether to use poured concrete. (It was not used.) As a result of inflation and debate, the music recital hall, once planned for capacity seating of 1200, was scaled back to an almost pitiful capacity of 260. So rapidly did prices rise in the early 1970s that each week of delay meant lopping off another row or two of seating. Thus did the community of Bozeman lose what it lacks yet, an auditorium built specifically to the highest musical and acoustical standards, and of size sufficient to entertain the university's and community's largest audiences.

Sherrick Hall, a new nursing building, was named for Anna Pearl Sherrick, first director of the School of Nursing. A delightfully designed structure nestled among the conifers west of Reid Hall, it was dedicated in 1973. Both Sherrick Hall and the Creative Arts Complex replaced old "temporary" wooden structures and quonset-hut af-

The Creative Arts Complex

Sherrick Hall

fairs that had been moved to the campus by Roland Renne directly after the World War II and were now real eyesores. Another wooden eyesore that came down in 1975 was the "Montana Hall Annex," the public relations and information building situated between Montana and Hamilton halls. Wilson Hall, or CLOB (Classroom Office Building) as it was ungracefully known for many months, was constructed between Montana and Herrick halls, and is named for Milburn Lincoln Wilson, Montana's first county agent, later head of agricultural economics at MSU and undersecretary of agriculture during the 1930s. This structure for the first time enabled the congregation of almost all of the humanities and social sciences in one building, including sociology, history, government, philosophy, English, theatre arts, speech communications, and math-

The Role of the Rails

May 1, 1971, was a black day for Montana, for on that date the merger between the Northern Pacific, Great Northern, and Burlington railroads that created the Burlington Northern effectively ended passenger service on the state's lower line—the old NP route that had served Bozeman for more than eighty-eight years. Although service would be partially restored in July 1971 when Amtrak would for a time add three trains a week to its schedule, for all practical purposes in-

The MSC debate team about to board the NP's Mainliner, 1965

state travel was mortally wounded that spring day of '71. All subsequent efforts to restore service on the old NP route failed, although this route was by far the most significant to Montana. Whereas the northern line, which retained passenger service under Amtrak's management, served only a miniscule percentage of the state's population, the old Northern Pacific railway passenger service was within eighty miles of 96 percent of the state's population and forty-four of the state's fifty-six county seats. Taken just from the standpoint of the university system, the impact was crippling: the high line served Northern Montana

College only, while the low line served Eastern, MSU, Tech, and UM directly, and offered a short rail link via the Union Pacific with Western. The abandonment of the old Mainstreeter passenger service was, and remains, one of Montana's greatest tragedies.

While rail travel is now quite remote to Montanans living south of the high line, its history is not. Rails first reached Bozeman on March 21, 1883, and most assuredly the College of Montana personnel who constituted MSC's first staff and faculty, in order to make the move, availed themselves of the NP's passenger service and the Gallatin Valley Electric Company's trolley system, which connected the train depot with the city. Once the college began to grow, so did the trolley service, eventually extending to the intersection of South 7th and Cleveland. Until this service was terminated in the late 1920s, MSC students used the trolleys regularly to commute to downtown, even doing so between classes just to get a cup of coffee—and for the fun of it.

The construction of the Milwaukee Railroad just before World War I was important to MSC, as a spur from its valley line enabled the delivery of coal to the power plant on the southeast side of campus. For a number of years during and following World War I, the engineering college had its own locomotive as a hands-on laboratory. The engine was situated on a siding by the power plant and served as a play center for town kids and a hangout for MSC students who smoked. Use of the Milwaukee spur ceased in the 1950s when the power plant was converted from coal to gas, but during the transition a large steam locomotive was hooked up to provide the campus with heat. For that short period of time this locomotive also provided power for the plant's awesome steam whistle, which up into the 1950s blasted the community awake each workday at the ungodly hour of 6:30 a.m. Rivaling anything ever installed on the great ocean liners, the whistle not only functioned as a daily alarm for the campus, but also had ceremonial uses, blaring its approval for Bobcat victories over the Griz, for example. Pranksters occasionally blew it on a dare, but high jinks resulted in tragedy once when, just after World War II, students trying to break into the power plant were caught in the act and one was shot and killed by a security guard. Other than for occasional testing, the whistle's most recent use was on New Year' Eve, 1991 to mark the retirement of "Swede" Erickson, power plant supervisor. Surely Founders Day, February 16, 1993, will afford another appropriate use of its stupefying sound.

The heating plant blowing its whistle, 1956

How many thousands of MSC students employed the trains for travel cannot be known, but up into the 1950s large numbers from rural Montana commuted to school by rail. The trains were also employed for school events, most of them associated with athletic contests. For example, the football and basketball teams used conventional train service for their road trips. When MSC was part of the Rocky Mountain Conference in the 1950s, the basketball team would leave via the NP on Wednesday afternoons for weekend games in Colorado and not return to Bozeman until Monday. Special trains were always run to accommodate students who wished to attend Bobcat-Grizzly athletic contests. Sometimes as many as ten cars would constitute these trains, the cars being beat-up coaches since the NP had learned from experience not to sacrifice good rolling stock to such events.

Today few vestiges remain of the former linkage between MSU and the rails. Perhaps one might still observe an old Northern Pacific boxcar passing through Bozeman on a Montana Rail Link hookup, or appreciate the fact that the city's new eastside linear park was once the roadbed of the old Interurban/Milwaukee valley line. But the Milwaukee's line, and its spur to the college, was torn up in 1979 and the right-of-way itself obscured in the landscaping for the new Museum of the Rockies.

MSU's president, Carl McIntosh, spoke for many when he lamented in a 1971 letter to Senator Mansfield the passing of this era in Montana history:

> The Railpax route decision appears to be the last in a long series of repudiations of any interest in or attention to passenger rail service. I am ill prepared to say how much my protests are based upon nostalgia alone for I confess freely to being influenced by the remembrance of days past when travel by rail embodied so much that was associated with hope and promise; new vistas, new acquaintances and a sense of the sweep and scope of this great country through glimpses of its small towns seen briefly in the night and its broad lands rolling past in the sun or storm of summer and winter days.
>
> It seems to me that a conspiracy of intransigence has brought about the destruction of this experience. I cannot think of any other well developed country that does not have a reasonably good passenger train service. [1]

1. McIntosh to Mike Mansfield, 2 April 1971, 79026/16, "United States Congress" file, MSUA.

Wilson Hall

ematics. It was also home to the dean of the College of Letters and Science, and eventually housed Native American Studies, University Honors, and the Center for Intercultural Development. At the insistence of its planners, the building was designed in a U-shape to preserve an exquisite grove of spruce, pine, and ash trees. But inflation and limited funds hit here as well, and a classroom-auditorium capable of seating roughly 400 was scrapped in the end.

The construction of Leon H. Johnson Hall, the life science building of eight floors situated between Montana and Lewis halls, rounded out this impressive list of new campus edifices. The various disciplines composing this branch of inquiry could be now housed under one roof, including plant and soil science, plant pathology, biochemistry, biology, entomology, and the WAMI program. As in the case of Wilson Hall, unfortunately, faulty brick was employed in construction, and lengthy litigation and years of re-

Leon H. Johnson Hall

pairs have been invested in maintaining the attractive exteriors of these two buildings.

Student organizational activities during the early-to-mid-1970s seemed to lift everybody's spirits. In the early '70s MSU's sophomore honorary groups, the Spurs and Fangs, participated in Project Concern, a national Spurs service project supporting hospitals and clinics in Hong Kong, South Vietnam, and Mexico. In 1971-1972, ASMSU was quite involved in the campaign for a new constitution, and created a special task force to implement it. In the same academic year MSU students created MontPIRG, the Montana Public Interest Research Group, a research organization initiated and supported by students for the purpose of promoting public interest in Montana. Student concern for foreign affairs still prevailed, but these concerns were not expressed in disruptive ways. In April 1972, when the Nixon administration stepped up bombing of North Vietnam and demonstrations broke out once more on college campuses across the nation, MSU was not among these. McIntosh was pleased to report that the school had suffered no "building occupations, 'sit-ins' or destruction of property." MSU students were "restrained," and did not channel their energies into "destructive demonstrations." [61]

Fraternities and sororities, after a tough decade of declining interest, began to revive as the war wound down and the antiorganizational tendencies of the 1960s youth movement softened. The Greeks began to integrate their activities and interests through the Interfraternity and Pan-Hellenic councils. Efforts were made to corral boozing, and philanthropic activities were emphasized. When student John Spitzer developed muscular dystrophy in 1973, the Pan-Hellenic Council sponsored a dance marathon and raised over $6000 to assist in the eradication of the dread disease. It could be said with some assurance that fraternal organizations were developing a new vitality. As the editors of the 1972 *Montanan*, the student annual, put it:

> [One] connotation of Greek life is the parties, the wild, all-night, crazy things that go on. They have not left. It would be sad if they did. It is a characteristic and even a tradition in Greek circles. Jungle parties, roaring '20s parties, cowboy parties,—all are a distinct part of the party circle. But Greeks are more than that. Greeks are getting along together—studying together—solving each other's problems together—failing together—and achieving together.
>
> No one sees fraternity life for what it really is. Everyone sees it. . . as Greeks playing and having a good time at activities such as Sigma Chi derby days, Greek week, the SAE olympics or at their own Greek houses. But no one sees fraternity men spending hours stuffing and pasting labels on envelopes for the March of Dimes; no one sees the Greeks going door to door on the Kathy Pitino drive; no one sees the little boy who learns to walk under the donations of a sorority; no one really sees [that] the money that comes out of Greek week goes to muscular distrophy; no one sees that a sorority adopts a local family; nor sees that Greeks care, because Greeks want to, not because they seek publicity.
>
> No one claims that fraternities and sororities are not without disadvantages. No one will claim that fraternities and sororities are for everyone. What is claimed is that they contribute to campus and community life, and they can be and are meaningful and relevant experiences for their members. [62]

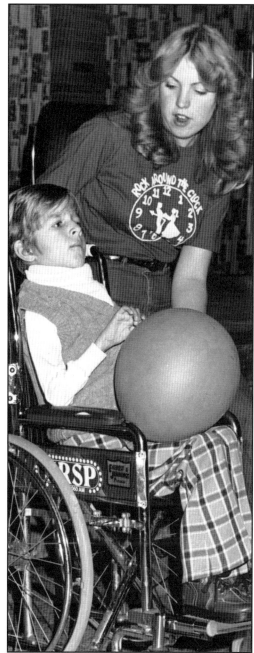

Muscular dystrophy dance marathon, 1978

On-campus living continued to reflect the liberalizing impact of the previous decade. In 1972-1973, the Associated Women Students and Men's Residents Association cooperated in instituting a plan for coeducational dormitories. Plebiscites were held with the result that four dorms were converted into coed residence halls: Hedges North and South, Roskie, and Johnstone/Mullan. Other rule changes included the relaxation of hours for male visitors in women's residences and the abolition of hours for freshmen women. [63] Then the central administration agreed to permit the use of liquor in the dorms. President McIntosh's reflection upon the change merits attention:

> Drinking is regulated more by custom than by law. . . . I do not expect students to be more or less sensible about drinking than non-students

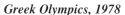

Greek Olympics, 1978

or other adults. . . . The University will have neither the time nor the desire to police the halls; the students must decide, themselves, the difference between acceptable and unacceptable practices. . . . If drinking is to be legal in the halls, it should be with the understanding that the change in regulation is not a licence to produce Dionysian festivals. . . . In general, only the students can make a "liquor in the halls" policy acceptable. I think they will, if we give them the chance, but we will need their help also in persuading the general population that life at the University is not just one long tax-supported beer bust. [64]

Throughout this period the Associated Students of MSU continued to undertake creative programming. The 1975-1976 ASMSU year serves as a good example. Under the leadership of student president Jim McLean, VP Taylor Brown, business manager Peggy Pascoe, and many others, ASMSU initiated a legal aid fund, a tutorial program, a "Community University," and a consumer affairs committee. The legal aid fund, underwritten by a small quarterly student contribution ($1.50), provided support for students involved in lessor-lessee issues (the most), consumer complaints (second most), traffic violations, bill collection, in-state residency issues, property taxes, employees' contracts, and even a criminal proceeding. The Community University offered thirty noncredit courses and required only a small registration fee to cover expenses. ASMSU officers attended a number of out-of-state conferences to improve their governing skills, including an academic affairs workshop in Logan, Utah, and a student rights symposium in San Francisco. [65] At the request of the commissioner of higher education, ASMSU took legal action against the Montana state department of administration in order force the issue on a controversy between that department and the Board of Regents. [66] During the 1975 legislative session, ASMSU sent busloads of students to Helena to demonstrate in favor of increased budgeting for higher education. When the regents visited the MSU campus, better than a thousand students showed up at a public meeting. ASMSU was still active in its criticism of athletics, conducting a campus poll on the subject, urging the downgrading of football to a lower division, and pushing strongly for the strengthening of women's athletics. [67] But this was not an all-work, no-play group of student leaders. ASMSU's cultural affairs board, under the direction of Jim Gee, offered an excellent 1975-1976 slate of ten concerts—from classical and dance to folk and jazz. ASMSU's support for concert series such as this was outstanding. To guarantee that visiting pianists had at their disposal the finest instrument, ASMSU had, the previous year, purchased a Steinway concert grand piano for the music department. [68]

The Lion and the Lamb

The constitutional creation of a powerful new commissionership for higher education was viewed with mixed feelings by university system administrators, and perhaps especially by those at MSU. For twenty-three years prior to 1973, or dating back to the abandonment of the chancellorship in 1950, the old Presidents Council, in the absence of strong centralized authority, had exercised considerable decision-making capability. This the presidents preferred, as under the old system they had resented the relinquishment of their prerogatives to a single officer. After 1950, MSU's presidents had done exceedingly well, particularly Roland Renne, whose seniority and forcefulness put him in a position of influence that was tantamount to a chairmanship within the council. Leon Johnson had profited from the same system.

In 1973 the new constitution seriously undercut the influence of the Presidents Council. Although not termed a chancellorship, this new office for higher education constituted in many ways a resuscitation of the old system. Understandably, the campuses were apprehensive about what this would mean. The smaller campuses, for example, were concerned that a commissioner might be disposed to favor the larger units. The larger units, UM and MSU, were understandably concerned that the commissioner might favor one or the other, or, just as bad, force a policy of leveling upon them. It also stood to reason that the smaller units might be strengthened at the expense of the two universities. All told, it was clear that the former independence of the units within the university system would be circumscribed.

These issues also concerned the new commissioner of higher education, Lawrence K. Pettit. Not only was Pettit obliged by the new constitution to assert his authority over the university system's fourteen units, he had a major task on hand to protect the newly won authority of the office from the Office of Public Instruction and from the legislature. The former had once exercised considerable influence in higher education and had given it up reluctantly. The latter, while still possessing considerable power—the power of the purse, for example—contained numerous members who resented and connived against the authority granted to the new Board of Regents. It would take an extraordinarily strong personality in the commissionership to protect these new regental prerogatives.

Larry Pettit unquestionably possessed the strength of purpose and courage necessary to make the higher educational system function as mandated by the new constitution. Determined to maximize his chances of success, he set about vigorously to increase the authority of his office. In many ways he was successful, particularly for the first two to three years of his term. With some difficulty the legislature was held at arm's length, feuding in the university system was limited, and the regents, under the chairmanship of Ted James, became a cohesive unit with a cohesive purpose such as had not been seen for many a year. But as Pettit worked to maximize his authority—upgrading the commissionership to a full chancellorship is clearly what he had in mind—resistance increased. So intense was opposition from the legislature that the regents were compelled to bring suit against it, a suit the regents won. But it was a Pyrrhic victory, as legislative foes of regental autonomy found other ways to exert their influence. In time, the executive branch, led by Governor Thomas Judge, came to share legislative apprehensions for regental independence. Resistance from within the university system was a further restraint the commissioner had to live with, as the campus presidents much preferred to report to the Board of Regents through the commissioner, rather than directly to the commissioner as chief executive officer. [69]

How Montana State University related to Pettit's determination to subordinate the campus administrations to his will is of particular interest, since Pettit had been elevated to the commissionership from a faculty position at MSU and since during his two-and-half year tenure at the Bozeman school he had developed an adversarial relationship with Carl McIntosh and his staff. Consequently, Pettit's ascendancy to the highest-ranking educational post in Montana's postsecondary system was viewed apprehensively in Bozeman, for there was reason to believe he harbored antagonisms toward the university. How Pettit impacted MSU, and how MSU responded, is an important facet of the university's history in the early to mid-1970s. It also offers important commentary on the difficulties of the administration of Carl McIntosh.

Larry Pettit came to MSU in the fall of 1969 as an associate professor in political science in the department of history, government and philosophy. (It is interesting to note that he and Ronald Perrin joined the same department simultaneously.) A native of Lewistown, Pettit had graduated from the University of Montana just ten years earlier. Subsequently he had obtained a Ph.D. in political science from the University of Wisconsin. This was followed by a position in the political science department at Penn State University. At the time of his appointment to MSU he was assistant director of federal relations for the American Council on Education in Washington, D.C. He had also been active in committee work for the American Association for University Professors (AAUP). Pettit came to MSU with the understanding that he was to shape up political science and steer it toward eventual independence from history and philosophy.

Pettit was exceedingly bright, highly organized, and aggressively ambitious. He possessed an extraordinary, some thought excessive, self-confidence in his own intelligence and organizational capabilities, both of which inclined him strongly toward administration. A consuming interest in politics, and a thirst for political power, drove him. Those close to him knew of one passion above all—he had his mind set on a major political post; probably nothing less than a senatorial position would have satisfied him. Some would argue that Pettit was overly controlled by political ambition, but others saw it as the natural outlet for his desire to secure a base from which to bring about meaningful educational reform. Always a strong advocate for efficiency in educational administration, the political scientist had also demonstrated a decided predilection for involvement with organizations dedicated to the protection and broadening of academic and personal liberties.

Pettit's willingness to utilize political pressure to secure his ends was early discernible. When he applied for the MSU position in political science, for example, he made it clear that he was the brother-in-law of Lieutenant Governor Thomas Judge, an acknowledged aspirant for the governorship itself. As political as Pettit was, it was hard not to conclude that his return to Montana related to Judge's interest in the governorship. Certainly, as politicians are wont, Pettit eagerly sought visibility. He quickly acquired it. Within months of his arrival he had revitalized the MSU AAUP branch, and within the year was elected state president of AAUP. At the same time he sought to improve his position within the department, pushing aggressively for promotion to full professor. Here he ran up against a roadblock. Pettit's capabilities and energies were fully appreciated, but his insistence upon promotion to full professor after hardly a year's residency at MSU represented to many of his colleagues, and to certain important administrators, an act of excessive expectation, a lack of sensitivity to traditional norms of promotion, and possibly even arrogance. His request for promotion was denied.

Pettit did not take setbacks easily. He made careless, vituperative remarks and angrily demanded a review. He held McIntosh and Irving Dayton particularly accountable for his defeat. Whether Pettit's remonstrances were justifiable or not, those privy to his disappointment were inclined to believe that if and when he had the chance, he would retaliate. This perception became pervasive on campus and played a role in how one interpreted Pettit's work as commissioner; it is a perception that remains strong at MSU to this day.

In April 1971, within the context of campus disillusionment with President McIntosh, Pettit led an attack on Montana Hall, charging the administration with having made "deleterious and high-handed decisions," and for having "scapegoated" the causes for such poor decision making to the dictatorial influence of "punitive, anti-intellectual regents and legislators." Everyone knew, the political scientist argued, that the "legislature, regents [and] taxpayers" were, in the large part, "sympathetic to the aims of higher education." McIntosh and his staff were the real culprits, and Pettit urged faculty, staff, and students to transfer their antagonisms from Helena to where they belonged, Montana Hall. [70] Pettit's attacks on McIntosh (based on an assessment of the 1971 legislature remarkably unlike McIntosh's) could have stemmed from any one factor, or a combination of factors. For instance, during Pettit's first year at MSU, he had expressed distress over the hiring of the new president. His personal review of McIntosh's record convinced the political scientist that the Californian had been hired by Governor Forrest Anderson and the regents in a deliberate effort to slow down MSU's rapid pace of development. In this context, one might interpret Pettit's actions as a reflection of his concern to strengthen MSU and the educational system by strengthening its administrative leadership. But one must also take into consideration that Pettit's charges mirrored campus concern about garbled lines of communication with Montana Hall. Then there was Pettit's natural proclivity for attention-getting; the political scientist seemed to be perpetually running for office. Finally, Pettit could have been retaliating for having been snubbed in his effort to be promoted. Though the observer wants always to emphasize the altruism in a leader's motives, it is difficult to sort through those of Larry Pettit. At the minimum, they were complex. In the end, one is reduced to the truism that perceptions are frequently more important than reality, and perceptions of Pettit's motives were generally not laudatory.

That Pettit was interested in Montana public affairs was immediately evident upon his appointment at MSU. He became intensely interested in the rewriting of the constitution, taught courses on the constitution, and spent many a day in Helena supervising legislative interns (supplied from his classes) and offering his counsel where appropriate. Where and when he made public statements, they dealt in the main with higher education. During the fall of 1971 he visibly stepped up his public involvement, both on campus and in the state. As state president of AAUP, he publicized the work he had undertaken personally to "further . . . the economic interests of the profession and guard . . . the integrity of the university." [71] As one interested in educational reform, he strongly supported centralized authority and the developing drive to constitutionally "separate governmental authority in higher edu-

cation from that over elementary and secondary education." [72] In December 1971 Pettit requested and received a year's leave of absence from MSU to run his brother-in-law's political campaign. He did his work capably, and Thomas Judge handily won the governorship in the November 1972 election. Pettit did not return to MSU, but stayed on in Helena for seven months as a governor's aide. Then, when the new constitution went into effect on July 1, 1973, Pettit was appointed Montana's first commissioner of higher education, an appointment strongly supported by the governor. Understandably, the defeated Republican Party saw this as an act of cronyism. Ed Smith, the unsuccessful Republican candidate, took it even farther, calling it "both unethical and illegal." [73] Despite such accusations, Pettit was a capable administrator, and his goals for higher education transcended political considerations; as expressed shortly after he took office they warrant strong consideration:

> To provide an "opportunity structure" so people cannot only improve themselves economically, but so they can derive greater satisfaction from the appreciation of esthetic and intellectual things.
>
> To provide a resource—a repository of useful knowledge and expertise—that can be used beyond the classroom to solve the problems of society such as health, economic, environmental, political and educational.
>
> To be a social critic, since the campus is the only place in society where new ideas and concepts can be freely tested and old ideas reevaluated.
>
> To be accountable to its sources of support and to be responsible to public decision makers, taxpayers and its students. [74]

While Pettit was convinced, as had been the Con-Con delegates before him, that the establishment of regental authority required autonomy and strong, assertive leadership, he knew that he could not do this entirely alone. While he saw the university system administrators as subordinates, he also expected them to demonstrate capabilities at vigorous leadership.

It is a fact that Carl McIntosh did not meet his expectations; Pettit felt the Californian's style of reflexive rather than proactive leadership left much to be desired. Perhaps because of this, and perhaps because Pettit harbored resentment at the treatment he had received at MSU, the new commissioner of higher education frequently intervened in MSU affairs, making life regularly difficult for the president and his staff. This is not to say that Pettit reserved his interventions for MSU—the University at Missoula also had much to complain about, as did some of the other units. But MSU seemed, when all was said and done, to have received an inordinate amount of Pettit's attention. One can perhaps better appreciate the burden of Carl McIntosh's presidency by examining a few of Pettit's actions.

In 1974 the commissioner, citing a procedural irregularity, reversed an MSU administrative decision to strike a student from the graduation list, even though the registrar argued he was seriously short in requirements. [75] The following year Pettit overturned an MSU decision to deny admittance to an out-of-state student. The student's grades did not meet MSU's out-of-state admissions standards, but Pettit ordered the university to accept the student on a provisional basis. The student's father, the press discovered, was a friend of the governor's. Harry Cockrum, director of admissions, was astounded, remarking that the case was the first instance of state administrative intervention he had experienced in thirty-four years at MSU. Pettit's response was right to the point: "I think some of the oldtimers at MSU can't accustom themselves to the new government structure, they don't understand it for one thing." What he meant by this was that as chief executive officer of the Board of Regents he had the authority to intervene at any time and at any level. Specifically, the 1972 constitution had given the commissioner's office the right to review appeals of campus decision making, and Pettit exercised this new authority quite freely. [76] As one can imagine, Pettit's liberal application of this authority frayed nerves throughout the system and caused much antagonism toward the commissioner's office.

Pettit's attempt to take over the Montana Tech-Montana State magnetohydrodynamics project (MHD) is another case in point. The reader will recall Senator Mansfield's determination to save and strengthen Tech by securing for it several millions of federal dollars for coal research. But Tech's staff was not strong enough, nor sufficiently versed in grant writing, to prepare the required proposal. Consequently, MSU, with a much stronger staff and experience in grantsmanship, was brought into the project in an administrative relationship. A board composed of representatives of the two units, along with an impressive list of outsiders, was put in place. At this point the commissioner of higher education stepped in, declaring that the project fell under his authority, and then requested that a sum of money be written into the grant proposal to enable his office to hire a director and establish an office. This miffed Mansfield and the MHD board. The end result was a compromise: Pettit was placed on the board, but denied the directorship. [77]

Another case involved MSU's and the state's effort to tap Saudi Arabian petrodollars for the establishment of a Cooperative Extension Service program in the Middle Eastern kingdom. The project was the brainchild of the Montana International Trade Commission (MITC), an office set up with Governor Judge's support. The MITC made the contacts, and the Saudi Arabian government provided the resources to fly over a team of MSU agricultural experts who investigated the possibility of building a network of agricultural experiment stations (wheat production being the main interest) composed of structures built with Montana plywood, an industry that was in decline at the moment and which the MITC also wanted to help. [78] Once again the commissioner's office attempted to obtain a place of significance in this enterprise but was frozen out. Eventually, the project fizzled, but it provided another example of the commissioner's constant interventions in the university's affairs. It was felt by Montana State administrators that circumscribing the influence of the commissioner's office in their projects was extremely important, and they took pride in having succeeded in these two instances. [79]

Setbacks such as these did not discourage Pettit from continuing to augment his authority. On one occasion he placed a gag rule on the unit presidents, angry because one of them, he believed, had tried to end-run his office. When fiscal considerations recommended an austerity budget for 1975-1976, Pettit and the regents put a freeze on hiring. In the spring of 1975, each and every case involving the hiring of a new employee and the replacement or promotion of a current employee had to be cleared, via extensive documentation, through his office. Then the commissioner ordered McIntosh to conduct an extensive self-evaluation of his own office. [80] These procedures were most uncommon, and accentuated the commissioner's willingness to go to extreme lengths to force the presidents into acknowledging his authority.

That summer of 1975, the Board of Regents made an extraordinary decision. Believing that MSU was not being governed effectively, and convinced that McIntosh would not take action on his own, the regents ordered the president to fire several members of his staff. This represented a remarkable departure from the norm, as the general responsibilities of the board were to direct broad policy, not campus personnel matters. But there was a great concern that MSU was "adrift at sea," that it did not have dynamic leadership at the top. The regents believed that McIntosh's lack of dynamism was hurting the public image of the university and, consequently, the entire system. Hence, they decided to shape up McIntosh by shaking up his staff. [81] The most prominent target of the regents' ire seemed to be Irving Dayton, vice president of academic affairs—a straight-shooting sort whose bluntness had gotten under their skin and who, it was also reported, was a source of conflict within the MSU administration itself.

McIntosh was alarmed at this intervention; he did not want to be pressured into censoring his own officers. Consequently, he obtained permission to appoint an investigative committee. In granting this permission the regents made a mistake, for the committee, working on the assumption that the review had been ordered by Pettit, rather than the Board of Regents, sympathized with Dayton and determined to prevent the commissioner from harassing the university. The committee's report slapped Dayton on the wrist and then devoted itself in part to an examination of practices in Pettit's office that made the vice president's job difficult, such as the commissioner's failure to encourage open discussion of academic issues and his failure to prevent pirating of programs within the system. Dayton was saved, and the committee concluded its work in the satisfied belief that it had also thwarted another effort by Pettit to embarrass the school. [82]

Roberts Hall and the Student Union Building, 1972

The capstone of the commissioner's intervention in MSU affairs took place in March and April of 1976. Known as the "million dollar" or "hidden million" controversy, the case involved Pettit's confiscation of slightly more than $1 million in MSU surplus student fees, monies he accused the McIntosh administration of having hidden from his office. These funds had been accumulated from greater-than-predicted 1974-1975 MSU enrollments. The controversy broke on March 1, 1976, when Pettit held a press conference in Helena and accused MSU of having "concealed" from him the presence of these funds and of having squirreled the money away in a local bank—a charge that translated into an accu-

sation of dishonesty. McIntosh and his staff were absolutely stunned, for these funds had been properly deposited in the state treasury and their presence reported to the regents as early as the previous July. Pettit also knew quite well that these monies were accumulating as MSU's 1975-1976 enrollments continued to increase.

Pettit's explanation of his charge further shocked MSU's staff. Three weeks earlier the commissioner had requested an estimate of carryover funds, meaning monies the university did not plan to utilize in 1975-1976 that would be carried over into the following academic year. Because MSU had anticipated making immediate use of the student fees—that is, for the ongoing 1975-1976 year—McIntosh's response did not list the million as a carryover account. But Pettit had chosen to interpret the absence of this million in the carryover account as a purposeful evasion of responsibility. Although he did not accuse McIntosh and his staff in public of criminal conduct, in private he seemed determined to treat the action as such, requiring McIntosh, Bill Johnstone, VP for administration, and Tom Nopper, business manager, to come to Helena, forcing them to take oaths, tape-recording their testimony, and advising them of their legal rights and entitlement to counsel. Pettit might have possessed a flair for the dramatic, but to the MSU administrators it was a humiliating and infuriating experience. [83] But all their protestations were without effect; Pettit confiscated the monies and allocated almost all of the million to the University of Montana, which had run into a fiscal crisis because of declining enrollments. Pettit also reserved a small portion for the use of his own office.

The loss of the surplus student fee fund severely penalized MSU. What the public could not know was that the 700 additional students enrolled at MSU above the legislative budget expectation (which budgets were formula-driven and almost always lower than MSU projections) had put MSU in a serious fiscal bind. Nor could the public know that the accumulated fees would cover only 25 percent of the actual cost of those 700 students to the university. MSU was not richer by $1 million at all; it needed this money to cover essential costs brought on by increased enrollment. The McIntosh administration had argued for two years that the legislature's funding formula did not account adequately for anticipated growth. But these protests had been ignored. The money was there in the state treasury, but was frozen until a legislative budget amendment was passed. There was a long history of allowing institutions the use of income that exceeded budgeted income. But technicalities born of a suit against the 1976 legislative budget were holding up the process. The McIntosh administration had been awaiting the resolution of the issue to make its request. McIntosh had not pressed for this amendment earlier because he felt that it was untimely and because he had been asked by the commissioner's office "to not rock the boat." [84] McIntosh's team, in fact, was finally prepared to make that request, but Pettit had anticipated it and his press conference had then mooted the request.

McIntosh could not get over how the commissioner's office would not acknowledge the difficulty faced by an institution so seriously underfunded because of increased enrollments. Now the monies had been transferred to UM because its enrollments were declining. "I know of no instance when student fees collected on one campus have been diverted to another campus for expenditure," McIntosh lamented. "I have had no personal experience with or personal knowledge of instances in which surplus student fees were withheld from the institution impacted by under-projection of enrollment." [85] This was McIntosh's generous and gentle way of expressing absolute astonishment and utter discouragement at what had happened. Johnstone and Nopper had urged McIntosh to confront Pettit head on, to "blow the case open." But McIntosh, true to his character, "was too much of a gentleman" and would not adopt this policy. [86]

When Johnstone and Nopper later recalled the affair, their perceptions of Pettit's duplicity had not mellowed. Johnstone concluded facetiously that MSU had indeed made a mistake—by foolishly building itself into an institution of excellence it had attracted too many students and grown too good under management that penalized growth in order to sustain less able units. [87] Tom Nopper echoed Johnstone's sentiments: "Of all the time I spent at the University, that was probably the shabbiest treatment the administration ever received. . . . That was a bum rap. The funds were fully accounted for, and the way that the commissioner's office treated the administration down here was unforgiveable . . . . I've never been as frustrated or felt that my integrity was questioned as much as at that point in time. . . . I think it was aimed at Carl so that it would reflect upon his performance as president." [88]

McIntosh understood this. At the Helena inquisition he had attempted to shield Johnstone and Nopper from interrogation, believing that the issue reflected solely upon the personal relationship between him and Pettit. McIntosh did not feel vindictive; instead he was prepared to take the heat. [89] To an old friend he wrote, "We have been having a flap here about $1,000,000 that everyone knew about but which was "discovered" in order to set in motion an interesting chain of events—the last of which we have not yet seen." [90] McIntosh did not know it, but the last in the chain of events would take place only months later, that very summer, when the Board of Regents would ask him to submit his resignation, effective June 30, 1977.

But the "million dollar" episode had not enhanced Pettit's influence and standing as commissioner of higher education. The commissioner's effort to set himself up as the "Zeus" of higher education, as one legislator expressed it, worked to his disadvantage. Pettit's penchant for power, and his willingness to manipulate to achieve it, undercut his success. The press, thriving on his vanity and oversensitivity to criticism, painted him in a very negative and often unjust light. Serving as Montana's first commissioner had been an extremely difficult task; by asking for authority Pettit had become the point man for every sort of grievance with higher education. Legislative resistance, always there, increased each year as hostile lawmakers intensified their efforts to circumvent the constitution and micromanage the university system in an extraconstitutional manner. [91] Even Pettit's own board began to resist his authority. In 1976, two new regents had taken office with an apparent mandate from the governor to curb Pettit's effort to remake his office into a chancellorship. [92] A vote of confidence was taken and Pettit survived by a margin of one. Although Montana's first commissioner of higher education had left behind a handsome list of accomplishments, most important of which was his success in getting the new educational governance system defined, launched, and stabilized, [93] the controversy over his leadership role tended to obscure this legacy. In 1978 Pettit tendered his resignation, effective the first day of the new year.

Governor Judge's evaluation of Pettit's commissionership was instructive. It was important to realize first of all, the former chief executive pointed out, that Montana's first commissioner of higher education, no matter who that person might have been, would have had a burdensome time, as it was extremely difficult for the college and university presidents, having run the show for so many years, to bow gracefully before a new authority. But Pettit had himself exasccerbated the problems, not from lack of capability, of which he was handsomely endowed, but from flaws in his character. Had Pettit learned to "walk softly," he might have survived and made a great commissioner. But he was a "controversial sparkplug" who "stepped on toes" and was unable to gain the confidence of the college and university presidents. [94]

Carl McIntosh looked back at these years in a nonjudgmental manner, as was his wont. When asked to explain Pettit's motives, he likened any attempt to do so to "chasing a black cat in a darkened room." This, of course, was a statement in itself. But ever the gracious loser, he would find fault with no one. As for Pettit's effort to accumulate authority, and his alledged animus toward MSU, McIntosh pointed out that UM had as often been at odds with the commissioner's office.

Opposition from the campuses had put Pettit in a no-win situation. [95] In effect, resistance within the system had been a major impediment to his efforts to solidify his authority, and in later years Pettit would lament that for all his toughness on the university system's units, because of their defiance he had not been tough enough. [96]

Pettit was simply too ambitious and too political. In much the same manner that the Blue Ribbon Commission had, in the early 1970s, its strongest opportunity to effect consolidation within the higher educational system, so too at the same time did Pettit have a chance to establish unimpeachable authority for the commissionership of higher education. Both came close to succeeding, but both fell short of purpose. Pettit tried hard to be a good ex-officio officer. But commencing in the mid-1970s, the authority of his office, and

that of the regents, began to erode as the legislative and executive branches gradually regained their influence over higher education. This would have important implications for the university system in the following decade.

The Pettit and McIntosh administrations, two very different styles of administration, bore striking resemblances nonetheless. The one did not fully succeed in its purpose because its director's grasp for power was inordinate and insensitive. The other did not fully succeed because its chief would not, and could not, excercise power. There was a middle ground, but neither Lawrence Pettit nor Carl McIntosh was capable of achieving it. It was a great disappointment to see them fall short of expectation. But the problems they faced, given their personalities and the political conditions, proved difficult to control.

North Seventh, 1977

Chapter Seven
Good Times, Hard Times, 1977-1993

Almost Halcyon Years

Montana State University's ninth president was William J. Tietz, who came to Bozeman the summer of 1977 from Colorado State University where he had been dean of the College of Veterinary Medicine and Biomedical Sciences and assistant director of the agricultural experiment station. The contrasts between Tietz and his predecessor were extraordinary. Whereas Carl McIntosh had offered a gentle and low-keyed form of leadership, Bill Tietz was aggressive, cocky, outspoken, and dynamic. Observers remarked that he "came on like gangbusters." The agencies reviewing him—the Board of Regents and the staff and faculty of MSU—were enthused over this brand of active leadership and warmed to him at once. Other factors were at play. The university, having chafed under the restraints of the

William J. Tietz, president of MSU, 1977-1990

McIntosh years, was permeated with a sense of resurgence. Enrollments were burgeoning and research activity was increasing at a remarkable rate. In June of 1977, MSU had graduated 1686 students, granting 30 doctoral and 200 master's degrees. That academic year the institution matriculated 9340, the largest enrollment in the state. The freshman class contained 44 percent of the state's first-quarter freshmen and 55 percent of the state's designated honor scholarship recipients. The school's grant and contract research totaled nearly $7 million. [1] And such figures were predicted to increase significantly in the next few years. To add to this, the state's economy was making a comeback, and the 1977 legislative session had proven generous in its funding of the university system. In sum, Bill Tietz was coming in on the crest of a wave.

The new president brought with him credentials abundantly suitable to MSU's scientific and technological character. Born in Chicago in 1927, he graduated from high school in 1945, served a stint in the U.S. Navy, and then enrolled in Swarthmore College, one of the "little Ivy League" schools, from which institution he received a bachelor's degree in zoology in 1950. Two years later he earned an M.S. degree in the same discipline at the University of Wisconsin. Following an arctic research trip, a stint in Alaska where he worked with metabolic adaptation by small animals, and an interim job in pharmacology at Baxter Laboratories in Illinois, he entered the veterinary school at Colorado State, graduating in 1955. From there he went to Purdue University for a doctorate in physiology and pathology, earned in 1961. After three years on the staff at Purdue, he accepted a position back at Colorado State. In 1967 he was appointed chairman of the department of physiology and biophysics. Then he became vice president for student-university relations (a position specially created to deal with student discontent at CSU during the late sixties and early seventies), and finally dean of the College of Veterinary Medicine and Biomedical Sciences.

Bill Tietz was attracted to MSU for a number of reasons. For one, his travels through the northwest, sometimes to visit old Swarthmore classmates, had led him to a consuming appreciation of Montana's environmental beauty. He was an avid outdoorsman, had his own stable of horses, and in his spare time loved to pack into the mountains. He had also become familiar with MSU's WAMI program, having worked with John Jutila and Frank Newman to piggyback onto WAMI a similar program for veterinary students, wherein Montana students would take a first year of study in Bozeman and then transfer to the Fort Collins program. So he knew much about, and respected, MSU's scientific accomplishments. Another factor that appealed to Tietz was that three of the four vice presidencies at MSU were open. Roy Huffman, vice president for research, and Bill Johnstone, vice president for administration, had just retired; Irving Dayton, vice president for academic affairs, had moved to Helena as deputy commissioner for higher education. The graduate dean's position was also vacant. The only top administrative position occupied at the time was the vice presidency for continuing education and extension, which was held by Carl Hoffman, who had previously been at Colorado State and with whom Tietz was familiar. Virtually the whole upper echelon of central administrative positions was open and could be shaped by a new president. [2]

If Tietz liked Montana and MSU, the feelings were reciprocal. MSU faculty and staff were impressed by his determination to augment funding for faculty research, travel, sabbatical leave, and instruction. Tietz also pledged strong support for programs favoring minorities and the disadvantaged, with particular interest in improving educational opportunities for Native Americans; he brought experience in similar endeavors instituted at CSU. Above all, Tietz emphasized scholarship, research, and creative activity. When queried as to where he thought he would get the financing to underwrite his platform, he replied that in a university of MSU's size there were assuredly available resources. To locate and earmark these resources would be one of his first priorities. The point was that MSU was geographically and informationally isolated and that research and creativity offered the strongest bases for broadening the institution's work and reputation. But the school had to be willing to take risks, Tietz said, if it hoped to attract outstanding scholars and researchers. The reaction on campus was good, and the search team gave him its highest rating.

The Board of Regents responded to Tietz in much the same manner. Ted James, chairman, believed that what was needed in higher education in the state was "aggressiveness and toughness"; he had grown impatient, even exasperated, with the previous administration's laid-back leadership and looked forward to the possibility of working with someone who enjoyed making decisions. [3] Other regents responded in the same manner. There was an eagerness on the board to find "assertive leadership, a strong prexy, and a representative who would effectively present MSU's case before the regents, the legislature, and the public." [4] Tietz seemed to fit the bill; "he had all the qualities that had been missing." [5]

The upbeat mood was apparent when the new president arrived on campus in August 1977. But there were also major tasks to be undertaken. The first task to confront Tietz was the framing of a role and scope statement for the institution. For many months the Board of Regents had discussed the need for statements clarifying the lines of program responsibility at the state's fourteen units; now that the presidency of MSU had been filled, they called for the project to go forward. In Bozeman that fall Tietz appointed a task force to develop role and scope statements for each division and office. Simultaneously, the other units in the system initiated the same self-surveys.

The fulfillment of "campaign" pledges now occupied the president's office. High on Tietz's list of concerns was the Native American studies program. Immediate support, generated by the W. J. Estelle, Jr., Fund, a Texas-based endowment established for use at the president's discretion, went to the Indian Club to get its annual powwow on good footing. Affirmative action received his attention: it was "more a state of mind than a set of rules and regulations," Tietz informed his staff. "I am asking that you treat minority and female candidates as you would personally like to be treated were you in the same situation." Concern for the disadvantaged had the same priority: MSU was to become handicap-friendly, "a more aware, sensitive, and accessible institution for all." [6]

Perhaps the most rewarding development for faculty that first year was Tietz's immediate allocation of $300,000 to faculty teaching development, research development, and sabbatical leaves. Taken right off the top of the university's annual budget, with virtually every area of the university contributing a share, including grounds and maintenance, the money was divided equally between the three target areas. Particularly attractive was the new commitment to sabbatical leaves. There had been much talk about instituting a sabbatical-leave policy back in the 1960s, when Leon Johnson and Bill Johnstone had been its major advocates. But the number of leaves allotted on a competitive basis to faculty who had completed a minimum seven-year residence at MSU was initially quite small, and the support, half pay for an academic year's leave, made it impossible for most faculty to even consider applying, since it meant securing hard-to-find supplementary funding to cover living expenses. Another factor served to discourage applicants. Scientists, especially experimental scientists, could likely conduct their sabbatical-leave research projects in their own laboratories on campus. But for theoretical scientists, social scientists, and humanists, a "laboratory" might be thousands of miles away—at the National Archives in Washington, D.C., in the British Museum in London, at Cal-Berkeley, or M.I.T. In short, a sabbatical leave at half pay, with added travel expense, was virtually inconceivable for many faculty before 1977-1978. Even when fiscal support for a full year's leave was raised to two-thirds pay by the Board of Regents during the McIntosh administration, this block remained.

Then, in the fall of 1977, the policy changed. Successful applicants for sabbatical leaves were informed by the acting vice president for academic affairs, physicist Georgeann Caughlan, that they were eligible for a full two-thirds pay over two quarters, rather than over the full academic year, and that they could work the third quarter full time at MSU in order to make ends meet. This enabled a successful applicant to receive full pay for the entire academic year, although only two quarters of actual leave would be granted. The boost in morale this generated among faculty can hardly be measured. It was one of the great breakthroughs in MSU faculty services.

During the winter and spring quarters, a collective-bargaining effort occupied the energies and emotions of the MSU faculty. Despite the fact that most faculty at the University of Montana supported unionization, MSU's faculty was split on the issue. The liberal arts, for the better part, favored collective bargaining, as did faculty in nursing and education. But the engineers, scientists, and faculty in agriculture were strongly opposed. So was President Tietz, who argued that recognition for merit—and the ability of the university to negotiate flexibly with the legislature and regents—would suffer in a unionized bargaining relationship. He asked his faculty to have faith in his abilities to negotiate for better budgets rather than give over that responsibility to any particular union. The large majority of MSU's faculty wanted to believe in Tietz, and they gave him what appeared to be a resounding vote of confidence, overwhelmingly defeating

the collective-bargaining proposal on May 18, 1978. The vote against unionization underlined once more the differences between MSU, with its emphasis upon occupational skills, particularly in business, engineering, and agriculture—schools that had for decades been cold toward faculty governance—and UM, with its strong liberal arts emphasis and tradition of resistance toward Renne-type decision making.

Yet the defeat of collective bargaining had implications beyond the issue of unionization. Granted, Tietz might well secure better budgets through the power of persuasive personal negotiation, but the question of faculty representation in university governance was still at hand. One professor, who actually voted against union affiliation, made this abundantly clear to the new president:

I voted against collective bargaining in yesterday's election. You are surely entitled to see the result as expressing confidence in you and your ability to make a good case for the University. But at the same time it would, in my view, be a mistake to think that those who voted against collective bargaining voted against the AAUP platform. The faculty is not yet adequately involved, as a group, in matters that primarily concern them: formulation of university-wide criteria of hiring, termination, and merit, review of promotion and tenure decisions, control of educational policy, development of academic budgets and establishment of priorities on the basis of which university resources are allocated. At many of the best schools across the country these rights and responsibilities are commonplace. Not here. We have no budget committee, no educational policy committee, faculty are only by grace included in the review of promotion and tenure decisions across the campus . . . . The University Council, whose underlying motive is admirable, simply does not take the place of an Academic Senate . . . . The will is here and the talent. But faculty as a group need to be much more actively involved. Your leadership on the issues listed in the AAUP goals statement would be a good place to begin. [7]

For some, a measure of the new presidency would be the degree to which that office incorporated faculty into campus decision making.

By graduation of 1978, three of the open vice presidencies were filled. The new vice president for academic affairs was Stuart Knapp, former dean of undergraduate studies at Oregon State University. John Jutila, dean of MSU's College of Letters and Science, became the vice president for research administration. Both men were scientists. Jutila was a microbiologist who before taking the deanship of Letters and Science had been head of the WAMI medical program. Knapp

Stuart Knapp, vice president for academic affairs, 1978-1988

*John Jutila, vice president
for research, 1977-1990*

*Thomas Nopper, director
of administration, 1977-1983;
vice president for university
services, 1983-1985*

had degrees in biology and parasitology and experience in university honors and faculty development. The third top administrative position was filled when Tietz appointed Thomas Nopper director of administration, a slot left vacant by Bill Johnstone's departure. Nopper, a native Montanan from Sunburst, an MSU graduate, and a seasoned expert in university fiscal affairs who had joined Bernard Copping's staff as assistant business manager in 1959, brought the administration budgetary expertise that would become almost legendary. Another administrator who joined the Tietz team early on was Michael P. Malone, head of the department of history and philosophy, who was called to fill the graduate

deanship. An American historian who came to MSU in 1967, Malone in short order established himself as one of the nation's rising scholars in the history of the trans-Mississippi West. His commitment to scholarship would prove a valuable asset in a graduate dean.

Overall, MSU's new president felt good about his first year at the helm:

> We have just finished another academic year at Montana State University and it was a most successful one. We enrolled the highest number of students ever and we are projecting a considerable additional growth for next fall. We have also selected two new vice presidents, one from within and one from without, and defeated by a 2-1 vote an attempt of a collective bargaining unit to organize our faculty. MSU new graduates continue to be employable above the national norms and, all in all, it has been a most happy and productive year for me as MSU's president. [8]

The good feelings were sustained through the fall of 1978 when Tietz and the university passed a critical test. There had been some concern over the six-mill levy—as there inevitably was each time it became a ballot issue. Some, and the MSU president was among them, sensed a growing tax resistance across the state and feared the voters would defeat the levy essential to sustaining Montana's system of higher education. Many residents seemed to believe that the levy constituted a new tax, and levy advocates feared that the "overburdened taxpower" mentality, bolstered by the stunning success of Proposition 13 in California, which rolled back property taxes to the mid-1960s level, would prevail in Montana. Throughout the spring and summer, Tietz had devoted himself to the campaign to convince voters how small a burden a six-mill levy imposed upon the individual taxpayer, yet how important it was for higher education. [9] Despite the fears, and because of concerted efforts, the six-mill levy was approved by a 2-to-1 majority in the general election of November 1978.

The overwhelming nature of the endorsement—the measure passed by 93,000 votes—was perhaps easily explained in retrospect. The absence of campus unrest helped, but likely the most telling factor was the voters' recognition that Montana's support of education was already minimal by every standard and that without the levy it would be come outright inadequate. [10] In 1978—indeed, as it had since the 1968 levy vote—Montana ranked last in the United States in increase in appropriations for higher education. In 1968, 29.9 percent of the state's general fund had been allocated to higher education; ten years later, despite the increased number of students and increased costs, higher education was receiving only 20 percent of Montana's general fund appropriation. [11]

Another factor in the voters' support for education in the late 1970s was a relative increase in disposable income. Fiscally speaking, the very end of the '70s, and the commencement of the 1980s, brought a period of good fortune for higher education. The summit of success was the extraordinary legislative session of 1981, when Montana's legislators provided support for higher education (and the school foundation program) on a level unrivaled since the 1960s. This is not to say that other legislative sessions did not provide significant support, but the substantial increase in educational aid approved by the 1981 legislature was absolutely extraordinary; it has not been matched since, nor is it likely to be for many a biennium.

The generosity of the 1981 legislative session stemmed from two factors. One was an acknowledgement of the woeful situation in which the Montana higher educational system found itself in relation to peer institutions throughout the West. Tietz documented the situation in a special report he put out for MSU alumni and friends just prior to the opening of the 1981 legislative session. The report reiterated his concern that the legislature adopt a new funding formula, since the one in place was seriously deficient in providing for increased enrollments, and detailed the physical plant problems, the inadequacy of classroom space and facilities, the dreadful budgetary scenario in library services, and the termination of several programs—marching band and the social-work option in sociology, for example—because of lack of funds. To make ends meet, course offerings had been reduced for the spring quarter in both 1979 and 1980 and the 1980 summer school budget had been seriously pared. Tietz also wrote of his concern over funding for agricultural experiment station and Cooperative Extension Service salaries, which had national rankings of forty-fourth and dead least, respectively. Although MSU's enrollment had increased 31 percent during the 1970s, the state's contribution to the cost of educating students at MSU had decreased 17 percent. Despite the increase in enrollment, faculty positions had been cut through the '70s by nineteen full-time equivalents, and faculty salaries had declined 23 percent in purchasing power. In a comparison with university salaries nationwide, MSU and UM were in the bottom 10 percent. On the basis of these statistics, the requests Tietz made weren't unreasonable—they were the simple basics required by a modern university attempting to provide a quality education. [12]

The other units in the system published their own needs and expectations, and it is reasonable to say that the legislators, for the most part, understood and empathized. The result was the implementation by the 1981 legislature of a new funding formula based on a peer analysis of fifteen plains and Rocky Mountain institutions. Although many legislators, and even university officials, were uncomfortable with the new formula as a final solution, it passed muster in Helena as a reasonable alternative to previous unsatisfactory methods.

But what made this particular legislative session unique was the fact that a strong economy and a healthy tax system now provided an unusual treasury of funds. At the commencement of the '80s Montana's economy was reaping the rewards of a gratifying boom in oil, coal, cattle, grain, and timber prices. So flush were the state coffers in 1981—there was a budgetary surplus of near $100 million— that the legislature approved a 35 percent increase in state spending for the following biennium, including large increases of 15-to-17 percent for public education and the Montana university system. On top of this, the 1981 legislative session also adopted tax cuts that amounted to over $140 million for 1981-1983. At the same time, Montana's voters adopted a tax-indexing system that adjusted income tax rates downward to compensate for inflation. [13]

As the result of the 1981 legislature's increased allocations to higher education, MSU faculty salaries rose an average 15 percent, and thirty new faculty positions were added to the instructional staff. Taken together, the university's instructional and operational budgets increased almost $10 million above the 1980-1981 level. "All-in-all," MSU's news service reported following an interview with the president, "the [1982-1983] school year is shaping up to be one of the most interesting and dynamic sessions in the history of the university." [14]

Bill Tietz was just the man to capitalize on the opportunity handed him by the legislature's largesse. He loved the challenge of risk taking, thrived on creative ideas, and had a well-deserved reputation for assertive decision making. His administrative manner was characterized by aggressive "run and gun" tactics and a brusque "can do" mentality. He liked and favored people and programs with similar qualities. Faculty learned quickly that a particularly good idea was worth a direct trip to the president's office, rather than a delayed, up-the-ladder approach, with every likelihood of endorsement. While this ofttimes dismayed the president's lieutenants, who were caught off guard and had to scramble to dig up the resources, significant new ideas that might have been caught in a web of bureaucratic paper and fiscal logic met approval and became actualities.

Tietz's philosophy of the power of positive thinking was complemented by more than just the availability of dollars. The times were flush for MSU in many ways. Defying national predictors,

Museum of the Rockies

The tri-state region of Montana, Idaho, and Wyoming is an area rich in size. Its combined square mileage makes it larger, for example, than the original thirteen colonies. While marvelous vistas abound for the relatively few fortunate enough to reside in the Northern Rockies, the vast spaces between communities have made cultural outlet and expression more difficult than in the more populated regions of the nation. Many efforts have been made to overcome this handicap, one of the most successful of which has been the development of state, county, and community museums. Leaders among these have been the state historical societies, our own Helena museum ranking with the best. And by every measure the county historical museums of the Northern Rockies are outstanding examples of this effort to celebrate and perpetuate regional history.

But two regional museums rise above all others in special significance. One of these is in Wyoming, the other in Montana. Of the two, the Buffalo Bill Historic Center in Cody is clearly, in terms of dollar supports, structural capacity, and sheer value and size of collection, the premier facility in the tri-state area. But the other, the Museum of the Rockies in Bozeman, has the distinction of being the only comprehensive museum. Unlike the Buffalo Bill Historic Center, which concentrates on cultural historical expression, with special emphasis on the "Wild West" of the nineteenth and early twentieth centuries, the museum accents not only historical culture, but the extraordinary natural history of the region as well. In fact, the Museum of the Rockies not only has the region's ranking paleontological exhibits, it has one of the most distinguished paleontological curatorial capabilities in the world. Moreover, the Museum of the Rockies is strong in prehistoric and historical archaeology and is on track to exceed all area museums in its research and educational capabilities.

The evolution of the Museum of the Rockies is the story of many dedicated persons laboring tirelessly over many years. The founders of the regional museum concept were Butte physician Caroline McGill and MSU historian Merrill Burlingame. Dr. McGill had distinguished herself as Montana's first pathologist; she was also, by Dr. Burlingame's description, a "compulsive collector" of Montana antiquities, and when she offered her sizable collection to MSC in 1956, president Roland Renne allocated three World War II quonset huts north of Herrick Hall. Dr. McGill accompanied her collection to Bozeman and served as its first curator. Volunteers from town and campus pitched in to make the huts serviceable. The "Quonset Museum," as it was

often called, opened formally in 1957. Dr. McGill's concept of its mission was clear—it would be a museum geared not only to the college, town, and county, but to the entire state and region embracing it. [1]

Merrill G. Burlingame and Caroline McGill

The quonset-hut setting proved a short one. Within a year President Renne's decision to build a dormitory on the site forced the museum to relocate. An enormous old 1904 dairy barn, located on South 11th, became available, and McGill's growing collection was moved there in the fall of 1958. Unfortunately, Dr. McGill did not live to see the formal opening; her health failed rapidly during that winter, and she died in February 1959. The museum, renamed The McGill Museum, opened officially the following December with Dr. Burlingame as interim director. The first exhibit featured homes of early Montanans, including a Victorian room and Crow Indian tipi, a ladies fashion showcase, an agricultural display, and southwest and plains Indian collections intended to provide a "unique insight into Indian culture." [2]

Although the historic barn and its fascinating collection were received enthusiastically by the public, a move to resite the museum's holdings began almost as soon as the facility opened. No matter how hard staff and volunteers worked, the barn was saturated with dust and chaff from over fifty years' use, and constant labor was required merely to keep the collection clean. More critical were problems involving fire safety and security. In the mid-1960s, friends of the museum, including representatives from nineteen community

*The McGill Museum
and Museum of the Rockies,
1958-1972*

organizations, incorporated as the "Museum of the Rockies" and commenced a $250,000 fund-raising campaign to build a new facility. The response was encouraging—generous contributions were made, prominent among them those from Montana pioneer families. [3]

In the meantime, the college, now renamed MSU, and under the presidential leadership of Dr. Leon Johnson, agreed to create a full-time museum directorship, which was filled by entomologist Leslie C. Drew. President Johnson also pledged acreage for a new facility, which after much debate was allocated at the present site. A one-story, eight-module complex design was adopted, and groundbreaking took place in November 1971. The first module was opened to the public a year later, and a second module the year after that. But expectations for rapid growth were to be disappointed in the mid-1970s; funding slowed, outreach did not materialize as anticipated, staffing remained sadly minimal, and the size of the facility static.

Prospects changed for the better in 1977

*The Museum of the Rockies
in its modular form,
1972-1989*

when William Tietz became MSU's president. Tietz and his new VP for research, John Jutila, saw in the museum an excellent, if unrivaled, mechanism for off-campus public service and on-campus instructional and professional stimulation. When the directorship opened in 1978 they brought in Michael Hager to develop that potential. Hager was Tietz's kind of man—a "can-do" dynamo. A paleontologist, Hager commenced at once to reorganize and expand the museum staff, promoting Judith Weaver to assistant director, and adding some excellent curatorial personnel. He also broadened the Board of Trustees into a larger state and regional council. While the staff was being reorganized and the board metamorphosed, Hager went after the monetary resources necessary to provide the museum with the means to function. A rewarding breakthrough occurred in the flush year of 1981 when a $100,000 planning grant was obtained from the state's Cultural and Aesthetic Projects coal tax funds. These dollars enabled the board to do much needed concrete planning. It was critical, for example, that a strategy be mapped out that didn't duplicate existing programs elsewhere in the region, especially those at the Montana State Historical Society Museum, the Buffalo Bill Historic Center, and even the Gallatin County Historical Society's own Pioneer Museum. [4]

Hager's major concern was to create a facility oriented to travelers. He and his staff concluded that a time-sequential concept would best meet this goal. Visitors would have choices, but museum layout would encourage a chronological approach to its exhibits—a multimedia format that walked people through time. Hence, the adoption of the theme "One Place Through Time." Hager and the new board then wisely planned expansion needs into the design, for it was a proven fact that museums shortly outgrew their capacity. Moreover, new exhibit space would be critical to implementing exhibits designed around time change.

The coal tax grant was not contruction money, however, and a major drive was required to raise the $9.5 million necessary to create a truly comprehensive museum facility and program. From the very beginning, the involvement and support of the Jim and Bea Taylor family of the Gallatin Valley was critical. Once the Taylors were convinced of the probability of success, they made a substantial commitment through the Ruth and Vernon Taylor Foundation. Thereafter they devoted considerable amounts of time, money, and energy to strengthening the museum and keep-

Michael Hager, director of the Museum of the Rockies, 1978-1990

The triceratops in the lobby of the new museum

ing the campaign on track. Another major devotee of the museum expansion effort was Phyllis B. Berger, an MSC alumnus and native of Whitehall. Ms. Berger had a lifelong interest in paleontology and Native American studies. She made an early financial commitment to the campaign, and when she died shortly thereafter left her entire estate to MSU, $1.6 million of which was earmarked for

the museum. It could only be regretted that she did not live to witness the opening of the museum's Phyllis B. Berger Dinosaur Hall. [5]

A third factor stimulating the success of the campaign was the decision to sell bonds in support of the museum. These were authorized by President Tietz and masterminded by Tom Nopper, vice president for administration. During this period too a national advisory board was appointed, broadening the museum and its appeal beyond regional borders. Bids for construction came in under expectation, and once construction actually commenced, financial support increased substantially, including significant contributions from the National Endowment for the Humanities and the Kresge, Burlington Northern, and Murdock foundations. [6] The striking new structure, some two times larger in size than the modules it incorporated, was opened with much fanfare in 1989. [7] One of its major opening exhibits, "Wolves & Humans: Coexistence, Competition and Conflict," underlined the museum's determination to field topics of highly controversial content as part of its mission to broach issues of regional significance. In 1992 a symposium built around the question of bison and the environment attracted nearly as much attention, although not as much vituperation.

While building was underway, staff and board energies were shifted into programming. The creation of an outstanding photoarchives has been one exemplary result. Another has been the archaeological program, with important digs begun at numerous prehistoric and historic sites, including dinosaur digs throughout the tri-state region, and work at Barton Gulch, Red Bluff, Fort Ellis, and the Lewis and Clark portage site downriver from Great Falls. The planetarium program has been conspicuously successful. The Taylor Planetarium is at present the superior facility in the Northern Rockies and features a state-of-the-art Digistar system that allows transfer of MSU programs to other Digistars worldwide and vice versa. To complement the facility at MSU, a traveling, inflatable planetarium exhibit circulates throughout the state, much to the delight of tens of thousands of Montana school children.

An additional programming development, considered to be the museum's greatest success, has taken place in paleontology, with the dinosaur dig at Choteau's "Egg Mountain" the most visible manifestation of it. Developed by museum curator Jack Horner, one of the world's leading authorities on dinosaur ecology and taxonomy, the dig features Horner's discovery of the world's most extensive clutch of dino-

Moving the Tinsley House to the Museum of the Rockies from Willow Creek, 1986

saur eggs. In 1986 the site was purchased by the Montana Nature Conservancy and developed into a paleontology field school. Each summer enthusiasts from all over the world arrive to take part in museum workshops held there. One remarkable result of the paleontological program has been the development of a relationship with Japan. When Japanese technology was engaged to create the museum's almost life-like robotic triceratops that sways, snorts, and scares kids in the main lobby, the museum exported in return a tremendously successful traveling dinosaur exhibit to Japan in 1990. Although the interrelationship is essentially musological, no one could deny that it was an excellent means by which to cultivate Japanese interest in Montana beyond the purely cultural.

Finally, the museum has integrated much of its programming with MSU's academic departments, which provide valuable input, their faculty serving as advisors and even functioning as appointed curatorial staff. At the same time, many academic disciplines, including anthropology, archaeology, geology, history, paleontology, and physics (planetary studies), have been able to

The Museum of the Rockies today

make excellent use of the museum's superb facility for university and public instruction. [8]

All told, the growth, scope, and public and private support of the Museum of the Rockies have been truly remarkable. While its founders always intended it to be more than a purely local institution, few could have foreseen the manner in which their dreams and designs would be expanded, not only into the state and region but into the national and even international arenas as well. The Museum of the Rockies has become one of the university's crowning achievements, both in the application and extension of its scholarly resources and as a major expression of its comprehensive outreach mission.

1. A major source for the early history (circa 1956-1977) of the Museum of the Rockies is Carol Jo Thompson's, "Museum of the Rockies," a graduate history seminar paper (1990). Thompson's study is valuable for its use of the McGill Museum file in the Montana State University Special Collections, MSU Libraries, and for interviews of persons privy to the early years of development, including Merrill Burlingame, Jim Goosey, Roy Huffman, Herbert Kirk, Charlotte Koch, David Swingle, and Judy Weaver.
2. Ibid.
3. Ibid.
4. Michael Hager interview, 26 July 1988.
5. Ibid.
6. The museum's ability to attract national funding support has continued. The National Science Foundation provided substantial support for paleontological research, and on the eve of the centennial grants from the [Ted] Turner Foundation, Dwight David Eisenhower Foundation, and the NASA-funded Montana Space Grant Consortium were being applied to museum projects covering history, archaeology, and the planetarium. However, even the availability of outside funding has not covered constantly rising costs, and the museum has had to resort to admissions fees and additional state aid to make ends meet.
7. "Museum of the Rockies Grand Opening Events," 90033/2, "Museum of the Rockies Grand Opening" file, MSUA.
8. Museum of the Rockies, Inc., Annual Reports.

both graduate and undergraduate enrollments were at an all-time high, and the projections pointed to even greater heights. Enrollment in the fall of 1981 approached 11,000; the following fall it topped that figure—10,574 undergraduates and 737 graduates. As ever, the huge proportion— 83 percent—were Montanans. Of students recruited from the state's fifty-six counties, MSU led in forty-one and was second in all the rest. [15] By comparison, UM had fallen behind by over 2000 in student numbers, even though Missoula's figures were bolstered by a roughly 30 percent out-of-state enrollment. MSU was riding the crest of unprecedented popularity in the state.

Signing in at a dorm

Impressive construction projects on campus served to enhance the school's image and energy. These projects included a film and TV center on the corner of Grant and South 11th, a new animal laboratory north of Lewis Hall, and major additions to the Student Union building and the physical education center. Enthusiasm enfused every area of campus activity. Each department, college, and service was asked to provide the administration with proposals for use of the new formula-generated appropriations. For some this was primarily an opportunity to restore courses, programs, and positions cut during the '70s. Others devoted the appropriation to new responsibilities. One such department was Student Services. Despite the increase in enrollments, Student Services had experienced very little increase in support during the 1970s. Federal regulations and financial aid programs put in place in the previous

two to three years had overburdened clerical and professional staff; placement services had been strained to the breaking point as more and more students matriculated in professional schools. Demands on the counseling staff had increased to the point where students often had to wait up to three weeks to secure appointments, and intramural and recreation programs lacked sufficient supervisory personnel. Handicapped students, all but invisible on campus a decade earlier, now numbered over 200, and those students required special facilities. There was no end to what Student Services could do with increased appropriations. [16] And so it was with any number of other administrative offices, now given the opportunity to launch programs previously denied or abandoned because of the lean budgets of the 1970s.

One of the major beneficiaries of the 1981 appropriation was the Office of Academic Affairs under Stuart Knapp. Vice President Knapp took two faculty development programs—one in support of research and one in support of instruction—and organized the research creativity program and the teaching-learning committee, respectively. The latter successfully secured a large grant to underwrite a teaching and writing project across the curriculum. Out of this project, and monies made available by the 1981 legislative appropriation, came the current writing center, administered by the English department. A new line was created for a full-time director, Mark Waldo, and space was secured in Hamilton Hall. Literally thousands of students make use of the center annually, and the experience has given rise to numerous English department publications. In all probability, the establishment of the writing center, spearheaded by Paul Ferlazzo, Jack Folsom, John Bean, and John Ramage, has been one of the most important developments in the history of the English department, and one of the most innovative and successful teaching aids available on campus today. [17]

The university's new writing center became the hub for another major improvement—an experimental freshman writing program. Heavy teaching loads and the "threat of midlife burnout" among English faculty, who had no graduate program to provide teaching assistants, virtually compelled the department to develop alternative means for meeting the compositional needs of more than 11,000 students. "Relying on [the] progressive writing center, a coordinated sequence of assignments, an elaborate network of upper division tutors, and a commitment to collaborative learning," the program enabled the department to raise the size of freshman English sections from twenty-five to sixty students, without increasing full-time faculty equivalents. The program enjoyed immediate and continued success, and was copied by a number of colleges and universities across the country. [18]

Increased budgets also made possible the reestablishment in 1981 of the university honors program. The first director of the new program was Arthur Coffin, head of English, and he was followed by another professor in English, Alanna Brown. Unlike honors programs in many other colleges and universities, where the affiliation is decidedly with Letters and Science, MSU's program was intended to be an all-university program, and from the outset the response across the campus was extremely gratifying. A large number of the initial enrollees were from colleges other than Letters and Science, most notably the College of Engineering. Participating students had to enroll in at least eight honors courses during their academic career, and two of these courses had to be honors seminars focusing on the exploration of complex issues from multidisciplinary standpoints. A committee of faculty from across the campus provided advice and helped select and prepare outstanding students for major national scholarship competitions, including Rhodes, Marshall, Truman, and Fulbright awards. In 1984 the decision was made to give honors increased support by hiring a full-time chair on a split-academic appointment. [19]

Students didn't have to be in the honors program to receive academic guidance. General studies, established in 1958, came into its own in the late '70s and early '80s, assisting undergrads who were not yet ready or willing to commit themselves to a specific curriculum. As a nondegree program, general studies became an increasingly desirable niche for incoming students, and at times a full quarter of the freshman class partook of its services. Under the direction of Margaretha Wessel, the office administered additional programs, including the national student exchange and academic advising support services.

Another by-product of Stuart Knapp's dedication to developing teaching effectiveness was the plan to improve the general education of the student body by initiating a core curriculum. Previously, each college or department had determined the general education requirements of its own students. In 1983 a program review committee, assisted by the undergraduate studies committee, went to work on what would emerge three years later as a basic fifty-six-credit requirement for all MSU undergraduates. Because the new core curriculum promised to increase costs—added writing assignments would be one result—the university provided extra dollars to support services specific to the new plan.

Critical to all instructional, research, and outreach improvement was the strengthening of MSU Libraries. During the 1950s and '60s, the library had managed to sustain itself under the able direction of Leslie Heathcote, but in the early '70s its acquisitions and staffing capabilities seriously declined. In 1976, the school was chagrined to report to the commissioner's office that the collection of books and periodicals in Renne Library was a wretched 40.6 percent of national standards. Actually, the deficiency was even greater, since a certain percentage of the library's acquisitions came from outside funds, such as WAMI and other research programs. [20] But increased revenues in 1981 made it possible for Renne Library, now under the direction of Noreen Alldredge, to dedicate more than $800,000 to the acquisition of new books and journals, an act that helped the library regain some of the lost ground. The generous appropriations of 1981 also made it possible for MSU libraries to hook up with the National Library of Medicine Network and the Washington Library Network, the latter a coalition of libraries whose catalogs are fed into a database that enables each member of the network to draw on the resources of the others. The library was now moving quickly into computerization. All new library acquisitions were catalogued in machine-readable form, as was the traditional card catalog. Such automation, combined with the installation of electronic mail and telefacsimile machines, made the MSU libraries more accessible to users on campus and at the state's public libraries, thus enabling the school to improve the delivery of information to the citizens of Montana. [21]

Renne Library

Culinary delights at the 8th Annual International Street Food Bazaar, 1989

One of Vice President Knapp's primary interests upon joining the MSU administration was the international studies program. The logical director for such a program was Donald Clark, assistant to the president, political scientist, and retired air force officer. Clark himself was so enthusiastic about the potential of an international study program for MSU students that he undertook much of the organizational work voluntarily. President Tietz subsequently gave the position official status by shifting the funding for his assistant into the new program, which was then able to expand significantly on resources made available by the healthy economy of the early 1980s. At Clark's urging the university became a member of the Northwest Interinstitutional Consortium for Study Abroad and placed students in schools in Cologne, Avignon, and London. In addition, Clark was successful in securing teaching appointments at these locations for several MSU Letters and Science faculty. MSU also joined the International Student Exchange Program and brought in Stephanie Becker to assist in its administration. At various times that program had as many as forty students involved, sending Montana students to cooperating universities all over the world, while hosting students from foreign instititutions. Together, Clark and Knapp set as their goal the involvement of at least 10 percent of MSU's student body in an exchange program, and they had reasonable success in achieving that goal. They also had success in attracting foreign students; by 1983 340 such students were enrolled at MSU. They were aided greatly in their orientation to the country and the campus by the international education office. [22]

A natural aspect of the Tietz administration's concern with raising the level of international awareness in the MSU community was the development of an institute to foster closer ties with Canada. Despite sharing an international boundary with three Canadian provinces—Saskatchewan, Alberta, and British Columbia—Montanans possessed only the vaguest notion of Canada and its resources. To Lauren McKinsey, head of the political science department at MSU, the times seemed propitious for the state to seek closer relationship with its neighbor, particularly as the center of Canada's economic wealth shifted from the central provinces to the west. In the summer of 1981 the Montana-Canadian Relations Institute was formalized. Tietz jumped at the idea of supporting the venture. No such agency existed between the Mississippi and the Pacific Coast, and the institute could expand MSU's research efforts and extend the school's commitment to Montana's economic welfare, in addition to fleshing out the international studies program.[23] In short order the institute organized a seminar in Canadian studies in Helena for state government employees and published a handbook of Montana-Canada border relations for use by state, federal, and local officials. The Helena seminar was run in conjunction with the recently authorized MSU/UM masters of public administration degree program centered in the capital city.

From this initial venture came the 49th Parallel Institute, formally approved by the Board of Regents and affiliated with state government in April 1983. The new institute's purpose was "[t]o improve the general level of mutual Canadian-American understanding and to facilitate the exchange of information and ideas on economic and trade matters among government officials, the business community, journalists and community leaders in Montana and the adjacent region."[24] To accomplish its goals, the institute commenced a series of workshops and conferences and published source books and a newsletter. The state and MSU were not the 49th Parallel's only underwriters; two-thirds of the institute's initial $100,000 budget support came from twenty different private-sector sources in Canada.[25]

MSU's desire to broaden its sphere of interest internationally took another step in the formalization of sister relationships with Kumamoto National University and Kumamoto University of Commerce, situated in the city of that name located about fifty miles east of Nagasaki on Japan's southern island of Kyushu. In the summer of 1983, twenty Montana university system students, led by MSU business professors Jim Lee and Bob Swinth, went to Kumamoto for a four-week management seminar at the University of Commerce. The following summer, twenty Japanese students came to MSU. An exchange of faculty also took place that year and the next, and these exchanges, student and faculty, continued on an alternating basis.[26] With this as the start, Don Clark broadened the program substantially, arranging exchanges with Kansai Gaidai University (also in Japan), Wollongong University in Australia (an engineering student exchange), Jilin University in China (a faculty exchange), Kunsan University in Korea (faculty and student), and Aberdeen University in Scotland (faculty and student).[27]

One of Bill Tietz's goals for the university—some would argue his major goal—was to build it into a "high quality research institution." Just after the passage of the six-mill levy in 1978, Lawrence Pettit, commissioner of higher education, had put forth a role and scope statement for the two universities that fully recognized the critical nature of research. Tietz applauded the statement, for it spoke his mind emphatically:

> Each campus should hold to the principle that a community of scholars and teachers can achieve its goals only if it maintains an atmosphere conducive to free inquiry, unfettered exploration of the unknown, and honest examination and evaluation of hypotheses and accepted bodies of knowledge. . . . A special mission of the two universities is to provide state, regional, and in some cases national leadership in the exploration and discovery of new knowledge; to impart such knowledge to students; and where appropriate to apply research findings to the solutions of the state's problems.[28]

Montana State's new vice president for research, microbiologist John Jutila, quickly adopted this goal of developing the university into a truly comprehensive research institution. The agricultural and engineering experiment stations already provided a research base and infrastructure. Coupled with the outreach mentality of the land grant institution and a positive working relationship between administration and traditional research faculty, the ag and engineering experiment stations had enabled the institution to develop its research capabilities and sustain itself even during hard times.

Organized scientific research had beginnings at the college in the immediate postwar years, and the scope of research grew impressively under the direction and inspiration of Leon Johnson during the 1950s and '60s. In these early years there was no institutionally defined direction to research, the tendency being for projects to follow opportunities where they arose and wherever faculty had an interest. In the late 1960s and early 1970s, however, this began to change as the university recognized the value of programmatic development in research. Between 1970 and 1975, organized research at MSU doubled, and doubled again in just another two years, reaching $7 million in support by 1977 at the commencement of the Tietz administration. In terms of federal support, which constituted the great bulk of the research budget, MSU ranked in the top 5 percent of the nation's more than 2500 colleges and universities (and continues to do so). Many of these research-based programs were quite significant—WAMI, the Gallatin Canyon Study, and MHD. (See Chapter 9.) Other projects featured in the university's annual report to the governor in 1977 included substantial research progress in animal diseases, grain productivity and disease resistance, water research, land reclamation research, and energy research.[29]

MSU's ability to increase its research capacity was aided greatly by Tietz's 1981 success in persuading the legislature to refund to the institution 15 percent of those portions of federal grants covering indirect costs (IDCs). Many indirect costs covered by federal grants were already accounted for by state funding—space and utilities costs, for example. Quite rightfully, the state requested the transfers of IDCs to its own general fund, but it was sympathetic with Tietz's argument that these monies could be used very profitably for research incentives. Beneficiaries would include all sorts of programs related to research creativity, support for speakers programs, and matches for grants. When hard times hit Montana and higher education in the middle '80s, Tietz got the state to increase the IDC refunds to 50 percent. The president's ability to retrieve these monies played a very important role in the great surge of MSU's research program during the 1980s.[30]

In view of the history of periodic hard times in Montana, research was deemed particularly important, not only as an adjunct to the instructional program, but as a hedge against declining enrollments, reduced state budgets, and possible reductions in staff. A philosophy of gathering importance at MSU was that a department with a strong research program would be in a much better position to offset reductions in its academic program, and hence minimize overall disruption, than a department without a research commitment. It stood to reason therefore that all sectors of the university, including the nontraditional areas of research—the humanities, social sciences, and performing arts—would profit from their involvement in quality research and creative activity. Assisting the nontraditional areas of research to upgrade and increase their efforts to secure grant support became a major function of the office of research administration during the 1980s. [31]

Another source of research support was the Endowment and Research Foundation (ERF), established in the late 1940s, but separated from the university in the 1970s. A non-profit organization like the university, ERF assumed increasing significance as the repository for funds obtained outside of state support. That such support was absolutely necessary, even after the great success of the 1981 legislature, was outlined in a letter from President Tietz to the state's new

governor, Ted Schwinden, that same year. For all that the state provided higher education, Tietz informed the governor, there were no state monies allocated for scholarships, for visiting lectureships, for seed money to encourage new research and other creative activities, or to provide adequate funding for such important activities as rodeo, Shakespeare in the Parks, Theater of Silence, and the Community Design Center. "[To] make MSU the kind of institution we believe Montanans...want it to be," Tietz told Schwinden, "[it] depends wholly or in part upon resources solicited from outside the [state] funding system." [32]

The extent of outside support was increasing impressively. At roughly $3.5 million in 1975, and then $7 million in 1977, by1980-1981 it had reached a total of $11.4 million—$7.7 million going to support research and $3.7 million to support other academic endeavors. These dollars were employed wherever they were needed: to purchase equipment and supplies, to underwrite a variety of faculty projects and institutional programs, to bring to the campus specialists and speakers to enhance the intellectual climate of the university. Some of the advances and opportunities derived from studies and projects supported by outside funding in 1980-1981 included treat-

Dedicating the Roy Huffman Building, 1982. From left to right: Carl McIntosh, Bill Johnstone, Roy Huffman, Bill Tietz, Roland Renne

ment for Dutch elm disease, development of new grain varieties and grain products, development of genetically engineered microorganisms that enhance the nutritive value of both animal and human foods, the new writing and reasoning skills project, student assistance in mathematics and English, studies of the Fort Assiniboine and Red Bluff historical sites, and fellowships for the faculty to study in the best laboratories, studios, and libraries of the world. Each of these programs was made possible by support external to the state funding formula. Without ERF, Montana State University and its students and faculty would have been deprived of important instructional and research opportunities, and the state of Montana would have been much the poorer for it. [33]

Not one to rest on laurels, Tietz broached an innovative proposal to put MSU's resources to maximum use toward the end of 1982. This was the development of a high-technology research center. He wasn't talking about another Silicon Valley, but a "modestly designed and developed high technology" center for the Northern Rockies that could play a major role in improving the Gallatin Valley's and Montana's economy and in putting to positive use the "great untapped reserve of talent and expertise" MSU had in its labs and classrooms. [34] As a follow-up to his proposal, Tietz petitioned for and received from the regents a six-month leave of absence for the first half of 1984 to study how other universities related to private enterprise while avoiding conflicts of interest.

These were heady times. When the Bobcats won the national NCAA IAA football championship that fall, it was merely a kind of capstone to a remarkable period in MSU's history.

MSU campus, 1982

Hard Times

On the morning of March 13, 1987, Billings' pride, the Sheraton Hotel, the state's second-highest building, only seven years old, was put up for sheriff's auction and sold for but three-quarters of its value—a victim of the region's softening economy. That evening in Bozeman, the MSU women's gymnastics team performed for the last time before a home crowd, another casualty of the fiscal austerity of the middle '80s. Ironically, the night before in Bozeman, David Halberstam, prize-winning political analyst and author and twelfth annual Burkon K. Wheeler lecturer, had figuratively prophesized the next day's events in a speech outlining the end of the American age of affluence. What existed in the 1980s, Halberstam argued, was at best the afterglow of a long age of prosperity that had ended sometime in the previous decade. Americans had best reconcile themselves to new realities, relinquish their fetish with leisure life, and tighten their belts. Taken together, these three seemingly disconnected events symbolized a return to hard times and reminded Montanans of how transitory wealth is in a state so dependent upon revenues from natural resources and so stubbornly unwilling to remedy the problem by other than piecemeal tax tinkering.

Compared with the 1970s, a "boom" period, the 1980s were a "bust" period. During the first years of the decade, the state enjoyed a continuation of the relative prosperity of the '70s. But then a severe economic depression set in. Some would mark the symbol of decline as the closure of the awesome Berkeley copper pit in Butte in 1983, but the slump was much broader—encompassing the timber, coal, oil, and agricultural industries as well. Montana was not alone in feeling the loss; other energy-dependent states, such as Wyoming and Alaska, suffered similarly. By the end of the '80s, Montana's natural resource tax revenues had fallen by 57 percent: to $28.3 million in 1989 from a high of $66.3 million in 1982. [35]

The shortfall in natural resource taxes exposed yet other shortcomings in the state's system of revenue raising. Although the six-mill levy vote of 1978 had withstood the fallout from a growing national rebellion against state taxes, subsequent fiscal decision making in Montana was increasingly impacted by a strong antitax movement that saw its first major success in the 1981 legislative decision to cut over $140 million in taxes. Granted, this was a biennium of extraordinary surpluses—as noted before, over $100 million worth; but when the economy turned sour in the middle '80s, and the state found itself in the red, rather than reconstitute the former tax base, the executive office and the legislature turned to even more tax cutting. The most extreme expression of this approach, which holds to the theory that the lesser the taxes the greater the possibility of recovery, came in 1986 when an irresponsible attempt was made by a citizens' group to eliminate all property taxes, including the six-mill levy for education. Tax indexing, another manifestation of conservative fiscal policy instituted in the early 1980s, simply exacerbated the state's economic woes by denying it a quarter of a billion dollars in the decade. Taken together, the various tax eliminations and rollbacks inaugurated in the 1980s cost state government an estimated $70 to $80 million annually. [36]

Rather than face the formidable task of rebuilding the state's tax base, or creating a new one based on, most logically, a state sales tax, fiscal conservatives, aided by a sympathetic executive branch, pointed to the 1981 decision to increase state spending as a major source of the state's fiscal woes. To be sure, there was truth in their criticisms. The additional millions in revenues advanced in 1981 to state services, including the educational systems, had created a substantially enlarged base that in subsequent years proved increasingly difficult to sustain. As the state slid into recession, the consequences of having built that base became clear. With respect to higher education, fiscal conservatives of both parties became increasingly critical of the 1981 decision to institute a funding formula that increased, rather than decreased, revenues for the university system. Enlarged enrollments and a new funding system based on peer comparison with other Rocky Mountain colleges and universities had created a budget base conservatives felt was costly beyond Montana's capabilities.

How formula funding became part of higher education's budget equation is of vital importance to understanding the complexities and difficulties the university system faced in the 1980s. The history of the formula stems from the mid-'70s during Carl McIntosh's presidency when the education subcommittee of the house appropriations committee called upon commissioner of higher education Larry Pettit and the Board of Regents to provide the legislature with a funding standard. An agreed-upon student-faculty ratio of 19 to 1 emerged from the analysis and was applied to the 1977 appropriation for the university system. As the University of Montana at that time had a student-faculty ratio substantially less, it caused considerable hardship to that institution, forcing it to plan a cutback of sixty faculty positions. Moreover, UM was suffering simultaneously from a serious decline in enrollment revenues, from which plight it had been partially rescued as the result of Pettit's 1976 confiscation of MSU enrollment increase revenues. (See Chapter 6.) To compound matters, there was evidence that the monies transferred from MSU to UM in 1976 had been employed in Missoula to increase or maintain faculty positions that should have been pared. Needless to say, UM's decline caused great concern, and it was determined that a new kind of formula was necessary to save the school from further debilitating losses.

What resulted was a study conducted jointly by the offices of the legislative fiscal analyst and commissioner of higher education during the months between the 1979 and 1981 sessions, a study that gathered data and developed a funding plan based on information provided by peer institutions. The finance committee held hearings throughout the summer and fall of 1980 and presented its funding formula to the regents in October. The regents and the campuses agreed, not without reluctance, to the formula in November 1980. The education subcommittee, also reluctant because it promised to be expensive, but presented with no better alternative, applied the formula to derive the 1981 appropriations for the colleges and universities. At the outset, several of the units—MSU, Tech, and EMC, especially—objected to all or significant parts of the derived formula. But saving UM was high in the priorities of many regents and legislators. Faculty-student ratio and enrollment budgeting was hurting the university in Missoula badly, and the peer formula was deemed necessary. Probably nothing would have resulted from the debate had not certain legislators thrown their full weight behind the formula. Of all, the most effective and forceful spokesman was Gene Donaldson, a veteran representative from Helena, who kept the formula moving through the various hearings and who was able to convince the legislature to accept the level of appropriations called for.

Although Tietz initially faulted the formula—in effect, it shored up an institution that had, as MSU administrators viewed it, failed to keep pace with changing times—he came to accept the formula for a number of reasons. For one, it served MSU well by enabling a more appropriate distribution of resources between high-cost and low-cost programs. The formula also served to effectively eliminate squabbling between the institutions and counterproductive lobbying. Moreover, the formula gave the central administration the ability to plan and predict major changes caused by enrollment shifts. "All in all," Tietz argued in 1986, "the formula has provided an equitable mechanism for funding the University sytem." [37] Almost from the start, however, numerous members of state government felt that what Tietz had come to believe was an equitable mechanism for funding the colleges and universities was, in fact, a bad mistake. It was simply too expensive. A concerted sniping action (some called it guerilla warfare) commenced on the part of fiscal conservatives throughout government that resulted almost at once in cutbacks in formula funding. The policy adopted was not so much to jettison the formula, although that was favored by

some, but simply to refuse to fund it in full. Instead of getting parity support, then, the university system found itself with only a portion of what it should have received. In 1983 Governor Ted Schwinden, who felt that the university system constantly asked too much, submitted an executive budget calling for funding at 95 percent of formula. This set a pattern. As the consequence, the Montana university system has never come up to the Rocky Mountain peer institution parity level. Among peer institutions, by the mid-1980s only North and South Dakota fell below Montana in the percentage distribution of resources to higher education. Nationally, Montana ranked fortieth in the nation on an expenditure-per-student basis. Wyoming, in contrast, ranked fourth. Even educationally impoverished states like Mississippi and Alabama were moving ahead. The figures tell the story: In 1969 Montana had assigned 25.36 percent of its total revenues to all its educational needs, in 1985 that percentage had been reduced to 17.60 percent, a full 30 percent decline. With respect to higher education's portion of these totals, in 1969 the university system had been allocated 27.88 percent, while in 1985 it had fallen to 21.31 percent, a 24 percent decline. [38]

To understand how the formula worked within the university system is extremely important. In reality, the legislature does not have the constitutional right to allocate monies to specific units and their specific programs, but it does make recommendations. Constitutionally, the Board of Regents has the final authority to distribute legislative budgets within the university system. But the regents, beginning in the late '70s, proved reluctant to exercise this authority, and repeatedly deferred to the budgets prescribed for each unit by the legislative branch. This system of line-iteming, as it is known, has hindered administrators, who have pushed the regents for "lump-sum" funding—an idea Tietz advocated in 1983-1984—but efforts to get the regents to accept the principle have failed, even when forwarded by the legislature itself. It should be added parenthetically that the executive branch has helped to limit the autonomy granted the Board of Regents by the 1972 constitution. Starting with Governor Judge, and continuing with Governor Schwinden, gubernatorial appointments of regents throughout the late 1970s and much of the 1980s tended to reflect executive desires to restrain regental authority, rather than to encourage it. Consequently, legislative, not regental, prescriptions determined the distribution of resources to the various units. [39]

One indisputable outcome has been preferential treatment for certain smaller units within the system. Northern Montana College, for example, has been a conspicuous beneficiary of the legislature's apportionment of revenues under formula funding. On one occasion it received more than 100 percent of formula; seldom has it received much less. In 1987, for example when MSU, UM, and Tech were funded at 67 percent, NMC was funded at 92 percent. This differential applied as well to EMC, with 84 percent of peer average, and Western, with 74 percent. The reason for this is not so much that there was hostility toward the universities in the legislature—although that did exist—but that the peers by which Montana's smaller colleges are funded were accelerating less rapidly in cost than the universities' peers. In terms of actual dollars allocated to the smaller units, the results were not that dramatic. It might take, for example, only $100,000 to keep or bring Northern up to peer, but it would take millions to do so for UM and MSU. Nevertheless, the results created a perception that the legislature was placing a premium upon support for the colleges units at the expense of the universities.

There is much more to the diminution of support for the universities than is explained merely by legislative formula funding. Various political, economic, and philosophical factors constitute a potent force when meshed together. That politics played a part went without saying; many detractors of the two universities were simply acting out of the logic that has historically supported the existence of fourteen units—that is, they represent valuable cultural and economic resources in different areas of the state. These legislators recall regental and executive branch attempts in the 1970s to terminate or scale back the smaller units, and they could cite university support of those failed efforts. Moreover, the actual number of units in the system served in itself to dilute legislative support for the two universities. There was an increasing tendency for legislators to think of the colleges and universities as regional entities, rather than state institutions, so that legislators from Beaverhead County, for example, did not feel compelled to support educational appropriations for Gallatin County. Increased parochialism, stemming from the 1969 creation of single-member districts, also contributed to the situation. No longer could legislators from nonuniversity districts be counted on to cast their votes for the major institutions.

Another factor, largely hidden from public awareness, has been the impact of federalization on legislative decision making. During the 1970s and '80s, the federal government handed over to state government many expensive programs. These new fiscal responsibilities vied with education for attention and funds. Also, as the federal government increased its regulation of society, particularly in matters relating to social institutions, state legislatures across the country gradually lost control of much of what had formerly been their exclusive domain. With more and more decisions subject to federal guidelines, including

funding requirements, legislatures found themselves with fewer and fewer areas of unfettered fiscal authority, for in numerous cases a cutback in state appropriations was matched by loss of federal dollars. But one area of authority that remained relatively unregulated was higher education, and legislators, restrained from acting freely in other areas, seized their powers to control higher education. A much closer and a much more critical scrutiny of public spending for the university system was the inevitable result.

Even though on every scale of economy the universities are much cheaper to operate than the smaller units, some legislators voted against the universities because they honestly believed that MSU and UM were inefficient users of public resources and weren't as effective in meeting educational needs as the smaller colleges. Still others believed sincerely that Montana, a state of diminishing resources, simply could not afford to subsidize so large a university system, and, unwilling to pare back the system in terms of units, pared it back in terms of support. Arguments that Montana, like any state in the union, deserved the best educational system possible fell upon deaf ears. Montana was unique in its difficulties, they responded; what was good for Wyoming or Idaho had little relevance for an impoverished state. Some legislators held to the defeatist attitude that all of the good students went out of state no matter how much was pumped into the system.

Of growing strength was the view that the university system was just one more claimant in a vast array of social services the state was responsible for—no more, no less. The very notion that education was a universal good and a public responsibility was being questioned. In place was a growing attitude that viewed higher education as elitist, as basically unnecessary except to those who felt they could or should afford it. This also reflected a swelling movement toward an economic philosophy of support that emphasized user fees as a supplement, if not a replacement, for taxes. It was a matter of fact, for example, that Montana was one of an increasing number of states that endorsed the notion of home schooling, a clear concession to those who lacked confidence in public education. Then too an unsettling streak of anti-intellectualism surfaced periodically in Big Sky country, a residual resentment of higher education, which is perceived as having gotten too big for its britches and deserving of a good financial spanking. That mentality prompted critics to put down the universities as too theoretical, too remote, from the people. In the mid-1980s these sentiments combined with other factors to impose a series of restraints on the growth of the university system. [40]

Signs of legislative displeasure with higher education in the 1985 session coincided with a downturn in mining and agriculture, the main-

Former ASMSU student body presidents serving in the 1987 state legislature: Bob Brown, Kelly Addy, Fred Thomas

stays of the state's tax base. Unfortunately, rather than confront the economic crisis on a bipartisan basis, the two parties made education a bone of contention. On votes on bills relating to the state's university system, those for higher education were overwhelmingly Democrats from the state's urban centers, while those opposed tended to be Republicans from rural Montana. In MSU's own legislative districts, the three Democratic representatives gave MSU and the university system strong support, while the three Republicans ranked in the lower half of those behind higher education.[41] The inability of Gallatin County to give bipartisan support to MSU was demoralizing, to say the least, and pointed out a serious problem particular to the Bozeman institution. Conservative local legislators have frequently failed to rally to the university causes. They might well marvel at Butte's remarkable ability to "circle the wagons" on local issues, but they themselves maintain a dogged detachment. This independence has been a burden to MSU throughout its history.

So it was that the 1985 legislative session proved unable to resolve the appropriations issue, and a temporary hiring freeze was adopted at MSU until the budget could be sorted out in a special session. In the meantime, it was decided to convert the department of veterinary science into a lab in the Cooperative Extension Service, to drop skiing from NCAA-level competition, and to consider closing the clinical nursing program in Butte. In June the special legislative session mandated another 5 percent cut in appropriations

for higher education, and President Tietz reported that MSU would "barely [be] able to stay even with last year's financial allocation."[42]

But this development was only preliminary to the fiscal crisis of the following year. In January 1986 Governor Ted Schwinden called for a 2 percent spending reduction. This was compounded that fall when the Montana university system suffered serious enrollment declines. Loss of students meant loss of tuition revenues, specifically for MSU in 1986-1987 a loss of $655,728. Then in November, with classes well into the fall quarter, Governor Schwinden called for a 2.55 percent reduction in MSU's general fund, while most other elements of state government were recommended for cuts of 2 percent or less; for some there were no cuts at all. The 2.55 percent reduction represented almost $700,000 to MSU. No sooner had that cut been enacted than the governor released his executive budget proposal for 1987-1989, which recommended an additional 6 percent reduction in appropriated funds for the system—or approximately $7.3 million. Accepting Schwinden's recommendations, the Board of Regents ordered the institutions to adjust their budgets accordingly.

Tietz's philosophy in a fiscal crisis—"to concentrate our resources in our highest quality, most productive programs"—brought drastic changes.[43] MSU memberships in the Center for Research Libraries and the Consortium for International Development (an eleven-university consortium to strengthen education, training, research, and extension programs of faculties of agriculture in Africa) were terminated, as were wrestling and women's gymnastics. Skiing, already downgraded, was abolished entirely. Engineering science was dropped, while undergraduate degrees in business education and industrial arts were discontinued. The Butte nursing campus and a two-year program to train administrative assistants were both phased out. Wholesale departmental and college reorganizations were announced. The number of departments in the College of Education was reduced from five to two, home economics and physical education were combined, agricultural engineering was joined with civil engineering, theater arts and film & TV were made one, and the office of institutional research was closed. Tietz also announced plans to terminate the international studies program, but backed off when confronted with a significant expression of campus support for its continuation. Other programs were put under review. These adjustments, serious in every respect, were overshadowed, however, when the president announced that the School of Architecture would be phased out. The resultant furor over the announcement drew statewide attention as Tietz worked to make his decision stick, and architecture and its allies staged a campaign to reverse it.

Many suggestions have been made as to why Bill Tietz chose architecture for elimination. The president had seriously weighed the possibility of terminating nursing, for example, since it entailed much higher costs and its elimination could provide greater savings. But nursing was integral to MSU's health science mission. Tietz also concluded that any decision to close the program, with its nursing clinics in four major cities (Butte, Billings, Great Falls, and Missoula), each with a cadre of nurses involved with human health and welfare, would produce dangerous political fallout. He was already in trouble for considering the closure of the Butte clinic, and no one had forgotten the attempt in the late '70s to eliminate that same clinic, an attempt that had failed at the last minute because of strong-armed politicking by Governor Judge and Ted James, chairman of the Board of Regents. Neither Tietz nor Anna Shannon, dean of the School of Nursing, wanted to borrow that kind of trouble again.

Architecture, by comparison, was more vulnerable, or so it seemed. The university's policy and priorities committee had not earmarked it as a candidate for elimination, but Tietz had his own agenda. Architecture was, after all, something of an exotic; at the time only eighty-eight programs existed in the nation, and Tietz honestly questioned whether architecture had real relevance to the future of Montana. He certainly wondered if the program fit MSU's role and scope. It wasn't into subjects he felt were significant to the state, like environmental and urban planning. He also felt that within the university architecture existed in a somewhat isolated state. Its program seemed of relatively little interest to other students, and few of the architecture students took classes outside of Cheever Hall. In addition, out of the last class of forty-five graduates, forty-two had left the state. In sum, architecture was much less critical to Montana than the health sciences, and unlike nursing, because it didn't have tentacles

out into the state, its closure shouldn't cause as much fuss. The program couldn't be terminated at once, but phasing it out over a four-to-five year period would ultimately save MSU $500,000 per annum. [44]

Later, when the battle had subsided, the smoke had cleared, and architecture still resided in Cheever Hall, more likely healthier than when it had been singled out for elimination in 1987, Bill Tietz could reflect on his failure to close the school. By his own admission, he had not been clear on the significance of the national accreditation standards that governed architecture. Had MSU not maintained its accreditation during the entire four-year phaseout period, architectural students could have sued for damages. Hence, the costs of phasing out architecture would have been formidable and would not have provided a savings for several years. Tietz's position was also eroded when the students, in order to save their own program, followed the recommendations of department head Robert Utzinger and volunteered to pay a supertuition of $190 per quarter—in effect, matching the savings supposedly gained in the first year of phaseout. [45]

However, this was in retrospect. In fact, Bill Tietz fought hard for over two months to make his decision stick. But the support generated in Montana for architecture was strong and had surprising political ramifications. Architecture, no less than nursing, had tentacles throughout the state. Montana's licensed architects came to the program's assistance. The overwhelming percentage of Montana's newspapers took a position in favor of the program, and sentiment against Tietz's decision inexorably built in the state legislature, then in session. The president, it seemed, inadvertently had a tiger by the tail. Only the student agreement to accept supertuition and Tietz's subsequent change of mind saved further damage to architecture's and to the university's reputation. [46]

Architecture students building a geodesic dome

Bill Tietz did not like losing, and he took this loss hard. It could be argued that it represented a major shift in his tenure as MSU president. In the years since 1977 Tietz had enjoyed remarkable success in Helena, gaining the respect of the legislature as a forceful and principled spokesman for higher education, not only because he was naturally endowed with qualities of leadership, but because Missoula offered only a merry-go-round of presidents and because the regents were increasingly unwilling to exercise their constitutional authority in the face of hostility from the legislative and executive branches. Now he had been successfully challenged. More than that, he had been forced to fight for the dismantling of his own institution. It was hard for him to countenance the dissolution of so many of the programs he had worked for since 1977. His toughness of character and mind, his determination to see things through—to bull them through, if need be—became increasingly apparent. Some of his patience, never very thick, had worn thin in the budget battles of '85, '86, and '87. At the same time his combativeness had intensified. During the '87 legislative session he had made clear his concern that the legislature was failing in its responsibility to "bring balance to the Montana tax system." In his opinion, only the combined passage of a sales tax and income tax surcharge, and the use of the coal trust—in other words, full reform—could rectify the problem. But prospects for such appeared dim. [47]

It is a matter of record that the 1987 legislature neither transcended partisan politics nor provided adequate resources to support higher education. A two-year salary freeze for the entire system was one result; another, totally unexpected, hit Montana State exclusively. A last-minute, early-morning legislative decision cut an additional $850,000 out of the Bozeman university's budget. The 1987 legislative session was a near disaster for MSU—the worst fiscally since the Nutter cuts of 1961.

Tietz was particularly upset with the governor's failure to give higher education firmer support. He had never gotten on well with Ted Schwinden, whose conservative approach to government, and particularly to higher education, rankled MSU's progressive president. Tietz felt that he and MSU deserved better. He had worked

Ted Schwinden, governor of the state of Montana, 1980-1988

175

hard for the state, and not just as an executive officer in its system of higher education. He had also put in many hard and frustrating hours trying to help the governor rebuild Montana's economy. Few had worked harder than he for Schwinden's "Build Montana" campaign and the Council of Economic Development. Schwinden's failure to give more than cursory acknowledgement to Tietz's efforts, and to the important role higher education played in addressing the state's failing economy, was hard for MSU's president to endure.

To add to these difficulties, none of the economic recovery programs had been very successful, and Tietz felt that the executive branch was at least partly to blame. In January, Schwinden had come out against the sales tax in his State of the State message and had announced his support for a substantial reduction of the lucrative coal tax as a means of creating investment incentives. To Tietz this was mere stop-gap policy and did not represent a dynamic solution to the growing fiscal crisis. When the governor in subsequent weeks criticized Tietz's handling of MSU's Tech Park and his proposal to terminate architecture, and continued to refer disparagingly to higher education, the president reached the end of his patience and informed the governor accordingly: "I want to express my growing concern that as Governor you have, I believe, increasingly omitted any reference to the University System as positive elements in the economic future of Montana," Tietz wrote Schwinden.

> Every outside consultant has emphasized the importance of university participation in human resource development, basic research and technology transfer. Yet in the totality of your interview in the Great Falls Tribune's look at Montana's future you do not once refer to elements of the University System. This approach persists in the Exponent interview. In addition, comments attributed to you in Missoula indicate your belief that the Universities' failure as agents of economic development are at least partially responsible for our current economic condition. . . . In other states, the alliance between higher education and the Governor's Office and staff has been strong, productive, and a key element of economic success. In a State with so few fiscal resources and such great need we cannot afford to be otherwise.
>
> [L]et me argue that it is my conviction that the majority of the people of this State <u>want</u> a strong responsive University System. The supporting vote for the "6 mill levy" in 1978 was in excess of 60%. A 1980 poll taken at the time of your gubernatorial race again showed that over 60% of respondents favored a strong University System. Polls taken by the two major state newspapers during the recent legislative session

continued to demonstrate that over 60% of the people wanted no reduction in the University System. A poll conducted by the center for Public Surveys at MSU recently found that over 79% of the 398 respondents would again favor the 6 mill levy in 1988. A UM poll showed over a majority supporting either a sales tax or more income tax for university support.

> I would argue that criticism of the University System comes from a vocal minority and that such voice is being used as an excuse not to support the system. It seems incredible to me that with every index showing salaries and support for Montana colleges and universities at rock bottom in the nation, the executive and legislative branches of our government continue to feel that we are somehow fat and unresponsive. In an effort to revitalize a productive relationship between the University System and your office, I would urge that our public statements take on a more mutually supportive tone.[48]

Little occurred in the following months to satisfy Tietz that a change was in the offing. When that summer MSU, Bozeman, and the state failed to convince U.S. West Communications Corporation to move a significant part of its operations from Colorado to MSU's Tech Park, the president was extremely discouraged. Although many factors explain U.S. West's decision to reject Montana's bid, Tietz felt that a major hindrance to success was the failure of the legislative and executive branches to send out strong proeducation signals. On one occasion during the campaign to court the communications company, the governor had openly criticized the universities for their "duplicity"—for claiming bad times before the legislature, while putting up a good face for their constituents. To Tietz this was an incredible accusation. Declaring weakness to those who sought to utilize the university's resources seemed so obviously a suicidal course that to criticize the laudatory comments as dishonest showed an astounding inability to grasp reality. [49] Once U.S. West saw the reluctance in Helena to support education, Tietz wrote a ranking Republican, the state lost its opportunity. "The dismal numbers on Montana's commitment to higher education were there for all to see and though we were able to counter with some impressive success stories, it is clear that potential businesses will measure Montana's viability by its educational system throughout this decade and into the new century." [50] In effect Tietz was echoing the logic of Colorado's own governor, an argument that helped to keep U.S. West in Denver: "The state that is second best educationally, will be the second best economically." [51]

In a way, Tietz had now declared war on the executive and legislative branches. In return, there was growing ambivalence toward the MSU president among members of the state legislature the summer of 1987. Yes, there was great admiration for his forcefulness, grasp of matters, and ability to manage affairs for the university and the university system. But his brusque and impatient manner was beginning to alienate some legislators. Perhaps they had gotten sick of reality and simply didn't want to hear Tietz's message anymore, loath to be reminded of the difficulty of the problems facing them. Some legislators simply couldn't stand up to Tietz's communicating and debating skills. Some legislators resisted Tietz because he was so forceful a personality, so confident of his facts. Fiscal conservatives saw his persistent advocacy for increased educational appropriations as unrealistic, needlessly uncompromising, and a major impediment to balanced budgets. Talk about the possibility that Bill Tietz might make a good governor raised hackles even higher among his critics. The adversarial relationship that had developed between Roland Renne and the legislative and executive branches in the early 1960s had surfaced again in the late 1980s.

Years of Frustration

Ted Schwinden's criticisms of MSU's new Tech Park touched nerves already sensitized by controversy in Bozeman and around the state concerning the institution's land grant mission. Was high tech a suitable enterprise for an institution historically associated with agriculture? Some thought so; some thought not. That Bill Tietz held to the former stance was more than clear.

MSU's Advanced Technology Park, situated on ninety acres that stretches west from the corner of College and South 19th, was conceived early in the 1980s. Debated in public meetings in 1984-1985, the enterprise took material shape in 1987 when Phase I, including streets, water, sewer lines, and an "incubator" building housing over 60,000 square feet of space, was completed late that year. Designed as a technology-transfer arm of the MSU Foundation, which was charged with moving new ideas from the campus laboratories to the commercial sector, Tech Park would also serve as a home for technology-based industry and companies that used systems complementary to campus resources. "A constructive opportunity to meld the skill and resources of the university with the needs and interests of private industry" is how it was described in the first annual report. [52]

Tech Park was likely the most visible example of Bill Tietz's concept of what a land grant institution ought to be doing in an age of depressed economies. "Encouraging the establishment of high tech business and industry in the state will keep Montanans in Montana," he remarked in November 1986. "Economic and technical growth go hand in hand and to solve Montana's economic development problems we must remain farsighted. The construction of the Advanced Technology Park through the Foundation instead of tax support is a major milestone in the university's quest to provide economic development that will not only benefit Montana State University and Gallatin County, but the entire State of Montana as well." [53] To an inquirer from Miles City, Tietz wrote, "We are trying to send strong signals to Montana and the rest of the nation that this is a state worth fighting for and worth investing in." [54] When a company employing biological techniques to detoxify or destroy hazardous waste and closely affiliated with MSU's chemistry department and a precision instruments firm in electro optics and connected with the electrical engineering department, expressed interest in becoming Tech Park tenants, it seemed as though Tietz's dreams of enhancing research opportunities for MSU faculty and creating employment opportunities for the region would be handsomely realized. [55]

Advanced Technology Park

Tietz made much of the fact that Tech Park, as a function of the MSU Foundation, was run without public assistance. Tech Park would exemplify Tietz's conviction that MSU become increasingly independent of state-tax revenues. It seemed a plausible plan. By 1987 MSU, a $95 million operation, received roughly 42 percent of its funding from state-tax based revenues, while the bulk, 58 percent, came from student fees, auxiliary operations (dorms and food service, for example), designated operations (intercollegiate athletics and motor pool, for instance), federal support (ag extension and experiment stations), and grants and contracts (federal and private-sector support). Thus it was not inaccurate to say that MSU was not so much a "state-funded" institution as a "state-assisted" institution. To Bill Tietz, MSU's strategy, if the school hoped "to be the intellectual and technical center of the Northern Rockies," should be to change the funding structure so that it would be less and less dependent upon the taxpayers of Montana. [56]

But some politicians, including Governor Ted Schwinden, questioned whether MSU's business orientation was its primary role; they wondered whether the school hadn't drifted away from its core mission. Schwinden was not entirely convinced that high tech would remedy the major problem, which, as he saw it, was a growing "skepticism" in the public's trust of the university system and the system's ability to make wise use of its state-supplied support. The governor felt that the Montana university system had developed a poor image in the state—one of "intellectual arrogance"—and that it needed to redirect its energies to salvage its standing. If anything, Schwinden was on the side of the legislators who decried the constitutionally mandated "insularity" of the university system and who would put it "back into the political process." They hoped to amend the 1972 constitution to bring the system "in line with public accountability," to compel it "to reenergize its outreach capabilities." To Schwinden, Tietz's effort to remove MSU from public restraints was *causing* tension, not *relieving* it. [57] He accused the institution and its administrators of bad faith by not acting within the spirit of entrenchment required by the state's huge budget deficits. And he wondered aloud if high tech was really doing what the schools should be doing—"getting out into small town Montana." Schwinden's peregrinations about the state had led him to conclude that the university system, while demanding ever-increased support, was providing neither adequate services nor proper contact with those who needed them. [58] As a former wheat farmer from Wolf Point, Governor Schwinden was giving voice to the conviction of the grain growing and livestock industries that high tech was somehow ignoring problems associated with the land and its use. Such was the

nature of the conflict between Helena and MSU.

A similar conflict had been brewing for years in Bozeman. Tietz's adoption of high tech was met grudgingly by those with a stake in the old land grant emphasis of the university's Cooperative Extension Service. In the mid-1980s a group of retired MSU land grant devotees organized to debate whether MSU was carrying out its historic mission. Prominent among the group were Roy Huffman, Max Worthington, Bill Johnstone, Joe Asleson (former dean of the College of Agriculture), Jim Krall (former superintendent of the branch experiment stations), and Bob Bucher and Torlief Aasheim, the latter two veterans of the Cooperative Extension Service. Dubbed the "Gray Foxes" by alumni director Sonny Holland, the group was split along many lines. Its membership had one thing in common, however—they feared that Tietz was not maintaining the old bonds with rural Montana. The most outspoken critic was Aasheim, director of the Cooperative Extension Service from 1958 to1974. Aasheim had a penchant for emotionalizing his position, but his grievances do make clear how deprived the extension service felt under MSU's ninth president.

First of all, Tietz had inherited a service that had been reorganized under Carl McIntosh and made independent of its old parent, agriculture. That experiment, to provide the state with extension services of all kinds and not just agricultural, had a meritorious objective, but it had not succeeded to the president's satisfaction. During the fiscal crisis of the mid-'80s, Tietz made the decision to transfer the service back into the College of Agriculture; July 1, 1987 was set as the date of transfer. This decision had incensed Aasheim and others devoted to an independent role for extension. The agency had also been lobbying for years for a new building to house its many services, still scattered haphazardly about the campus. Tietz had opposed this building, preferring to place his budget priorities in a new multimillion dollar structure for engineering and the physical sciences. Aasheim's efforts to go over Tietz's head to the governor, the legislature, and the regents only exacerbated the animosity between them. "We don't need bricks and mortar," Tietz informed Aasheim, "what we need to do is do a better job." [59] There was no question that Tietz felt that the "hands-on" extension agent mentality was a thing of the past. That aspect of the extension service, Tietz believed, had outlived its usefulness. His view of 4-H, for example, was one of skepticism: "You'll have to prove to me that 4-H is a viable effort," he informed Aasheim. [60] Needless to say, this irked those who had put their lives into 4-H activities. Tietz's message, moreover, that the College of Agriculture was not moving fast enough to adjust to the new scientific age— was spending too much time pushing quantity, or agricultural production, and not enough on quality, in molecular biology and genetics research, for example—was received without enthusiasm in Linfield Hall. It was hard for MSU's agriculturalists to give up what they had excelled at for so many years. [61]

Future Farmers of America

Merino breeding project, 1990

When Tietz had designated College of Agriculture acreage west of campus for Tech Park, it confirmed the fears of those who were convinced he was moving away from the school's age-old commitment to the soil and those who toiled there. [62] The controversy came to a head during the 1987 legislative session when Aasheim attacked Tietz for failing to demonstrate an understanding of the traditional value of extension: "In your emphasis on high tech, a new engineering building, research and graduate emphasis, you are deserting those fundamental programs which have gained support for MSU," the former director of the service wrote Tietz. [63]

Bill Tietz was not deserting extension, but he was unquestionably intent upon leading MSU on new paths. He felt that those hostile to his plans were taking much too literally the old Smith-Lever Act that had created the Cooperative Extension Service back in 1914, that they were trying to apply the literal interpretation of a World War I act in a modern context. The act had to be interpreted in the light of today's problems. Cooperative extension could no longer be "all things to all people." There simply weren't resources sufficient to enable extension to have a 4-H program, a broad homemaker program, an agricultural program, and a natural resources program all at the same time. In addition, the old information services so successfully conducted through the years by extension were now rivaled and even bettered by private industry and by advanced communications. Moreover, a vast element of Montana not touched by extension were the people who were the main source of the criticism registered toward higher education. If extension wanted to help the state, then it had to "change its structure." One way of making cooperative extension more relevant would be to apply "new mechanisms for reaching new audiences." New communications concepts, particularly the use of electronic media, is what Tietz had in mind. He had tried to integrate extension into the communications revolution only to find it a painful process. But Tietz saw it as the only way to go. "Some of the old walls have got to be knocked down," he said. "I think there's a realization that you can't ever go back . . . that we have to be a progressive institution." [64]

How Tietz applied progress to one department long affiliated with agriculture indicates the kinds of changes he hoped to put in place. In 1986 the department of agricultural and industrial education underwent a major transformation—a "new adventure into the area of technology," as Max Amberson, department head, described it. Whereas formerly students had concentrated almost wholly on developing skills in the operation of tools and machines from a microperspective and had gone on to careers in woodworking, metal working, and automobile mechanics, for instance, the newly titled department of agriculture and technology education prepared students "to understand the technological world they and we live in [as] part of the technology education movement nation wide." Students in the curriculum now would take a macroapproach to industry, looking at the big picture by "studying the technical means by which things are produced and . . . the scientific, social, economic and environmental impacts of these technological changes." A major involvement in math, science, economics, and the social sciences would be required while the students developed "technological literacy through problem solving/decision making activities with the use of tools, resources and machines." Under a systems approach using "modern communication, production and transportation knowledge and processes," students in technology education would conduct "group activities and projects" to satisfy marketable needs. They would become involved in design, economic studies, technological processes, labor and production management, and marketing. All of this was a far cry from the old discipline that described its methodology as one of students designing and making "individual projects and exercises such as tables, lamps, gun racks, etc." [65] For some this change was almost revolutionary in nature, but to Bill Tietz it was the way to prepare for the future.

The development of an MSU telecommunications system was another means by which central administration hoped to update MSU's outreach capabilities. "Telecommunications" involves the use of an electronic system in delivering instruction to students at locations removed from the physical presence of the instructor. Delivery systems include TV, cable TV, low-power TV, communication and/or direct broadcast satellite, satellite master antenna system, microwave, videotape, videodisc, or phoneline microcomputer programs, including on-line computer access. Beginning in the early 1980s, when Tietz's new special assistant and director of communications, Marilyn Wessel, was charged with developing such a system for MSU, the program was quickly broadened, particularly in the area of academic affairs. MSU's Renne Library, under the direction of dean of libraries Noreen Alldredge, moved rapidly into the use of new technology, and by 1983 was employing electronic mail and telefacsimile machines to make its collections more accessible to state users. Under a Kellogg Foundation grant project, begun in 1986, MSU cooperated with the state library system in the electronic delivery of informational and educational resources to Libby and Hamilton. In the same year, Stuart Knapp, vice president for academic affairs, took a six-month leave to work up a grant for a regional educational telecommunications study and to conduct a cooperative academic planning project through telecommunications for WICHE, the Western Interstate Commission for Higher Education (a thirteen state consortium). Knapp also used his sabbatical to study library delivery systems in the Northwest; some of the techniques he looked at were then applied at MSU.

In the meantime, the state legislature, grasping the significance of these developments, and coupling this with the intensifying interests of both the public and university school systems, empowered a special task force, chaired by the commissioner of higher education Carrol Krause, to develop telecommunications options for delivery of educational materials statewide. Future possibilities for this medium were given a widely publicized test at MSU in early 1988 when two-way video and two-way satellite communication demonstrations took place between MSU and Great Falls and between MSU and Boise, Idaho. The moral encouragement received from the state legislature was gratifying; the catch, still unresolved, was that the legislature was predictably unwilling to accept the high up-front costs associated with the telecommunicative process. Back in the 1950s and 1960s, MSU's nationally noted rural sociologist Carl Kraenzel had made clear the costs of communicating with a sparse population in a state of such territorial magnitude, but many legislators could not grasp the tremendous costs associated with delivery systems. To microwave a video signal to Fort Peck, for example, would cost hundreds of thousands of dollars, and the cost per student in such a low-population area would be enormous. Despite these problems, the Tietz administration felt strongly that the future outreach ability of MSU would depend upon the success of the telecommunications effort. While the university had no intention of abandoning the traditional approach, symbolized for so many years by the work of the Cooperative Extension Service, it was daily becoming more and more obvious that the demand for information could be met best through electronic transmission. [66]

MSU's commitment to faculty and student scholarship continued unabated. In 1986 Michael Malone, dean of graduate education and acting vice president for academic affairs, recommended, as a "very good way in which to stress our commitment to excellence," a special chair for a senior faculty member who had distinguished himself or herself beyond the ordinary through "cumulative achievement, national-international scholarly recognition, and breadth of scholarly commitment." [67] Titled a Regents Professorship, the honor would hold for a period of five years, was renewable, and was accompanied by an additional salary and travel support stipend. [68] The concept of a regents professorship was not new; in 1977 commissioner of higher education Lawrence Pettit had pushed for something along

MSU and Public TV

The muted sounds of the chopper blades could be heard in the distance as the first symbols of public television arrived in Montana. It was December 20, 1983, a time picked more for its windless, cloudless conditions than for consideration of any historical significance.

With 11,000 students gone for the holiday break, only a scant group of MSU faculty and staff were on hand to watch the chopper sweep into view with a twenty-foot television tower dangling below its belly like a giant swizzle stick.

A few workers paced back and forth on the ground trying to forget that despite the sun, the thermometer at midday was stuck at minus eleven degrees. The engineers and photographers up on the roof of South Hedges dormitory where the pilot aimed to plant the tower were also aware of the bitter cold and how the approaching helicopter wash would make it that much colder.

No one talked much about the hazards of such an operation, but fortunately the tower was firmly anchored after only two passes above the 11-story dormitory. Working slowly with numb fingers encased in heavy gloves, the crew secured the last of the tie lines and retreated inside to thaw out.

The tower itself would remain unused for another 10 months as a small cadre of MSU faculty, staff and students struggled to bring Montana's first public broadcasting station on line. They were determined that however small the start, Montana would not go through another year as the last of the 50 states without a public television station. [1]

If ever an act passed that fit the role and scope of MSU as a land grant institution, it was the Public Broadcasting Act of 1967. Pushed hard by President Lyndon B. Johnson as part of his Great Society and Frontiers of Excellence programs, the purpose of the act, as Johnson intended it, was to extend the principles of the 1862 Morrill Act into the modern telecommunications age. As he expressed it in his dedication speech, "In 1862, the Morrill Act set aside lands in every state—lands which belonged to the people—and it set them aside in order to build the land grant colleges of the Nation. So today we rededicate a part of the airwaves—which belong to all the people—and we dedicate them for the enlightenment of all the people." [2]

Given the purpose of the act, it would seem logical that MSU would have moved rapidly to implement its intent. The school certainly had the capability of doing so. Building on the Board of Education's 1957 decision to authorize a B.S.

degree in film and television production for MSU (UM got radio and television performance), the department grew rapidly, and on the eve of the passage of the Public Broadcasting System offered three options—motion picture, television, and still photography—servicing more than 150 majors. Although the program's facilities were scattered all over campus, department head Fred Gerber headed up the enterprise with all the expertise and energy required to take advantage of the federal supports mandated by the act. But before the university could act, the state had to act, and it proved disappointingly slow in doing so. Authority had been vested initially with the state superintendent of public instruction, but the 1972 constitution had transferred higher education to the new Board of Regents. Much valuable time was lost, and it was not until 1974, when deadlines to receive federal startup monies were expiring, that the state acted. But the state Commission for Educational Television, after initially designating MSU's campus for the primary studio facility, decided, for reasons yet unclear, to bypass MSU, with all of its professional expertise, equipment, and facilities, for a totally separate operation located on Bozeman's North 7th Avenue. This unexplained reversal of plans was then accompanied by a public flap in which conflicts of interest and purported insider shenanigans resulted in not only a grand jury investigation, but a complete withdrawal from the project by the state legislature. [3] In fact, the "ed-TV" issue became so political that the legislature would not touch it for many years. In the meantime, Montana received its educational programming from Utah's public broadcasting station, KUED, located in Salt Lake City.

A combination of factors explained the more successful ed-TV effort of the late '70s and early '80s. Significant among these was the continued ability of MSU's film and TV department not only to attract students but to place them after graduation. In 1978, for example, the department had so many students in limited space it had to impose an enrollment cap of approximately 250, the only curriculum at MSU so obliged. Still, 89 percent of its majors were landing jobs directly or indirectly related to production. The department's ability to attract good faculty was noted as well. After overcoming a harrowing confrontation with the regents over duplication problems covering the radio and television performance program at UM, President Tietz, film and TV department head Fred Gerber, and assistant dean of the College of Arts and Architecture Edward Groenhout were able to convince the 1979 legislature to authorize the planning of a new film and television building. Two years later the remarkably beneficent 1981 legislature appropriated the actual monies, $4.6 million worth. The new visual communications building, located on the corner of Grant and South 11th, was occupied in time for the 1983-1984 academic year. The state's most modern television facility was now in place.[4]

Three other hurdles were overcome when the station's call letters were approved, programming arranged, and monies secured for programming and delivery. KMSU call letters were not available—Mankato State University in Minnesota already had them—but professor Jack Hyyppa's recommendation of KUSM was approved. Then permission was granted graciously by KUED, the PBS station in Salt Lake City, to allow KUSM to re-broadcast the Utah signal to the Gallatin Valley. When the Burlington Northern Foundation awarded a grant for the purchase of microwave equipment the station was on its way, albeit a low power station serving only the immediate vicinity of Bozeman. At 7 a.m., October 1, 1984, KUSM officially signed on with the *Electric Company*, followed immediately by *Sesame Street*.[5]

During the 1980s the state did little to support KUSM and public television. The station did use MSU offices, but the bulk of its funding came from private sources, raised arduously by periodic subscription. In the meantime, other states were doing considerably more. New York in 1988 provided $19 million for public television, South Carolina $17 million. South Dakota, not

content with one public TV station, set up a network of eight. KUSM was as embryonic as they come: Chief engineer Tom Jenkins remarked that he had "never seen a station go on the air with less equipment," but added at the same time that he had never seen one "with more people rooting for its success."[6]

Slowly, KUSM extended its signal. Park County came on line when a new translator brought in the Shields River and Paradise valleys. Then the entirety of the Gallatin Valley was reached. Both extensions were made possible by substantial private grants-in-aid. By 1987 MSU felt strong enough to apply to PBS for true affiliation. The application was approved, and KUSM became the state's first and only CPB and PBS affiliate, receiving its first checks for more than $300,000 in PBS community service grants. This was followed by the cutting of the umbilical relationship with KUED by arranging for a unique three-year phasing out of the Salt Lake City's Montana programming so as to soften the Utah station's loss of revenue.[7] Phaseout was completed in 1991. KUSM now exclusively reached almost the entirety of Montana east of the divide. That same year the state legislature finally recognized the significance of public television by appropriating $400,000. Three-quarters of this went to PBS headquarters at KUSM, while the remainder went to UM to set up a sister station serving western Montana. Thus was the entire state to be serviced by one network.[8]

It would be wrong to assume that KUSM's financial needs are satisfactorily covered by federal and state support. Far from it. Only twenty-to-thirty percent of the station's annual budget is provided by public funding, while the rest is derived equally from MSU and private sources. KUSM's early ability to attract strong support from a local group interested in better children's programming, and now incorporated as Friends of KUSM with over 5,000 members, has been one of its greatest blessings. KUSM's monthly program guide, for example, is one product of this support group's work.

As important as all the aforementioned has been the unique relationship developed between KUSM and the students and faculty of MSU. From the very beginning KUSM has been a working lab for students in the film and television department, since 1985 under the headship of Paul Monaco. Students operate the cameras, the master control room, the editing, engineering, and planning at KUSM. Students from other campus departments provide art work, theatrical production, and educational pieces for delivery by the station. Research work in many MSU labs and departments is regulary reported on the station, as are school activities. MSU faculty and staff double as program producers and writers, secretaries cover phones for both the department and KUSM, and the managers of the station also teach campus courses in film and TV. [9]

Film & TV

Above all, KUSM's dedication to the delivery of programming beyond campus boundaries—to some 200,000 households on the eve of the centennial—carries on MSU's mandate to provide educational enrichment to Montanans as part of its land grant mission. No one doubts that this accomplishment represents only the barest beginnings of a much instir telecommunications interface to be developed between MSU and its widely dispersed public.

1. KUSM Draft, 3 December 1984, 87023/18, "KUSM" file, MSUA.
2. As printed in James MacGregor Burns (ed.), *To Heal and to Build: The Programs of President Lyndon B. Johnson* (New York, 1968), 390-393.
3. Michael Bilyeu, "A Short History of the Film and Television Department at Montana State University," graduate history paper (1990). See also, "Educational Television Comes to MSU," *MSU Collegian* (Fall 1974), 4-5.
4. Bilyeu, "A Short History."
5. KUSM Draft.
6. Ibid.
7. Edward G. Groenhout to Donald K. North (president, Burlington Northern Foundation), 24 February 1988, courtesy of Michael Bilyeu.
8. Paul Monaco interview, 9 March 1992.
9. "KUSM Channel 9 PBS: Who, What, and Why," undated, 87023/18, "KUSM" file, MSUA; "Students Gain Experience Working at KUSM," 1988, courtesy of Michael Bilyeu.

similar lines, but had not been able to secure the necessary funding. In 1986 the Tietz administration picked it up and made it work. The Board of Regents endorsed the proposal and made it official the same year. MSU's first recipient of this prestigious new faculty award was Gordon G. Brittan, Jr., a philosopher who had achieved an international reputation for his scholarship in the philosophy of science and the history of philosophy and who had built up a regional reputation for his involvement in public service in a wide range of activities. In 1991, Brittan was rehonored and awarded a second five-year term.

The university honors program continued to receive the administration's blessings, and its quality was upgraded immensely by three developments in 1985-1986. One was the creation of twenty new scholarships for incoming freshmen. Recipients did not have to be enrolled in honors, but the large majority were. Called Presidential Scholarships, they provided a four-year grant yielding $1250 per year, renewable to a total of $5000. The scholarships also provided fee waivers. Presidential Scholarship holders enrolled in the honors program could supplement their awards, also on a competitive basis, in the form of University Honors Program Scholarships valued at an additional $500 per year. Funding for Presidential Scholarships was provided by the Phyllis (Beamer) Berger Trust, the extraordinary benefi-

cence of an MSU alumnus originally from Whitehall, who had left the university its largest bequest ever in 1985.

All students enrolled in honors were required to take part in the second major change—a first-year core seminar entitled "Texts and Critics: An Introduction to Knowledge, Love, and Power." Intended as a rigorous and imaginative introduction to university-level studies across the board, Texts and Critics became highly successful. A new set of expanded and improved requirements for an honors degree was also inaugurated. Enrollments in honors mushroomed; in 1985, 139 students representing twenty-four departments were active. Two years later those numbers had increased to over 300 students from forty-three different departments.

A third factor encouraging student participation in university honors was the administration's decision to convert sections of Atkinson Quadrangle, better known as the Quads, to honors use. This was excellent use of space made available by the increasing transfer of resident students (the Quads are dorms) to private accommodations. Honors now had not only an invigorated core curriculum and greatly enhanced scholarship program to attract students, but a classy facility that provided the program with an instructional and residential base and a newfound sense of community. [69]

A Student's Assessment of Honors

In 1988, Edis Schneider, twelve years out of high school—in MSU admissions jargon, a SOTA student, or "student over traditional age"—submitted the following essay in applying for acceptance in the honors program:

I had spend the past 12 years since high school traveling the country, enjoying various experiences. I did everything from herding sheep in Wyoming to working casinos in Las Vegas; I bused tables in Pennsylvania and cleaned barns in Minnesota; I served people drinks in bars and money in banks; I jack hammered concrete on a road construction crew and harvested corn on a farm crew; I drove school buses in New Jersey and tractors in Nebraska; I played with Blue Grass bands in North Carolina and danced the cowboy swing in Montana; I rode English Jumpers in Virginia's hunt country and moved cattle on high western plains; I rafted the Colorado River through the Grand Canyon and hiked the Wind River mountains in the Rockies.

Often I've felt awed and inspired by the beauty of this country. I've also felt frustrations at my own limitations. I sought meaningful employment and instead was handed a shovel or a typewriter. At 30 years old, I've returned to the formal education environment, thrilled with the prospect of exercising my brain as much as I've exercised my limbs in the past. So far school has been everything I'd hoped and more. I enjoy learning; even some of the so-called boring subjects are interesting to me because I can relate them to my life experiences.

I'm finding my base of understanding expanding and that I have more informed opinions about current issues. For instance, classes like Economics and World Regional Geography have allowed me to better understand the various factors that influence the political state of affairs in the Middle East. I also feel my horizons expanding culturally as well as academically. I've attended plays, symphonies, opera, films, etc. My experiences with MSU Chorale has taught me a new appreciation for classical music. I now enjoy a more expanded range of music and theatre.

I'm also feeling frustrations, however . . . . I especially dislike the large lecture classes wherein I am treated as a mindless Freshman with nothing to offer the class. Many times I am instructed by a Teacher's Assistant who clearly is learning from the mistakes he/she makes while teaching us. Particularly disheartening is when only one instructor teaches a required class and I hear nothing but horror stories about his/her teaching techniques.

I'm hoping the Honors Program can alleviate some of the frustrations I'm experiencing. I have taken one class so far: "Creating the World" with Clark Llewellyn and Ralph Johnson. For me the class has been like a first spring flower after a long, cold winter—a wonderful break from the usual regimen. We do a lot of sharing of ideas and brainstorming. I feel like a human being with something to contribute. The readings we do are very thought provoking as well as informative. The instructors seem equally as enthused and each has such interesting experiences and knowledge to share.

I think the Honors program will allow me to get the most out of my time at MSU. My priority is not merely to get a diploma, but to get a worthwhile education while still enjoying the entire learning process. The Honors program seems to promote interest and excellence. As an older student, these qualities remain foremost in importance to me. [1]

The Quad, home of the University Honors Program

1. Undated (1988), 90024/1, "Honors Program" file, MSUA.

Campus politics, having hibernated for a number of years, was in evidence again in 1988 when Bill Tietz and his staff were compelled to schedule a round of visitations with departments across campus to answer to various complaints, most of them stemming from concern over the cutbacks in university appropriations. From most accounts, not a great deal of satisfaction was gathered from these get-togethers; Tietz's old ability to operate flexibly, responsively, and creatively for his faculty's scholarly and research needs and aspirations was more and more circumscribed by revenue shortfalls and by the growing perception that while the president meant well, he simply wasn't able to deliver like he used to. In much the same way that the legislature had constructed in 1981 a base it couldn't sustain, President Tietz had built a base at MSU that was now frayed at the edges.

In 1989 the MSU faculty held another referendum to decide whether to unionize. As they had eleven years before, they again voted resoundingly against collective bargaining. The vote demonstrated anew the antiunion stance of a university dominated by professional schools affiliated with national professional organizations. But the fact that the vote was taken at all is significant, for this time the push for unionization reflected a growing resentment of the president's managerial style.

Controversy surrounding the presidency surfaced again in April 1990 when an audit by the state charged MSU with mishandling nearly $1.2 million in federal grant money. At the root of the problem was the revelation that grantees in certain departments had badly overspent their awards by hundreds of thousands of dollars and that the central administration had not taken appropriate remedial action. One angry legislator went so far as to call the MSU administration's failure to blow the whistle another "Watergate . . . the top people knew for months and months and months and let it go by." [70] It was said that MSU would lose future federal and private grants as a result. Tietz did not believe that, and in the end he proved to be right. But the incident further depreciated MSU's credibility in Helena and on campus. It was obvious that MSU had run up some hefty debts which would have to be serviced at the expense of other programs.

As it turned out, the problem would be bequeathed to a new administration, for Bill Tietz had already concluded that it was time for someone else to take up the challenge. Ever since the commencement of the state's economic decline in the mid-1980s, he had been bucking hard

The Rocket That Almost Wasn't

The Class of '58's rocket

Many have marveled at the striking twenty-foot sculpture shaped in the form of a rocket that inhabits the entrance to campus at the intersection of South 8th and College, but prior to 1990 only a select few knew where it came from and what it meant. In that year a decision by the University Facilities and Planning and Utilization Board brought the rocket and its background into clearer focus when the board and the president's office announced that a decision had been made to destroy the white sculpture with its sky blue letters—MSU.

No way, spoke the graduates of 1958, who weren't about to see their hard-earned memorial to their alma mater and the age of space blasted off into nothingness. A group of them, led by George Mattson, Carol (Mathews) Roehm, and Wayne Gibson raised cain; they recalled the effort they had put into organization, design, and fund-raising and resented MSU's insensitivity to what they had created. They put together an effective petition calling for a halt to such nonsense. Other classmates acted independently, calling in their protests, or writing letters. One of the latter was Forsyth's Wally McRae, one of the West's better known cowboy-poets and longtime benefactor of the Museum of the Rockies.

The rocket's primary value was that it recalled a spectacular year in the history of space. In August of 1957 the Soviets had successfully test-fired the first ICBM and in October had launched Sputnik, the world's first satellite. Despite the successful launching of superior U.S. satellites starting in January of 1958, a concern that the country had somehow allowed a "missile gap" to develop gripped America's conscience and stirred a determination to push hard for improvement in science and technology programs in the nation's schools. One product of that was the National Defense Education Act of 1958, which poured money into training teachers, particularly in science, math, and foreign languages. Understandably, MSC's students emotionalized these developments and the Class of '58 decided to erect a memorial to the promise of American technological and scientific supremacy in the form of a rocket, designed by art students in the shape of a stylized M, and crafted in concrete by students in the College of Engineering. Thirty-two years later the members of that class were not about to allow the university to obliterate what had become, whatever its esthetic value, a part of campus history. They raised a storm of protest. Enough, said central administration. Science and sentiment had proved an unbeatable team. [1]

So the next time you drive up South 8th and pass by that unique sculpture, just think of what history and college spirit, mixed with some wholesome agitation, can do. Don't mess with the alums it says. Get involved, it says—for involvement can be fun—and constructive.

1. *Bozeman Daily Chronicle*, 16 April 1990; interviews with Carol (Mathews) Roehm and Sonny Holland, 9 March 1992; Wayne Gibson, 10 March 1992. The lettering on the rocket originally spelled out MSC, but in 1965, when MSC became MSU, it was a simple matter to turn the "C" on its side.

against burgeoning fiscal restraints and their inexorable impact upon university affairs. Now he was war-weary. More important, he felt he had done much good for the university; he had turned it toward the future, and he felt confident the path he had laid out was the appropriate one. A month before the audit issue became public, Tietz announced his retirement to the college community. "Although we have faced some very difficult times during the last 13 years," he informed a large gathering in the SUB main ballroom, "we have also made tremendous progress. I truly believe that the people of Montana can be proud of Montana State University. Through it all we have not compromised our academic standards." [71]

For all of the decade's problems, Bill Tietz left behind a remarkable and enduring list of achievements. He cited among major rewards his pride in the nationally recognized performance of MSU's students and faculty, the university's research preeminence, and its leadership in the area of state economic development. Ranking equally among his accomplishments, as he himself saw it, were the success of MSU graduates, the services inaugurated for handicapped students, the university's support of Native American studies, and the expansion of its land grant philosophy through technology transfer to all of the people of Montana. He felt strongly about groups which he had helped organize or strengthen, including the Museum of the Rockies, the MSU Foundation, KUSM-Montana Public Television, the Bobcat Boosters, the University Alumni Association, Shakespeare in the Parks, and the Vigilante Players. Tietz drew attention to the physical growth of the campus during his tenure as president. The university arboretum, the visual communications

building, the plant growth center, the laboratory animal facility, the remodeling and expansion of Strand Union, new married-student housing units, and major remodelings of the field house and dormitories were yet other achievements in which he took pride. [72]

Tietz did not claim it, but all of Montana, even those at odds with him, had to admit that he had been the state's major force in higher education throughout the thirteen years of his presidency. Like Roland Renne before him, his staying power and his ability to present his arguments with courage, force, and conviction, earned him respect at every level. Some were put off by his bullishness, but none could question his willingness to take the bull by the horns. His success in aggressively pushing MSU to the forefront in the state's higher education system was openly, and even jealously, recognized. Above all, Tietz's insistence that Montana could not sustain a quality education without radically altering the state's ill-suited public funding base was vindicated repeatedly throughout the decade as Montana fell in ranking against virtually every national funding average. That he did not succeed in effecting necessary change constituted his major disappointment. But it was a shared failure, as every indicator corroborated what Tietz perceived but what the legislative and executive branches could not or would not address.

Strong public validations of his position persisted right to the end of the Tietz administration. In the fall of 1988, as it did every tenth year, the Montana university system had faced another six-mill levy measure, or Referendum 106, as it was known that year. Skeptics who argued that Montanans would not tax themselves for the sake of

Plant Growth Center

higher education were soundly defeated, as every county, and almost two-thirds of the state's voters, approved the measure. Of all counties supporting units in the university system, Gallatin County, MSU's home county, provided the strongest backing, 72.9 percent. Although the county's legislative delegation was still split partywise on matters relating to appropriations for the school, the overwhelming majority of the district's voters were clearly supportive of higher education.

In 1989, a new governor, Stan Stephens, took office and immediately appointed a commission to examine postsecondary education in Montana and to recommend changes for the future. Entitled the "Education Commission for the Nineties and Beyond," its bipartisan and independent membership "held nearly 100 public meetings, visited all campuses, [spoke] with faculty, staff, students and administrators, conducted a statewide poll of Montana citizens, consulted with nationally recognized specialists, and considered hundreds of written comments." [73] The commission's September 1990 report validated much of what Tietz and his administrators had

been arguing for more than a decade. Montanans wanted "more than a collection of separate educational units serving local needs." They wanted an integrated system serving the entire state, "not just those who live near a campus." They didn't want a system "with programs teetering on the edge of minimal standards," but desired "a system with a reputation for high quality." Most important, Montanans had emphasized to the commission that they were "willing to pay for that kind of system." [74]

Unfortunately, Montana's funding system, still beset by poor economic conditions and inadequate revenue, was doing precisely what the commission said the state had to avoid—lowering legislative assistance to a point where the university system was threatened with becoming a mere conglomerate of community colleges, with funding "at about three-quarters of the national average figure." "Montana is at a crossroad," the commission concluded, "but whichever road it chooses, it cannot pursue the present route: hard choices await us. These choices must be confronted." [75]

Native American Studies

A Native American Studies program for Indian college students did not exist in Montana until 1967, when Montana State University president Leon H. Johnson inaugurated a special program to provide "help and guidance" to Indians enrolled at the Bozeman school, and to increase the number of Indians who graduated. Dan Voyich was hired to counsel students in the new program, and Barney Old Coyote (Crow) was hired as the first coordinator. [1] Although Old Coyote's appointment represented the first ever made of a Native American to the administration of an Indian education program at MSC/MSU, concern at the Bozeman school to provide services for Native Americans had been in effect for many decades, as the Smith-Lever Act creating the Cooperative Extension Service required land grant institutions to provide outreach to all residents of the states. This early phase of Indian education was carried on primarily by volunteers on the staff of the college, and represented a labor unsupported by formal programming. It was not an easy task, and would have discouraged less committed servants to the cause. As Martha Harroun Foster points out in her 1990 study of Indian education at MSU, those who engaged themselves in the effort before the late 1960s "struggl[ed] against . . . almost insurmountable odds of Indian poverty and White prejudice and indifference." [2]

Two MSC instructors were conspicuous above all others in their commitment to Indian

education in the decades before the 60s. One was Harriette Cushman, who came to MSC in 1922 from New York and Idaho as one of the nation's few women specialists in agriculture. Cushman became interested in Indian affairs early on when she was required to provide Montana's seven reservations with poultry projects. Her interests were given strong support in 1947 when Verne Dusenberry, an MSC graduate, joined the faculty of the English department. Dusenberry, who was an adopted member of the Pend d'Oreille tribe, had wide

Harriette Cushman and President McIntosh

extracurricular interests, particularly in Indian youth and educational programs. In short order he established MSC's first anthropology program under Merrill Burlingame in the history department, introduced courses on Indian subjects, served as Indian Club advisor, and invigorated the school's Indian affairs program in the Cooperative Extension Service. But Dusenberry died in 1966, and although Cushman continued in her implacable way to attract federal aid for Indian education at MSU, she had retired ten years earlier and was in the twilight of her life. [3]

So it was that Leon Johnson, recognizing the value of Dusenberry's work, and reflecting on the national pressures for minority programs and the availability of federal monies to support them, agreed to the establishment of an educational program for Indians at MSU in 1967. Initially, the program was put under the authority of the International Cooperation Center, administered by Robert Dunbar, professor of history, and one of the campus directors of the Peace Corps training program. As Foster observes, "the irony of being placed in a program with 'foreign' students was not lost on the Indian students"; but the decision to place the program with other bilingual efforts was understandable. The first Indian advisor to the program was Dan Voyich, appointed in 1967 and still in that position today. Voyich has been a Rock of Gibraltar to the program for twenty-five years and is referred to as the "Indian Slav" by the many who hold an affection for him. He received much help in the early days not only from Harriette Cushman, but from Elnora Old Coyote Wright of elementary education and Herbert Kirk, a retired ceramist and philanthropist. [4]

In the five years Barney Old Coyote coordinated the program he barnstormed the state in successful efforts to publicize the MSU program and develop a rapport between the reservations and the Bozeman institution. Ever at the front was Old Coyote's goal—Indian involvement. The program had to be fit to specific Indian needs, he argued. "We wanted to get away from the idea of 'experts' bringing programs to the Indians and deciding what the Indians needed." [5] The result was increasing effectiveness as the state's Indian population developed the trust that was needed to make the program work. When Old Coyote resigned in 1973 to assume the presidency of the Indian Bank of America, there was a recognition that he had done well in meeting his goals, despite the austere budgets of that decade, which had handicapped his efforts.

Robert Peregoy (Flathead), Old Coyote's assistant, took charge in 1974 and was responsible for the creation of the present Center for Native American Studies. Peregoy profited from new sources of federal money for minority programs and the passage in the state legislature of the Indian Culture Master Plan, which, among other things, required that Montana teachers complete six postsecondary educational credits in Indian subjects. As the Indian program now had teaching responsibilities, it was reorganized into the present Center for Native American Studies and shifted from intercultural studies to the College of Letters and Science.

As a consummate writer of grants, Peregoy was able to secure support for numerous programs covering Indian education, health, and cultural awareness. When Peregoy left MSU in 1981 he had established the bulk of the programs that would carry the program through the decade. The best testimony to Peregoy's—and Old Coyote's—success was in the numbers: in 1956, twenty-three Indian students had been enrolled at MSC. Under Old Coyote the number had increased to seventy-six by 1973, and to 208 under Peregoy in 1977.

CNAS fortunes received a terrific boost in 1977 with the appointment of a new president, William Tietz. Tietz had had good experiences with Native Americans at Colorado State, something he was determined to repeat at MSU. First he pumped money and resources into the Indian education program. He had a spacious room in Wilson Hall set aside for Indian Club, he diverted discretionary funds into the annual powwow, and threw his weight into Indian efforts to secure federal and state support. He was also aided by Phyllis Berger, who set aside a significant portion of her bequest for NCAS. Perhaps the most impressive demonstration of Tietz's determination to bring Indians into the university mainstream came when he had them made a part of Montana State's expanded health science and biomedical educational programming. In 1980 MSU tapped into a Minority Research Apprenticeship Program; four years later it secured a Minority Biomedical Research Support grant from the National Institutes of Health. In 1988 the university was awarded another NIH grant to support minority access to research centers. In that same year, MSU's development of a regional health science program included a component devoted to American Indian Research Opportunities. Combining state and federal monies, the total amounted to over $2.4 million in support of Indian education at MSU. [6]

Tietz's unrivaled support for Native Americans drew raves from the Indian community. "Your understanding of the cultural and educational needs of Indian people is most unique among university presidents and I laud

Barney Old Coyote

5th Annual PowWow, 1980

and encourage your continued efforts in support thereof," wrote a former coordinator. [7] Others in the department referred to Tietz as a "hero" and as one of the "most important figures in Indian education in the country." [8] Outsiders registered their own applause. "Montana can take pride in having a college president who is truly interested in the betterment of the educational system and programs for the Indian population," wrote the president of the Montana Indian Education Association. "Many administrators verbalize their concern and desire to promote and pursue relevant programs for the Indian population; few ever actually demonstrate that commitment." [9]

With strong administrative and private support, the CNAS program continued to prosper during the 1980's under Walter Fleming (Kickapoo, Oneida, Cherokee) and director Irvin "Bobby" Wright (Chippewa-Cree). The '80s saw several changes in CNAS administrative personnel, but the presence of Fleming, who filled in several times as acting director, provided the continuity the program needed. One of the successful services Fleming and Wright provided was the creation of a link between MSU and Montana's seven tribal community colleges. Established between 1974 and 1984, the tribal colleges were able to attract growing numbers of students and to bridge two cultures—"teaching tribal history, language and culture as well as math, computers and Shakespeare." From the beginning, MSU's central administration made a formal commitment to the colleges' success. [10]

Other programs instituted during the '80s on the MSU campus to aid Native Americans were the Center for Bilingual/Multicultural Education; the Advance By Choice program and other tutoring services, which gave important assistance to Indian students; the Native American Women's Project, which deals with the needs of Indian women at MSU; and the Native American Task Force, organized to tackle discrimination against minority faculty and students. Yet another program is the International Indian Exchange, energized by Patrick Morris, which arranged student exchanges with Italy, Norway and Sweden.

Perhaps least noted, but exceedingly important for Native American students at MSU, has been the Indian Club room in Wilson Hall. A "home away from home," the room provides an "extended family" atmosphere of great value, especially for rural Indians. MSU's current director of CNAS, Wayne Stein (Turtle Mountain, Chippewa), surmised that likely 50 percent of MSU's Indian students would leave the institution were they to lose that facility. [11]

*Indian Club Room,
Wilson Hall*

The University of Montana has also been successful in educating Native Americans, though Missoula's program puts almost exclusive stress on academics, preparing Indians for careers in law, for example, rather than on practical education and service, the emphasis that pertains at MSU. Important programs also exist at the other branches of learning. Northern Montana's student population is fully 10 percent Native American, and Eastern's is 6 percent. While MSU and UM service a smaller percentage (approximately 2 percent each), their total numbers, roughly 200 to 250 at each institution, exceed Indian student populations at the smaller units.

MSU's commitment to prepare Indians for science continued into the new administration of Michael Malone. In 1991 the National Science Foundation designated MSU as the center of an eight-state regional effort to attract American Indians to scientific careers. A five-year grant totaling $4.6 million, the project was proposed by David Young, coordinator of biomedical research programs at MSU, and Patrick Weasel Head (Blackfeet, Gros Ventre), assistant director of MSU's American Indian Research Opportunities Program. It is the first NSF program to focus on American Indians, and Montana's in-place network of tribal colleges and MSU's strong relationship with them made the Bozeman institution the logical center of administration for the grant. [12]

MSU's success in graduating its Native Americans bears mention. Whereas fifty years ago the prospect for successful matriculation of Indians was virtually zero, today roughly 20 percent who enter MSU graduate— approximately the same average as for the MSU student body as a whole. Instructionally, the impact of the Native American Studies program at MSU has been such that, on the eve of centennial, the administration introduced a fund-raising campaign to endow a professorship in Native American literature. [13] Indian education at Montana State has come a long way since Harriette Cushman visited her first reservation and recognized the need in the early 1920s.

1. This outline of Indian education at MSU is in large part based on a superb 1990 graduate history paper, "Education, Service, Research: Indian Education at Montana State University," by Martha Harroun Foster. Foster's work received high praise from the MSU Native American Studies program; it is based on primary research and extensive interviewing of principal participants.
2. Ibid.
3. Merrill G. Burlingame, "Verne Dusenberry: 1906-1966," from Leslie B. Davis (ed.), *Lifeways of Intermontane and Plains Montana Indians*, Museum of the Rockies Occasional Papers, No. 1 (1979). Cushman crusaded for years after Dusenberry's death to memorialize his work as a fighter for Indian causes in the form of a Museum of the Rockies Plains Indian research center.
4. Foster, "Education, Service, Research."
5. Ibid.
6. "Health Science Programs at Montana State University," 15 June 1988, 90033/11, MSUA.
7. Peregoy to Tietz, 28 April 1983, 87023/7, "General Correspondence" file, MSUA.
8. Foster, "Education, Service, Research."
9. Ed Parisian to Tietz, 20 September 1983, 87023/7, "General Correspondence" file, MSUA.
10. Pamphlet, American Indian College Fund; Foster, "Education, Service, Research."
11. Ibid.
12. *Bozeman Daily Chronicle*, 8 October 1991.
13. Ibid., 5 March 1992.

Toward the Centennial

One less fortunate hold-over from our more remote past is the University's time-worn motto: "Education for Efficiency," This would be better applied to a vo-tech center than a university, and I have ordered it interred. As part of our centennial enterprise, we shall find a better statement of purpose . . . .

In much the same way that this beautiful mountain valley gives life to the headwaters of a great river, I have come to think of Montana State University as the cultural and intellectual headwaters of this Treasure State. And because we are a headwaters, we have a special responsibility that goes far beyond training our graduates to get a job. We strive to instill in these men and women a sense of the principles that bind us together as a nation. . . . Of course, not all our graduates will make history . . . , but as President of this institution, it is my goal that each will be a good citizen. As the headwaters of our mighty Missouri springs forward to nurture and renew vast parts of our nation clear to the sea, so our students must be prepared—each in his or her own way—to help a tired and sometimes frustrated state and nation find a higher path toward a finer day. I want our graduates to leave here with the clear understanding that ethical purpose and the pursuit of knowledge are higher life goals than the pursuit of profit. [76]

John Hutchinson, commissioner of higher education, confers the presidential medallion upon MSU's new president, Michael Malone, 1991

On October 25, 1991, Strand Union Building was the scene of a presidential inauguration, MSU's first in almost half a century. It was a novel experience for the vast majority of the audience, as only a very limited number could recall the last such ritual, a war-delayed ceremony for Roland Renne in 1945. In the interim years, no inaugurals had been held, as presidents Leon Johnson, Carl McIntosh, and William Tietz had declined the pomp and circumstance associated with a formal installation. But the new president was of a different mind, and the inaugural, held in the main ballroom before an estimated 1100 persons, was impressive. A musical fanfare and processional performed by the MSU Wind Ensemble, directed by Jonathan Good, and the University Chorale, directed by Lowell Hickman, ushered in a regalia-clad column of 150 faculty, staff, and notables—including Governor Stan Stephens who had been hassled during the procession from Romney Gym by a small group of students protesting his university budget cuts. Following an invocation by Father Tom Haffey of Resurrection Parish, greetings to the new president were made by representatives of the campus community—Arthur Coffin, president of Faculty Council; Todd Casey, president of ASMSU; Craig Roloff, speaking for university classified and professional staff; and Donald Cheever, president of the MSU Alumni Association. Representing the Montana public was Ivan Doig, the noted Montana author, who creatively linked MSU and its new president with Thomas Jefferson and his ideals. The governor offered brief remarks; William Mathers, chair of the Board of Regents, presented the new president with a bible once owned by MSU's second president, James Reid, and, bestowed in turn to each succeeding president; and John Hutchinson, commissioner of higher education, performed the actual investiture of office, conferring on the president a handsome new presidential medallion cast by Richard Helzer, head of the school of art. Following the new president's inaugural address and a benediction in native tongue by William Tall Bull, a Cheyenne elder and professor at Dull Knife Memorial College, faculty and friends wound their way to Leigh Lounge for an informal reception. That night several hundred enjoyed a sold-out inaugural dinner and danced 'til midnight to the big-band tunes of MSU's Swing Band, directed by Glen Johnston.

The decision to reinstate the inaugural tradition after a half-century hiatus said much about the new president and his philosophy of leadership. Michael P. Malone, MSU's tenth chief executive, was determined that the university forge ahead; that it become, as his immediate predecessor had envisioned, a progressive institution. Malone's determination to cast off the school's old motto, Education for Efficiency, as represen-

Michael P. Malone, president of MSU, 1991-

talked about new electronic delivery systems that would "revolutionize" off-campus instruction and about KUSM Public Television and the Museum of the Rockies as major outreach agencies. And he talked about MSU's unrivaled position as the state institution best suited to lead in economic-development initiatives recommended by the governor and the state's congressional delegation. This inaugural was not only a signal for change but a reminder of the significance of established traditions and responsibilities. [77]

Michael Malone was born in 1940 in Pomeroy, Washington, a tiny agricultural town situated among the rolling hills contiguous to the Idaho panhandle. After graduating from Gonzaga University in Spokane, he flirted with law, but then gravitated to his real love, history, and earned a Ph.D. in American Studies from Washington State University. Following a year at Texas A&M, he came to MSU in 1967 as the successor to the legendary Merrill Burlingame. Less than two years later, Malone's first publication, *The Montana Past: An Anthology*, coedited with Richard Roeder, was adopted for classroom use. The following year his dissertational study of Idaho and the New Deal was published. This book was succeeded by *Montana: A History of Two Centuries* (1976), also coauthored with Richard Roeder, and *The Battle for Butte: Mining and Politics on the Northern Frontier, 1864-1906* (1981). His expanding interests then resulted in *Historians and the American West* (1983). In 1989 his sixth book, *The American West: A Twentieth Century History*, coauthored with Richard Etulain, was nominated for a Pulitzer prize and was the History Book Club's main Christmas selection for that year. On the eve of his inaugural, yet another major work was in the offing, a biography of the great western empire builder, James J. Hill. This body of work had earned him status as one of the nation's premier historians of the American West.

Malone's prolificacy was all the more remarkable when one considers that for the better part of his employment at MSU he was an administrator as well as a teacher. The transition from full-time teaching took place in 1975 when he became head of his department. Then in 1979 he moved up to the graduate school as dean. Between 1984 and 1990 he served as acting academic vice president on three separate occasions. During these years he also served as president of the Montana Historical Society and as a founder and first executive director of MSU's Burton K. Wheeler Center, a foundation created by the former Montana senator's family to foster discussion of public policy issues pertinent to Montana and the Northern Rockies. Upon Bill Tietz's resignation, Malone was appointed by the Board of Regents to serve as acting president of MSU, and was subsequently selected from a large list of candidates to become the school's tenth chief executive.

tative of conditions no longer applicable, was one measure of that determination. At the same time, Malone made clear in the inaugural address that he was determined to continue the university's double commitment to instruction and research and to its land grant mission. He talked about plans to create a new architectural unity and improved public image for the university campus in the form of a centennial mall, about public seminars to increase human interrelationships, about his dedication to MSU's Native American studies programs, about his determination to improve the university's relationship with Montana's agricultural community. He talked about improvements in undergraduate instruction and student advising, and about the need to find a "balance between teaching and research," achieving a "maximum symbiosis between the two at the undergraduate as well as the graduate level." He

Michael Malone's attachment to Montana's development and the important role MSU played in it as the state's land-grant institution weighed heavily on his mind, and one his first actions was to visit the university's agricultural experiment stations at Lewistown, Winnett, Malta, Glasgow, Culbertson, and Sidney. This was an important statement on Malone's part; he was determined to demonstrate that MSU cared about its ties with the land.

Malone's plans to fashion a brighter future for MSU were engaging and ambitious, but they had to share attention at the outset with some pressing administrative issues. One of these was the conversion of the Montana university system from quarters to semesters. While Montana Tech and Western already operated on a semester calendar, Eastern, Northern, and the two universities adhered to the old quarter system. Talk at MSU about converting to semesters had come up as early as the McIntosh years. A poll taken by student affairs in 1975 revealed mixed results; faculty, staff, and administration were virtually deadlocked on the vote, but the students opposed it 3-to-2. [78] A decade went by without much further discussion. Then in 1987, following a national trend, the Montana Board of Regents began a serious study of the feasibility of a state-wide conversion. A directive ordering the conversion was issued early in 1988. MSU, with acting graduate dean Henry Parsons in charge, moved rapidly to implement the transition by the appointed date—fall 1991. In contrast to MSU, where protest was minimal, at UM opponents of the semester system were far greater in number and much more vocal. One outcome was regental dispensation given to the Missoula campus to delay implementation of the semester system until 1992, one full year after MSU's conversion.

Objection to the semester system was not taken capriciously; there was serious reason to prefer the long-established quarter system. The transition to semesters, for example, would result in far fewer class offerings, increases in class size, and high conversion costs. At MSU there was much concern, moreover, that the transition would cause difficulty for the just-implemented core curriculum. In addition, the quarter system, with its late September commencement and early June dismissal, was far better suited to Montana's climate and seasonal employment than a system that started in August and ended in May.

But advocates for change had counter-arguments. They maintained, for example, that with semesters faculty preparation time was reduced as was the number of exams to be graded. A semester, they pointed out, allowed students more time to assimilate data and more time to arrive at understandings. Also, textbook costs would be reduced, transfers made easier (since most colleges and universities in the nation were on semester systems),

and as the early semester system coincided more closely with public school schedules, student teachers would be better served.[79] Athletic departments at both universities also favored conversion, as the students would now be able to attend early home football games, formerly played to half-empty stands. In any event, debate was concluded with the regents' decision; a last-minute effort by UM in early 1991 to throw out the whole idea failed.

Thus do the patterns of the past change. On August 26, 1991, following four days of orientation and registration, classes began at MSU almost a full month in advance of the familiar late-September commencement. Although MSU made the transition to semesters with relative ease and in keeping with the Board of Regents' deadlines, UM's ability to postpone its conversion until 1992 undoubtedly had some impact on enrollment patterns at the two universities. Whether UM officials had this in mind when they requested permission to put off conversion is not clear. What is clear is that UM's enrollments went up significantly in fall 1991, while MSU's declined. When enrollments were tallied in September, for the first time since the mid-1970s the University of Montana had the larger student body—10,700 to 10,100. Analysts of the situation cautioned against a hypothesis based purely on transfers from MSU to UM because of the semester conversion, pointing out that UM's central administration, smarting from the drastic student declines of the 1970s, had recruited heavily with much success during the following decade. In any event, the unexpected switch in enrollment patterns became quite significant when the Board of Regents, in January 1992, ordered the entire university system to freeze the upcoming 1992-1993 enrollments at the fall 1991 levels.

The regental decision to freeze enrollments had been in the making for some time. But its major impetus came from a new fiscal crisis associated with the 1991 legislative session. After all monies had been allocated for state services, Governor Stephens revealed new data forecasting a major shortfall in tax revenues, and he ordered a rescinding of many millions in these appropriations, including $13 million from higher education. This created a crisis reminiscent of the 1986-1987 period. Antagonism toward these belated cuts was intense, as it was obvious that the governor had exceeded his constitutional authority. When the Board of Regents, composed mostly of Stephens appointees, proved unwilling to challenge the governor, a citizens coalition principally composed of and funded by the MSU Associated Students and members of MSU's Faculty Council, and driven by a member of the Board of Public Education, Alan Nicholson, sued Montana's chief executive in the fall of 1991. The coalition won its case in the courts and achieved part of its objective when the governor called a special legislative session. In that session, the legislature reduced the executive cut by several millions, but the outcome pleased few. In order to raise monies for state services, the legislature had dipped deeper and deeper into its reserves, borrowing from here and taking from there. If ever a legislature resorted to piecemeal funding, the special 1992 special session provided the model. Proposals for a meaningful resolution to the state's impending bankruptcy were, predictably, not taken up.

Stan Stephens, governor of the state of Montana, 1988-1992

The regental call for downsizing the system followed logically from the fiscal crisis. Adopting the recommendations of the Education Commission for the Nineties and Beyond, and reflecting the inability of the state to appropriate sufficiently, or tax properly, for higher education, the regents concluded that the only way the state could afford excellence would be to downsize the system—to require the universities and colleges to cut back enrollments to the number they could actually afford to educate at desirable levels with available funds. Since in 1991 the state was willing, or able, to provide only 75 to 80 percent of the revenues required by peer-analysis formula, the logical move was to downsize the system proportionately. Accordingly, the Board of Regents mandated a five-year plan to shrink all university system campuses to match actual budgets, or to put it another way, to match those dollars available to ensure quality educational conditions.

On paper, the cuts would be dramatic. MSU's enrollments would be reduced by 19.8 percent, UM's by 27.6 percent, EMC's by 16.8 percent, Northern's by 14.3 percent, and Western's by 6.3 percent. Montana Tech would be the biggest loser at 40 percent. But the regents did not intend to mandate a "straight-forward, simplistic, crude and clumsy reduction" in student numbers. Each campus would have free rein to chose its own downsizing method. There would be no requirement, for example, that the universities make their adjustment solely by cutting enrollment. Increasing tuition, raising admissions requirements, rearranging programs, finding other funding sources, or reevaluating comparisons with peer colleges in the region were all possibilities. [80] In other words, a combination of increasing tuition and finding alternative funding sources would enable an institution to maintain enrollments larger than those predicted by pure percentages. That lessened the threat that MSU might have to cut back to as few as 7500 students.

President Malone took these developments in stride. MSU did not want to be a party to yet another student tuition increase, nor did it delight at regental hints at higher admissions requirements for the two universities. Central administration also harbored serious doubts as to whether the legislature would fund higher education at the same level once the university system made its adjustments. Malone had talked with members of the legislature and could get no promises. [81] The new president was also mindful that MSU's physical plant had been built to accommodate a fairly large enrollment. As he expressed it, "We are a better campus at a little over 10,000, although we are fiscally happier at over 11,000." [82]

Whether intended or not, downsizing was closely linked with a disturbing new phenomena—the growing exodus of Montana's students to out-of-state schools. Since the mid-1980s, more and more of Montana's high school graduates had been enrolling in out-of-state colleges and universities. Statistics released in the summer of 1991 revealed, for example, that an all-time-high 26 percent of Montana's high school students were enrolling out of state. This was a reflection of both intensified recruiting by out-of-state schools and of bad publicity related to the decline of Montana's support for higher education. The relationship between student exodus and hard times for Montana's system of higher education was irrefutable. [83] The figures were especially depressing when related to the state's best students. A late 1991 poll released by the Board of Public Education indicated that only 21 percent of the state's top-ranked high school students were committed to a Montana college or university, while 42 percent intended to leave. The remaining 31 percent were undecided. [84]

Unquestionably, downsizing would impact enrollments. But which way wasn't clear, as there were two sides to this coin. On the one side, downsizing suggested a reduction of every aspect of an institution's instructional and research capability and might hasten the exodus. On the other side, an argument could be made that downsizing would stem it. This position held that a sensible way to keep Montana's best and brightest was to improve the university system's educational quality. A downsizing philosophy might accomplish that.

MSU's central administration was sensitive to both arguments. But it was much more comfortable with the logic of quality in ample, rather than, minimal, numbers. Extremely confident that it could maintain higher levels of enrollment by supplementing MSU's budget with private and federal support, it pushed ahead. A privately endowed chair in American history and literature honoring the great western author Wallace Stegner was announced in the spring of '92. A significant endowment in support of MSU Libraries accompanied the award. The new administration's commitment to the long-held dream of the '80s, the construction of a $22 million engineering, physical sciences, and research complex, was finally approved for state funding, with groundbreaking announced for mid-1993 and completion for 1995. The new building would replace old Ryon Lab and rearrange many of the research facilities in other campus buildings. As one of its promoters remarked, "[The building] will be able to accomodate research that is not even pronounceable today." [85]

MSU had every reason to construct such a complex. In 1990, for example, the National Science Foundation awarded a five-year $7.5 million grant to MSU to establish an engineering research center for biological and chemical study of industrial and environmental problems. This only presaged another achievement: the following year NSF rated MSU's research effort ninety-first out of 595 public universities. This marked the first time MSU had broken into the top 100. (Missoula, by contrast, ranked 148th.) MSU physics and chemistry fared even better, ranking seventy-fourth and eighty-eighth, respectively, which standing placed them in the company of such institutions as the University of Nebraska and Iowa State. [86] Montana State University, with almost $20 million in annual federal and private grant support, in addition to another $10 million received by the agricultural and engineeering experiment stations, was determined to strengthen its reputation and its ability to serve the public by greatly improving its research capacity.

This held as well for MSU's Tech Park and the Research and Development Institute. As Robert Swenson, new research vice president, expressed it, "A university's distinguishing characteristic—the creation of knowledge—bears with it a public trust to transmit that knowledge." The new engineering and physical science complex, Tech Park, and RDI were important parts of both MSU's and the state's concern to "target technology transfer as a critical component in strengthening Montana's economy." [87] The development and maintenance of these MSU services was hardly compatible with the philosophy of downsizing, yet the university could not envision cutting back its research program. Research at MSU was alive and well, and the state legislature and executive branches, in giving the go-ahead for the new engineering complex, were in full agreement, even while they provided funds for other educational needs only grudgingly.

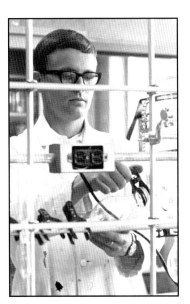

The Research Spirit

Few could have put the significance of research to Montana State University so succinctly as did John Jutila, who presided over its spectacular growth as vice president for research, 1977-1990. On his retirement, Jutila left this poignant tribute to the inquisitive spirit on the Bozeman campus:

> Montana State University has evolved from a small, relatively unremarkable university to a highly respected institution known for its clusters of outstanding programs and for a general excellence among the faculty that surprises those who evaluate us. This distinction has been accomplished at a time of scarce resources and in a state environment that would have discouraged a lesser

institution. How does one explain, then, such an amazing growth in the intellectual quality of a university?

The answer is found, I am convinced, in the character of the faculty and the spirit of inquiry that leads to the discovery of truth. In other words, this growth is attributable to something more than the normal drive for scholarly achievement. The spirit of MSU's research and creative efforts has had qualities of entrepreneurship, unselfishness, energy and commitment that exceed what I have observed in the faculties of many other campuses. It is truly remarkable and drives the entire institution towards excellence. [1]

1.   MSU Report on Research, 1989.

As much as Mike Malone was determined to give attention to research, his commitment to instruction was every bit as intense. "A lot of people would tell you research has been emphasized at the expense of instruction," he remarked when the university's NSF ranking was announced. "I wouldn't go that far. I think the whole point of research is [that] good research and good instruction go together."[88]

Evidence was abundant that MSU's instructional capabilities could produce students with

MSU's 1992 USA Today All-Academics, Sonja Short, Andy Bayramian, and Jan Wright

national rankings, just as its research labs merited national attention. During the1980s, MSU undergrads had succeeded in winning recognition for extraordinary scholarly achievement based on research initiatives. In the four years preceding the centennial year, eleven MSU students won prestigious Truman or Goldwater scholarships, a figure topped in the nation only by Harvard University's thirteen. Then in 1991, Jeff Kommers and Jennifer DeVoe were honored as two of *USA Today's* All-USA College Academic Team, which honored the top twenty undergraduates in America. A third MSU student, Jan Wright, made the third team. The following year, MSU placed two more in the top twenty, Jan Wright and Andy Bayramian, while Sonja Short was selected for the second team. The honor gave MSU a unique distinction: "No other school has ever had six people make [the team]," *USA Today's* education editor reported. "No school has had two people make first team in consecutive years." Even Harvard couldn't compete with that achievement.[89] All five of MSU's best and brightest were enrolled in the honors program and were MSU presidential scholars, and their majors—physics (2), chemical engineering/political science, nursing, and pre-health (a conglomerate of disciplines)—underlined the extraordinary quality of MSU's instructional capabilities across the board.

A Student Profile on the Eve of the Centennial

In the fall of 1991, the most significant change in the MSU student body reflected not only a sizeable decrease in students generally, but a very visible decline in in-state enrollment, and a marked increase in out-of-state enrollment. The old 82-83 percent instate enrollment figure that had held for decades had decreased precipitously to 76 percent. MSU continued to enroll more students than any other university-system school in thirty-five of the state's fifty-six counties—and was second in enrollments in eighteen of the remaining twenty-one counties. But this was down from 1980 when MSU led in forty-one counties and came in second in all the rest. A profile of county representation in the early '90s demonstrated that Montana's students were in increasing numbers matriculating at the unit closest to them, convincing testimony to the state's depressed economies.[1]

The current 24 percent out-of-state enrollment constitutes, then, the largest MSU non-Montana enrollment ever. Of the 24 percent, 21 percent come from the states, 3 percent from foreign countries. The bulk of the out-of-state non-foreign students come from, understandably, Wyoming (321); less obviously, Minnesota ranks second (214). States supplying more than 100 students are Colorado, Washington, North Da-

kota, Alaska, California, and Idaho—in that order. Only one state isn't represented—Mississippi. Out-of-state statistics are impacted by MSU's membership in WUE (Western Undergraduate Exchange), which enables students at WUE-affiliated states from the Mississippi River to the Pacific Coast to attend MSU at one-half again the fee charged an in-state student. This has the excellent result of bringing in a wider range of students who have much to offer in the way of cultural cross-fertilization. But WUE, which has supplied nine percent of MSU's enrollment in 1991-1992 (933 students), is under fire on the eve of the school's centennial, its preferential fee structure criticized by revenue raisers and the state's taxpayers who resent subsidizing non-residents. The mandate issued by the Board of Regents to downsize the university system also impacts WUE's prospects for survival, and it appears probable that this program may be killed for fiscal rather than educational reasons.

A breakdown of the 3 percent foreign student enrollment reveals significant differences from that of 1980. At the beginning of the '80s, MSU enrolled approximately 100 foreign students, who constituted less than 1 percent of the student body. Roughly 50 percent of this 1 percent were from Canada, while the remainder were from Taiwan, India, the Middle East (mostly Iran), and Norway. During the decade, then, the Middle Eastern and Norwegian students left to be replaced mostly by Malaysians, and by a growing number of Chinese students, more of whom now come from the mainland than from Taiwan. In the fall of 1991, of MSU's 257 foreign students, 30 percent came to Bozeman from Canada, 17.5 percent from India, and 16 percent from the People's Republic of China, while the remaining 36.5 percent came from fifty different countries, the largest contingent of which was only five in number. Except for the Canadian enrollment, the foreign makeup of MSU's student population reflects governmental support established in Washington D.C. with other world capitals . While some foreign students are beginning to look at MSU's film and television offerings, the vast majority came to Bozeman for physics, chemistry, computer science, and engineering.

Students over traditional age, or SOTAs, did not changed significantly in number over the previous decade, and the average age of MSU's student body continues to hover around 25. Enrollment by sex has also been constant in its ratio—55 percent male to 45 percent female. A small number, twenty-nine, of MSU students are actually studying elsewhere, enrolled in the National Student Exchange program. Another twenty-two are overseas on international exchanges spread out among thirteen nations, with small concentrations in the United Kingdom, Australia, and the Netherlands.

The most recent attitudinal study of MSU's student body covered freshmen entering the school in the fall of 1989. This was the class of '93—the centennial graduating class. Politically, better than 50 percent of these young men and women identified themselves as "middle-of-the-road," but differed left and right of center, with more men favoring conservative causes than women, and more women claiming liberal interests than men (about 10 percent each way). Twenty years before a much larger number of incoming freshmen males had claimed liberal leanings. On social matters, approximately two-thirds of '93's class, both men and women, favored the legalization of abortion, but they were much cooler toward the legalization of marijuana than were their peers of twenty years before. Opposition to the death sentence had also waned. Predictably, for every female opposing premarital sex, two men did not oppose it. On ecological matters, roughly 85 percent of both men and women believed that state and federal governments were not doing

enough to clean up the environment. These patterns reflected what one might expect nationally from a small state university with a large rural base. [2]

Although motives for choosing MSU were exceedingly hard to define, the largest justification of the incoming freshmen of '89-'90 cited MSU's academic reputation and the encouraging employment record of its graduates—motivations that had not changed measurably from the previous decade. The courses of study enrolled in by all of MSU's students said much about MSU's educational emphasis: [3]

Engineering	1858
Letters & Science	1761
Education, Health & Human Development	1186
Business	1106
Graduate Studies	1033
Arts & Architecture	1032
Nursing	567
Agriculture	<u>553</u>
	10,111

On campus, students could hardly complain of being bored. Ten fraternities and four sororities provided homes away from homes for 8 percent of the student body. The majority contributed regularly to a variety of campus and community service and charitable undertakings. Campus honoraries, like the scholastic honorary Phi Kappa Phi, and a host of disciplinary honoraries, societies, and clubs kept students engaged. Student government offered numerous outlets for the politically zealous. On-campus social events were staged so regularly one could hardly keep up with them. The Procrastinators, a group out of media and theatre arts, sponsored economical films in the newly refurbished Linfield Hall auditorium. ASMSU was strong into entertainment, bringing in big-name attractions on a regular basis. KGLT, the Associated Students' alternative public radio station, had developed into one of the finest in the Northern Rockies. The *Exponent* continued to cover the news capably and engagingly. For those desiring high-class culture, MSU's theatre arts department offered stage performances of the first order, and in Howard Hall, music department concerts, many of them free of charge, took place sometimes three to four nights a week. *Infinity*, the student literary magazine, catered to yet another interest.

For those who needed to work off energies, the Marga Hosaeus Health and P.E. Center had many activities, and even more users—

Floating the Madison

In the field

so many that it looked on occasion like New York's Broadway at rush hour. SOB Barn contained a wealth of outdoor equipment for reasonable rental fees. In good weather the university's intramural fields were literally overrun with competitors. Car-aficionados could work up a sweat at the student auto repair facility. The more sedate could enrich themselves by browsing in the student-owned bookstore. If students couldn't find an organization to meet their needs—a rare event—they formed their own. Finally, of course, the Strand Union Building and Renne Library each offered amusements of a special sort. The campus was a dynamic place, to say the least. And we havn't even considered the offerings of the Bozeman community as a whole, with its own organizations—cultural, religious, recreational, and educational.

MSU's graduates at the start of the '90s—at least those who took jobs or went to graduate school—leaned heavily toward business and industry, education, and government or military employment. From the class of '91, forty eight percent went into business or industry, 22 percent into education, and 13 percent took jobs with the government or pursued military careers. Almost half of the class managed to find employment in Montana, another 12 percent in Washington, and 6 percent in California. Better than one-third obtained their jobs through MSU Career Services or department and faculty contacts. Interestingly, the single largest employer of MSU graduates was Boeing Aircraft in the state of Washington. Those who determined to further their education could be found at the nation's finest graduate schools—from Princeton to Cal-Berkeley and from Wisconsin to Texas. [4]

A not insignificant number of graduates, sixteen, had been accepted by the Peace Corps and were assigned to such third world countries as Belize, Bolivia, Botswana, Costa Rica, Ecuador, Gabon, Honduras, Hungary, Kenya, the Marshall Islands, and Paraguay. Half of the sixteen had teaching degrees in various subjects, while the others possessed backgrounds in business, bee keeping, crop extension, forestry, health and human development, parks and wildlife, small animal husbandry, and water and sanitational engineering.

In yet other ways Montana State University's students have done more than merely graduate; they have become contributors to society in a big way. For instance, if you have been hospitalized recently, chances are an MSU-trained nurse attended to your needs; if you have required tax assistance recently, chances are an MSU-trained accountant provided the service; if you have enjoyed a meal recently, chances are the grains, dairy products, and meats were produced by an MSU-trained agriculturalist; if you enjoyed a drive through the country recently, chances are that an MSU-trained civil engineer designed, surveyed, and assisted in the construction of the road. Extend this list to teachers, architects, physicians, dieticians, veterinarians, wildlife management specialists, horticulturalists, bankers, businesspeople, government officials . . . . Well, you get the idea.

In 1972, then-president Carl McIntosh spoke of a higher mission when he addressed that year's graduating class. "We ask that you respect the people of Montana who established and who have maintained this University," McIntosh told the graduates, "and if you have the chance to enhance their lives or welfare, do not neglect the opportunity to do so." [5] MSU's students have more than lived up to that charge.

1. Comparison of Montana University System Autumn 1980 and 1990 Enrollments by County, as figured from enrollment reports provided by the Office of the Commissioner of Higher Education.
2. "Montana State University: Trends for 1971-1989," courtesy of Rolf Groseth (vice president for student affairs). For additional data for this profile the author is indebted to Celia Allard and Stephanie Becker, representing administration and international affairs respectively.
3. "Montana State University: Facts and Figures, 1991-1992."
4. "Summary of 1990 Graduate Survey," MSU Career Services. That only half of MSU's graduates remained in Montana matches almost precisely the percentage for the late '60s and early '70s. See Paul E. Polzin, "Why They Leave," *Montana Business Quarterly* (Autumn, 1972), 11-38.
5. Commencement remarks, 10 June 1972, "1972" file, MSUA.

Student honors were inextricably connected with faculty guidance. Despite arguments nationally that higher educational instruction had seriously degenerated, was "Killing the Spirit" or bringing about a "Closing of the American Mind," as critics Page Smith and Allan Bloom contended, MSU's faculty could demonstrate innumerous success stories that belied these contentions. [90] Critics who asserted that America's university system failed to reward, and even penalized, those who took teaching too seriously, would find few believers in MSU's classrooms. Research, while increasingly emphasized as a positive measure of faculty worth, was seen at MSU as interrelated with good instruction, not separate from it. The Burlington Northern Foundation Faculty Achievement and Phi Kappa Phi awards for teaching excellence were as coveted as the Wylie award for outstanding accomplishments in faculty research.

Faculty also demonstrated a slow but steady progress toward the assumption of decision-making responsibility in university affairs. In the late 1970s faculty had complained of having little input in the formulation of university policy. To some extent this was still true. On the eve of the centennial, a faculty senate, such as existed at UM, was still nonexistent. And the administratively appointed planning and priorities committee put in place in 1986 had been disbanded once Tietz felt its immediate mission had been accomplished. On the other hand, a faculty council had replaced the university council, and promotion and tenure decisions were firmly in the hands of the faculty. So was educational policy. The level of participation in governance throughout the faculty was up measurably. For example, whereas fifteen years prior, research policy and fund allocation had been the sole prerogative of the research vice president, in 1992 a faculty-composed university research committee made these decisions. University governance was moving slowly, but firmly, in favor of increased faculty input. [91]

One measure of the caliber of MSU's faculty was its marketability. Actually, this was both good and bad. It was good because the instructional staff had a wide reputation and was sought after nationally, bad because it was hard to maintain such quality when other institutions could offer salaries at 10 to 30 percent higher than those offered at MSU. The institution had to struggle to retain its best in the midst of Montana's depressed economic climate and the state's continued inability to adequately fund the university system. This applied as well to MSU's faculty recruiting program. It might have been worse were MSU not blessed with quality students, quality faculty, and a most beautiful natural environment, characteristics that worked against the dispersion of faculties occurring at other hard-pressed institutions. But there was a limit to institutional endurance, and the continuation of hard times promised to make the school's effort to attract and hold good students and faculty, not to say staff, a problem of ever-magnifying proportions.

The continued success of MSU would depend not only on the resources granted it by the state, but on the strength of the relationship between school and state. All knew, as one legislator made clear, that "there are no great universities run by governors or budget analysts or legislators." [92] At the same time, it was fully understood that a state university that lacked a commitment to its public funding sources would evolve toward self-interest rather than public interest. Michael Malone seemed to have a grasp of these realities as MSU embarked upon its second century:

> It is as true today as it was 100 years ago, at the time of its birth, that there is really only one way to understand Montana State University, its mission, its role and scope. That is in the context of the State of Montana. The University, of course, relies upon the state for its sustenance, although this reliance has often been an insecure one. Less obviously, the state has relied upon the University—for educational opportunities for its citizens, and for the basic research and development that are so vital to its economy. This mutual dependence has never been greater than it is today, and if Montana is to escape its spiral decline in the spectrum of American states, this institution must play a key role. [93]

MSU graduation, 1991

Chapter Eight
Sport as Symbol

Shaping the Tradition

"I don't care what you think," argued a UM administrator's wife in 1979, "student enrollments at Bozeman and Missoula are determined by who wins the Bobcat-Grizzly football game." [1]

This lamentation, uttered in distress at MSU President Bill Tietz's home after a UM 21-38 grid loss to the Bobcats, the seventh loss in the decade, and coupled with, if not caused by, a disappointing drop in enrollments at Missoula, reflects the remarkable degree of competitive emotion this contest generates off the field as well as on. How many have heard fans, players, coaches, perhaps even regents and legislators, remark that no matter how good or bad a season might be, its outcome would be measured by who emerged victorious in the annual intrastate struggle! There are, to be sure, not a few who could condone a virtually winless season as long as their team prevailed in The Game; it wouldn't be idle talk to say that the contest breeds a degree of intensity bordering on the fanatic. Fan turnouts for football and basketball contests between the two schools are remarkable, often 50 percent and better over customary attendance, and it might be said with some validity that, at least in football, the capacities of Sales and Washington stadiums were designed not for regular season games, but for the single crowd that fills each only once every other year—the big one between the Cats and the Griz.

The "Aggies" in action at the turn-of-the-century

While among the coaching staffs many refer to "Save Your Job Week," there isn't much evidence that any recent prexy in Bozeman or Missoula has put inordinate pressure on his football staff to win the big one "or else." At least none seem to have taken seriously the prescription of acting MSU President Bill Johnstone at the 1969 Cat-Griz booster breakfast when he advised head coach Tom Parac that if he didn't win, there was a train leaving town at 9 p.m. and that he and his assistants had better be "under it." [2] Nevertheless, one has to sympathize with the president who informed his grid staff that it would sure make it a lot easier on him during the banquet circuit and legislative session if MSU could pull off a victory. Because the outcome of the game does have a tendency to govern the rights of the winning institution to make claims of excellence in other fields as well as sport, one can indeed conceive of enrollments as tied to athletic prowess.

All of this is overdone, of course. State collegiate rivalries are legendary across the country, and Montanans' claim to uniqueness in this regard is possibly as much a reflection of our geographic and informational isolation as it is our propensity for thinking of ourselves as out of the ordinary. And most Montana high schools graduates are far too sophisticated, one likes to believe, to allow a single football contest to determine their collegiate preferences. Still, the enthusiasm generated by the contest is, unquestionably, healthily invigorating, and the contest itself is one of the state's annual "events." Let an MSU representative mosey into virtually any town in Montana at virtually any time of the year, and after a few cosmetic remarks covering the weather, conversation will invariably turn to speculation, perhaps even a wager, on the outcome of the upcoming Bobcat-Grizzly game. Athletic directors at both MSU and UM aver that if all those who desired a seat were to be accommodated, the stadiums in Bozeman and Missoula would have to be expanded sizably.

All of this intensity has come a long way—from when enrollments in Bozeman were, at the turn of the century, less than a hundred and teams played at the county fairgrounds on the north side of town, to the late 1940s when student figures reached 3000 and competition took place in Romney Gym and mostly wooden Gatton Field, to today's figures of 10,000-plus students with copious seating in Breeden Field House and Sales Stadium. The Bobcat sporting tradition is the product of many years.

In 1897 the Montana State "Aggies," as they would be known until 1916, inaugurated the school's intercollegiate athletic program with grid losses to Butte High and the university in Missoula.

The 1905 MSC football team

quired athletes to be legitimate students, the early years of intercollegiate athletics in Montana were not so rigidly governed. Football coaches, some of them professionally employed by the college, were expected to play one or more positions, and, when the occasion called for it, "ringers" were recruited to increase chances of success. There also seemed to be no limitation on the number of years of eligibility. The famous Flaherty family sent six sons to MSC, five of whom played varsity football. Two of them, Will (an outstanding end) and Charles (the team's quarterback), each played six straight years. [4] Although an MSC rule of 1901 banned nonmatriculated students from athletic participation, and expected the same from its opponents, the rule was not always taken seriously. In 1904, the university in Missoula, having lost five consecutive years to MSC, turned the tables, 79-0, allegedly with the aid of professionals. Presumably, the formation of the new Northwest Intercollegiate Association in 1905, which MSC joined, would eliminate such practices, but in the very same year MSC was charged with using four ineligible players in the Utah State game. When, in protest, the remaining players refused to show up for the next contest—a Thanksgiving Day encounter with Missoula—a faculty committee abolished MSC football for two years. Slowly but surely MSC athletics, paralleling national patterns, was coming under institutional control. [5]

The first victory that season came over Helena High School, 8-0. It was not unusual for the college to play high schools; a number of them had larger enrollments than MSC, and the competition served the Bozeman school well for recruiting and public relations purposes. Enthusiasm for sport was intense from the start, enough to prompt the first editor of the *Exponent* to caution that "athletics [should] not be encouraged to such an extent that the acquisition of knowledge shall be materially impaired." [3]

Rules and regulations governing participation in athletics were few and far between. Although in the 1890s many eastern schools had barred professionals from competition and re-

In 1908 football was started up again from scratch with poor results. Over a four-year period the team had a record of 4-11-4. When in the middle of the 1911 season MSC suffered a 97-0 loss to Utah and player Charles Lange died of injuries received in the season's opener against the School of Mines, the student body voted to cancel the remaining games. In the meantime a quarter-mile, on-campus cinder track enclosing a football and baseball field had been built, including a grandstand for 500, some of the costs of which were covered by community contributions and student fees. In 1915 MSC's grid fortunes took a turn for the better when Bozeman's Cyrus Gatton starred at halfback. The next year, Gatton, 145 pounds of muscle and inspiration, was voted team captain, but he transferred to the University of Wisconsin. When the United States declared war in 1917, Gatton enlisted in the air force and served in France, where he was killed in aerial combat only a week before the armistice. Although Gatton had left MSC, his class, the class of 1917, later persuaded the college to name the athletic field in his memory.

An early MSC baseball team

Gatton Field Court

BOZEMAN (3/6/72)—Gatton field, Montana State University's football stadium for 40 years, has disappeared from campus. First to go were the temporary bleachers. Then the cement and steel grandstand was torn down. . . . Any day now equipment will be moved onto the old playing field and work will begin on a new health and physical education center. [1]

fall of 1913 and quickly established himself in four sports—football, baseball, basketball, and track. In three of these sports he served as captain. In 1916 Gatton transferred to the University of Wisconsin, and then volunteered for the army when the United States entered the war in April 1917. Subsequently, he was trained in the air corps and flew over two

Gatton Field, 1971, with Romney Gym in the background

Today, at the university's centennial, all that physically remains of four decades of sporting memories, some of them absolutely remarkable, is Gatton Field Court, composed of the original brick-arched gateway and a more recently constructed monument, all situated about fifty yards east of where the main grandstand formerly stood. The two plaques bolted onto the monument warrant inspection. One is dedicated not only to "that host of athletes who participated here over the years," but very specifically to the memory of MSC and MSU athletes "who gave their lives for their country" in World War II and beyond. Poignant are the memories associated with those losses. Perhaps one stands out especially—the loss during World War II of thirteen members of the MSC football teams of 1940 and 1941: Orin Beller, Newell Berg, Dana Bradford, John Burke, Bernard Cluzen, William Coey, Karl Fye, John Hall, Joseph McGeever, John Phelan, Richard Roman, Wendell Scabad, and Alton Zempel. The extent of this loss was traumatic beyond the norm, and received national attention when several of the nation's top sportscasters picked it up, including Bill Stern who made these MSC athletes his "All-American Football Team of 1944."

The second plaque is dedicated to the old field's namesake, Cyrus J. Gatton, outstanding athlete at MSC between 1913 and 1916, and much-bemedaled member of the army air corps during World War I. "Si" Gatton was born in Iowa in 1894 and came with his family to Bozeman in 1908. A star athlete at Gallatin County High School (he held the state high jump record for many years, and as a halfback led his team to the state football championship in 1912), he entered MSC in the

dozen combat missions with the Eleventh Aero Squadron. The last, his twenty-sixth, he might have avoided, as he was officially still out on a leave. But he volunteered— "anxious to get back into the game" was how his fellow pilots recalled his mood—and hastening to catch up to his squadron, was pounced upon by three German planes and shot down just one week before the armistice of November 11, 1918. Back in Bozeman his distraught classmates proposed that the athletic field at MSC be named Gatton Field in "memory of an athlete, who, when he gave, gave all to his school, and in memory of a man who gave his life for his country." [2]

Gatton Field Court

1. MSU sports news release, by Ken Nicholson, 6 March 1972, 79026/43, "Gatton Field and Memorial Gate" file, MSUA.
2. "Gatton Field at MSC Named in Memory of One of College's Greatest Athletes," *Bozeman Daily Chronicle*, 13 March 1949. See also "Gatton Field and Memorial Gate" file, 79026/43, MSUA.

1916 saw not only "Si" Gatton's departure, but the departure of the old nickname—"Aggies." In its place the school took its current athletic tag—"Bobcats." *The Exponent's* editor and sports editor, Lester Cole and Fred Bullock, failing to get any inspiring ideas from the student body, simply compiled their own list of all the fighting animals not yet claimed by other schools and settled on "Bobcats." Cole sold the name in a clever front-page editorial:

G. Ott Romney

At last, what promises to be a splendid name for the various teams of Montana State, has come to light. This name is "Bobcats" and fills the bill in every respect. . . . The ideal name should have a touch of the western, a trace of the Aggie and should be related to the mountains. Now, just analyze bobcats. It fits doesn't it? . . . The question arises as to whether this animal has the necessary characteristics. He certainly has. There is more fight and pep in a bobcat than there is in all the rest of the animal kingdom. He is not large, but is highly respected by his enemies. As for being wild, there is nothing wilder than a bobcat. His fighting tools consist of sharp claws and teeth with which he has developed some wonderful teamwork. He does not depend on brute strength alone but upon headwork and cunning . . . Just try to softly warble that name, Bobcats. It can't be done. You have to spit it out.[6]

Although football rebounded for a while after World War I (no games were played in 1918), it was steadily eclipsed by basketball. Basketball was, in fact, arguably the most successful sport over MSC's first seventy-five years. Between 1901 and 1930, for example, the basketball team suffered only three losing seasons, achieving an amazing record of 343 wins as against only 99 losses. During the same period MSC dominated in the intrastate rivalry with Missoula, winning thirty-nine of fifty-three contests. Bozeman was a hotbed of basketball enthusiasm. Even before Romney Gym was built in 1922, MSC was reputed to have had the state's best basketball floor in its drill hall, and many of Montana's earliest high school championships were held on the Bozeman campus.

Schubert Dyche

What really put MSC basketball in the limelight was the remarkable performance of the Golden Bobcats, the teams coached between the 1922-1923 and 1929-1930 seasons by George Ott Romney and Schubert Dyche. Over those eight seasons MSC had a record of 202 wins against only 42 losses. The pinnacles of success were reached in the 1926-1927 through 1929-30 seasons when the Bobcats were 129 and 21. In 1928-1929 the team compiled a record of thirty-six wins against only two losses, in the process capturing the Rocky Mountain Conference title, for the third successive year, and the 1929 Helms

Award, emblematic of the national collegiate championship in those days. J. Ashworth "Cat" Thompson and Orland Ward started for this team at forwards; Frank Worden at center; and John "Brick" Breeden and Max Worthington at the guard positions. Thompson and Orland Ward were selected as All-Americans. "Cat" Thompson was simply outstanding—in the 1950s the Helms Foundation named him as one of its all-time All-American selections. These Bobcats perfected—some argue originated—the fast-break offense so characteristic of basketball today. Thompson, called "Cat" because of his amazing speed, led an offense that literally ran other teams ragged. And Frank Ward, who stood six feet two inches, could dunk the ball easily and was one of the nation's first players to perfect the hook shot. Breeden and Worthington went on to distinguish themselves as alumni, serving for decades as MSC coaches and administrators. As a coach, Breeden led Bobcat basketball teams to 283 wins between 1935 and 1954, a record likely never to be bettered. Worthington filled in one year for Breeden in 1947-1948 with an 18-6 performance. Worthington's most notable work came as dean of students, a position he held as late as 1973. The naming of the field house in 1981 in Breeden's honor, and four years later, the naming of the arena within in Worthington's honor, were fitting rewards for their many years of service. [7]

The Golden Bobcats: Recollections of Max Worthington

No mention of Montana State basketball is complete without inclusion of the Golden Bobcats, the extraordinary teams coached by George Ott Romney and Schubert Dyche during the 1920s. During the eight seasons between 1922-1923 and 1929-1930, the Cats won 202 games against only 42 losses, or an average year's record of 25-5. Romney built the foundation for these teams, but when he left at the conclusion of the 1926-1927 season, the reins were picked up more than ably by Dyche, who two seasons later, 1928-1929, managed the team to a national championship and the Helms Award for a record of thirty-six wins against but two losses.

The following year, the now nationally famous Bobcats were invited east during Christmas vacation to play some of the toughest teams in the country. Max Worthington, who later served many years as dean of students at Montana State, recalls some of the highlights of the four seasons from 1927 to 1931, including the trip east:

[In 1927] Ott Romney, who was the director of athletics and coach of everything in those days, came to Billings . . . and invited me to come to MSC. He said he could give me some help. At that particular time help was of interest, because banks had failed. Our family's funds were in a bank that had failed. So things were pretty tight in terms of financing. So I [came to MSC] and started in agriculture, and played freshman football. Then came basketball, and that's what Romney wanted me for. Frank Worden, from

Butte, and I were competing for the guard job that had opened as the result of the graduation of Val Glynn. Worden was a fine athlete. . . . We . . . split the time for a while, and then all of a sudden I was the one getting the start as a freshman.

Well, that was a great thing, because we went all the way, and played Wyoming here for the conference championship. In the meantime, my education broadened because we traveled into Washington, Idaho, Colorado, Utah, and places where I'd never been before. Our coaches would contact alumni in those areas, and we got tours of industry at various places. It added to the books we weren't reading that we took on these trips.

Earlier I had decided that if I was going to be in athletics . . . for two-thirds of the school year, I better get out of agriculture. So I enrolled in the physical education program and practically had to start over. I have to say that the PE program, which many thought was a snap, was heavily scheduled into the science courses. And so we were getting a good background. . . .

[When I was] a junior we made an extensive trip. Coach Dyche received various invitations from the Middle West and eastern schools for games. Our winning reputation apparently made many newspapers. . . . During the Christmas holidays we . . . [went] to Indianapolis where we played Butler University. From Butler we went to Milwaukee

The 1928-1929 Golden Bobcats

and played Marquette. We lost to Butler, but won at Marquette. Next we played Purdue. John Wooden, of great later fame in California [UCLA], was part of that squad. We won at Purdue. Came back to Chicago on New Year's eve and played Loyola of Chicago. They were probably the best we saw on this trip; they beat us. But we pretty well had our minds on the Loop that night. We'd never been in a metropolis, and on New Year's eve. We were awed by all the traffic, people, noise, etc.

We grabbed the train from there. We went to Pittsburgh, where we played the University of Pittsburgh. . . . And we had a real close one; we lost by one point in the last seconds. One of the Pittsburgh players, Charles Hyatt, was an All-American, and he showed us that he was good. We went from there to Penn State at State College, the end of the line. Won a game up there that got us back on track. On the way home we played Nebraska. Of course, I was looking forward to this because we'd been thumped there in

football. . . . [W]hen we got . . . there we were ready for them. The strange part of that was, according to the news . . . we drew the largest basketball crowd they'd had in years. . . . But we won that one, to get revenge, so to speak, after playing football against odds.

In Worthington's senior year, he was the "only one left out of the whole crew." "It was a whole new team," he recalled. "I think we lost more than we won, but the games were pretty close." And Worthington was philosophical; it was just one more learning experience, he concluded, one in which he "learned to accept the losses"—a lesson he had no way of learning in his first three years when the Golden Bobcats won eighty-three of ninety-seven contests. [1]

1. Max Worthington interview, 17 August 1987.

In contrast, football did not do well during the 1930s and '40s. Over nineteen seasons between 1931 and 1953 (football was canceled during the war years, 1942-1945), the college enjoyed only one winning season, that of 1946 when its team won the Rocky Mountain Conference championship and tied New Mexico on New Year's day in San Diego's Harbor Bowl. But that season was definitely aberrational; in the '50 and '51 grid seasons the Bobcats were a combined 1-15. Following the winless season of '51, President Roland Renne decided to turn things around. An intense competitor in his own right—many

are those who remember him as an absolutely ferocious handball and tennis player—Renne hired Tony Storti in 1952 and thereby inaugurated the most successful presidential grid reign in school history. In the succeeding eleven seasons, or until Renne retired as president in 1964, his football coaches—Storti, Wally Lemm, Herb Agocs, and Jim Sweeney—would have only one losing season, compiling a remarkable record of 71-32-4. This included Storti's undefeated team of '56, which concluded its season in a scoreless tie for the national championship in the mud and rain at the Aluminum Bowl in Little Rock, Arkansas.

The 1958 Bobcat-Grizzly Goalpost Fight

November 18, 1958
Andrew C. Cogswell, Dean of Students, MSU, to Val Glynn, Dean of Students, MSC:

I feel obliged to make some sort of report to you on the activities of the past week end, which I am sure you know by now were a bit rough in spots. We did have the fight around the goal posts that I feared, but it was not as extensive as it might have been. . . For the most part, the episode on the field was a pushing and shoving proposition. However, as always happens in affairs of this kind, individual fights did break out. We sewed up seven or eight youngsters, mostly ours, at the Health Center. . . . I understand there were others who turned up at the emergency wards down town. . . . Probably the most serious potential injuries [were the result] of a fight in the stands [a concussion and broken leg]. . . . [M]ost of the

worst fighting occurred down town Friday night between what you have called the "fringe elements" of both schools. . . . I believe the tensions of the previous week brought about by the raids and rumors of raids had a lot to do with the edginess of both student bodies. . . I also believe that in most cases serious fights broke out where one or both contesting individuals or groups had been drinking pretty heavily. . . .

All in all, the majority of our two student bodies have an enjoyable time mingling. The Fangs and the Bear Paws had a fine meeting as did the student government groups. We used all the empty beds we could find in our halls to accommodate Bobcat students who were friends of our residents. There was wide mingling of fraternity members from the two schools, and youngsters from common home towns had pleasant reunions. These associations are the great values of Bobcat-Grizzly competition. Unfortunately, however, they are the covert phases of the event. The raids and battles are the overt ones.

Our student body, at the moment at least, is quite disgusted with many of the happenings. I hope to capitalize on this for the game next year, but student bodies change and "traditions" of raiding and fighting have a tendency to reoccur from time to time. [1]

November 20, 1958
President Roland Renne, MSC, to Acting President Gordon B. Castle, MSU:

I am writing concerning certain events which occured in connection with the Grizzly-Bobcat football game Saturday, November 15. . . . [S]pecifically, I am informed that students from your campus visited the Montana State College campus three weeks before the game. . . . While no great damage was done by this visit outside of painting grizzly bears with gold paint on various walks, including my own porch, the fact that the visit was made and some painting and other work done encouraged a feeling of retaliation and, of course, was followed by a visit to the Montana State University campus by some Montana State College students, I understand. Parenthetically I might mention that Grizzly students apparently were on the roof of our Women's Dormitory and events might have developed that could have been embarrassing.

I understand that in Missoula on Friday evening there was a considerable amount of horseplay and some undesirable activities, particularly some fighting, including cars being stopped by Grizzly students, and a general attitude of trying to pick a fight seemed to prevail. . . . Immediately following the game, there seemed to be a great deal of individual fighting which some feel was encouraged by Grizzly students who had previously placed a water hose in front of one of the goal posts and were congregating immediately after the game with the idea of preventing the goal posts coming down. I recall my reaction two years ago when we won at Missoula for the first time in my Montana existence and when our students rushed out to take out the goal posts. . . I suppose if the loser would accept this in principle and just permit the goal posts to be taken down by the winners, the strong feelings would not develop because there would not be so much challenge in the whole affair. This might be one way of handling this. . . . We have won so little and only until very recently that I am not very familiar with this tradition.

In addition to the fights which developed around the goal posts, I understand the Grizzly

football team stayed on the field after the game was over and when the Bobcat band was marching down toward the other goal posts, the players assumed some band members were going to try to take their goal posts and clashed with the band. This seems to have been a very embarrassing and unnecessary development . . . . I certainly do not wish to convey the impression that I think your students were anymore to blame in general than ours. . . . I am writing in the hope that we can work out something to make these football games in the future more the types of events which I am sure you and I would both favor. [2]

MSC Student Senate Policy, February 6, 1959:

Tempers have apparently cooled and the MSC-MSU rivalry appears dormant until next football season. Unless, however, action is taken by the student governments of both schools, it is extremely probable that a re-enactment of last year's post-game festivities will occur. In years past, the rivalry grew so bitter that the game was no longer held on either of the campuses, but in Butte. If the present trend continues it is very conceivable that the contest would again be played on neutral territory.

Student Senate adopted...the following policy concerning the problem:

1. That the goal posts shall be the rightful property of the victors.
2. That no organized defense or the use of law officers to protect the goal posts shall be allowed.

The reasoning behind this is that the main cause of the battle this year was the organized defense set up by the Grizzlies. If no defense was presented and the winning side had easy access to the posts there would be no fights.

This action by Senate has placed the final responsibility squarely in the lap of MSU. If the student government of MSU adopts this or a similar policy, it is very probable that the post-game bitterness will not result in physical clashes as in the past. [3]

Until their victory in 1956, the Bobcats had not won at Missoula since 1928. There had been a serious battle for the goal posts at the 1956 game as well, with Grizzly fans fighting to preserve the posts with a high-pressure water hose that got loose and hurt numerous students. Bobcat fans won this war and hauled many pieces of the goalposts back to Bozeman on the special train.

(By the way, back in the Renne years it was a practice for the president of the winning school to cancel classes on the following Monday.)

1. Andrew C. Cogswell to Val Glynn, 18 November 1958, Box 46, "MSC" file, University of Montana Presidential Papers, UM Archives.
2. Roland R. Renne to Gordon B. Castle, November 1958, ibid.
3. *Exponent*, 6 February 1959.

But Renne was not satisfied simply to win football games. In every way he sought to upgrade the men's athletic program. Storti was authorized to bring in four assistants, three of whom, Herb Agocs, Gene Bourdet, and Tom Parac, would play significant roles in the continued development of athletics and physical education on the Bozeman campus. The wrestling program, already well established under Keith Bowen, was strengthened. And basketball was put in the able hands of Dobbie Lambert, who brought in with him a young assistant from Kansas who'd make his mark in the '60s, Roger Craft.

The successful athletic program of the 1950s was supplemented and strengthened by new facilities, among them "Rollie's Folly," or "Rollie's Roundhouse," the remarkable domed sports arena on the south side of campus now familiarly known as the Brick Breeden Fieldhouse. Renne's field house, designed by Bozeman's Oswald E. Berg, Jr., and Fred J. Willson, was one of the architectural wonders of the world—the largest wooden arched roof structure in existence, and the second-largest building of its type in America. [8]

Brick Breeden Fieldhouse

Anyone contemplating the construction of this 300 foot circular indoor stadium, ninety feet in height, cannot help but marvel at Renne's foresight, while at the same time perhaps chuckling at the guile with which the man pushed through a project many thought extravagant in cost and ridiculous in size. Here was a huge domed 8400-seat facility, built for a cow college of less than 3000 enrollment in a rural town of perhaps 12,000 to 13,000 residents. Who would pay for it, and how would it be filled? Realizing that he would have great difficulty in attracting legislative fiscal support for the structure, Renne, as he did repeatedly with the general campus building program,

finessed the construction with independent, private-sector funding, in this case "balloon" bonds, whose periodic payments would be less at the start and larger in time. To provide backing for the bonds, Renne was extremely innovative. As was his style in an age of few restraints on presidential authority, Renne took unilateral action, instituting a student fee for campus building. He did this not only because it promised to provide a sure and predictable source of income for the field house and other structures, but because statistical evidence forecast a doubling of enrollments, at the minimum, within a decade. Although critics viewed Renne's figures with skepticism, his prognostications were more than realized—within ten years the enrollment had reached 7000. Consequently, the balloon payments, linked to enrollment increases going beyond even Renne's expectations, were readily financed. Renne pulled every stop to get the field house; his staff recall he went so far as to back the bonds with the revenue from campus soda pop machines and from the pay washing machines in the dormitories. [9]

Once "Rollie's Folly" was up and functioning, Renne luxuriated in his success by showing off the facility to the state legislature. Those who were there at the unveiling recall the awe with which the politicos viewed it. Perhaps rancher-legislator Jack Brenner from Horse Prairie expressed that amazement best when he observed that it was likely to cloud up and rain inside the huge structure someday. And not a few agriculturalists looked lasciviously at it, if with tongue in cheek, as one whale of a bin for the storage of surplus grain. [10]

Overnight, the new field house revolutionized not only MSC athletics, but much of the school's capacity for extending its services to the state. Spectator capacities for arena sports were more than quadrupled. Whereas old Romney Gym seated less than half of the college enrollment in 1956, and precious few of the community's sports enthusiasts as a result, the new field house could accommodate not only the entire student body, but thousands of nonstudents as well. Basketball now had, for that time, a world-class facility and the Bobcat staff responded by producing even better teams and by attracting better competition. Some truly great basketball squads from the West came to play in Renne's new facility, perhaps none sparking more the enthusiasm of Bobcat buffs than the extraordinary rivalry that developed between the local school and Seattle University with its All-American forward Elgin Baylor. MSC-Seattle games were absolute sellouts, and continued to be for years after Baylor had graduated and moved up to the pros.

The huge capacity of the field house provided an attraction for many other events. In 1960 the world middleweight boxing championship between Gene Fullmer of Utah and Joey Giardello, which ended in a bloody fifteen-round draw, was held here before a crowd of over 10,000, the largest attendance for an indoor sporting event in the state's history. As the primary surface of the field house was originally dirt—and would not be converted to hardwood for two decades—the facility proved perfect for rodeos, for circuses, and for football and baseball practices. The Montana High School Association found the facility much to its liking for state track and field meets and basketball tournaments. On one occasion, an eight-man high school football game was played under its dome. For years, students, musing on the joint use of the field house for both equestrian and administrative functions, could claim the dubious distinction of being probably the only collegians in the world who registered for classes on "horse manure," as some of the more civilized delicately put it. With staging installed and large audiences assured, big-name bands and performers came to MSC—Bob Hope, Louie Primo, Victor Borge, and the Satchmo himself performed to capacity crowds.

Another significant, in fact, the culminating, athletic development under President Renne was MSC's participation in the chartering of the Big Sky Athletic Conference. During the late 1940s and early '50s, the school competed in the Rocky Mountain Conference, an NAIA conglomerate composed of MSC, Idaho State, and several Colo-

rado schools. By 1956, following its undefeated football season, MSC had clearly outgrown the league, and became an independent. Seven years later, in 1963, MSC, soon to become MSU, joined Idaho State, Weber State, Idaho, Montana, and Gonzaga as charter members of the new Big Sky Conference. Subsequently, Boise State, Northern Arizona, Nevada (Reno), and most recently Eastern Washington, joined the conference, while Gonzaga, without a football program, withdrew. It would not be an exaggeration to say that the Big Sky Conference is one of the strongest NCAA 1AA football conferences in the nation, placing one or more teams in the national playoffs on an annual basis. And its level of basketball competition has been rewarded with a guaranteed slot in the postseason NCAA tournament. At the outset, MSU dominated the conference in football, basketball, and wrestling, and over the years has won or tied for individual team titles in those sports numerous times.

It would be a mistake, however, to assume that Renne's new emphasis on athletics meant the program of those days paralleled that of the present. Far from it. Herb Agocs' first impression when he arrived on campus in 1956 merits our attention. While football was the first priority, the Pennsylvania steeltowner recalled, compared to what he had experienced back east, MSC's program was by every comparison miniscule. High school

The circus comes to MSU

MSU's ground attack, 1967

games in the mid-Atlantic states attracted crowds of 10,000 to 20,000, and Franklin Field, where Agocs had played for the University of Pennsylvania, held 79,000 fans. In contrast, Gatton Field, with many of its seats temporary wooden bleachers, held 6000, mostly for the Cat-Grizzly game. Competition was also limited; the better teams at MSC's level performed at what would likely be a good Division II level today. Frankly speaking, only a limited number of players could have, given the performance required today, "cut the mustard" in MSU's current football program. [11]

Budgeting, despite Renne's commitment, was extremely tight, particularly for minor sports. Baseball operated with almost no scholarship assistance, and wrestling, one of the college's best varsity programs, was run on $3000 annually. To conserve on resources, whenever the team was on the road Bobcat grapplers were put up in private homes as frequently as possible,

often two to a bed. Meal allotments were $2 a day. These limitations extended deep into the 1960s, and staff and wrestlers often likened their existence on trips as akin to what they had heard about life in the Peace Corps. Despite these limitations, the MSC/MSU wrestling program under Agocs was superb, winning or placing near the top in the first four Big Sky Tournaments. [12]

President Renne's departure in 1964 for a post with the U.S. Department of Agriculture did not mean a reduction in the administration's interest in athletics. Dr. Leon Johnson, an enthusiastic outdoorsman, horseman, and hunter, gave continued support to what Renne had initiated. MSU dominated action in the Big Sky Conference throughout Johnson's tenure, 1964-1968. Four sports had marked success—football, basketball, wrestling, and skiing. MSU won the conference All-Sports Trophy, awarded on the basis of records in all league competition, in both 1964 and 1966.

Allyn "Sonny" Holland

Don Hass

In 1966, for example, MSU took the conference titles in football and skiing, tied for the title in basketball, and placed second in wrestling and baseball.

The school's success in the 1950s and 1960s was complemented by the outstanding contributions of native-grown athletes. It was not easy to recruit locally; the college's sport scholarship program, based upon limited scholarship grants and work opportunities, simply could not compete with large, out-of-state institutions capable of flying recruits to their campuses and offering them "free-ride" scholarships. [13] And the Bobcats were competing for athletes within the state with the university in Missoula, which for years had played at a higher level of competition and possessed a better line on locals. Nevertheless, the college did remarkably well in securing some of the state's finest athletes; that degree of success increased markedly in the 1960s, while Missoula began to lose its former recruiting edge and looked increasingly to junior colleges in California, Washington, and even Hawaii.

Conspicuous among MSU's in-state recruits were student athletes from both the industrial towns and the rural agricultural regions. Hardened and determined young athletes, nurtured in the tough and demanding environs of the state's mining centers and on its farms and ranches, prided themselves, as did their coaches and families, in their work ethic, desire, and commitment to perform at high levels. There was something special imparted to competition by being Montanan, the argument went. Montanans were believed to be overachievers, and for many years the records they piled up seemed to validate that belief.

One has only to think of the two great "Hs" among the college's pantheon of athletic greats—Holland and Hass—to understand the influence of Montana's "character" on the success of Bobcat athletics. Allyn "Sonny" Holland, from Butte, the three-time mid-bracket All-American center and MSC's first selection to the annual East-West Shrine Bowl game in San Francisco in 1959, symbolized the rich interrelationship between the working-class ethic and the teaching of skills offered on campus. Holland's no-nonsense approach to the game, carried through into the 1970s when he became MSU's most successful football coach, was meshed with a paternalistic care and consideration for his players and staff that reminded many of the unique sense of family so pervasive in the social history of Montana's laboring communities. Although Holland was but one of many contributors to MSU athletics, he became the most visible and celebrated example of the combination of commitment, care, and loyalty that residents of Butte, Anaconda, Great Falls, and other industrial communities found much to take pride in.

Rural Montana's contribution had its symbol in the remarkable Don Hass. A native of Glendive, one of Montana's leading ranching and farming communities, Hass was twice a Little All-American halfback. Arguably the greatest Bobcat gridder of all time, Hass holds virtually every school rushing record. He was the nation's second leading ground gainer in 1966 and its fifth in 1967, compiling a total of 2702 yards in those two seasons alone. He led the Bobcats to two unbeaten Big Sky Conference titles, plus a berth in the Camellia Bowl at Sacramento in 1967, capping that off with an invitation to the East-West Shrine Bowl. The epitome of Montana's earthy legacy of hard work and determination, Hass acquired from his admirers the sobriquet "The Iron Tumbleweed," which, intentional or not, appropriately and symbolically linked the industrial and agricultural nature of the state's contributions to MSU's athletic fortunes. This unique implantation of a kind of Montana frontier spirit upon MSU athletics has added a great deal of excitement to the program and has made the contributions of native sons quite gratifying for Bobcat fans.

Montana's unique environment influenced the football program. Weather, wind, and natural turf combined to dictate an offense based on a ground attack, and with perhaps a seasonal exception or two—such as in 1968 when head coach Tom Parac unleashed the Dennis Erickson-to-Ron Bain passing attack, or in the early '70s when Sonny Holland was fortunate to have Sam McCullum at split end, MSU football teams be-

Larry Chaney

tween 1952 and 1981 emphasized earthy, rather than aerial, efforts. It stood to logic, the strategists held, that tough MSU teams were better adapted to a game philosophy based on trench warfare in adverse climatic conditions. Few fans will ever forget, for example, the two remarkable losses on Gatton Field in 1968 to San Diego State and West Texas State, visiting teams that sported between them four All-Americans who would make good in the pros. Even though MSU failed to win these games, it was clear to all who attended that while skill on the part of the visitors provided them with the scoring edge, where it really counted, meaning in the trenches, MSU won decisively. To the satisfaction of MSU's fans, the Aztecs and Buffaloes each seemed happy just to escape the mayhem—with wins as mere consolation. The fans' reaction typified—in the same way as does the

value placed on the Bobcat-Grizzly fracas—the attitude by which Montanans can interpret a game to suit their own concept of what is and what isn't important.

Basketball did not differ greatly in its philosophy. Coaches Dobbie Lambert and Roger Craft worked hard to recruit the best Montana players. Their argument was that Montana kids had an excellent work ethic, were tough, and of good character. [14] The crowning achievement of this approach was the successful recruitment of Fairfield's Kermit Young, Butte's Don Rae, and the golddust twins from Great Falls, Tom Storm and Jack Gillespie. Wrestling had its Bill Spring, a local lad. Grappling enthusiasts still talk about the legendary matches in the late '60s and early '70s between Spring and ISU's John Caccia, matches many a fan drove miles to see. [15]

Of course, no Montana team ever turned down the opportunity to secure out-of-state talent either, and it is a fact that the emotional commitment given to in-state recruiting tends to obscure the extraordinary accomplishments of those nonresidents who stud MSU's pantheon of athletic greats. Few will forget, for example, the contributions of Larry Chaney in basketball and Jan Stenerud and Bill Kollar in football. Chaney, who came from Seattle, remains MSU's all-time scoring great, averaging over twenty points per game over a four-year career in the late 1950s. Stenerud, recruited from his native Norway as a skier, was discovered accidentally by MSU basketball coach Roger Craft, and honed his skills for football under head coach Jim Sweeney. Stenerud revolu-

Jan Stenerud

Bill Kollar

*Coach Roger Craft
and Jack Gillespie*

ing a National Football League Hall-of-Famer. Kollar, from Ohio, became the greatest defensive lineman ever to play for MSU. He was an All-American selection in 1973 and a first-round NFL draft choice, going on to play nine years of professional football with Cincinnati and Tampa Bay.

The capstone of this era came in the 1970s when Sonny Holland, MSU's most successful grid coach, built the Bobcats into perennial contenders in the Big Sky Conference. In 1976, the year of the nation's bicentennial, MSU went 12-1, led the NCAA Division II in total offense, and captured the national title with hard-fought televised victories over New Hampshire, North Dakota State, and Akron. While Holland's most valuable plaudits went deservedly to Bert Markovich, Tim Nixon, Alan Reichow, Jerry Reisig, and Ken Verlanic, fans who followed the season could not forget quarterback Paul Dennehy's generalship and the hard, slashing ground game of Tom Kostrba, Don Ueland, and Delmar Jones. Bobcat boosters still talk of the colorful postgame remarks on national TV of All-American defensive end Les Leininger, who attributed the final victory to the rigorous conditioning required by rural Montana's eight- and six-man high school football leagues—images that underlined the perception of Bobcat teams as the epitome of frontier toughness, energy, and endurance. Understandably, there was a very special bonding on this squad—coach Holland coined it "Bobcat Pride."

tionized football nationally with his introduction of soccer-style place kicking, and went on to a long and spectacular stint in professional football, first with the Kansas City Chiefs and later with the Green Bay Packers, eventually becom-

Losses and Gains

Even as 1976 brought a national grid title to the Bobcats, it brought at the same time a challenge to athletic continuity at MSU, a challenge in the face of change on numerous fronts. From 1976 onwards, new approaches and new institutions would significantly reshape Bobcat athletics.

Signs of change were evident even earlier. Influenced in part by the energy radiating from the youth movement of the 1960s and early 1970s, students began to challenge the manner in which their financial support for athletics had been taken for granted, as they viewed it, by the MSU administration and athletic department. When the question came up in the mid-'60s of replacing old Gatton Field with a new modern facility of 150 percent greater capacity, the students balked, arguing that from the standpoint of desirable student services a physical education and recreational complex would be of infinitely greater value than an exposed stadium employed but minimally. The students, who, like collegians across the nation, had made contributions to athletics over the years in the form of special student fees, turned down one proposal for a new stadium in the late 1960s and continued to resist when the

Bill Spring

administration and athletic department tried to push it through again immediately thereafter. It was clear that the earlier arbitrariness with which Dr. Renne, for example, had levied fees upon the students for the construction of the field house and other buildings, was being challenged. The era of student acquiescence had come to an end. In the spring of 1970 the Board of Regents agreed with the students, ruling that they had full authority over their own funds and could allocate them as they chose. [16]

Vets against the stadium

As good as this ruling was for student self-respect, it was highly undesirable for MSU men's athletics. Though eventually the Marga Hosaeus Physical Education Center and the Reno H. Sales Stadium were both constructed, the latter came three years later than hoped for (1974) and was seriously modified in size and design because of student refusal to provide support for a stadium costing more than $750,000 and because of the effects of inflation while the debate dragged on. Advocates of the new stadium blamed the students for succumbing at any cost to a trendy, irrational resistance to established authority, while the students, including a number of Vietnam vets, were disturbed at the inability, or reluctance, of the administration to understand and respond to student motives. At one stage of the impasse, the students actually brought suit against the university, stalling procedures for many months. Ultimately, the student fee for men's athletics was steadily decreased during the 1970s, and finally

discontinued, shearing off a much-needed 12 percent of the athletic department's budget. The students did not stop at that, eventually voting to terminate subsidies for a whole series of activities, including music department programs. Indirectly, this hurt athletics again, as the marching band had its support cut by this action.

Throughout the confrontation, the students insisted that they would not support a stadium unless a physical education and recreational complex was guaranteed along with it. Inadvisedly, stadium supporters attempted to place the two structures together on the same ballot, making a vote against the stadium a vote against the PE complex and further alienating the students. Finally, the stadium was approved by a narrow margin. But the damage had been done; men's athletics now had a modern facility but had lost a valuable source of fiscal support. Students, on their part, had developed a cynicism toward men's athletics as the result of that department's and the administration's insensitivity to their cause, a cynicism, which, upon examination, appears justifiable. It should be noted that students at the University of Montana, replicating MSU's example, also abolished student-fee support for athletics, while all other Big Sky Conference schools continued to enjoy financial aid from student fees, some of them extensively. Students at the three Idaho schools, for example, continued to contribute substantial fees for support of athletics, in some cases more than double what Montana students once pledged. By 1991 Idaho was realizing $877,000 in student athletic fees, Boise $760,000, and ISU $592,000, while MSU and UM received nothing. This places a peculiar kind of funding burden on the Montana athletic programs, emphasizing user-fee and legislative appropriations as a substitute, a burden their rivals do not share on nearly so severe a basis. [17]

Although MSU students are aware of student athletic support policies on other campuses, they have put their monies to other uses, most notably to contracting big-name entertainment, and there appears to be little hope today for reinstating student support for men's athletics. This is not to say that MSU students have not stood behind their teams. Far from it. Since the decision to withdraw funding from football and basketball, the students through ASMSU have generously supported other athletic programs, particularly women's athletics and intramurals. And they have continued to give gratifying individual support to the major athletic events. In fact, the student sections in the stands at Sales Stadium and in the bleachers at Breeden Field House have been filled with fans of the most loyal and boisterous sorts. But with attendance now linked to the particular fortunes of any team in any year, and with football always pressured by weather in the computation of its gate, student financial support through the purchase of season passes or individual game tickets can be unpredictable at best. As a result, there is ever-greater pressure on the varsity athletic programs to find alternative sources of income.

Many assert that the single most important development in Bobcat athletics in recent years has been the emergence of women's athletics, citing the impact women now have on the use of facilities, on budgeting, and on how sport is viewed generally. The rise of women's athletics has been more than a necessary and proper accommodation to women, as women have developed the athletic abilities that make sport for them more than mere recreational outlet. This has been achieved despite much foot-dragging on the part of traditionalists who would have denied women their quest for athletic equality and opportunity.

Women who went through school in an earlier era can only envy the opportunities their sisters have today in athletics. President Renne, while making his mark for men's athletics, gave little support to the women. The new field house, for example, was designated for male use only. In the mid-1960s, the only competition afforded women was through the Women's Athletic Association (WAA), which supported a kind of women's intramural program. Definitely consid-

ered subordinate to men's intramurals, WAA was confined to the use of the old Romney Gym one night per week and was supported by the grand total of $500 per annum by the Associated Students. Equipment had to be borrowed from the women's physical education department. Once a quarter WAA sponsored a "play day," when teams from other state schools were invited to campus to compete. These were more or less pickup teams; none of them practiced formally, conditioned for their sport, or had professionally trained coaching—all of which attested to the primitive condition of women's athletics in the Northern Rockies. Varsity athletics for women simply did not exist. [18]

These conditions are not cited to suggest that the situation in this region was unique; across the country women desiring to compete had very few avenues open to them. A number of factors held them back. That the decision making and the pursestrings were in the hands of men was one reason. Another was the influence of old wives' tales—used as weapons by some, but believed sincerely by others. Whether employed tactically or argued from the heart, these myths held that competition was not good for women, that it could even cause physiological damage. Extremists went so far as to argue that physical activity,

particularly competitive physical activity, would harm female reproductive organs. The myth of female frailty supported a traditional view that sport was appropriately a masculine, not a feminine, expression. Activities incompatible with sustaining this myth were seen as a threat to the existing power structure in sport, based as it was on the assumption of male strength and female weakness. Myths aside, there were those who opposed the development of women's athletics because they feared its challenge to priorities in budgeting that were clearly dominated by men. [19]

At the same time, it should be pointed out, many women who labored against these obstructions, while discounting the physical harm detractors alledged would come from competitive athletics, were yet deeply concerned about the growing competitiveness that characterized men's athletics. They were also concerned with the emphasis placed by men on so-called major sports at the expense of so-called minor sports. Moreover, they worried about a growing neglect for academics they saw as attending the male competitive ethic. In short, these women raised points of issue with male administration and male philosophy in the field of athletics.

This was the environment that prevailed at MSU in 1965 when Ellen Kreighbaum was hired to teach activities classes and head up WAA. For Kreighbaum, who came to the campus from the University of Wisconsin-LaCrosse, it was like arriving on an "athletic frontier." Given lots of freedom, she decided to create a women's basketball team. Fifty students showed up for tryouts;

twenty-four were invited to return to practices that were held twice weekly between 9 and 10 p.m. at the conclusion of men's intramurals. With her fledgling team in need of competition, Kreighbaum enticed the university at Missoula and Carroll College to send teams to a tournament. For uniforms, the "Kittens" wore MSU T-shirts; the visitors paid their traveling expenses out of their own pockets. [20]

In 1966, a year after her arrival, Kreighbaum requested financial support from men's athletics and men's intramurals. Receiving no response, she made a pitch directly to ASMSU, which at that time provided a good portion of the athletic and intramural budget. When the Associated Students supported the request and allocated an additional $500, Kreighbaum created a permanent women's basketball program. At approximately the same time, she inaugurated a women's volleyball team. Women's gymnastics followed soon after.

Early efforts to get the university's athletic commission to support women's athletics were met with disappointment. Perhaps this could have been anticipated—the athletic commission was a faculty group composed entirely of males who oversaw the men's athletic program. Then aid came from another quarter; George Shroyer, who arrived in 1968 to head up men's physical education, assigned a graduate student assistant to women's athletics, which enabled the development of a women's track program. Over time Shroyer provided continual support to women's athletics, treating it as a bonafide varsity program. By 1970 women's basketball was firmly established, and volleyball, gymnastics, and track were off the ground. Two years later, in order to give organization to this fledgling operation, Kreighbaum, with Shroyer's approval, became the unrecognized, self-appointed women's athletic director. By now, Shroyer had mounted efforts to get women's athletics out of the physical education program, likely a tactic to ease budgeting woes in his department as well as to create an independent identity for the women. It was time, he said, to stop "sandbagging" the program and to provide them with the "same opportunity for varsity athletics as the men." [21] His efforts had results when the women's coaching staffs were augmented by qualified graduate students, and ASMSU allocated something like $3000 for uniforms and travel.

Further efforts to obtain support from the athletic commission failed, however. What progress had been made had come from much personal initiative and energy on a voluntary basis from within the women's intramural and physical education program, and was accomplished over the resistance of the men who had the authority to make budgeting decisions. This conflict only intensified as the women's demands for

1905 Women's championship basketball team. Women's teams were terminated after World War I

money increased. In late 1973, for example, the vice president for administration, who was also a member of the athletic commission, stated privately that "if equal opportunities mean the same type of program for girls as the varsity men's athletic program . . . I am opposed." [22] Then Bill Johnstone went public: "I personally would place intramurals above Women's Intercollegiate Athletics on the list of priorities." [23] Shortly thereafter, when the athletic commission voted anyway to recommend the appropriation of $2000 for women's athletics, it did so providing the "funding d[id] not curtail any other activity." [24] At approximately the same time, the commission was dealing with a men's athletic program supported by a budget of close to $200,000. Clearly, it was proving hard for men to accept the concept of women as athletes with demands as legitimate as the men's, a state of perplexity the rest of the country was also experiencing.

Ellen Kreighbaum, Marga Hosaeus, and George Shroyer at the dedication of the Marga Hosaeus Health & Physical Education Center, 1983

All of the women's frustration with male attitudes and discrimination was galvanized in 1972 when research by Mollie Hatch, a member of the women's physical education department, revealed the extent of the disparity between what men and women were paid at MSU. Ellen Kreighbaum and Betty Lowry, another member of the women's physical education department, discovered that they were paid at least $4000 less than each of three males they regarded as their peers. Further research built a prima facie case for what women had sensed for years: MSU not only discriminated against women in pay but in promotion and managerial opportunities as well. For example, while men reached full professorship in an average of seven years, it took women seventeen years to reach the same level. In 1973-1974 there were 144 full professors at MSU; only six of them were women. Only two departments were headed by women—nursing and home economics. The statistical data supporting the women's case were staggering. [25]

Initially the women sought a voluntary and nonlitigational solution to the problem, but the administration rejected their appeals and male department heads tried to discourage the women from acting on their findings and convictions. Although Montana had ratified the national Equal Rights Amendment and its new 1972 constitution included a similar amendment, the MSU administration responded with almost deliberate slowness to its responsibilities. The frustration that built on the part of the women was somewhat mitigated by their feelings of loyalty toward the university. But loyalty had its limits, and some of the women talked anonymously about their concerns with the women's editor of the *Bozeman Daily Chronicle*. As one of them put it:

It took us three months to get our way into the president's office. They [the administration] have attempted to handle it completely unilaterally, accepting no input from the women faculty. . . . No one will pay attention until their cage has been rattled. [26]

The women now saw the necessity for legal action. The cage would have to be rattled. Power, particularly male power, the women had concluded, conceded nothing without a struggle. In 1974, five women faculty members, including three from women's athletics and physical education, brought a class-action suit against MSU for violating the Civil Rights Act of 1964. After two years of litigation, *Mecklenburg et al.* vs. *Montana State Board of Regents of Higher Education, Montana State University, and Carl W. McIntosh* was won decisively by the plaintiffs and became a legal landmark as the first successful class action filed by women faculty within the United States. The findings of Federal District Court Judge W. D. Murray, issued on February 17, 1976, warrant citation, at least in part:

The evidence shows discrimination against women as a class by the defendants at Montana State University in that females are under-utilized as deans, vice presidents, department heads and as instructional faculty in many departments of the University. Women have also been discriminated against as a class in the areas of promotion, tenure, salary, and appointment to important university committees. [27]

The court then ordered the university to cooperate with the women in forging a plan that would eliminate these conditions. The resultant agreements brought about striking changes all over the campus, but perhaps none so conspicuously dramatic as those that took place in athletics, where women secured an equality none of the litigants even dreamed of at the outset of proceedings.

Even before the case was settled, the growing weight of the evidence, coupled with Ellen Kreighbaum's unflagging energy, brought about significant change for women's athletics. In 1974, or coincident with the commencement of the class action suit, Kreighbaum labored to convince the right people that a full-fledged women's varsity athletic program was not only justifiable, but that it deserved to be given official status alongside that of the men. Few believed, even during the case, that women at MSU could ever achieve complete independence. But the legitimacy of women's athletics had to be recognized in view of developing realities, and an incorporation of women's athletics into the men's athletic program under the men's athletic director, with a woman as an assistant AD, seemed plausible. While this was, from MSU's standpoint, a striking new direction, it was not particularly innovative if viewed from a national perspective. Where women's athletic programs existed in the United States they were being run almost entirely under the authority of the men's athletic program, with the director of the women's program serving as an

Women's soccer intramurals

assistant or associate director of athletics.

Although the MSU strategy sought to replicate national models, amalgamation with the men's program was not easily achieved. Each effort to acquire equality was met with grudging resistance. Opposition to any form of female-male balance was everywhere. Some of it related to the uniqueness of the land grant nature of MSU with its traditional absence of faculty governance. The reluctance of the school's faculty, particularly on the part of the colleges of Business, Agriculture, and Engineering, to accept the role of self-governance went back over decades, if not generations. Faculty new to MSU in the '60s, '70s, and even the '80s, invariably remarked on the absence of faculty input. MSU faculty not only had no appreciation of their responsibility to participate in governance, they even questioned their right to do so, which was exactly opposite the experience of many of the incoming faculty, particularly those who came from colleges and universities with strong liberal arts traditions. This same political inertia served to effectively muzzle the efforts of women to develop an athletic program. [28]

In general, opposition to women's athletics was based on the same rationalizations America had employed historically to discourage racial equality. Applied to gender discrimination now, the argument held that male athletes had worked for a century to achieve what women were demanding overnight. The old irresistible forces based on an addiction to the cult of individuality and the self-made man, to the cult of domesticity, and to the cult of Darwinian logic, again and again placed impediments in the way of women's athletics. On occasion, even the good Lord was invoked to thwart women's equality in sport.

But the evidence that emerged from the class action suit, coupled with more sensible administrative acceptance of the equal rights movement, finally broke through these obstructions. In late 1974, men's athletic director Tom Parac was persuaded to bring women's athletics under his authority, thereby granting women a degree of recognition. Cherry Spurlock was hired as the first women's athletic director, although officially she was an assistant to Parac. Two new women's varsity athletic coaches were hired. The staff was now composed of three full-time coaches, who between them covered basketball, volleyball, tennis, and gymnastics. [29]

On the face of it, these developments appeared to be positive ones for women's athletics. But although well intended, the incorporation with men's athletics proved to work against women's sports. There was serious grumbling about coaching proficiency, and administrative relationships did not mesh harmoniously. Moreover, their tie to the men's program did little to relieve women of their concerns with developments in athletics that they considered undesirable for women. Friction set in and morale dropped. In the meantime, the athletic commission continued to drag its feet. President McIntosh had asked the commission to create greater opportunities for women in the wake of the court decision, but concrete action had not resulted. [30] When in early 1977 Spurlock resigned under pressure, McIntosh, faced with a depressing climate, and pushed by Kreighbaum, concluded that incorporation wasn't working for women, that the program would best be split into two equal departments. In the spring of that year, Kreighbaum was relieved of her duties in physical education and assigned to the field house to direct women's athletics and head up the search for a new staff, including three new coaches and a full-time women's athletic director. These positions were filled for the fall quarter. In the meantime, President McIntosh had left office. When incoming President William Tietz lent his support to women's athletics as a necessarily separate entity, the program embarked on a wholly new course. MSU's women had not only joined the mainstream—they were redefining it.

The revolutionary nature of these decisions cannot be overemphasized. With independence, MSU women's athletics now enjoyed an extraordinarily privileged position. At the time, only six other independent women's athletic departments existed in the entire nation, nor has the number changed significantly since. Women at the University of Montana have not acquired the independence that women at MSU now enjoy; in the rest of the Big Sky Conference, only Eastern Washington's women can claim even a modicum of independence from male sovereignty. In assessing the uniqueness of these developments, certain things are clear. While women across the country generally have been forced to exist in collegiate athletic departments in a state of subordination, at MSU a precedent-establishing lawsuit, brought by women of remarkable courage and commitment, gave women the equality so much of society was championing in theory but paying mere lip service to in practice.

From P.E. to Health and Human Development

From the outset in the 1890s, and for many decades thereafter, physical education, today known as movement science, was subordinated to athletics and intercollegiate sports. In 1908, for example, the department was occupied primarily with coaching athletic teams and supervising training for athletes. The staff also conducted mandatory physical exams for newly enrolled male students, and on the basis of those physicals made exercise, dietetic, and hygienic recommendations. Women were first included in gymnasium work in 1909. Una B. Herrick, MSC's first instructor of physical education for women, and later dean of women, outlined her objectives:

> The aim of the Physical Education Department for women is to develop each girl to her highest economic value, as a unit of society, to the end that when she finishes her college work she may carry forth into life a sane, well balanced, logical mind, high moral character and a strong symmetrical, properly functioning body capable of assuming and performing cheerfully and well the duties of cultured womanhood. [1]

The formalization of physical education received a boost with the outbreak of World War I when military drill became mandatory. Although physical education was available on a noncredit basis, military drill and athletics were considered the core for male exercise. This changed in the early 1920s when physical education became required of all freshman and sophomore males.

The completion of the new gymnasium in 1922, later named Romney Gym, was the major impetus in these developments.

The following thirty years are identified with George Ott Romney and Schubert R. Dyche, both of whom also coached with remarkable success. Romney, who came to MSC in 1922, laid the foundation for a four-year course leading to a degree in physical education designed to "train men to assume professionally the responsibilities of positions in high schools which include coaching athletic teams and instructing in other branches of physical education." [2] In establishing this program, he followed the pattern taking shape at state institutions nationally. When, in 1928, he left MSC, he was replaced by his assistant, Schubert Dyche, who remained affiliated with the school's athletics and physical education until 1952. Dyche was a remarkable person; not only did he coach a variety of sports and teach numerous physical education courses, he served as an instructor of flute and cello in the department of music. He was also the first to suggest the separation of intercollegiate athletics from physical education, although in his early reports he advocated only fiscal differentiation.

The 1930s saw the development of a larger role for the men's and women's physical education programs in providing elective work for more and more students. As numbers increased, a minor was created in 1935 for women teaching aspirants, combining physical education theory classes with study in bacteriology and human physiology. This became a major three years later, with a variety of new courses added to the curriculum.

During World War II, the men's program declined in numbers, while the women's remained fairly steady. In both programs much energy was devoted to assisting the war effort. The first aid course became quite important, and male staff members were heavily engaged in providing physical training activities for military personnel stationed on campus. Dyche himself took a three-year leave of absence to join the American Red Cross. Terrific expansion followed the conclusion of the war. The department renamed itself Health, Physical Education and Athletics, and at graduation in 1947 presented degrees to fifty-three men and thirty-three women. In 1952 Dyche retired, urging once more the separation of physical education from intercollegiate athletics. John "Brick" Breeden, member of the famed Golden Bobcats, and head basketball coach since 1935, replaced him as department head. Following Breeden, the school's football coaches doubled as directors of physical education. During this same period Marga Hosaeus was director of women's health and physical education. [3]

In the mid-1950s, the department became part of the newly formed Division of Education, while athletics became accountable and responsible directly to the Office of the President. Though Roland Renne was high on athletics, he was not so enthusiastic in his support of physical education, and the male members of the department always understood that their prime responsibility was to varsity sports. As elsewhere in the nation, two years of physical education were required of all students, and faculty teaching loads were regularly sixteen to twenty hours a quarter. Nor was it uncommon for the P.E. faculty to have to help in fund-raising drives, run clinics, give speeches at graduations and banquets, lobby for legislation bearing on matters relating to physical education, and officiate at sporting events. [4]

A major breakthrough occurred in 1967-1968. The concept of a physical education complex was inaugurated, a P.E. graduate program was initiated, the two-year physical education requirement was dropped, the program was placed on a coeducational basis, and physical education and athletics were split into two separate departments. Much of this was the result of the direction of George Shroyer, who came to MSU in 1965 and immediately set about to energize the program, increase the staff, and, through the newly proposed graduate program, bring in students who would provide the department with new vitality. Shroyer also lessened the heavy professional loads of the faculty, deemphasizing the extensive service requirements for which faculty had received no pay. Professional development was now emphasized; high value was placed on publication and appointments of men and women with terminal degrees. For the first time, athletic coaches were not supervising physical education courses, an arrangement that in previous years had been too often detrimental to good teaching. Physical education was now standing on its own, even though phasing out the P.E. requirement had meant that the department had to do considerable marketing to keep up its enrollments. Shroyer and his staff did this by instituting such courses as slimnastics and weight training, and offering lifetime sports such as racquetball, bowling, badminton, dance, and golf. [5] The new departmental title assumed in 1975, Health, Physical Education and Recreation, reflected the new emphasis.

The physical education complex, now the Marga Hosaeus Health and Physical Education Center, completed in 1973, was a great boon to the program. At first the demands placed upon it by swimmers and tennis players were huge, but these tapered off in the mid-1980s and appropriate space has been given to aerobics, golf, and weight training. Skiing, which once enrolled as many as 1200 students each year, has fallen off in the last few years to better than half of that, a decline prompted by increased costs, less than optimum snow conditions, and declining enrollment generally.

In 1987 the department underwent still another name change when the College of Education reorganized and became the College of Education, Health, and Human Development. The health and human development half of the newly organized college was composed of three units: counseling, psychology and family sciences; home economics and consumer sciences; and health, nutrition and movement sciences. Movement science, or what had formerly been known as physical education, was only one part of the third unit, which itself comprised a variety of fields: biomechanics, community health, exercise science, food and nutrition, health promotion and wellness, physical education and home economics teacher preparation, sport medicine, physical therapy, consumer science, textiles and clothing, child and family science, and counseling. [6] The shift in emphasis represented a decided move away from recreation as an end in itself to a philosophy emphasizing human wellness in its broadest sense. As Alexander McNeill, department head, expressed it, "Sport and games are only a process

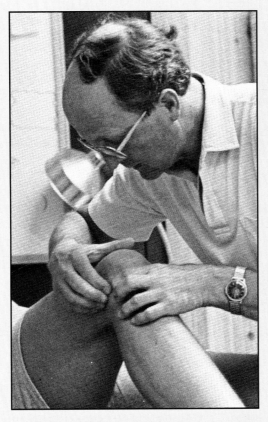

Sports medicine

become a major player in the university's overall outreach program, serving as a resource for wellness programs for schools and organizations across the entire state.

Consequently, the physical education curriculum today is quite unlike that of forty to fifty years ago. Whereas the old objective had been to prepare students for teaching, this has now become a much less important task as a whole new series of options has become the focus of the curriculum. In 1990-1991, for example, students in the K-12 health and physical education option constituted only 11 percent of the department's enrollment, while the largest number were in child and family science (18 percent) and sports medicine (15 percent). Moreover, the department of health and human development had increased enormously in size, having become one of the very largest in the university, with 604 undergraduate and 69 graduate students. This has been an amazing development, which, when combined with the change in philosophy, marks the evolution of the discipline as one of the more noteworthy and interesting stories in the university's history.

of fulfilling a complete life...."[7] Development of social values and emotional health was as important as physical training and recreation according to this philosophy of total wellness. The department's interest in gerontology and thanatology was a natural extension of this new commitment. Another was the decision to place the Cooperative Extension Service's nutritional and 4-H programs under the department's administration. Health and human welfare had now

1. Cited in William H. McAlduff, "A History of the Health, Physical Education and Recreation Department at Montana State University, 1893-1979," M.A. thesis, Montana State University, 1979, 39.
2. Ibid., 41.
3. Ibid., 48-49, 51-52.
4. Herb Agocs interview, 14 July 1988.
5. Ibid.; McAlduff, "A History," 57-59.
6. "Reorganization and Reconceptualization of the College of Education: A Report Submitted by the College of Education Management Team, June 23, 1986."
7. Alexander McNeil interview, 10 February 1992.

The Vicissitudes of Growth

Many will argue that the most critical issue encountered by collegiate athletics in the last fifteen years has been its movement toward professionalism and commercialization and the increased costs associated with attempts to maintain Division I status. Today not 8 percent of the nation's universities and colleges can turn an athletic profit. Spiraling inflation has hit hard. Many state legislatures have reduced their aid to athletics. At some schools, student supports have been lowered or withdrawn. The growth of women's athletics has created new and not insubstantial demands on budgeting. Playoffs in basketball and football, rather than regular season play, often provide the difference between black-and red-ink accounting. Everywhere, these factors have pressured schools to increase their level of competition in the so-called major sports. In turn, increased levels of competition

have served to boost costs by surprising magnitudes. And the costs have not been solely monetary. In an age of declining resources, an unnerving fee-based economic philosophy drives programs inexorably away from individual skill sports to those group activities favored most by spectators, namely football and basketball. The need to enlarge the recruiting base to provide talent adequate for high levels of competition has introduced sociological and academic problems. The effort to remain competitive generates a relentless momentum that in turn generates enormous pressures.

The results have not always been salutary. All across the country, colleges and universities desiring competitive athletic programs have had to resort to extraordinary means, some of them undesirable. So-called minor sports have suffered badly in the wake of efforts to maintain and improve the major sports. Scheduling has been prostituted. Recruiting has become institutionalized and professionalized. High-pressured commercialism has entered the scene in a variety of innovative, sometimes overly influential, ways. Athletic boosterism has gone beyond merely providing fan and dollar support. There have been alarming increases of recruiting violations and lowered academic standards. The media report regularly on big-time collegiate athletics as a major source of public scandal.

Since the mid-1970s, all of the aforementioned problems have in some way, in some degree, been experienced at MSU. Elevation to more competitive brackets, big-game scheduling, big-time boosterism, crises in recruiting and academic standards, the elimination of nonsolvent sports—all of these have shown up at MSU in the last fifteen years. And although the school can look proudly at its record in meeting the challenges, the struggle to balance the books and maintain a program of academic integrity has not always been an easy one. Progress, the reader of

history appreciates, isn't always inexorably forward; periodic steps backward are as much a part of the process. Understanding how the university bridged the gaps, filled the fissures, and worked to smooth the road can serve as a means of appreciating MSU's success in dealing with the issues.

The NCAA's creation in 1978 of a new IAA bracket for football, and the Big Sky Conference's decision to move up from Division II to compete in it, had significant consequences for MSU athletics. What the NCAA had done was to take the least competitive Division I teams and couple these with the most competitive Division II teams to create a wholly new league. From the outset, the Big Sky Conference was a dominating factor in IAA, winning the national title twice—including MSU's remarkable crown in 1984—and placing two and even three teams annually in the championship playoffs.

The MSU 1984 National Football Championship

Code Blue! Code Blue! The cardiac care units around the state go on alert—the Montana State Bobcats are behind and only 4:20 is left in the game. [1]

On December 8, 1984, the 'Cats had their backs to the wall against Rhode Island in the semifinals of the NCAA IAA football playoffs. But let Fred White, voice of the Kansas City Chiefs, who called the game that bright, crisp day in Bozeman, pick it up from there:

Rhode Island; they lead by two. They're at the thirteen yard line. Ehrhart into the end zone. It's intercepted. A big defensive play for Montana State. They're at the forty; they're at midfield; and they're going to go. For Montana State that's. . . . Joe Roberts, who intercepted near the end zone, takes it all the way back. It's Joe Roberts who made the play, the strong safety.

Look at this crowd; look at them piled up in the snowbank in Bozeman. Talk about electricity. Down by two points, shoved back against their own goal line. Joe Roberts, a senior strong safety from Missoula, Montana, just made the biggest play of the year for the Bobcats. [2]

After the game, the team members needled defensive lineman Tex Sikora about his near-collision with Roberts on the way downfield. "Tex was just slowing down to let Joe pass," someone quipped. Bruce Parker, MSU sports information director, remarked that Roberts had confided to him before the game that he had dreamed the night before of intercepting a Ram pass.

As a matter of fact, 1984 had been a season for dreams. Coming off a sad 1-10 record the previous year, and then picked by some scribes and coaches to finish dead-last in the Big Sky Conference, the Bobcats, under head coach Dave Arnold, instead tied the school's record for most wins in a season (12), established its longest winning streak (10), and then made the biggest turnaround in NCAA football history, winning a national championship.

At the outset, the road to Charleston, South Carolina, and the IAA championship hadn't seemed paved with such gold. Early losses to Eastern Washington and Idaho State suggested a so-so season at best. But then the 'Cats walloped Weber to set the stage for the season's turning point—a quadruple OT win in Bozeman over Nevada-Reno. Following the next week's lopsided victory over Portland State, PSU's head coach Don Reid explained what made the '84 'Cats tick: "They're just an offensive machine," he said. "They're devastating with the football. You've got to play big plays with them because they play big play all the time." [3]

Now 5-2, the 'Cats continued to roll as they came from behind to beat Boise and the Griz, and then crush NAU to claim the Big Sky championship and a place in the playoffs. No one really figured the 'Cats would win the final regular season road game over Fresno State, a Division I team led by former MSU coaches Jim Sweeney and Cliff Hysell. But down 24-7 in the third quarter, the Blue and the Gold came back to win 34-31 with only 27 seconds

The 1984 Cats host Boise

*1984 national champions.
From left to right:
co-captains Joe Roberts,
Mark Fellows, and Joe
Bignell; head coach Dave
Arnold; president Bill Tietz*

left on a 20-yard pass from quarterback Kelly Bradley to tight end Joe Bignell. This win gave MSU a high seed in the playoffs and the home field advantage for round 1.

The quarterfinal game against Arkansas State started very much like most of MSU's regular season contests, with the visitors bolting to a 14-0 lead. But then ASU wilted as the Bobcat defense adjusted to the wishbone offense and the team won going away. The semifinal game against Rhode Island, also at Bozeman (described above), was the game of the year, bar none. While the team made extraordinary plays throughout the season, Roberts' interception was arguably the most electric play in MSU's entire grid history. Like the offense, which prided itself on the big play, Roberts' decision to depart from his normal pass defense responsibility, to "not play it by the book," as Rhode Island's head coach lamented

after the game, typified the way the 'Cats performed all season. [4]

The championship 19-6 win in Charleston over Louisiana Tech, a team that had averaged 42 points a game in its two previous playoff contests, proved indisputably that MSU was not only offensively potent, but was defensively devastating as well. Louisiana Tech ran up against a stone wall and was held scoreless until the last minute of the game. Against the Bobcat's most formidable defensive showing of the season the Bulldogs rushed for minus 25 yards, were intercepted four times, had two punts blocked, and lost three fumbles; their quarterback was sacked eleven times, five of them by defensive end Mark Fellows. "Their strength and aggressiveness surprised us," remarked a stunned LTU offensive tackle after the game. "Their defensive pressure was the key to the ball game," added LTU's head coach. "We just couldn't keep them out." [5] "Swarming 'Cats Shut Down 'Dogs," was the appropriate observation of the *Bozeman Chronicle*.[6] As Dave Arnold put it: "Our defense came to play. That's [been] their characteristic all year. They're just a tough hard-nosed bunch from Montana who love to play the game." [7]

The personal records set during this season were as remarkable as those compiled by the team. Bradley's passing stats for 1984 were awesome—642 passes attempted, 367 completed, for 4477 yards and 38 touchdowns. To give that achievement its proper perspective, compare it with the next best set of seasonal figures, also set by Bradley—383 passes attempted, 222 completed, for 2431 yards and 16 TDs. Those on the receiving end of Bradley's passes in '84 set marks as well, particularly Joe Bignell, who caught eighty-eight for 1149 yards.

There were plenty of stars on this team. Mark Fellows, punter Dirk Nelson, and offensive tackle Bill Schmidt made first-team All-America, while Bradley was picked for third team. Honorable mentions went to Bignell, noseguard Lonnie Burt, safety Doug Kimball, and guard Bruce Randall. Fellows was drafted by the NFL and played in the East-West Game in San Francisco.

It was a great season, a story-book season, one of the best ever in MSC/MSU grid history.

1. *Bozeman Daily Chronicle*, 9 December 1984.
2. Transcript of game video.
3. *Bozeman Daily Chronicle*, 21 October 1984.
4. Ibid., 9 December 1984.
5. *Charleston News and Courier/The Evening Post*, 16 December 1984.
6. Ibid.
7. Ibid.

Big Sky membership did not come without additional cost, however, and these costs have increased markedly over the years. While an additional twenty football scholarships composed the immediate added expense, it soon became obvious that in order to compete at the IAA level, coaching staffs would have to be increased and that the competitition for good coaches who would be willing to come to as remote a region as the Northern Rockies would be intense. Within a few

Craig Finberg airborne

years, salaries for coaches had increased sharply, almost doubling. Costs of travel also skyrocketed in the late 70s and early 80s as inflation gripped the nation. As the conference is geographically one of the most widespread of any in the country, lengthy and expensive road trips are the rule, some of them approaching 1000 miles in each direction. Moreover, within the conference individual school ambitions drove competitive levels and costs yet higher. One or two institutions made no secrets of their desire to eventually move up to Division I level of performance and recruited and improved their facilities accordingly, forcing the rest of the conference to do so as well.

Consequently, recruiting in the Big Sky Conference became big time. Trips to recruit out-of-state athletes increased in number and proved exceedingly costly as MSU's coaching staffs felt compelled to extend their networks from Montana and the Northwest to the Midwest and, most recently, to the Deep South. The decision to draw on more non-Montana athletes was not made capriciously. As athletic director Doug Fullerton pointed out, "Virtually every coach in the nation knows that the closer to home you can recruit the better off you are. 'Home grown' talent creates more fan support and quite frankly costs us less to educate." [31] But changing circumstances can no longer justify the former commitment to predominately Montana-based teams. Although MSU coaches still draw consistently from Montana, the increasing level of skill required by Big Sky Conference play simply can't be found in its entirety within the old recruiting base. This dictum applies to both football and basketball.

In football, speed has become the impelling factor. In a conference that is overwhelmingly patterned on an exceedingly mobile passing strategy, speed—and speedy defenses against speed—are requisites. It is a fact that Montana cannot provide adequate numbers of players with this skill; the all-time Montana high school 100-meter-dash record, for example, will not qualify for the Big Sky Conference track meet. Looking at it this way, once MSU and UM moved up to IAA with the Big Sky Conference, the pool of football players available in Montana with appropriate skill levels declined. The hard reality of a declining regional pool has been psychologically very difficult for many of MSU's football fans to face. Few forget that there was a time when MSU could field a football team of competitive Montana athletes—the 1976 and 1984 national championship teams were heavily in-state—and the inclination is always there to stay at home, to cultivate, recruit, and work with those young regional athletes who have a long record of having both excelled and overachieved when put up against good competition. Times have changed, however, and in some sports the new demands are understood. The realization, for example, that the need for quality players transcends the significance of regional talent is accepted in basketball, where individual capability, or lack of it, is conspicuous. But the old ethic dies hard in football, where the rock 'em, sock 'em concept of a team stocked with raw-boned, tough, committed Montana mining and ranching kids can subvert the logic of crossing state borders. Nevertheless, it is a fact that MSU's football fortunes began to decline in the early '80s, and that the administrative analysis of that decline credited it to a recruiting philosophy too heavily reliant upon a pool of local talent. For example, advocates of change pointed out that this entrenched, underlying loyalty to Montana athletes, and to the hiring of Montana assistant coaches, was so well recognized in the conference that opposing coaches often exploited it, convincing likely out-of-state prospects that they would never play for MSU if Montana kids were competing with them for the same positions.

The 1981 decision to fire popular, Butte-born head football coach Sonny Lubick, who had an overall winning record but had experienced two consecutive losing seasons, brought this issue to the forefront. Critics, right or wrong, took the position that he had taken the Montana-first ethic too far. More important, and over the long run far more serious in its implications for Bobcat athletics, the forced departure of Lubick alienated many of MSU's most avid supporters, and overnight transformed MSU's regional recruiting from a basically successful process to a difficult one. For the sacking of Lubick, and his connections with the legendary Sonny Holland, and before that with Jim Sweeney, represented the severance of an almost umbilical relationship with the state's mineral cities, particularly Butte. Butte would not forgive MSU that decision, it seemed, and the automatic path the mining city's athletes once took to Bozeman turned increasingly in a westerly, rather than an easterly, direction. Loyalty in Montana, particularly in a union town, is taken seriously; to many the firing of a native, with his commitment to the family ethic, was a reprehensible act. Since Lubick left, the critics point out, and despite a national championship in 1984 (achieved with a senior class of Lubick-recruited athletes), MSU has won less than one-third of its football games.

This whole question of how many in-staters an MSU football roster should be composed of is a subject that simply will not go away; it is pervasive in alumni conversations and has been for decades. Other schools in the Big Sky Conference must wonder at the intensity of it. It is likely a mark of the extraordinarily parochial character of Montana that of the six states represented in the Big Sky Conference, only the Treasure State puts so much emphasis on the need for its teams to be predominately home-grown. Idaho, Nevada, and Boise State, in contrast, have sported generally fewer than 25 percent natives on their football rosters. But Montanans seem dissatisfied with less than 50 percent. Support for this situation has been voiced at every level since time immemorial and is best summed up by the statement of a member of the Board of Regents in 1961: "I want to see all Montana boys on Montana athletic teams. I think we should give the scholarships all to Montana boys." [32] The strength of this argument has been felt continually in Bozeman. Inquire of a coach or an athletic director about the state of affairs, and very likely the discussion will shortly proceed to a breakdown of the number of in-state and out-of-state players on the teams. Too often, when a team loses, a scapegoat is found in these numbers; when a team wins, a justification appears instead. Inevitably, it appears that only a winning record will quell the controversy. It is a fact that these complaints have festered precisely because MSU football has not been a successful program in the past decade.

The verdict is much clearer on MSU's determination to field teams composed of high-quality scholar-athletes. Save for one lapse in the late 1970s and very early '80s, no Big Sky Conference team has come close to rivaling MSU's record of recruiting good scholar-athletes who graduate on time. MSU's admittance and matriculation standards have always been high. They became even higher following the so-called Bernard Madison case of 1979-1980, an exceptional development that helped MSU reaffirm its commitment to the scholar-athlete.

In the intense Division I basketball competition of the late '70s, MSU's coaching staff became convinced that in order for Montana State to compete successfully it would have to set aside MSU's time-honored standards and recruit inner-city athletes who may have marginal academic skills. At least one other Big Sky school had done this repeatedly—and with notable success, so long as one measured the results purely on a won-and-loss record. Bernard Madison was a promising freshman basketball player from Chicago. He was a fine young man, but he came to MSU with limitations as a student, limitations which the Bobcat basketball staff sought to compensate for by enrolling him in a less-than-challenging curriculum his first quarter. The classes Bernard was placed in by his coaches included basketball fundamentals and techniques, basketball philosophy, physical conditioning, wrestling theory, general biology (a remedial course in health), and safety with hand power tools. The young man made a B average, and having been led by his high school advisors back in Chicago to believe that he possessed scholarly skills superior to those required in, for example, wrestling theory, and worried that this sort of curriculum would hardly earn him a degree, he requested, for the second quarter, a course load of solids that included English, math, and general economics. He dropped out just before the end of the quarter, however, arguing that MSU had "destroyed" his motivation.

It is an unfortunate reality that cases such as Madison's rarely receive more than passing attention, so often do instances of this kind occur on American college campuses. Academic subterfuge in the athletic arena has been going on for decades, to such a degree that eyebrows scarcely rise anymore at the latest revelation of another All-American "majoring" in basket weaving, badminton, or folk dance. But in the Madison case, the young man was placed in the public spotlight by being cited in *Sports Illustrated*, with numerous others, as a tragic victim of academic corruption in collegiate athletics. [33]

The article caused a flap in Montana, of course, and President Tietz called immediately for an investigation to reveal and remedy the conditions suggested by the expose. Although the basketball coaching staff justified Madison's program, and similar programs for at least four other marginal students, all of them junior college transfers, as necessary to ensure the players' "survival," the investigation concluded that the coaches unfortunately considered the recruiting and covering up of unqualified student-athletes as necessary to their own survival. What was starkly revealed in the investigation was not only the way in which academic deficiencies were being covered, but the ridiculously easy and academically unsound manner in which junior college athletes with subpar scholastic records could transfer without penalty to four-year institutions. By matriculating heavily in Mickey Mouse courses, some of which were even more content-free than those Madison had taken, and by avoiding at all costs solid courses outside of athletics and recreation, junior college athletes could transfer in grade point averages high enough to sustain themselves through a year of additional competition, even when they did poorly at their new school. As could be predicted, few, if any, of these transfer students ever graduated. [34]

While Bernard Madison never did make any scholarly or athletic contributions in Bozeman, his case did result in substantial improvement of the enrollment and counseling of student-athletes at MSU. Academic advising was removed from the province of the athletic staffs and reassigned to the major academic areas in which the athletes matriculated, and the athletic director was directed to oversee that process. MSU admission standards were strengthened. Junior college transfers now had to have a grade point average of at least C, based solely on solids, and the number of core courses for all incoming freshmen was fixed at fourteen, or three more than required by the NCAA. These upgradings gave MSU the tough-

Kral Ferch slams one

est entrance requirements of any school in the Big Sky Conference. [35]

Some lamented these developments, branding them impediments to the success of Bobcat athletics by diminishing the customary recruiting pool and by creating, as a consequence, another cause for increased dollar expenditures from having to increase the geographic parameters of the pool. Others saw the developments as very positive moves and made the most of the higher standards. In time, MSU coaches in every sport came to realize that Montana State's loftier standards appealed to many prospects, that MSU could use to great advantage its reputation as an institution that recruited quality student-athletes, and that MSU graduated them and prepared them to be competitive in the national job market. The results are revealed in the statistics. No Big Sky school can rival the graduation rate of MSU's men and women athletes, and no Big Sky school has come even close to matching MSU's All-Academic Athlete achievement—better than twice as many as the nearest conference rival. On campus, the athletic departments take pride in graduating athletes at a GPA 25 percent higher than that of nonathletes. Between 1988 and 1992, MSU athletes won more major post-graduate scholarships than any other NCAA Division 1 program in the intermountain West. MSU's scholar-athlete record has been outstanding by every standard. [36]

That Bernard Madison was an Afro-American spoke to yet another of the significant changes MSU athletics underwent in the 1970s and '80s. It is only recently, since the early-to-mid '80s, that MSU has seriously recruited black athletes. To be sure, the 1950s and '60s did produce their Larry Chaneys and Bill Brickhouses, but MSU teams in those decades were otherwise virtually all-white. At the very end of the 1960s, however, the basketball program brought in a number of players who, unfortunately, not only failed to provide the breakthrough talent MSU sought, but who also roused local alarm by becoming associated with radical campus politics. That these young men were black placed them in the spotlight. That they espoused the cause of black nationalism compounded things badly on a conservative campus and in an even more conservative community. It mattered not that these blacks were simply local actors in the national civil rights movement, and that they felt quite naturally compelled to assert their independence of white protocols while claiming their rights to white privileges. Bozeman, and not a few campus administrators, looked at these developments with ill favor. Some members of the community even tried to restrain faculty from becoming associated with, or to buy up the contracts of those who were associated with, black protest, among numerous other causes.

A decade later the Madison case raised the old issues once more. With only one exception, the MSU athletes cited in the internal review prompted by the expose were black. Not one of them ever graduated; some, like Madison, didn't even complete one academic year. In retrospect, Bobcat basketball did not do well in the 1970s and early '80s, and likely much of it was MSU's failure to recruit competitively for good black student-athletes.

The experience of the early '70s and '80s was instructive, however. In recent years black athletes have been incorporated with much greater success in the basketball program and, increas-

Bobcats 58, Grizzlies 57 (1982)

ingly so, in football. Black athletes have made their mark scholastically as well as athletically. The success of basketball coach Stu Starner's three great seasons, 1986-1988, was due in no small part to the leadership of three superb black guards, Tony Hampton, Ray Willis, and Chris Conway, all of whom graduated (Willis with honors) and went on to succeed in the private or public sectors. The integration of blacks has been so successful that the athletic departments can say with some pride that their coaches have recruited people, not color. Nevertheless, this has not been easy. The white homogeneity of our state and campus makes it more difficult to bring blacks to MSU. Ninety-nine percent of the student body is Caucasian. Those few blacks who are on campus are predominately athletes, and predominately male. Moreover, memories are long, and the need to recruit blacks of a calibre good enough to offset lingering community skepticism forces upon the coaches yet another condition they must add to their recruiting objectives. These are not things coaches like to talk about, but they have to be considered. It was only a few years ago, for example, that the women's track coach felt compelled to advise a prime Jamaican sprinter to enroll elsewhere because of MSU's social environment. And more recently, women's athletics had to suffer the indignity of booster complaints about the candidacy of a woman for the head coaching position in basketball, not only because the boosters favored male coaches for all sports, but because she was oriental, and worse, Japanese. The resistance of the Montana legislature to proclaim a Martin Luther King day as a commemoration of the civil rights breakthroughs of the 1960s was another kind of message. Montana finally adopted the holiday in 1991, the forty-eighth state in the union to do so. But the footdragging underwrote a distasteful reality: racial narrowness has had a long history on the frontier, and while our senior citizens aver it has abated greatly over recent years, it still crops up too often for the likes of most, and helps to complicate the ability of MSU to strengthen its athletic program with the best talent, regardless of color or gender.

Meeting the Challenge

By the mid-1980s, the main challenge facing MSU athletics was no longer gender or race, or even so much a winning record. Rather, it was budgeting—the worst fiscal crisis athletics had possibly ever faced. There was very little flexibility in facing the lean years, as over 90 percent of the budget was fixed. External factors threatened to and then succeeded in unbalancing the books. Periodic increases in student enrollment fees impacted the athletic scholarship program. Health insurance costs skyrocketed. As women's athletics grew, so did its budgetary needs. Inflation and higher academic standards forced travel and recruiting costs ever higher. The need for new and more sophisticated equipment added to the burden. New facilities had to be constructed, and older ones rehabilitated. To compound matters, MSU was one of only two schools in the Big Sky Conference lacking dedicated student athletic fee support.

Then the worst blow hit—in 1985 the state legislature cut its aid for athletics by 30 percent, reverting to a figure below its 1981 appropriation, and the cut was not reinstated. All of the administrative offices controlling the resources, including those at MSU, seemed to be saying that while they expected Montana State to remain competitive, they expected it to be done on fewer dollars. MSU athletics found itself on the fiscal ropes. Adjustments simply couldn't be made fast enough. Although scholarships and staff were cut, a big deficit emerged, running to over $200,000, or 10 percent of the total athletic budget. The worst hit in 1986-1987. It was a time of real crisis, calling for emergency measures. Anything that didn't pay for itself was in jeopardy. Even rodeo was in trouble. [37]

Three strategems came, more or less, to the forefront. On surface, the easiest alternative would have been to drop out of the Big Sky Conference and down to Division II competition, perhaps along with two or three other conference schools. Presumably the costs would be reduced significantly at this level. Burgeoning salaries could be contained, the number of scholarships cut back, and the tremendous expenses of national game travel and recruiting could be reduced substantially. Moreover, Division II status would enable MSU to provide more regional services, as a greater number of Montana athletes could now find a place for themselves at a state university.

This was not a new alternative, or one unique to MSU. In the midst of a similar crisis in 1976, President McIntosh had ordered the athletic department to draw up a scenario in which only football and basketball would be retained, the former at a Division II status. [38] Fortunately, it had not been necessary to adopt such a radical policy. By the late 1980s, however, several other schools in the Big Sky Conference were experiencing the same difficulties and discussing the advantages that might be had from moving down. Idaho State, for example, openly discussed this alternative, and officers from several other schools, including Eastern Washington and the University of Montana, hinted at their theoretical support. [39] The action taken by Montana's state legislature to reduce its commitment to athletics seemed to suggest the necessity for such thinking.

A second alternative suggested a shift in exactly the opposite direction—moving football up to the Division I level. Basketball had long enjoyed this advantage, and at one time skiing at MSU had provided some of the nation's finest collegiate performers. Rodeo had always performed with the very best of the nation's competitors, and there had been talk in recent years about moving the wrestling program beyond the conference into the truly big time, bringing in teams with national reputations, such as those from Iowa and Oklahoma. Other schools in the conference were weighing these possibilities—Nevada (Reno), and Boise, for example, were beginning to more than hint at their desire to move up to the big time. (In 1990, Nevada did take the step, announcing that it would leave the Big Sky Conference at the conclusion of the 1991-1992 season. There was consequent talk of creating two conference divisions, north and south—the southern division including Northern Arizona and a number of California schools.)

It did not take long for MSU's athletic staff to reject these two alternatives, however. A move down would not reduce costs sufficiently, the staff observed. The budget was now dependent to a large degree on big-game guarantees with Division I opponents and on TV contracts, including especially the NCAA Division I postseason basketball tournament, which guaranteed better than a quarter of a million dollars for qualification alone. Booster support and game attendance would decline inevitably, perhaps drastically. The result would be a greatly enlarged dependence on what was already an inadequate and unreliable state general fund capability. Only a drop all the way down to Division III, or the total elimination of scholarship aid, would be fiscally reasonable. But the matter of pride and politics was also at stake. MSU had reached a certain plateau of competition from which a withdrawal would be almost psychologically impossible.

As for the second alternative, it was really no alternative at all—its implausibility was guaranteed by the immense costs associated with Division I football competition, compounded by the absence of an adequate spectator base, profitable media market, and sufficient state support. These were advantages Reno and Boise had, but assuredly not Bozeman.

Predictably, MSU chose a third alternative, a decision to remain where it was—to commit itself fully to a competitive Big Sky Conference level, to do so by aggressively establishing a sound fiscal base sufficient to support a winning program and to become as independent as possible from state funding. Although there was implicit in this decision the potential that the state would interpret a move toward fiscal independence as justifying further general-fund reductions, the risk was accepted and the decision to forge ahead was made. Critical measures were immediately undertaken, some of which paid good dividends, but none of which were without cost. [40]

The most drastic step taken by the central administration was its decision to drop three sports—men's wrestling, women's gymnastics, and men's and women's skiing. All three sports, especially wrestling and skiing, had strong Montana roots, and their termination not only cut off opportunities for regional wrestlers and skiers, but stood to weaken MSU's image as a concerned, service-oriented institution. Internal opposition to the termination of these sports was fierce, particularly on the part of the women, who were already handicapped by the enormous inequity of athletic opportunity given men by football. The women's athletic department decried especially the loss of gymnastics, as it represented a critical individual skill sport perfectly suited to women. Rather tennis than gymnastics, they protested. All arguments to the contrary were rejected, however, on the reasoning that none of the minor sports targeted for termination produced revenue sufficient to justify their continuation. Besides, tennis was required by the conference, was less injury-prone than wrestling, and was one of the least expensive of the minor sports. These decisions left intact very few sports at MSU. Men had football, basketball, rodeo, tennis and track, while women retained basketball, rodeo, tennis, track, and volleyball. This was a tragic commentary on what the fiscal crisis had done, especially to those sports emphasizing individual skill and performance. Dollars were now clearly driving athletic decision making at every level.

Debates over what sports MSU should support have always been part of athletic planning. In 1971, baseball and golf were dropped. Some said that the Gallatin Valley's wet spring weather prohibited the continuation of these sports (the baseball team had been rained out or snowed out of virtually every home game that spring), but the real factor was dollars. Swimming might have been a logical alternative varsity sport, especially following the construction of the Marga Hosaeus Physical Education Center. But it was not supported because of cost. Soccer and ice hockey, both highly suitable sports for Montana, as they defy weather, have never been instituted at MSU, presumably because the former would be non-revenue producing and would potentially deplete the pool of high school football players, while the latter, a great spectator sport, would compete for basketball's audiences in addition to requiring far-flung road scheduling. In short, the influence of the business ethic on sport, or "corporate athleticism" as it is known in the trade, [41] speaks loudly, and never with greater influence than in the present; the decision to focus MSU's fiscal energies even more directly on the so-called major spectator and revenue-producing sports—football and basketball—by dropping wrestling, gymnastics, and skiing has a lengthy and unfortunate legacy.

The "Minor" Sports

For all the attention given to the gridiron and the hardwood at MSU, the school's so-called minor, or nonrevenue, sports have attained some remarkable heights. The 1960s brought the heyday of the minors, as MSC/MSU repeatedly won Big Sky Conference titles in skiing and wrestling and performed more than creditably in baseball and golf. Sadly, all four of these sports would later be dropped for fiscal reasons—baseball and golf in 1971, skiing and wrestling in 1986.

Montana State's downhillers, under the direction of coach Bob Beck, dominated the conference in the '60s and produced many standout athletes, including Jan Stenerud who was an NCAA All-American jumper in 1964. Throughout the 1970s and early '80s, MSU's ski teams were among the nation's finest, competing with the likes of Colorado, Utah, Vermont and Wyoming. This proud era in MSU athletics produced the school's best alpine skier, Dan Brelsford, who in the late '70s ranked among America's top collegiate racers. Under head coaches John, and then Gary, Shampeny, Brelsford was a three-time All-American and the 1978 NCAA national slalom champion. Another giant slalom and slalom racer who distinguished himself during the same period was Rusty Squires. In 1981 Brelsford became head coach of MSU's women's and men's alpine teams and served in that capacity until skiing was dropped as the result of the 1986 budget cuts. Under Brelsford the women's team boasted some exceptional talent—Carol Clauser in the early '80s and Ingrid Gustafson and Sylvia Bonfini in the mid-'80s were regional standouts. Another woman who made her mark in the mid-'80s was Kari Swenson, an outstanding bi-athlete (cross-country skiing and shooting) who achieved national ranking.

Wrestling too enjoyed the limelight. Herb Agocs' teams during the 1960s were the envy of the conference, with Bob McIntyre winning conference championships in both '65 and '66. Agocs coached another outstanding grappler in the late '60s and early '70s, Bill Spring, who was a Big Sky champion in 1970. Spring's accomplishments were all the more remarkable because he suffered from asthma; had the medical profession known in 1970 what it knows now about the malady he assuredly would have vied for national honors. In the middle '80s, or just before the sport was dropped, MSU wrestlers, coached by Lanny Bryant, were led by All-American Wade Ayala, two-time Big Sky champion.

Despite their low visibility, tennis and track and field have also produced some remarkable athletes at MSU. Unfortunately, the same kind of unpredictable weather that helped justify the ter-

mination of golf and baseball in the early 1970s beleaguers tennis and track and field. Bozeman's mountain climate discourages other universities from coming to MSU in the spring, forcing the Bobcat teams to schedule almost all of their matches and meets on the road, thereby depriving them of the home-field advantage in addition to adding a travel fatigue factor. It is not uncommon for both teams to host a single match or meet at home each year.

Despite such a disadvantage, MSU tennis has produced numerous standouts. In the late '60s, Dave Harmon qualified for the NCAA national championships at singles, and the sport was revitalized in the early '80s when Jerry Peach, once an MSU standout himself, became head coach. Between 1986 and 1989, Todd DeVries won 125 matches, and, with a 3.9 undergraduate GPA, made the NCAA All-American, All-Academic Tennis Team. No sooner had DeVries graduated than Tarn Callis stepped forward; in the spring of 1992, Callis set an MSU standard in winning his 150th match, obliterating the old record held by Robin Coverdale, who had won 140 matches between 1981 and 1984. Coverdale was simply outstanding. In her freshman year she teamed with another of MSU's greats, Jeannie Rogers, who went to the NCAA national championships in both 1982 and 1983. A third Lady 'Cat who rose to stardom was Michelle Cutler, class of '91.

Track and field has known its own days of glory at MSU. Prior to the mid-1980s when drastic cutbacks in athletics eliminated half of track's scholarships, MSU teams more than held their own in the Big Sky Conference. In 1964, Ken Christison was the conference's javelin champ and went on to place sixth in the NCAA nationals. In the early 1980s another field-event man, Lance Deal, burst into prominence as one of the nation's best weight men. Four times conference champion at the discus, Deal eventually became the world record holder in the indoor weight throw and a member of the 1988 Olympic team. Brian Schweyen in the late '80s and early '90s won six Big Sky Conference championships in the high jump and pole vault. In 1991 Schweyen became the world's first performer ever to clear seven feet in the high jump and seventeen feet in the pole vault. In the same year he placed fourth in the NCAA high jump finals. Likely the greatest of all MSU track athletes was Shannon Butler, a long-distance runner who won twelve indoor and outdoor league titles and the 1990 NCAA crowns in the 5000- and 10,000-meter runs.

Dan Brelsford

Wade Ayala

Shannon Butler

MSU track has also produced some superb women performers. Commencing in the late 1970s under the tutelage of first Neil Eliason and then Dale Kennedy, Bobcat women did remarkably well. Laurie Adams, 1978-1980, was one of the school's all-time great distance runners. A three-time qualifier for the AIAW national championships, she set marks in the 3000- and 5000-meter runs that would still qualify her for the nationals in 1992. During the 1982-1984 seasons Janet Buntin, a stellar long jumper, accumulated the second greatest point total ever scored by an MSU team member in championship competition, earning All-American honors in the process. Annette Hand distinguished herself as a distance runner in track and cross-country in the mid-'80s, qualifying four times for NCAA championships. Hand kept running after graduation, even as a mother of three and a teacher of first-graders. On the eve of the centennial she was a good bet to make the 1992 Olympic team as she ranked among the nation's top five distance runners in the 1500-, 3000-, and 5000-meter runs. Theresa Zacher and Kathleen Monaghan, both engineering students with superb scholastic records, were yet other distance runners of note. Zacher came in twelfth in the NCAA indoor mile in 1988, and Monaghan holds the school record for most points accumulated in Big Sky championship competition. In 1989 she placed ninth in the NCAA cross-country nationals. In the same year she was named Big Sky scholar-athlete of the year.

Women's gymnastics, while having a short life, produced some long talent. One of the early greats was Kathy King, who came in second in the 1979 NCWSA regional all-around competition. Another was Christy Ross, who in 1982 duplicated King's feat, placing second in the AIAW regional as an all-around performer.

Women's volleyball, inaugurated in 1970, remains a strong program today. Bill Newell, coach of the Canadian national men's team, came to MSU in 1977 and over a ten-year period produced some excellent talent. Three players who performed together under his direction in the late '70s and early '80s were especially outstanding. These were Barbara Moe, setter, and Diane Terrall and Moyra Ditchfield, outside hitters. During their playing years, MSU's volleyball team was almost without equal in the AIAW's northwest region; rivaled only by only Portland State.

Before golf was dropped in the budget cuts of 1971, it had produced the likes of Nick Fullerton, who came in second in the Big Sky

Annette Hand

Lance Deal

Butler set six indoor and outdoor MSU records during his undergraduate days, and as the result of his national prominence head track coach Rob Stark was able to recruit two of the nation's top ten high school distance runners in 1991.

*Coach Dale Kennedy
and the 1986-1987 MSU
cross country champions*

Conference championships in 1969 and qualified for the NCAA nationals. The sport is under consideration for reinstatement in the fall of 1993, and possibly Nick Fullerton's feats will be linked in time to the feats of future Bobcat golfers.

Although the lack of strong financial support has handicapped the ability of MSU's minor-sport teams to produce consistently in conference play, individual performers have risen to remarkable heights over the years to leave their mark in regional and national competition. [1]

1. Interviews with Doug Fullerton, Ginny Hunt, Chuck Karnop, Dale Kennedy, Rob Stark, March-April 1992.

Women's athletic director Ginny Hunt and women's track coach Neil Eliason

In recent years, some of the most effective argumentation against professionalization in athletics has come from the women, who continue to attempt to resist the market mechanisms driving men's athletics, and who invoke their legal rights to demand equity in athletic opportunity. Even then, their resistance has not always met its objectives. MSU's women's efforts to resist being swallowed up by the male-dominated NCAA provides an example. Commencing in the mid-70s, the National Collegiate Athletic Association, fearing the effect of equal rights legislation, and believing that women's sports programs could well curtail, if not mortally wound, men's athletics, decided it would have to control the growth of those programs. The NCAA's objective was to place women's athletics under the men's athletic directorship. Nationally, critics saw this as seriously limiting women's independence. MSU's first independent director of women's athletics, Virginia Hunt, was one of those who took an aggressive stance against the NCAA. Why else, she reasoned, would men desire to control women's athletics except to prevent women from commanding too much of the budget and from obtaining equity in athletic opportunity. [42]

Hunt's form of protest was an effort to prevent the NCAA from absorbing the AIAW, the Association of Intercollegiate Athletics for

The 1979-1980 women's volleyball team

Women, of which she was national president. President Tietz agreed that the women had special needs and that the AIAW represented for women a suitable alternative to the NCAA's growing emphasis on professionalism in athletics, witness the AIAW's opposition to the categorization of women's sports as either major or minor. When the AIAW brought suit against the NCAA, President Tietz testified on behalf of the value of AIAW for women. [43] Unfortunately, the AIAW lost its suit, and what resistance remained was broken down by the NCAA's successful proselytizing, with all sorts of pecuniary benefits and inducement, of certain key AIAW members. In 1982 the AIAW lost its sponsorship of championship events to the NCAA, and in 1985 the organization was dissolved. Though women at MSU were not coopted into men's athletics, their major national lobbying organization was now defunct.[44] But the full effects of the NCAA's victory were mitigated at MSU by Tietz's support for continued administrative independence for women's athletics.

In yet other ways women have not fared so well. Although independent administratively, they do not enjoy an equitable situation in athletic opportunities. Equal rights, to women, means equal opportunity. If MSU's student population was composed of 55 percent men and 45 percent women, as it has been for many years, then by law athletic opportunities should have been available for women athletes on a pro-rata basis. But men's football, with ninety scholarship openings, or more opportunities than existed in the entire women's program, completely disarranged the equity equation. MSU's women labored throughout the late '70s and all of the '80s without much success to offset the unequal relationship created by men's football. [45] Their position was made more difficult by the NCAA, which lobbied to have football placed in a special category outside the formula.

The Reagan administration's conservative interpretation of law added to the women's burden. In 1984, a court in western Pennsylvania declared in Grove City [College] vs. Bell that an entire institution could not be penalized if one of its programs failed to comply with Title IX of the Civil Rights Act. In other words, if the athletic department, as it did at Grove City College, violated Title IX by failing to provide an equitable number of athletic opportunities for women, federal monies could be denied only to athletics, and not, as Title IX had intended originally, to the entire college. As the Grove City athletic department had not been the beneficiary of federal funds, the college was essentially immune to the law, and the court ruled the college could not be compelled to require compliance in athletics. The Reagan administration approved of the decision; this represented a major shift in the legal applica-

bility of Title IX and seriously crippled the efforts of women to secure athletic equity. In effect, the Civil Rights Act of 1964 had been reinterpreted and severely handicapped. For four years, from 1984 to early 1988, women's efforts to tackle the problem were hampered by the fact that there was no legal way to bring athletics into compliance.

Then the pendulum swung back the other way as Congress sought to repair the damage. The passage of the Civil Rights Restoration Act in March 1988 reintroduced the legitimacy of the sex-equity issue in university and college athletics. MSU women did not wait long to act. In early 1989, MSU's affirmative action officer, Corlann Bush, notified President Tietz that under the new law, MSU's athletic departments were out of compliance with Title IX. The president, who was mulling over several other problem areas in athletics, added the Title IX issue to his concerns and called for a special review conducted by outside referees. In the meantime, the U.S. Department of Education rejected the NCAA's argument for a special status for football. [46]

Judging by what other institutions and legislative bodies across the nation were doing to meet the objectives and spirit of the Civil Rights Restoration Act, MSU's women stood to gain favorably. Action taken in the state of Washington served as an inspiring example. In May 1989, a bill was passed enabling the state's colleges and universities to waive 1 percent of their tuition to help finance more opportunities for women athletes. Under this bill, the athletic departments of the two major universities, Washington and Washington State, would benefit by almost $1 million. WSU moved immediately to enlarge the value of women's athletic scholarships and to add women's soccer as a competitive intercollegiate sport. Two more women's sports were to be added in succeeding years, most likely softball and crew. Other institutions, although fewer in number than anticipated, were reaping the rewards of similar action. There was every reason to believe that MSU's women would benefit similarly. [47]

The Title IX issue was convenient for President Tietz to incorporate in his review, as virtually all of his concerns touched upon the economics of athletics. These included the advisability of maintaining two separate men's and women's athletic departments, the status of MSU's athletic facilities—their care, maintenance, utility and function—and the relationship of the Bobcat booster organization to the health of athletics. Of these, the rise of big time boosterism and the programs and pressures associated with it commands our attention.

The Bobcat Booster club, officially known as the MSU Athletic Scholarship Association (MSU-ASA), originated in the early 1950s simultaneously with the hiring of Tony Storti and President Renne's increased commitment to MSU athletics. Erv Hintzpeter from Gallatin Gateway was its first president. At the outset, the boosters raised perhaps $2000 to $3000. By the late 1960s their efforts had increased funding to $30,000. By the mid-1980s booster contributions were ten times that, or $300,000. As formidable a leap as that might seem, in 1990 an annual goal of from $500,000 to $1 million per annum did not seem, by any measure, out of line. Although the support of men's athletics has always been its major cause for existence, the Bobcat Booster organization has continually allocated a percentage of its funds to academic scholarships. The boosters also line-item small annual sums to the women's athletic program, about 10 percent of what they dedicate to the men. [48]

Under the leadership of men's athletic director Doug Fullerton, many other programs were inaugurated to boost revenues for men's athletics, including a basketball Dunk Club, a new athletic newsletter ("Cat Tracks," with paid advertising), estate planning, life insurance, and improved TV and radio contracts. A foray into corporate sponsorships provided gratifying yields in return for large-scale advertising. Big-game guarantees had long been attractive fund providers, and in recent years football away games with Florida, Kansas, and Colorado State and basketball games with Indiana, Minnesota, and Nebraska provided good returns, despite the ever-present fear of season-ending injuries from playing Division I football opponents. Most recently, the men's athletic department has become concerned enough with debits to venture into what might be called literally a "show-biz" operation. In 1991, after a thirty-one-year hiatus, the field house became the site of another major boxing event, a sellout card of five fights, the main event featuring Montana's rising middleweight boxer, Todd Foster. Another new form of fund-raising has been the fruitful sponsorship of rodeo-concert combos, highlighting the championship MSU men's and women's rodeo teams along with top-rank country western groups. Rodeo's continued success in attracting the annual National Collegiate Rodeo Association championships, and the Big Sky Conference's automatic qualification in the extraordinarily profitable postseason NCAA basketball tournaments, monies that are shared within the conference, have produced no small amount of revenue.

MSU Rodeo: The Most Successful Program

A hundred cowboys and cowgirls race their horses into the [Worthington] arena, the riders forward in their saddles urging the horses faster, circling the arena on the run before forming two parallel lines that stretch from one end of the space to the other. The riders, representing the 11 regions of the National Intercollegiate Rodeo Association, lift their hats to the audience and 5,000 people applaud. The lights dim. Miss College Rodeo enters carrying the American flag. Wearing a red, white and blue sequined shirt, her blond curls cascading out from under her cowboy hat, she circles the darkened arena in a spotlight as "the Star-Spangled Banner" is sung by a cowboy from Missoula. She smiles into the audience, her smile immediate and warm. In that moment, whoever you are, you are an American, a westerner, a cowboy bred on the vast Montana plains. [1]

Many are the thousands who can identify with this colorful description of opening night ceremonies at the CNFR, the College National Finals Rodeo held each year at Brick Breeden Fieldhouse on the MSU campus. Rodeo has a remarkable appeal, and, more than any other MSU activity, successfully couples Montana's rich cowboy heritage with the earthy ideals of the land grant institution. To boot, rodeo is unquestionably MSU's most successful varsity sport. Since its birth as a student club just after the conclusion of World War II, MSU's cowboys and cowgirls have produced more national team championships and national individual title holders than all of the other varsity sports combined.

MSU rodeo became a reality in 1947 when a group of students held an all-school event down at the Bozeman fairgrounds. Any student, experienced or not, could compete, and there were no entry fees. Each event at-

Janet Bignell, MSU's 1977 CNFR rodeo queen, heads the ceremonial procession

tracted a dozen or so entrants, and the undertaking was well attended. The following year competitors from the university at Missoula and from North Dakota State Teachers' College were invited. This was an historical moment, as it represented the Northwest's first intercollegiate rodeo competition. In the same year, MSC rodeo club members, led by Gene Pederson, went to Texas to the foundational meeting of the National Intercollegiate Rodeo Association. A year later in 1948, MSC, as a founding member, sent a team to the first national collegiate competition at San Francisco's famed Cow Palace, establishing itself competitively when Bob Sauke won the wild-cow milking event (a category since eliminated) and Gene Pederson placed fourth in steer wrestling. [2]

MSU rodeo at Belgrade, 1953

During its first five years the rodeo club operated on an absolute shoestring. Its practice capabilities were primitive, and practice stock was almost nonexistent. A bucking barrel simulated bronc or bull riding. When Bozeman closed down its fairground rodeo facilities in the late 1940s, competitions had to be run in Belgrade. Conditions improved somewhat during the 1950s; the club became more formally organized in the College of Agriculture, obtained faculty advisors, and partial ASMSC financial support for travel. Then President Renne provided partial funding for, among other necessities, practice stock. But the bulk of rodeo's financial backing throughout the early years continued to come from gate receipts and other fund-raising events. [3]

The completion of the MSC field house in 1957 gave rodeo an enormous boost. Overnight Bozeman had one of the country's premier arenas, and the annual spring rodeo, no longer fettered by the uncertainties of Montana's fickle and often fierce weather, became one of the largest in the nation. In the mid-1960s, rodeo received another lift when President Leon Johnson and rodeo advisor Bob Miller built rodeo practice facilities, including bucking shoots and roping

boxes, into the design of a new livestock pavilion, completed in 1968. Now MSU enjoyed the luxury of permanent year-round indoor practice facilities. [4]

A crowning achievement of the rodeo program was the selection of the MSU field house in 1970 as the annual site of the College National Finals Rodeo. Other communities across the nation applied to host the event, but they couldn't match the facility—nor the terrific support given to CNFR by local and state rodeo boosters. Although this event diverted attention from the popular spring rodeo, it gave MSU's overall rodeo program enormous prestige. Rodeo grew so successful it ran into an unusual problem. So many aspirants were enrolling spring quarter only in order to compete in the annual spring rodeo and CNFR that the team imposed academic eligibility standards more stringent than those for any other student activity. [5]

The question of entry fees and prize money was long contended within the rodeo program. In the 1950s and 1960s, MSU rejected fees and monetary prizes, although the national trend was running toward professionalism. Then, in 1973, when the huge northwest region was divided into smaller sections, and the Big Sky rodeo region, almost entirely Montanan, was established, MSU's rodeo team changed its position and supported the mandatory entry fee and prize system. The decision has had a major impact. At the 1991 CNFR, for example, MSU's team and team members won $28,000 in awards. [6]

Ironically, the rising costs of rodeo almost simultaneously changed the character of the sport at MSU. By the early 1980s, the Associated Students and the College of Agriculture were no longer willing to continue their sponsorship of rodeo. When ASMSU terminated its support in 1981, rodeo was transferred from the College of Agriculture to the department of men's athletics, and John Larick replaced Sandy Gagnon as head coach. [7] The jump to varsity status was unique—hardly duplicated elsewhere in the nation. It also transformed what had been a club activity with more than 250 members into a varsity program designed for perhaps thirty competitors. This represented something of a social loss, as the old club atmosphere with its warm informality became a thing of the past. [8]

On the other hand, the elevation of rodeo to a varsity sport brought certain advantages, including full-time coaching, a more predictable budget, and a substantially enlarged scholarship aid program. These factors, combined with superb facilities, and the contract to host

1972 MSU national champion men's rodeo team

the annual CNFR, made MSU rodeo one of the top four-year college rodeo programs in the country. Some would argue convincingly that MSU's is the best. Whatever its exact status, MSU's rodeo staff is able to recruit with great success in the Northern Rockies and the Plains region,

thereby ensuring its continued ranking in national competition. [9]

The record of MSU's young rodeo performers has been absolutely outstanding. Together, the men's and women's rodeo teams have won six national championships—the men's team in 1972, '75, '88, '90, and '91; the women's team in 1986. MSU teams have come close to winning on many other occasions. All told, over twenty-nine national championship years (1963-1991), MSU teams have placed first, second, third or fourth nineteen times! To add to that remarkable record, MSU team members have won dozens of individual titles, and at the regional level they have exceeded even those numbers. It has been a rare occasion indeed when the Big Sky regional trophy hasn't been awarded to MSU. While MSU rodeo greats are too numerous to all be acknowledged, a certain number demand recognition. Consider, for example, the exploits of Jim Carrig, Carol O'Rourke, Carol Daley, the outstanding husband/wife team of Terry and Jan (Walter) Wagner, Bob Schall, Jock McDowell, Jim Solberg, Dave Griffith, Rex Phillips, Mary (Melany) Salmond, Carrie (Munson) Bignell, Stacy (Waldhauser) Baumann, Ken Lensegrav, Shawn Vant, Chris Witcher, and Dan Mortensen.

1986 MSU national champion women's team

CNFR, 1989

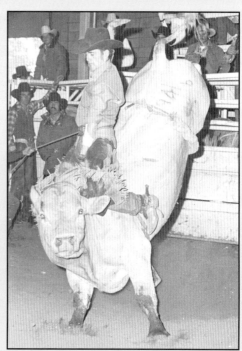

Dave Griffith on #79

1. Ruth Rudner, "Rodeo Days at the Old College Corral," *The Wall Street Journal*, 28 August 1987.
2. Matthew J. Wald, "MSU Rodeo: 1947-1989," history seminar paper (1989). Wald was a member of the rodeo team.
3. Ibid.
4. Ibid.
5. Irving Dayton to Tom Parac, 11 December 1975, 81033/1, "Athletics" file, MSUA.
6. Records of rodeo advisor John Larick.
7. James R. Welsh memo, "MSU Rodeo Team: Rationale for Change," 22 April 1981, 84031/3, "Rodeo" file, MSUA.
8. Wald, "MSU Rodeo."
9. Ibid.

To get an idea of how central these nonlegislative elements are to the men's athletic budget, a comparison with 1970 would be instructive. In that year approximately 50 percent of the men's athletic budget was provided by the state, 12 percent came from the students' athletic fees, and the remaining 38 percent came from boosters, gates, and guarantees. By 1990, these percentages had completely reversed. The state now provides only 34 percent of the men's $2.1 million budget, or less in actual dollars than what it allocated to MSU for athletics in the early 1980s. Student-dedicated-fee support no longer exists, having been withdrawn in the '70s. The remaining 66 percent, or $1.4 million, was raised entirely by means disassociated from the state, the greater bulk of it coming in roughly equal amounts from the boosters and from basketball and football gate receipts. While substantial, such gate receipts would, on their own, hardly help men's athletics turn the corner without all the booster-type programs that are run simultaneously.

The success of the effort to increase MSU's athletic funding has been mixed. In 1990 men's athletic director Doug Fullerton was able to report that the big deficit of 1985 had been wiped out, and that for the first time in years men's athletics could look forward with some optimism to the prospect of balanced books. But only one year later, inflationary costs, legislative cutbacks, and flagging gate receipts pushed the men's program back into the red, and it had to be bailed out by the central administration. NCAA 1991 funding formulas for the sharing of tournament TV revenues only exacerbated MSU's difficulties. Based upon a scale that rewards schools that have extensive scholarships and a maximum number of sports in both men's and women's athletics, the funding formula penalizes a school like MSU, which has the minimum number of sports allowed, twelve. As a result, MSU received only 20 percent of what Boise State received from NCAA tournament

Head football coach Cliff Hysell, president Mike Malone, men's athletic director Doug Fullerton, and alumni director Sonny Holland, in Great Falls, 1991

receipts in 1991, a difference of over $75,000. This creates a catch-22 situation for the Bobcats, for, as Fullerton noted, "if you have enough money for additional grants and sports, the NCAA will give you more. If you don't have the money, the NCAA will give you less and keep you where you are." [49] Knowing that they would have to add sports to qualify for more NCAA funds and to meet increased conference requirements, MSU considered golf for both men and women, but as a fall sport, the experience of fickle spring weather and the conversion to the semester system being the major determinants. Any additions, of course, would bring about new costs, and with assurances that costs generally would continue to spiral in every area, all acknowledged that the struggle to stay solvent would take unflagging energy and that the ability of Bobcat teams to produce winning seasons would be absolutely critical to that.

The December 1991 hiring of former Bobcat Cliff Hysell to reshape the floundering football program seemed to be one step in that direction. A native of Helena, Hysell was an outstanding defensive lineman for Jim Sweeney in the mid-1960s. After a successful stint as head coach at Great Falls High, he returned to MSU in 1972 to assist Sonny Holland, and then Sonny Lubick. In 1981 Hysell went to Fresno State as defensive coordinator under his old MSU mentor, Sweeney. In becoming MSU's twenty-ninth head football coach, Hysell was hired in hopes that he could restore to MSU what it had given up in '81—the old MSU sporting interface with Montana and its people. Men's athletic director Doug Fullerton put it this way: "We're going back to what we know," he announced. "Cliff Hysell bleeds Blue and Gold. We're going back to what Montana State represents and we're getting that tradition without sacrificing what it takes to win at this level." [50] When Hysell immediately succeeded in recruiting some of the state's outstanding prep players, including several from the industrial towns, it seemed as though everything was back to normal. But Hysell was a realist; while roughly a third of his scholarships went to Montanans, the other two-thirds went to out-of-state players. Bobcat fans waited anxiously on the eve of the centennial in hopes that the new head coach would bring about the materialization of their aspirations for a return to the good old days.

MSU's basketball teams under coach Stu Starner provided a prime example of what winning could do. Led by Chris Conway, Tom Domako, Kral Ferch, Tony Hampton, and Ray Willis, the Cats won big in the conference in 1986 and 1987 and qualified for the NCAA and NIT postseason tournaments, narrowly losing to St. John's University and the University of Washington. St. John's head coach Lou Carnesecca's assertion that World War II would have ended months earlier if the U.S. armed forces had had

NCAA tourney bound—MSU's 1986 Big Sky champs

shooters like the Bobcats epitomized their exciting run-and-gun style. But Starner's teams were more than just a collective of outstanding players, they were class act people as well. The fans warmed to them, the turnstiles clicked at Brick Breeden Field House, and Max Worthington Arena experienced crowds reminiscent of the good old '60s. By the late 1980s basketball enthusiasm was paying big at the gate and inspiring the boosters to even bigger contributions. When Starner departed after the 1989-1990 season, his position was filled, and the excitement perpetuated with the appointment of former Bobcat Mick Durham.

While the extraordinary growth and fundraising success of the Bobcat Booster Club poured new heart into MSU athletics, it also raised natural concerns about the extent to which the boosters would be allowed, or would demand, athletic decision making privileges. The degree to which boosters have influenced and even damaged athletics when left to their own enthusiastic ways is an open page in the history of American sport. Conservatively speaking, every month seems to bring another revelation of booster over-zealousness. Fortunately, MSU has not suffered similarly, but there are symptoms sufficient to cause alarm. Montanans rue, as noted, the loss of every Treasure State athlete to another school. Alums bewail the failure of the athletic department to recruit their favorite natives. The selection of coaches undergoes close scrutiny by the boosters, and on occasion there have been real tiffs over hiring. The decision to play or not play a particular athlete is sometimes taken to issue, and on occasion Bobcat supporters have questioned decisions to suit up or not suit up injured athletes. As long as there are people who will pay good dollars to support athletics, there will always be on the part of a few some subtle, or not so subtle, efforts to contribute their opinions, especially if these will, they believe, help win games. MSU's goal has been to sublimate those energies into a posi-

tive and cooperative relationship with the university's over-all educational goals. So far that relationship has not gotten out of harness, but has been productive and commendable.

Women in athletics at MSU will seemingly never enjoy the same degree of fiscal independence as the men. In contrast to the men's program, which produces 66 percent of its own funding, the women's produces but 6 percent. Only women's basketball returns any revenue, and despite the success of the Lady Bobcats, led most recently by head coach Judy Spoelstra who led the team to the Big Sky Conference playoffs in 1991 and '92, and over the years by such standouts as Marcia Topp, Vicki Heebner, Kathy McLaughlin, Lynn Andrews, Liz Holz and Sarah Flock, the almost total inability of women's athletics to raise its own dollars perpetuates the relative inferiority, or dependence, of their program. Naturally, the increasing tendency to balance budgets by retaining only those sports generating self-supporting revenues is deplored by the women as destructive of the broad original intent of intercollegiate athletics. That so much emphasis has to be placed upon women's basketball, merely because it produces gate receipts, represents to them a form of prostitution. MSU's women also realize that the existence of two separate athletic departments is viewed by many with jaundiced eyes, and that on the basis of economies it might be necessary for the women to relinquish the one deciding advantage they presently have—their administrative independence. The 1990 external review arranged by President Tietz recommended this, [51] but the decision to amalgamate failed because of resistance on the womens' part. In the meantime, a general cooperative effort to arrange an efficient joint use of facilities and services with the men has been effected.

There is a stubborn tendency among women's athletic departments across the nation, however, to believe that athletic funding should be governed by the same principles governing academic funding—wherein all revenues raised by women's and men's athletics would be deposited with the university's general funds, and thence reallocated to athletics on the basis of what is soundest for the academic programming of the institution, and not on the basis of spectator support. In the past, this approach would have been considered exclusively a feminists position, but it is now being discussed by some men's programs and has even had a place on the NCAA's agenda. Some programs are going beyond that to advocate an across-the-board sharing of all the astounding millions raised by basketball and football playoffs and bowl games. However, as MSU's women's staff acknowledge, most university and collegiate athletic departments, ever male-dominated, would

Marcia Topp and Kathy McLaughlin, 1980

Liz Holz, 1990

inevitably resist such reasoning, hardly being disposed to give up control of their often huge budgets to academic managers for redistribution to nonspectator sports and noncompetitive athletic programs. While MSU's women have come a long way since the mid-'60s, their position is still in many ways insecure, and their concept of what is preferable for athletes of both genders is not materializing according to plan. When Ginny Hunt was elected in 1989 as the first woman president of the MSU Faculty Council, it represented not only the women's rise in equality and their continued belief in athletics as an adjunct to academics, it also spoke to women's recognition that those positions can be maintained only by aggressive advocacy in the political arena. [52]

MSU's men's athletics does not differ from the women's in recognizing the need to be politically active. Doug Fullerton's membership on the same council attests to his firm belief in the link between athletics and academics and in the fact that the athletic departments must sell their importance to the campus and to the state. On both scores, and for both women and men, MSU athletics runs a sound, honest, and creditable program—absolutely the most creditable in the Big Sky Conference and one of the most creditable in the entire country. The concern of the athletic

directors is to sell the significance and importance of that to those with decision-making capabilities. Convincing seemingly unreceptive legislators and regents to rethink their positions and acknowledge athletics as a legitimate academic program is the primary goal. Like many programs across the nation, MSU men's athletics has taken that concept one step farther, hoping to persuade the public that big-time intercollegiate athletics is not just another costly form of entertainment. Rather, it has become a performing art, if not a religious experience, and as such is a part of the nation's cultural fabric. [53]

Consequently, the argument continues, intercollegiate athletics should be funded just as other academic programs are funded. Perhaps the men's athletic department had in mind the European university experience, where sport is traditionally incorporated with art and music in the same academic division. That Montana's decision makers are prepared to accept this reasoning appears doubtful on the eve of MSU's centennial, but that the argument itself is worthy of being taken seriously cannot be questioned, given the extraordinary changes that have taken place in athletics in recent years.

Chapter Nine
The Tradition of Science at MSU

The Creation of "Big Science"

Since World War II the relation of the federal government to the practice of science has been recognized as an issue of profound importance. The development of the atomic and hydrogen bombs represents only one aspect of this dynamic relationship. The government has emerged as a great user of science and a great support to many lines of research, and institutions in which science exists have found that the actions of the government in contracting for and conducting research are factors of first importance. [1]

Animal science in action

In the custom of the land grant college, engineering and agriculture were the foundations upon which Montana State University was built, and the sciences, both theoretical and applied, were from the beginning the school's primary focus. Four major influences, one working upon the other, have largely shaped the tradition of science on campus:

1. International scientific inquiry has always largely defined the focus of the school's scientists. Though regional and local concerns have played a part in shaping some of the departmental programs, the college faculty have generally dealt with the same problems as have their colleagues around the world.
2. The mix of state and federal funding changed dramatically after World War II, with federal agencies becoming increasingly central to the kind and quality of science practiced on the campus.
3. With this shift, individual scientists began to give more and more attention to federally

funded projects that were only marginally related to contemporary university concerns.
4. As a result, science departments have experienced increasing tension as faculty members have become more and more deeply involved in their own research and less and less concerned with both the undergraduate and graduate teaching missions of the university. [2]

World War II constituted a watershed in the relations between science and the federal government. The war generated an enormous amount of scientific research—everything from atomic energy to penicillin to microwave radar. Thousands of gadgets, products, and techniques evolved under the stress of wartime schedules and demands. It was indeed a heroic period for American science. Cold War hostility then drove the lesson home: only technical and scientific superiority could keep America in the race against the "Soviet menace."

As politicians took cognizance of Russian scientific progress, Congress routinely appropriated more and more money for scientific research and development. Specifically, federal science policy aimed at a comprehensive national research effort, and the National Science Foundation (NSF) eventually emerged from lengthy Congressional debate. The debate was based on some issues of long-standing. As a result of its experience in two world wars, the nation was agreed that a federal science program was necessary to our national defense, but there were questions as to the propriety of creating a scientific elite and sustaining it with taxpayers' money. As early as the Constitutional Convention of 1788-1789, there had been common agreement that science was important to the new republic. "Federal science" was viewed as an internal improvement, like canals and roads. Benjamin Franklin, an important scientist in his own right, saw that to raise the issue of centralized versus local policies regarding internal development would only hinder the effort to create a new nation. It was better not to insist upon a strong Federalist position and to work with those who would seek ratification of the new constitution.

That position undoubtedly aided in gaining ratification, but it created something of a problem at times when science needed to be done. For example, when Thomas Jefferson sought to explore the newly acquired Louisiana Territory and to determine its wealth in natural resources, he employed what would become a favorite presidential artifice for some time to come. When Meriwether Lewis and William Clark were sent west, the expedition was paid for and supplied by army appropriations, since the cause of scientific research alone would never have justified such a costly project. Subsequent government explorations followed the same pattern. But an approach like this would not have served the nation as well in the twentieth century. Although the Manhattan Project that developed the atomic bomb resembled this early constitutional mix of monies, in peacetime it would become much more difficult to justify continued military secrecy and to attract competent scientists to the project. It was clear that national consensus would have to be developed for any coherent science policy to work well in the new age of scientific technology.

When Congress took up the issue of national science policy after the war, a collective memory was at work. The old problem of states' rights—now so closely connected with the divisive issue of racial integration—took on a new urgency. From the perspective of science, that meant that representatives from those states which did not have a strong research tradition feared that they would lose out in the funding competition. The "old-boy" network that served the interests of the major universities could hardly be expected to offer more than crumbs to the less prestigious institutions. Wartime research had centered on campuses like M.I.T., Berkeley, and Cal Tech. From a democratic point of view it seemed unwise to base the nation's research effort on such a narrow—and elitist—foundation. [3]

Vittal Rai (left) and Gary A. Strobel

But custom carried and, as it turned out, the major universities continued to receive a lion's share of the available monies from the new National Science Foundation. Soon recognizing the disproportionate funding pattern, NSF initiated a program to stimulate in-state competitions and to help habituate researchers to the grant-writing process. The Experimental Program to Stimulate Competitive Research (EPSCoR) was organized to grant money to those states that evidenced little grant competitiveness. In 1979, Dr. Gary Strobel, a plant pathologist at MSU, secured such a grant for Montana and established MONTS (Montanans on a New Trac for Science). Any researcher in the state could now apply for funding if his or her area of research was a normal part of NSF activity. To date, 250 of the state's scholars have received funding, and three-quarters of them have gone on to submit nationally competitive grants. Montana's success ratio (33 percent) is well above the national EPSCoR average. [4]

But that is to get ahead of the story. As the national patterns of funding were evolving in the years just after World War II, so was Montana State College. In the closing months of the world war, President Roland Renne, newly installed, took cognizance of the patterns of change. In a letter to an east coast friend he outlined what he hoped would develop on his campus in the wake of the changes. While the student body had been reduced in numbers to little more than a thousand in the last two years of the war, Renne foresaw that the school's strong foundations in science, engineering, and agriculture would attract many new students in the postwar years. In order to accommodate them, the president proposed to construct new facilities, update and improve older ones, and structure the curriculum to take advantage of the future opportunities. Specifically, Renne envisioned tearing down some of the temporary facilities dating back to World War I and building a new mathematics/physics center. In his mind, bricks and mortar would be visible symbols of the state's commitment to the Bozeman campus. He wanted these visible symbols and he wanted them quickly.[5]

This would seem an ambitious plan, but there was good reason for Renne's optimism. The nation had committed itself to helping its veterans—about 12 million women and men had been in uniform at one time or another during the war—so that when Mary and Johnny came marching home they would have a solid opportunity for a higher education. The G.I. Bill was a comprehensive response to postwar conditions, and it had great impact on the campus in Bozeman. Montana State College attracted a great many veterans, and the boost in enrollment proved the wisdom of Dr. Renne's plans. Furthermore, the veterans who came on campus represented a new breed of students, and former faculty members recall the postwar period with nostalgia because of the seriousness of the mature students and the level of instruction and interaction they demanded. For most of these students, college was clearly a means to an end. Seeking solid careers, they tended to matriculate in engineering, agriculture, and the physical and life sciences. This postwar boom provided a new plateau on which the various branches of scientific instruction would expand.

But expansion required money, and budget constraints still restricted the kind and the amount of research that could be done on campus. The incorporation of new technology would require new instrumentation and new buildings, or, at the very least, extensive remodeling of older buildings. Ironically, at the very time these needs were being identified, the level of state funding was declining. It was readily apparent that federal funding would have to be secured to finance the expansion that Renne envisioned. Fortunately, the school's needs coincided with the

government's increased interest in supporting scientific inquiry.

The needs and the interest that surfaced in those postwar years have mutually expanded over the course of the last forty-some years as the university's science curriculum has become more and more dependent upon federal funds for its advancement. Today MSU receives about $20 million annually in terms of federal support for scientific research. [6] This money has spillover effects that benefit the school as a whole, since some of the dollars designated for overhead costs are distributed to faculty and students in the humanities who would not otherwise have access to supplementary monies. But as noted earlier, the influx of federal funds for research projects has been a mixed blessing, since faculty members have necessarily given more and more time to research and less and less time to teaching. Thus each administration has had to address the issue of how to balance research activity against the teaching mission of the university.

The Tradition in the Life Sciences

From the beginning the life sciences were organized along disciplinary lines; the fact that there has been constant reconfiguration of divisions and departments within the sciences at the college reflects the history of scientific development over the last century. Particularly in the past fifty years has work in the life sciences changed dramatically. Most notably, new technology and a more fundamental understanding of basic science have made possible the manipulation of genetic material.

In the biological sciences and in agriculture these new techniques have provided a tremendous set of tools that are changing our world. For example, the work of plant pathologist David Sands is primarily in the field of biological control. "We look for genes which will do exactly what we need to have them do and then we put them where they are needed" Sands points out. "I am Doctor Death!" he likes to say. "I study death in order to enhance life. If I can find a fungus which will kill leafy spurge and then cause that fungus to shut itself down and die after it has done its job I will have used death wisely." [7] Sands and his fellows reflect the present trend in life science to seek out and utilize genetic material, DNA or RNA, so that serious problems affecting human and animal well-being can be solved, always mindful that these solutions must not damage the environment and must be affordable.

Other methods of biocontrol are being used on campus too. In cooperation with federal entomologists, campus scientists are working on grasshopper control using protozoa. It appears at present that, used in conjunction with low levels of insec-

David C. Sands (left) and Robert F. Eslick studying barley genetics

ticides, these organisms can be made increasingly lethal to the pest.

In the past decade plant pathologists on campus have made great strides in the area where biochemistry meets life forms. For example, it became possible in the 1970s to regenerate complete plants from protoplasts—that is, a viable, phenotypic plant can now be grown from germ cells. These cells can be cloned, or divided in such a manner that identical plant materials are generated. In such a way the genetic differences that underlie the array of variations in the real world can then be observed. So it was that the work at Montana State University first gave rise to a

virus-free seed-potato industry in southwest Montana. This cloning system then gave way to a more easily manipulated system called meristem culture—largely the work of James Shepherd—which utilized the meristem tips, not the eye of the tuber. The results of eight years of research costing $105,000 have meant increased yields, better prices, and more widely planted acreage in Idaho, Washington, and Oregon—dividends that have been valued at $53 million. Indeed these techniques are now widely used around the world, and plant materials so constructed run the gamut from bananas to rice. [8]

MSU'S "Chain Saw Massacre"

As a youngster in Ohio, Gary Strobel nurtured a passion for conserving the environment. He pursued this interest in college, where he concentrated in forestry, botany, and chemistry. In 1963 he received his doctoral degree in plant pathology from the University of California, Davis, where his research centered on nematodes, organisms that play a crucial role in helping or hindering plant growth. That same year he came to Bozeman and joined the college's plant pathology group. His work soon won national recognition, and in 1969 he received a prestigious five-year career development grant from the General Medical Division of the National Institutes of Health. [1]

In 1977 the Freshwater Biological Foundation in Minnesota asked for assistance in combatting Dutch elm blight, which was reducing once-graceful trees to bare hulks in towns and cities across the East and Midwest. Strobel responded quickly to the challenge. On the basis of his wide experience with plant disease, he concluded that although plants do indeed succumb to fungi and other microorganisms, there are in plant systems other, helpful bacteria capable of countering the disease-causing organisms. He saw the model as similar to that of the human immune system's ability to attack outside invasive agents. Strobel and his departmental colleague David Sands devoted the summer of 1979 to injecting one of these helpful bacteria, the *Pseudomonas syringae*, into Dutch elms in Washington, D.C., Rhode Island, Minnesota, South Dakota, and Montana. A surprising 80 percent of the inoculated trees survived.

The advantage of this treatment was that it was biological—it did not require chemicals, which might have negative side effects. Several companies were interested in the process, and MSU applied for a patent. Some years later, Strobel and Sands sought to improve the efficacy of *Pseudomonas syringae* by genetically altering

the bacterium. Similar material was in wide use in Holland, where it had been tested on 15,000 trees.

Strobel's work with *Pseudomonas syringae* would likely have caused little controversy, had it not been for earlier events in the field. By the late 1960s, when genetic engineering was becoming an increasingly common laboratory practice, some important scientists became concerned about the possible effects of the escape or release of genetically altered organisms into the natural environment. A 1970 conference in Asilomar, California, addressed these issues and created a tremendous stir in the public press. Governmental agencies decreed that only a few laboratories would be allowed to pursue recombinant DNA research. Throughout that decade and into the eighties, concern with the issue of genetic engineering mounted.

Gary Strobel was well aware of the public apprehension, but he was determined that regulatory red tape not retard his work with the elm blight. In the spring of 1987 he contacted the Environmental Protection Agency to determine exactly what permits he needed in order to inject an altered strain of *Pseudomonas syringae* in an experimental plot of trees he had planted for research purposes on the Bozeman campus, just southwest of Reno H. Sales Stadium. EPA informed him that he would indeed have to initiate a formal application process through the agency, a process generally requiring a ninety-day review before permission was granted or denied. [2]

There was the rub. If Strobel was to take advantage of the short growing season in Bozeman, the test plot would have to be inoculated when the flow of sap began in mid-June. A ninety-day delay would cost him the opportunity of performing this small-scale test, which was necessary before a nationwide effort could be mounted. Strobel weighed his priorities, and then, on June 14, 1987, he injected the altered bacteria into fourteen Dutch elm trees in his test plot. Having done that, he made formal application to EPA for permission to perform the experiment. The fourteen trees, along with thirteen control elms, had been previously injected with the infectious Dutch elm fungus. All thirteen control trees died, while the fourteen that had received the protective bacteria all lived. Unfortunately, the striking success of Strobel's experiment was not what called national attention to his work.

blight, he was keeping a sharp eye out on the introduced Dutch elm disease, because it was not present in Bozeman at that time. He testified that he had applied pesticide to the trees to prevent the spread of the blight by beetles and other insects.

Within hours of that hearing, the Strobel incident was front-page news around the world. Two major issues were brought forward. When is an organism genetically engineered and was this such an organism? And when and how should the use of genetically engineered substances be controlled by the government and

The chain saw in action with interested reporters on the scene

Strobel had made no attempt to conceal the experiment, and in July, a team from EPA came out to investigate the illicit procedure. At this point, the university, which was in the process of structuring four major oversight committees in accordance with new federal regulations, belatedly called a meeting of the biosafety committee, an on-campus group of scientists who were to review proposals like Strobel's to ensure that all federal guidelines were followed. Since this committee was only partially up and running, it had conducted no review. Indeed, nothing had been submitted to it. Now, on August 12, 1987, the committee held a formal hearing in the Student Union Building to consider Strobel's actions and their implications. Gary Strobel was represented by counsel, all proceedings were videotaped, and a stenographic record was kept. The professor admitted that he knew it was not legal to release the bacteria. However, he had performed this experiment at his own expense and had no intention of letting any biological agent spread to the surrounding environment. While the altered material posed no threat to anything except the

through what agency? Some scientists agreed with Strobel that his material was not genetically altered but consisted of a bit of naturally migratory genetic material. Most agreed that current rules and regulations were muddy and imprecise.

In an interview with the *Bozeman Daily Chronicle*, Strobel admitted that he was fed up with federal red tape and declared, "I am expressing civil disobedience. We can sit and talk about Dutch elm disease, or we can do something about it. I chose to do something about it." He received some support from the press, particularly from papers like the *Wall Street Journal* that shared his opinion of federal regulations.

In mid-August, the university's biosafety committee handed down its finding: Dr. Strobel had erred in not following the federal guidelines in performing his experiment; however, those guidelines were all but "unfollowable." In effect, the committee of his peers at MSU exonerated Strobel. Then, three weeks after this decision was announced, on September 3,

1987, the "Great Chain Saw Massacre" took place when Strobel himself cut down the fourteen treated elm trees. The man was emotionally exhausted: "This has been fourteen years of my life," he told a reporter. "Watching this go would be like seeing one of my kids die." [3]

Generally, Strobel received campus and public support, though some of his fellow scientists were concerned that his actions might prejudice federal agencies against proposals generated thereafter at MSU. A strong supporter of Strobel and his research, President William Tietz gave him a private reprimand and directed him to obtain permission from the biosafety committee before pursuing this line of research further. The January 1988 finding of a ten-member committee of NIH scientists vindicated Strobel to some extent when it expressed the judgment that he had not violated federal rules, since his experiment had not involved recombinant DNA. But the committee was concerned about the deliberate release of altered organisms and pointed out that the overlapping federal jurisdictions needed clarification.

In the case of the Chain Saw Massacre, the competing interests of science, society, and national policy had combined to create an incident that prompted the various federal agencies engaged in regulating research eventually to streamline their procedures and coordinate their efforts. Even beyond Bozeman's borders, the Strobel incident resulted in a new international policy concerning the use of genetically altered substances in scientific research.

In retrospect, the message is clear. MSU has attracted a cadre of superior scientists in a variety of fields. Their research sometimes crosses into sensitive and previously unexplored territory that happens to be a matter of public concern. Recognizing the import of the moment, President William Tietz noted, "We have... a major set of circumstances coming together at MSU, and I'm not sorry to see that. It's an issue that has to be dealt with somewhere, and it might just as well be here." [4]

1. Gary A. Strobel interview, 25 January 1990; background information from a brief summary of Strobel's previous work in *Great Falls Tribune,* 12 February 1980, 4-A.
2. William E. Brock, "Bozeman Chain Saw Massacre," *Discover,* November 1987; William E. Brock, "Campus Reacts to Strobel," *The Scientist,* vol I, no. 2, 7 September 1987.
3. "Tearful Scientist Halts Gene Test," *New York Times,* 4 September 1987, 1; Gary A. Strobel, "Fundamental Science in the States," *Science,* vol. 223, 17 February 1984, 651.
4. *The Scientist,* vol. I, no. 2, 7 September 1987.

New viral-detection techniques in plants, perfected at MSU, have changed Montana's economic landscape. Barley stripe mosaic, once a dreaded grain disease, is now controlled by applying a serological test to seeds before they are planted. The school's veterinary science program has also impacted the state's economy. The veterinary science program originally served a dual purpose: clinical veterinarians looked after the college herds, and diagnostic veterinarians, based in Helena, identified problems in commercial herds. After World War II and the construction of Marsh Laboratory on the Bozeman campus, the laboratory staff of the Bureau of Livestock in Helena moved their base of operations to Montana State College.

Hadleigh Marsh, for whom the new facility was named, was the personification of the dedicated veterinarian-scientist. In the 1950s he worked with other western states to target some common problems, focusing primarily on the diseases of sheep. For example, did selenium deficiency correlate with urinary calculi? Were sheep parasites to be found in the soil or in the vegetation? What was the parasite's life cycle? What was its host? Even after Marsh retired he continued to work nearly full time at the laboratory, thus providing continuing leadership and inspiration.

But Marsh did not confine himself, nor his laboratory staff, to the study of diseases in sheep. They were also involved in the elk-reduction programs of Yellowstone National Park in the 1950s, which provided ample material for the study of health problems in populations of wild ungulates. The important issues of brucellosis in bison and the cross transmission of diseases or disease-causing organisms between wild and domesticated species were pioneered here. The isolation facility made it possible to study dangerous diseases in animals, including rabies and scrapie. For example, parasitologist Stuart Knapp has been collecting varieties of snails from the river basins of the state to examine the spread of various parasites that packinghouses report at slaughter.

In 1990 Marsh Laboratory changed its primary focus to molecular biology, where research crosses the boundaries of veterinary science and enters the domain of human biomedicine. Especially important now are the diagnostic and detection techniques being developed by the lab's staff and the preventive vaccines being formulated to protect various types of animals. [9]

Similar progress is in train across the spectrum of the life sciences. Biochemists have done extensive research on insects; indeed, many of their doctoral students have done advanced work on pheromones, or sex hormones in insects, using nuclear magnetic resonance techniques. This kind of research, the extreme costs of which are sup-

Agronomy staff in the field

ceeded in creating a team spirit such as is characteristic of few scientific projects. One of Pepper's doctoral students, Saralee Van Horn (Visscher), devised a theory to account for the strange fact that egg counts in the autumn had little or no predictive value concerning the spring hatch. Other members of the team worked on chemical physiology. Ironically, in the very act of studying this pest, the team discovered that *Aulacara elliottii* was spontaneously disappearing, and to the present day this species exerts only a minimal impact on Montana agriculture. It would be pleasant to assume that the team of entomologists studied the bigheaded grasshopper out of existence. While their work may not have had that effect, it did substantially increase understanding of the life cycle of grasshoppers, and one legacy of this project is the huge federal locust project being conducted on campus in the centennial year in which researchers are pursuing a problem that has global implications. [11]

In 1935 another aspect of biological research began on campus. Realizing the importance of fish and wildlife to the state of Montana, scientists at the college pushed for the development of a program on campus to study these resources. As a result, the regents gave permission to MSC in 1936 to grant a graduate degree in fish and wildlife management. It was one of the few such programs in North America, and it took as its province fish and game populations and the attendant habitat in the area east of the divide and on privately owned lands. As such, the program separated its field of inquiry from that of the forestry program in Missoula, which was concerned with large blocks of land in the public domain. From the outset, members of the departmental team concentrated on structuring the curriculum so that students would have a solid undergraduate foundation in basic life science, in contrast to later programs that would stress graduate-management techniques in wildlife populations. At first there was only one undergraduate course in this option, a clear signal that students would have to have a thorough background in the biology of organisms before moving into fish and wildlife studies.

Amicable relations with state and federal agencies created solid financial and staff commitments to the college fish and wildlife program. A mid-1980s survey revealed that over 60 percent of professional-level personnel in the Montana Department of Fish, Wildlife and Parks were MSC/MSU graduates. Further evidence of the symbiotic relationship is the fact that well over 200 student theses have been written on research supported by $7 million channeled to the department from state and federal agencies. [12]

Given the importance, and the political sensitivity, of hunting and fishing in Montana, the faculty's insistence on a science-based rather

ported largely by federal funds, has worldwide applicability.

The historical roots of such intensive research reach back to just after the turn of the century when Robert A. Cooley, an entomologist in the fledgling science program at the Montana College of Agriculture and Mechanic Arts, became involved in working out the biology of the wood tick, *Dermacentor andersonii*, the vector for transmitting Rocky Mountain spotted fever. Eventually Cooley left the college to manage the federal laboratory in Hamilton that was built to carry on his work. [10]

But the tradition of research he established continued under James H. Pepper. The target this time was the bigheaded grasshopper, *Aulacara elliottii*, a pest that had devastated crops around the state in the 1930s and became a scourge again after World War II. Pepper assembled a team of researchers and graduate students and focused their work on the fundamental biology of the species. This work encompassed everything from cell biology and genetics to chemical physiology and habitat studies. Begun against the background of concern about the environmental dangers of unrestricted DDT use, the project was designed to become a model for biological control. It suc-

than a management-based curriculum has paid handsome dividends, basic science serving as a solid barrier between academic concerns and political pressures. Such vision has created an international reputation for the program, a reputation based on the work of Robert Eng, Don C. Quimby and C. J. D. Brown, who developed an outstanding collection of native fish. The fishes represent every watershed, every important habitat in the state and thus constitute a massive archive of baseline data. The collection is recognized as a priceless DNA pool, which will prove invaluable when it becomes possible to extract nucleic acids from single cells and to reproduce that material at will. [13]

Crucial to serious study of the life sciences are such collections of plant and animal material. The school maintains several important libraries of these materials—not only the archive of fishes built up by C. J. D. Brown but the herbarium, which is a splendid collection of regional plant materials; a vertebrate museum; an invertebrate collection; and a mycological library, all housed in Lewis Hall and all providing important reference material for those who focus on the life sciences.

One can hardly look at the history of the life sciences on the Bozeman campus without being impressed by an almost constantly shifting intellectual map. Plant pathology became an important area in the College of Agriculture; botany moved from microbiology to zoology, and entomology became an increasingly important federal program in agriculture.

Science, Politics, and Big Sky: MSU and the Gallatin Canyon Study

The fact that Montana State University lies within the greater Yellowstone ecosystem has prompted a close connection between the school's faculty and local environmental concerns. For example, the fish and wildlife management program at the school has been consulted many times concerning elk migration from the park and fishing pressures in the blue-ribbon trout streams. But one of the most significant projects in regional research began in 1968 when several faculty members pulled together to form the Center for Environmental Studies. John Wright, a botanist, became its first director and set the center upon its avowed course—to develop a curriculum for students interested in ecology and in outreach programs that would help both the community and the region.

One of the center's earliest projects focused on plans for developing a major ski resort near Lone Mountain, a multimillion-dollar project backed by television personality Chet Huntley. The resort, to be called Big Sky, would be financed by Chrysler Realty Corporation, Montana Power, Northwest Airlines, Burlington Northern, Continental Oil Company, Meridian Company of Georgia, and General Electric's Retirement and Pension Fund. The aim was to create a high-quality recreational center that would attract condominium and home buyers and vacationers from around the world. While Montana, the Gallatin Valley, and Bozeman itself all stood to gain from the project, there was no question that the resort would impact some pristine country in the Spanish Peaks area. The Center for Environmental Studies at MSU was contracted to study the nature and extent of that impact. It seemed a highly appropriate activity for the center, presenting MSU faculty with a rare opportunity to conduct a series of baseline studies that could become a model for other studies of similar recreational developments. And with Chet Huntley involved, the study was sure to command the front pages of American papers and bring attention to the work being done at MSU.

Initially $11,000 was set aside to fund the Gallatin Canyon Study, but that sum went instead to planning and zoning studies. Then MSU officials discovered that a block of National Science Foundation funds was available to conduct the studies they envisioned. Research Applied to National Needs (RANN) funds were to be granted to a project requiring interdisciplinary approaches. Center director John Wright and his new associate, James Jezeski, submitted a proposal to NSF in May of 1970. Entitled "The Impact of a Large Recreational Development upon a Semi-Primitive Environment: A Case Study," the proposal argued that the study envisioned would provide hard-science information in assessing significant impacts of the proposed construction in the west-fork drainage of the West Gallatin River. The academic participants would work with the state fish and game department, the state environmental health bureau, the National Advisory Committee to the Bureau of Land Management, the Governor's Advisory Council, and the city and county planning boards. Scientists would work in harmonious tandem with Huntley's partners, with the government, and with the community. [1]

NSF agreed to fund the project, and to implement it four major teams were formed—one to concentrate on aquatic environment, one on terrestrial environment, one on socioeconomic impacts, and one on data management. Soon the overall project included twenty such substudies that involved twenty-three investigators, eleven departments, three colleges within the university, and two centers.

From the beginning, the Big Sky development project posed two major concerns. The first was based on fears of the State of Montana that any exchange of Burlington Northern lands to accommodate the proposed recreational center could adversely affect the state's tax base: the Montana treasury had long relied heavily upon property taxes paid by major corporations, and BN was its largest taxpayer. The second major concern was reflected in a survey of Gallatin Canyon residents, private landowners who feared that an environmental impact study of the canyon might lead to restrictions on their rights to develop or sell their holdings. At the same time, they feared that Big Sky would become a big-money project from which they could conceivably be excluded.

Because of the suspicious attitudes of many canyon residents, MSU investigators took to driving their own vehicles, rather than readily identified state cars and trucks, when they conducted on-site research. The goal of their initial data gathering was to establish as effectively and as rapidly as possible the statistics needed to measure the resort's probable impact. College researchers studied the canyon's air, water, vegetation, geology, soils, and traffic patterns—even the canyon's history. Nearly half a million dollars went into the studies in the first thirty months. During this time Huntley and Big Sky proponents found themselves in numerous confrontations with the natives, who were justly concerned about everything from air pollution to a proliferation of hot-dog stands up and down the Gallatin River.

Since work to date indicated that the resort could actually enhance the local environment, Gustavus Raaum, president of Big Sky, characterized those opposing the development as isolationists, not ecologists. And Roger Houseman, the director of design and construction for Big Sky, reassured the public that his office was working closely with the ecologists. [2]

The MSU administration, caught in the political cross fire between boosters of the local economy, canyon residents, and sports and conservation groups, backpedaled. The Gallatin Canyon Study, they argued, was sparking more criticism of the school "than was called for." After all, it was science that MSU was providing expertise in, not planning and zoning. An indicator of the rising intensity of the debate was a letter Governor Forrest Anderson sent to the Center for Environmental Studies. Opposition to development, even science-based opposition, was not viewed with favor by the state house, Anderson wrote, and canyon residents who held land privately should not be subject to regulations that shut them

out of the potential bonanza. Citing as his primary concern the long-range tax implications of the proposed land exchange, the governor asked for a copy of any correspondence bearing on it.

Even the Watergate scandal got into the land-exchange picture when the *Great Falls Tribune* reported that the White House wanted to block the exchange because of hostile comments that Huntley had made regarding President Nixon.[3] Yet the White House staff subsequently phoned the U.S. Department of Agriculture urging that the exchange go through, thinking that the president might receive public support from Huntley in exchange for the favor.

In August of 1973, as the word "environmental" became increasingly politicized, the Center for Environmental Studies became the Center for Interdisciplinary Studies. Within a few months, CIS renamed itself again, becoming the Institute of Applied Research, but even that entity was soon to disappear as the school was subjected to national criticism for its role in the controversy. An Andy Rooney segment on *60 Minutes* ridiculed some of the social and behavioral science aspects of the Gallatin Canyon Study. In a stinging presentation, Rooney pilloried MSU and its researchers before millions of television viewers, though he apparently had second thoughts about the attack against the university and later said as much in a magazine article. [4]

In spite of all the unfavorable publicity, some very solid science was done under the Gallatin Canyon Study. The geology of the area was studied thoroughly, and its flora and fauna carefully examined and cataloged. Unfortunately, negative publicity meant that valuable follow-up studies on hydrology, geology, and biology were never undertaken.

The disappointments associated with the Gallatin Canyon Study did not end the environmental concerns of scientists at MSU. Nor did they lessen the university's belief in the importance of keeping the public mindful of the interrelatedness of activities in the Yellowstone ecosystem, a task currently falling to one of the newest environmental studies groups on campus, the High Elevation Studies Institute. Despite all the controversy, the Big Sky research project was a valuable pilot study, and it set an important precedent in scientific inquiry into the potential impact of development upon pristine lands.

1.   John Montagne interview, 12 September 1991
2.   Charles Bradley interview, 2 November 1987.
3.   Ibid.
4.   *The Environmental Professional* (1987), vol. 9, no. 3.

Clifford V. Davis, zoologist/ ornithologist, with young friends on a birding walk

A major figure in the reorganization of departments and the new environmental focus in the life sciences was Professor David Cameron, who had originally come to the campus from the University of Alberta, Edmonton, to work on the genetics of the bigheaded grasshopper under James Pepper. As chair of the old department of zoology and entomology and later as chair of the department of biology, Cameron sought to follow the successful example of the Pepper project by focusing departmental research on a common area of endeavor—in this case, environmental concerns. New coursework and research were thus based on environmental biology, an approach that had the merit of combining ecological studies, population dynamics, and evolutionary biology.

Politically, the very use of the term "environmental" raised hackles around the state, but from a scholarly point of view, the new emphasis afforded a multidisciplinary approach to everything from limnology to weather modification. The legacy remains, though at present ecological foci in biology are scattered in a way that reflects the many-faceted aspects of societal concerns with environmental problems. [14]

This same environmental focus—as well as shifting intellectual alignment—is seen in the evolution of the microbiology group from bacteriology, which had originally been introduced to the MSC curriculum after World War I under Deane B. Swingle. Swingle organized the initial courses around subjects pertinent to conditions and problems found in Montana, and for many years his bacteriologists worked alongside their colleagues in botany. But in 1945 the bacteriology group began a period of dramatic growth that moved them closer and closer to the microbiologists. During that period, an internationally known anaerobic bacteria expert, Louis DeSpain Smith directed the group. Smith's work periodically brought headlines to the campus, as, for example, in 1963 when he became integrally involved in the investigation of the fatal botulism cases in San Francisco that were found to have resulted from improperly canned salmon.

William Walter, an environmental microbiologist, joined with Smith and a specialist in rumen flora, Richard H. McBee, in 1961 to apply for a grant from the National Institutes of Health and the U.S. Public Health Service to develop a strong graduate program in microbiology, expand their course offerings, and fund three new faculty. These same monies made it possible for the school to remodel Lewis Hall and to create Cooley Laboratory. [15]

During the 1960s the microbiology program acquired a strong medical emphasis while retaining its environmental component. An outstanding doctoral program was soon attracting graduate students to the study of immunology and other medical specialties. John Jutila and his student Norman Reed, who eventually became a professor in his own right, achieved international recognition for their research on the immune system, basing their studies on a rare variety of mice born without a thymus. Others in the department worked on fungal infections and basic medical microbiology. Federal funds provided the first electron microscope on campus, and Thomas Carroll came from the University of California, Davis (a training ground of some significance in life science programs at MSU), to operate it. In related developments, the department designed and provided workshops and training sessions for sanitarians, and a newly instituted medical technology program quickly attracted a significant number of students.

Animal scientist Oscar Thomas in the field

Hayden Ferguson

campus was supplemented by applied research carried on at seven experiment stations, the results of which were brought to the farming and ranching communities through the Cooperative Extension Service.

It is a matter of record that the work done at the college has made a phenomenal difference to the agricultural development of the state. Hayden Ferguson, a soil scientist, has argued forcefully that "in relation to the total state economy, research and development here at the College of Agriculture has contributed so much that it has probably had the greatest in-state impact of any such program in the nation." [17] Those contributions have been evident from the school's earliest history. Augustus Ryon worked on irrigation problems as early as 1894; not much later, Frank Traphagen fostered the development of the beet sugar industry, working closely with Montana growers. At the turn of the century, contemporaneous with Traphagen's work, Howard Welch from the veterinary science area found the cause of necrosis in horses and other animals, diagnosing the thyroid malfunction and tracing its etiology to a phosphorus deficiency in the soil. Welch's work was of international importance.

MSU's contributions to the general economy of the state have continued into the modern period. Right after World War II, college scientists began the work that produced the Yogo wheat variety, a hardy, high-yield winter wheat well suited to Montana's harsh climate. Sown with a deep-furrow drilling technique, Yogo moved the winter-wheat belt from a baseline just south of Great Falls to a line almost 300 miles farther north. In other words, Yogo winter wheat created a new crop for the rich glacial soils of the famed Golden Triangle area.

The botany side of the microbiology group also experienced rapid growth during the sixties, as Mitrofan Afansiev, Gene Sharp, and Edward Booth laid the foundations for plant pathology, which would soon move into the College of Agriculture to form its own department. The logic of this development was in keeping, of course, with the land grant tradition, by which a great deal of work in the various branches of the life sciences was performed as a service to agriculture. [16]

The College of Agriculture was, from its earliest days, organized in the classic four-part land grant manner: (1) crops and soils, (2) animal and range science, (3) agricultural mechanics and vocational agriculture, and (4) agricultural economics and rural sociology. And, again in the land grant tradition, basic theoretical research on

The 1957 Moccasin Agricultural Field Day

The authority to establish the first off-campus Montana agricultural experiment station was given in House Bill No. 405 passed by the state legislature in 1907 and signed by Governor J. K. Toole in March of that year. The station was to be located on 160 acres of land in the Judith Basin—near Moccasin—that had been donated by S. S. Hobson of Lewistown. Hobson augmented his donation to the state with a gift of $2500 to MSC, which, with the U.S. Department of Agriculture, was to administer the station. The money was to be used for the erection of a farmhouse on the property. Hobson's largesse was greatly appreciated, since the original legislative appropriation was only $2000—$1000 for the operational support of the station in 1907 and $1000 for 1908. Subsequent legislatures provided funds for a horse barn, a granary, and other outbuildings on the property.

The station's first superintendent was John M. Stevens, an employee of the U.S. Department of Agriculture. He was soon joined by other federal employees, a cereal scientist and a forage crops investigator. Following World War I, the station's staff grew to as many as five federal and twenty state employees.

Early on, the station undertook projects involving potatoes, shrubs, trees, and milk. It ran carcass tests on cattle, poultry, and hogs, and it tested the latest agricultural techniques—notably, crop rotation. Though agronomists initially studied crops thought to prosper in the region's harsh climate—broom, oats, spelt, and Emmer wheats—the work eventually expanded to include the introduction of crested wheatgrass in eastern Montana and of Yogo winter wheat in central Montana, the production of grass seed on dryland ranges, and the use of dryland tillage with small grains.

With the unwelcome introduction of exotic weeds into the state, the station pioneered in herbicide testing. The shelterbelt, an innovation that was to become a familiar landscape feature and wildlife habitat, was the subject of much early

study. Over the years the station tracked progress in mechanical technology, planting and cropping methods, fallowing techniques, fertilization methods, and trash management.

Beginning in 1909, the Moccasin station hosted field-day celebrations intended to showcase its work. Governor Norris attended the first "Experimental Farm picnic," along with about 1200 other Montanans who came by wagon, buggy, and train—two of the Great Northern trains stopped at the north side of the farm to discharge and take on passengers—and twenty-six newfangled automobiles. That first celebration even included a baseball game between Hobson and Moore.

The first event of its kind, that 1909 celebration was followed by many more. The annual picnics generally began with guided tours of the various experimental plots. Demonstrations of the latest mechanical equipment followed. After World War I, free airplane rides were even offered to the day's participants. FFA and 4-H judging contests were a part of the activities, as were all kinds of games—three-legged races, sack races, ladies' nail driving, hog calling, pie eating, and greased pig contests. In some years trap shoots and boxing matches entertained the crowds. Traditionally, both dinner and supper were served, with packers and others donating food for the occasion. Speeches by prominent politicians were always on the program, and a dance in Moccasin concluded the day's events.

Perhaps the grandest of all these celebrations came in 1957, on the occasion of the Central Montana Station's golden anniversary. Governor Hugo Aronson was there, as were 12-year-old Duane Peterson of Coffee Creek, who took the prize in pie eating, 11-year-old Anne Baker of Bozeman, who won the trophy for watermelon consumption, and 15-year-old Richard Delaney of Winnett, who literally carried off the greased pig. The governor's wife presided over a fashion show, and modern tractor races vied for attention with demonstrations of vintage steam-powered threshing equipment.

What amazed everyone was the turnout for that golden anniversary celebration. Superintendent Jim Krall and his staff had planned on a couple of thousand visitors, but twice that many showed up. When all was said and done, the sunburned assembly agreed that it had been a wonderful day.[1]

Central Montana Agricultural Experiment Station, Moccasin, Montana

1.　*Great Falls Tribune,* 18 July 1957; *50th Anniversary Celebration,* Experiment Station Publication, 18 July 1957; James Krall interview, 16 April 1990.

Work in the College of Agriculture has also given farmers across the state new varieties of barley. The first good dryland barley to be developed was Compana, a variety realized largely through the work of Robert Eslick at the Central Montana Agricultural Experiment Station at Moccasin. During dry cycles, varieties of barley used earlier tended to produce a plethora of individual kernels having little weight. Compana was bred to produce fewer but plumper kernels under drought conditions. Eslick and his associates moved on to study other barley varieties, including Betses, a strain preferred by the malting industry, and thereby provided one more option for farmers pressed with increasing costs and declining income. Even more recently, an MSU chemist, Kenneth Goering, developed a waxy barley that has industrial uses, and a plant to process this special variety has been built in Dillon.

Custom combines, 1948

Agronomists on and off campus have always worked closely with buyers, millers, and bakers in efforts to develop and disseminate new grain varieties. David Davis for many years headed the grain laboratory and the associated facilities for testing gluten and other grain properties before the laboratory was moved to Great Falls. [18]

Like other scientists, researchers from the College of Agriculture have often worked with their counterparts in federal agencies. One example of this fruitful cooperation is the work done on Line I Hereford cattle at the Miles City experiment station, where the research done by Ray Woodward and his colleagues led to the creation of the Hereford gene pool that dominates the national beef-cattle scene today. It is estimated that at least 90 percent of Herefords in the country have germ plasm originating in the Miles City project, which is being continued today at the Havre station.

But the school's most important contribution to the beef-cattle industry did not derive from the development of a specific breed or even of a specific technique like artificial insemination. The most critical development in the beef industry since 1960 has been the advent of beef indexing, or performance indexing as it is more widely known. Ray Woodward and many other scientists on and off campus had a hand in bringing ranchers around to the view that the most profitable operation could be attained only by accurate record keeping of the performance characteristics of their herds—and by ruthless culling of those individuals that were not up to standard.

Performance breeding had long been practiced in the dairy industry and in other countries, but there was strong resistance to it in Montana and in the American West in general. Western ranchers liked to see a herd of uniform and, above all, attractive animals. They were convinced that what they saw—the phenotype—was what counted, and they bred for the characteristics that produced what they wanted to see. What they failed to realize was that what really counted was not what the animal looked like, but what the animal was genetically—the genotype. Performance records, if based on the appropriate genetic traits and if accurately kept, can give breeders solid data on the economic value of their herds.

Until the development of the electronic computer, such record keeping was tiresome and difficult, but as the power of the computer became available, the beef-performance movement prospered on campus, despite intense opposition to this sort of research from ranchers who had a personal commitment to a uniform herd of Hereford or Angus cattle and who felt their investment in purebred herds was being threatened.

Despite such tension, the work done in the 1960s yielded a valuable economic by-product. After World War II, some ranchers recognized the need for new germ plasm for their herds. At first they imported semen from breeds from Canada. (At the time federal law prohibited the importation of the bulls themselves.) Eventually they looked to Europe, specifically Switzerland and France, and brought two new breeds—the Simmental and the Charolais—to Montana. Because of the leadership of the College of Agriculture in bringing the Simmental to this country, the national headquarters of the American Simmental Association is located in Bozeman. [19]

Agricultural research, often conducted with other state and federal agencies, has paid handsome dividends across the board. New fallowing methods for grain growers, new products like safflower, and new fertilizing and weed control methods all contributed to Montana's agricultural economy at a time when it was under tremendous pressure. Because Jerald W. Bergman developed specialty safflowers for oil qualities, a new safflower oil industry was created in the northeast corner of the state. The work of dedicated and talented scientists in soil-water-fertilizer interactions led to enhanced fertilization techniques that boosted crop production remarkably. New range management approaches have been pioneered by MSU's range scientists, and increasing interest in holistic management techniques promise substantial gain for western ranchers. There is no doubt that as more young Montanans are exposed to the work of university researchers, the more knowledgeable they will become in solving the problems faced on farms and ranches every day.

The Tradition in the Physical Sciences

Just as the life sciences formed an integral component of an agriculturally oriented land grant institution, so did the physical sciences form the core of the engineering and mechanic arts curricula on campus. As industrial America came of age, the demand for scientists, engineers, and technicians placed substantial responsibilities upon the college. The undergraduate curriculum had to provide a spectrum of preparatory courses that would feed students into either basic sciences or career-oriented degree programs in agricultural and engineering areas. In keeping with national trends a century ago, courses in physics, chemistry, and geology formed the heart of the curricula in physical science studied at the new college in Bozeman.

A natty early chemistry laboratory class

Professors Frank Traphagen and William Cobleigh laid the foundations for degree programs in physical science and taught most of the original offerings. Four-year programs in physics and chemistry began in 1901-1902, but academic reorganization in 1913 eliminated them. Physics, then linked as an administrative unit with mathematics, resurfaced in 1921-1922 as a curriculum in the division of engineering, where it was to remain until 1957, while chemistry was allied with the division of science and had close ties to agriculture through experiment station funding for agricultural chemistry. This source of support proved critical during the Great Depression and allowed the department to develop a strong faculty at a time when other areas suffered. [20]

The crisis of the depression laid a pall over the campus. Internal debate concerning the propriety of agricultural reform efforts being conducted by some college staff at that time touched the very nature of scientific research. The college reacted to both internal and external criticism by pushing programs that would have an immediate impact on the state. Deane B. Swingle, who came to the campus as a bacteriologist and who stayed on to organize the nursing curriculum and to lay the foundations for the student health services (that center is now named in his honor), was hardly optimistic in assessing the scene: "This state is more interested in the superficial and spectacular things incident to the college than in the deeper and more fundamental things that give colleges their value and we are not doing much to dispel that attitude," he said. [21]

Against this background, then, World War II proved a turning point in the story of the physical sciences. Training programs offered on campus during the war brought new seriousness to the enterprise and helped to prepare some departments for leadership roles in the postwar era. For example, chemistry burgeoned in the forties. Because its foundation was solid, its faculty moved ahead rapidly in strength and numbers. Standard courses in analytical, qualitative, and physical chemistry provided a springboard for the recruitment of strong new faculty, and as grant money flowed in, new laboratory facilities followed.

In order to build professional programs, chemists pushed for and received permission to offer a doctoral degree in 1955. Thus chemistry, along with microbiology, was among the first departments to support a Ph.D. program on campus. Chemists occupied a central position at MSC. Their relations with engineering areas were good, their service courses were a requirement for many other curricula, and their faculty were well known and well respected on campus. A chemist, Leon Johnson, headed up the new office of grants and contracts in the mid-'50s, and by the mid-'60s chemists were numerous enough, experienced enough, and ambitious enough to move into the upper echelons of central administration.

With people in high places and with federal grant monies, emphasis was placed on expanding department facilities. Spectroscopic analysis was vastly enhanced by new electronic equipment, and Charles Caughlan secured a state-of-the-art X-ray crystallography laboratory. The growth

Hands-on science

continues today; in the past decade, nuclear magnetic resonance equipment and other expensive analytical tools have been acquired. Most recently, scientists with off-campus funding have leased space and laboratory facilities in the department, attracted by Bozeman's climate, environment, and working conditions. The Environmental Protection Agency has long helped fund the fisheries bioassay laboratory, which is essentially a water chemistry facility under the leadership of Robert Vance Thurston. With the dawn of nucleic acid research, biochemistry offered significant new technologies as well as important new scientific insights. [22]

In 1930 Arthur J. M. Johnson and James Kiefer constituted the physics group in the combined mathematics-physics department in the engineering division. Johnson had remarkable success in identifying and preparing students for graduate school. But despite this, and some other areas of distinction—for instance, the college's engineering physics curriculum was one of only three in the world, the University of Illinois and McGill University in Montreal having established programs earlier—the physics program was limited by the weaknesses of the mathematics program, and Johnson fought regularly with mathematicians to offer more sophisticated courses. He was eventually obliged by William Tallman with a course in differential equations, and from the mid-1920s such courses were part of math offerings.

By the postwar period, physics had achieved a strong position on campus, and faculty recruitment was focused on securing individuals capable of submitting successful grant proposals. Professors Kurt Rothschild and Hack Arroe (an Austrian and a Dane, respectively) brought in

Atomic Energy Commission and National Science Foundation grants to purchase equipment. Unfortunately, personality conflicts in the small group led to internal departmental difficulties, which the Northwest Association accrediting committee noted. When Arthur Johnson retired as department head in 1960, Irving Dayton, educated in physics at Swarthmore and Cornell, replaced him. Dayton came with a mandate from President Leon Johnson to update the undergraduate curriculum, to develop a doctoral program so that faculty interested in high levels of research would have an opportunity to work in their areas of expertise, and to augment the weekly physics colloquium. He was also to acquire vigorous new staff to push the department forward.

Dayton had the advantage of beginning with a basically strong program and a clean slate. Faculty recruitment was at the top of his list of priorities. "It was a very tough time to recruit because there was a shortage of physicists. We decided to concentrate upon solid state and atomic/molecular physics as these fields were where we could reasonably expect to get support; there was a niche there." [23] Professors Hugo Schmidt, Gerald J. Lapeyre, and John Drumheller constituted the foundation for an energized program. Building upon their commitment and skills, Dayton went on to strengthen the areas of relativity, quantum physics, and astrophysics.

As the department expanded in numbers of students and faculty, more emphasis was placed upon cooperative research projects with faculty in other areas. Most notably there was a strong interaction with engineering and chemistry faculty in the magneto-hydrodynamics (MHD) program, which was developed in the sixties. When he was still majority leader of the Senate, Mike

Mansfield used some of his political muscle to favor Montana Tech with a project that would provide substantial funding for a research program based on the concept of generating electricity using a very high temperature and high pressure plasma field. The concept was not a new one—containing tremendously volatile plasma had long posed formidable problems—but practical solutions had proved elusive. The school in Butte was made the home base of the MHD program, but the project was of such scope as to draw in faculty from other units, most notably MSU. The Montana Power Company was interested in the work for obvious reasons and lent support. After nearly two decades of work, the project has generated much new knowledge, most notably in the area of materials science. Perhaps its most tangible result to date, however, is the strong commitment to interunit cooperation that it represents.

The physics department affords another example of advance in the sciences: the entry of women into the field. Georgeanna R. (Jan) Caughlin, a master's-prepared physicist, first came to Bozeman with her chemist husband. In 1955 the department asked her to begin teaching sections of the introductory physics courses; two years later, she took a full-time position, though she was offered considerably less than her male colleagues. Studying astrophysics in summer sessions at California Institute of Technology, she again faced discriminatory rules that barred her from staying overnight in the Mount Palomar Observatory to take advantage of the optimum conditions for studying the skies. Completing an NSF fellowship in 1964, Caughlan took up the teaching of astrophysics at MSU. The subsequent development of a strong doctoral program in that area largely reflects her pioneering efforts. She was later to teach courses in nuclear physics. Even so, when she was recommended for promotion from assistant to associate professor, a woman on the Board of Regents raised some pointed questions about "housewives in the classroom." But her faculty colleagues found strength in her example as they attacked issues of sex equity. [24]

There may be no better example of the quickening pace of scientific research at MSU than the surface physics laboratory housed in the basement of A.J.M. Johnson Hall. Since the mid-1960s this facility has attracted international attention. Gerald J. Lapeyre began modestly with Air Force funding, expanded gradually with other sources, and by 1979 had received an NSF regional facility grant, one of only thirteen in all science, and one of two in surface science. The laboratory is used by researchers from around the world and has generated enormous revenue for the university and the state.

The surface physics lab calls attention to an aspect of university science too easily overlooked.

Sophisticated machines require sophisticated management. The care and calibration of such equipment is itself a specialized skill, and those who tend to it are often the forgotten people. Many have doctorates, yet because they are not employed in tenure-track positions, they enjoy little academic security. The range of benefits and salary that they do command is contingent solely upon the success of the principal grant writer in securing continued funding. James Anderson, who oversees the CRISS (Center for Research in Surface Science) lab, is one of those unsung and generally invisible figures and is representative of so many others who contribute heavily to basic scientific research, but who fit no particular niche in teaching and research and whose work therefore all too often goes unnoticed. [25]

Unnoticed, too, in its early history was the fact the MSC was located in the heart of a vast natural geological laboratory. This resource went untapped when geology as a discipline became a part of the trade-off with the university in Missoula early in the century and later with the School of Mines in Butte, both of which offered curricula in that science. In time, Pascual Gaines and Raymond Woodruff would offer occasional work in chemical geology, and Nicholas Helburn laid the groundwork for introducing more geology when he formed a new department of geography in 1946. (At one time the college had offered geography courses through the secretarial science department.) When, after World War II, Helburn brought in the first professional geologist, Charles E. Bradley, there was considerable resentment throughout the university system—it being perceived as an encroachment on another's turf—and at least one regent persistently attempted to thwart the growth of the geology curriculum at Bozeman. Nevertheless, the department did grow, and in the mid-1950s, when meteorology was first offered, the department of geography became the earth sciences department.

President Leon Johnson, in particular, admired the multidiscipline departmental arrangement in earth sciences, which allowed the development of some unique courses. Because the department was committed to exploiting all that was offered by the local environment, its faculty members undertook studies and courses in snow dynamics, avalanche control, cloud-seeding techniques, and field geology. (In fact, the field trips led by Charles Bradley, John Montagne, Robert Chadwick, and William McMannis have become part of local folklore.) Research in snow dynamics, in particular, gained international attention. Geologists worked closely with colleagues in a number of engineering disciplines to develop instruments and techniques for managing snow safely. In 1982 the International Snow Science Workshop was held on campus, its aim being to translate theory and data into applied management techniques for those responsible for managing ski areas and other snow recreation sites. [26]

Another direct descendant of this multidisciplinary approach is the high-elevation studies group which today supports graduate-level work and involves representatives from a spectrum of the sciences and engineering as well as public administration, business, and history and philosophy. At present this group is forging strong ties with the National Park Service naturalists and with other scientists interested in the Yellowstone region. Other practical applications of the work from earth sciences include the computer-generated microclimate maps that are increasingly popular with farmers, business people, and researchers in general who need meteorological information of economic or environmental importance.

In contrast to the eclectic, evolutionary nature of the department of earth sciences is the history of the College of Engineering. As the former dean of the college, Byron Bennett, recalled,

> I came in 1960 to a traditional hierarchical administrative operation. The faculty did not have a great deal to do with governance. . . . The department head . . . was responsible for the total operation of the department. And however he could best do what he was instructed to do, he did. The deans operated the same way. They reported directly to the president. It was an industrial model, frankly. We did not have to have full state support because we generated our own outside work . . . with such firms as Technical Material Corporation, the Naval Research Laboratory in San Diego, the Bonneville Power Company, the Signal Corps Laboratory, and Montana Power Company. . . . We did not do a lot with the National Science Foundation because we found we could do a better direct job by working contractually with companies. [27]

Into the early sixties the majority of faculty of the College of Engineering did not have doctoral degrees, and Bennett placed a major upgrading of faculty high on his administrative agenda. For the most part, MSU's engineers kept one foot

Steam tractor moving bleachers just before construction of Gatton Field; locomotive used for extra steam in winter and as an object of study by engineering students

in the academic world and the other in the particular technological industries of their specialties, finding that consulting with private firms was a good way to keep in touch with the field as professionals. In fact, by the mid-1960s it was state law in Montana that in order to teach advanced courses in the classroom, the faculty member be licensed by the state as a professional engineer. Because that requirement did not square with the traditional idea of academic freedom, it brought engineering administrators into conflict with central administration from time to time.

Lloyd Berg - Mr. Chem. E.

But from the point of view of the engineering staff, the effect of straddling both worlds was generally positive, since it kept them in close relationship with colleagues around the state and nation. For instance, because of all his contacts Lloyd Berg was able to vastly improve research in chemical engineering, begging and borrowing materials from various companies. Berg and his colleagues and students also secured any number of patents dealing with petrochemical technology. The power laboratory in electrical engineering similarly profited from private donations of equipment, by-products of a close relationship with a consortium of private companies for whom the power lab provides a nationally important consulting service.

Student enrollments in engineering exploded throughout the 1970s and 1980s. In 1982-1983 there were 3000 student-engineers, nearly triple the enrollment in 1973. At present there are about 1850 engineering students who are taught by about 70 faculty. At any one time one-fifth of the entire MSU student population will be engineering majors. Certainly one of engineering's attractions is the conspicuous success various departments have in placing their students. The majority of faculty attribute much of this success in placement to the intensive laboratory experience their students acquire over their undergraduate years. Every senior electrical engineering student, for example, is responsible for a specific design project. Other engineering curricula offer college summer internships and industrial experience, all of which provide links to future employers.

A continuing thrust in the college is to assist in whatever ways it can to develop resources. Water resources programs, obviously important to the state and region, have long been part of engineering outreach, largely orchestrated through the Water Resources Center. The Rural Technical Assistance Program, centered on campus and working with local officials on transportation structure, is affiliated with the federal highway program. The University Technical Assistance Program, which assists budding industries, is "set up along the lines of producing the better mousetrap," in the words of longtime college administrator Ted Williams. [28] The electrical engineers have a similar cooperative program to assist northwest and west coast firms. The campus technology park, created by President William Tietz in the late '80s (see Chapter 7) is a logical extension

A trio of perplexed engineers! From left to right: Theodore C. Lang, Robert L. Brown and Robert G. Oakberg

of science and engineering commitments to these technical outreach efforts. Many of the small technological industries characteristic of the Bozeman area had their genesis in various components of the engineering school. The electronic research laboratory spawned Montronics and several other firms. The fiber-optics firms located in the area regularly employ students and faculty from the college. An example of this symbiotic relationship is the Toomay-Mathis Company, founded by two retired air force generals, engineers themselves. The company has an international market for its high-technology products. The profits generated go to support Eagle Mount, a philanthropic program to offer the terminally ill outdoor recreational opportunities. Students and faculty in engineering areas work with the company and company personnel are often lent back to departments on campus, at no cost to the university. [29]

The engineers played a key role in developing the campus central computing service. When discussions about acquiring a control mainframe system began in the early 1960s, accessibility for individual faculty from terminals in buildings across campus was a prime consideration, since personal computers were not available then. The initial machine, an IBM 650, used a revolving magnetic drum with 2000 cells, a very limited storage capacity. Because of limitations in the campus electrical system, as well as in machine storage capacity, only a minimum number of students could be accommodated initially, even though facilities were open around the clock to take advantage of slack time in the middle of the night. In 1965 the school acquired a Sigma 7, and in the early 1970s a Honeywell. Then, in 1985 the College of Engineering prepared a five-year computer plan based on partnership with industry. The result is the new DEC that now handles the bulk of the mainframe computing demands from the central campus computing center in the basement of Renne Library.

The curriculum for the computer science program itself originated with Louis Schmittroth and was first affiliated with industrial and management engineering. Later moved to electrical engineering, then temporarily abandoned, it is now institutionally a separate department in the College of Engineering.

Engineers of all disciplines on campus now look ahead to a multimillion-dollar facility that will soon replace the badly overextended Ryon Laboratory and Roberts and Cobleigh Halls. Where now the entrance to Roberts Hall is graced by the symbols of electrical engineering (the dynamo), of civil engineering (the compass and square), and of mechanical engineering (the scissors arrangement of the ball governor), the industrial and computer science logos will surely have their own place of prominence in the new facility. [30]

The Tradition in the Outreach Sciences

The professional schools have served the university as a link between the sciences and the public. The College of Nursing offers certainly one of the most visible of these outreach programs. The care of the sick in Montana is a reflection of the high cost of open space. The state is large, the population scattered. Though several orders of Roman Catholic nuns and the Methodist Deaconesses movement historically served the health needs of some of this population, by the turn of the century it was clear that a training program for nurses would be necessary to fully provide for the needs of the state. E. Augusta Ariss, R.N., established the first nurses' training program in Great Falls in 1902. Then, in 1916 Montana State College inaugurated a one-semester program in nursing based on a curriculum ordained by the state. This program was ex-

A nursing practicum

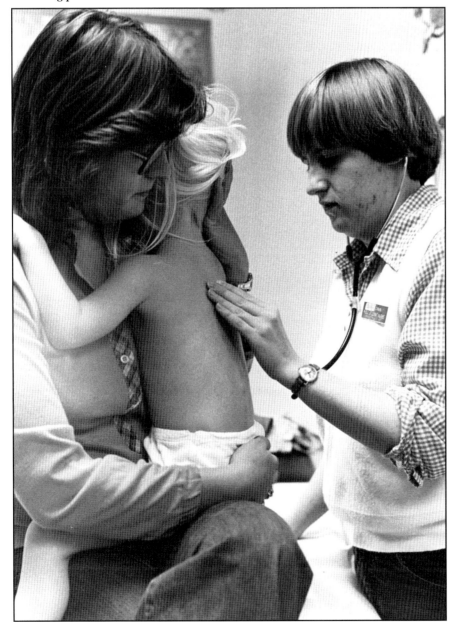

panded in 1917 with America's entry into World War I. [31]

By 1935 several hospital-based nursing schools in the state were seeking consolidation and a campus location. The Deaconess group sent out inquiries to northwest regional schools asking if there was interest. That inquiry prompted a new level of commitment on the part of the administration at Montana State College to build a consolidated program. In May 1938, President A. L. Strand contracted with the Consolidated Deaconess School of Nursing in Great Falls to offer college credit for work done there, implementing a bachelor of science degree in nursing and collecting appropriate fees from their students. Professor Pascual Gaines of chemistry, Frank B. Cotner, then dean of the division of science and a microbiologist, Deane B. Swingle, and Louis True, director of college publications formed, along with Anna Pearl Sherrick, the initial leadership group. Professor Sherrick, a dynamic nurse-educator, led the charge for a strong nursing program. But the group had come together at a difficult time, for tax-supported funding for nursing, which nurses wanted in order to sustain their autonomy, was almost nonexistent. Although the nurses set up a revolving fund, independent of the college budget, to attract private donations, the greatest financial assistance to the program came from the Cadet Nurse Corps which was sponsored by the federal government during the war and brought with it a massive infusion of new money. From 1937 to 1965 there were five separate nursing curricula administered from Bozeman. This variety of off-campus, mostly Deaconess-based programs ranged from a five-year baccalaureate course to a one-year practical nursing option.

By 1964 the administration of the nursing school had set up a teleconferencing facility which enabled them to maintain contact with the off-campus training sites. The potential for televised instruction seemed so worthwhile that Fred Gerber, new head of film and television, and Lee Good, a technical director under Gerber, joined with Anna Pearl Sherrick to submit a proposal for a five-year television project to the Division of Nursing, U.S. Public Health Service. The accepted proposal brought nearly $5 million to the campus to buy equipment and support salaries. It was a big boost for nursing instruction and a very important one for the film and television center as well. Originally eleven nursing courses were taught over TV; soon other disciplines like history were using the network for some of their large-section courses.

By the middle of the 1980s nursing was experiencing some of the same financial difficulties as were the other areas on campus. In particular, the costs of the off-campus segments of the nursing program had skyrocketed. In need of imposing economies, university administrators opted to close the nurses' extended campus in Butte, touching off a painful struggle. (See Chapter 7.) MSU extended campuses remain open for upper-division course work in Missoula, Great Falls, and Billings. Student demand is high and the program is fully accredited. [32]

The home economics program, principally because of its close ties to the Cooperative Extension Service, represents another key area of the practical application of science and science outreach. Offerings in what was first called "domestic economy" were important for women students in the early days of the campus. The first instructor in the curriculum was a tough-minded New York native, Eliza Owens, who had resigned her position at Iowa State in protest against underfunding of the program there. In Bozeman she soon moved into a leadership position in the community, being one of the few female members of the Contemporary Club, a group of town-gown elites. As the feminist movement took hold nationally in the dawn of the twentieth century, domestic science courses increased in popularity and in stature. Employment for domestic science graduates of the college increased as the demand for teachers in the state grew.

In 1911, President James Hamilton, concerned that the college offer young women new opportunities and yet that students on campus be properly supervised, invited Una B. Herrick, a home economist, to join the faculty as the first dean of women. Among her other innovations, Dean Herrick called a women's vocational conference. Underwritten by funds from local women's clubs, the first conference was held in November of 1913 with sixty-seven girls in attendance. The program, which a few years later was opened to young men, evolved into High School Week, a program that now annually attracts hundreds of students from around the state. [33]

Jessie Donaldson of the English faculty worked closely with Dean Herrick to build the home economics curriculum. From an institutional point of view, the real impetus to the growth of the program was the Purnell Act of 1925, which provided funding through the agricultural experiment station to encourage experimentation in foods, clothing, health, and the domestic economy. The new energy generated by the Purnell Act prompted Frederic Linfield, dean of the College of Agriculture, to bring in Gladys Branegan in 1925 to direct the department. Jessie Richardson joined the staff at the same time.

Gladys Branegan's career illustrates the close link between the extension service, the experiment station, and the home economics faculty. She served as an extension home economics liaison, supervised the state's high school programs, and helped set up local councils for improving nutrition and domestic management. She always encouraged staff to take leaves of absence to acquire terminal degrees in the field, and through her world travels encouraged her colleagues to take an interest in international affairs. In 1931 when Robert A. Cooley moved to Hamilton to direct the new federal laboratory there, Branegan persuaded the college to acquire his house at the corner of Grand and Cleveland and to use it for a home management course.

When bell bottoms were in vogue: painting the "M"

New staff like Bertha Clow provided strong links to the medical community because of interest in nutrition, specifically the newly discovered vitamin content of foods. At that time—the early 1930s—improved diets were only beginning to be seen as a means of preventing some diseases and providing treatment in others. Child development programs expanded when Marjorie Paisley joined the faculty in 1944. Facilities for youngsters had been in existence for some time, but now they were enlarged as interest in the program intensified. The overall strength of the entire department, as well as world conditions, is reflected in the fact that in June of 1945, half the graduating seniors were home ec majors.

After World War II, the national hot lunch program became popular, and in 1951 Gladys Roehm joined the faculty to supervise that development. The family life option, added to the curriculum in the mid-60s, brought men to the home economics faculty; Clark Swain came in 1965, followed a few years later by Robert Lind and Howard Bushing.

In 1965 the School of Home Economics received a $600,000 five-year grant from the Kellogg Foundation for a leadership program; that same year home economics initiated a program to assist those working on or near the state's Indian reservations. Both of these programs added depth to the curriculum and provided a pool of community leaders who visited the campus regularly. As time passed, curricular changes were recognized in a campuswide reorganization that made the School of Home Economics a department in the College of Education. [33]

Reconfiguring the Tradition

In the centennial year, significant transformations in certain areas of the sciences are clearly seen. While the focus remains on undergraduate instruction and graduate research, the old philosophy—"stack 'em deep and teach 'em cheap"— is dying. Doing science today requires tremendous capital expenditures. For a variety of reasons the State of Montana has not had the resources necessary to support these expenditures, and all areas of the campus have been searching for alternative sources of funding, usually within the context of a land grant tradition of outreach and service. Three examples of this reconfiguration can be used to illustrate the directions the university will likely take in the new century.

The first example is that of the SIMM (Systemic Initiative for Montana Mathematics) project, an understanding of which is best gained in reviewing the history of the college's mathematics program. Mathematics has been at the heart of the academic curriculum since the days of Plato's academy, and almost every student who has matriculated at the Bozeman academy has taken some mathematics along the way to a degree. Historically, relations between the mathematicians, who were service-oriented, and the departments they served were sound. But during the height of the Renne regime, as the Cold War intensified and the college moved toward more research emphasis, it was clear that mathematics would have to be upgraded to provide some critical support to the scientific disciplines. John Hurst was hired as department head in 1957 to do just that. Building upon existing staff strengths— faculty like Robert Lowney, William Swartz, Eldon Whitesett, and James Simpson—Hurst set out to recruit as energetically as did his peers in chemistry, physics, and microbiology. He quickly acquired a stable of sound talent and in 1959 received permission to offer a doctoral degree.

Adrien Hess, a new instructor, was placed in charge of the teaching option in mathematics. Recognizing the need to upgrade at the local school level, Hess applied for and received an NSF grant for summer instruction that led to the founding of the Montana Council of Teachers of Mathematics in 1961. This Montana group was to become known as the strongest math education group in the nation. So the department moved forward as quickly in teacher preparation as in top-level research.

When John Hurst left, Louis Barrett became department head and focused on expanding undergraduate offerings; courses in statistics, algebra, differential equations, analysis, and topology were now listed in the college catalog. Succeeding Barrett, Robert Engle conducted a joint review of math programs at both state universities. As a result, emphasis now shifted to statistics and applied areas. Applied mathematics led naturally to emphasis in numerical analysis and dynamical systems—the corollaries of sophisticated computing systems.

In 1974 the department spearheaded the establishment of the Montana chapter of the American Statistical Society, a parallel group to the math teachers' council. By virtue of both organizations, the MSU math department was connected with a cadre of the state's teachers—not just those working on the high school level but also instructors in Montana's community, tribal, and private colleges. In the late 1980s these connections became the basis for a joint math-education doctoral program at MSU. The program's emphasis on classroom instruction and curriculum development has intensified the need for new teaching materials and techniques in the math classroom. One result of this intensified need was a grant from Exxon in 1989 that enabled MSU, UM, and the teachers' council to consider jointly the design of an integrated mathematics curriculum. The effort was aimed at developing a northwest-area consortium to improve mathematics instructions in the high school. MSU mathematician Maurice J. Burke, himself an MSU graduate and a Rhodes Scholar, led the effort, in conjunction with Dan Dolan of the Office of Public Instruction and Johnny Lott of the University of Montana.

After two years of careful planning and assessment, the Montana Mathematics Coalition submitted its proposal for a revitalized education program—the Systemic Initiative for Montana Mathematics (SIMM) Project—to Governor Stan Stephens to be forwarded to NSF. When the federal agency gave $9 million to the project, the governor pledged an additional $5 million in state support.

The project is designed to be truly systemic: the new curriculum will use an integrated, interdisciplinary approach and incorporate the best technology in all facets of math instruction. Once implemented, SIMM will fundamentally change the ways in which we study the world of numbers. If it achieves its potential, Montana will become a national leader in renewing math education. It is quite likely that a parallel component that would fundamentally reconfigure high school science curricula will eventually be joined to this project. [35]

Another program developed at MSU and representing this same fusion of internal academic interest, national or international need, and private- and public-sector funding is the Center for Interfacial Microbial Process Engineering

William G. Charackalis and Keith E. Cooksey in the lab

(CIMPE). Established on campus in 1990 under the leadership of William G. Characklis, the center, in partnership with the National Engineering Laboratory in Idaho, received $7.4 million from NSF for research in the area of environmental biotechnology. To date, the center is the only NSF site in the field of environmental engineering.

William Characklis received a doctorate from Johns Hopkins and taught engineering at Rice

University before President William Tietz and the College of Engineering, wanting to develop their environmental engineering program, brought him to Bozeman. In 1983, the Institute for Biological and Chemical Process Analysis, Characklis' program on campus, established itself as a recognized leader in the business of microbial interfaces. The success and momentum of that institute led in turn to the establishment of CIMPE, where research is focused on understanding the complex dynamics of microorganisms that collect at surfaces. Industrial production involves square miles of surfaces in pipes, vents, distribution systems, and production machinery. For example, the high temperatures and the nature of the oil flowing through Alaska's pipelines make the lines conducive to harboring bacteria that eventually form balls—in many cases, balls the size of a golf ball. The various private associates of the center face similar microbial problems. One industrial associate, a petrochemical company, estimates that it will invest about $300 million in the next decade to treat wastewater and bioremediate hazardous contaminates in its downstream effluents.

In its work, the Center for Interfacial Microbial Process Engineering is integrally involved with several associated programs administered by Johns Hopkins University; the Naval Oceanographic Research and Development Activity; Rensselaer Polytechnic Institute; California State University, Long Beach; University of Idaho; University of Wyoming; and Montana College of Mineral Science and Technology. At these sites as well as at MSU, biologists and microbiologists, biochemists, engineers of all kinds, and students from every conceivable scientific discipline are at work on research projects. The vision of Bill Characklis, who died in 1992, continues to drive the center, and that vision embraces more than a project involving microbial research. In its organization, its support, and its outreach, "the Center is at the heart of cultural change in our research universities," Characklis said. [36] If this vision is compared with that of the mathematics initiative, then one can begin to see the impact of the university's contributions to the world of science and technology.

By all accounts, a major watershed in the history of the sciences at MSU has been the WAMI program, which began in the early seventies from roots that were deep and mostly invisible. The accretion over time of a dedicated staff, a talented faculty, better laboratories, better library and computing resources, and strong support services had moved the school to the point where, with everything in place, the University of Washington selected MSU as the site for its extended medical school program. [37]

There was a national consensus in the early seventies that a serious shortage of medical doc-

*In Dillon, Montana,
Dr. Ron Lodge makes a
house call at the home of
Hans Christian Anderson.*

tors was in the making, especially in rural areas, and the University of Washington School of Medicine began serious inquiry into the possibility of establishing a regionalized medical school that might help offset the predicted shortage. The school invited Alaska, Montana, and Idaho to experiment with them in offering a year's preclinical medical instruction at state universities in the three collaborating states and at Washington State University in Pullman, followed by a three-year course of study based in Seattle. This system was enthusiastically endorsed by all invited participants, and in 1971 the group obtained $1 million in start-up monies from the Commonwealth Fund of New York. The program, named WAMI in acknowledgement of the participating states, was, and remains, unique in that it is the only decentralized basic science and clinical program in the United States.

The proposal raised a basic question in Montana: Where would the satellite program be located—in Bozeman or in Missoula? Recognizing the competition that lay ahead, John Jutila and Frank Newman of the microbiology faculty took the lead in preparing the MSU proposal. They stressed the educational goals of the land grant institution and emphasized the school's commitment to service and outreach. They documented the strength of campus science programs, the solid achievements of the applied-science areas, and the vigor of the school's humanities programs as applied to medical education. Jutila and Newman also focused on associated health fields, including nursing, dietetics, medical technology,

physical therapy, environmental health, veterinary science, and the programs in premedicine and preveterinary medicine already strongly in place on the campus. In particular, they called attention to the eminently successful premed advising program established by Dr. Harold Watling.

In late 1971 a review team from the University of Washington School of Medicine visited both Missoula and Bozeman. They were favorably impressed with the University of Montana program proposal and from all accounts had concluded to recommend locating the program there. However, Jutila and Newman were determined to secure the program for MSU, and they spared no effort when the review team arrived in Bozeman. The two men introduced the team to faculty from across the campus, stressed the excellence of the basic sciences at MSU, noted the strong research programs in the allied health areas, and detailed the comprehensive support groups that would be available to the program—like the then-state-of-the-art mainframe computer system housed beneath Renne Library. It was a vigorous and a well-planned presentation. And a convincing one. The review team selected Bozeman as the WAMI site.

The campus became integrally involved in UW's experiment in regionalized medical education in September of 1973, when ten medical students from Montana enrolled at Bozeman for the first quarter of instruction in a pre-WAMI program in basic medical studies. A second class of ten matriculated in 1974, and the actual operational phase of WAMI at MSU began on July 1, 1975, with the naming of twenty Montana residents to the program and the initiation of full state funding for the costs of their medical education. Though the Commonwealth Fund and federal grants, notably from the U. S. Bureau of Health Manpower, continued to support the project through the mid-seventies, the Montana legislature, since 1975, has provided for the basic educational costs of eighty students each year, that is, twenty students for each of four years in medical school. [38]

The aims of the WAMI program have been modified somewhat over the years, but basically the major goals remain the same: (1) to increase the number of primary-care physicians practicing in Montana; (2) to redress the maldistribution of physicians in Montana, attracting more physicians to small communities and areas of need; (3) to make the resources of the Seattle school available to MSU and to Montana generally; and (4) to avoid having to build, staff, and operate a medical school in Montana. The program has been quite successful in meeting all its goals. Since graduating its first class in 1977, WAMI has produced 164 physicians from Montana who are currently in practice, and eighty-eight additional graduates are doing their residency work. The bottom line is that, to date, seventy-six WAMI graduates have returned from their various residencies to practice in their native state. Another measure of success of the program is that 66 percent of Montana's WAMI students have entered primary-care practice, about double the national average for those specialties.

As can be expected, some areas of Montana still have great difficulty finding and retaining physicians, but without the WAMI program it is safe to suggest that this situation would be even more critical. By any standard, the regionalized concept that underlies the medical education program has served Montana communities and taxpayers well.

WAMI has also had a profound impact on the MSU campus. Its presence has fostered the development of several other programs, notably the genetics institute begun under Palmer D. "Dave" Skaar, which became a model for others across the nation, pulling together as it did the many divergent constituencies that focus on DNA research. The institute not only represented the wave of the future in the broader world of research, it also provided educational and research opportunities for personnel and students from other disciplines on campus—for instance, animal science, which had no doctoral program of its own. Unfortunately, recent budget cuts have undermined the institute.

Nevertheless, WAMI continues to provide a tremendous resource to faculty and students outside the curriculum itself; in the effort that brought it to Bozeman, the program focused the various science groups on their own research and opened lines of communication regarding that work on regional, national, and international levels. WAMI was, and is, not just a medical program. It has legitimized what the science faculty knew all along: Montana State University had come of age. [39]

Chapter Ten
The Tradition of the Humanities and Professional Schools at MSU

Multidisciplinary Departments as the Foundation

The Morrill Act of 1862, under which the university was originally established, specified that the "leading object" of any land grant institution should be "to teach such branches of learning as are related to the Agricultural and Mechanical Arts"— yet "without excluding the scientific and classical studies. " But confusion as to exactly what constituted "such branches of learning" was evident from the very beginning as the Local Executive Board established the curriculum at the Montana College of Agriculture and Mechanic Arts in Bozeman. Latin, English, ethics, music— these were certainly "classical studies." But what of history, political science, sociology, and economics? The Local Executive Board, in its statement of rules for the new school, claimed that "economic science" lay within the province of the college. That apparently opened the door for history, political economy, and constitutional law. [1]

Max Worthington, Golden Bobcat, MSU stalwart, dean of student affairs and services, 1946-1972

The versatile Benjamin F. Maiden, previously an instructor at the Bozeman Academy, taught a sequence of ancient, medieval, and modern history the first year of the school's existence, while also teaching logic and ethics. In the following year the president of the school himself, James Reid, taught sociology. Because engineering was still in a formative stage and student interest in agricultural courses was not strong, this catch-all liberal arts curriculum became increasingly important to maintaining enrollments.

By the end of the century, the student could choose a "scientific course" that included history, the English language, and literature. The course was ostensibly designed so that any student completing it would be "thoroughly equipped for the duties of life and fitted to enter successfully upon any chosen career." [2]

Maiden and Reid were succeeded quickly by William Brewer, and Brewer in turn by his sister, Helen R. Brewer, an Iowa (Grinnell) College graduate and, until her retirement in 1932, a dynamo on campus. Helen Brewer it was who essentially built the curriculum, only to see a major part of it traded away by President James Hamilton in 1913. Hamilton felt strongly that if students were seriously interested in pursuing a four-year degree in the humanities and social sciences they ought to go west to Missoula. The ag college offered "service courses;" the university offered degrees.

World War I offered the Brewers—William having returned from graduate school and joined his sister on the faculty—an opportunity to capitalize on the importance of historical and social studies as background to the war. Increasing enrollments after the war brought new faculty to teach expanded offerings. The most notable addition to the faculty in this era was Merrill G. Burlingame, who would become a premier historian in the state before his retirement some forty years later. The Great Depression occasioned staff reductions, but offerings in the "service department" remained comprehensive and popular.

The end of the Second World War, like the end of the First, brought growing enrollments and consequent faculty additions, like Professors Robert G. Dunbar and Alton B. Oviatt, who came in 1947. An innovation during this period was the extension courses offered by the history department to meet the needs of public school teachers as credential requirements changed. Courses were offered from Three Forks to Livingston, and many a young assistant professor augmented his or her salary by teaching night classes in history.

By the mid-fifties departmental offerings included philosophy and political science courses as well as history. From an administrative perspective such humanities courses were good for the college because they were economical to offer. In 1958 a study submitted to the legislature showed that in Bozeman a history course could be taught at a cost of $4.47 per student, while the institutional average for coursework was $11.34 and at the university in Missoula, a similar history course would cost $10.31 per student. Riding on the strength of such statistics, the department

History student Ron Nemec holding forth

Freshmen taking a break at the SUB, circa 1947

expanded dramatically, doubling its faculty between 1960 and 1970. Total student enrollment in the department reached an astounding 6264 in 1975. This was "service" with a vengeance.[3]

Interest in graduate-degree work in the humanities and social sciences kept pace with growth in undergraduate courses. History offered its first graduate degree in 1954—a master of science in applied science, the generic degree across the campus. The department received permission to offer a master of arts degree in 1970; for some time it was the only M.A. offered on campus.

Philosophy courses benefitted from the presence of two dynamic professors. Ernest Lauer had joined the faculty in 1945 and quickly became a very popular instructor. Upon his retirement, Harry E. Hausser, fluent in Spanish and one of the editors of *Encyclopedia Britannica*, was invited to join the staff. He took up Lauer's mantle, offering lively courses. In 1960 Hausser and historian Alan Kittell first established an honors section for the better students in the history of civilization sequence. When Kittell left, Hausser assumed sole responsibility for honors and expanded it campuswide in 1965.

The honors program is just one example of the university's support of the various interests of its faculty members. International awareness was Helen Brewer's special interest. Upon her retirement, Merrill Burlingame expanded her efforts and focused on acquainting Montanans with Latin American culture when Mexican sugar-beet workers became an important economic factor in the state during World War II. Under Burlingame's guidance, the campus produced films and pamphlets to familiarize Montana with the nation to the south. After the war, Robert Dunbar picked up the torch, forming a Foreign Students Club, a Model United Nations, the Center for International Studies, and ultimately the Peace Corps program. Merrill Burlingame and H. G. Merriam of the University of Montana joined forces to work with rural sociologist Carl Kraenzel on his Great Plains project. At the time that important study was reaching the publication stage, the question of water rights on the upper Missouri and a plan for damming the river were being debated nationally as well as regionally. It was not long before courses on the Great Plains found a place in the curriculum.[4]

The Peace Corps at Montana State

Robert Dunbar, professor of history, founded the International Studies Center on campus in 1955 to further the goal of bringing the world's people together peacefully. Then, in 1963, intrigued by President Kennedy's volunteer program to help people in other countries, Dunbar began to explore the possibility of inaugurating a Peace Corps training program in Bozeman that would focus on helping agricultural projects in Ecuador, Bolivia, and Paraguay. His application was readily approved, and in the summer of 1964, he began training Peace Corps volunteers on campus. The curriculum emphasized Spanish, interpersonal relationships, history, and cultural attitudes.

As the program matured, it began to incorporate feedback from Peace Corps volunteers who had returned from the field. Eventually, Dunbar moved his training program off campus, having found a site that was primitive enough to simulate the isolation of work in Ecuador. He leased a run-down guest ranch located on the east flank of the Crazy Mountains near Melville, Montana. There, one cold, drizzly night in June of 1969, he greeted his first group of trainees, welcoming the volunteers to the roofless, sagging log cabins that would be their homes while they acclimated themselves to conditions that they would soon have to cope with in South America. He allowed only Spanish to be spoken in camp while he and the volunteers worked to make the site as comfortable as possible and to learn the skills that would make their service of value to the people of the Latin American countries.

That they learned their lessons well from Dr. Dunbar is attested to in a letter from David Wilson to his congressman from Ohio:

This is just a brief letter to openly express my appreciation to the Peace Corps for the tremendous training program that Montana State University provided this summer at Melville, Montana. Things that had to be done at the training site (an abandoned dude ranch) had to be done by the trainees. It was an environment where they had to learn how to adjust ... to new ... and rapidly changing situations. It was the same type of environment with which they now find themselves confronted ... in Ecuador.... I am writing this letter to you because I want to say one more time that I feel that Dr. Dunbar and these people should be congratulated for a job very well done.[1]

In his seven years as Peace Corps advocate, Robert Dunbar trained hundreds of volunteers. While the program began with a strong orientation toward peasant agriculture, it evolved into more complex community-building enterprises: electrical engineers built and maintained power facilities; volunteers showed villagers how to set up and monitor credit unions; animal science and agronomy students showed farmers how to care for their stock and their fields. It was testament to volunteer effort and the quality of their instruction that they were able to accomplish so much.

The volunteers returned on a regular basis over the course of the years to honor their mentor. Trainee Donna Gray wrote to Dunbar at Christmas time 1970, three months after her arrival in Ecuador:

This has been a great cultural shock for me both mentally and physically. A new language, different customs, food and lack of time schedule and promptness. My system has had some bugs to fight, my mind has had a lot of time to think and decisions to make.... I'm the only nurse and now the only girl in our group here in Cuenca so my work in health is "solo." I work about three weeks out in the jungle villages, living and working among the colonists, and return to the city for a week or two for medicines, teaching aids, and a good meal.... So far it has been challenging, colorful, depressing and frustrating, and I hope it will be a self-learning experience through the little bit of good that I may do.[2]

Gray's success in achieving "self-learning" while doing a "little bit of good" is due in no small part to the success of Robert Dunbar's training program for Peace Corps volunteers, a program that began because the university was open to the idea that the citizens of Montana can impact the larger world.

1. Robert G. Dunbar interview, 18 September 1990.
2. Ibid.

Without doubt, Merrill Burlingame was the driving force of the history department. And nowhere was his energy more evident than in his work with Caroline McGill to create the Museum of the Rockies. McGill was a remarkable woman who had traveled widely over the years; in 1956, newly retired from her medical practice in Butte, she offered her extensive collection of antiques, books, and other items to the college. Recognizing the value of the acquisition, Burlingame secured three quonset huts on campus, and the historian and the physician began the work of sorting through the material. Eventually the collection was moved to a dairy barn on campus, which was refurbished as a museum and named in Dr. McGill's honor, though she did not live to see its completion. As others began to donate materials and the regional nature of the growing collection became obvious, the McGill Museum became the Museum of the Rockies. (See Chapter 7.) Merrill Burlingame served as the museum's director until his retirement from the university in 1967. A decade later, another director, Mick Hager, launched a fund-raising campaign that resulted in the beautiful facility that graces the campus today.

The museum effort alone would have been testimony to the drive and the vision of Merrill G. Burlingame, but it was really only one of many interests that captured the man and benefitted the school. Burlingame fostered a western focus in the department of history; he and K. Ross Toole of Missoula collaborated on a territorial history of Montana and both worked hard to develop library resources at their respective units. [5] Burlingame's efforts were richly rewarded in 1965, when the Special Collections department of the university library secured the extensive collection of rare Montana and western Americana materials amassed over the years by Alexander Leggat of Butte. Gonzaga University had offered $50,000 for the collection when it came on the market, but in the midst of the negotiations, Gonzaga had to withdraw its bid, and Leggat's widow offered the collection to MSU for $25,000. Head librarian Leslie Heathcote and Professor Burlingame agreed that it would be proper to use some of the $35,000 Dr. McGill had left the museum to buy the collection. However, in the end, the museum was able to retain its funds and the library was still able to secure the Leggat collection when the President's Office, the library fund, and a donor from White Sulphur Springs, Mrs. Walter Donahoe, provided the necessary monies. Subsequent additions to Special Collections came from Milburn Lincoln Wilson, an MSC agricultural economist and an important figure in New Deal farm legislation, and from the Burton K. Wheeler family, who, with a close friend, Edward Craney of Butte, also provided funds for the annual Wheeler lecture. [6]

In his focus on western Americana, Professor Burlingame first introduced the story of the Plains Indians to students in his history of Montana courses and then brought in Verne Dusenberry of the English department to develop a course on the Indians of Montana. Carling Malouf, a noted archeologist at the University of Montana, taught popular summer courses in Bozeman before anthropology and archeology became regular offerings in the sociology department. Throughout these years, the Cooperative Extension Service worked to promote studies that would improve relations between the seven Montana reservations and the surrounding communities. The Bureau of Indian Affairs commissioned Edward Barry and Thomas Wessel of the history department to write reservation histories, and ultimately, in 1972, the university became home to a full-fledged Native American studies program.

The history department under Dr. Burlingame also supported the establishment of Religious Emphasis Week which indirectly connected MSU to the Danforth Foundation and eventually brought about the construction of the Danforth Chapel on campus. When Leon Johnson, who with Merrill Burlingame had been an advisor for Religious Emphasis Week, became president of the college, he promoted the hiring of a religious studies scholar. An intensive and far-ranging search brought a new Ph.D. out of Columbia, Marvin Shaw, to campus. It was under Shaw that academic coursework in religious studies took root, and those studies continue to be an important and popular area of the general philosophy offerings.

As the history department expanded, its faculty became involved in major political movements in the state. In 1972 MSU historians, most especially Richard Roeder, contributed their expertise to the 1972 Constitutional Convention. Roeder served as a delegate to the convention and edited the newsletter that publicized the new constitution and helped assure its passage. Upon Burlingame's retirement, Richard Roeder and Michael Malone continued the western emphasis in the history department. The two collaborated on a series of texts and readings that have largely defined the subject of Montana history. Most recently Malone's contributions to western history have brought national recognition, including a Pulitzer Prize nomination.

When the historians elected Michael Malone their chair in 1975, it signaled a new direction for the department. Malone's supporters for the hotly contested election were those who sought to place greater emphasis upon research and publication. In the wake of Malone's election, the department aggressively recruited research-oriented faculty. [7]

It can be said that the curriculum in the social and behavioral sciences at MSU has derived from one of two sources: the agricultural focus of the early institution or one of the multidisciplinary humanities areas. That the social sciences share

Religious studies professor Marvin Shaw in class

this hybrid origin reveals itself in the shifting organizational structures of departments. In the early years of the century, under President James Hamilton, the college offered almost all the courses now included under a social science heading: ethics, psychology, economic history, and rural sociology. In the 1916-1917 academic year, the strong rural character in the state was obvious in the restructuring of economics courses into agricultural economics, economic sociology, engineering economics, and rural sociology—courses aimed at assisting students in confronting the influx of homesteaders and all the economic realities of a rapidly changing farm frontier. By 1922 farm-management programs were high on the academic list; farmers needed to learn to keep books accurately and to assess their economic status clearly. [8]

Congress responded to rural pressure with the Purnell Act in 1925, which granted an initial $20,000 to the agricultural experiment station to solve some perennial agricultural problems. Over the next half-decade that sum would increase to $60,000 per annum. In response to the federal emphasis, the school organized a new department of agricultural economics and rural sociology. Though M. L. Wilson was designated to head the department, James Hamilton, newly resigned as college president, served as interim administrator until Wilson's return from postgraduate studies. Roland Renne, the earliest of the professionally accredited economists, joined the staff in 1930, and R. B. Tootell of the Cooperative Extension Service was appointed land economist in 1931. In 1935 Carl Kraenzel was added to the faculty.

By the time Kraenzel arrived, economics had developed a two-tier approach, Renne having moved into the more classical areas of economic inquiry in attacking the state's problems and Elmer Starch concentrating on purely agricultural aspects. Despite the different foci, the studies complemented one another and were applied to larger economic areas, with campus economists cooperating with the U.S. Tariff Commission to assess production costs on which to base tariffs. In the meantime, economic sociology generally focused on the areas of community development, human resources, and economic education. The extension service coordinated demonstration work, offering programs in problem identification, problem solution, and consolidation of education and experience. [9]

Economics and sociology became integrally aligned with production agriculture under M. L. Wilson, who had long been concerned with maximizing yields, whether of grains, grasses, or animals. When the limits of horse-drawn equipment were reached after the war, economists began to evaluate capital inputs necessary to operate tractors capable of plowing a given number of acres per unit of time. From the onset of the Montana homesteading movement to the depression, a gospel of efficiency dominated economic thinking at MSC. This view had substantial national impact as Starch worked to ameliorate state problems and Wilson persuaded national leaders of the efficacy of the Montana experiments. And there were many experiments, ranging from demonstration units like the Fairway Farms and the Pumpkin Creek-Mizpah grazing district to irriga-

A clutch of sociologists, from left to right: (seated), Wayne Larson, Anne S. Williams; (standing), Patrick C. Jobes, C.J. Gilchrist and D'Albert Samson

tion studies. Wilson and his Montana State colleagues came to play an important role in shaping legislation on acreage limitations, price supports, conservation techniques, and loan guarantees. [10]

One of the great social experiments instituted by economists was the land reclassification survey undertaken initially in Teton County. Here all the elements of social science policy meshed with rural politics and reality. The survey was used to identify suitable and unsuitable lands for the various types of agriculture in that large county. This land reclassification was the *sine qua non* of the proposed allotment system, which would set limits on production in order to increase prices. The Teton County tax assessor, Otto Wagnild, a hero in Joseph Kinsey Howard's *Montana: High, Wide, and Handsome,* cooperated with the various members of MSC's sociology department to create a model in land reclassification for the state and ultimately for the intermountain West. The study, much refined, remains the basis of the Montana land classification system and the resulting taxation structure to the present day. [11]

Both before and after the Second World War, projects involving river-basin development required economic as well as political skills. The growth of irrigation districts associated with increased water availability meant pooling considerable economic and political resources. Multiple-use concepts evolved here and soon spread to other environmentally sensitive areas. In the Missouri basin, the multiple-use concept brought into consideration rural development, small industries, tourism, recreation, and public policy education. The field of rural sociology now shifted its focus to a more demographic emphasis. The study of population trends raised important rural health care issues. By the late 1950s certain communities had plenty of hospital bed space, but insufficient numbers of health professionals. Mental health issues also loomed in these areas of isolated and aging populations.

With university status in the mid-'60s came structural reorganization. The new College of Letters and Science became the administrative home for economics and sociology, though the close ties between agricultural economics and the College of Agriculture remained intact. When sociology split off to form its own department, its main focus continued to be rural and medical sociology, even as new faculty members knowledgeable in organizational theory worked to move forward the existing programs in general sociology. Anthropology and social justice became visible components of the new department, anthropology providing a junction between the biological and social sciences and soon spawning an archeology curriculum. There had long been support for archeology among professors of history and geology, and now that a departmental structure existed to house it, the discipline burgeoned. As the Museum of the Rockies matured, archeology found there a solid base of support for its research on fossil remains, including the internationally recognized program centering on the work of Jack Horner. [12]

The social justice program reflected the political activism of the 1960s. Belief in Lyndon Johnson's Great Society, a concern with the imprisoned, the impoverished, and the alienated fueled students and faculty. But the social justice program was short-lived; when federal financial support evaporated, the group was disbanded, though criminal justice, an offshoot of the social justice program, continued to receive federal support. One of its concrete symbols of success was the location of the state's Law Enforcement Academy in Bozeman, and courts and law enforcement agencies came to value their contacts with the academic community.

As the sociology department itself came of age, one of its largest projects was a regional and national migration study conducted through the agricultural experiment station. Beginning in 1972, this study tracked demographic change in employment patterns and eventually compiled a database covering over 1 million workers. While Census Bureau statistics offered gross statements regarding work patterns, this new system, keyed into MSU's CP-6 program, fined-tuned the data. The software developed here, sometimes sarcastically referred to as GRASP (Generating Revenue And School Prestige) could evaluate patterns that would have otherwise remained undetected, but it soon became clear that the potential for interactive access to other bases could result in the dissemination of heretofore confidential information that might endanger the status of individual workers. When the Freedom of Information Act was passed by Congress, social security identifiers associated with the data raised issues of confidentiality, and the researchers aborted the project. The group had long fought against the grain, keenly aware of what they felt was lack of support from the central administration. [13]

It was not a new scenario. The various options in sociology had merely recreated a situation familiar to the older multidisciplinary departments—that is, active, aggressive faculty inevitably moved in directions not envisaged by the administration, thereby creating tensions. Despite, or perhaps because of these tensions, dedicated and gifted faculty like Wayne Larson, Jack Gilchrist, D'Albert Samson, Thomas Roll, John Saltiel, Robert Harvie, David Fabianic, Anne Williams, Pat Jobes, and Leslie Davis moved the group into the mainstream of social science work on campus.

Sociology provided a home on campus for the emerging discipline of archeology. In the beginning, archeology enjoyed strong support from the history side and later from the Museum of the Rockies as well. Les Drew, the first director of the museum, stated his reasons for fostering a close relationship with campus archeologists: "We deal with physical articles, and there is a great demand for these things. If we want the best, we have to go out and dig for them." The MSU Foundation supported the early digs conducted by Larry Lahren, a research associate for the museum.

In late July 1966, Joe Walker, a rancher moving his combine down a county road in eastern Montana, noticed what he suspected was a huge tusk near the edge of the road. He reported the find to Dawson County Commissioner Don Gibson, who passed on the information to George Arthur, an MSU archeologist. Soon Les Davis and his team had uncovered an almost complete skeleton of a wooly mammoth. Building on these efforts, the department of sociology and the Museum of the Rockies put together an internationally recognized program centered on the work of Jack Horner, whose research on the Maiasaurus, conducted both at Egg Mountain north of Choteau and more recently near Fort Peck, have made him and the Museum of the Rockies world-famous. If archeology was a late-comer to the campus, it has certainly burgeoned in spectacular fashion. [14]

Social science methodology found wide-ranging applications. Dean of Agriculture James Welch used the department to compile annual farm surveys that were invaluable to him in framing policy. (One of these surveys showed considerable dissatisfaction with some agricultural credit systems; as a result, the Production Credit Association came under heavy fire, which led it to modify some of its procedures and policies.) Other surveys were targeted to specific problems, including rural crime patterns, which were important in budget allocations for equipment and personnel, and the attitudes of Native Americans toward higher education and access to education, which were critical to building bridges between the university and the reservation. Studies in the sociology of work connected the department to the College of Engineering, and studies in medical sociology connected the department to the WAMI program.

At the same time that sociology gained its autonomy, the government, or political science, section of the history group aspired to the same goal. Considerable discussion, and some agitation, finally established a separate political science presence on campus in 1970. Lawrence K. Pettit was brought in to head the newly created department, though he took leave in 1972 to manage the successful gubernatorial campaign of Thomas Judge and subsequently became the first commissioner of higher education in the state. (See Chapter 7.)

Because the political science department emerged from a group that contained philosophers as well as historians, there was initial indecision as to which direction to pursue: a more philosophical or a more practical political science. Perhaps the first indication that the department would orient itself toward the practical needs of local and state government was the establishment of the master's degree program in public administration, a degree that clearly trained students for governmental administration. Krishna Tummala, Loren McKenzie, Jerry Calvert, and others in the department encouraged an outreach program that would take students to Helena and align them with those already working there. The MPA quickly brought the campus visibility in the state capitol. If MSU students could achieve status in important governmental niches, then benefit would redound to the faculty and the school. This view is also obvious in the fact that the political science curriculum was made mandatory for prelaw students, ensuring, in time, a fair number of lawyers who would become influential in the state.

The visibility of MSU's political science department statewide was enhanced by a $500,000, three-year grant from the W. K. Kellogg Foundation of Battle Creek, Michigan, to establish a Local Government Center. Set up by Ken Weaver, former head of the political science department and chief administrator of the grant, the center soon incorporated elements of the entire university system in a program that brought together state officials and clients from all branches of municipal and county government to review local governmental procedures. In 1990 the Northwest Area Foundation of St. Paul, Minnesota, offered a new grant of $400,000 to assist in this community development program, which has evolved to the point that it provides not only basic research, often undertaken by graduate students in the MPA program, but technical assistance as well for the twenty or so local government entities requesting it each year. Generally this technical assistance amounts to instruction in personnel matters, budgeting procedures, computer optimization, and the writing of clear and understandable ordinances. Judy Mathre, former mayor of Bozeman, has conducted the training sessions since inception of the local government review process. The 1991 legislative session commended the center for its work in consulting with communities in funding infrastructure improvement, compensation of county officials, solid waste management, and consolidation of local and county governments. [15]

A library is the all-important laboratory for those in humanities and social sciences, and the library facilities have grown as the school has grown. The Renne Library is the legacy of Lois Payson and Lieslie Heathcote, dedicated librarians who worked to build collections and provide for academic needs. Located in the center of campus, and architecturally one of the more attractive buildings, Renne Library is a key facility in the university.

Significant to the humanities on campus was the creation of the Montana Committee for the Humanities in 1972. This federally funded program is aimed at providing Montanans with a maximum opportunity to interact with faculty from the humanities. The committee sponsors programs dedicated to exploring such themes as the ecology of the greater Yellowstone area (the Cinnabar Symposium directed by philosopher Gordon G. Brittan); celebrations of Bach and Mozart directed by historian Jeffrey J. Safford; and the nationally acclaimed Eclipse '79 and LOGON '83 celebrations directed by Lynda Sexson of philosophy and Michael Sexson of English. MSU faculty have been active in all aspects of the Committee for the Humanities' efforts to ensure that quality of the programs offered to the state's citizens has been consistently high. MSU scholars have won more grants from the Montana Committee for the Humanities than any other unit in the state.

The Humanities Come of Age with Eclipse '79 and LOGON '83

1979 brought a total eclipse of the sun, which occurred in Bozeman at 9:24 a.m. on February 26. In observance of the rare event—we will not have another such for more than three and a half centuries—Professors Lynda Sexson of the philosophy staff and Michael Sexson of the English department, put together a four-day program that was a fine mix of science and humanities, centering upon new visions in darkening light. The totality of the eclipse became a metaphor for the idea that totality is an imaginative construct in which we entertain the infinite possibilities of imagination and the infinite imagination of possibility.

Presentations were given by physicists, folklorists, dancers, and novelists. There was everything from a holograph exhibit to a Unitarian-Universalist snow sculpture contest.

The day of the eclipse itself was cold, a typical February day in Montana. Great piles of snow lay heaped up on the perimeter of the parking lot west of the Museum of the Rockies, where hundreds of people were gathered for the ceremony beautifully orchestrated by the project directors. It was not only cold, it was cloudy. Indeed, it appeared that the momentous event might be obscured by the cloud cover. At the north edge of the lot, John Woodenlegs, former president of the Northern Cheyenne Native American Church, busied himself at a little wooden altar, paying little heed to the crowd assembled. He never so much as glanced skyward. A few minutes before totality, as the moon slid into the disk of the sun, he broke into prayer, releasing a

puff of smoke and brandishing an eagle feather. As he did so, as if by command the clouds parted and an audible sigh went up from the gathering. In the darkening sky, Mars became visible just above the sun; the corona, beads of Bailey, and other phenomena grew awesomely clear; the city street lights came on.

The diamond ring effect - Eclipse'79

In moments, the great event was over. But its legacy was a continuation of that lively forum on questions of the human and divine. From it came *Corona*, a journal edited by the Sexsons and supported by the office of the vice president for research. From it, too, came the inspiration for LOGON '83, which renewed Eclipse '79. Supported, like its predecessor, by the Montana Committee for the Humani-

English, like history and mathematics, has been offered at the college since the Local Executive Board drafted the school's first curriculum. From the beginning, freshmen were required to take a year of English composition. Later, speech courses were added to give an oral dimension to the intensive reading and writing regimen. For the first two decades, English courses were heavily impacted by the demands of the preparatory department, but by 1913 the growing strength of the state's public schools made it possible for the college to end its remedial courses.

Initially, the "service courses" offered in English began with the obligatory year of grammar followed by a series of courses offering literature, drama, and public speaking. The campus also hosted a smattering of drama, journalism, and literary clubs. The development of the curriculum reflects a utilitarian pattern. As the demand for teachers grew around World War I, a course in methodology for English teachers became available. Then pressure from agriculture and home economics brought a journalism course. A parallel course in forensics, or debate, was offered to satisfy the growing demand for that subject.

Retrenchments in the depression years followed the general institutional pattern. With fewer funds available, the group struggled to offer a decent curriculum. The integration of English, speech, and theatre became even tighter when Burt Hansen, member of the English faculty, was appointed "director of entertainment," in which capacity he coordinated music, drama, and speech.[16]

English shared in the general growth accompanying the end of World War II. John P. Parker, a 1934 MSC graduate, joined the faculty in 1946. He was soon followed by Howard Dean, one of the keenest practical intellects the department ever had. As a shipbuilder during the war, Dean had been exposed to what was called "the communication principle," and he brought this theory with him to Bozeman where he wrote the texts for the freshman English course that stressed writing and speaking. A constant effort to rehabilitate the poorer students dominated faculty discussion, and staff members were required, it seemed, to maintain a sort of fix-it shop of remedial courses. Eventually this evolved into a Writing across the Curriculum program, first institutionalized as a writing laboratory in 1982. Operating under the

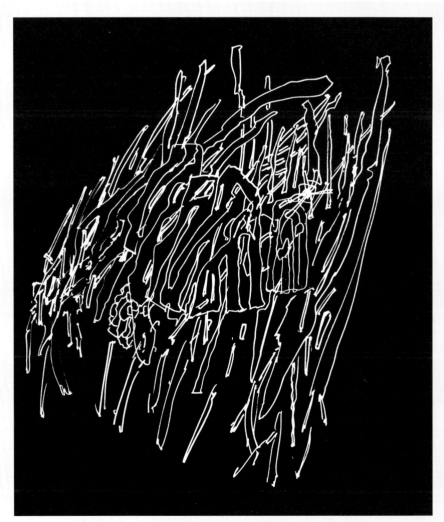

"Making the Edges of Many Circles," by Robert DeWeese

ties and local contributions, LOGON '83 was a week's dialogue on technology, mythology, and literacy in a computer age that was spawning new ways of thinking, speaking, and writing. Over 1000 humanists and scientists participated in the program; over 5000 attended the presentations.

The conference received national recognition. *Technology Illustrated* spoke of it as "the first conference of its kind." "If the density of passionate intelligence and excitement evident [at LOGON] is to be taken as characteristic of the future of human involvement in the new technologies, we can all leap forward to the future with confidence," the article's author said.[1] The National Endowment for the Humanities honored the Sexsons and LOGON '83, with the Schwartz Award, the highest national prize offered for this type of state-based program.

Whatever significance might be assigned to Eclipse '79 and LOGON '83 these programs brought together all elements of the campus community. Faith and reason were no longer seen as mutually antagonistic, nor were scientific and humanistic perspectives.

The two major celebrations, held within a brief span of four years, offered proof that the humanities had attained maturity at the ag and engineering school.[1]

1. NEH Certificate of Citation, made available by Michael and Lynda Sexson.

motto drawn from E. M. Forster, "How do I know what I think until I see what I say," the lab's staff collaborated with disciplines as diverse as ceramics, physics, and nursing to design tests and writing components for their students. John Bean, Mark Waldo, and Adele Pittendrigh put together a program which became nationally prominent because of its quality and success. [17]

Just as there had been tensions between political scientists, philosophers, and historians in the old history department, so too did discord surface between English and speech teachers. The latter wanted to see more emphasis on the new techniques in their field; they wanted, in fact, their own department. They were supported by national pressures. The National Council of Teachers of English had a communications section, which embraced the concept that language in spoken or written form was part of the "communications process." When the English department set up a radio course right after World War II, it was merely the precursor of a course in television that evolved in the early 1950s under James Duderstadt. These new media courses formed the "communications" group. President Leon Johnson was supportive of this initiative, and the speech group began to see the outlines of their department.

Even so, English itself continued to grow; in the late 1970s and early 1980s the department faced the problem of trying to accommodate over 10,000 students in sections small enough to give each one individual attention. The service responsibility remained paramount.

When speech separated in 1970, the communications courses went with them, and so did technical writing, which had been important to engineers since the English faculty had introduced it in the 1920s. As speech matured during these years, the intellectual gulf between the more traditionally oriented English instructor and his or her speech colleague became more pronounced. As Kenneth Bryson, the first head of the new speech department, recalled:

> Howard Dean had written his first edition of *Effective Communication* which used the radical approach of combining speaking and writing, focusing upon the product rather than the process. It was an attempt to focus upon a more functional approach to expression. In the second edition, I got involved and we tried to integrate oral and written communication. [18]

That led to the speech emphasis in the English curriculum and eventually to the creation of the television and theatre departments. It also led indirectly to the option now available in sign language and to the Theater of Silence, a perfectly logical result of the trends in communications. The goal of the Theater of Silence was not only to entertain the deaf in their own language but to perform for hearing audiences as well. Jack Olson, the founder of the troupe, recalls:

> The Theater of Silence was formed in 1970 as part of a summer language camp for the deaf offered at Hyalite youth camp.... In 1973 we started touring out of state with MSU students primarily making up the cast. Until 1983 we toured all twelve western states and Canada during spring quarter, giving sixty-five shows. Since 1986, we have been primarily touring internationally: we have performed in Hong Kong, the Philippines (twice), New Zealand, Australia, France, Germany (twice), Norway, Czechoslovakia, and Austria. And we're planning a trip to Central America. [19]

The story of theatre also includes a rich tradition of drama clubs, which appear to have been spontaneous student initiatives. In 1922 a group performing a play named *Loot* took the name Looters and put on a lively musical. Their rivals, performing more serious pieces, named themselves the Tormentors. Faculty from music and English wrote texts for them and assisted with direction and performance. After World War II, the Loft Theater, located in the loft of a barn on West Main (now the Red Barn), played summer stock. Joseph Fitch promoted this work, and solid casts consisting of faculty, students, and townspeople gave memorable performances. In one of the several remodelings of the Student Union, a theatre was built, encouraging the growth of the art. Theatre arts was also invigorated when Ben Tone arrived to complement Joe Fitch's talents. Their influence is seen today in companies such as the Vigilante Theatre Company, which works its magic all over the intermountain West.

A feisty duo from Shakespeare in the Parks

Filming a scene in a mine. From left to right: John Knutson and Salah Sayed Ahmed

words, folk theatre at its finest. (The added merit of playing Shakespearean comedies was that there would be no royalties to pay.) The first performances in 1973 were rather tentative and amateurish, but the enterprise survived and grew popular throughout the state. Indeed, the town of Birney, population 20, draws a crowd of 200 for Shakespeare in the Parks, the highlight of their summer season. Excitement rises as the caravan containing the players, costumes, and simple sets first comes into view across the dusty prairie. When all is readied, the play begins. At play's end, audience and actors gather together around picnic tables laden for a feast, and all spend the evening in good Elizabethan style. Grants from the Montana Arts Council, private donations, consistent support by successive MSU presidents, and the fine art of cliffhanging have kept the program alive for two decades. [20]

When theatre is mentioned, the first thing that comes to a Montanan's mind is likely to be Shakespeare in the Parks, the brainchild of Bruce Jacobsen. The son of an MSC extension agent, Jacobsen wanted his brand of Shakespeare to approximate conditions existing in sixteenth-century England. That meant outdoor theatre with a stage of modest dimensions, minimal costume changes, and broad acting technique—in other

Shakespeare in the Parks and the Vigilante Theatre Company are now housed in media arts in a new configuration. Still and motion picture photography and television had long been established on campus. The early radio work in the English group then spawned the first television effort, which soon blossomed under James Duderstadt. President Renne supported film and television because he could see it as a valuable adjunct to the college public relations effort; the Office of Information, the experiment station, and the extension service were supportive for the same reasons. Eventually the department acquired space on the third floor of Montana Hall to construct a TV studio. From the beginning, students were involved in every aspect of production, a system which gave them valuable practical experience. Even though nationally it was rare to have motion picture and television instruction conjoined, the system worked well for MSC. Too well. By 1957 conflict between UM and MSC over the media arts became a subject of regental discussion. As a result, Missoula received a mandate to concentrate on the radio side, MSC on television. In 1958 the first curricular offerings appeared in the school's course catalog. The following year the Office of Information and the chemistry department received a $25,000 Ford Foundation grant to install equipment for classroom TV reception. In 1961 Fred Gerber joined the department to direct film and TV productions and to manage the group. John M. Stonnell, Paul Jesswein, Rudi Dietrich (in still photography), Jack Hyyppa, and more recently, Paul Monaco, have been at the heart of this work. Its success was apparent quite early when an MSC production, *Vision Quest,* was selected for the Venice Film Festival. [21] In 1984, the department also brought Montana's first full-service public television station into existence. With the advent of KUSM - Montana Public Television, Montana became the last of the fifty states to enter the PBS family.

The Campus ROTC Program

The Morrill Act of 1862 establishing land grant colleges required that all male students under the age of 26 receive two years of military training. By the provisions of the law, the U.S. Army was to provide the equipment and instructors for this training, but until the eve of the Spanish-American War the army was basically a frontier constabulary and had no extra personnel to spare for student instruction at the new school in Bozeman. So it was that in 1896, three years after Montana State College was founded, William Cobleigh, a member of the faculty and later

William Wylie Galt, B.S., general agriculture, 1942; ROTC Commission, 1942;Congressional Medal of Honor; Geyser, Montana. Citation: G.O. No. 7; 1 November 1945: "For conspicuous gallantry and intrepedity above and beyond the call of duty. . . He volunteered, at the risk of his life, personally to lead the battalion against the objective (German positions near Villa Crocetta, Italy, 29 May 1944). . . A few minutes later an 88-mm. shell struck the tank destroyer and Captain Galt fell mortally wounded across his machine gun."

head of the College of Engineering, took on the challenge of beginning the required military program, rounding up forty students, putting them in military formation, and marching them from downtown Bozeman out to the campus as part of the ceremonies that marked the laying of the cornerstone at Main (Montana) Hall.

And the wonderfully energetic Professor Cobleigh continued to drill those students and instruct them in military science to the best of his ability until the army was able to staff the program. Lieutenant George Ahern of the 25th Infantry, U.S. Army, was detailed to the college in 1897, where he not only took over instruction in military science, making use of the newly constructed drill hall, but also taught forestry and served as an assistant football coach. The lieutenant's deployment to the Spanish-American War a year after his arrival initiated an eigh-

teen-year hiatus in the program, during which time the army was unable or unwilling to appoint another instructor. During that period, the college faculty provided what instruction they could, the most visible contributor being Joseph Thaler of the electrical engineering department, who had served with the Austro-Hungarian army as a young man.

Then, in 1916, Congress passed the National Defense Act, which, among other things, established the Reserve Officer Training Corps, and in its wake, the war department assigned a senior-division ROTC program to MSC. The early curriculum for military science at the college reflected the program's present educational goals. The basic course, required of all able-bodied freshmen and sophomore males, provided instruction in military drill, tactics, and courtesy. A senior course was organized for students who excelled in the program as underclassmen; those who completed this course received their commission as U.S. Army officers upon graduation. Students enrolled in this "advanced course" received 30 cents a day toward living expenses and $30 toward the purchase of their uniforms, which were required apparel. They were also required to attend a six-week summer camp, for which they received 75 cents a day while in camp and 5 cents a mile in travel to and from camp.

Within a year of the program's revitalization, however, the country's entry into World War I meant that military instructors were again called away from the school, though a unit of the Special Army Training Corps was billeted on campus. College instructors again staffed the program, which contributed its share of personnel to the war effort. More than 200 MSC graduates and undergraduates were called into the service. Sixteen of them were killed in action and six died later of their wounds. Given the size of the school's student body, these numbers represented a major contribution to the American war effort. [1]

By 1919 the ROTC program was resurgent at MSC. In the years immediately thereafter, two barracks were constructed, as was an indoor shooting gallery, which stood at the corner of College and 11th until the site was converted to a minipark in 1989.

As the program and the campus had contributed personnel to the World War I, so did they to the Second World War. Ninety-nine sons of MSC gave their lives. Through the war years, the college hosted the 312th College Training Detachment, and a unit of the Specialized Training Corps was again billeted on campus while the soldiers were given concentrated courses in engineering.

In 1952, with the Korean war as an impetus, the MSC ROTC program began to shift focus. Whereas the department had once trained its cadets for the infantry, now its graduates were commissioned in any of the several branches of the army. It was at this time that the Bobcat Battalion was formed, a unit that trained in mountaineering warfare. Another development in the program was the elevation of the air unit, which had been established in 1947, to full departmental status.

A new era in ROTC was ushered in in 1964 when Lyndon Johnson signed into law the ROTC Vitalization Act, which made the program voluntary rather than obligatory for college men at land grant institutions and provided a higher pay scale for cadets and scholarships for outstanding students. Almost simultaneous with the implementation of the Vitalization Act was the escalation of the war in southeast Asia. Enrollment in ROTC dropped drastically, not only because the program was now voluntary, but because of the increasing unpopularity of the war—though the conservative atmosphere of the MSU campus meant that the cadets, highly visible in their uniforms every Thursday, continued to be regarded in a good light. [2]

Lt. Col. Lones Wigger, Jr., two time Olympic gold medalist, director, U.S. Olympic shooting team, BS, agronomy, 1960

The student body once again gave its members to the military effort, and those members paid a high price for their service. The campus was especially touched by the return of Earl Martin, an English major who was severely wounded during the Tet offensive of early 1968. Under Sergeant Major Jack Greenway, the army ROTC unit built an outstanding rifle team. Lones

Wigger, a cadet from Carter, Montana, emerged as an Olympic marksman, and the MSC team carried off national marksmanship honors in 1967.

In 1973, yet another significant shift in military policy brought change to the ROTC program on campus, as women were accepted into the program for the first time. Colonel Raymond Amenson, professor of military science at that time, carried out the difficult task of ensuring that MSU did not experience the negative reaction toward women cadets that was found on other campuses. Indeed, women quickly took their places in the corps and even carried on the tradition of national ranking in marksmanship.

In 1986, in the ninetieth year of its presence on campus, the cadet command was reorganized. A new shoulder patch, a shield divided into quadrants, each representing a stage in the development of an officer, replaced the old patch that featured a Greek temple. The newly reorganized command gave its personnel in the support of Desert Storm, the allied action against Iraq in 1991. An MSU alumnus and former cadet, Major General Paul Funk, commanded the Third Armored Division, which spearheaded the allied ground assault. Six cadets were activated to serve with the 420th Military Police unit, processing Iraqi prisoners of war, and a newly commissioned officer, Lieutenant Jacqueline Chambers, served with an antimissile unit in Saudi Arabia.

The U.S. military has long relied on ROTC programs for the vast majority of their officer personnel, and both the army and the air force ROTC programs at MSU have served the country well. The healthy, symbiotic relationship of the campus and the military is illustrated in the fact that the first book to be published by the MSU Endowment and Research Foundation, under the Big Sky Books imprint, was *A Poet Goes to War*, a book of poetry written by Earl Martin upon his return to school after a long hospitalization. Through his poetry, Martin exorcised the ghosts of his war experiences and reflected on his work in the English department under Rolfe Olson [1]:

I reach back to touch the self
that was that went
away to war it seems so far
to reach
beneath the scar.

1. A History of the Bobcat Battalion, 1967, MSUA; Lt. Col. Mark Yrazabel interview, 7 September 1991.
2. Cdt. Mike Scarlett paper, Army ROTC, MSU.
3. Earl Martin, "Once I was an Evening Shadow," in A Poet Goes to War, (Bozeman, MT). 1970.

Psychology had been taught in a variety of settings from the beginning of the century. Generally it was tied in some way to philosophy or to educational theory, but when a separate department of education was created in 1954, psychology became an independent department as well. Like all of the social and behavioral sciences in the college, it began as a service department. The original faculty were basically educational psychologists but, at the time the school gained university status, psychology was staffed by professionals with doctorates and with experience with experimental approaches to the discipline. While service remained important, especially for those seeking a major in education, greater opportunities for psychology majors developed as the university itself grew. In 1963 a practicum enabled students to visit some of the state's custodial institutions. As instruction stressed work in experimental and theoretical psychology, students began to acquire more knowledge in the biological and behavioral science. For example, J. Daniel Duke introduced the study of suggestibility by using hypnotism in the classroom, constantly reminding students of the ethical issues of suggestibility. Some of his other colleagues introduced biofeedback techniques; yet others worked on addictive behaviors. [22]

From the beginning the "classics" mission of the land grant institution was fairly clear. Latin was taught along with English in 1893 at the Montana College of Agriculture and Mechanic Arts. Five years later German and French appeared in the catalog. One instructor, Aaron H. Currier, taught both languages; he also offered music courses. Enrollment in the languages grew to the point that, when Currier left in 1911, two instructors were hired to replace him. Carrie M. Cehrs taught German in Bozeman until the wave of hysteria that struck the state during the Great War sent her on to California. Montana was one of twenty-eight states to prohibit instruction in German. Spanish was offered in its place until 1923, when German reappeared in the MSC catalog without comment.

Although Russian became important after World War II, it was offered only sporadically; German, Spanish, and French remained the major offerings of the language department. In order to improve language laboratory facilities for individualized instruction, electrical and industrial engineers on campus were called in to design the listening laboratory.

In more recent years, courses in language have been cross-listed with disciplines like history and English so that the great literature of these western European cultures could be made available to students who were not proficient in specific languages. While the language group never received enough support to offer the spectrum of languages necessary for close economic ties with Pacific Rim nations, faculty from other departments, usually business, from time to time have offered Japanese, Korean, and Chinese. On occasion, faculty from religious studies and history have offered special courses in Greek, Latin, and Hebrew. Now, as foreign student enrollment continues to grow, the interested person can find tutorial assistance in just about any of the world's major tongues, a sign of the growing sophistication—and sensitivity—of the university. [23]

The universal language of music is often included in a liberal arts curriculum. However, from the beginning, instrumental instruction was the narrowly defined focus that obtained at MSC. In 1908 President Hamilton reported to the state Board of Education that

> teachers in the school of music receive no salary ... the director is paid to prepare and furnish music at the weekly assembly and at all college functions. The director trains the glee clubs and takes charge of all music recitals. Students in domestic science and general science courses above the freshman year have been allowed to elect not to exceed four credits in music. These are mostly young ladies in the home science course. [24]

Though obviously not an essential element in an industrial college, music nevertheless had its uses.

Louis Howard had organized a band—The Bozeman Free Silver Kid Band—shortly after the school was founded. The group played for the cornerstone-laying ceremony at Montana Hall in 1896. Aaron Currier, a language instructor, formed a glee club a year later, but the group was evidently regarded so skeptically that they didn't

H. Creech Reynolds in an instrumental class

make their first public appearance until 1900. In 1906 Howard formed the group that has evolved into the present-day Bobcat Band. Sponsored by the Associated Students of MSU, that band, as well as the symphonic band, the chorale, and the Montanans, toured the state regularly.

The music program itself developed gradually over the years. Despite the fact that its instructors were unpaid, the program first offered a "diploma in music" in 1908. The director of entertainment, Burt Hansen, established a minor in music in 1937, and a major was first offered in 1945.

Jesse Wilber and Frances Senska receiving the governor's citation

Through these years, music bounced about in terms of institutional relationships and in terms of housing. Leora Hapner, director of the educational program for many years, invariably concluded her annual reports by expressing the hope that someplace decent would soon be found to house music. Often practice sessions were conducted at the homes of faculty; rehearsals were held in buildings across campus. While the peripatetic nature of the department provided enjoyment for others, it hampered the development of a rigorous program in music. The department finally reaped its reward when the creative arts complex was built in the early '70s. Even then, music suffered, as what might have been a fine, large recital hall shrank bit by bit in the process of designing the building. Faculty continued to be frustrated because successive administrations never seemed to understand the special needs of

music—the high cost of simply keeping pianos tuned, for one thing. But a boon to the faculty, and to the community of music lovers in Bozeman, was the attractiveness of the area for musicians like Pablo Elvira and like Christopher Parkening, whose many recordings carry labels proclaiming his adjunct affiliation with the university.

In spite of a heritage of deprivation, faculty and students in music have offered a great deal to the campus community and to the greater public. The Bozeman Symphony, the Bozeman Symphonic Chorus, the Chamber Music Festival, and the Intermountain Opera Company rest upon the efforts and dedication of music department staff— Charles Payne, Creech Reynolds, Edmund Sedivy, Mary Sanks, Lowell Hickman, Henry Campbell, Lorna Nelson, Alan and Karen Leech, Karl Overby, and the others who have worked so hard for so long. [25]

Art, like music, has made profound contributions to the campus and the state. That Bozeman today is a locus of great artistic attainment is indisputable; that it would be so without the richness of campus-based art is unlikely. Art was offered from the beginnings of the school, and for the first three decades, instruction included every aspect of the arts and crafts. Art history courses were not offered as such until after World War II, but specific faculty and student interests had periodically prompted a variety of short courses, say in ancient Egyptian art. Other aspects of art history, like the history of costume, reflected interests of home economics students. The craft tradition continued in areas like furniture making as a shop culture pervaded the early years of art offerings.

For the first fifty years, the majority of the art faculty were female, although a fair number of male students signed up for art courses. Graduates generally went on to teach in high schools in the region, although a few became heads of advertising departments or even connected with manufacturers like the American Crayon Company. Olga Ross Hannon dominated the art scene for many years. Because her interests lay in community service and education, she was oriented toward a practical, applied curriculum. She made no apologies for her views when speaking on the occasion of the school's fiftieth anniversary:

> The aim of the Art Course is to insure a broad foundation of art culture and to enable students to make practical uses of this training. The purpose of this training is three-fold: To cultivate an appreciation of art; to prepare students toward a commercial profession, such as costume design, interior decoration, poster advertising; and to prepare students for supervising and teaching art. The ultimate aim of the applied arts course is to prepare students for a practical realization of their talents. [26]

So much for *ars gratia artis*. But the nature of the art enterprise at MSC was changing dramatically even as Hannon spoke. Jessie Wilber, Cyril Conrad, and Frances Senska began to move the program into a more openly academic environment. A guest artist program began; Wilber's interest in American Plains Indian, particularly Blackfeet tipi art, spurred a connection with the Smithsonian; art history became a serious curricular area; ceramics took on a new life; and the number of national exhibitions featuring MSC artists rapidly increased.

Robert DeWeese joined the staff in 1949 and added his talents and energy to the art program. The flood of World War II veterans brought new and enthusiastic students into art, some of whom achieved artistic fame. Less obvious but significant work was done at the thesis level. On the eve of university status, enrollments in the department skyrocketed as the reputation of the art faculty spread. By the mid-1960s, former students like Peter Voulkos and Rudy Autio returned to conduct workshops. Strong outreach efforts brought MSU art programs within reach of Montana communities. A fine example of selfless drive and talent was the program directed by Ray Campeau through the Bozeman public school system. In 1979, when the department received permission to offer the master of fine arts degree, Missoula reacted strongly. But as Willem A. Volkersz, then director of the school of art, later noted in testimony before the regents, MSU had the only accredited program in the six neighboring states. [27]

The strength of the program was easily traced to its founding faculty. In January 1988, Governor Ted Schwinden presented the annual Governor's Award for the Arts to two of those artists, Jessie Wilber and Frances Senska. Giving the award, he attempted to summarize the depth of the women's contributions to the arts:

> On the eve of our Centennial Celebration, this annual tribute to Montana artists is particularly important. As we prepare to strike up the bands, light fireworks and drive 10,000 head of cattle over our prairies in honor of our 100th year as a state, the contributions of our artists deserve to be in the forefront. In a time of great world troubles and difficulties to be faced at home as well, Jessie Wilber and Frances Senska seem to live with an attitude that breeds solution and peace. [28]

"Solution and peace" were the sought-after qualities when the economic shock of the mid-'80s threatened the art department. At the time of the cutbacks, there were 200 art majors working in the fine arts, art education, and graphic design. As the administration struggled to trim the budget, supporters of the art program rallied to salvage as much as possible. Art and music were both stepchildren of the land grant institution's concern for the practical and the applied. That they prospered despite the lack of strong institutional support was due mainly to the hard work and talent of their faculties.

Though frequently linked with art and music, architecture has a different background from those disciplines at MSC. It was at first closely allied with civil engineering, architectural engineering being a natural product of the gospel of efficiency that marked the early twentieth century not only in Bozeman but across the country.

Architecture first appeared in the 1910-1911 catalog, although the only specific course offered in the discipline then was drafting, which could be taken as a substitute for woodworking and foundry. But by World War I a fair number of architecture-related courses were available: highway construction, geodesy, and concrete construction, for example. With homesteaders moving to the state in substantial numbers, architecture rode the crest of the wave of optimism that permeated the economy. "The rapid increase of population in the State of Montana will result in a healthy growth of our cities and towns," the college catalog proclaimed. "Homes, factories, office buildings and public buildings will be erected. Ancient and modern architecture is studied in all its phases in order that the student may become acquainted with proper architectural forms." [29] Architecture, as taught at MSC, would provide the professionals who would build the new utopia.

And students were attracted to the program, even though they knew it was tough to complete in four years. By 1920 architects were graduating and setting up shop around the state. In that year the noted Bozeman architect Fred Willson joined the faculty as an adjunct. H. C. Cheever joined the group in 1921, making it his focus to improve the architecture library and to build a sense of the culture of great architecture.

In order to maintain enrollment during the depression period, the architecture program offered a home planning course for home economics students. The device worked well enough, but after World War II, when increasing professionalism led the department to seek national accreditation, such peripheral courses were dropped. In 1948 the curriculum was split into a five-year architecture course and a four-year architectural engineering course, the duality being necessary to gain accreditation from both the American Institute of Architects and the Engineers' Council for Professional Development. Hugo Eck and David Wessel, both alumni, joined the faculty right after the war as student enrollments increased.

The national accrediting committee in 1957 granted the program its seal of approval on the condition that the library be upgraded, the curriculum reexamined, and the school made autonomous. The administration conceded these arrangements the following year, but because tradition dies hard, architectural engineering remained as an option. The school grew rapidly on the eve of university status and engaged in important local initiatives. The historic buildings survey by John DeHaas not only provided the foundation for the Bozeman historic district, it also catalogued important Montana ghost towns. MSU architects also designed low-cost housing for Lame Deer and other reservations.

An influx of architects from Rensselaer Polytechnic Institute in New York enriched the faculty in the early '70s. Ilmar Reinvold, Francis Woods, and others brought new strengths to the faculty. Student quality also improved. Women were no longer automatically advised to enter the four-year interior design program rather than the five-year architectural program, and they now constitute about a third of the total enrollment in architecture. The success of the program as a whole is seen in the fact that the percentage of MSU architectural graduates taking and passing the architectural registration exam is the highest of any program in the country. Despite that statistic, the central administration decided to terminate the program during the budget massacres of the mid-1980s. The decision met with an outcry that surprised many. The strength of support for the architectural program throughout the state astounded even architects themselves, and it saved the program from extinction. (See Chapter 7.)

In point of fact, the first class offered at the new college in 1893 was a business course offered by Homer G. Phelps, who had been conducting business institutes in Bozeman and Livingston. He and the acting president, Luther Foster, shared eight students in the ten-week course, which commenced April 17. The prescribed study covered basic secretarial skills, bookkeeping, and standard business practice, vocational skills much in demand at the time and so quite attractive to the school's prospective clientele. Commercial subjects were also considered desirable because they offered courses that would attract young women. After home economics courses multiplied, other avenues for women were open, but initially the business curriculum was supported by the college to ensure that women would enroll. [30]

Economics and agricultural economics would eventually provide a more theoretical approach to some of the business subjects, but in the beginning typewriting, shorthand (usually Pitman and Gregg), business machine operation, and office management constituted the basic courses. The secretarial/business options maintained a strong attraction for years, but in time, Leona Barnes, Bernice Lamb, John Blankenhorn, Alfred Day, and Harvey Larson presided over the transition to a truly professional business curriculum. As might be expected, their efforts were opposed by the accredited school of business in Missoula. As the reorganization proceeded in the waning years of the Renne era, business found itself administered under the umbrella of "Household and Applied Arts," a mix that included home economics, music, art, and nursing in addition to secretarial science and reflected the sense of indirection in areas that represented a threat to Missoula.

In 1958-1959, a department of commerce emerged to join with the new College of Professional Schools. But the issue of duplication of business course offerings at Eastern Montana College came to the front and caused the cancellation of several advanced accounting and CPA-

A turn-of-the-century secretarial class

Daniel C. Hertz and class

preparation courses. In response to such issues, to current needs, and to internal staff patterns, business offerings increasingly stressed business education. Potential high school business teachers in particular were targeted as students, although the associate degree program in secretarial science remained popular. By 1970 the business school began to reflect national trends that had dominated professional thinking a decade or so earlier. This was a familiar pattern in the social science areas across campus, but the inevitable lag in adopting the most current theory and technology could be laid to funding and staffing realities. A continuing problem was adequate staffing. Once faculty attained their doctorates they became eminently marketable and left. "A total of 185 individuals have taught in our School of Business over the years", noted Harvey Larson, "yet it was not until 1974 that we were able to hire the first individual who came 'with degree in hand,' fully qualified for the teaching assignment with a Ph.D. from a major university in the field for which we were recruiting." [31]

While general business remained the most popular option, accounting attracted an increasing number of students. A master's in business education brought in high school teachers during summer sessions. In 1975 the core areas of the school were realigned and emphasis was placed on accounting, finance, management, marketing, and international trade. In 1981 the School of Business received accreditation, and when the data first became available in the early '80s, it was discovered that Harold Holen's accounting program had achieved top ranking nationwide in the percentage of students taking and passing the CPA exam. The program has remained in the top ten in that category ever since.

Accreditation and national recognition helped in making the School of Business "a player on campus," but business still faced the same problems as did every other department on campus—for example, a heavy undergraduate load that discouraged research-oriented faculty. For business too there was the handicap of being located in a rural state that boasted only one large employer—the Montana Power Company. Not being able to offer its students the kind of hands-on experience they would find in an urban area, business had to find a focus to fit its rather isolated niche. By dovetailing its efforts with other disciplines—engineering, for example—business has been able to find its focus, or better, to rediscover its focus in the land grant mission of outreach. Today MSU's College of Business directs its education efforts toward helping various types of organizations, small businesses, and communities at the state and local level. One joint program with UM and EMC links all university system resources to the business community through a database available on each campus. This Montana Entrepreneurship Center provides counseling and information to growing businesses. Another program, the Small Business Institute, a joint effort of MSU and the federal Small Business Administration (SBA), assigns seniors in business options as unpaid consultants to small firms to assist in everything from marketing to direct mail campaigns. An international-business program directed by Sitki Karahan seeks to enhance Montanans' role in the global economy.

But the learning experience is not one-directional. A Business Advisory Council, composed of outstanding business leaders from the state and the region, advise on current business conditions and practice and provide a link between faculty, students, and community needs. In order to translate such sources of information into action, a brand-new effort, a joint venture involving the extension service and KUSM - Montana Public Television, broadcasts a weekly TV program. Every other week there is a call-in segment of the show during which time panelists address the specific needs of a community/business group, sort of a "sack-lunch seminar" with immediate feedback. Such programs address one of the fundamental requirements of this university: "We are expected to be creative in addressing ... problems and are responsible for sharing ... knowledge." [32]

That the college is able to do this demonstrates its commitment to its mission, despite the austerity of more recent years. In 1986 the regents mandated that the school phase out its business education and office systems options in a bona fide attempt to reduce duplication across the university system. The school lost some of the 1650 students enrolled in business at that time, though none of the staff were sacrificed since instructors from those options were assimilated into the mainstream program.

In 1986, in the midst of the gloom, the college experienced a stroke of good fortune. David Orser, class of '66 in accounting and president of Occidental Petroleum, contacted Marilyn Wessel of the University Relations office. He had been a nontraditional student, Orser told Wessel, one of a type increasingly found at MSU. He had had trouble maintaining an interest in freshman-level courses, amd he wanted to help change that for others, to try to engage them in the world of ideas from their first day on campus. He proposed establishing a chair that would be offered each year to a person of both academic excellence and solid practical business background, who would interact with entering students. Wessel immediately saw the benefits of bringing in a figure of international reputation to inspire young people. The Orser chair now each year supports a distinguished lecturer who addresses freshman seminars and keeps faculty in touch with the "real world." During a period of sustained economic difficulty, it has been a boon to the College of Business. [33]

Just as interest in business grew from the changing needs of a young state, so did an interest in public education. The need for a preparatory department at the college was a simple recognition of the scarcity of educational resources in a large and undeveloped land. The early history of teaching in the state, whether in public or private schools, was largely the story of individual interest and initiative. Farmers' institutes were first established in 1884 in response to grass-roots demands for information on the new techniques of agriculture. Parallel boys' and girls' groups soon sprang up. The Smith-Lever Act of 1914

specifically enjoined states to "diffuse information on subjects of agriculture and home economics." By July of that year, MSC was working through the Cooperative Extension Service to assist youth groups. Augusta Evans brought some order into the organization of these groups, which numbered several hundred, and gave them a sense of direction. She was succeeded by M. J. Abbey, who organized a vocational program for agricultural and home economics students. The need for teachers to serve in the rapidly expanding public education sector of the state all but guaranteed employment for the student who finished the program. In 1917 the Smith-Hughes Act expanded teacher preparation to include industrial subjects, shifting the focus to include urban education.

The first summer session for teachers in Bozeman was held in 1917; completion entitled the student to a "certificate of credit" equal to that given by the state normal college. The Gallatin County superintendent of schools designated the college summer session as the official county school, that is, a place where appropriate credit for certification could be earned. Over the years other counties followed suit. By 1918 education coursework was offered by M. J. Abbey of vocational agriculture, Lilla Harkins of home economics, and Ralph T. Challender of mechanical engineering, who picked up the industrial courses.

At this time, and for two decades to come, the college held the right to grant teaching certificates, but on the eve of World War II, the superintendent of public instruction in Helena took over the licensing procedure and retains it to the present day. Criteria for teaching were moral as well as academic: "Candidates must be in good health and free from such defects as would prevent successful teaching; his character must be above doubt or question ... finally he must possess such favorable attitudes, interests, and ideals as to justify certification." [34]

The first statement of objectives for the Montana State College department of education and psychology appeared in 1944. The department's primary goal was to prepare well-trained teachers for junior high and high school work. The teaching candidates were to acquire an "understanding of the place of the school in our democratic society; a philosophy of education based upon democratic and Christian principles." The school also offered refresher courses for teachers returning from the armed forces and placed considerable emphasis on retooling other veterans for careers in teaching. This "retooling" was based on tests that assessed aptitudes and intelligence, and the testing and counseling service that exists on campus today grew from this focus in the education department.

Applicants for teaching certification had to pass through a series of bureaucratic hoops, and because of this, more courses became necessary in the education curriculum. Growing emphasis upon graduate work led to the reintroduction of an applied master's degree with an emphasis in education. Agricultural education and home economics shared the degree. A sustained and successful lobbying effort led to the doctorate of education, first given in 1954, only a year after the first-ever doctorate on campus—in chemical engineering—was authorized. This illustrates the clout now enjoyed by education; it was getting to be a very big business indeed.

All this must be seen against the backdrop of a nation building schools at a frantic pace and facing a serious shortage of teachers. Between 1955-1970, 5 million new public school teaching slots were created. The Montana State Board of Education not only recommended doctorates for Missoula and Bozeman but requested that a division of education headed by a dean be established at both schools. Concurrently, psychology, until now linked with education, spun off to form its own department in a different division, one which ultimately became the College of Letters and Science.

Leroy Casagranda and advisee

The new doctoral program (actually there were two doctoral degrees given for a time—a Ph.D. and an Ed.D., the former dropped because the latter was more appropriate) reflected a dual purpose: to train public school administrators and to develop administrators for higher education. By the 1960s, education had developed a series of programs for everything from a four-year elementary degree to a doctorate designed for superintendents and college/university administrators. The academic part of the curriculum was under the control of the various subject-matter departments. For administrative purposes educa-

tion from time to time embraced business, library science, music, film and TV production, various physical education options, including health, and a mathematics-science resource center. Several thousand teachers have graduated from one or the other of education's programs, and chances are good that every school district in the state has at least one MSU alum on its staff.

As public schools become the focus of public frustration with social problems, they are forced to respond with special-emphasis programs—courses in sex education, drug and alcohol, abuse and suicide prevention—and programs to incorporate those with disabilities. That means that the education rubric must subsume a great many different options and programs. Students may select from a menu that includes courses across the spectrum—education, counseling, health, physical education/movement science, recreation, biomechanics, sports management and medicine, and a host of subfields. Supplementing the various curricula leading to undergraduate and graduate degree programs are a number of special services like the Center for Community-School Development and Field Services, the Center for Research in Rural Education, and the Adult Learning Center, all housed in the College of Education, Health and Human Development. Basically the idea is to offer students, and returning professions, whatever tools they need to work in their home communities. [35]

The long history of curricular development at MSU—particularly in the area of the humanities—endorses the observation of Jacques Barzun, a noted scholar:

> Finally, the university must make up its mind and choose between two attitudes.... One is "Behold our eminence—it deserves your support and affectionate regard after you have attended and shared our greatness." The other is "We are a public utility like any other—drop in any time."... Let it be clear: The choice is not between being high-hat and being just folks. It is not a question of hospitableness—a university should be hospitable; it is a question of style, reflecting the fundamental choice as to what a university thinks it is. [36]

The various pressures on each of the curricula, and on their faculty, have molded and shaped their distinct characters. The university has often vacillated between compliance and academic apartness, but if anything has become clear from this history of the instructional framework, it is that undergraduate concerns have always been primary, that the faculty of the "service departments" must remain mindful of their obligation to service, and that in time of economic stress, and there have been many, the university must look to alternative sources of support.

Lest They Be Forgotten: Recognizing MSU Staff

It's recalled in campus lore as "The Night the Lights Went Out." On Friday, January 24, 1987, with the 'Cats leading the Idaho Vandals by three points and with just over three minutes left to play, the lights went out in the Brick Breeden Fieldhouse, leaving not only the players on the court, but thousands of spectators in the bleachers in semi-darkness. Howard Ross, the fieldhouse director, acted quickly to avert disaster. Knowing that the university's head electrician, Kenneth Ostermiller, was a basketball fan and season ticketholder, Ross quickly found his man in the stands. Thirty-five minutes later Kenneth Ostermiller and his colleagues had restored power to the fieldhouse. The 'Cats went on to defeat the Vandals 64-63. Ostermiller himself missed the end of the game. Having brought the fieldhouse out of darkness, he had moved on to pinpoint the source of the outage experienced across campus that cold, clear winter's night. With the help of his assistant, Dan Emig—and of Montana Power Company personnel and equipment—Ostermiller located the source of the problem, a blown transformer in the Brannegan Court area, replaced that transformer with a spare, and by 3 o'clock Sunday morning, some six hours after the breakdown, had power surging again through campus buildings.

Ken Ostermiller's skills and cool-headedness had served the school well in a crucial situation. Hundreds of people in staff positions, both professional and classified, serve the school equally well on a day-to-day basis, though admittedly in less dramatic situations. In effect, Montana State University is the seventh largest city in Montana. The operation of such an enterprise requires the skill and dedication of many different people—accountants and attorneys, clerks and cooks, secretaries and security police, sanitarians and health-care specialists—all caring people who bring skill, experience and dedication to their jobs. And far more often than not they serve in positions that are all but invisible to the casual observer on campus.

That MSU is truly a user-friendly campus is a tribute to the staff which handles the countless needs of this city within a city. The first contact prospective students and their parents usually have with the school is through an admissions counsellor or a departmental secretary. Student financial needs are assessed and aid disbursed by personnel trained to provide the best guidance possible in helping students meet the monetary strain of a college education. Physicians, dentists, and counselors provide medical, dental, and psychological services at Swingle Health Center; physical therapists and trainers provide conditioning tips for athletes, whether they compete on the intercollegiate or intramural level; skilled technicians run the sets at KUSM-TV; agronomy specialists run test plots at both on-campus and off-campus sites; nutritionists provide advice in food choice and preparation for the food service staff who provide more than 10,000 meals a day for campus residents; day-care workers tend to the needs of some 400 children who are brought to the center each morning; a host of clerks, secretaries, and accountants provide the information needed in a single legislative audit; grounds crews and building custodians maintain the beauty of the campus, even in the face of student carelessness. . . .

It is such people who present the human face of the university to the students and the public who make constant demands on them. In situations that sometimes create great tensions, the professional and classified personnel of MSU play a pivotal role. And they play it with grace and wisdom. The failure of the electrical transformer in January 1987 that left the fieldhouse without power occasioned a vivid example of how power-less this university would be without the services of trained and dedicated staff.

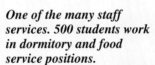

One of the many staff services. 500 students work in dormitory and food service positions.

Conclusion

Facing the Future

As this centennial celebration implies, Montana State University was officially founded 100 years ago, yet it has actually experienced three "foundings" over the course of its history, and it may well be poised on the brink of a fourth. The first founding, the formal establishment of the college, occurred in 1893 when Governor Rickards signed the document authorizing its creation. That document mandated that the institution be molded in the tradition of the land grant college. The second founding occurred in 1910 when President James Hamilton reformed the institution around a cluster of beliefs that emphasized industrial efficiency in training and thinking. The third occurred in 1965 when Montana State College took on the status and identity of a university.

Each of these founding events left powerful imprints on the institution in the form of physical structures and, more subtly, of philosophical constructs—habits of thinking and acting that have persisted with varying degrees of influence into the present time.

Chief among these imprints is the legacy of the land grant concept. But that concept has hardly been static. Over the years, many land grant colleges have been transformed from agricultural and technical training institutions into multipurpose universities, and MSU is no exception.

Another imprint, no less important, is the legacy of President Hamilton's emphasis on "education for efficiency." That philosophy influenced the school's concept of itself throughout the early and middle years of the century but was gradually called into question by a community of scholars who were not convinced that efficiency and productivity should be the primary focus of an institution of higher learning.

This questioning brought about a major philosophical shift that paralleled the movement that resulted in the transformation of Montana State College into Montana State University, an institution dedicated to the generation of new knowledge as well as the transmission of received wisdom. That legacy remains a dominant influence in the closing years of the school's first century.

But as a human institution that reflects the changing economy, demography, and culture of its setting, MSU finds itself facing a fourth "founding," one necessarily influenced by the lingering legacies of the first three. The land grant concept, the Hamiltonian creed, and the school's increased focus on research are all being reexamined in light of the pressing social and environmental concerns facing Montanans—and all humanity. Indeed, in his inaugural address, MSU's tenth president, Michael Malone, questioned once and for all the long-standing philosophy of "education for efficiency" and called for the adoption of a new motto, one more expressive of the university's evolving vision of its mission for the twenty-first century.[1]

But what words will take the place of Hamilton's slogan? What vision will underscore those words? If not "for efficiency," then what *will* be the purpose of education at MSU in the next century? In seeking the answers to these questions, the university that Ivan Doig described as destined to "help take Montana into its future" would do well to accept that author's challenge and "look both at the face of the land and into the dreams of its landsmen and landswomen."[2]

Endnotes

Introduction

1. Robert M. Pirsig, *Zen and the Art of the Motorcycle Maintenance* (New York, 1974), 129.
2. Merrill G. Burlingame, interview with Jeffrey Safford and Robert Rydell, 30 June 1987.
3. Jean Baudrillard, *America* (London, 1988), 1.

Chapter One

1. On Lewis and Clark in Montana, see Bernard DeVoto, *The Journals of Lewis and Clark* (Boston, 1953); Ernest S. Osgood, ed., *The Field Notes of Captain William Clark* (New Haven, Conn., 1964). The original name of the Gallatin Valley is noted in Marjorie Smith, "Common Ground," *Bozeman Daily Chronicle,* 30 July 1989.
2. Alan Trachtenberg, *The Incorporation of America* (New York, 1983).
3. Joseph Kinsey Howard, *Montana; High, Wide, and Handsome* (New Haven, Conn., 1943).
4. Information about the land grant acts is from *The Land Grant Fact Book* (Washington, D.C., 1962).
5. Among the historical works that attest to the changed circumstances of American life are Sean Wilentz, *Chants Democratic* (New York, 1984); and Douglass C. North, *Economic Growth of the United States, 1790-1860* (New York, 1966). Abraham Lincoln, "Speech At Springfield, Illinois, Accepting the Republican Senatorial Nomination," 16 June 1858, in T. Harry Williams, ed., *Abraham Lincoln. Selected Speeches, Messages, and Letters* (New York, 1957), 76.
6. *Land Grant Fact Book,* 4-5, 23-24.
7. The best account of these developments is provided by Eric Foner, *Reconstruction* (New York, 1988).
8. *Land Grant Fact Book,* 25.
9. *Historical Statistics of the United States* (Washington, D.C., 1975), 1083.
10. *Land Grant Fact Book,* 29.
11. On the struggle to secure statehood, see Michael P. Malone and Richard B. Roeder, *Montana: A History of Two Centuries* (Seattle, 1976), chs. 5 and 8; and Clark C. Spence, *Montana: A Bicentennial History* (New York, 1978), 73-106.
12. Malone and Roeder, *Montana,* 147-151.
13. James Hamilton, "History of the Montana State College of Agriculture and Mechanic Arts," 1930, 1-3, in Merrill G. Burlingame Papers, Acc. 84014, Box 2, f. "Hamilton's History," Montana State University Archives (hereafter cited as Hamilton's History, 84014/2, MSUA); and Merrill G. Burlingame, "Montana State College, 1893-1919: A Preliminary Sketch," 1943, 5-6, Acc. 71043, Box 1, MSUA (hereafter cited as Burlingame, "Montana State College," 71043/1, MSUA).
14. Quoted in Hamilton's History, 84014/2, MSUA, 5-6.
15. The best account of these struggles is William Lang, "Spoils of Statehood," *Montana the Magazine of Western History* 37:4 (Autumn 1987), 35-45.
16. Roger Lotchin, "The Darwinian City: The Politics of Urbanization in San Francisco between the World Wars," *Pacific Historical Review* 48 (1979), 357-381.
17. Lang, "Spoils of Statehood," 42-43; Burlingame, "Montana State College," 10-11, 71043/1, MSUA.
18. Lang, "Spoils of Statehood," 43.
19. Ibid.
20. James Bruce Putnam, "The Evolution of a Frontier Town: Bozeman, Montana, and Its Search for Economic Stability, 1864-1877," M.A. thesis, Montana State University, 1973, 1-13; Merrill G. Burlingame, "The 'Un-Natural' History of Bozeman," 18 November 1975, unpublished paper, Coll. 1026, Records of the Q.K. Club, Box 4, f. "1975-1976," Montana State University Special Collections (hereafter cited as Burlingame, "'Un-Natural' History," 1026/4, MSUSC).
21. Putnam, "Evolution," ch. 2.
22. Burlingame, "'Un-Natural' History," 1026/4, MSUSC.
23. Putnam, "Evolution," 20-21.
24. Details of Koch's life are from Malcolm Story, "Bozeman's Early Business Men," File 889, MSUSC.
25. Details of Story's life are from "Nelson Story," *Progressive Men of Montana* (Chicago, 1901), 1256-1257; and Story, "Bozeman's Early Business Men," File 889, MSUSC. Concerns of army officials are contained in "Brisbin's Report of Indian Frauds Made to General Sheridan," 21 December 1878, File 1064, MSUSC (original held at Montana Historical Society, Helena).
26. "Brisbin's Report," ibid.
27. *Progressive Men of Montana,* 440-442; Story, "Bozeman's Early Business Men"; and "Walter Cooper File," Caroline McGill Papers, Coll. 945, Box 1, MSUSC.
28. *Progressive Men of Montana,* 1871-1872.
29. Women's cultural activities in the American West are discussed in Dee Brown's much-criticized *Gentle Tamers: Women of the Old Wild West* (New York, 1958) and the important corrective offered by Sandra Myres, *Westering Women and the Frontier Experience, 1800-1915* (Albuquerque, N.M., 1982, A good overview of the importance of cultural concerns in the American West is Robert V. Hine, *The American West: An Interpretive History* (Boston, 1973).
30. Information about Emma Willson's activities is from an interview with Merrill Burlingame, 11 August 1989.
31. "Bozeman the Literary," *Bozeman Weekly Chronicle,* 27 January 1898.

Chapter Two

1. James Hamilton, Commencement Address, James Hamilton Papers, Acc. 74001x, f. "Addresses," Montana State University Archives (hereafter cited as 74001x, MSUA).
2. Merrill G. Burlingame, *A History: Montana State University* (Bozeman, 1968), 9-13.
3. William F. Brewer, *Higher Education* in Montana (Bozeman, Mt., 1946), 6-7.
4. Ibid., 7.
5. Ibid., 9. See also minutes from the Local Executive Board, 74001x, f. PR2, MSUA.
6. Brewer, *Higher Education,* 10; Merrill G. Burlingame, "Montana State College, 1893-1919: A Preliminary Sketch," 1943, 13, Acc. 71043, Box 1, MSUA (hereafter cited as Burlingame, "Montana State College," 71043/1, MSUA).

7. Ibid., 14.

8. Burlingame, *A History,* 12, quotes Thomas McKee; see also Merrill G. Burlingame Papers, Acc. 84014, Box 2, f. "McKee," MSUA (hereafter cited as Burlingame Papers, 84014/2, MSUA).

9. Laurentza Koch to [Christian Koch], 22 July 1893, Christian Koch Family Papers, Microfilm 652, Montana State University Special Collections (hereafter cited as MSUSC).

10. Lawrence A. Cremin, *American Education: The Metropolitan Experience, 1876-1980* (New York, 1988), 555-565; Laurence R. Veysey, *The Emergence of the American University* (Chicago, 1965), 264-268. On the College of Montana, see Merrill G. Burlingame and K. Ross Toole, *A History of Montana,* vol. 2. (New York, 1957), 381; *Eighth Annual Catalogue of the Colleqe of Montana* (Butte, Mt., 1891), at the Montana Historical Society, Helena (hereafter cited as MHS); and the editorial in *New Northwest,* 27 January 1894. 4.

11. James Hamilton, "History of the Montana State College of Agriculture and Mechanic Arts," 1930, in Burlingame Papers, 84014/2, MSUA.

12. The best overview of this development is found in Veysey, *Emergence.*

13. John S. Brubacher and Willis Rudy, *Higher Education in Transition* (New York, 1958), 261.

14. Ibid., 261-262.

15. Robert C. McMath, *Engineering the New South: Georgia Tech 1885-1985* (Athens, 1985).

16. This notion of a land grant college was far from unique. See Veysey, *Emergence,* 112n168.

17. Information on Ryon is from the Burlingame Papers, 84014/2, f. "Ryon," MSUA.

18. Ibid.

19. *First Annual Catalogue of the Montana College of Agriculture and Mechanic Arts, 1893-1894,* passim.

20. Ibid., 6-7.

21. Ibid., 12.

22. Ibid., 4.

23. Ibid., 13, 41. On the early history of the School of Business, see Harvey Larson, "A 90-Year Metamorphosis: The School of Business at Montana State University, " 1984, File A.3.8, MSUA.

24. Ibid., 25. On the early history of home economics at MSC, see Gladys Roehm, "The History of Home Economics at M.S.U.," Departmental Histories Drawer, f. "Home Economics Department." MSUA.

25. *First Annual Catalogue,* 10-11; Burlingame, *A History,* 19.

26. Ibid., 21.

27. Burlingame, *A History,* 25.

28. Brewer, *Higher Education,* 3.

29. Ibid., 25.

30. For information on Reid, see Mary Ellen Fitzgerald, "Dr. James Reid: The Second President's Influence on the Montana College of Agriculture and Mechanic Arts," unpublished seminar paper, 1988.

31. Fitzgerald, "Dr. James Reid," 12.

32. David Hollinger, "Inquiry and Uplift: Late Nineteenth-Century American Academics and the Moral Efficacy of Scientific Practice," in Thomas L. Haskell, ed., *The Authority of Experts* (Bloomington, Ind., 1984), 142-156.

33. James Reid, "Education! What Is It?" *College Exponent,* December 1896. See also Reid's "The Teacher's Mission," *Montana Educator* 1:6 (September 1895), 10-12.

34. Burlingame, "Montana State College," 29-33, 71043/1, MSUA.

35. Ibid., 33.

36. Descriptions of the cornerstone-laying ceremony are from "Laying of the Corner Stone of the M.C.A. and M.A.," *College Exponent,* 1:6 (October 1896); "The College Corner Stone," *Avant-Courier,* 24 October 1896; "The Corner Stone," Bozeman Chronicle, 29 October 1896.

37. "Laying of the Corner Stone of the M.C.A. and M.A.," College Exponent 1:6 (October 1896); "The College Corner Stone," Avant Courier, 24 October 1896.

38. "Laying of the Corner Stone of the M.C.A. and M.A.," *College Exponent,* 1:6 (October 1896).

39. "Montana State College History," Montana State University Quick Facts, MSUSC.

40. James Reid, "Report to the Executive Board," 27 May 1896, 74001x, f. PR2, MSUA.

41. Brewer, *Higher Education,* 6.

42. Burlingame, *A History,* 27-28.

43. Ibid., 27; Edward Byron Chennette, "The Montana State Board of Education: A Study of Higher Education in Conflict, 1884-1959," Ed.D. thesis, University of Montana, 1972, 96. This episode also shocked contemporaries. "The board should either say that it has no charges to make, or, if it has any charges it should make them," declared an editorial in the *Inter-Mountain Educator* 1:11 (March 1896), 10.

44. James Reid, "Report to Executive Board," 20 May 1897, 74001x, f. PR2, MSUA.

45. *Montana State College of Agriculture and Mechanic Arts* (Bozeman, Mt., 1902).

46. "Laying of the Corner Stone of the M.C.A. and M.A.," *College Exponent,* 1:6 (October 1896).

47. Reid, "Report to the Executive Board," 20 May 1897, 74001x. f. PR2, MSUA.

48. Fitzgerald, "Dr. James Reid," 15-16.

49. Chennette, "Board of Education," 156.

50. Reid to Ella Holden, 18 May 1904, quoted in Fitzgerald, "Dr. James Reid," 20.

51. Reid to Ella Holden, 9, 15, and 25 January 1903, quoted in Fitzgerald, "Dr. James Reid," 12.

52. Ibid., 12.

53. Ibid., 22.

54. Reid's letters to Ella Holden in 1903 and 1904 are particularly helpful in reconstructing Reid's reasons for resigning. See also Fitzgerald, "Dr. James Reid," 18.

55. "Montana State College History," Montana State University Quick Fact, MSUSC.

56. *Twelfth Annual Catalog, 1904-1905;* Burlingame, "Montana State College," 33-35, 71043/1, MSUA.

57. Fitzgerald, "Dr. James Reid," 14.

58. *The "Dean Hamilton Tradition,"* University of Montana Booklet, State College Series No. 74 (Bozeman, 1929), 4.

59. In 1895, Frederick W. Taylor presented a paper to the American Society of Mechanical Engineers entitled "A Piece-Rate System, Being a Step toward a Partial Solution of the Labor Problem." Taylor's paper, arguing that "'an honest day's work' could be fixed scientifically" and that the factory should be a place for producing character as well as goods, helped launch the scientific management crusade to transplant ideals of efficiency into the culture of everyday life. Samuel Haber, *Efficiency and Uplift: Scientific Management in the Progressive Era 1890-1920* (Chicago, 1964), 55.

60. Quoted in Raymond E. Callahan, *Education and the Cult of Efficiency: A Study of the Social Forces That Have Shaped the Administration of the Public Schools* (Chicago, 1962), 8. 61. This informa-

tion is derived from the Hamilton Papers, 74001, Biographical Files, MSUA.

62. Henry F. May, *End of American Innocence* (Chicago, 1964), 132.

63. Haber, *Efficiency and Uplift,* 55.

64. Edwin Norris, "The Duty of the State towards Education," *Inter-Mountain Educator* 3:1 (September 1907), 3-8.

65. James Hamilton, "The Educational Policy, 1904-1919," in the Burlingame Papers, 84014/2, f. "Hamilton," MSUA.

66. Burlingame, *A History,* 44.

67. Hamilton, "The Educational Policy," 84014/2, MSUA.

68. Ibid.

69. Ibid.

70. "Exponent Greetings," *Weekly Exponent,* 15 August 1911.

71. "Education for Efficiency," *Weekly Exponent,* 2 June 1911. See also James Hamilton, "Getting in Touch," *Weekly Exponent,* 14 April 1911; "President Speaks," *Weekly Exponent,* 30 September 1910; and Charles W. Eliot, "Education for Efficiency," *Journal of Pedagogy* 17 (1904), 97-113.

72. Blankenship developed into a "professional witness" for smelter companies around the country. See Donald Macmillan, "A History of the Struggle to Abate Air Pollution from Copper Smelters in the Far West, 1885-1933," Ph.D. dissertation, University of Montana, 1973, 154.

73. See Chapter 1.

74. Brewer, *Higher Education,* 8-10, provides an eloquent defense of specialized Montana system of higher education. For a contrary perspective, see Cassius J. Keysere, *Mole, Philosophy & Other Essays* (New York, 1972), 72-85. The debate is also addressed in "Consolidation of the University, the Agricultural College, and the School of Mines," *Inter-Mountain Educator* 10:2 (October 1914), 7-20.

75. H. G. Merriam, *The University of Montana. A History* (Missoula, Mt., 1970), 37-38. See also the Hamilton Papers, 74001x, f. "Biography—Craighead Controversy," MSUA.

76. Burlingame, *A History,* 50-54; Merriam, *University of Montana,* passim.

77. The hand-in-glove relationship between efficiency in education and the rise of corporate power is addressed in Callahan, *Education and the Cult of Efficiency,* passim.

78. Edward C. Elliott, "The University and Public Service," quoted in Frank K. Burrin, "Edward Charles Elliott, Educator," Ph.D. dissertation, Purdue University, 1956, 106.

79. "War Cloud Threatens Whole of Europe; Austria at War," *Bozeman Weekly Courier,* 29 July 1914.

80. "College Notes," *Weekly Exponent,* 11 September 1914, quoted in J. D. Pike "Fighting on All Fronts: Montana State College during World War I," unpublished seminar paper, 1988.

81. Pike, "Fighting on All Fronts," 2.

82. Michael P. Malone and Richard B. Roeder, *Montana: A History of Two Centuries* (Seattle, Wash., 1976), 208.

83. Burrin, "Edward Charles Elliott," 129.

84. "Will Place M.S.C. on War Footing by Next Fall," *Bozeman Weekly Courier,* 23 February 1916.

85. Susan D. Moeller, *Shooting War* (New York, 1989), 3-25.

86. Burlingame, *A History,* 116-118; "College Emblem Looms Large on the Landscape," *Bozeman Weekly Courier,* 17 May 1916.

87. "M.S.C. Students Leave with Second Montana,"

Weekly Exponent, 16 April 1917, cited in Pike, "Fighting on All Fronts," 9.

88. "Student Body in Patriotic Parade," *Weekly Exponent,* 5 October 1917, cited in Pike, "Fighting on All Fronts," 9.

89. "Intense Interest in War Shown by Men and Women Students at College," *Weekly Exponent,* 7 December 1917, quoted in Pike, "Fighting on All Fronts," 7.

90. David Noble, *America by Design* (New York, 1977), 217.

91. Ibid., 215. For evidence of the War Department's efforts to shape curricula at MSC, see the Hamilton Papers, 74001x, f. "SATC, 1918," MSUA.

92. Advertisement, *Bozeman Daily Chronicle,* 13 June 1918.

93. "Grading Men On Character, *Bozeman Weekly Courier,* 29 March 1916

94. *Home Economics* (Missoula, Mt., 1918), 2, quoted in Sandra J. Anderson, "World War I and the Women of Montana State College," unpublished paper, 1984.

95. "College Women Will Conserve Sugar Supply," *Weekly Exponent,* 9 November 1917; "College Girls Cut Down on Their Candy," *Bozeman Chronicle,* 10 November 1917, quoted in David R. James, "Passivity and Motherhood? An Analysis of Women's Responses to the World Wars at Montana State College," unpublished seminar paper, 1988.

96. James, "Passivity and Motherhood?" 4-5. On the history of nursing at the college, see the files of Anna Pearl Sherrick, Acc. 83042, MSUA. See also Chapter 9 of this text.

97. James, "Passivity and Motherhood?", 7-8.

98. *The Montanan 1922.*

99. Una B. Herrick, "Twenty Years at Montana State College," typescript, A5.8, 44, MSUA.

100. Ibid.

101. "War Courses for Summer Session," *Weekly Exponent,* 29 March 1918, cited in Anderson, "World War I."

102. Roehm, "History of Home Economics," 42.

103. Malone and Roeder, *Montana,* 213; Nancy R. Fritz, "The Montana Council of Defense," M.A. thesis, University of Montana, 1966; Charles S. Johnson, "The Montana Council of Defense, *Montana Journalism* Review 16 (1973), 2-16; [Elliott to Hamilton], 29 December 1917, RS 72, f. 12, MHS; Arnon Gutfeld, "The Levine Affair: A Case Study in Academic Freedom," Pacific Historical Review 39 (1970), 19-37.

104. "Organize Student Council of Defense, *Weekly Exponent,* 15 February 1918.

105. "Slackers," *Weekly Exponent,* 22 March 1918.

106. "A Short History of the Modern Languages at M.S.U.," Departmental Histories Drawer, f. "Modern Language History," MSUA.

107. O. R. Rhoads to William Cobleigh, 14 April 1943, Departmental Histories Drawer, f. "Military Service," MSUA. The letter notes that Hamilton was a member of the Council of Defense.

108. Carol Gruber, *Mars and Minerva: World War I and the Uses of Higher Learning in America* (Baton Rouge, La., 1975), makes clear that loss of intellectual independence was a national phenomenon during the First World War.

109. "Sub Discovered near Main Hall," *Weekly Exponent,* 10 May 1918, cited by Pike, "Fighting on All Fronts," 11.

110. "Riggt [sic] Here at Home," (Miles City) *Daily Star,* 18 June 1918, clipping, RS 72, Box 12, f. 12-16, MHS; J. A. Gilluly to Edward Elliott, 22 July

1918, ibid., f. 12-22, MHS.

111. "Dr. Reid Speaks at Quarter Centennial Celebration," *Weekly Exponent,* 29 March 1918.

Chapter Three

1. Atkinson to M. A. Brannon, 2 February 1937, Records of the Office of the President, Acc. 00001, Box 1, f. "Report of Progress (unofficial)," Montana State University Archives (hereafter cited as ROP, 00001/1, MSUA).
2. Atkinson to H. S. Cannon, 16 December 1930, ibid.
3. Ray Bowden to Atkinson, 20 March 1933, ibid.
4. Merrill G. Burlingame interview, 30 June 1987.
5. Among the best introductions to America's interwar years are William Leutchenberg, *The Perils of Prosperity* (Chicago, 1958); Warren A. Susman, *Culture as History* (New York, 1984); and Roland Marchand, *Advertising the American Dream* (Berkeley, Calif., 1985).
6. The two best accounts of Montana during the 1920s and 1930s are Michael P. Malone and Richard B. Roeder, *Montana: A History of Two Centuries* (Seattle, 1976), ch. 12; and Joseph Kinsey Howard, *Montana High, Wide, and Handsome* (New Haven, Conn., 1943), 19-26.
7. David O. Levine, *The American College and the Culture of Aspiration 1915-1940* (Ithaca, N.Y., 1986).
8. "A Brief Biographical Sketch of Dr. Alfred Atkinson...," in Merrill G. Burlingame Papers, Acc. 84014, Box 2, f. "Atkinson," MSUA (hereafter cited as Burlingame Papers, 84014/2, MSUA).
9. On the Levine case, see Howard, *Montana,* ch. 23. Regarding the case, MSC professor M. L. Wilson recalled that the Company was "as mad as boiled owls..., stories were started that... the university had become infiltrated with socialists . . . that Chancellor Elliott had . . . begun importing a bunch of socialists from Columbia University to knock out the industries of the state." ("The Reminiscences of M. L. Wilson," Columbia Oral History Collection, vol. 1, 293-294.
10. Merrill G. Burlingame, *A History: Montana State University. Bozeman, Montana* (Bozeman, 1968), 68.
11. For Strand's description of Atkinson, see Burlingame Papers, 84104/2, f. "Atkinson," MSUA.
12. "Alfred Atkinson Formally Installed as President of Montana State College," *Exponent,* 16 January 1920; "Inaugural Address of Alfred Atkinson at the State College," Bozeman Daily Chronicle, 15 January 1920; "Our New President," *Bozeman Daily Chronicle,* 14 January 1920.
13. "Proceedings as Published by the *Bozeman Daily Chronicle* of the Montana Implement and Hardware Association, Feb. 26, 27, 28, 1923, Bozeman, Montana," clipping in Faculty Biographies Drawer, A5.8/Atkinson, MSUA.
14. Westinghouse's H. F. J. Porter quoted in David Noble, *America by Design* (New York, 1977), 45.
15. Ibid., 46.
16. "Who's Who in the Engineering School," *Weekly Exponent,* 17 March 1923.
17. Norris to Atkinson, 4 December 1923, ROP, 00001/5, f. "Activities of Various Divisions, Depts, etc.," MSUA. Norris was fully in sympathy with Alfred H. White, professor of chemical engineering at the University of Michigan, who drew an analogy between "the college and the manufac-

turing plant which receives partially fabricated metal, shapes it and refines it somewhat, and turns it over to some other agency for further fabrication. The college receives raw material.... It must turn out a product which is saleable. . . . The type of curriculum is in the last analysis not set by the college but by the employer of the college graduate." (Noble, *America by Design,* 46.)

18. Norris to Wickendon, 8 April 1924, Records of the College of Engineering, Acc. 89026, Series 2, Box 1, f. "S.P.E.E.," MSUA (cited hereafter as RCE, 89026/2/1, MSUA).
19. Noble, *America by Design,* 130.
20. *Twenty-eighth Annual Catalogue.* 1920-21, 66.
21. *Twenty-ninth Annual Catalogue.* 1921-22, 59; *Thirtieth Annual Catalogue.* 1922-23, 58.
22. "The General Criteria of the Status of a Profession" (memo, 1924), RCE, 89026/2/1, f. "S.P.E.E.," MSUA.
23. Ibid.
24. Norris to George W. Hobbs, 5 October 1925, RCE, 89026/2/1, f. "Norris Correspondence, H," MSUA.
25. That the College of Engineering remained in the mainstream of racist thinking throughout the interwar period is apparent from Professor E. W. Schilling's remarks at a Quest for Knowledge Club meeting: "It seems unique and to me almost incredible that the Portugese should have intermarried with the negro people. The English speaking countries have not done that. In our own country we think of people who would marry into the black race as amongst the lowest type of our own civilization. Even the negroes themselves, those who have no white blood, look with disdain upon those of their own race who would marry a white man." See RCE, 89026/3/9, f. 19, "Discsussion, 'The Portugese', a Paper by Mr. Plew," MSUA.
26. An important exception to this rule was Arthur C. Ford. Ford, an African-American graduated from Helena High before attending MSC, where he finished in mechanical engineering in 1916. He went on to a distinguished career in New York City, becoming Commissioner of Water Supply, Gas and Electricity. In 1956, he received an honorary doctorate from MSC. See "Commencement," *Collegian,* July 1956, 3; and *The Montanan 1916,* 51.
27. "Sigma Epsilon Secures National Tau Beta Pi," *Exponent,* 10 November 1925.
28. Norris, "The Blue and Gold, To the Engineer," *The Montanan 1925,* 33, cited in Tim Arnaud, "Education for Efficiency," unpublished seminar paper, 1981.
29. Norris, "Dean of Engineering," The Montanan 1927.
30. Norris to F. B. Linfield, 27 June 1928, RCE, 89026/2/1, f. "Correspondence from President, 1927-1928," MSUA.
31. Biographical information is from Faculty Biographies, f. "Cobleigh," MSUA.
32. Cobleigh to Atkinson, 19 December 1929, ROP, 00001/15, f. "1929-30 Cobleigh, William," MSUA; "Annual Report of Committee on Personnel and Placement, 1929-30," ROP, 00001/7, f. "Personnel and Placement, Counsellor System Testing," MSUA.
33. *Catalogue Number Thirty-Seven. . .1929-30,* 60.
34. *Catalogue Thirty-Eight for 1930-31,* 62.
35. "Personality Rating Scale," ROP, 00001/7, f. "Personnel and Placement, Counsellor System Testing, Engineering 1930-1936," MSUA.

36. "Personality Rating Scales," RCE, 89026/3/8, f. "Personality Ratings, 1932-36," MSUA.

37. Cobleigh to Atkinson, 5 June 1933, RCE, 89026/3/1, f. "President Atkinson," MSUA.

38. Merrill R. Goode, "Personnel and Placement Service," *The Montana Engineer* 1:1 (May 1936), 8. There is a sample personnel leaflet on the following page. By 1932, Atkinson was so pleased with the personnel service in the engineering college that he sought to implement its procedures across the institution. See Atkinson to Cobleigh, 6 August 1932, ROP, 00001/7, f. "Personnel and Placement, Counsellor System Testing, Engineering, 1930-36" MSUA; and "Summary of Personnel and Placement Service, 1932-1933 [College of Agriculture]," in ROP, 00001/7, f. "Personnel and Placement, Counsellor System Testing, Agriculture, 1930-1933," MSUA.

39. Louis Bender to Cobleigh, 17 April 1931, RCE, 89026/3/1, f. "Administration General (A1) 1929-31," MSUA.

40. "List of Firms Who Have Received the Complete Personnel Booklet," 6 April 1931, RCE, 89026/3/2-3, f. "Personnel and Placement General, 1931-32," MSUA.

41. J. A. Thaler to R. M. Dolve, 1 May 1931, RCE, 89026/3/1, f. "B," MSUA.

42. Cobleigh to Atkinson, 9 February 1933, RCE, 89026/3/7, f. "President Atkinson 1933," MSUA.

43. Atkinson's spells are noted in Burlingame, *A History,* 68.

44. Atkinson to J. M. Hamilton et al., 14 February 1933, RCE, 89026/3/7, f. "President Atkinson 1933," MSUA.

45. Engineering was not alone in keeping tabs on students through the personnel service. As Clyde McKee, dean of the College of Agriculture and director of its personnel department, reported: "[A] student who had made an excellent scholastic record during the autumn quarter was interviewed at the end of the first 'roundup' period of the winter quarter to determine 'why' the low grades in certain subjects. The young man did not look well and the condition of his face suggested that he needed to consult the Student Health Director. Without knowledge on the part of the student, Miss Barnes was advised of the case, and she called him in for examination. Violet ray treatments cleared up his face, but quite as important was the fact that the student was greatly impressed with the interest of the institution in his personal welfare." See Clyde McKee, "Summary of Personnel and Placement Service: 1932-1933," ROP, 00001/7, f. "Personnel and Placement, Counsellor System Testing, Agriculture, 1930-33," MSUA.

46. Cobleigh, "You are Wrong About That," 17 October 1939, Records of the Q. K. Club, Coll. 1026, Box 2, MSUSC (hereafter cited as 1026/2, MSUSC). For Cobleigh, the blame for the nation's depression rested squarely with financiers, and it was up to engineers to wrest control from them. See his "Annual Report 1930-31," May 1931, Annual Reports Drawer, MSUA.

47. "Techno-Campus News," *The Montana Engineer,* 1:1 (May 1936), 4.

48. Atkinson to M. A. Brannon, 11 January 1933, ROP, 00001/1, f. "Report of Progress (official), 1920-1936," MSUA; and Clyde McKee, "Occupation Record of Agricultural Graduates of Montana State College (1896-1927)," 1 September 1927, ROP, 00001/1, f. "President's Annual Report," MSUA.

49. The best account of the MSC experiment stations and extension service remains Burlingame, *A History,* ch. 6. For additional information, consult Ralph Mercer, "History of the Montana Extension Service" folder in Burlingame Papers, 84014/2, MSUA.

50. F. B. Linfield, "Starting an Experiment Station in the West," Records of the Q. K. Club, 1026/2, MSUSC.

51. Malone and Roeder, *Montana,* 180.

52. Ibid.

53. F. B. Linfield, "A Talk Prepared for the Quarter Century Club But Not Given," Burlingame Papers, 84014/2, f. "Linfield, F. B.," MSUA. See also Paul Brailsford, "Frederic Bertil Linfield, 1866-1948," unpublished paper, 1990.

54. Press release, 13 April 1937, Faculty Biographies Drawer, f. "Linfield, F. B.," MSUA.

55. H. C. Gardiner to Beatrice Freeman Davis, 12 November 1946, History of MSU 75th Anniversary, Acc. 71043, Box 1, f. "H. C. Gardiner letter to Mrs. Davis," MSUA.

56. Malone and Roeder, *Montana,* 182, 184.

57. Surprisingly, there is no full-length biography of Wilson. Useful starting points include Burlingame, *A History,* 136-141; William D. Rowley, *M. L. Wilson and the Campaign for the Domestic Allotment* (Lincoln, Neb., 1970); and "Biographical Sketch of M. L. Wilson," 3 January 1949, M. L. Wilson Papers, Coll. 1434, Box 1, "Wilson, M. L., Home Office Collection, 1935-1971," f. "Wilson, M. L., Pictures & Publicity," MSUSC.

58. Burlingame, *A History,* 138.

59. Ibid., 157-181.

60. Richard S. Kirkendall, *Social Scientists and Farm Politics in the Age of Roosevelt* (Columbia, Mo., 1966), 11-29.

61. Ibid.; David A. Hollinger, "The Problem of Pragmatism in American History," *Journal of American History* 67 (1980), 88-107.

62. M. L. Wilson, "Dry Farming in the North-Central Montana Triangle," *Montana State College Extension Service,* no. 66, June 1923, quoted in Burlingame, *A History,* 138.

63. Kirkendall, *Social Scientists* 12-14. See also Ronald Lee Kenney, "The Fairway Farms: An Experiment in a New Agricultural Age," M.S. thesis, Montana State University, 1969.

64. Russell Lord, "Look Out for the Engine," *The Country Home,* February 1931, clipping in Records of Agricultural Economics, Acc. 00002, Box 35, f. AD-1, "Publicity on Fairway," MSUA (hereafter cited as RAE, 00002/35/AD-1, MSUA).

65. Ibid.

66. Malcolm C. Cutting, "Farm Relief by Factory Methods," *Nation's Business,* clipping in RAE, 00002/35/AD-2, f. "Publicity on Fairway," MSUA.

67. Kenney, "Fairway Farms," 51-69; Roy E. Huffman, "Montana's Contributions to New Deal Farm Policy," *Agricultural History* 33 (1959), 164-167.

68. After he moved into the Roosevelt administration, Wilson's own enthusiasm for mechanized agriculture evidently began to wane. "As technology progresses," he wrote in 1948, "it can be developed to provide an economy of abundance. In so doing, the physical insecurities of life may be overcome. But, there must be a balance between physical well-being and spiritual and psychological well-being." See "M. L. Wilson" in *American Spiritual Autobiographies: Fifteen Self-Portraits* (New York, 1948), 20.

69. Atkinson to R. O. Wilson, 20 February 1933, ROP, 00001/1, f. "Report of Progress (unofficial), 1920-1937," MSUA; Atkinson to R. E. McConnell, 13 February 1933, ibid., f. "University System Chancellorships, 1920-37," MSUA.

70. Atkinson to M. A. Brannon, 2 February 1937, ROP, 00001/1, f. "Report of Progress (unofficial), 1920-1937," MSUA; Atkinson to R. E. McConnell, 13 February 1933, ibid., f. "University System Chancellorships, 1920-37," MSUA; M. L. Wilson, "Annual Report: Farm Management Demonstration Work in Montana, 1922," Acc. 78036, Box "Extension Service, Harriette Cushman," f. "Farm Managment/1922 Annual Report, and First Quarter Report, 1923," MSUA. Typical of opposition sentiments was F. E. Benepe, Jr., to Senator Armstrong, 17 February 1933, Records of the Agricultural Experiment Stations, Acc. 71021, Box 1, f. "Linfield, F. B., Taxes," MSUA: "[Y]ou will probably have the entire strength of the University thrown down on you in the next day or two. . . . They will produce figures showing where the County Agents have made millions of dollars for the farmers and other producers, . . . and so on down the line, but in the long run it is only propaganda to hold their jobs."

71. Burlingame, *A History,* 78-80.

72. A. L. Strand, "Report of the Committee on State Problems and College Policy," 5 March 1936, ROP, 00001/1, f. "Reports of 'Philosophy of Education' and 'State Problems and Policy' Committees, 1934-1936," MSUA.

73. F. B. Linfield, "A Philosophy of Education for Montana State College," ibid.

76. Atkinson to J. O. Huff, 1 June 1921, ROP, 00001/1, f. "M.S.C.—Scholastic Standing, 1921-36," MSUA. Montana State College's standing was so low that one eastern college evidently refused to accept student credits earned at MSC.

75. Atkinson to M. A. Brannon, 12 November 1932, ROP, 00001/3, f. "Library Correspondence 1919-1937," MSUA. According to Atkinson, the head of the library had been disposing of library materials without appropriate consultation with faculty. "I find on investigation," Atkinson wrote, "that she has been throwing out Experiment Station bulletins and material of that sort. The woman seems to be without a sense of values so far as library material is concerned, and she remarked in our discussion that if they had publications which were not asked for for a few years, there didn't seem to be much point in keeping them." Atkinson came to the appropriate conclusion: "In light of the whole situation, I am convinced that she's utterly unsafe to leave in the library. . . . In my judgment, the woman really deserves to be dropped summarily today, but she can do us useful service by straightening out these division libraries, which are in need of attention, and since this is the case, we'd probably better leave her on the payroll until the end of the present year."

76. Burlingame, *A History,* 197, 83-84. In 1929, Matt Pakkala earned MSC's first Rhodes scholarship.

77. Paula Fass, *The Damned and the Beautiful: American Youth in the 1920s* (New York, 1977), 375.

78. Keith Walden, "Hazes, Hustles, Scraps, and Stunts: Initiations at the University of Toronto, 1880-1925," in Paul Axelrod and John G. Reid, eds., *Youth, University, and Canadian Society: Essays in the Social History of Higher Education* (Kingston, Quebec, 1989), esp. 116.

79. Burlingame, A History, 96-102.

80. Ibid.

81. Ibid.

82. Harvey P. Griffin, "An Objection to Exponent Stand," *Exponent,* 16 December 1910, quoted in Mike Fanning, "The Development of Fraternities at Montana State College," unpublished seminar paper, 1982.

83. "Traditions," editorial, *Weekly Exponent,* 1 October 1929. See also Michelle Meese, "Popular Culture at M.S.C. in the 'Roaring Twenties,'" unpublished seminar paper, 1988.

84. Una B. Herrick, "Twenty Years at Montana State College," typescript, A5.8, 80-81, MSUA.

85. "Necking—Chief Campus Sport," *Montana Exponent,* 4 December 1934.

86. "Coed Social Survey Shows Campus Moral Standards to Be High," *Montana Exponent,* 1 February 1938.

87. Brannon to Atkinson, 1 April 1932, and attached correspondence, ROP, 00001/4, f. "Students, Student Problems, Discipline, etc., (General), 1919-1937," MSUA.

88. "Work for Initiative Measures 18 & 19," ROP, 00001/2, f. "Finances 1918/1919-1929/1930," MSUA, cited in Brian Devine, "Romney Gymnasium: A By-Product of World War I," unpublished seminar paper, 1988.

89. "Dedication Exercises Start Twelfth Annual Event," *Weekly Exponent,* 8 March 1923.

90. Burlingame, *A History,* 107-108.

91. Atkinson memo, 26 May 1930, ROP, 00001/16, f. "Dyche, Schubert," MSUA, cited in Pat Dringman, "Schubert Dyche," unpublished seminar paper, 1989. Grade lists and grade deficiency lists give no indication that the student made up the grade or that the grade was changed.

92. "Dyche Traces Growth of Present Athletic Scandals," *Bozeman Daily Chronicle,* 15 August 1951, clipping in Faculty Biographies Drawer, f. "Dyche, Schubert," MSUA.

93. Henry T. Murray, "Some Recollections of Montana State College," May 1969, Burlingame Papers, 84014/2, MSUA. See also Atkinson to G. H. Vande Bogart, 1 October 1932, and Atkinson to Division Superintendent, Great Northern Railway Co., 20 December 1921, both in ROP, 00001/4, f. "Students, Student Problems, Discipline, etc., Marriage, 1924-1932," and f. "Students, Student Problems, Discipline, etc., Hoboing, 1922-1923," MSUA.

94. Burlingame, A History, 75-76. There is a great deal of information about the strike in ROP, 00001/4, f. "Students, Student Problems, Discipline, etc., Student Strike, 1930," MSUA.

95. Ralph S. Brax, *The First Student Movement* (Port Washington, N.Y., 1981).

96. Burlingame, *A History,* 77.

97. Walden, "Hazes, Hustles, . . .," 116.

98. Biographical information is from Faculty Biographies Drawer, f. "Strand, A. L.," MSUA.

99. The Student Union Building, later to be named the Strand Union Building, opened with the fall quarter of 1940. Construction costs were covered entirely by the students themselves. Mildred Leigh, the director of Hamilton Hall, was named the first director of the facility, which saw major additions and renovations in 1956, 1968, and 1983. (Montana State University Quick Facts, MSUSC.)

100. Burlingame, *A History,* 88-89. On the beet harvest, see Ray B. Haight Papers, Coll. 491, MSUSC.

101. "Trained Men Needed in All Engineering Fields Immediately," *Bozeman Daily Chronicle,* 6 July 1941, clipping in RCE, 89026, MSUA, cited in James Sander, "Engineering, Science, and Man-

agement Defense Training Courses: Dean W. M. Cobleigh and His Department's Contribution to the War Effort," unpublished seminar paper, 1989, 5-6.

102. Sander, "Engineering, Science, . . .," 8.

103. Official Program: 1942 High School Week, ROP, 00001/26, f. "High School Week," MSUA.

Chapter Four

1. Polly Renne (Mrs. Roland R. Renne) interview, 12 August 1987.

2. Lawrence A. Cremin, *The Transformation of the School: Progressivism in American Education, 1876-1957* (New York, 1961), 161.

3. Ibid., 162.

4. Ibid., 165.

5. Renne's "MSC as a Land-Grant Institution and the Development of Montana," 30 November 1961, is an excellent example of his application of this ethic. See the Papers of Roland R. Renne, Montana State University Archives, Montana State University Libraries. 81002, Box 1, "MSU as a Land-Grant Institution" File (hereafter cited as 81002/1, MSUA).

6. Robert T. Handy, ed., *The Social Gospel in America: Gladden, Ely, Rauschenbusch* (New York, 1966), 174-175.

7. Russel B. Nye, *Midwestern Progressive Politics: A Historical Study of Its Origins and Developments, 1870-1959* (Lansing, Mich., 1959), 140.

8. Cremin, *Transformation*, 164.

9. Ibid., 164-165.

10. Nye, Midwestern *Progressive Politics*, 141.

11. Samuel Haber, *Efficiency and Uplift: Scientific Management in the Progressive Era, 1890-1920* (Chicago, 1964), 141, 148-149.

12. Renne to E. E. Agger, 16 May 1930, 81002/1, "R. R. Renne - Personal 1930-1943" file, MSUA.

13. Merrill G. Burlingame, "Roland Roger Renne: A Personal Reminiscence," June,1985, Merrill G. Burlingame Papers, file 1046, Montana State University Special Collections (hereafter cited as Burlingame, "Renne," 1046, MSUSC).

14. Unsigned letter to "Governor," 23 August 1943, 81002/1, "R R. Renne-Personal 1930-1943" file, MSUA.

15. Renne, "The Future of the Land-Grant College," 10 April 1945, 81002/7, folder BO (342), MSUA.

16. Ibid.

17. Ibid.

18. Merrill G. Burlingame, *A History: Montana State University, Bozeman, Montana* (Bozeman, 1968), 184.

19. Ibid., 185.

20. Edward H. Ward interview, 9 September 1991.

21. Marjorie Paisley interview, 28 October 1991.

22. Edward Ward interview.

23. Renne, "Are We Ready?," statement prepared for the Collegian, Fall 1953, 81002/10, folder AS (692), MSUA.

24. Ibid.

25. Polly Renne interview.

26. Charles Bradley interview, 2 November 1987.

27. "Orientation," undated, 81002/10, "Orientation" file, MSUA.

28. Kenneth Nicholson interview, 26 June 1987; Polly Renne interview.

29. Edward Ward interview.

30. Edward Ward and Charles Bradley interviews.

31. Finding Aid for acc. 81002, MSUA.

32. Charles Bradley interview.

33. Ibid.; Kenneth Bryson interview, 19 August 1987.

34. Renne memo to the Board of Education, 21 December 1960, Box 46, MSC File, Presidents Papers, University of Montana, Mansfield Library Special Collections. (Hereafter cited as UMA).

35. Edward Ward interview.

36. MSC Staff Bulletin, 18 June 1951.

37. Robert Pantzer interview, 3 September 1991.

38. Roy Huffman interview, 12 September 1988.

39. Charles Bradley interview.

40. Irving Dayton interview, 27 June 1988.

41. Burlingame, *A History*, 186-188; H. G. Merriam, *The University of Montana: A History* (Missoula, 1970), 104-105.

42. Burlingame, *A History*, ibid.

43. "The Reminiscences of William Groff, "Montana Oral History Project," Montana Historical Society Archives (hereafter cited as MOHP, MHSA).

44. Robert Pantzer interview.

45. Merriam, *The University of Montana*, 139.

46. Robert Pantzer interview.

47. Richard Roeder interview, 7 September 1991.

48. Ellen W. Schrecker, *No Ivory Tower: McCarthyism and the Universities* (New York, 1986), 3-4.

49. Schrecker, *No Ivory Tower*; David Caute, *The Great Fear: The Anticommunist Purge under Truman and Eisenhower* (New York, 1978); Michael Paul Rogin, *The Intellectuals and McCarthy: The Radical Specter* (Cambridge, Mass., 1967).

50. Joseph McCarthy, *The Retreat from Victory: The Story of George Catlett Marshall* (New York, 1952).

51. *Bozeman Daily Chronicle*, 13 February 1951.

52. Nicholas Helburn interview, 6 September 1991.

53. *Bozeman Daily Chronicle*, 17 February 1951.

54. Edward Ward and Nicholas Helburn interviews; Maurice Kelso interview, 10 September 1991.

55. Charles Bradley interview.

56. Schrecker, *No Ivory Tower*, 308.

57. Robert G. Dunbar interview, 3 August 1987.

58. Ibid.

59. *Great Falls Tribune*, 15 October 1952.

60. Merrill Burlingame interviews. The authors interviewed Dr. Burlingame numerous times between 1987 and 1992.

61. Harvey M. Matusow, *False Witness* (New York, 1955). See also William D. Miller, "Montana and the Specter of McCarthyism, 1952-1954," M.S. thesis, Montana State University, 1969.

62. Charles Bradley interview.

63. Ibid.

64. Merrill Burlingame interviews.

65. Polly Renne and Robert Dunbar interviews; James M. Edie interview, 6 July 1987.

66. Robert Dunbar interview.

67. Ibid.

68. Merrill Burlingame interviews.

69. Robert Dunbar interview.

70. Kenneth Bryson interview.

71. Ibid.

72. Alonzo L. Hamby, *Liberalism and its Challengers: F.D.R. to Reagan* (New York, 1985), 103-105.

73. "The Reminiscences of Ted Schwinden," MOHP, MHSA.

74. "Objectives, Responsibilities, and Scope of the Montana Cooperative Extension Service," Circular 1065, August, 1960.

75. Merrill G. Burlingame and Edward G. Bell, Jr., *The Montana Cooperative Extension Service: A History, 1893-1974* (Bozeman, 1984), 253-254; Torlief Aasheim interview, 5 September 1991; William Johnstone interview, 30 June 1987. The Ford Foundation incorporated many granting cat-

egories, some of which, conservatives surely noted, lent strong emphasis to civil liberties issues.

76. *Great Falls Tribune*, 12, 13 April 1960.

77. *The Exponent*, 22 April 1960.

78. Ellen Missall, Letter to the editor, *The Exponent*, ibid.

79. A. B. Guthrie, undated, uncited, Letter to the editor, courtesy of Edward Ward.

80. "Resume of the actions of AFT #1005 relating to the 'Fiedler Affair,'" undated, as compiled by acting secretary K. D. Bryson, courtesy of Kenneth Bryson.

81. Charles Caughlin to Renne, 15 April 1960, 00030/111, Fiedler file, MSUA.

82. Renne to C. R. Jeppesen, 25 April 1960; Renne to Robert S. Hoffman, 25 April 1960, ibid.

83. Leslie Heathcote to Renne, 21 April 1960, ibid.

84. Duane Hill to Renne, 15 March 1960, ibid.

85. Howard Dean, "AFT: A Brief History," undated, courtesy of Kenneth Bryson.

86. Polly Renne interview.

87. The Nutter-Renne feud is covered in Judith B. Rollins, "Governor Donald G. Nutter and the Montana Daily Press," M.A. thesis, Montana State University, 1963.

88. Burlingame and Bell, *Montana Cooperative Extension Service*, 254.

89. Torlief Aasheim interview.

90. Robert Dunbar interview.

91. "The Reminiscences of William R. Mackay," MOHP, MHSA.

92. "The Reminiscences of Clyde Hawks," MOHP, MIISA.

93. Roy Huffman interview.

94. Polly Renne interview.

95. Renne, "Report on Montana State College," 25 April 1961, 81002/1, "MSC Cuts, etc." file, MSUA; Johnstone interview.

96. Minutes of Meetings, Board of Regents, Meeting of 11-13 March 1961, 79026, "Board of Regents" file, page 46, MSUA.

97. Reminiscences of Clyde Hawks," MOHP, MHSA.

98. Burlingame, *A History*, 193-194.

99. Michael P. Malone and Richard B. Roeder, *Montana: A History of Two Centuries* (Seattle, 1976), 299.

100. Burlingame, "Renne" f. 1046, MSUSC.

101. Renne, "Report on Montana State College," 25 April 1961, 81002/1, "MSC 1961 Cuts, etc." file, MSUA.

102. Ibid.

103. Burlingame, *A History*, 196.

104. *The People's Voice*, 19 January 1962, as quoted in Jerry R. Holloron, "The Montana Daily Press and the 1964 Gubernatorial Campaign," M.A. thesis, Montana State University, 1965, 26.

105. Renne to Perry Roys, 16 December 1963, 81002/1, "R. R. Renne Personal Correspondence" file, MSUA.

106. John L. Fischer to Renne, undated, late 1963, ibid.

107. Gene Mahoney to D. A. Nash, 25 February 1964, 81002/1, "Answered Correspondence" file, MSUA.

108. Thomas Judge to Lee Metcalf, 17 June 1964, Senator Lee Metcalf Papers, Box 636, Folder 1, Montana Historical Society Archives.

109. *Billings Gazette*, 14 September 1964.

110. "The Reminiscences of Jack Brenner," MOHP, MHSA.

111. Renne, *Land Economics*, 1st ed. (New York, 1947), 109.

112. Polly Renne interview.

113. Renne campaign speech in Conrad, 24 September 1964, 81002/3, "Sept.-Oct. Speeches" file, MSUA. James Battin was a candidate for the U.S. House of Representatives, Alex Blewitt was running against Mike Mansfield for the Senate seat, and "Barry" was, of course, Barry Goldwater, the Republican presidential candidate.

114. Robert Dunbar interview; Merrill Burlingame interviews.

Chapter Five

1. Leon Johnson to Charles Bradley, 10 February 1966, Acc. 70427, Box 2, "College of Letters and Science" file, Montana State University Archives (hereafter cited as 70427/2, MSUA).

2. Rev. Herbert Strom interview, 2 August 1988.

3. Johnson to J. Russell Larcombe, 29 December 1967, 77065/9, "L" file, MSUA.

4. Merrill G. Burlingame, *A History: Montana State University, Bozeman, Montana* (Bozeman, 1968), 203-204.

5. John Jutila interview, 28 August 1987.

6. John Parker interview, 4 August 1987.

7. Joe Asleson interview, 11 August 1987.

8. An excellent profile of Leon Johnson was written by William D. James, editor of the *Great Falls Tribune*. See the Tribune, 21 July 1968.

9. Roy Huffman interview, 12 September 1988.

10. See, for example, Gordon B. Castle, acting president, MSU, to Virgil M. Hancher, president of Iowa State University, 24 February 1959, Box 59, Presidential Papers, UMA.

11. William Johnstone interview, 21 July 1988.

12. John A. Hannah, president of Michigan State College, to the Michigan legislature, 15 February 1954, Box 59, Presidential Papers, UMA.

13. Ted James interview, 9 July 1987.

14. Minutes of Meetings, Board of Regents, 14-15 November 1963, 79026/4, MSUA.

15. Richard Roeder interview, 14 November 1991.

16. Johnson to Merrill G. Burlingame, 23 September 1965, 70427/2, "History, Government, and Philosophy" file, MSUA.

17. Minutes of Meeting, MSU Advisory Council, 3-5 December 1967, 77035/6, "Advisory Council, Fall Meeting" file, MSUA.

18. B.A. in History Degree Proposal, Statement of Emphasis, undated, 73050/1, "B.A. Degree in History" file, MSUA.

19. B.A. in English Degree Proposal, Statement of Emphasis, undated, 73050/1, "B.A. Degree in English" file, MSUA.

20. Irving Dayton interview, 13 November 1991; Carl Issacson interview, 1 August 1988.

21. Carl Isaacson interview.

22. Robert Pantzer interview, 3 September 1991.

23. Johnson to Babcock, 29 June 1964, 73050/1, "Governor" file, MSUA.

24. Johnson to Maurice E. Richard, 6 October 1965, 74027/4, "Board of Regents, General" file, MSUA.

25. John D. French interview, 23 September 1991.

26. Johnson, "MSU Administrative Structure," undated, 77035/3, "President Leon H. Johnson" file, MSUA.

27. Carl Isaacson interview.

28. Johnson, "MSU Administrative Structure."

29. Johnson to C. Mansel Keene, 29 June 1966, 70427/2, "President Leon H. Johnson, Personal" file, MSUA.

30. Allen J. Matusow, *The Unraveling of America: A History of Liberalism in the 1960s* (New York, 1984); and William L. O'Neill, *Coming Apart: An Informal History of America in the 1960s* (Chi-

cago, 1971).

31. Irving Dayton interview, 27 June 1988.

32. Edward Hanson interview, 25 August 1988.

33. Marge Paisley interview, 28 October 1991.

34. *Stiletto*, 20 January 1964.

35. David Swingle interview, 24 October 1991; James Goetz interview, 21 October 1991.

36. Edward Hanson interview.

37. See, for example, *Billings Gazette*, 2 August 1967. The *Gazette* did a series of articles in late July and early August on the arrests.

38. The intensity of this anger is illustrated superbly in Theodore Roszak's *The Making of a Counter Culture; Reflections on the Technocratic Society and its Youthful Opposition* (New York, 1969).

39. An excellent examination of the relationship between black writing and black nationalism is provided by Morris Dickstein in *Gates of Eden: American Culture in the Sixties* (New York, 1966), chapter 6.

40. Douglas H. Lien to Leon Johnson, et al., 30 November 1967, 77035/7, "English, Speech and Theatre Arts" file, MSUA.

41. Carl Isaacson interview.

42. Kenneth Bryson interview, 19 August 1987; John Parker interview.

43. Johnson to W. P. Fidler, 22 February 1968, 77035/ 9, "AFT-AAUP-AAUW-MEA" file, MSUA; Johnson to Mrs. Dretta Van Delinder, 23 February 1968, 77035/7, "English, Speech and Theatre Arts" file, MSUA.

44. Johnston to A. A. "Buddy" Arras, 8 March 1968, 77035/10, "Board of Regents—General" file, MSUA.

45. *Exponent*, 9 February 1968.

46. Ibid., 26 April 1968.

47. Ibid., 10 May 1968.

48. Robert Pantzer interview.

49. Johnson to June Berg, 18 April 1969, 79026/3, "Johnson General Correspondence" file, MSUA.

50. "War Correspondent Reports from College Battlefields," Max Lerner column, *Great Falls Tribune*, 7 May 1969.

51. Johnson to I. Wayne Eveland, 3 October 1968, 77035/10, "Johnson General Correspondence" file, MSUA.

52. *Exponent*, 27 January 1967.

53. Rick Freeman, "The Rehumanize Movement in Bozeman," history seminar paper, 1987.

54. Gene Bourdet to J. J. McLaughlin, 17 September 1968, 79026/1, "Athletics" file, MSUA.

55. Johnson, "Comments on the Stadium Controversy," 14 February 1969, 79026/3, "General Correspondence" file, MSUA.

56. Dayton to Wayne Cooper, 2 April 1969, 79026/1, "ASMSU" file, MSUA; William Johnstone, "Notes for President Leon Johnson," covering the period 18 April-22 May 1969, 79026/4, "VPA" file, MSUA.

57. Ibid.; Johnstone to Mrs. Leon Johnson, 9 May 1969, 79026/4, "VPA" file, MSUA.

58. Freeman, "The Rehumanize Movement."

59. Johnstone public statement of 9 May 1969, 79026/ 4, "VPA General Correspondence" file, MSUA; Johnstone to Mrs. Leon Johnson, 9 May 1969, ibid.; Johnstone interview; Marjorie Langenbach Ennes interview, 11 October 1991.

60. Johnstone to Loren M. Furtado, 23 May 1969, 79026/4, "VPA" file, MSUA.

61. Johnstone to Howard J. Axtman, 27 May 1969, ibid.

62. Lindy Miller interview, 22 August 1988.

63. Matusow, *The Unraveling of America*, 324.

64. Ibid., 325.

65. Ronald Perrin interview, 28 March 1988.

66. Robert Dunbar interview, 3 August 1987.

67. October 15th Peace Committee announcement, distributed 10 October 1969, 79026/10, "Vietnam Moratorium" file, MSUA.

68. Johnstone statement, 10 October 1969, ibid.

69. Marjorie Langenbach Ennes interview.

70. See "Statement of Purpose for a Radical Student Union," undated, but distributed during spring quarter 1970, 79026/14, "Student Affairs & Services" file, MSUA.

71. Lindy Miller interview.

72. Ronald Perrin interview, 24 March 1988.

73. Johnstone to Richard H. McBee, et al., 30 October 1969, as printed in the *Exponent*, 5 November 1969; petition form in the *Exponent*, 19 November 1969.

74. "Report of the Montana State University Committee on Service Concerning the Non-Renewal of Contract of James E. Myers...," 28 January 1970, Mansfield Papers, Series XVII, Box 196, MSU file, UMA.

75. Lindy Miller interview.

76. The author has interviewed numerous participants, including Bill Johnstone, Irving Dayton, and Ronald Perrin; also Samuel Curtis, James Goetz, Lindy Miller, Pierce Mullen, John Parker, and Milt Vanderventer.

77. Johnstone interview.

78. Jan H. Lynch to Senator Mike Mansfield, 9 April 1970, Mansfield Papers, Series XVII, Box 196, MSU file, UMA.

79. Johnstone to Ervin D. Hintzpeter, 13 April 1970, 79026/9, "H" file, MSUA.

80. Johnstone to Budget Committee, 10 April 1970, 79026/6, "Budget Committee" file, MSUA.

81. Johnstone to Forrest Anderson, 17 April 1970, 79026/10, "Governor's" file, MSUA.

82. Johnstone to Harvey Griffin, 27 April 1970, 79026/ 9, "G" file, MSUA.

83. William Shawcross, *Sideshow: Kissinger, Nixon and the Destruction of Cambodia* (New York, 1979), 152.

84. William Johnstone and Rev. Herbert Strom interviews; Robert Brown interview, 26 July 1987; Johnstone announcement, 6 May 1970, 79026/8, "Campus Unrest" file, MSUA; Johnstone to Willard E. Frazer, 15 May 1970, 79026/9, "F" file, MSUA.

85. Robert Brown interview.

86. Johnstone telegram to Mansfield, 5 May 1970, 79026/8, "Campus Unrest" file, MSUA.

87. Johnstone memo, 6 May 1970, ibid.

88. Ronald Perrin interview.

89. Johnstone interview.

90. Johnstone and Robert Brown interviews; Kelly Addy interview, 13 August 1987.

91. Robert Brown and Kelly Addy interviews.

92. Minutes of Student Senate Meeting, 18 May 1970, 79026/6, "Associated Students" file, MSUA.

93. Patrick C. Jobes and Robert A. Harvie, "A Case Study of Conventional Student Activism and the Small State University," *College Student Journal*, 22:2 (Summer 1988), 160-170. Portions of this article were written in 1973, but not published until 1988, when the authors concluded that their profile and conclusions were still valid, even after fifteen years.

94. Johnson to I. Wayne Eveland, 3 October 1968, 79026/3, "General Correspondence" file, MSUA.

95. Marge Paisley and Irving Dayton interviews.

96. Jobes and Harvie, "A Case Study."

Chapter Six

1. Mike Mansfield to Raymon E. Dore, 13 August 1974, Series XVII, Box 199, "MSU" file, Mansfield Papers, University of Montana archives (hereafter cited as UMA).

2. Johnstone to Carl McIntosh, 4 June 1970, Acc. 79026, Box 8, "Acting President General" file, Montana State University archives (hereafter cited as 79026/8, MSUA).

3. MSU Report on Audit, Fiscal Year Ended June 30, 1970, 79026/16, "Audit Report" file, MSUA.

4. Carl McIntosh interview, 11 August 1987; McIntosh to John H. Bunzel, 5 May 1972, 79026/19, "Civil Rights Audit" file, MSUA.

5. McIntosh memo to MSU Advisory Council, 25 January 1971, 79026/13, "President's Forum" file, MSUA.

6. Ibid.

7. McIntosh to Robert Pantzer, 28 June 1971, 79026/23, "UM" file, MSUA.

8. Comments to Faculty, 12 March 1971, 79026/13, "Faculty Meetings" file, MSUA.

9. Author's personal experience.

10. These views are the result of interviews with MSU faculty and staff.

11. McIntosh to Jennifer Evans, 2 December 1970, 79026/11, "Associated Students" file, MSUA.

12. *Bozeman Daily Chronicle*, 18 April 1971.

13. John M. Wylie to Robert Woodahl, 17 April 1971, Record Group RS 111, Montana Attorney General's Office Records, Box 17, Montana Historical Society archives (hereafter cited as MSIIA).

14. Faculty Policy Advisory Council Resolution, undated, April 1971, 79026/13, "Faculty Meetings" file, MSUA.

15. Michael McNeil to Mike Mansfield, 13 May 1971, Series XVII, Box 196, "MSU" file, Mansfield Papers, UMA.

16. R. L. Sanks to McIntosh, 22 February 1971, 79026/11, "ASMSU" file, MSUA.

17. McIntosh memo to FPAC, 19 April 1971, 79026/13, "Faculty Meetings" file, MSUA.

18. Irving Dayton remarks, Student Senate Workshop, 8-9 May 1971, 79026/11, "ASMSU" file, MSUA.

19. Robert Pantzer interview, 3 September 1991.

20. *Billings Gazette*, 30 May 1971.

21. Pantzer to McIntosh, 7 June 1971, 79026/23, "UM" file, MSUA.

22. McIntosh to Pantzer, 28 June 1971, ibid.

23. *Billings Gazette* editorial, 21 December 1986.

24. Michael P. Malone, Richard B. Roeder, and William L. Lang, *Montana: A History of Two Centuries*, rev. ed. (Seattle, 1991), 393.

25. Ibid., 393-394.

26. Richard B. Roeder, "The 1972 Constitution in Historical Context," *Montana Law Review*, 51:2 (Summer 1990), 260-269.

27. Malone, Roeder, and Lang, *Montana*, 395.

28. "Constitutional Convention Booklet—Objective Analysis for Montana Citizens," MSU Community Services Program, June 1972.

29. Malone, Roeder, and Lang, *Montana*, 395.

30. Richard B. Roeder interviews, 15 and 16 November 1991; Dorothy Eck interview, 15 December 1991.

31. Statement by Ted James, undated, but circa 1976, courtesy of Ted James; Ted James interview, 9 July 1987.

32. Richard Roeder and Dorothy Eck interviews.

33. Thomas Judge statement, *Montana University System Newsletter*, 1:3 (June 1973). See also Judge's "Statement on Postsecondary Education," undated, but forwarded August 1973, 79026/35, "Commission on Post-Secondary Education" file, MSUA.

34. McIntosh, "Remarks to the Post-Secondary Commission," 7 February 1974, Record Group 88, Montana Commission on Post-Secondary Education Records, Subject Files, Misc., Public Hearings, Bozeman, February 1974, Folder 2/8, MHSA.

35. *Congressional Record*, 5 June 1974, 120:13, 17668-17672.

36. Mansfield to Thomas Judge, 7 June 1974, Series XVII, Box 199, Mansfield Papers, UMA.

37. KBOW radio editorial, 11 June 1974, ibid.

38. Patrick Callan statement, *Great Falls Tribune*, 18 June 1974.

39. James H. Albertson to Mansfield, 11 June 1974, Series XVII, Box 199, Mansfield Papers, UMA. Emphasis in the original.

40. Mansfield to Mary Fenton, 22 June and 26 July 1974, ibid.

41. Mansfield to Raymon E. Dore, 13 August 1974, ibid.

42. Mansfield to Ted James, 19 September 1974, ibid.

43. Lawrence Pettit to Brian Mertz, editor of Dillon's *Daily Tribune Examiner*, 15 July 1974, ibid.

44. Ted James to Mansfield, 1 October 1974, ibid.

45. *The Montana Standard*, Butte, 24 October 1974. It is important to note that the controversy over Tech and Western obscured other important commission recommendations that ultimately were adopted.

46. Background for this analysis was enhanced by interviews with Jo Ellen Estenson, 17 August 1988; Ted James, 9 July 1987; Thomas Judge, 23 February 1990; and Lawrence Pettit, 19 June 1990.

47. Thomas Nopper interview, 6 August 1987.

48. Ibid.

49. McIntosh to John H. Bunzel, 5 May 1972, 79026/19, "Civil Rights Audit" file, MSUA.

50. Quoted in "Jane Doe Settlement," a document prepared by Central Administration for Members of the Board of Regents of Higher Education, 1977, 13.

51. Carl McIntosh interview; Donald Clark interview, 1 July 1987.

52. "Master Plan for M.S.U. Compliance with Court Orders Concerning Sex Discrimination," 7 June 1976, 81033/2, "Class Action Suit" file, MSUA. See also Donald L. Clark, "Discrimination Suits: A Unique Settlement," *Educational Record*, 58:3 (Summer 1977), 233-248.

53. Sharon Dunn, "Montana State University and Women, 1975-1990," history seminar paper, 1990.

54. McIntosh to Dayton, 5 June 1972, 79026/20, "Honors Program" file, MSUA.

55. 1973-1975 "Hold the Line" Budget, 18 December 1972, 79026/36, "Montana State Legislature" file, MSUA.

56. McIntosh to Regents of the Montana University System, 13 March 1973, Box 193, "MSU" file, Presidential Papers, UMA.

57. "Social Justice Studies at Montana State University," 7 March 1973, 79026/30, "United States Congress" file, MSUA.

58. Charles Bradley interview, 2 November 1987; John Jutila interviews, 13 August 1987 and 28 August 1991.

59. John Jutila interview, 13 August 1987.

60. Carl McIntosh interview.

61. McIntosh to Mansfield, 14 June 1972, Series XVII, Box 193, "MSU" file, Mansfield Papers, UMA.

62. *Montanan* (1972), 254-255: Edward Hanson interview, 25 August 1988; McIntosh, "Message to Interfraternity Council, June 1975, 79026/41, "Student Affairs and Services" file, MSUA.
63. 79026/41, "ASMSU" file, MSUA.
64. Angie Burnham, "MSU Residence Halls," history seminar paper, 1990.
65. McIntosh to Max Worthington, 31 May 1972, 79026/21, "Student Affairs file," MSUA.
66. Donald Clark Memorandum for Record, undated, circa 24 April 1976, 81033/1, "ASMSU" file, MSUA.
67. Jim McClean to McIntosh, 12 April 1976, 80133/1, ibid.
68. Creech Reynolds interview, 2 July 1987.
69. Lawrence K. Pettit interview, 19 June 1990; Pettit to Jeffrey J. Safford, 9 July 1990.
70. *Bozeman Daily Chronicle*, 18 April 1971.
71. "Memo to MSU Faculty," undated, Fall 1971, 79026/22, "AAUP" file, MSUA.
72. Pettit to Dolores Colburg, 15 November 1971, ibid.
73. *Great Falls Tribune*, 13 July 1973.
74. Ibid., 25 July 1973.
75. *Bozeman Daily Chronicle*, 23 May 1974.
76. *Great Falls Tribune*, 20 January 1975; *Bozeman Daily Chronicle*, 20 April 1975.
77. Roy Huffman interview, 12 September 1988.
78. Roy Huffman interview; Huffman memo to McIntosh, "Saudi Arabia Contract and Agreements," 17 August 1976, 82031/5, "Saudi Arabia" file, MSUA; Joe Asleson interview, 11 August 1987.
79. Roy Huffman interview; William Johnstone interview, 21 July 1988.
80. McIntosh Self Evaluation Report, 30 July 1975, A5-8, MSUA.
81. Mary Pace Ellerd interview, 7 July 1987; Sid Thomas interview, 14 August 1987.
82. Statement of Evaluating Committee, 10 December 1975, "Review-Dayton" file, 81033/1, MSUA; Sid Thomas interview. The author served on the evaluating committee.
83. *Bozeman Daily Chronicle*, 2 March 1976; McIntosh to MSU Advisory Council, 17 March 1976, 80040x/2, "Outgoing Correspondence" file, MSUA; McIntosh to William Krutzfeldt, 21 May 1976, ibid; Thomas Nopper interview, 6 August 1987.
84. Carl McIntosh interview.
85. McIntosh to Faculty Committee of Inquiry, 18 March 1976, 80040x/2, "Outgoing Correspondence" file, MSUA; William Johnstone memo, "The $1,000,000 'Scandal'," undated, courtesy of William Johnstone.
86. Thomas Nopper interview, 17 December 1991.
87. William Johnstone interview, 30 June 1987; Johnstone memo, "The $1,000,000 'Scandal'."
88. Thomas Nopper interview, 6 August 1987.
89. Thomas Nopper interview, 19 December 1991.
90. McIntosh to Myron L. Coulter (president, Idaho State University), 14 April 1976, 80040x/2, "Outgoing Correspondence" file, MSUA.
91. Lawrence Pettit interview.
92. Personal matters may have impacted politics here; in the mid-1970s Pettit had gone through a divorce and was no longer related to the governor.
93. Pettit outlined his achievements in a final report to the Board of Regents, "Implementing a New Governance System for Higher Education in Montana," 31 December 1978, 84031/4, "Board of Regents" file, MSUA.
94. Thomas Judge interview, 23 February 1990.
95. Carl McIntosh interview.
96. Pettit to Dennis Lind (chairman, Board of Regents), 22 August 1990, courtesy of Lawrence Pettit.

Chapter Seven

1. "Report to the Governor for Fiscal Year 1977," Acc. 82031, Box 6, "Governor's Budget" file, Montana State University Archives (hereafter cited as 82031/6, MSUA).
2. William Tietz interview, 12 August 1987.
3. Ted James interview, 9 July 1987.
4. Mary Pace Ellerd interview, 7 July 1987.
5. Sid Thomas interview, 14 August 1987.
6. Tietz memorandum, 28 April 1978, 84001/1, "Affirmative Action" file, MSUA.
7. Gordon G. Brittan, Jr., to Tietz, 19 May 1978, 84001/3, "History & Philosophy" file, MSUA.
8. Tietz to Henry M. Rockwell, 10 July 1978, 84001/1, "Outgoing Correspondence" file, MSUA.
9. Tietz to MSU Faculty and Administration, 23 May 1978, ibid.
10. Hal Stearns, "How the War of 1978 Was Waged," undated, 84001/5, "Six-Mill Levy" file, MSUA. MSU's members on the levy team were Max Worthington, Sonny Holland, and alumni director Joe May.
11. Editorial, *Exponent*, 3 October 1978.
12. Tietz memo to alumni and friends of MSU, October, 1980, 86005/11, "MSU Information" file, MSUA: "Faculty Salary Comparisons for MSU and Peer Institutions, 1979-1980," 91017/2, "Salary Information" file, MSUA.
13. John Vincent interview, 10 January 1992; *Bozeman Daily Chronicle*, 12 January 1992; Michael P. Malone, Richard B. Roeder, and William L. Lang, *Montana: A History of Two Centuries*, rev. ed. (Seattle, 1991), 398-399.
14. "President Sees Years of High Productivity, Change at MSU," undated, 84031/2, "Publications and News" file, MSUA.
15. Joseph Frazier (registrar) to Tietz, 18 October 1983, 87023/2, "Enrollment Breakdowns" file, MSUA.
16. Budget Allocation Narrative, 91017/3, "1981-1983 Biennium" file, MSUA.
17. Stuart Knapp interview, 24 September 1987.
18. John C. Bean and John D. Ramage, "An Experimental Program to Increase the Efficiency of Freshman Composition at Montana State University: An Initial Report," *WPA: Writing Program Administration*, 7:1-2 (Fall/Winter 1983).
19. "University Honors Program Assessment," 1 February 1984, courtesy of Alanna Brown.
20. Dayton to Freeman Wright, 5 May 1976, 81033/1, "VPAA" file, MSUA.
21. Noreen S. Alldredge to Senator John Melcher, 15 August 1983, 87023/2, "Library" file, MSUA; Patricia A. Deeg, "Montana State University Libraries: A History," history seminar paper (1990).
22. Stuart Knapp interview, 24 September 1987; Donald Clark, "International Education: Five Year Plan," 1985, 88019/5, "International Education" file, MSUA; Andrea Yang, "International Education at Montana State University," history seminar paper (1990).
23. Prospectus, "Montana-Canadian Relations Institute," 1 June 1981, 84031/2, "Montana/Canadian Relations Institute" file, MSUA; McKinsey to Tietz, 10 June 1981, ibid.
24. "Proposal to the Business Fund for Canadian Studies in the United States," 1983, 87023/7, "49th Parallel" file, MSUA.

25. Annual Report, 49th Parallel Institute, 3 April 1984, 88001/10, "49th Parallel" file, MSUA.
26. Clark to Knapp, 14 February 1983, 87023/2, "Japan Exchange" file, MSUA.
27. "International Education Programs at MSU," April, 1988, 90024/1, "VPAA" file, MSUA.
28. Pettit, "Role and Scope of the Montana University System," 15 November 1978, 91017/1, "Role and Scope Statements" file, MSUA.
29. "Report to the Governor for Fiscal Year 1977," 82031/6, "Governor's Budget" file, MSUA; John Jutila interview, 13 August 1987.
30. Bruce Shively interview, 11 February 1992.
31. Ibid.
32. Tietz to Schwinden, 13 October 1981, 98005/8, "Governor's Office" file, MSUA.
33. "President Sees Year of High Productivity, Change at MSU," summer, 1981, 84031/2, "Publications and News" file, MSUA.
34. *Bozeman Daily Chronicle*, 21 October 1982.
35. Malone, Roeder, and Lang, *Montana*, 398.
36. Ibid., 398-399.
37. Tietz to Francis Bardenouve, a letter not sent, 26 November 1986, 89027/9, "General Correspondence" file, MSUA; William Tietz interviews, 12 August 1987 and 24 September 1991.
38. Peer Comparison Data, 1986-1987, 91017/4, "1980s" file, MSUA; Carrol Krause to Judy Rippingale, 26 August 1986, ibid.
39. Lawrence Pettit interview, 19 June 1990; Pettit to Jeffrey J. Safford, 9 July 1990.
40. Most of these examples are the result of empirical observation made during the author's twenty-five years in Montana. The author's perceptions, however, were made clearer in interviews with Marilyn Wessel, MSU director of communications, and Bruce Shively, MSU budget director.
41. 1985 Legislative Session-Votes on Bills Relating to the Montana University System, 89027/9, MSUA.
42. Tietz to Dick Gray, 5 August 1985, 88019/1, "1986" file, MSUA.
43. Tietz to Carrol Krause and Board of Regents, 26 November 1986, 89027/9, "General Correspondence" file, MSUA.
44. Tietz to Ted Schwinden, 10 June 1987, ibid.; William Tietz interview, 24 September 1991; Robert Utzinger interview, 2 November 1989.
45. William Tietz and Robert Utzinger interviews.
46. Robert Utzinger interview; Utzinger memo for the *Exponent*, 25 April 1988, 90024/2, "College of Arts and Architecture" file, MSUA.
47. "Draft for Exponent from William Tietz," 1 April 1987, 89027/9, "General Correspondence" file, MSUA.
48. Tietz to Schwinden, 10 June 1987, 89027/9, "General Correspondence" file, MSUA.
49. William Tietz interview, 1 February 1992.
50. Tietz to Robert L. Marks, 20 October 1987, 89027/9, "CFLW" file, MSUA.
51. Quoted in Frank Newman, *Choosing Quality: Reducing Conflict Between the State And The University* (Denver, 1987), 4.
52. "The Advanced Technology Park at Montana State University," Report of November 1987, 90024/9, "Research Technology Park" file, MSUA.
53. "Technology Park, It's a Go!," MSU Foundation Press Release, 20 November 1986, 89027/5, "Research Technology Park" file, MSUA.
54. Tietz to Nancy W. McDonagh, 13 October 1986, 89027/9, "General Correspondence" file, MSUA.
55. "Technology Park, It's a Go!"; "Proposed Research-Technology Park," 20 November 1984, 88019/7, "Public Meetings on Research Park" file, MSUA.
56. William Tietz interview, 12 August 1987. For budget data and clarifications the author is indebted to Bruce Shively, budget director in the MSU office of administration.
57. Ted Schwinden interview, 2 October 1991.
58. Ibid.
59. Torlief Aasheim interview, 5 September 1991.
60. Ibid.
61. John Jutila interview, 28 August 1991; James Welsh interview, 8 August 1988.
62. In return for the College Street acreage, the MSU Foundation transferred two Big Timber ranches to the College of Agriculture. The College of Agriculture thought that it had lost in the exchange.
63. Aasheim to Tietz, 14 April 1987, 89027/9, "General Correspondence" file, MSUA.
64. William Tietz interview, 12 August 1987.
65. Max L. Amberson to Beatrice McCarthy, 11 November 1986, 90042/10, "Build Montana" file, MSUA; Max Amberson interview, 8 July 1987.
66. Marilyn Wessel interview, 1 February 1990.
67. Malone to Tietz, 3 January 1986, 88019/5, "Regents Professorships" file, MSUA.
68. Tietz to Board of Regents, 7 May 1986, ibid.
69. Saul Benjamin report, "Looking Backwards, Looking Ahead," 17 June 1987, 89027/4, "Honors Program" file, MSUA; Tietz to Benjamin, 31 December 1986, ibid.
70. *Exponent*, 1 May 1990, *Billings Gazette*, 20 April 1990. MSU's official response is contained in *Discovery*, 2:2 (May 1990).
71. Office of the President release, 28 March 1990.
72. Ibid.
73. John O. Mudd (chair) to Governor Stan Stephens, 26 September 1990, contained in "Report of the Montana Education Commission for the Nineties and Beyond."
74. "Report of the Montana Education Commission for the Nineties and Beyond."
75. Ibid. At almost the same time, the evaluation committee for MSU's 1990 accreditation review by the Northwest Association of Schools and Colleges: Commission on Colleges arrived at many of the same conclusions. See report of 16-19 October 1990.
76. Michael P. Malone, inaugural address, 25 October 1991.
77. Ibid.
78. John A. Stefferud to McIntosh, 2 June 1975, 79026/41, "Student Affairs and Services" file, MSUA.
79. "MSU Quarter/Semester Transition '91," No. 1 (8 March 1991).
80. *Bozeman Daily Chronicle*, 6 December 1991.
81. Michael Malone interview, 25 August 1991.
82. *Great Falls Tribune*, 8 December 1991.
83. Ibid.; Michael Malone interview, 25 August 1991.
84. *Bozeman Daily Chronicle*, 6 December 1991.
85. Ibid., 6 February 1992
86. Ibid., 12 September 1991.
87. Ibid., 12 January 1992.
88. Ibid., 12 September 1991.
89. Ibid., 31 January 1992; *MSU Staff Bulletin*, 7 February 1992.
90. Page Smith, *Killing the Spirit: Higher Education in America* (New York, 1989); Allan Bloom, *Closing of the American Mind* (New York, 1987).
91. Gordon G. Brittan, Jr., to Jeffrey J. Safford, 2 February 1992. The October 1990 MSU Institu-

tional Self-Study Report, Instructional Staff Section, contains much valuable information on faculty representation in university governance (see 337-358).

92. Quoted in Newman, *Choosing Quality*, 10.
93. Michael Malone, inaugural address.

Chapter Eight

1. Author's notes of conversation, 3 November 1979.
2. William Johnstone interview, 21 July 1988.
3. Merrill G. Burlingame, *A History: Montana State University, Bozeman, Montana* (Bozeman, 1968), 102.
4. *Kalispell Times*, 7 April 1938, courtesy of Marg Paisley.
5. Burlingame, *A History*, 105; Ronald A. Smith, *Sports and Freedom: The Rise of Big-Time College Athletics* (New York, 1988), Epilogue.
6. Burlingame, *A History*, 106.
7. Giles E. Parker, "A History of the Rocky Mountain, Skyline, and Western Athletic Conferences: 1909-1976," Ed.D. dissertation, Brigham Young University, 1976, 179-181. MSC/MSU basketball and football statistics have been obtained from annual press guides.
8. *Bozeman Daily Chronicle*, 11 January 1957. The University of North Carolina at Chapel Hill had the largest, made of steel.
9. William Johnstone interview, 21 July 1988.
10. "The Reminiscences of Jack Brenner," Montana Oral History Project—Legislative, Montana Historical Society, Helena.
11. Herb Agocs interview, 14 July 1987.
12. Ibid.
13. Renne to Boynton G. Paige, 21 February 1961, Box 46, Presidential Papers, University of Montana Archives.
14. Roger Craft interview, 2 November 1989.
15. Chuck Karnop interview, 1 August 1988.
16. Gregory O. Morgan, "Memorandum Re Student Activity Fee," January, 1974, Accession 79026, Box 30, "ASMSU" file, Montana State University Archives (hereafter cited as 79026/30, MSUA). This is a review of student fee support for athletics at MSC/MSU. Other sources for aforementioned developments are cited in Chapter 5.
17. Doug Fullerton interview, 16 September 1991.
18. Ellen Kreighbaum interview, 9 August 1988. There is a very good masters thesis covering the history of women's athletics at MSC/MSU up to 1979. It is rich in interviews and understanding, even without access to presidential papers. See Jo Ann Marie Buysse, "An Historical Analysis of Women's Athletics at Montana State University from 1893-1979," M.A. thesis, Montana State University, 1979.
19. The literature available for study of this issue is excellent and rapidly growing. See, for example, Helen Lensky, *Out of Bounds: Women, Sport and Sexuality* (Toronto, 1986), and Mary A. Boutilier and Lucinda SanGiovanni, *The Sporting Woman* (Champaign, Ill., 1983).
20. Ellen Kreighbaum interview.
21. George Shroyer to Carl McIntosh, 11 October 1972, 79026/34, "Women's Intercollegiate Athletics" file, MSUA; Buysse, "Women's Athletics at MSU," 72.
22. William Johnstone to Ellen Kreighbaum, et al., 15 October 1973, 79026/34, "Women's Intercollegiate Athletics" file, MSUA.
23. *Exponent*, 30 October 1973.
24. Robert VanWoert to Carl McIntosh, 4 December 1973, 79026/34, "Women's Intercollegiate Athletics" file, MSUA.
25. George R. LaNoue and Barbara A. Lee, "The Feminist Implosion: Mecklenburg v. Montana State University," from "Lawsuits and Litigants: The Impact of Academic Discrimination Cases on the Parties and Their Institutions," a report submitted to the Carnegie Corporation, 1985, Chapter VII.
26. Ibid.
27. Quoted in "Jane Doe Settlement," a document prepared by Central Administration for Members of the Board of Regents of Higher Education, 1977, 13.
28. Ginny Hunt interview, 5 August 1987.
29. Ellen Kreighbaum interview; Buysse, "Women's Athletics at MSU," 73-74.
30. Ellen Kreighbaum to Athletic Commission, 8 February 1977, courtesy of Ellen Kreighbaum.
31. Fullerton to Dave Lloyd, 28 May 1987, 89027/4, "Men's Athletics" file, MSUA.
32. *Helena Independent Record*, 15 February 1961.
33. John Underwood, "The Writing is on the Wall," *Sports Illustrated* (19 May 1980). Underwood's subtitle reads as follows: "The rash of phony transcripts and academic cheating spells out the fact that athletics are now an abomination to the ideals of higher education. Victims: the student-athletes. Culprits: the system and those who run it."
34. The report of the Men's Basketball Review Committee was presented to President Tietz on 13 June 1980, but was never made public. The chairperson of that committee is the author of this chapter.
35. The upgrading of admissions standards that followed the investigation was outlined in the *Bozeman Daily Chronicle*, 24 June 1980. The title of the article, "Bobcats cleared in report," is not an accurate description of the Men's Basketball Review Committee's findings.
36. Interviews with Doug Fullerton, 28 July 1988, 16 October 1989, 16 September 1991; Stu Starner, 19 October 1989; and Earl Solomonson, 19 October 1989.
37. Doug Fullerton interview, 28 July 1988; Fullerton to Thomas B. Robinson, 18 June 1987, 89027/4, "Men's Athletics" file, MSUA.
38. Carl McIntosh to Tom Parac, 22 April 1976, 80040x/2, "Outgoing Correspondence" file, MSUA.
39. James Koch (president, UM) to William Tietz, 18 May 1987, 89027/4, "Big Sky Conference" file, MSUA.
40. Doug Fullerton interview, 28 July 1988.
41. Nand Hart-Nibbrig and Clement Cottingham, *The Political Economy of College Sports* (Lexington, Mass., 1986), 1-5.
42. Ginny Hunt interview, 16 October 1989.
43. "Responses from William J. Tietz, President, Montana State University, AIAW/NCAA Testimony", 1982, 84031/3, "AIAW versus NCAA 1982" file, MSUA; Hunt to Tietz, 26 April 1982, ibid.
44. For the conflict between the AIAW and the NCAA see R. Vivian Acosta and Linda Jean Carpenter, "Women in Sport," as contained in Donald Chu, Jeffrey O. Segrave, and Beverly J. Becker, eds., *Sport and Higher Education* (Champaign, Illinois, 1985), 313-325.
45. Ginny Hunt interview, 16 October 1989.
46. Corlann G. Bush interview, 25 October 1989.
47. Ginny Hunt interview, 16 October 1989.
48. Tom Parac interview, 21 July 1988.

49. *Bozeman Daily Chronicle*, 4 September 1991.
50. Ibid., 8 December 1991.
51. "External Review of the Intercollegiate Athletic Program at Montana State University," August 15-18, 1989; William Tietz interview, 14 November 1991. Overall, the review was a disappointment, offering little beyond what was known and what had already been weighed carefully by both the central administration and the two athletic programs.
52. Ginny Hunt interviews, 16 October 1989, 16 September 1991.
53. Doug Fullerton interview, 16 October 1989. Seymour Kleinman argues that "there is increasing evidence indicating that this society is beginning to accept the possibility of athletic performance as an art form." See Kleinman, "The Athlete as Performing Artist: The Embodiment of Sport Literature and Philosophy," *Somatics* (Spring/Summer, 1988), 13-17.

Chapter Nine

1. A. Hunter Dupree, *Science in The Federal Government* (Baltimore, MD, 1989); David Reisman, "A Changing Campus and a Changing Society," in William W. Brickman and Stanley Tehner, eds., *Conflict and Change on the Campus: The Response to Student Hyperactivism* (New York, 1970), 69.
2. For the international and national perspective, see Joshua Lederberg, compiler, *The Excitement and Fascination of Science: Reflections by Eminent Scientists*, vol. 3 (Palo Alto, CA, 1990); introduction; Victoria A. Harden, *Inventing the NIH: Federal Biomedical Research Policy, 1887-1937* (Baltimore, MD, 1986); interviews with campus administrators Max Amberson, 8 July 1987; Byron Bennett, 26 July 1988; Charles Bradley, 2 November 1987; Max Amberson, 15 October 1991, Maurice Kelso, 21 September 1989, Robert Swenson, 12 July 1989.
3. Dupree, *Science*, I Stephen Cole, *Peer Review in the National Science Foundation phase 1 of a study* (Washington, DC, 1978); David E. Drew, *Strengthening Academic Science* (New York, 1985); General Accounting Office, *Engineering Research Centers: NSF Program Management and Industry Sponsorship* (Washington, DC, 1988).
4. Gary A. Strobel interview, 19 September 1991.
5. R.R. Renne to Alvord Johnson, Cape May, NJ, 14 April 1944; President's paper CN, 376, Box 38, esp. f. AO-306.
6. In the fiscal year ending 30 June 1991, expenditures for research totaled $18,900,085. Multi-year grants and other carryover funding commitments would raise that figure significantly if added to these expenditures. Whatever the means of calculating these monies, they are now critical to the university's survival.
7. David Sands interview, 14 September 1991.
8. Interview with Johan A. Asleson, 11 August 1987; Max Amberson, 15 October 1991; Hayden Ferguson, 21 September 1991.
9. David Worley interview, 23 January 1992.
10. Pierce C. Mullen, "Howard Taylor Ricketts and the Early Struggle against Rocky Mountain Spotted Fever," *Montana: The Magazine of Western History,* vol. 32, no. 1 (Winter, 1982); Cooley is memorialized in a mural by Professor Jessie Wilber on the west wall of the main, or south, entrance to Lewis Hall. In an interesting artistic error, Cooley's famous log school house and laboratory is placed on the wrong, or east, side of the Bitterroot River.
11. David Cameron interview, 23 August 1991; Theodore Weaver interview, 25 August 1988.
12. Harold Picton interview, 1 February 1990; Robert Eng interview, 19 September 1991.
13. David Cameron interview.
14. Theodore Weaver interview.
15. William Walter interview, 23 October 1991; Richard H. McBee interview, 16 May 1989.
16. John Jutila interview, 12 November 1991; Northwest Accreditation Self Study, 1960, MSUA.
17. Hayden Ferguson interview, 21 September 1991; Max Amberson interview, 8 July 1987. For a complete evaluation of 4-H work nationally, see Thomas Wessel and Marilyn Wessel, *4-H: An American Idea 1900-1980* (Chevy Chase, MD, 1982).
18. Northwest Accreditation Self Study, 1960, MSUA; Maurice Kelso interview, 12 June 1989.
19. Pierce C. Mullen, *A Record of Performance: A History of the American Simmental Association* (Bozeman, MT, 1989).
20. Irving Dayton interview, 20 June 1988; Gerald Lapeyre interview, 21 July 1988; Hugo Schmidt interview, 29 June 1988; "A Proposal to the Montana State Board of Education, Ex Officio Regents of the University of Montana Requesting Authorization for the Degree of Doctor of Philosophy in Physics at Montana State College, n.d., introduction.
21. Merrill G. Burlingame, *A History: Montana State University,* (Bozeman, MT, 1968) 80.
22. Charles Caughlin interview, 22 June 1989; Kenneth Emerson interview, 24 June 1989; Georgeanne Caughlin interview, 19 June 1988.
23. Irving Dayton interview; John Drumheller interview, 15 July 1989.
24. Georgeanne Caughlin interview, 29 June 1988.
25. Gerald Lapeyre interview; James Anderson interview, 20 November 1991.
26. Charles Bradley interview, 2 November 1987; John Montagne interview, 12 September 1991.
27. Byron Bennett interview, 26 July 1988.
28. David F. Gibson interview, 4 August 1988; Theodore Williams interview, 14 July 1987; Northwest Accreditation Self Study, 1960, MSUA.
29. Robert C. Mathis interview, 16 March 1992.
30. Byron Bennett interview.
31. Anna Pearl Sherrick with Jeanne M. Claus and John P. Parker, *The Montana State University School of Nursing: A Story of Professional Development,* (Bozeman, MT), 1976; Anna Pearl Sherrick, 2 December 1989, Oral History Archives, Montana Historical Society, O H 1308.
32. Anna Pearl Sherrick oral history; for the importance of the Florence Nightingale tradition in nursing nationally see Ethel Johns and Blanche Pfeffenkorn, *The Johns Hopkins School of Nursing 1889-1949* (Baltimore, MD) 1954.
33. "From Domestic Economy to Home Economics: 85 Years of History at Montana State," Department of Home Economics, 1980; Bertha Clow interview, 4 December 1991; Marjorie Paisley interview, 7 December 1991.
34. Diane Schroeder, "Home Economics at Montana State University 1980-1990," history seminar papers.
35. Maurice L. Burke interview, 21 October 1991; SIMM document; Northwest Accreditation Self Study, 1960, MSUA.
36. David F. Gibson interview; brochure issued by MSU Center for Interfacial Microbial Process Engineering, 1991.

37. *Report of the WAMI Review Committee for Reconceptualization of the WAMI Program,* November 1987; Frank S. Newman, "WAMI Program: Regionalized Medical Education in Montana," courtesy of Professor Newman, see esp. 300-301.
38. *Report of the WAMI Review Committee,* 22-25.
39. David Cameron interview.

Chapter Ten

A Note on Sources: This chapter is based largely on the fifty-year and seventy-five-year histories submitted by the respective departments, on the annual reviews once required of each department, on various accreditation reviews, and on the 1960 self-study conducted as the college was moving toward university status. Taken together, this material provides a good picture of faculty, curriculum, and facilities. All sources are available in the MSU archives.

1. Merrill G. Burlingame, *A History: Montana State University* (Bozeman, MT, 1968) 196-200.
2. Burlingame, "A History of the Department," 3.
3. Ibid., 11.
4. Robert G. Dunbar interview, 12 August 1989.
5. M. G. Burlingame and K. Ross Toole, *A History of Montana,* 3 vols. (New York, 1957).
6. Burlingame, "A History of the Department" 17-18.
7. Author's personal records.
8. Departmental histories, "Agricultural Economics," A. H.-2, MSUA.
9. We have not attempted to review the rather considerable materials relating to the history of the Cooperative Extension Service. A very good history is M. G. Burlingame and Edward J. Bell's, *The Montana Cooperative Extension Service: A History , 1893-1974,* (Bozeman, MT, 1984).
10. "Agricultural Economics," A.H. -2, MSUA; a straightforward statement of Wilson's program is his own *Democracy Has Roots* (New York, 1939), preface by Charles A. Beard. This book provides a sample of his thinking: "The Jeffersonian ideal of an agrarian America definitely belongs to the past. That being so, the question then arises: Can democracy operate in a country whose manner of life and whose manner of making a living differ with all the difference between industry and agriculture? The farm affords the independent farmer opportunity for daily experience in policy-making; what has the factory to offer? Specialization division of labor, has precluded the possibility of anyone kind of life being typical of the America of today; what does that mean for the concept of the general welfare?" Ibid., 31.
11. Joseph Kinsey Howard, *Montana, High Wide, and Handsome,* (New Haven, 1943); "Agricultural Economics," A.H.-2, MSUA.
12. Ed Mohler, "Making the Acquaintance of Early Man," *Montana Collegian,* Summer 1970, 18-20.
13. Jack C. Gilchrist interview, 5 March 1992; E. J. Bell, Jr., *Agricultural Economics and Economics at Montana State University, Bozeman, Montana, 1893-1970,* Agricultural Experiment Station Research Report No. 7.
14. Jack Horner's work is the subject of considerable literature; see, for example, "Dinosaur Fever...," *The Wall Street Journal,* 3 October 1983.
15. Kenneth Weaver interview, 16 February 1992; Burlingame, "A History of the Department."
16. Paul A. Grieder, "Notes on the History of the Department of English, Speech and Theatre Arts, 1893-1963," A.H.-2, MSUA.

17. "MSU Writing Center," A.H.-2, MSUA; *"Writing Laboratory Newsletter ,* vol. VI, no. 8, 9.
18. John P. Parker interview, 4 August 1987; Kenneth D. Bryson interview, 19 August 1987.
19. Jack R. Olson, 14 February 1992 memorandum; *Bozeman Daily Chronicle,* 24 January 1992.
20. Bruce Jacobsen, "USO Sponsors Pacific Tour for MSC Drama Students," *The Montana Collegian,* January 1962; Paul Brailsford, "A History of Shakespeare in the Parks," history seminar paper (1990); *The Stage Door,* Summer 1990.
21. "A History of the Department of Film and Television Production," A.H.-2, MSUA.
22. William A. Miller, Jr., memorandum to Louis G. True, 6 November 1967, A.H.-2, MSUA.
23. "75th Anniversary History of Modern Languages," A.H.-2, MSUA.
24. Louis L. Howard, "A History of Music at Montana State College, 1893-1946," A.H.-2, MSUA.
25. Creech Reynolds interview, 2 July 1987; William J. Rost interview, 10 August 1988.
26. "The Art Department's Fiftieth Anniversary Report, Montana State College, 1943;" "School of Art: 75th Anniversary History, 1943-1967, The Years since the Fiftieth Anniversary," A.H.-2, MSUA; H. G. Merriam: *The Arts in Montana* (Missoula, 1977), covers many facets of art creativity.
27. Frances Senska interview, 29 January 1988, and 28 February 1992; Mary Laura Klausing, "MSU Centennial History Project: A History of the School of Art, 1893-1990," history seminar paper (1990).
28. Governor's Citation, 18 February 1992.
29. "A History of the School of Architecture/Draft," A.H.-2, MSUA; Francis Woods interview, 21 February 1992.
30. "A History of the Business Department of the Montana State University," by H. G. Phelps, supplemented by William F. Brewer, A.H.-2, MSUA.
31. Harvey A. Larson, "A History of the School of Business," A.H.-2, MSUA.
32. James Lee interview, 5 March 1992; *Business Insight,* vol. 3, issue 12, 5 March 1992; "Fact Sheet," College of Business, 1992.
33. James Lee interview.
34. William F. Brewer, "A History of the Department of Education," A.H.-2, MSUA.
35. Mary Pace Ellerd interview, 7 July 1987; Newsletter, College of Education, 1989.
36. Jacques Barzun, *The American University: How It Runs, Where It Is Going,* (New York, 1968), 285.

Conclusion

1. Michael Malone, inaugural address, 25 October 1991.
2. Ivan Doig remarks at the inauguration of Michael Malone as president of Montana State University, 25 October 1991.

Appendix A

The Presidents of Montana State University

Augustus M. Ryon
1893

The Rev. James Reid
1894-1904

James M. Hamilton
1904-1919

Alfred Atkinson
1919-1937

Dr. A.L. Strand
1937-1942

Dr. Roland R. Renne
1945-1964

Leon H. Johnson
1964-1969

Dr. Carl W. McIntosh
1970-1977

Dr. William J. Tietz, Jr.
1977-1990

Dr. Michael P. Malone
1991-

Acting Presidents at MSU (MSC)

Luther Foster
April-June 1893

F.B. Linfield
1928-1929
while Atkinson traveled abroad

Deane B. Swingle
1930s
occasional absence of Atkinson

William Cobleigh
October 1942-August 1943
for Strand who resigned to accept presidency at Oregon State College

R.R. Renne
September 1943-April 1945
followed Cobleigh, acting, and was inaugurated in 1945

P.C. Gaines
1951-1953*
for Renne who was on an economic mission in the Philippines

Leon H. Johnson
1963-1964
followed Renne and was inaugurated February 1964

William Johnstone
October 1968-June 1970
during illness and subsequent death of Leon Johnson

Michael P. Malone
1991
followed William Teitz and was inaugurated October 1991

(bold type indicates acting presidents who then became presidents)
*Gaines was acting president on several occasions while at MSC

Appendix B

Campus Buildings

Atkinson Quadrangle, residence halls, social center, and home of the honors program, completed in 1935, and named for Alfred Atkinson, fourth president of the college during whose term it was built.

Branegan Apartments, built in 1978 and named for Gladys Branegan, dean of home economics, who introduced the fields of child development and family relations to the department.

Breeden Field House, built in 1958 to replace the old Romney Gym and named for John "Brick" Breeden, a member of the Golden Bobcat basketball team, later head coach for seventeen years of the basketball team, athletic director, and career placement officer.

Cheever Hall, the architecture building, a part of the Creative Arts Complex built in 1974, named for Hurlbert Cheever, a member of the architecture faculty for forty-four years, and head of the school for nineteen.

Cobleigh Hall, the engineering building, built in 1970 and named for William Cobleigh, who joined the faculty in 1894 to teach chemistry and physics. Cobleigh served as head of the chemistry department, dean of the College of Engineering, and acting president (1942-1943).

Cooley Laboratory, built in 1960 and named for Robert A. Cooley, head of the department of zoology and entomology for thirty years and senior entomologist for fifteen years at the U.S. Public Health Service Rocky Mountain Laboratory in Hamilton.

Danforth Chapel, built in 1950-1952 with the financial help of the Danforth Foundation.

Dyche Field, the practice field named for Schubert Dyche, MSC baseball, football, and basketball coach during the 1920s and 1930s.

Fisher Court, named for Wallace Fisher, an electrical engineering graduate of MSU who received an honorary doctor of engineering degree from the school in 1975.

Gaines Hall, the chemistry building built in 1961, named for Pascual Gaines, a faculty member for forty-three years, head of the chemistry department, dean of the university faculty, and acting president on four different occasions.

Gatton Field, laid out in 1929 and named for Cyrus Gatton, captain of the 1915 Bobcat football team who was killed in action in the First World War; today only Gatton Field Court remains as a memorial.

Grant-Chamberlain Apartments, built in 1975 and named for Nancy Grant Chamberlain, killed in a plane crash with her husband and her four children, whose memory was honored by her parents, Eugene and Mildred Grant, MSU alumni.

Hamilton Hall, built as a woman's dormitory in 1910 and named two years after her death for Emma Hamilton, wife of James Hamilton, third president of the college, during whose tenure the building was erected.

Hannon Hall, student residence, built in 1954-1955 and named for Olga Ross Hannon, faculty member and head of the art department from 1931 to 1947.

Hapner Hall, student residence, built in 1959 and named for Leora M. Hapner, faculty member and head of the department of education and psychology from 1932 to 1947.

Harrington Park, named for Frank M. Harrington, head of the department of horticulture.

Haynes Hall, one of three buildings in the Creative Arts Complex, opened in 1974 and named for Jack Ellis Haynes who, like his father, was famous for his pictorial record of Yellowstone National Park and was awarded an honory doctor of letters degree by MSC in 1960.

Hedges Halls, twin residence halls (North and South Hedges), built in 1964-1965 and named for Cornelius Hedges, who served four terms as territorial superintendent of schools and is sometimes call "the father of education in Montana."

Herrick Hall, built in 1926 to serve the needs of the home economics department, was named for Una B. Herrick, who joined the college staff as supervisor of the women's dormitory in 1911 and became the first dean of women and director of the College of Household and Industrial Arts.

Hoseaus Health and Physical Education Center, completed in 1973 and named in 1983 for Marga Hoseaus, longtime director of women's health and physical education.

Howard Hall, the music building that is part of the Creative Arts Complex, was built in 1974 and named for Louis Howard, who joined the faculty in 1908 and served as band director for thirty-eight years.

Huffman Building, home of the Endowment and Research Foundation, built in 1969 and named for Roy E. Huffman, dean of the College of Agriculture, director of the agricultural experiment station, vice president of research, and executive director of the Foundation.

Arthur J. M. Johnson Hall, the physics building, named in honor of the man who headed the physics department from 1938 to 1968.

Leon H. Johnson Hall, the life sciences building, was named for the professor of biochemistry, executive director of the Endowment and Research Foundation, dean of graduate studies, and president of the university from 1964 to 1969.

Peter Koch Tower, married student residence, built in 1968 and named for Peter Koch, early Bozeman banker and member of the first Local Executive Board, the committee appointed to oversee the college in its earliest days.

Langford Hall, student residence, erected in 1960 and named for Nathaniel P. Langford, Montana pioneer and first superintendent of Yellowstone National Park.

Lewis Hall, the biology building, erected in 1923 and named for Meriwether Lewis, naturalist and co-leader of the Lewis and Clark expedition of 1804-1806.

Lewis and Clark Dormitories, built in 1955 and named to honor Meriwether Lewis and William Clark, leaders of the historic expedition to the West in 1804-1806.

> **Colter Wing** named in honor of John Colter, an explorer who traveled with Lewis and Clark.

> **Culbertson Wing,** now mostly office space, named for Alexander Culbertson, an early agent for the American Fur Company and responsible for the building of Fort Benton.

Mullan Wing, dormitories, named for Captain John Mullan, a member of the Isaac Stevens expedition that charted a transcontinental railroad route across the northern United States and a roadway linking the headwaters of the Missouri and Columbia rivers.

Pryor Wing, named for Nathaniel Pryor, a member of the Lewis and Clark expedition.

Johnstone Center, offices, named for William A. Johnstone, former vice president of administration.

Linfield Hall, the agricultural building, built over several years and completed in 1909; for years called either Morrill Hall (for the Morrill Act that established America's land grant colleges) or the ag building. It was renamed in 1968 for Frederic B. Linfield, director of the agricultural experiment station and dean of the College of Agriculture from 1913 to 1937.

Marsh Laboratory, the veterinary research station, built in 1953 and named for Hadleigh Marsh, director of the laboratory from 1929 to 1959.

McCall Hall, the chemistry analytical lab, erected in 1952 and named for William H. McCall, professor of English and vocational mathematics and college registrar from 1926 to 1947.

Miller Stock Pavilion, built in 1968 and named for Robert W. Miller, who developed the horse program at MSU and served as rodeo coach.

Montana Hall, the original Old Main, built in 1896-1897, and renamed in 1914.

Museum of the Rockies, built in 1973 and expanded to 90,000 square feet in 1989, presents a "living history" of the northern Rockies through fossil displays, photography, Indian artifacts and western art.

Nelson Dairy Center, established in 1936 and named for John A. Nelson, first head of the dairy department and later the first dean of the graduate school.

Perry Swine Testing Station, established in 1970 and named for Clarence H. Perry, Fort Benton rancher who for years operated the only swine testing facility in the state.

Plant Growth Center, completed in 1987, houses climate-controlled areas for agronomic experiments and insect quarantine areas.

Plew Physical Plant, built in 1952 and named for William R. Plew, acting head of the architecture department and supervising architect of the campus.

Post Field Research Laboratory, built in 1968 and named for Arthur H. Post, member of the faculty and the agricultural experiment station staff for forty-five years.

Reid Hall, the business and education building, erected in 1958-1959 and named for James Reid, the second president of the college.

Renne Library, opened over Christmas break 1949-1950, named in 1978 for Roland Renne, head of economics and sixth president of the college.

Roberts Hall, the engineering building, built in 1922 and dedicated in 1923 to the memory of William Milnor Roberts, chief engineer for the Northern Pacific Railroad and president of the American Society of Civil Engineers in the late 1800s.

Romney Gymnasium, built in 1921-1922 to replace the old drill hall and named in 1973 for G. Ott Romney, head basketball and football coach at the college in the 1920s.

Roskie Hall, student residence, built in 1966 and named for Gertrude Roskie, instructor in home economics, head of the home economics department and later dean of the professional schools.

Ryon Laboratories, houses engineering laboratories and shops, built in 1922-1923 and named in 1939 for Augustus M. Ryon, first president of the college.

Reno H. Sales Stadium, built in 1973 and named for a member of the first Bobcat football team.

Sherrick Hall, home of the College of Nursing, built in 1973 and named in honor of Anna Pearl Sherrick, first director of the School of Nursing.

SOB Barn, recreational center for the campus, built in 1926 as a cattle barn and saved by a student-sponsored campaign in 1968-1971 from destruction.

Nelson Story Tower, family housing residence, built in 1968 and named for Nelson Story, Bozeman pioneer and banker, member of the first State Board of Education, and donor of the site on which the school opened in 1893.

Strand Union Building, opened in the fall of 1940 and named in 1978 for Augustus LeRoy Strand, president of the university from 1937 to 1942.

Swingle Health Center, built as an addition to the SUB in 1957 and named for Deane B. Swingle, who came to Bozeman as a professor of botany in 1906, founded the department of botany and bacteriology, later played a primary role in establishing both the student health service and the nursing education program, and served as acting president on several occasions.

Taylor Hall, the original agricultural experiment station and now the home of the Cooperative Extension Service, the first building on campus, erected in 1894 and named in 1983 for J. C. Taylor, leader of the Montana Extension Service in the 1920s through the 1940s.

Traphagen Hall, the earth sciences and psychology building, erected in 1919 to replace the old chemistry and physics building that had been destroyed by fire three years earlier, and rededicated in 1968 to honor Frank W. Traphagen, member of the school's first faculty as instructor of chemistry and natural sciences and staff member of the ag experiment station.

Visual Communications Building, completed in 1982, houses the media and theatre arts department and the Montana public television station KUSM.

Welch Veterinary Clinic Annex, built in 1960 and named for Howard Welch, professor of veterinary science for thirty-eight years.

Wilson Hall, the liberal arts building, opened in 1976 and named for Milburn L. Wilson, an agricultural economist who was a member of the college faculty from 1914 to 1933 and who later served as undersecretary of agriculture in the Roosevelt administration.

The Montana State University Campus

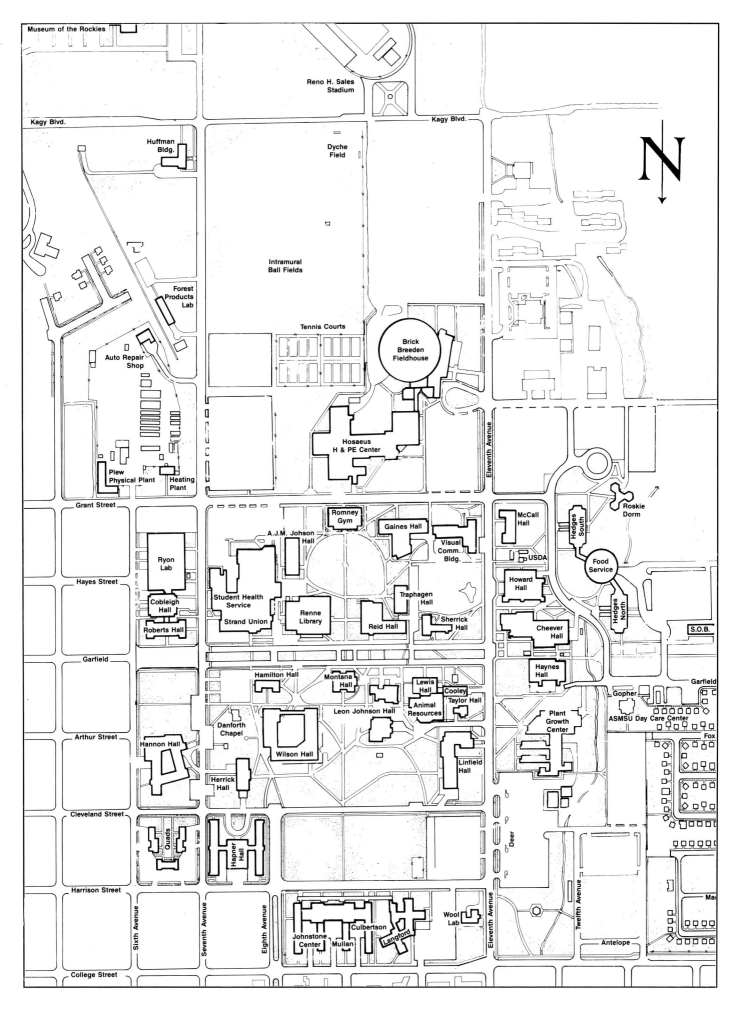

Index